Mapping Diversity in Latin America

Mapping Diversity in Latin America

Race and Ethnicity from Colonial Times to the Present

Edited by
MABEL MORAÑA AND
MIGUEL A. VALERIO

VANDERBILT UNIVERSITY PRESS
Nashville, Tennessee

Copyright 2025 Vanderbilt University Press
All rights reserved
First printing 2025

Library of Congress Cataloging-in-Publication Data

Names: Moraña, Mabel, editor. | Valerio, Miguel Alejandro, editor.
Title: Mapping diversity in Latin America : race and ethnicity from colonial times to the present / edited by Mabel Moraña and Miguel A. Valerio.
Description: Nashville, Tennessee : Vanderbilt University Press, [2024] | Includes bibliographical references and index.
Identifiers: LCCN 2024023128 (print) | LCCN 2024023129 (ebook) | ISBN 9780826507259 (hardcover) | ISBN 9780826507242 (paperback) | ISBN 9780826507266 (epub) | ISBN 9780826507273 (pdf)
Subjects: LCSH: Latin America--Race relations--History. | Latin America--Ethnic relations--History.
Classification: LCC F1419.A1 M36 2024 (print) | LCC F1419.A1 (ebook) | DDC 305.80098--dc23/eng/20241028
LC record available at https://lccn.loc.gov/2024023128

Cover image credit: Jorge González Camarena (Mexico, 1908–1980), *Presencia de América Latina*, Casa de Arte José Clemente Orozco, Universidad de Concepción, Concepción, Chile, 1965. Courtesy of © Universidad de Concepción.

Contents

Introduction: Constructing the Other in Latin America   1
Mabel Moraña

PART 1. THE RACIAL OTHER IN COLONIAL TIMES

1. Foundations of Race and Colonialism in Latin America   31
   Amber Brian and Mónica Díaz
2. Race and the Baroque: Social Actors and Christian Subjects in Seventeenth-Century Lima and Mexico City   56
   Stephanie Kirk
3. African Slavery in Latin America   82
   Miguel A. Valerio
4. Race in Eighteenth-Century Spanish America   99
   Mariselle Meléndez

PART 2: RACE AND NATION

5. Genealogies of *Blanquitud/Branquitude:* From Critical Race Theory to Critical Whiteness Studies   127
   Ruth Hill
6. Indigenous Populations and Nation-Building Projects on the Central American Isthmus (1810–1930)   156
   Patricia Arroyo Calderón and Marta Elena Casaús Arzú
7. Reconsidering the "Racial Other": Nation Building, Citizenship, and Interracial Alliances in Latin America and the Caribbean   176
   Jorge Daniel Vásquez
8. Looking through Layers of Jewishness in Latin America   199
   Ariana Huberman
9. Race and Nationalism: Hierarchical Imaginaries, Institutional Racism, and Fantasies about the Mestizo   224
   Iván Fernando Rodrigo-Mendizábal and Marcel Velázquez Castro

10. Interethnic Conflict and Sociocultural Contributions of Asian Diasporas
    in Latin America and the Caribbean   250
    Ignacio López-Calvo

11. Mobilizing Black Culture against Racism: The Negritude Movements
    in Latin America   279
    Carlos Alberto Valderrama Rentería

12. Beyond Binaries: Genealogies of *Mestizaje* and *Mulataje* in Améfrica Ladina   302
    Agustín Laó-Montes

13. Genealogy of Indigenist Translations: From Colonized Methodologies to
    Indigenous Self-Determination in Peru, Twentieth and Twenty-First Centuries   348
    Christian Elguera

14. On Democratic Imaginaries in a Discriminatory Society: The Colonial
    Foundations of Racialization and Land Struggles in Contemporary Brazil   379
    Tracy Devine Guzmán

PART 3. CONCEPTUALIZING DIVERSITY

15. From Creolization to *Créolité*: Creole Subjectivities and Racial Divisions in
    Caribbean Societies   415
    Ariel Camejo

16. Race Relations in Contemporary Central America: From State Violence to
    Indigenous Empowerment (1940s–2021)   433
    Patricia Arroyo Calderón and Marta Elena Casaús Arzú

17. Racializing Arabs in Latin America   458
    Bahia M. Munem

18. Ethno-Racial Landscapes in Argentina, Uruguay, Paraguay, and Chile: From
    Assimilation to Contestation   475
    Gonzalo Aguiar Malosetti

19. Chicanos, Hispanos, and Latinos   502
    Bárbara I. Abadía-Rexach

Acknowledgments   523

Contributors   525

INTRODUCTION

Constructing the Other in Latin America

MABEL MORAÑA

We offer this collective volume to the reader in an attempt to update and refocus the study of race and ethnicity in Latin America from a new perspective, one in which historical developments and cultural contexts interact in a productive manner. The cultural studies approach followed by the contributors to this book allows for an integrated analysis and interpretation of social and political processes without leaving aside matters related to the formation of collective imaginaries, the configuration of subjectivity, and the symbolic struggles that accompanied the construction of identity and the figurations of racial and ethnic "otherness" in the so-called New World. To this end, the diachronic approach has been combined with geo-cultural perspectives, thus bringing together regional studies that provide a solid basis for comparative analysis. In this respect, this book hopes to contribute to the field of racial and ethnic studies with an overarching examination of historical processes, textual materials, and cultural practices from the early stages of conquest and colonization to the period of nation formation, the organization of the new republics, and the development of modernization until the present. The abundant bibliography on race and ethnicity in Latin America, which has established the basis for current incursions in this field, usually approaches the vast array of historical processes and the manifestations of racial conflicts in partial studies that introduce the reader to specific areas, periods, and facets of social and political developments that surround the conceptualization and regulation of interracial relations. Some examples are *Race and Ethnicity in Latin America,* by Peter Wade, a classic book in this area of study, first published in 1997. That volume provides a useful and thorough introduction to the topics at hand from the perspective of anthropological and sociological analysis and focuses basically on Indigenous and Black populations. Another point of reference has been the collection of essays *Race and Nation in Modern Latin America* (2003), edited by Nancy P. Appelbaum, Anne S. Macpherson, and Karin Alejandra Rosemblatt. The volume approaches issues of collective identity and debates on race and nation formation, showing the conceptual changes to those concepts from interdisciplinary perspectives. *Mapping Diversity in Latin America* adds to those efforts a more comprehensive overview, both from historical and cultural perspectives. It covers, for instance, ethnicities not included so far in critical readers on racial developments, such as Jews, Sirio-Libaneses, and members of Asian diasporas. The book also includes a chapter on Brazil, a country not often included in overarching studies, and a final chapter on Latinx populations in the United States in order to supplement the emphasis on Latin America with the consideration of the vast Mexican population that has migrated to the United States in numerous waves, and their descendants, most of whom are now part of US society. Finally, it is worth mentioning the attention that contributors to this book have paid to ethnic classifications such as *mestizaje, mulataje, creolization, negritud, blanquitud,* and the like, a testament to the dynamic nature of Latin American societies in all stages of their development.

The complex processes of identity formation and the organization of societies cannot be grasped in all their intricacies and developments without considering issues related to racial and ethnic interactions, particularly in postcolonial societies. Questions of race and ethnicity traverse Latin American history, with each subregion presenting geo-cultural, political, and economic particularities that need to be considered in order to understand how power and resistance operated in colonial times and the postindependence period, as well as in our contemporary age. Latin American history has been marked, from the very beginning, by conflicts inherent to interracial relations in contexts characterized by extreme inequality and sustained exploitation. The "construction of the Other" names, within those parameters, the processes of social and political (self-)recognition, in which the conceptualization of sameness and alterity followed the patterns intrinsic to imperial domination while responding creatively to the unprecedented challenges of the New World.

Colonial societies were, as it is well known, highly stratified social formations, something that did not preclude the constant intermixing of individuals, languages, and beliefs. However, racial hierarchies were overwhelmingly present both in the practices of daily life and in political and religious discourses.[1]

Foundational critical works, elaborated from the perspectives of history and anthropology, provided important bases for a critical study of racial and ethnic interactions in America. However, it is worth noting that some of the best-known books on these topics, Peter Wade's and the collective volume coedited by Nancy Appelbaum, concentrate on modern and contemporary times, prioritizing issues of race in the processes of nation formation and modernization in Latin America. Such a focus leaves much room for an overarching study of the diachronic changes that the concepts of race and ethnicity have gone through in different periods and regions since the Conquest, and also of the conflicts and advances registered at the level of racial and ethnic integration over the centuries. At the same time, central issues pertaining to the situation of Indigenous peoples, as well as African and Afro-descendants in America, often overshadowed the presence, contributions, and struggles of other racial and ethnic minorities that have been an integral part of Latin American societies from the beginning, only increasing in importance and diversity from the nineteenth century on. This book, then, constitutes an attempt to offer a historical, social, and political overview of race and ethnicity in Latin America from the colonial period until postmodern times, paying attention to the great variety of cultures that, in addition to Indigenous and Afro-descendant cultures, have also nurtured the highly diversified societies in the region.

Authors of the chapters included in this volume deal with issues of race and ethnicity in their own way, including the changing definitions of those terms and the debates such resignifications have inspired in different disciplinary fields. According to Cornell and Hartmann, the term *race* refers to "a human group defined by itself or others as distinct by virtue of perceived common physical characteristics that are held to be inherent. . . . Determining which characteristics constitute the race . . . is a choice human beings make. Neither markers nor categories are predetermined by any biological factors."[2] Ethnicity, in contrast, is traditionally understood as a cultural term that denotes a common ancestry (a shared language, religious beliefs, and phenotypical characteristics).[3] However, the meaning, and especially the social significance, of these concepts have been modified and refined multiple times in different historical and cultural contexts, and consequently, their definitions and political connotations have varied and evolved.[4]

Racial issues were not limited to social and political interactions but projected themselves at all levels of intellectual inquiry. The need to conceptualize—and legitimize—racial and ethnic classifications influenced the development of biological sciences, anthropology, historical studies, sociology, and psychology. It also inspired, over the centuries, the exploration of a variety of theoretical approaches and methodologies that could illuminate the intriguing field of racial differentiation and its presumed correlation with human abilities, propensities, and deviations.

As Aníbal Quijano indicated in his studies on social classification in Latin America, the notion of race was tightly linked in the colonial period to issues of labor (particularly mining and agricultural work, but also construction, transportation, and domestic services). However, it is well known that "in European thought, the identification of Africans with inferiority was already common at the time of the Renaissance."[5] In America, the need for cheap laborers certainly was one of the factors that consolidated the conception of society as a stratified realm in which privileges and obligations were distributed depending on skin color, a distinction of strong discriminatory potential. That did not mean that assigning hard work and overexploiting certain sectors of society involved ethical, philosophical, and religious issues that the interest of colonizers could not fully dissipate. A variety of arguments were used in the attempt to legitimize the exploitation of Indigenous and African populations. One had to do with the concept of slaves "by nature," supposedly taken from book 1 of Aristotle's *Politics*, a controversial assumption that has been the center of academic and ecclesiastical disputes.[6]

In the nineteenth century, racialization was stimulated both by scientific advances and by the expansion of capitalism, which required the massive incorporation of laborers into different kinds of productions and manufactures. Processes of racialization incorporated findings in the fields of human diversity and evolution as valid arguments for the subalternization of human beings by dominant classes. The ideas of Carl von Linnaeus (*Systema naturae*, 1758) and Charles Darwin (*The Origin of the Species*, 1859, and *The Descent of Man*, 1871) were interpreted as reliable sources legitimizing racial division and human exploitation. But it was the philosopher Herbert Spencer who would have the most incisive influence on racial politics and the correlative ideological models of social organization.[7] The notion of survival of the fittest and the idealized concept of evolution permeated scientific and political discourses, thus providing a supposedly incontrovertible argument in favor of the perpetuation of social hierarchies and the exploitation of the "inferior" races. The idea of "whitening" the nations was popular in many countries in their attempt to emulate European notions of progress and social sophistication. Different versions of this ideology can be seen in Sarmiento's work, particularly *Conflicto y armonía de las razas en América* (1898), but also in his *Facundo* (1845) and in that of authors from Brazil, Mexico, and other countries.[8] In the twentieth century, debates on race concentrate on topics such as miscegenation, whitening, *negritud*, and *indigenismo*, all oriented toward the ideals of social integration, but the well-rooted legacy of racialization that originated in the colonial period has remained, just under new appearances and at different degrees.

Racial classification was evident in colonial times in the caste system, the distribution of labor, and the ways different sectors participated in public life and integrated the domestic sphere. The organization of societies and the distribution of wealth, both in colonial times and during the formation and consolidation of national projects, also responded, to a great extent, to hierarchical criteria. Arguments in favor of the superior value of the "purity of blood," as well as notions such as the Aristotelian idea of slavery by nature, were part of extended debates that discussed the "humanity" of Indigenous subjects, their "dubious" spirituality, and the connections between Christianization and social recognition.

As it is well known, the subalternization of Indigenous and Black populations on the basis of racial and ethnic considerations justified the exploitation of "inferior" and "primitive" races for the benefit of colonizers first, then Creole elites after independence. Similar notions were also used to legitimize the dominance of some nations over others. Some of the ideas that informed this process had their roots in Spain's long wars against Islam (religion, associated with ethnicity and skin color, being the official justification for the "holy war" against the Moors), and even in the Old Testament, where dark-skinned peoples were sons of Ham.[9] Even Aristotle's notion of natural slavery was adapted to the framework of colonialism in order to justify the exploitation of Indigenous and Black people in the New World.

For the dominant groups, the use of racial differentiation for the enjoyment of social and economic privileges and for the exploitation of supposedly inferior social sectors trickled down in society, thus creating a generalized hierarchical system in which Creoles, mestizos, and mulattoes ranked above Indigenous and Afro-descendant populations, thus enjoying some advantages and opportunities that were denied to "colored people." But without a doubt, the link between race, labor, and capital accumulation constituted one of the pillars of the relations of domination established by Peninsular powers in transoceanic territories.

Among other authors, the Peruvian sociologist Aníbal Quijano analyzed the specific forms of labor adopted in America and the process of social classification they prompted in colonial times as part of the historical development of capitalism. Such racial and economic compartmentalization of society constituted the basis of the all-encompassing system of radical inequality that characterized the organization of colonial societies and the formation of national states. In his study "Coloniality of Power, Eurocentrism, and Latin America," for instance, Quijano elaborates on the perpetuation of structures of domination and exploitation that transcended their colonial origin and were embedded in the process of modernization. He refers to the social, economic, and political continuity of the colonial matrix using the expression "coloniality of power," emphasizing the crucial role of labor in the configuration of modernity:

> In the historical process of the constitution of America, all forms of control and exploitation of labor and production, as well as the control of appropriation and distribution of products, revolved around the capital-salary relation and the world market. These forms of labor control included slavery, serfdom, petty-commodity production, reciprocity, and wages. In such an assemblage, each form of labor control was no mere extension of its historical antecedents. All of these forms of labor were historically and sociologically new: in the first place, because they were deliberately established and organized to produce commodities for the world market; in the second place, because they did not merely exist simultaneously in the same space/time, but each one of them was also articulated to capital and its market. Thus they configured a new global model of labor control, and in turn a fundamental element of a new model of power to which they were historically structurally dependent. That is to say, the place and function, and therefore the historical movement, of all forms of labor as subordinated points of a totality belonged to the new model of power, in spite of their heterogeneous specific traits and their discontinuous relations with that totality. In the third place, and as a consequence, each form of labor developed into new traits and historical-structural configurations.[10]

As argued by Quijano, such a distribution of roles consolidated the notion of race among Spaniards and Creoles as a founding criterion for the economic development and the organization of the social, thus instituting inequality, injustice, and discrimination as "natural" conditions of existence: "The new historical identities produced around the foundation of the idea of race in the new global structure of the control of labor were associated with social roles and geo-historical places. In this way both race and the division of labor remained structurally linked and mutually reinforced in spite of the fact that neither of them were necessarily dependent on the other in order to exist or change."[11]

The caste system constituted an official attempt to regulate and normalize social control and exploitation of "inferior" sectors of American populations, compartmentalizing society and imposing pigmentocracy as a criterion for marginalization, exploitation, and invisibilization of individuals and communities other than Spaniards and Creoles. Personal whiteness and progressive social whitening became the ideals of stratified societies eager to institutionalize the power of the elites and legitimize privilege and exclusion.

Simón Bolívar clearly perceived the shattering effects of social hierarchies based on a combination of class and race considerations. In 1819, in his address at the Congress of Angostura, Bolívar made reference to "a matter ... of vital importance":

> Let us bear in mind that our people are not European, nor North American, but are closer to a blend of Africa and America than an emanation from Europe, for even Spain herself lacks European identity because of her African blood, her institutions, and her character. It is impossible to say with certainty to which human family we belong. Most of the indigenous peoples have been annihilated. The European has mixed with the American and the African, and the African has mixed with the Indian and with the European. All born in the womb of our common mother, our fathers, different in origin and blood, are foreigners, and all differ visibly in the color of their skin; this difference implies a bond and obligation of the greatest transcendence.[12]

Quijano's synthetic concept of race suggests the convenience of a pluralist (multiethnic) paradigm in order to overcome the binary system that opposed Europeans and Creoles to Indians and populations of African descent, but his influence on these matters did not prevail. For Bolívar, race is a matter of clear political implications and strategic value, a fundamental element that would prove crucial for the development of independent nations. He speaks of civic responsibility and moral inequality, pointing to racial justice as one of the pillars for the construction of the new republics.

Thus, with these facts, it would be accurate to indicate that, in addition to other forms of social categorization (e.g., class, gender, sexuality), the new republics emerged as stratified and exclusionary systems in which the control and subalternization of certain sectors served the purpose of consolidating Creoles' hegemony, thus perpetuating the power relations of colonial times in modern scenarios. Since the nineteenth century, the formation and consolidation of nation-states have confronted issues of race, given the resistance of ethnic communities to the homogenizing and exclusionary practices that characterized Creole domination from independence. In Argentina, for instance, dominant classes believed in the need to overcome the "primitivism" and "barbarism" of vernacular sectors, with injections of Nordic blood through immigration policies, in order to purify and strengthen the belligerent and untamable nature of autochthonous populations. Questions of race were also prominent among the humanists reunited in the Mexican Ateneo de la Juventud. Across Spanish America, mestizaje would become the racial pillar of the ideology of progress, projecting the idea of a harmonious racial/ethnic synthesis that would erase sociocultural differences and economic inequalities. José Vasconcelos attempted, along those lines, a mythification of mestizaje as "the cosmic race" that would redeem the human species. That gives us evidence of the tight entanglement of issues of race and ethnicity in the advancement of the national projects and in the organization of civil society in Latin America. By the last decades of the nineteenth century, the processes of modernization presented a new social and political scenario, characterized by industrial growth and the strengthening of international relations, thus creating new conditions for the gradual integration of popular sectors of society in the dynamics of massive production, expansion of national markets, and cultural transnationalization.

In the twentieth century, José Martí, Manuel González Prada, José Carlos Mariátegui, and many others started to take a different perspective on the immense political potential of racialized sectors, whose marginalization Creole elites had perpetuated. Society became increasingly aware of the complex racial/ethnic interactions that traversed modern societies, in which colonial structures of domination continued to impose their privileges over the vast majority of national populations. Aníbal Quijano's concept of coloniality of power provided a name and a qualified analysis of the extended strategies of control and exploitation of the "other" and of the prolonged validity of social imaginaries shaped by the perversities of elite hegemony.

Mestizaje is an umbrella concept in Latin America that covers a wide array of historical and political processes and encompasses a rich combination of lineages. It also suggests a number of ideological connotations, symbolic values, and practical applications in different societies. Peter Wade approaches mestizaje mainly as a "lived experience." In his own words, "I address mestizaje not just as a nation-building ideology—which has been the principal focus of scholarship on the issue, but also as a lived process that operates within the embodied person and within networks of family and kinship relationships."[13] However, he recognizes that, academically, mestizaje has triggered two basic concerns: "First, that nationalist ideologies of mestizaje are essentially about the creation of a homogeneous mestizo (mixed) future, which are the opposed to subaltern constructions of the nation as racially culturally diverse; and second, that mestizaje as a nationalist ideology appears to be an inclusive process, in that every one is eligible to become a mestizo, but in reality it is exclusive because it marginalises blackness and indigenousness, while valuing whiteness."[14] In reality, as Wade indicates, mestizaje also leaves room for differentiation, although its final goal is to homogenize the population in order to avoid social conflicts originating in racialization. Other societies characterized by multiculturalism and multiple ethnicities have also elaborated other versions of miscegenation. According to Wade, "In the USA and Europe increasing attention has been paid to processes of racial and cultural mixture, usually referred to by a series of different terms, such as hybridity, syncretism, *métissage, mélange* and creolisation, all or some of which may be related to other concepts, such as diaspora, which evoke the kinds of migrations and movements that lead to mixture."[15]

It is clear, in any case, that the phenomenon of mestizaje provides clear evidence of the fluid nature of society and of the uselessness of classifications and stratifications of an ever-changing reality whose internal dynamic overtakes any kind of compartmentalization. But if *mestizaje* is a keyword for the study of Latin American racial history, particularly in the case of Indigenous-Creole relations, *blanqueamiento* also is a crucial concept for the understanding of racial policies related to populations of African descent and their perceived resistance to participating in the liberal implementation of Europeanized "order and progress." At the end of the nineteenth century, Brazil confronted the contradiction between the ideal of modernization and the lingering institution of slavery, considered them an obstacle to development. Being the country that had received more slaves than any other nation in the Americas, and that still depended on them at many levels, the existence of a large mass of illiterate and unskilled Afro-descendants constituted an unresolvable problem even for abolitionists. Whitening became a social and political ideal that could result in the "upgrading" of the Brazilian population.[16] The sociologist and anthropologist Gilberto Freyre (1900–1987), author of *Casa-grande e senzala* (1933), was a key figure in these debates. His work represented interracial relations in the Northeast's sugar plantations, where he illuminated social problems that had been ignored by Brazilian elites while emphasizing Indigenous and Black contributions to the country's development and social enrichment.[17] In 1934, he organized the first Afro-Brazilian Congress in Recife and continued to stress that the nation's identity was that of a multiracial society. However, the ideal of a whitened society did not cease to exist.

The Négritude movement emerged in the first decades of the twentieth century, propelled by the ideas and transformative impulses of thinkers such as Léopold Senghor (Senegal), Frantz Fanon (Martinique), and Aimé Césaire (Martinique), intellectuals who instilled racial debates with a humanist, emancipatory perspective that illuminated the impact of colonialism as one of the most important factors in the racialization of the world and the degradation of colonized peoples.[18] Some of them proposed "cultural miscegenation" as a way to overcome racial struggles. Others considered more direct and belligerent practices of resistance and social transformation. The work of the above-mentioned intellectuals passionately and effectively deconstructed the notion of colonization, removing from the concept all religious legitimizing rhetoric and showing colonialism, instead, as an indefensible practice of devastation, plundering, and dehumanization.

When talking about race in Latin America, the consideration of regional processes is of key importance, as each geo-cultural area has received, at different times (and in addition to the original impact of autochthonous populations), descendants of European conquerors and African slaves as well as migrant communities from Asia, Arab countries, and many other areas, all of whom have enriched its demographic composition, its history, and its culture, making Latin America one of the most diverse parts of the world. Bernasconi and Lott indicate in their introduction to *The Idea of Race* that in the historical formation of the concept of race, some critics could argue against "the obsessive focus on the black race, often to the neglect of the other races, and of the unique association of the white race with racial purity."[19] The authors suggest, then, that other perspectives could illuminate different aspects of the

Latin American racial spectrum, such as those resulting from Asian migrations and, in general, of non-European ethnicities. This side of the issue, much less explored than those of populations of Indigenous and African descent, shows how much of this crucial aspect of Latin American cultures and societies is still an undefined and elusive object of inquiry and how slippery the concept of race still is today at an interdisciplinary level.

The Racial Other in Latin America

Taking into consideration the multifarious nature of the issues at hand, this volume constitutes an attempt to complement, expand, and elaborate aspects related to the history of power relations in connection to race in the postcolonial societies that emerged from the experience of colonialism in the so-called New World. Latin American peoples endured imperial domination and fought for their independence, and they continue to struggle today for their actual decolonial emancipation. The editors of this volume recognize in race and ethnicity one of the crucial fields of intellectual and political debate and socioeconomic transformation. The construction of the racial Other involves the complex interweaving of historical practices and beliefs, economic conditions, political negotiations, and subjective positions. The culture of racism exists as much in obvious (aggressive, offensive, and demeaning) forms as it does in subtle (ironic, patronizing, and duplicitous) behaviors, as much in prejudices that are embedded in the fabric of society. It is present in lexical habits, in official history, and at institutional levels as much as in the microhistories of daily life. We understand that to change canonical historical narratives that erase or minimize the contributions and even the actual existence of vast sectors of Latin America's diverse population, it is necessary to know its developments, its struggles, and its achievements. We are making reference here to official discourses of political or historiographical nature that have traditionally ignored, erased, or rendered invisible whole sectors of national populations, such as the invisibilization of Mapuche cultures that long took place in Chile, the myths of Argentina and Uruguay as homogeneously white countries of almost exclusively European descent, the erasure of Indigenous Amazonian communities, the reduction of many other autochthonous or Afro-descendant ethnicities to the stature of insignificant minorities, and the negation of the role of Asian descendants in national cultures in several Latin American regions.

We also believe that, to a large extent, emancipation happens at the epistemic level, and decolonial thinking begins with the vindication of marginal subjectivities, the recuperation of silenced voices, and the retrieval of forgotten subjects. Race studies need to rehumanize the arid territories of official national or continental histories written from the perspective of those who have traditionally occupied positions of dominance and exercised their own regimes of truth as if they were universal laws. Race and humanity, race and gender, race and class, race and sexuality—these are only a few of the multiple articulations that need to be explored to offer a more complete and plural history of Latin American societies. The studies that compose this book have benefited immensely from the ample bibliography already existing in the field of Latin American racial history. Without this corpus of archival research, critical elaborations, and theoretical approaches, our work would have been an impossible task.

All chapters of this book, elaborated by international specialists in the field of race studies and cultural theory/criticism, are offered to the reader following a flexible chronological and regional order. The ambitious objective of covering the vast Latin American region from colonial times to the present and, at the same time, including most racial/ethnic aspects of racial developments and ethnic struggles proved particularly challenging, not only because of the immense bibliography on these topics, but also because of the changing nature of social developments and subject positions. We understand that Latin America is a conceptual unit whose multiple realities cannot be reduced through geo-cultural or historical generalizations. For this reason, we opted for a double diachronic and regionalized outlook, destined to analyze the particularism of each area of study, which, in turn, presented differential realities in diverse localities. This, without losing sight of Latin America as a complex and extremely diversified object of study. Our plan was to present the reader with an overarching view of Latin American racial history in which historical perspectives work in combination with localized processes of interracial coexistence, social conflict, resistance, integration, and change. We are confident that with the contributions of our very qualified team of scholars, we managed to do that.

The book opens with two important chapters that cover the initial stages of the process we are following in this book: the so-called discovery of transoceanic territories and the foundations of both the concept of race—as it would be experienced in the colonized world—and the imposition of relations of imperial domination. Amber Brian and Mónica Díaz focus on Christopher

Columbus's writings and incursions in the new lands to analyze the inaugural European gaze over the savage and voluptuous landscapes across the ocean and to reflect on issues of representation and cultural translation as a discursive between European invaders and Native peoples. As Brian and Díaz indicate, "The creation of the *indio* in the early years of the colonization of the Antilles was the first step in racial formation in colonial Latin America." But from the beginning, racial nominations were fluid, and their connotations varied depending on the purposes of the speakers and the locus of enunciation.

In this manner, this chapter establishes as a point of departure the inextricable link between colonialism, the construction of racial discourses, and the praxis of spoliation and cultural submission imposed on autochthonous populations. In "Race and the Baroque," Stephanie Kirk analyzes the development of interracial relations in viceregal societies in the Andean region and in New Spain, emphasizing the struggles that were inherent to heterogeneous populations. Imperial hegemony and marginalization of subaltern sectors characterized colonial society. In an in-between social, economic, and political position, *criollos* continuously negotiated their hybrid descent to gain institutional access both in governmental and ecclesiastical domains. In the sixteenth century, African slaves started to arrive to the New World, and by the times of the baroque era, they had already established their presence, thus exposing the complexity of a highly stratified society. Multiple ethnicities traverse the baroque cities and leave their imprint in social and economic spaces. Each ethnic community had its own traditions, beliefs, and legal status, and on those bases, alliances and hostilities became conspicuous, contributing to the instability of Creole and Peninsular sectors. In addition to the intricacies of city life in times of the baroque, Kirk analyzes the alternative spaces of confraternities and the impact of heterodox practices such as witchcraft, which gave evidence of the existence of other subjectivities and lifestyles. Kirk's study of Indigenous intellectuals is of particular interest, as it shows the parallel development of the subaltern knowledge that flourished in the margins of canonical discourses.

While baroque culture flourished in viceregal societies through the reproduction of political, ecclesiastical, and administrative institutions, and through the development of courtesan relations and the dissemination of European humanistic knowledge, African slavery was a rampant practice in the New World, in Spanish and in Portuguese colonies, since the beginning of the sixteenth century. Miguel Valerio's chapter on this topic provides an array of quantitative information about the processes of transportation and trade of

African slaves, as well as their distribution in America. He also engages in the discussion of ideological positions about race from religious and political fronts. In particular, he refers to Alonso de Sandoval's works on the salvation of Africans, which would be crucial in colonial and postcolonial debates on racialization and slavery. Valerio elaborates on various sources (both biblical and Islamic) that influenced Sandoval's concepts of Blackness and informed his elucubrations on hereditary racial traits, ancestry, and parentage, although the Spanish *letrado* avoided a direct discussion of slavery, a practice that, according to him, was religiously justified. The chapter on slavery illustrates different aspects of the complex identity of Africans in the New World, as well as their resistance against domination and exploitation. Finally, it refers to the abolition of slavery in both continental and Caribbean regions.

Mariselle Meléndez's "Race in Eighteenth-Century Spanish America" offers a key approach to the dissemination of new ideas in colonial societies. This chapter discusses the history of the word *race* in connection to notions such as purity of blood and the caste system. She makes reference to the definition provided by Sebastián de Covarrubias in his *Tesoro de la lengua castellana* (1611), Carl Linnaeus's taxonomies, and other sources to retrieve some of the most received explanations of race (racial traits as the expression of Nature's determinations, the adaptation to climate, the influence of lineage, physicality, and other theories). Meléndez's comprehensive discussion of primary works of the eighteenth century provides very valuable information that allows us to understand in a new light the formation of racial stereotypes and the position of well-known authors such as Francisco Javier Clavigero, Francisco Eugenio Santa Cruz y Espejo, Juan de Velasco, and others in the conceptualization of race and ethnicity. As Meléndez states, "In the eighteenth century, race as a concept and as an idea resisted universal applications in the Americas because race was and remains a social construction prone to subjective interpretations."

When colonial societies advanced toward independence, the political scenario influenced by the ideas of freedom, equality, and republicanism that was found in popular sectors was at the same time, an obstacle and a motivation. On the one hand, illiteracy, multilingualism, and lack of participation in political life made it impossible to disseminate the ideas and the ideals of emancipation among Indigenous populations and communities of African descent. On the other hand, many members of these segments of society who in fact joined the movements against Spanish domination just by enrolling in armies or following masters or local leaders inspired *libertadores* to struggle for a more open and comprehensive model of social and political organization. However,

Creoles were, without a doubt, the central actors in the transition from colonial rule to nation-states. Their leading role, as well as their particular political and economic interests, has been well analyzed by historians, sociologists, and political scientists, although there are still many more aspects of their interracial relations to be explored in different regions of Latin America.

A particular version of Creole cultures and ideologies can be found in the processes of Caribbean creolization and in the aesthetic movements that represent their collective identities. Ariel Camejo offers in this book a comprehensive analysis of *créolité* in the Caribbean islands, where the original population was almost completely annihilated by colonial domination. Camejo's study illuminates the particular ways Creole society emerged in the region from the implementation of imperial patterns of colonization, in which colonies of settlement coexisted with plantation systems. Due to the islands' strategic geo-cultural location, the models of domination were somehow less restrictive than in continental territories. Widespread social heterogeneity did not preclude Creole elites from exercising total control over material and symbolic productions. British, French, and Dutch interests in the exploitation of the lands also contributed to the diversification of Caribbean societies and to the escalation of the slave trade, a situation that would change with the Haitian Revolution (1791–1804).[20] This major historical and political event would trigger a series of social and economic transformations that, as Camejo indicates, strengthened the resistance of Caribbean societies to Western hegemony. The critic analyzes Négritude and *créolité* in the Caribbean region through the works of Kamau Brathwaite, Jean Bernabé, Patrick Chamoiseau, Raphaël Confiant, Edouard Glissant, Frantz Fanon, and others to show the philosophical, aesthetic, and political processes that lead to a redefinition of humanism as an emancipatory platform against imperial domination and in favor of radical "diversalism."

The case of Central America deserves particular attention in the study of race and ethnicity due to the region's rich diversity and the devastating aggression Indigenous communities suffered in many instances of their colonial and independent history. Marta Elena Casaús Arzú and Patricia Arroyo Calderón were assigned two chapters on Central America, given their proven expertise in the region and to ensure the continuity of the critical perspective used for the study of this area. In their first chapter, the authors emphasize the historical intricacies of race struggles between a wide array of racial/ethnic sectors of society: whites, Ladinos, Indigenous, and Afro-descendants. Power relations have always been characterized in Central American countries by extreme socioeconomic inequality and political authoritarianism, conditions that have been, and continue to be, particularly detrimental to subaltern sectors of society. The difficult concurrence of multiple cultures, traditions, and language registers constituted obvious obstacles in the processes of social integration or, at least, pacific coexistence in national territories. The authors of this chapter analyze the instrumentality of race and the role of ethnicity in the configuration of hegemony from colonial times to the formation of nation-states. Strategies such as the racialization of society contributed, without a doubt, to intensifying antagonisms and igniting violence. At the same time, the effects of racism strengthened ethnic identities, thus contributing to the advancement of political resistance. Arroyo and Casaús refer to the ethnic antagonism between Indigenous and Mestizo/Ladino sectors of society. Discourses on the primitivism of Indigenous populations, a rhetoric of idealization of pre-Hispanic history, projects of whitening the nation, and many other discursive strategies go hand in hand with the intensification of highly racialized social struggles. After 1870, and in the first decades of the following century, liberal reforms would gradually introduce changes in collective imaginaries, incorporating the notion of heterogeneous Central American societies. Nevertheless, Indigenous and Afro-descendant populations would continue being the object of ethnic persecution, genocides, and radical marginalization.

The transition from the praxis of colonial compartmentalization to the utopia of national unification took different routes in Latin America depending on many factors, such as the particular history of colonial domination in each region, the colonies' geo-cultural locations, their particular social constitution, and their economic power. Jorge Daniel Vásquez studies questions of national formation, citizenship, and interracial relations, showing the tensions that emerged from the opposing interests of Creole elites and popular communities. Vásquez studies the "construction of the racial Other" vis-à-vis the exclusionary notion and practice of citizenry, showing the importance of interracial alliances in the configuration of national imaginaries, and in the institutional order of state politics. In this way, Vásquez overcomes traditional perspectives restricted to the role of mestizaje as the dominant ideology of the new republics. His chapter focuses on struggles for equality in Haiti, Cuba, and Colombia; the role of Afro-descendant populations; the myth of racial democracy in Cuba; the articulation of Indigenous, mestizo, and peasant populations in Bolivia and Ecuador; and the impact of racial genocides in the Dominican Republic and Guatemala. Vásquez sheds new light on key social and political processes in Latin American history, allowing the reader to perceive interracial relations as a dynamic force whose coordinated efforts produce emancipatory energy, thus resisting the homogenizing and exclusionary forces of national projects.

Ariana Huberman discusses key moments in the history of Jews in Latin America through the lenses of intersectional and social justice pedagogy. The level of interaction between Jews and non-Jews, which has included waves of antisemitism and self-segregation as well as a steady integration into their host countries, informs how Jews experienced being part of Latin American daily life. This is why it is essential to study their history through the lens of intersectionality, as Huberman contends. Awareness of social constructions of race, class, religion, sexual orientation, and gender of Jews in Latin America will provide a more accurate understanding of their history. The concept of foreignness is also central to the Jewish experience in the Diaspora; therefore, the historical perception of the Jew as Other is discussed in tandem with the Christian myth of the wandering Jew. Huberman discusses historical instances in which Jews were targeted, interrupting what otherwise has been a long history of integration into the social, political, and cultural fabric of Latin America.

In the Andean region, race and nationalism also followed a particular direction in the nineteenth century. Iván Fernando Rodrigo-Mendizábal and Marcel Velázquez Castro concentrate on the tensions between race, nationalism, and modernity, particularly in Bolivia, Ecuador, and Peru in the second half of the nineteenth century. "Scientific racism" adds new arguments to the practice of social classification and to the notion that miscegenation was the only possible solution to the "problem" of racial and ethnic heterogeneity. The authors analyze the demographic constitution of Andean societies in the nineteenth century and the differences that characterized each one of them to provide a regional perspective that also considers national differences. The series of rebellions they register gives an idea about the extent and frequency of racial confrontations due to the deep inequalities embedded in Andean societies and the lack of efficient political responses to social upheavals. On the one hand, with the development of Romantic imaginaries associated with racial stereotypes, Indigenous sectors are the object of symbolic appropriations that attach political and social value to ethnicity and race. On the other hand, xenophobia and eugenics go against any kind of idealized figuration of racialized subjects, particularly of those of African descent. An interesting aspect of this issue has to do with linguistic nuances and semantic connotations in the language used to refer to racialized sectors of society. Entering the twentieth century, the "problem of the Indian" would be seen from a very different perspective, as in the works of Manuel González Prada, José Carlos Mariátegui, and a number of writers who represent racial interactions through a critical lens. However, new perceptions are far from being politically and culturally unified; thus, there is a wide range of perspectives for the construction of the racial Other in the Andes and in Latin America in general.

The chapter devoted to Asian diasporas offers a documented and insightful perspective on the contributions of Asian immigrants in Latin America and the Caribbean and the conflictive coexistence they endured in societies that resisted, in variable degrees, the cultural difference they represented. Ignacio López-Calvo analyzes the ways Asians were perceived and depicted in Latin American collective imaginaries to illustrate cultural clashes, alliances, and antagonisms between individuals of Asian descent and other ethnicities. Among the different literary representations of Afro-Asian, interethnic, sociocultural interactions in Latin America and the Caribbean, López-Calvo mentions two recurrent ones: the eroticized image of the *china mulata* and that of the Black ally who expresses sympathy or even marries the Asian protagonist. In the chapter, however, he focuses on the animosity and clashes between people of African and Asian descent as represented in Latin American and Caribbean cultural production. More specifically, he studies instances in which members of the Chinese community were empowered by denying Black accomplishments, which López-Calvo considers an antecedent of the model minority myth in Latin America. In any case, according to the critic, both these alliances and the animosity between Asians and Blacks contributed to challenging the stereotype of the Chinese as an isolated community, as well as the official discourses of mestizaje and *mulataje* that ultimately favored whiteness over Indigenous, Black, or Asian worldviews.

Négritude movements constitute another key chapter in Latin America's history. As a response to centuries of exploitation, marginalization, and racist exclusion from public life, Black movements emerged in Latin America in the 1970s and 1980s, replicating the impulses of civil rights mobilizations in the United States. Carlos Alberto Valderrama maps the rise and fall of Négritude, covering the organizations against racism in Brazil, Colombia, Ecuador, Peru, and Panama, as well as the transnational connections that linked activism in these and other countries. The movements would be the basis for struggles against racism and in favor of ethno-racial citizenships in the following decades. The author emphasizes the heterogeneous nature of the academic, intellectual, and political processes that contributed to the reevaluation and strengthening of Black culture and identities at a continental level. Valderrama shows the connections but also the tensions between this Négritude activism and the African diaspora and antiracist projects. He focuses on racial formations in Latin America, issues of purity of blood, notions of eugenics, and other factors that, as other chapters in this book demonstrate, were common to discrimination of Black, Indigenous, and Asian populations. The ideological and intellectual components of Négritude were, as recalled by Valderrama, Pan-Africanism, socialism, and psychoanalysis. Also, it is important to remember that Negritude is not a homogeneous movement but a diverse configuration of tendencies and positions of political and humanistic value. As Valderrama shows, the movement evolved through decades of debates and definitions of agendas and methodologies in support of social transformation. Valderrama's mapping efficiently summarizes Négritude's ambiguities, contributions, and legacies.

Complementing this chapter, Agustín Lao-Montes works on the genealogies of mestizaje and *mulataje* in what he calls Améfrica Ladina, thus proposing, through a modification of the continent's name, a perspective centered on the struggles of social actors of African and Indigenous descent. He focuses on an analysis of mestizaje as a complex and controversial category, taking back the origins and meanings of the term and making reference to distinctive nuances of the concept (carnal mestizaje, mestizaje of blood, structural mestizaje, good/bad mestizaje, and so on). He also elaborates on the notion of *mulataje*, again going back in time to pursue original meanings of the term in a variety of sociocultural contexts. Caste systems are another nucleus of this chapter. The numerous etymological, semantic, and historical distinctions Lao-Montes displays in his erudite study offer an extensive and sound analysis of the topics at hand, giving evidence of the complex development of the ideas and the terms that articulated, at different times, some of the most heated and politically charged debates in Latin American history.

Christian Elguera undertakes the study of *indigenismo* through a comprehensive review of the main cultural and ideological positions that have articulated, over the centuries, issues of political and symbolic representation of Indigenous sectors in the Andean region and in Mexico. As in the study of other conceptualizations of race included in this book, *indigenismo* includes an ample scope of stereotypes and misrepresentations and is based in the reduction and generalization of cultural, ideological, and physical traits, as if the Indigenous "condition" could be captured in an ahistorical and essentialist construction. Elguera defines *indigenismo* as a form of "cultural translation that perpetuates colonial relationships," reminding the reader that, "in the process of translation, the original Indigenous culture lost its sovereignty." The author discusses multiple opinions on the notion of *indigenismo* as a rhetorical and political dispositive used to control differences and reinforce the idea of the *mestizo* nation. Elguera's perspective is well documented and innovative, and it constitutes a serious attempt to insufflate new energy to the connotative field of *indigenista* studies by reading Andean struggles from a point of view that leaves behind Romantic and essentialist interpretations of the Indian in favor of a materialist reading of Indigenous agency. He also provides an interpretation of the identity politics in the Andes under different political rulings, analyzing indigenist translation vis-à-vis indigenous self-translation and emphasizing the need to "reinforce the empowerment of Indigenous voices."

The importance of Brazil in the study of Latin American race and ethnicity—and of racial issues around the world—should not be minimized. In the chapter "Democratic Imaginaries," on Brazil, Tracy Devine Guzmán offers a solid analysis of the colonial legacies that projected a history of racial discrimination in modern times regarding both Indigenous and Afro-descendant populations. In tracing this ambiguous and constantly shifting demographic scenario from its colonial roots to the neocolonial present, Guzmán's essay examines the interwoven social, cultural, and political processes through which Brazil's "white" minority has come to control not only the country's power structures but also its preferred modes of imagining itself—collectively appropriating Black, "brown," and Indigenous cultural products (and sometimes imagery) as markedly Brazilian while at the same time relegating those sectors of the population to social invisibility or political irrelevance. In light of this historical "inclusion by exclusion" (Agamben), she argues that the historical and present-day mobilization of Indigenous and Afro-descendant Brazilians for social justice represents a long-standing struggle for political and social representation as reflected in national census data. At the same time, Guzmán proposes that those struggles also constitute a fundamental demand for visibilization as racialized and heterogeneous subjects, in the nation's homogenizing, racist, racially "democratic" national imaginary.

As a continuation of the previous chapter on Central America, "Race Relations in Contemporary Central America" covers the year 1940 until today, with particular emphasis on the ways Native populations have been able to preserve and rebuild strong ethnic identities in the region. Patricia Arroyo Calderón and Marta Elena Casaús Arzú explain that, despite the fact that different processes of state violence disproportionally affected (and still affect) the Indigenous peoples of the isthmus, it is important instead to recognize instances of resistance, as well as the capacity of communities to imagine alternative futures and to organize and mobilize in that direction. The chapter is divided into two sections. The first concentrates on the decades from the 1940s until the 1980s, particularly the political and economic reforms—such as those advanced by the governments of Juan José Arévalo and Jacobo Árbenz (1944–1954) in Guatemala—that were frustrated by the increased intervention of the United States in the internal affairs of Central American nations. This period was also characterized by high levels of social and political conflict, the emergence of strong popular and revolutionary movements, and the unleashing of extreme forms of state violence against Indigenous people. The second section examines the period initiated by the "democratic transitions" of the 1990s, when the open conflicts that had ravaged the isthmus during previous decades (the Sandinista Revolution and the Contra War in Nicaragua, the civil wars in El Salvador and Guatemala) mutated into new types of low-intensity violence disseminated across the Central American social fabric. The authors study the "democratic transitions" in which collective rights were recognized and Indigenous communities expanded their representation in the public sphere. They also refer to the challenges presented by extractivism and the criminalization of Indigenous activists.

Alongside elaborations on Négritude (as well as on mestizaje, *indigenismo*, *criollismo*, and the like), the concept of *blanquitud*, *blanquitude*, or *branquedade*, equivalent to the English meaning of *whiteness*, emerged by the end of the eighteenth century as an approach to the racial paradigm and referred to white individuals of European origin and lineage. As Ruth Hill explains in her study of the genealogies of the term, *whiteness* was considered, in all uses, a synonym for cultural, economic, and political power. Inspired by the writings and interventions of the Black American writer James Baldwin (1924–1987), critical race theorists analyzed whiteness as an ideological concept aimed at the critique of social hierarchies and applicable to the domains of economics, law, education, and more.[21] The notion of *blanquitud*, or whiteness, has also made its way into Latin American studies on race (although not via critical race theory), particularly through the analysis of Aníbal Quijano and Bolívar Echeverría, as part of the critique of coloniality and modernity, respectively.[22] The concept of *blanquitud* has also been key for the articulation and affirmation of Négritude and, in general, of Blacks' resistance to white supremacy. While Bolívar Echeverría's approach to the topic connects whiteness to the critique of capitalism and modernity, Quijano's reflections emerge from his general study of racial discrimination as a distinctive trait of colonial domination. Hill analyzes the impact of critical race theory in Brazil, as well as the concepts of *blanqueamiento*, *branqueamento*, and *blanchiment*, or whitening. Her chapter provides readers with the historical density needed to understand the development of the cultural and ideological nuances of *blanquitud* and its relevance for the study of racial struggles in Latin America from colonial times to the present.

In the chapter titled "Racializing Arabs in Latin America," Bahia Munem focuses on Arabs' most significant migratory waves to the Latin American region: in the late nineteenth and early twentieth century, in the midtwentieth century, and from the beginning of the 1970s on. The critic refers to the composition of these diasporic movements and to the processes of racialization of Arabs (sometimes referred to as *sirio-libaneses* or *turcos*) in the countries where they established new residency. Munem pays particular attention to the intersectional categories of gender, labor, religion, and nation building in countries such as Argentina, Mexico, Columbia, Honduras, and Brazil. The examination of the political and economic ascendency of Arab immigrants in specific contexts, viewed through the prism of these categories, challenges Orientalist narratives about this population. It parses specific ethnicities nested into the classification of *sirio-libanés* and the integration challenges many individuals had to endure in their new destinations.

In the chapter devoted to the Southern Cone, Gonzalo Aguiar analyzes major events in the history of displacements, resistance, and cultural and social reappropriations brought about by Indigenous and Afro-descendant populations in Argentina, Uruguay, Paraguay, and Chile. The goal of this study is to identify the main tendencies of racial interactions in the region from a sociohistorical standpoint, as well as to explain how rewriting hegemonic discourses is at the center of the political and cultural agenda of these historically relegated communities. In some cases, both Indigenous and Afro-descendants have developed strategies to counter—and sometimes dismantle—racialized spaces where ideologies of whiteness had for centuries dominated national cultures. The chapter starts in the colonial period and covers main racial issues in the nineteenth century, focusing on the contemporary efforts of ethnoracial communities to break away from discrimination and exclusion through struggles for recognition and social justice.

In the final chapter of this book, Bárbara Abadía-Rexach approaches the distinction and commonalities in the concepts of Chicano/as, Hispanics, and Latinos (Latinx) to extend the reflections of this book also to racial/ethnic configurations related to Latin American cultures flourishing in the United States as the result of migratory movements, including the search for labor markets, as well as exiles and diasporas. Closely related to the topic of voyage and de- or reterritorialization, this chapter implicitly connects to the idea of nomad subjectivities developed by Linda Martin-Alcoff. As part of the discussion of the political implications of social classification and the ways academia and public opinion conceptualize this issue, Abadía-Rexach focuses on racism "as a system of oppression and white privilege that has normalized violence and racial harassment." Although this working definition functions in most contexts, it does not seem to cover cases in which racism is also practiced at other levels of stratified societies (for instance, between Indigenous sectors toward Blacks). In any case, the goal of this study is to illuminate the ways race is seen as a political/ideological dispositive for social (self)recognition, a process that is implemented in different manners in Latin America, depending on the region, the social sector and the historical period in which race is being scrutinized. As the author indicates, the difference between race and ethnicity is not evident to members of the general public, who treat these notions as interchangeable categories. The core of this chapter has to do with the history of emigrants coming to the United States from Mexico, Central America, Puerto Rico, the Dominican Republic, and other nations of Hispanic and Brazilian origin, and the denominations they received in the process of economic, social, and political integration. The critic analyzes social movements, struggles for civil rights, and official attempts to homogenize the great variety of nationalities and ethnicities that have been converging for centuries in the United States. These processes entail a continuous reconfiguration of identities and alterities, usually affected by different forms and degrees of racism, xenophobia, and stereotyping of the Other.

The readers of this book will be immersed in the intricate processes and strategies implemented by those in power in colonial and contemporary times in order to achieve, consolidate, and perpetuate economic, political, and social domination. They will see the notions of race and ethnicity utilized, redefined, manipulated, and negotiated innumerable times, to the point that they became a shadow, a ghostly presence, and a mirage but also an unavoidable reality for the victims of discrimination. It will not be difficult to recognize in today's (still) racialized social scenarios the continuities of power relations imposed centuries ago against the Other in order to subjugate bodies and souls, profit from cheap labor, abuse the vulnerability of subaltern positions, and dominate emotions and desires. The reader will also corroborate the perseverance of oppressed sectors of society in their resistance to despotism and marginalization, to genocides, exclusion, and erasure of vernacular cultures. In this sense, this book should be not only a learning tool but also an inspiration in the struggle for justice, equality, and decolonization.

All contributors to this book worked under the difficult conditions imposed by pandemic scenarios and cooperated in the advancement of this project with dedication and professionalism. The editors are indebted to them and grateful for their scholarly efforts, friendship, and intellectual acumen. We wish to thank Dr. Anna Valerio, who helped copyedit the volume, and Yamile Ferreira, who helped us format the notes and bibliography.

NOTES

1. On the debate on the applicability of the term *race* to pre-1800 reality, see, e.g. Ruth Hill, *Hierarchy, Commerce and Fraud in Bourbon Spanish America: A Postal Inspector's Exposé* (Nashville, TN: Vanderbilt University Press, 2005), 197-238; Sinclair Thomson, "Was There Race in Colonial Latin America? Identifying Selves and Others in the Insurgent Andes," in *Histories of Race and Racism: The Andes and Mesoamerica from Colonial Times to the Present*, ed. Laura Gotkowitz (Durham, NC: Duke University Press, 2012), 72-91.
2. Stephen Cornell and Douglas Hatmann, *Ethnicity and Race: Making Identities in a Changing World* (Thousand Oaks, CA: Pine Forge Press. 1998), 24.
3. For an introductory discussion of these terms, see Michael James and Adam Burgos, "Race," particularly the section "Race and Ethnicity," in *The Stanford Encyclopedia of Philosophy*, ed. Edward N. Zalta and Uri Nodelman, Summer 2023), https://plato.stanford.edu/archives/sum2023/entries/race/.
4. Cornell and Hartmann, *Ethnicity and Race*, 19. In this respect, see José Antonio Mazzotti's discussion of race and ethnicity in Peru, particularly in connection with *criollismo*: "Race, Ethnicity and Nationhood in the Formation of *Criollismo* in Spanish America," in *The Routledge Hispanic Studies Companion to Colonial Latin America and the Caribbean (1492-1898)*, ed. Yolanda Martínez San Miguel and Santa Arias (New York: Routledge, 2020), 85-98.
5. Richard Graham, "Introduction," in *The Idea of Race in Latin America, 1870-1940*, ed. Richard Graham (Austin: University of Texas Press, 1990), 2.
6. On this topic, see, e.g., Nicholas Smith, who offers a thorough overview of these debates on the Aristotelian positions: "Aristotle's Theory of Natural Slavery," *Phronesis* 37, no. 2 (1983): 109-122. Another take on this topic is developed by Malcolm Heath, "Aristotle on Natural Slavery," *Phronesis* 53, no. 3 (2008): 243-270.
7. See Graham, *The Idea of Race*. Some studies on race and ethnicity in particular regions are José Vasconcelos, *La raza cósmica* (1925; rpt., Madrid: Verbum, 2021); Mervyn C. Alleyne, *Construction and Representation of Race and Ethnicity in the Caribbean and the World* (Kingston: University of the West Indies, 2002); Jorge Daniel Vásquez, *Transforming Ethnicity: Youth and Migration in the Southern Ecuadorian Andes*, Migration, Diasporas and Citizenship (Cham, Switzerland: Palgrave Macmillan, 2023); Luis Villoro, *Los grandes momentos del indigenismo en México* (1950; rpt., Mexico City: Fondo de Cultura Económica, 2022); George Reid

Andrews, *Afro-Latin America, 1800–2000* (Oxford: Oxford University Press, 2002); Niyi Afolabi, *Identities in Flux: Race, Migration, and Citizenship in Brazil* (Albany: SUNY Press, 2021).
8. Peter Wade analyzes the connections between liberal ideology, nation formation and racism in "Liberalismo, raza y ciudadanía en Latinoamérica," in *Debates sobre ciudadanía y políticas raciales en las Américas Negras*, ed. Claudia Mosquera Rosero-Labbé, Agustín Laó-Montes, and César Rodríguez Garavito (Bogotá: Universidad Nacional de Colombia, 2010), 467–486.
9. See David M. Goldenberg, *The Curse of Ham: Race and Slavery in Early Judaism, Christianity, and Islam* (Princeton, NJ: Princeton University Press, 2004).
10. Aníbal Quijano, "Coloniality of Power, Eurocentrism and Latin America," *Nepantla: Views from South* 1, no. 3 (2000), 535. On the connections between race and labor markets, see Charles W. Bergquist, *Labor in Latin America: Comparative Essays on Chile, Argentina, Venezuela, and Colombia* (Stanford, CA: Stanford University Press, 1986); and Quijano, "El trabajo," *Argumentos* 26, no. 72 (2013): 145–163.
11. Quijano, "Coloniality of Power," 536. On the importance of the connections between labor and race, see also Quijano, "El trabajo,"
12. Simón Bolívar, *El Libertador: Writings of Simón Bolívar*, ed. David Bushnell, trans. Fred Fronoff (New York: Oxford University Press, 2003), 38–39.
13. Wade, "Rethinking 'Mestizaje': Ideology and Lived Experience," *Journal of Latin American Studies* 37, no. 2 (2005): 239.
14. Wade, "Rethinking 'Mestizaje,'" 240. Wade refers to Stutzman's definition of mestizaje as an "'all-inclusive ideology of exclusion,' a system of ideas that appeared to include everyone as a potential mestizo, but actually excluded black and indigenous people," a definition that recognizes mestizaje as political strategy created as an expression of power relations, and as an attempt to control social dynamics.
15. Wade, "Rethinking 'Mestizaje.'"
16. On the "whitening ideal," see Thomas E. Skidmore, *Black into White: Race and Nationality in Brazilian Thought* (Durham, NC: Duke University Press, 1992), 200–204, 207. On whiteness, see the reader edited by Neil Hill, as well as Jensen. These books, as well as others published on the topic of whiteness, provide, for the most part, critical and theoretical elaborations useful for comparative approaches to the ways this notion has been used in different geo-cultural contexts.
17. *Casa grande e senzala* was first published in English 1933 under the title *The Masters and the Slaves*. It is the first of three volumes. The other two are *The Mansions and the Shanties: The Making of Modern Brazil* (1938) and *Order and Progress: Brazil from Monarchy to Republic* (1957). Gilberto Freyre's work is considered as important and influential as Fernando Ortiz's *Contrapunteo cubano del tabaco y el azúcar* (1940). On Gilberto Freyre, see Joshua Lund and Malcolm McNee, eds., *Gilberto Freyre e os estudos latino-americanos* (Pittsburgh, PA: IILI, 2006).
18. See Aimé Césaire, *Discourse on Colonialism* (New York: Monthly Review Press, 2001); Frantz Fanon, *Black Skin, White Masks* (New York: Grove Press, 1967); Frantz Fanon, *A Dying Colonialism* (New York: Grove Press, 1965); Frantz Fanon, *The Wretched of the Earth* (New York, Grove Press, 2005); Léopold S. Senghor, *Liberté I, Négritude et humanisme* (Paris: Seuil, 1964), Léopold S. Senghor, *Liberté II, Nation et voie africaine du socialisme* (Paris: Seuil, 1971); Léopold S. Senghor, *Liberté III, le dialogue des cultures* (Paris: Seuil, 1933). On the Négritude movement, see Reiland Rabaka, *The Negritude Movement: W. E. B. Du Bois, Leon Damas, Aimé Césaire, Léopold Senghor, Frantz Fanon, and the Evolution of an Insurgent Idea* (New York: Lexington Books, 2016).

19. Robert Bernasconi and Tommy L. Lott, *The Idea of Race* (Indianapolis: Hackett Publishing Co., 2000), vii.
20. On Haiti, see Tardeuz Lepkovski, *Haití*, 2 vols. (Havana: Casa de las Américas, 1969); Jean Casimir, *The Haitians: A Decolonial History*, trans. Laurent Dubois (Chapel Hill: University of North Carolina Press, 2020).
21. On James Baldwin's contributions to the visibility and study of whiteness, and to the resistance to it, see his *Collected Essays: Notes of a Native Son, Nobody Knows My Name, The Fire Next Time, No Name in the Street, The Devil Finds Work, Other Essays*, ed. Toni Morrison (New York: Library of America, 1998).
22. As Hill indicates, critical race theory has not been adopted, for the most part, in Latin American studies of race. This is probably due to the origins of this approach in US culture and academia, and its direct connections to the history of racial struggles in this country.

BIBLIOGRAPHY

Afolabi, Niyi. *Identities in Flux: Race, Migration, and Citizenship in Brazil*. Albany: SUNY Press, 2021.

Alleyne, Mervyn C. *Construction and Representation of Race and Ethnicity in the Caribbean and the World*. Kingston: University of the West Indies, 2002.

Andrews, George Reid. *Afro-Latin America, 1800–2000*. Oxford: Oxford University Press, 2002.

Appelbaum, Nancy P., Anne S. Macpherson, and Karin Alejandra Rosemblatt, eds. *Race and Nation in Modern Latin America*. Chapel Hill: University of North Carolina Press, 2003.

Baldwin, James. *Collected Essays: Notes of a Native Son, Nobody Knows My Name, The Fire Next Time, No Name in the Street, The Devil Finds Work, Other Essays*. Edited by Toni Morrison. New York: Library of America, 1998.

Bergquist, Charles W. *Labor in Latin America: Comparative Essays on Chile, Argentina, Venezuela, and Colombia*. Stanford, CA: Stanford University Press, 1986.

Bernasconi, Robert, and Tommy L. Lott, eds. *The Idea of Race*. Indianapolis: Hackett Publishing, 2000.

Bolívar, Simón. *El Libertador: Writings of Simón Bolívar*. Edited by David Bushnell. Translated by Fred Fronoff. New York: Oxford University Press, 2003.

Casimir, Jean. *The Haitians: A Decolonial History*. Translated by Laurent Dubois. Chapel Hill: University of North Carolina Press, 2020.

Césaire, Aimé. *Discourse on Colonialism*. New York: Monthly Review Press, 2001.

Cornell, Stephen, and Douglas Hatmann. *Ethnicity and Race: Making Identities in a Changing World*. Thousand Oaks, CA: Pine Forge Press. 1998

Fanon, Frantz. *Black Skin, White Masks*. New York: Grove Press, 1967.

———. *A Dying Colonialism*. New York: Grove Press, 1965.

———. *The Wretched of the Earth*. New York: Grove Press, 2005.

Goldenberg, David M. *The Curse of Ham: Race and Slavery in Early Judaism, Christianity, and Islam*. Princeton, NJ: Princeton University Press, 2004.

Graham, Richard, ed. *The Idea of Race in Latin America, 1870–1940*. Austin: University of Texas Press, 1990.

Heath, Malcolm. "Aristotle on Natural Slavery." *Phronesis* 53, no. 3 (2008): 243–270.

Hill, Michael. *Whiteness: A Critical Reader*. New York: New York University Press, 1997.

Hill, Ruth. *Hierarchy, Commerce and Fraud in Bourbon Spanish America: A Postal Inspector's Exposé*. Nashville, TN: Vanderbilt University Press, 2005.

James, Michael, and Adam Burgos. "Race." In *The Stanford Encyclopedia of Philosophy*, edited by Edward N. Zalta and Uri Nodelman. https://plato.stanford.edu/archives/sum2023/entries/race/.

Jensen, Robert. *The Heart of Whiteness: Confronting Race, Racism, and White Privilege*. San Francisco: City Lights, 2005

Lepkovski, Tardeuz. *Haití*. 2 vols. Havana: Casa de las Américas, 1969.

Lund, Joshua, and Malcolm McNee, eds. *Gilberto Freyre e os estudos latino-americanos*. Pittsburgh, PA: IILI, 2006.

Mazzotti, José Antonio. "Race, Ethnicity and Nationhood in the Formation of *Criollismo* in Spanish America." In *The Routledge Hispanic Studies Companion to Colonial Latin America and the Caribbean (1492–1898)*, edited by Yolanda Martínez San Miguel and Santa Arias. New York: Routledge, 2020.

Ortiz, Fernando. *Contrapunteo cubano del tabaco y el azúcar*. Madrid: Cátedra, 2002.

Quijano, Aníbal. "Coloniality of Power, Eurocentrism and Latin America." *Nepantla: Views from South* 1, no. 3 (2000): 533–580.

———. "El trabajo." *Argumentos* 26, no. 72 (2013): 145–163.

Rabaka, Reiland. *The Negritude Movement: W. E. B. Du Bois, Leon Damas, Aime Cesaire, Leopold Senghor, Frantz Fanon, and the Evolution of an Insurgent Idea*. New York: Lexington Books, 2016.

Senghor, Léopold. *Liberté I: Négritude et humanisme*. Paris: Seuil, 1964.

———. *Liberté II: Nation et voie africaine du socialisme*. Paris: Seuil, 1971.

———. *Liberté V: Le dialogue des cultures*. Paris: Seuil, 1933.

Smith, Nicholas. "Aristotle's Theory of Natural Slavery." *Phronesis* 37, no. 2 (1983): 109–122.

Thomson, Sinclair. "Was There Race in Colonial Latin America? Identifying Selves and Others in the Insurgent Andes." In *Histories of Race and Racism: The Andes and Mesoamerica from Colonial Times to the Present*, edited by Laura Gotkowitz, 72–91. Durham, NC: Duke University Press, 2012.

Vasconcelos, José. *La raza cósmica*. Madrid: Verbum, 2021.

Vásquez, Jorge Daniel. *Transforming Ethnicity: Youth and Migration in the Southern Ecuadorian Andes (Migration, Diasporas and Citizenship)*. Cham, Switzerland: Palgrave Macmillan, 2023.

Villoro, Luis. *Los grandes momentos del indigenismo en México*. Mexico City: Fondo de Cultura Económica, 2022.

Wade, Peter. "Liberalismo, raza y ciudadanía en Latinoamérica." In *Debates sobre ciudadanía y políticas raciales en las Américas Negras*, edited by Claudia Mosquera Rosero-Labbé, Agustín Laó-Montes, and César Rodríguez Garavito, 467–486. Bogotá: Universidad Nacional de Colombia, 2010.

———. *Race and Ethnicity in Latin America: How the East India Company Shaped the Modern Multinational*. New York: Pluto Press, 1997.

———. "Rethinking 'Mestizaje': Ideology and Lived Experience," *Journal of Latin American Studies* 37, no. 2 (2005): 239–257.

PART I

THE RACIAL OTHER IN COLONIAL TIMES

CHAPTER I

Foundations of Race and Colonialism in Latin America

AMBER BRIAN AND MÓNICA DÍAZ

> *Son de la color de los canarios, ni negros ni blancos* [They are the color of the Canary Islanders, neither black nor white].
>
> COLUMBUS, October 12, 1492[1]

In the early hours of the twelfth of October 1492, after departing from the Canary Island of La Gomera at the beginning of September and spending thirty-three days crossing the Atlantic, Christopher Columbus set foot on the island of Guanahaní. As reported in his *Diario*, with the royal flag of the Catholic Monarchs in hand, Columbus took in the landscape and inhabitants of the island, declaring the lands fertile and the people young and well disposed to be good servants and good Christians. Columbus's 1492 voyage to what he mistook for Asia opened the door to a centuries-long process of conquest and colonization of lands and peoples of the Western Hemisphere by the kingdoms of the Iberian Peninsula. The Genoese navigator's impressions of the people he encountered were foundational to the emergence of a racialized discourse around the Natives he named *indios*, which from its inception was coupled with the discourse on blackness from the centuries-long practice of African slavery already in place in the Iberian Peninsula. This chapter takes up the importance of race at the outset of European colonization of the lands Columbus named "the Indias," later named "America" by the cartographer Martin Waldseemüller. From his first day on land, Columbus's assessment of the people he called *indios* focused on physical attributes, as he painted a picture of the hair, body type, and skin color of the Natives, who he found to be "the color of the Canary Islanders, neither black nor white." Significantly, as this passage indicates, these descriptions were triangulated against known social groups, and the subordinated category of *indio* emerged in relation to prior Iberian colonial projects in the Atlantic, including most immediately the Canary Islands as well as sub-Saharan Africa. In many ways, 1492 represents a continuation of already-established processes of racialization and discourses of race, which became foundational to the emergent colonial social and administrative structures.

The supercategory *indio* (as it is described by Schwartz and Salomon) is a term that sheds little light on the history, cultures, and pre-1492 identities of the thousands of distinct ethnic and linguistic groups it boldly enfolds into its reach.[2] In its origin, it tells us much more about the Europeans and their notions of hierarchies and political structures than it does of the Native inhabitants of the Western Hemisphere. The scholar of Nahuatl Frances Karttunen has said quite frankly: "'Indian' is a word I would like to avoid. The name and idea were both mistakes imposed on the diverse peoples of two immense continents. But it forces itself upon us, because Spanish sources use the word *indios* constantly."[3] With time, those diverse Native peoples utilized this category, as it became inflected in juridical and religious contexts, as a means to assert their own projects and initiatives. As Stuart Hall has succinctly stated about identity as a category, it is "not an essentialist, but a strategic and positional one." Furthermore, "because identities are constructed within, not outside discourse, we need to understand them as produced in specific historical and institutional sites within specific discursive formations and practices, by specific enunciative strategies. Moreover, they emerge within the play of specific modalities of power, and thus are more the product of the marking of difference and exclusion, than they are the sign of an identical, naturally constituted unity—an 'identity' in its traditional meaning (that is, an all-inclusive sameness, seamless, without internal differentiation)."[4] Hall's emphasis on the specificity of identities as products of historical and institutional sites tied to discursive formations is illuminating for the study of early racialized identities that were formed in the crucible of colonialism, a context overdetermined by modalities of power. *Indio* as a category is constituted not by nature but through Columbus's mistaken understanding of geography, and it remained salient as a category through the exertion of colonial administrative power, which was inherently premised on marking and hierarchizing difference and exclusion.

Under Spanish imperial rule, racialized social categories were used as instruments of colonial domination, but they also provided means of resistance and self-determination by *indios* and other named groups, including *negros*, *chinos*, and *castas* such as *mestizos* and *mulatos*. As Ann Laura Stoler has suggested, racial discourses can affirm and contest state power and should be understood as providing a "'dense transfer point'—the site and idiom—in which relations of power are defended and fought."[5] Whereas the perspectives of Natives on their early experiences with colonization and enslavement in the Antilles are registered only in refracted form in the writings of Europeans, on the mainland, we have a rich array of pictorial and alphabetic materials authored by Natives that document their diverse experiences.[6] We find a striking example of this in the works of the Andean mestizo humanist and historian Inca Garcilaso de la Vega, who assertively assumed his identity as *indio* throughout his writings as a source of authority.[7] When addressing the broad issue of the construction of racial categories in the early colonial period, these sources remind us that racialization did not go unanswered by those subjected to colonial labels and hierarchies.

To understand the origins and impacts of racial difference in Latin America, it is necessary to explore the relevant social and political nodes that undergird the strategies and reference points of identification. The colonial administrative structures that emerged in the Western Hemisphere after 1492 were informed by Hispanic and Lusophone political, cultural, and economic practices developed and pursued in Europe and Africa. The more-than-seven-hundred-year Reconquista of Muslim-occupied regions of Hispano-Catholic Iberia, culminating in the 1492 retaking of Granada by the Catholic Monarchs Isabel and Fernando, laid the ground for the religiously inflected Spanish conquest of the Western Hemisphere. From the middle of the fifteenth century, Portugal's expertise in navigation, coupled with their active involvement in the African slave trade, established slavery as an odious cornerstone to Iberian imperial expansion. Additionally, for Columbus, the ongoing Castilian conquest of the Canary Islands was a model for the conquest of the islands of the Caribbean, including the enslavement of subjugated populations. The structures of power that emerged as settler colonialism took hold in Brazil and the Spanish viceroyalties were indebted to these earlier patterns of empire building, and the ways individuals and groups were marked and differentiated were intrinsically enmeshed in the burgeoning colonial state. This chapter addresses these early patterns of colonialism through the lens of race by surveying the incipient social categories and foundational inequalities that emerged in the decades after 1492 yet were informed by prior events and have been studied by historians, anthropologists, and literary scholars.

1492 and the Outlines of Race

Race is a slippery concept, and for however much, in the words of Henry Louis Gates Jr., it "pretends to be an objective term of classification," it has become, as Gates so incisively stated, "a trope of ultimate, irreducible difference between cultures, linguistic groups, or adherents of specific belief systems which—more often than not—also have fundamentally opposed economic interests. Race is the ultimate trope of difference because it is so very arbitrary in its application."[8] In our approach to the discussion of race in the first century of European occupation of the lands of the Western Hemisphere, we follow this treatment of race, including the more recent reaffirmation of Gates's basic framework offered by Geraldine Heng: "Race is a structural relationship for the articulation and management of human differences, rather than substantive content."[9] Heng's discussion and application of the study of race is especially useful in that she, as a medievalist by training and practice, emphatically demonstrates the relevance of a critical discussion of race to the premodern period. Gates's project of identifying race as a "trope of difference" and Heng's careful invocation of the study of race in the medieval period are illuminating stances for understanding race in the context of European imperial expansion in the late fifteenth and sixteenth centuries.

Columbus's first voyage has long been viewed as a point of rupture, signaling a new set of social and political relations that emerged from the European colonization of the lands and peoples of the New World. As Stuart Hall has noted in his essays on race, ethnicity, and nation, *The Fateful Triangle*, "racial discourses constitute one of the great, persistent classificatory systems of human culture," and "racial classification systems themselves have a history, and their modern history seems to emerge where the peoples of Europe first encounter, and have to make sense of, the peoples and cultures of the New World."[10] In studies by Latin American scholars such as Aníbal Quijano, 1492 is also viewed as a watershed year. Throughout Quijano's writings, the influential sociologist and theorist of coloniality links race to the events surrounding the European wars of conquest and acts of colonization, beginning with Columbus's landing in the Bahamas. He opens his essay "Questioning

'Race'" with the proposition that the "idea of 'race' is surely the most efficient instrument of social domination produced in the last 500 years."[11] He goes on to affirm that "the idea of 'race' was born with 'America'; it originally referred to the differences between 'Indians' and their conquerors (principally Castilian)."[12] Of course, later, it also implied the presence of enslaved people brought from Africa. Hall and Quijano emphasize the complementary roles of racialized discourses and colonialism, where, in turn, one process magnified the other.

The study of connections between 1492 and racialized social categories is evident in early and foundational historical studies, such as Magnus Mörner's *Race Mixture in the History of Latin America* (1967). Mörner acknowledged that though the prevalent, twentieth-century understanding of race was informed by phenotypic categories, which he designated as "Mongoloids, Caucasoids, and Negroids," "no basic biological differences have yet been found among contemporary races, all of which represent a parallel evolution from man's humble beginnings."[13] His focus was race mixture, or miscegenation, and his central proposition was that the European colonial projects in the Western Hemisphere beginning in 1492 "made possible large-scale miscegenation between geographically distant human groups."[14] Mörner's project was to make sense of categories of identity as part of processes of social stratification in colonial Latin America.

In her efforts to underline the importance of studying race in premodern periods, Geraldine Heng has explicitly recognized that we inevitably read the past through the prism of our own time and the term *race* performs important work as it "continues to bear witness to important strategic, epistemological, and political commitments," while "not to use the term race would be to sustain the reproduction of a certain kind of past, while keeping the door shut to tools, analyses, and resources that can name the past differently."[15] In Mörner's case, he openly states that his own historical moment left indelible marks on his research. Born in Sweden in 1924, Mörner came of age during World War II and worked as a professional historian at institutions in Europe and the United States. He wrote *Race Mixture* in a decade marked by social tumult and activism while on faculty at Queens College, City University of New York, and during visiting professorships at Cornell University and El Colegio de México. He witnessed the impact of racism on societies across the globe as a set of violent prejudices used to justify the Holocaust, Apartheid, and segregation in the United States.[16] Quijano also cites the horrors of twentieth-century racism in Europe and South Africa as part of the context of his probing study of "racist social relations" in Latin America.[17] Being attentive to race in our present moment enhances our ability to notice relevant patterns in the past. The reverse, we posit, also holds true: observing the emergence of race as an organizing concept in the early decades of Iberian occupation of the Western Hemisphere allows us to notice the ways in which racial discourses were foundational to the social, political, and economic processes embedded in colonialism and its many legacies.

To point at these legacies is not to establish a teleology. Rather, as Ann Laura Stoler has proposed, "race as a concept performs in a mobile field. It animates vacillating discourses with dynamic motility. Racial lexicons accumulate recursively producing new racial truths as they requisition and reassemble old ones."[18] These racial lexicons accumulated after Columbus's landing in 1492, just as they had accumulated in the preceding historical period. Stoler's insights prompt us to probe the racial lexicons that served as models and precedents for European colonizers. When Columbus landed, he, as the original narrator of the colonial project, was not a tabula rasa. In fact, he came to that experience with a very developed sense of the world as he and the other men in his company were formed in a context defined by, among other events, Atlantic voyages to Africa and the islands found off its shores for the purposes of trading in goods and human beings. At times, 1492 has become fetishized as the point of origin for European expansion—and with that, the racialized hierarchization of multiple social and linguistic groups, including Native inhabitants of the Western Hemisphere, forced migrants from Africa, travelers and enslaved people from Asia, Europeans (born in Europe and in the New World), as well as the offspring of men and women who belonged to more than one of these groups. Yet the ways these groups of individuals were identified, categorized, controlled by, or exercised autonomy within the structures of governance and discourse were informed by patterns of social organization present on the Iberian Peninsula well before 1492.

Before 1492: Precedents for Racialized Social Categories

Four interrelated and momentous events defined 1492 on the Iberian Peninsula: Antonio de Nebrija's publication of the *Gramática de la lengua castellana*; the end of the Reconquista with the conquest of Granada by the Catholic Monarchs Fernando and Isabel; the expulsion of the Jews; and Columbus's landing on islands in the Antilles. Individually and collectively, these events point to imperial impulses and the emergence of a political union built around linguistic and religious homogeneity after a period of more than seven hundred years defined by linguistic and religious heterogeneity. If we recognize Gates's insight that race is the "ultimate trope of difference," and Heng's assertion that race is a means for "the articulation and management of human differences," the growing tendency in the fifteenth century toward recognizing and purging linguistic, religious, and cultural difference from the dominant Iberian kingdoms provided fertile ground for social structures built around racialized social categories.[19]

Writing in 1998, the literary scholar George Mariscal expressed concern that US Hispanists, unlike their peers in English departments, were not engaging in "discussions of early modern racial formations."[20] In the article, Mariscal points out that Michael Omi and Howard Winant's influential *Racial Formation in the United States*, originally published in 1986 and updated in a third edition in 2014, provides a productive conceptual and theoretical framework, especially in their discussion of "racial formation," which he summarizes as "'a process of historically situated projects in which human bodies and social structures are represented and organized.'"[21] However, Mariscal contests their proposal that race as a modern concept does not emerge until 1492.[22] Mariscal points out that we find examples fitting their description of racial formations in fifteenth-century Spain, "at least as early as 1449 when the city of Toledo excluded under penalty of death all *conversos* from public office and certainly no later than 1480 when Rome granted the Spanish monarchs their own inquisitorial powers."[23] Furthermore, Portugal's role in the African slave trade is "crucial to an understanding of early modern European racist discourse," as is the treatment of Gypsies, who were disciplined in spite of their professed Catholicism and because of their "color, physiognomy, private language, and moral laxitude (that is, racial and ethnic difference)."[24] Mariscal sees a clear progression from the racialized categories and associated social structures that emerged in the Iberian context in the fifteenth century through overseas expansion in the sixteenth century and beyond. He concludes by noting that if the colonization of the New World had a decisive impact on racial projects, "it can be explained less by the encounter with previously unknown peoples than by the influx of wealth that began the slow reconfiguration of traditional European class structures."[25] For Mariscal, 1492 magnified already existent patterns of racialized social organization.

Still cited as a significant intervention on the topic, published in 1997 in the special issue "Constructing Race" of the *William and Mary Quarterly*, James

Sweet's article "The Iberian Roots of American Racist Thought" sought to dispel the argument that racism was not present in Iberia before 1492. Sweet established an important line of inquiry into the connections between the "racism that came to characterize American slavery" and "cultural and religious attitudes in Spain and Portugal in the fifteenth century."[26] Sweet finds antecedents for fifteenth-century Iberia in Muslim distinctions between white (*mamluk*) and Black (*adb*) enslaved people that informed the social hierarchies during the nearly eight centuries of Muslim presence on the Peninsula that are echoed in Christian sources, including the writings of the thirteenth-century king of Castile Alfonso, "El Sabio," to such an extent that, Sweet says, "though Christians and Muslims regarded one another as infidels, adherents of both faiths found common ground in their disparagement of black Africans."[27]

Patterns of enslaving people for service labor through cross-border raiding changed as the Christians overtook more and more Muslim-occupied territory and some kingdoms lost their frontiers to Arab enemies. Increasingly, the Portuguese sought opportunities to obtain enslaved people in Africa, first in the northern regions and then, as their maritime technologies grew, further down the West African coast. The 1441 slaving expedition, supported by the Portuguese Crown, near Mauritania brought back to the kingdom ten Muslim Idzagen and an enslaved Black woman. That signaled the beginning of raiding, capturing, and trade in Black Africans.[28] As Sweet points out, papal bulls issued between 1452 and 1456 endorsed the enslavement of Black Africans, providing, in essence, "divine approval for the conquest and enslavement of sub-Saharan Africans as a mission for Christ."[29] Sweet quotes Gomes Eanes de Zurara, the fifteenth-century chronicler of these expeditions, who wrote that in 1444, upon the arrival of 235 enslaved people from south of the Sahara, Prince Henry said he "'had no other pleasure than in thinking that these lost souls would now be saved.'"[30] Sweet notes in the documentation of these fifteenth-century slaving expeditions an overt denigration of the enslaved Africans based on their physical appearance, but that also extended to their overall inferiority. The condemnation was coupled with a rationalization of the violence of slavery imposed on Black bodies, which, as Sweet quotes Zurara, "liberated Africans from their bestial condition, introducing them to Christianity and European culture."[31]

The Portuguese established a firmer foothold in the slave trade when they created the first permanent trading post on the island of Arguim in 1448 and the first slave fort, São Jorge da Mina (in present-day Ghana), in 1482. Sweet notes that as a response to Castilian challenges to Portuguese claims, under the provisions of the Treaty of Alcáçovas (1479), "Castile renounced all claims to West Africa in exchange for unchallenged rights to the Canary Islands."[32] Historians estimate that before 1492, between 80,000 and 150,000 enslaved Black Africans passed through the Portuguese ports, with the principal market being Castile, where they performed all manner of hard labor from salt mines to brothels.[33] Sweet concludes by suggesting that the "treatment of black Africans from the Middle Ages to the early modern period appears to be racism without race" and that the "conquest of the Americas and the classification of the Indigenous peoples according to race may be understood as part of a process that began with the expulsion of the Muslims from Granada and continued with the Iberian invasions of the Atlantic islands and Africa."[34] Broadly, the social hierarchy based on religion, customs, and physical appearance was translated to the Western Hemisphere, where the model of conqueror-conquered and master-servant was applied in the aftermath of 1492 to the Natives of the Antilles.

The most direct antecedent for Columbus's initial interactions with the inhabitants of Guanahaní was the Castilian conquest of the Canary Islands and subjugation of the Guanches. Agents of the Crown of Castile undertook the conquest of the Canary Islands between 1478 and 1496.[35] Pedro de Vera, the grandfather of Álvar Núñez Cabeza de Vaca, the sixteenth-century conquistador-turned-wanderer of lands later occupied by the United States, completed the conquest of Gran Canaria in 1483.[36] Vera's methods were brutal, and in the aftermath of the military conquest of the island, he continued to brutalize the population, transporting *canarios* to slave markets in Andalusia for sale. In fact, continuing in the decade of the 1480s, Vera orchestrated further slaving, when there was presumably a ban against such activities, under the pretext of violent uprisings by the Natives of the islands.[37] Occurring in the decades immediately preceding Columbus's voyage, Castile's support of the violent conquest, subjugation, and enslavement of the Native inhabitants of the Canary Islands served as a template for activities in the Antilles in the years following 1492. The discursive structures used to explain and justify the brutal treatment of the *canarios* were part of a historical context that informed the violence of the wars of conquest in the Western Hemisphere. That context also included the wars of reconquest of Muslim-held lands on the Peninsula and the ensuing exclusionary policies against Muslims and Jews. We find patterns of racialized categories and racializing policies based on human difference that were intended to organize social structures and in turn were correlated to practices of violent domination. Although these patterns did not emerge in 1492, they did take on greater significance as the colonial projects came to impact millions of people who were previously unexposed to European imperial ambitions.

Stuart Schwartz's recent intervention on the topic of race in the early colonial context, *Blood and Boundaries: The Limits of Religious and Racial Exclusion in Early Modern Latin America* (2020), emphasizes the importance of the precedent of purity of blood, or *limpieza de sangre*.[38] While Schwartz recognizes that many scholars, Sweet and Mariscal being among the exceptions, have tended to avoid the term *race* as a critical tool in discussions of exclusion and discrimination in the Iberian and New World contexts, he observes in early modern Spain, Portugal, and their empires traces of racially inflected social organization and hierarchies. More specifically, Schwartz accepts "the argument that aspects of the purity of blood restrictions and the beliefs of the inheritability of cultural and moral characteristics have a similarity to modern racism," while he also asserts that other concepts played important roles in establishing Hispanic colonial social order in the Western Hemisphere, including "nobility, honor, legitimacy of birth, occupation, education, and accomplishment in ways that were quite unlike more modern forms of racial thinking."[39] In her analysis of the role of race and its mutability in the colonial context, Kathryn Burns also emphasized the centrality of customs around blood purity as a distinctive feature of colonial Latin American social categories and hierarchies.[40]

Limpieza de sangre was initially understood as the absence of Jewish and heretical ancestry. It emerged sometime in late medieval Castile but gained strength especially during the fifteenth century.[41] The role of *limpieza* became even more predominant with the adoption of the "statutes" or requirements of Old Christian ancestry by different secular and ecclesiastical institutions. As María Elena Martínez explains, people believed that "Jewishness" was transmitted in the blood, that it was an inheritable condition. In addition, "this naturalization of a religious-cultural identity coincided with the emergence of a lexicon consisting of terms such as *raza* (race), *casta* (caste), and *linaje* (lineage) that was informed by popular notions regarding biological reproduction in the natural world and, in particular, in horse breeding."[42] Biological reproduction, and therefore female sexuality, became central to the perpetuation of a social hierarchy in which Old Christians would be situated at the top. However, when Iberian notions of genealogy and purity of blood were transplanted into the Latin American context, new understandings of racial difference were born. While in the Iberian Peninsula, being an Old Christian was important in order to occupy the highest place in the social hierarchy, in the Americas, things became quite complex.

After 1492: Discourses of Racial Difference

Fifteenth-century political and economic developments, as well as historical events in the kingdoms of the Iberian Peninsula, served as critical precedents in establishing discourses of alterity before Columbus's voyage in 1492. In addition to the Christian, Jewish, *converso*, and Muslim inhabitants of the Iberian Peninsula in the fifteenth century, there was also a significant presence of peoples of African descent, some free, some enslaved. Slavery had existed for centuries and at its core was historically justified with a religious argument: captives of a "just war," one waged against "infidels," could be enslaved. During the second half of the fifteenth century, slaves came almost exclusively from Africa, and even though there was abundant proof of their acceptance of Christianity, papal bulls were issued justifying their enslavement. Clearly, it was not simply religion that informed their decision to enslave people from Africa, but other markers of difference. Certain cultural traits that were foreign and repulsive to Europeans, such as minimal clothing, religious practices, and diet preferences, became enough reason to be considered less "civilized" than their European counterparts. As James Sweet argues, behavioral patterns and lifestyles that Europeans considered inferior "were linked to genetically fixed qualities—especially phenotype and skin color."[43] This deeply rooted ethnocentrism informed how Europeans developed notions of difference when a whole new population was encountered in the Caribbean.

That ethnocentrism manifested in textual narratives as well. As Peter Hulme has so insightfully pointed out, one finds in Columbus's *Diario* two distinct discursive networks: first, "a discourse of Oriental civilization," and second, "a discourse of savagery." Both, as he says, are "archives of topics and motifs that can be traced back to the classical period" that influenced Columbus most immediately through his reading of Marco Polo and Herodotus, respectively.[44] In Hulme's analysis, as the *Diario* progresses, Columbus's descriptions of the Natives, and specifically of the gold associated with the lands of the Natives, become increasingly colored by language of savagery. His creation and depiction of the "indios" did not emerge out of nowhere. For Hulme the "savage gold" drives the narrative in the *Diario* just as it would drive the narrative of Castilian expansionism.[45] The binaries of good-bad, friends-enemies, and gentle-violent that operate in Columbus's initial reports seed the dichotomous representations of Native peoples of the Caribbean under the ethnographic labels "Arawak" or "Carib" that are found in later narratives. This is evident most poignantly in the emergence of the neologism *cannibal (caníbal)*, which was used for the first time in the entry for November 23, 1492.[46] Perhaps more than any other descriptor, the construction of specific groups of Natives as anthropophagi served to draw a clear line between the European colonizers and those represented as the aggressors, not only to Columbus and his crew but perhaps even more significantly—for rhetorical purposes—to the passive and innocent non-Caribs (construed as *taínos* and *arahuacos*).

Within a decade after Columbus's landfall, the populations of the Caribbean islands rapidly diminished due to war, enslavement, and disease, with the result that the Native polities of the Greater Antilles were usurped by colonial rule and the islands of the Lesser Antilles became a refuge for Native populations and eventually *cimarrones*, enslaved Africans who had escaped captivity.[47] The category of *caribes* was, from its inception, tied to the justification for colonial violence. Neil Whitehead has observed that it was projected "as an enduring source of resistance to colonial control" and, thus, "inextricably joined to the self-serving interests of colonial rule."[48] The representation of *caribes* as a source of violent resistance to colonial rule served as the very justification of violent acts against them by the colonizers, just as the image of *caribes* as hostile to nonconflictive Native groups, identified as *taínos* or *arahuacos*, justified the violent actions of the colonizers in presumed defense of those Natives represented as peaceful and compliant in the face of European occupation. What studies like Hulme's and Whitehead's have demonstrated is that Columbus's early characterization of the *indios* was both politically strategic and extraordinarily enduring. While at the same time, significantly, the image of the *indio* that emerges in Columbus's writings was simultaneously reflective of preceding discourses—Genoese mercantilism, slaving expeditions in Africa, and conquests of islands in the Atlantic—and the point of origin for a novel discourse of New World colonialism.

Beatriz Pastor has labeled Columbus's narrative production of the *indios* and their lands a "discourse of mythification," noting that the navigator from Genoa drew from a host of European sources, including Pierre d'Ailly's *Imago Mundi*, a 1489 Italian version of Pliny the Elder's *Historia Naturalis*, a copy of Aeneas Sylvius's *Historia Rerum Ubique Gestarum*, and a 1485 Latin version of *The Travels of Marco Polo*, as he described a land he mistook for Asia.[49] In what

Columbus drew from these books, he found images of gold, silver, monstrous creatures, and peace-loving and people-eating inhabitants. The result, Pastor has said, was that "rather than observing and acquainting himself with the concrete realities of the New World before him, he chose to interpret each of its components in a manner that would allow him to identify it with his imaginary model of the land he felt destined to discover."[50] Columbus's will to impose his own preconceived notions on the Natives of Guanahaní and the other islands of the Antilles reminds us that there was a larger context for the events and consequences of his voyage in 1492. He belonged to a historical moment increasingly defined by maritime and land travels to secure trading partners and goods, including enslaved peoples, as well as a fervent religiosity, such that his interactions and those of later Europeans with Natives of the Western Hemisphere were shaped by the religious, economic, and cultural discourses of Europe on the cusp of modernity.

After 1492: Racialized Social Categories and Colonial Administration

Natives became a conundrum for European invaders. Jurists and theologians were not convinced that *indios* were "natural slaves," a category derived from Aristotelian thought, but the argument that a "just war" could be waged against them was also not generally accepted. Ultimately, the Indies were claimed by the Crown, and *indios* were the Crown's vassals. Columbus captured a large number of Natives who were taken across the Atlantic to be sold in the slave markets of Seville; however, in 1495, Queen Isabel stopped the sale and ordered that all Natives in Seville be freed from their masters and sent back to their former home.[51] Isabel's posture toward these new vassals was not uniform. In fact, during the early decades of colonization, the association between *caribe* and cannibalism provided the legal pretext for unrestricted slaving of those deemed to fall into that category.[52] In August 1503, as part of a proclamation prohibiting the enslavement of *indios*, the queen provided an exemption allowing for the enslavement of *caribes* or *caníbales* (Caribs or cannibals) because of their violent resistance to Christian evangelization and colonial occupation. The position of the Crown toward the Natives was formalized in the Laws of Burgos of 1512, which recognized them as free vassals who should be treated well and pay tribute. Mendicant friars such as Antonio de Montesinos lobbied for the protections found in these laws; however, they meant nothing to the conquistadors-turned-colonizers who wanted to be rewarded for their efforts. Furthermore, even under these statutes, legal slave raids continued to be common throughout the circum-Caribbean especially after Queen Isabel declared that, while *indios* were not infidels, they could be enslaved if they resisted Christianity, again, as captives of just war (*guerra justa*) or if they were seen to be cannibals.[53]

The Crown also sought to legitimize acts of colonization with the Spanish Requirement, or Requerimiento, a legal document used to enact political authority over the inhabitants of the newly found lands during the years of 1512 and 1573. The Requerimiento, read aloud in Spanish to the Natives from a written text, represented an ultimatum for *indios* "to acknowledge the superiority of Christianity or be warred upon."[54] The ludicrous ritual was harshly criticized by some members of the religious orders who had had direct experience with the Natives of the Caribbean, such as Bartolomé de las Casas. Yet its existence can be best understood as a transposition of practices and a mindset that responded to Christians' interactions with Muslims, and vice versa. In fact, the long-held practice of slavery, and particularly the large numbers of enslaved Black people who had recently been brought from Africa to Portugal, and also Castile, was an important precedent that justified Native slavery and the creation of the encomienda.

The formal reward given to the invaders for their military success was an encomienda, which was similar to enslavement but differed in some important respects, the main one being that the Catholic Church was complicit with this arrangement. Groups of *indios* were assigned to the invaders, and the *encomenderos* received all the labor, service, and tribute from that group as long as they provided the Natives with religious instruction. This arrangement created great disruptions in terms of ethnic autonomy, as well as control over the natural resources that formerly belonged to the Natives. In many cases, Indigenous peoples were forced to relocate geographically for an encomendero and the missionaries to better manage them. These *reducciones* were meant to help colonial authorities control and govern Natives more effectively. Encomiendas were not land grants, yet possession of the land and removal of the original owners followed naturally. The encomienda soon became a disguised form of slavery; many *encomenderos* subjected the Natives to forced labor and precarious living conditions. The New Laws of 1542 were issued to abolish Indigenous slavery and put an end to the encomienda system; however, in practice, the encomienda continued to exist for years.[55]

Not surprisingly, Indigenous peoples learned how to survive and sometimes even thrive in a system that was created to subjugate them. The category of *indio* had inherent flexibility. Nancy van Deusen points to this flexibility, because in sixteenth-century Castile, *indio* could refer to people from "East and West Indies, China, the Moluccas, India, Brazil, Hispaniola, Mexico, and Peru," but most notably, from its inception, the label *indio* "constituted difference based on unequal power relations."[56] *Indio* became a legal category that defined Natives as *miserables*; this meant that they were regarded as in need of special legal assistance, and their cases and complaints would be taken under special royal and church protection.[57] Many Natives took advantage of the special status and learned to maneuver within the complex legal system to claim their ancestral rights to the lands that had been taken by the invaders. Not everyone was successful in these judicial battles, yet the frequency with which Natives went to court to fight for their rights has become commonplace in the history of Latin America. Nonetheless, the encomienda system did not end but rather morphed and allowed for a continuation of the differentiation of racial and power structures.

As colonial cities began to form, a sociopolitical system was put in place to maintain the differentiation of *indios* and non-*indios*. The Crown instituted two independent republics, the *república de españoles* and the *república de indios*, each with distinct legal rights and obligations. The separation of Europeans and Natives was not only made in juridical terms; there was also a physical separation of the republics. The *traza* was the area where the Spanish population resided in the center of the city, and outside the *traza*, the Indigenous population lived in different *barrios* or neighborhoods, and *pueblos de indios*, or Indigenous towns with a somewhat autonomous governing body.[58]

The dual republic was also conceived of as a solution to protect the Indigenous population from the abuses of the colonists and from their loose morals, some argued. Missionaries in particular believed *indios* to be, as Fray Gerónimo de Mendieta stated, "meek, gentle, humble, simple of heart, obedient, and content with poverty." In religious discourse, this was the image of Indigenous peoples that was championed to protect them under the law, yet it also helped in keeping them subjugated and with considerably fewer privileges than Europeans. The separation of the two republics could give the impression that there was a total separation of the two groups, but in fact, there was close contact between the two, primarily because the Spanish sector of society depended on the Indigenous one for goods and labor.

It is important to note that the system of difference that was established in the colony was constantly in flux. This was a new reality, and while the hierarchical system of power was transplanted from the Iberian Peninsula and strongly informed by notions of purity of blood, the Latin American context presented other challenges. For example, an important element in the way hierarchy was established had to do with the concept of nobility. The European mindset understood and highly regarded noble status; therefore, the invaders recognized the special place that Indigenous nobility had among their people. Indigenous nobles not only had political power; in many cases, they also owned property and other forms of wealth. Intermarriages between Spaniards and Native noblewomen were common in the first years of European presence in the Americas, and interestingly, the offspring of such unions were seen as "purer" because of the nobility status of the mother, even though they carried both European and Native ancestry.[59] Even though this perceived "purity" began to dissipate as miscegenation became generalized, a process in itself leading to the *sistema de castas*, the discourse of purity was pervasive, and Natives strategically used it to their advantage. Many nobles became intermediaries between colonial officials and the rest of the Indigenous population, and they learned to negotiate better conditions for themselves and their families throughout the colonial period.

People of African descent were part of the earliest expeditions of conquest and colonization in different capacities. They were brought to work in the Caribbean as early as the 1510s, though in small numbers.[60] The quick demise of Native groups in the Caribbean due to genocide, disease, and onerous labor conditions caused the colonizers to turn more and more to enslaved African people in order to continue exploiting the natural resources of the New World. Between 1521 and 1639, the number of forced migrants from Africa increased dramatically.[61] Current estimates would indicate that, before the abolition of slavery, of the ten million to eleven million people taken by force from Africa to North and South America, five million to six million of them disembarked in Spanish or Portuguese territories.[62] While slavery was prevalent, other Africans came to the Americas as free soldiers, cooks, and servants. The gender imbalance was perhaps one of the main reasons unions between Spaniards and Indigenous women were so common early in the sixteenth century, yet unions between Black men and Native women happened frequently as well. As Ilona Katzew explains, even though intermarriage among Spaniards, Natives, and Africans was rare until later in the seventeenth century, sexual contact between the three groups happened early in the sixteenth century, creating a large number of mixed people known collectively as *castas*.[63]

Africans and people of African descent also found accommodation within the colonial system in Latin America and were able to build communities that went beyond the shared experience of slavery. Free (and enslaved) Blacks and mulattoes drew on African culture, yet they also attained a certain degree of autonomy and power within the spaces opened by the Catholic Church. Confraternities and brotherhoods allowed them to foster a sense of community while at the same time providing financial and spiritual support for one another.[64] In recent years, scholars have relied more heavily on the role that the Catholic Church played in the lives of Africans and Afro-descendants, as canon law authorized certain forms of private life even among slaves, which in many ways stood at odds with civil law.[65] Therefore, we have been able to witness the shift in the scholarship that focuses on the Black experience in colonial Latin America.

In addition, immigrants from Asia also came to the Americas in the Manila galleons. Some came voluntarily, but many came as slaves; known generically as *chinos*, they came from many different regions of Asia, but especially Southeast Asia and, even more specifically, the Philippines. As Tatiana Seijas has illustrated, *chinos* became vassals of the Spanish Crown after 1672. This seemingly minor detail had enormous consequences: as *indios*, *chinos* could no longer be held as slaves. They, too, went to court, in their case, to claim their illegal enslavement.[66] Many mestizos (people of Spanish and Indigenous descent) were born of illegitimate unions and were usually absorbed into the homes of one of the parents. As time went by, mestizos of both genders formed unions with people of Spanish, Indigenous, and African descent or with other people of mixed ancestry, and this led to the social classification of people into the many different *castas* that were popularized later in the eighteenth century through a genre of painting (*cuadros de castas*). However, in real life, these categories of identification were quite flexible and mostly based on discourse that was used when appealing to the court or the church. Colonial subjects were not passive recipients of the racial categories that were created and imposed on them. In many cases, they used them to their advantage by claiming to belong to one racial group rather than another; for example, a person might claim to be *indio* instead of a particular *casta* in order not to be tried by the Inquisition.[67] It is also important to take into consideration the scholarship that has made evident that the racial categorization that made up the system of social stratification was a construct that "cut across other classificatory systems, notably those of class, estate, occupation, and culture."[68] As time went by, a plebeian class made up of diverse racial groups formed, particularly in urban centers. Class solidarity became more important than the racialized system of difference that was imposed on people to subjugate them.[69]

Conclusion

Following patterns of colonization and slaving in Africa and along its coastline, from Columbus's first voyage on, discourses of racial difference in the Western Hemisphere were tied to economic and political control of colonized lands and subjected people. The creation of the *indio* in the early years of the colonization of the Antilles was the first step in racial formation in colonial Latin America. Racialized social categories grew in the decades after 1492, as Europeans invaded the mainland and forcibly migrated more and more Africans and then Asians to the New World. Recalling Stuart Hall's discussion of identity, we recognize that racialized identities were produced in "specific historical and institution sites" within "specific discursive formations" and through "specific modalities of power."[70] The central significance of these specificities must be accompanied by the recognition that there was an ongoing fluidity in the expression of racial differences. To survey the foundations of racialized categories in the early decades of Iberian conquest and colonization of the Western Hemisphere, we are faced with a complex web of relevant historical and institutional sites and discourses that inform and produce the power relations enacted in the islands of the Caribbean and the mainland of the New World.

The hierarchies premised on racial differences were not static. Even the category of *indio*, the paramount invention by Iberian colonizers of racialized social categories, was interpreted and implemented in distinct ways. In the face of European invasion, if the Native group was compliant, *indios* curried protection from the Crown. Yet, if *indios* resisted or displayed violent behavior, they could be labeled "cannibals" and subject to slavery. Additionally, *indios* themselves at times embraced this category in their own efforts to regain autonomy and land through the court system. In each scenario, *indio* is used as a category to note differences, yet for distinct purposes and ends.

Our study of the foundational period of Latin America, in its origins overdetermined by the violent assertion of Europeans over Native inhabitants, is enriched by bringing greater focus to questions of race. Race, as the category has been so insightfully interrogated by scholars and theorists, is about taking note of human difference in order to reinforce power relations and hierarchies. To address the topic of race in the early colonial period is to look carefully at the ways in which social, economic, and political relations in the context of the wars of conquests and efforts to establish colonial systems of government were constructed around racialized categories of groups of people according to Iberian precedents and with the effect of establishing new models and vocabularies that left deep and enduring legacies.

NOTES

1. Cristóbal Colón, *Textos y documentos completos, relaciones de viajes, cartas y memoriales*, ed. Consuelo Varela (Madrid: Alianza Editorial, 1982), 31. Our translation.
2. Stuart B. Schwartz and Frank Salomon, "New Peoples and New Kinds of People: Adaptation, Readjustment, and Ethnogenesis in South American Indigenous Societies (Colonial Era)" in *The Cambridge History of the Native Peoples of the Americas*, ed. Frank Salomon and Stuart B. Schwartz (New York: Cambridge University Press, 1999), vol. 3, pt. 2, 443-501. Schwartz and Salomon discuss *indio* as an example of the phenomenon of "ethnogenesis," which represents "the ways in which new human groupings came to be, and how they were categorized in colonial cultures" (443).
3. Frances Karttunen, *Between Worlds: Interpreters, Guides, and Survivors* (New Brunswick, NJ: Rutgers University Press, 1994), xiii.
4. Stuart Hall, "Introduction: Who Needs 'Identity'?" in *Questions of Cultural Identity*, ed. Stuart Hall and Paul de Gay (London: Sage, 1996), 3-4.
5. Ann Laura Stoler, *Duress: Imperial Durabilities in Our Times* (Durham, NC: Duke University Press, 2016), 252.
6. Volumes such as Matthew Restall, Lisa Sousa, and Kevin Terraciano's *Mesoamerican Voices: Native-Language Writings from Colonial Mexico, Oaxaca, Yucatan, and Guatemala* (Cambridge: Cambridge University Press, 2005) have compiled writings from Native perspectives on wars of conquest, colonial political life, and colonial religious life.
7. Guaman Poma de Ayala and Fernando de Alva Ixtlilxochitl provide additional examples of authors who embraced their Indigenous ties as a means of asserting their own identities and projects in the colonial context.
8. Henry Louis Gates Jr., "Editor's Introduction: Writing 'Race' and the Difference It Makes," *Critical Inquiry* 12, no. 1 (1985): 5. Gates edited the influential 1985 special issue of *Critical Inquiry*, "Writing 'Race' and the Difference It Makes," which brought together essays by Anthony Appiah, Edward Said, Mary Louise Pratt, and Gayatri Spivak, among other scholars, and became a touchstone for later scholarship on race.
9. Geraldine Heng, "The Invention of Race in the European Middle Ages I: Race Studies, Modernity, and the Middle Ages," *Literature Compass* 8, no. 5 (2011): 319.
10. Stuart Hall, *The Fateful Triangle: Race, Ethnicity, Nation* (Cambridge, MA: Harvard University Press, 2017), 53.
11. Aníbal Quijano, "Questioning 'Race,'" *Socialism and Democracy* 21, no. 1 (2007): 45.
12. Quijano, "Questioning," 50. For Quijano, the hierarchization and categorization of groups on the basis of racialized social categories is intimately connected to what he has called the "coloniality of power." He offers this definition: "That specific basic element of the new pattern of world power that was based on the idea of 'race' and the 'racial' social classification of world population—expressed in the 'racial' distribution of work, in the imposition of new 'racial' geocultural identities, in the concentration of the control of productive resource and capital, as social relations, including salary as a privilege of 'White-

ness'—is what basically is referred to in the category of coloniality of power." Aníbal Quijano, "Coloniality of Power and Eurocentrism in Latin America," *International Sociology* 15, no. 2 (2000): 218.
13. Magnus Mörner, *Race Mixture in the History of Latin America* (Boston: Little, Brown and Co., 1967), 1, 4.
14. Mörner, *Race Mixture*, 4.
15. Heng, "The Invention of Race," 322.
16. Mörner's comments on the necessity for studying his academic subject ring true even fifty years later: "Nevertheless we know that the categorical opinions expressed on race by pseudoscientists have had much more influence—a nefarious influence, at that—than cautious statements made by serious scholars. I refer to the Nazis in Germany, the Afrikander in South Africa, the segregationalists in the American South.... The racists have successfully appealed to human envy, ignorance, and stupidity by confusing biological and sociocultural concepts under a veil of mysticism," Mörner, *Race Mixture*, 5.
17. Quijano, "Questioning," 46.
18. Stoler, *Duress*, 250.
19. Gates, "Editor's Introduction," 5; Heng, "The Invention of Race," 319.
20. George Mariscal, "The Role of Spain in Contemporary Race Theory," *Arizona Journal of Hispanic Cultural Studies* 2 (1998): 8. Interested in contributing to scholarship on race and culture broadly and Spain's role in racial formations more specifically, Mariscal reviews, in light of the Spanish example, the genealogy of racism found in two influential studies: Omi and Winant's *Racial Formation in the United States* (London: Routledge, 2014) and Étienne Balibar's essays in *Race, Nation, Class: Ambiguous Identities*, ed. Étienne Balibar, Immanuel Wallerstein, and Chris Turner (London: Verso, 1998), particularly the final one, "Racism and Crisis," 217–227.
21. Mariscal, "The Role of Spain," 9.
22. Omi and Winant demarcate the emergence of race firmly: "It was only when European explorers reached the Western Hemisphere, when the oceanic seal separating the 'old' and the 'new' worlds was breached, that the distinctions and categorizations fundamental to racialized social structure, and to discourse of race began to appear," thus creating a "ferocious division of society into Europeans and 'others.'" *Racial Formation*, 113–114.
23. Mariscal, "The Role of Spain," 9–10.
24. Mariscal, "The Role of Spain," 10, 12.
25. Mariscal, "The Role of Spain," 15–16.
26. James Sweet, "The Iberian Roots of American Racist Thought," *William and Mary Quarterly* 54, no. 1 (1997): 144.
27. Sweet, "The Iberian Roots," 152.
28. Sweet, "The Iberian Roots," 156–157.
29. Sweet, "The Iberian Roots," 157.
30. Sweet, "The Iberian Roots," 157.
31. Sweet, "The Iberian Roots," 161.
32. Sweet, "The Iberian Roots," 162.
33. Sweet, "The Iberian Roots," 163–164.
34. Sweet, "The Iberian Roots," 165.
35. Silvio A. Zavala, *Las conquistas de Canarias y América* (Las Palmas: Cabildo Insular de Gran Canaria, 1991). In 1936, Zavala first published a comparative study of the conquests

of the Canaries and the Americas. His meticulous analysis of the two cases emphasizes the significant connection between them while also taking into account the relevant differences.

36. In their three-volume study of Álvar Núñez Cabeza de Vaca and his experiences as one of only four survivors from the 1528 Pánfilo de Narváez expedition to La Florida, Rolena Adorno and Patrick Charles Pautz include a detailed study of Cabeza de Vaca's life and the history of his ancestors: Rolena Adorno and Patrick Charles Pautz, eds., *Álvar Núñez Cabeza de Vaca: His Account, His Life, and the Expedition of Pánfilo de Narváez* (Lincoln: University of Nebraska Press, 1999). The section addressing the Veras is found at 1:323-333.
37. Rolena and Pautz, *Álvar Núñez Cabeza de Vaca*, 1:326-329.
38. Schwartz has addressed the broad topic of social organization during the colonial period based on imposed or self-professed identities over the course of decades of research. This book presents his most current analysis of the topic and is organized around three essays addressing Moriscos, Conversos, and mestizos.
39. Stuart B. Schwartz, *Blood and Boundaries: The Limits of Religious and Racial Exclusion in Early Modern Latin America* (Waltham, MA: Brandeis University Press, 2020), 8-9.
40. Kathryn Burns, "Unfixing Race," in *Rereading the Black Legend: The Discourses of Religious and Racial Difference in the Renaissance Empires*, ed. Margaret Greer, Walter Mignolo, and Maureen Quilligan (Chicago: University of Chicago Press, 2007), 189.
41. María Elena Martínez states that the reasons for the shift in attitude toward Conversos (Jewish people who converted to Catholicism) remain a mystery. For more on the subject, see chapter 1 of her *Genealogical Fictions: Limpieza de Sangre, Religion, and Gender in Colonial Mexico* (Stanford, CA: Stanford University Press, 2008).
42. Martínez, *Genealogical Fictions*, 28.
43. Sweet, "The Iberian Roots," 144.
44. Peter Hulme, *Colonial Encounters: Europe and the Native Caribbean, 1492-1797* (London: Routledge, 1992), 21.
45. Hulme, *Colonial Encounters*, 38.
46. Hulme notes, as have other scholars, that we must remain circumspect when reading the text known as "el diario de Colón," given that the original was lost within fifty years of the voyage and the version we rely on was prepared by Bartolomé de las Casas and most likely itself based on a copy. For Hulme's purposes, and ours here, the *Diario* does not represent an accurate ethnographic record, but rather, as he says, "the first fable of European beginnings in America." *Colonial Encounters*, 18.
47. Neil L. Whitehead, *Of Cannibals and Kings: Primal Anthropology in the Americas* (University Park: Pennsylvania State University Press, 2011), 6-8.
48. Whitehead, *Of Cannibals and Kings*, 7.
49. Beatriz Pastor, *The Armature of Conquest: Spanish Accounts of the Discovery of America, 1492-1589*, trans. Lydia Longstreth Hunt (Stanford, CA: Stanford University Press, 1992), 12. Pastor notes that "copies of these books used by Columbus have been preserved, showing all the handwritten annotations made as he read them carefully over and over again" (12).
50. Pastor, *The Armature of Conquest*, 22.
51. Anthony Pagden, *The Fall of Natural Man: The American Indian and the Origins of Comparative Ethnology* (Cambridge: Cambridge University Press, 1982), 31.
52. Whitehead, *Of Cannibals and Kings*, 11.

53. Nancy E. van Deusen, *Global Indios: The Indigenous Struggle for Justice in Sixteenth-Century Spain* (Durham, NC: Duke University Press, 2015), 3.
54. Patricia Seed, *Ceremonies of Possession in Europe's Conquest of the New World, 1492–1640* (Cambridge: Cambridge University Press, 1995), 70.
55. These laws were particularly unpopular among the encomenderos and led to violent revolts, especially in Peru.
56. Van Deusen, *Global Indios*, 11.
57. Woodrow Borah, *Justice by Insurance: The General Indian Court of Colonial Mexico and the Legal Aides of the Half-Real* (Berkeley: University of California Press, 1983), 80–81.
58. For an analysis of the interrelated processes of colonial urbanization and racialization which impact the emergence of the *traza*, see Daniel Nemser, *Infrastructures of Race: Concentration and Biopolitics in Colonial Mexico* (Austin: University of Texas Press, 2017). Through a careful study of infrastructure and its associated material dimensions, including labor and the spatial concentration of colonized peoples, Nemser draws our attention to the structural character of race and ways it is inherently tied to the material practices of power (9).
59. There were systematic forced sexual relationships between European men and Indigenous women, as well as consensual relationships that did not end up in marriages but resulted in a whole generation of mestizos. Gender is another important category that should not be dismissed when thinking about racial identification. Ultimately, it is through an intersectional lens that we can better understand the complexities of a system of control that was more fluid and flexible than might at first seem.
60. For a recent study of the historiography of the slave trade to Latin America, see Roquinaldo Ferreira and Tatiana Seijas, "The Slave Trade to Latin America: A Historiographical Assessment" in *Afro–Latin American Studies: An Introduction*, ed. Alejandro de la Fuente and George Reid Andrews (New York: Cambridge University Press, 2018). For up-to-date data on numbers of enslaved Africans taken to the Western Hemisphere, see the website Slave Voyages (www.slavevoyages.org).
61. Ben Vinson III, *Before Mestizaje: The Frontiers of Race and Caste in Colonial Mexico* (New York: Cambridge University Press, 2018), 3.
62. Ferreira and Seijas, "The Slave Trade to Latin America," 28–29.
63. Ilona Katzew, *Casta Painting: Images of Race in Eighteenth-Century Mexico* (New Haven, CT: Yale University Press, 2004), 40.
64. For more on the topic, see Nicole von Germeten, *Black Blood Brothers: Confraternities and Social Mobility for Afro-Mexicans* (Gainesville: University Press of Florida, 2006), and the edited volume by Javiera Jaque Hidalgo and Miguel A. Valerio, *Indigenous and Black Confraternities in Colonial Latin America: Negotiating Status Through Religious Practices* (Amsterdam: Amsterdam University Press, 2022).
65. Herman L. Bennett, *Africans in Colonial Mexico: Absolutism, Christianity, and Afro-Creole Consciousness, 1570–1640* (Bloomington: Indiana University Press, 2003), 1.
66. Tatiana Seijas, *Asian Slaves in Colonial Mexico: From Chinos to Indians* (New York: Cambridge University Press, 2014), 1–2.
67. The chapters included in Fisher and O'Hara's *Imperial Subjects: Race and Identity in Colonial Latin America* (Durham, NC: Duke University Press, 2009) are a good case in point. They explore the many instances in which racial categories were put to the test and challenged in courts and other outlets, proving how flexible and transformable categories of identification really were.

68. David Cahill, "Colour by Numbers: Racial and Ethnic Categories in the Viceroyalty of Peru, 1532–1824," *Journal of Latin American Studies* 26, no. 2 (May 1994): 326.
69. Later in the eighteenth century, the notion of purity became replaced with concepts related to class and social status. We start finding concepts such as *calidad* and *condición* in the historical record. *Calidad* had multiple connotations, but it generally referred to occupation, wealth, honor, and integrity, among other characteristics pertaining to one's station in society. For more on *calidad*, see Martínez, *Genealogical Fictions*, and Magali Carrera, *Imagining Identity in New Spain: Race, Lineage, and the Colonial Body in Portraiture and Casta Paintings* (Austin: University of Texas Press, 2003).
70. Hall, "Introduction," 3-4.

BIBLIOGRAPHY

Adorno, Rolena, and Patrick Charles Pautz. *Álvar Núñez Cabeza de Vaca: His Account, His Life, and the Expedition of Pánfilo de Narváez*. Vol. 1. Lincoln: University of Nebraska Press, 1999.

Bennett, Herman L. *Africans in Colonial Mexico: Absolutism, Christianity, and Afro-Creole Consciousness, 1570–1640*. Bloomington: Indiana University Press, 2003.

Balibar, Étienne. "Racism and Crisis." In *Race, Nation, Class: Ambiguous Identities*, ed. Étienne Balibar, Immanuel Wallerstein, and Chris Turner, 217–227. London: Verso, 1998.

Borah, Woodrow. *Justice by Insurance: The General Indian Court of Colonial Mexico and the Legal Aides of the Half-Real*. Berkeley: University of California Press, 1983.

Burns, Kathryn. "Unfixing Race." In *Rereading the Black Legend: The Discourses of Religious and Racial Difference in the Renaissance Empires*, ed. Margaret Greer, Walter Mignolo, and Maureen Quilligan, 188–202. Chicago: University of Chicago Press, 2007.

Cahill, David. "Colour by Numbers: Racial and Ethnic Categories in the Viceroyalty of Peru, 1532–1824." *Journal of Latin American Studies* 26, no. 2 (May 1994): 325–346.

Carrera, Magali. *Imagining Identity in New Spain: Race, Lineage, and the Colonial Body in Portraiture and Casta Paintings*. Austin: University of Texas Press, 2003.

Colón, Cristóbal. *Textos y documentos completos, relaciones de viajes, cartas y memoriales*. Edited by Consuelo Varela. Madrid: Alianza Editorial, 1982.

Ferreira, Roquinaldo, and Tatiana Seijas. "The Slave Trade to Latin America: A Historiographical Assessment." In *Afro–Latin American Studies: An Introduction*, ed. Alejandro de la Fuente and George Reid Andrews, 27–51. New York: Cambridge University Press, 2018.

Fisher, Andrew, and Matthew O'Hara. *Imperial Subjects: Race and Identity in Colonial Latin America*. Durham, NC: Duke University Press, 2009.

Gates, Henry Louis, Jr. "Editor's Introduction: Writing 'Race' and the Difference It Makes." *Critical Inquiry* 12, no. 1 (Autumn 1985): 1–20.

Germeten, Nicole von. *Black Blood Brothers: Confraternities and Social Mobility for Afro-Mexicans*. Gainesville: University Press of Florida, 2006.

Hall, Stuart. *The Fateful Triangle: Race, Ethnicity, Nation*. Cambridge, MA: Harvard University Press, 2017.

———. "Introduction: Who Needs 'Identity'?" In *Questions of Cultural Identity*, ed. Stuart Hall and Paul de Gay, 1–17. London: Sage, 1996.

Heng, Geraldine. "The Invention of Race in the European Middle Ages I: Race Studies, Modernity, and the Middle Ages." *Literature Compass* 8, no. 5 (2011): 315–331.

Hulme, Peter. *Colonial Encounters: Europe and the Native Caribbean, 1492–1797*. London: Routledge, 1992.

Jaque Hidalgo, Javiera, and Miguel A. Valerio, eds. *Indigenous and Black Confraternities in Colonial Latin America: Negotiating Status Through Religious Practices*. Amsterdam: Amsterdam University Press, 2022.

Karttunen, Frances. *Between Worlds: Interpreters, Guides, and Survivors*. New Brunswick, NJ: Rutgers University Press, 1994.

Katzew, Ilona. *Casta Painting: Images of Race in eighteenth-century Mexico*. New Haven, CT: Yale University Press, 2004.

Mariscal, George. "The Role of Spain in Contemporary Race Theory." *Arizona Journal of Hispanic Cultural Studies* 2 (1998): 7–22.

Martínez, María Elena. *Genealogical Fictions: Limpieza de Sangre, Religion, and Gender in Colonial Mexico*. Stanford, CA: Stanford University Press, 2008.

Mörner, Magnus. *Race Mixture in the History of Latin America*. Boston: Little, Brown and Co., 1967.

Nemser, Daniel. *Infrastructures of Race: Concentration and Biopolitics in Colonial Mexico*. Austin: University of Texas Press, 2017.

Omi, Michael, and Howard Winant. *Racial Formation in the United States*. London: Routledge, 2014.

Pagden, Anthony. *The Fall of Natural Man: The American Indian and the Origins of Comparative Ethnology*. Cambridge: Cambridge University Press, 1982.

Pastor, Beatriz. *The Armature of Conquest: Spanish Accounts of the Discovery of America, 1492–1589*. Translated by Lydia Longstreth Hunt. Stanford, CA: Stanford University Press, 1992.

Quijano, Aníbal. "Coloniality of Power and Eurocentrism in Latin America." *International Sociology* 15, no. 2 (2000): 215–232.

———. "Questioning 'Race.'" *Socialism and Democracy* 21, no. 1 (2007): 45–53.

Restall, Matthew, Lisa Sousa, and Kevin Terraciano. *Mesoamerican Voices: Native-Language Writings from Colonial Mexico, Oaxaca, Yucatan, and Guatemala*. Cambridge: Cambridge University Press, 2005.

Schwartz, Stuart B. *Blood and Boundaries: The Limits of Religious and Racial Exclusion in Early Modern Latin America*. Waltham, MA: Brandeis University Press, 2020.

Schwartz, Stuart B., and Frank Salomon. "New Peoples and New Kinds of People: Adaptation, Readjustment, and Ethnogenesis in South American Indigenous Societies (Colonial Era)." In *The Cambridge History of the Native Peoples of the Americas*, ed. Frank Salomon and Stuart B. Schwartz, vol. 3, pt. 2, 443–501. New York: Cambridge University Press, 1999.

Seed, Patricia. *Ceremonies of Possession in Europe's Conquest of the New World, 1492–1640*. Cambridge: Cambridge University Press, 1995.

Seijas, Tatiana. *Asian Slaves in Colonial Mexico: From Chinos to Indians*. New York: Cambridge University Press, 2014.

Stoler, Ann Laura. *Duress: Imperial Durabilities in Our Times*. Durham, NC: Duke University Press, 2016.

Sweet, James. "The Iberian Roots of American Racist Thought." *William and Mary Quarterly* 54, no. 1 (1997): 143–166.

van Deusen, Nancy E. *Global Indios: The Indigenous Struggle for Justice in Sixteenth-Century Spain*. Durham, NC: Duke University Press, 2015.

Vinson, Ben, III. *Before Mestizaje: The Frontiers of Race and Caste in Colonial Mexico*. New York: Cambridge University Press, 2018.

Whitehead, Neil L. *Of Cannibals and Kings: Primal Anthropology in the Americas*. University Park: Pennsylvania State University Press, 2011.

Zavala, Silvio A. *Las conquistas de Canarias y América*. Las Palmas: Cabildo Insular de Gran Canaria, 1991.

CHAPTER 2

Race and the Baroque

Social Actors and Christian Subjects in Seventeenth-Century Lima and Mexico City

STEPHANIE KIRK

The capital cities of the two most powerful viceroyalties in the Americas adopted a societal approach whose underlying principle was the control and containment of a heterogeneous population of colonial subjects, all of whom, in theory, occupied stratified and codified positions and spatial allocations within each baroque metropolis. Society, however, proved difficult to control, as populations of different racial groups and social positions mingled freely, and cultural and epistemological exchanges were commonplace. Even in colonial institutions like the Catholic Church, interracial exchanges and the blurring of hierarchical lines took place in what were deemed the most controlled spaces. The baroque cities of Mexico and Lima were spaces of excess where those of "other" races, despite being judged of inferior *calidad*, coexisted with their superiors. In these urban areas, the "strange bedfellows" of "heterogeneity and hegemony" lived side by side and in a constant state of tension.[1]

The very development and constitutions of these two marvelous baroque cities provided the spaces for marginalized subjects to push back against their condition and develop strategies not only to explore agency but also to forge lives that held deep and personalized meaning in terms of community and kinship. The Crown's own policies created mechanisms—unwittingly at times—that allowed subjects with few rights to mobilize power. What made the New World baroque and the cities that stood as its most glittering manifestation such propitious spaces for the development of manifestations of racial plurality? A partial answer can be found in the marked difference between the Spanish baroque and its New World manifestation. As Nora Jaffary describes, while the Spanish baroque "was a manifestation of royal and elite attempts at social consolidation through a culture of order, hierarchy, and tradition," the New World baroque took on a far different character.[2] She identifies the baroque in colonial Latin America as a way for the creole population strove to "assert their independence from the competing controlling force of imperial Spain."[3] Simultaneously, these same *criollos* attempted to assert "domination over the other demographic groups that formed the colonies' demographic majority."[4] Not only did *criollos'* attempt to dominate other demographic groups change the character of the New World baroque, but those same groups' participation in and resistance to *criollo* society also endowed it with its particular character. Baroque Lima and Mexico City became sites of plurality where cross-cultural and cross-ethnic knowledges were shared and developed even within institutions that strove to impose hierarchy and ordering upon their diverse populations. For César Salgado, the New World baroque represented "an ironic reversal of the imperial project" in which "through hybridizing, the colonial subject took advantage of Baroque elements in the dominant system to create sites and terms for cultural resistance."[5] Engaging with Lezama Lima's famous essay on the Latin American baroque, "Baroque Curiosity," Salgado details how "a culture's specific image" is created "by means of 'appropriation, transformation, and reorganization,'" and by "poetic recycling and plutonism."[6] For her part, Stephanie Merrim anchors her analysis of the baroque New World city (specifically Mexico City) in two colonial cultural artifacts: Felipe Guaman Poma de Ayala's *El primer nueva corónica y buen gobierno* (1615/1616) and Cristobal de Villalpando's 1695 painting of Mexico City's *zócalo*. Guaman Poma, according to Merrim, invokes the "dynamic multiplicity of the Western world's most racially and ethnically complex society," where cities emerge as "contact zones, the essence of lived syncretism, spaces configured by cultural mixture, juxtaposition, exchange, fluidity."[7] Reading Villalpando's representation of "twelve hundred miniature figures" through the lens of Guaman Poma's urban evocations, Merrim shows how this "optic" liberates them from the "mercantile machine" instead "individuating them": "the dark faces of Indians swathed in ponchos and rebozos as well as those of acculturated Indians in sober European garb come forcefully into view."[8] According to Merrim, Villalpando's painting "vibrates with the energy of the assorted individuals who converge upon and pluralize the very center of Mexico City at the end of the seventeenth century, with the Baroque in full force."[9]

In the case of Mexico City, built upon the razed ruins of Tenochtitlan, the Indigenous presence could never be obliterated. Barbara Mundy has argued that if we look beyond the "triumphant accounts of Cortés and the despairing accounts of Las Casas" of Tenochtitlan–Mexico City and focus on those "created by and about its indigenous occupants," we can find "the endurance of the indigenous city" still present in the space of the so-called Spanish city.[10] Enslaved Africans began to arrive in New Spain in the sixteenth century, and by 1570, Mexico City was home to the largest African population in the Americas, radically transforming the city with their presence.[11] Enslaved people from Africa had begun to arrive in small numbers in Spain's American colonies in the Caribbean in the sixteenth century.[12] Following the conquests of Mexico (1519) and Peru (1532), the Atlantic trade in enslaved Africans greatly intensified after the acquisitions of large new territories and the tragic demographic decimation of the Indigenous populations.[13] The main period of trading in enslaved people took place during the sixteenth century and in the first few decades of the seventeenth. By 1622, the trade had become less organized in Mexico, and Africans were transported there only sporadically, with most of the seventeenth-century enslaved already in place.[14] Following the 1640 restoration of the Portuguese Crown, the "regular slave trade" to New Spain ended, inaugurating a "series of transformations within and for the population of African descent in the colony."[15] A similar situation occurred in Peru, which by the seventeenth century had become one of the "most important centers for slavery in the Americas" and slaveholding—begun as a luxury—became by 1650 a "necessity."[16] Lima also became an important distribution center for enslaved people to other parts of Spain's American colonies. Flush with Peruvian silver, Lima's merchants bought what they considered the best merchandise in Cartagena and sold it on to locations in the rest of Peru as well as Ecuador and Chile.[17]

In 1612, a traveler to Mexico City, Vázquez de Espinosa, estimated that there were around 50,000 Blacks and mulattoes, 30,000 Natives, and 15,000 Spaniards.[18] By 1646, 70 percent of the Black population of New Spain was creole, a pattern that was likely mirrored in Mexico City.[19] The origins of Lima were different from those of Mexico City. While the latter was built upon the ruins of a thriving city-state, the Indigenous past of Lima was more distant but nonetheless significant. As Emily A. Engel explains, while Lima was a city "built at the behest of European interlopers" it was nonetheless the result of a coming together of past and present settlements populated by a multiplicity of cultural actors."[20] For her part, in her monumental and aesthetically arresting study *Lima: Memoria prehispánica de la traza urbana*, Adine Gavazzi traces the five thousand years of pre-Hispanic civilization in the area where Lima now stands, detailing how, over millennia, Native inhabitants transformed the desert area into a habitable and cultivatable terrain whose vestiges are still visible today, which then allowed the Spanish colonizers to found their city.[21] Moreover, following the conquest, many Indigenous peoples migrated to the region, and the presence of other groups made the city a baroque contact zone. By 1636, there were 13,260 Blacks in Lima, 11,088 Spaniards, and 1,426 Indians. In addition, there were 861 mulattoes, 327 mestizos, and 22 "Chinese."[22]

The same institutions that organized and placed the inhabitants of Lima and Mexico City into restrictive hierarchies also offered mechanisms that allowed marginal subjects to strive for a level of autonomy. As Herman Bennett analyzes, these mechanisms arose from the fact that by subjecting converted Africans and their descendants to canon law, the Catholic Church "authorized certain forms of private life among slaves."[23] He offers one of the key tensions attending the figure of enslaved people in the Americas: "Even as civil law sanctioned the master's dominion over chattel, canon law simultaneously upheld the slave's personhood."[24] This focus on personhood and on a "social self" leads Bennett away from "an institutional history of bondage" and toward the forms the lives of Afro-Mexicans took "beyond slavery and racial oppression."[25] He deliberately focuses on "Black community formation" rather than "race relations"—that is, his book charts Blacks' relationships with other Blacks rather than looking at them in relation to whites and the colonial power they held.[26] While the Crown most often allowed Indigenous peoples to stay in their own communities, the experiences of Africans were, of course, radically different, and slavery destroyed all preexisting community bonds. Therefore, Bennett's focus on Black community formation and relations within these communities is essential for understanding how Blacks as individuals built their lives as colonial subjects and, in so doing, forged a "narrative of liberty."[27] Working with what he terms the "colonial archive" or "absolutist" archive, he demonstrates how Africans and their descendants "exploited the legal opportunities within absolutism to make claims to their social selves."[28] While looking, as do other scholars, at how these subjects "exploited the legal opportunities within absolutism," he does so to demonstrate how they made claims to "their social selves."[29] At the same time, he calls into question "the assumption that colonial and national elites had an "unrestricted ability to define the historical icons of colonial and national culture."[30]

Both enslaved and free Black male subjects were instrumental in constructing the marvelous cities that stood as the jewels in the crown of the Spanish Empire, working as "architects, craftsmen, and skilled artisans; they constructed the monasteries, municipal buildings, and other ecclesiastical as well as secular institutions critical to colonial cities."[31] Women, for their part, also provided essential labor to secure the success of colonial societies, such as "child and elder care in households and convents, as well as supplied markets with prepared foods, bread, and produce."[32] While it is important to recognize both free and enslaved Black subjects' assistance in the creation of these cities, it is far more significant to look at how they engaged in social and affective practices independent of their identities as laborers tied to the viceregal commercial economy. While Spaniards and Creoles relied on Black subjects as "vital cogs" in this economy, Afro-Hispanics also lived lives that were not imbricated into their commodified roles.[33] They were not defined exclusively by the type of labor they conducted or by the conditions of this labor but were also "fathers and mothers, husbands and wives, sons and daughters, siblings, lovers, friends, neighbors and co-workers."[34] As Bennett elucidates, the narrative of private life (romantic relationships, child-rearing, friendship) did not require a relational entanglement with whites as opposed to the narrative of social mobility and instead allows us to "glimpse the relations that defined freedom."[35]

María Emma Mannarelli sheds light on some of these relationships and private experiences through her study of marriage in colonial Lima. While marriage rates of enslaved people were low because of the interference of owners (marriage between enslaved people did little to benefit owners), enslaved subjects and free Blacks did marry. While the Crown declared that marriage did not dissolve the bonds of slavery, Mannarelli points out that the kinship links developed through these relationships "created new relationships and networks that at least symbolically eroded the stigma of slavery" and that, in the best cases, these "links could favor real liberation" in a variety of ways.[36] The destructive, imperial force that enslaved Africans, as Bennett tells us, "was a distinct political process from the analogous process that Native Americans experienced."[37] At the same time, both groups struggled to forge a new colonial identity within the narrow framework the deeply hierarchical Spanish system allowed them.

While Native peoples in Mexico and Peru belonged to a wide variety of pre-Hispanic ethnic groups, within the colonial administrative system, they all became *indios*, as the name of their "republic" indicates.[38] While *indio* was an imposed colonial category that had no resonance with Indigenous peoples' preconquest identities, they could strategically mobilize it as a "signifier to differentiate themselves vis-à-vis other ethnic or social groups in order to gain recognition and additional privileges."[39] Begun in order to classify the conquered peoples in a way that would both protect them and allow the state to exploit them, over time, *indio* began to indicate "a collective form of identification that responded to people's needs and circumstances."[40] The category required them to "learn to maneuver within the different laws, concepts and values imposed by Spanish rule."[41] For Mónica Díaz, however, Indigenous peoples' appropriation of aspects of European identity in New Spain and Peru does not "alter their identities as indios."[42] Within baroque society, racialized and marginalized groups leveraged their assigned identities within colonial structures and institutions to achieve agency.[43]

In what follows, my goal is to trace the instances in which Africans, Afro-Hispanics, Indigenous peoples, and mixed-race subjects were able to engage in social and epistemological practices that held meaning for them as individuals. I also evoke the colonial structures that attempted to circumscribe their freedom as social actors. In this chapter, I explore the manifestation of baroque tension itself as racialized subjects forged autonomous paths through the stratified institutions and urban spaces of Lima and Mexico City.

"The Political Fiction" of the Two Republics

To demonstrate how Indigenous, Black, and *casta* subjects functioned within society and how they attempted to engage with the organization of this society to their advantage, I would like to establish how these groups were positioned in various ways within the baroque societies of Lima and Mexico City. In a gesture that was distinctive of Spanish imperial rule, the Crown divided its newly conquered territories into two administrative and juridical republics: of Spaniards and of Indians.[44] Spaniards, of course, positioned themselves at the apogee of New World society. As Vinson elucidates, "what we categorize today as 'race' became a means of dividing the spoils."[45] The two republics had, as we will see, both spatial and juridical implications, and they were designed to impose a "persistent and vigilant exercise of maintaining racial purity."[46] In the seventeenth century, jurists overseeing the creation of the two republics were obliged to "negotiate changing demographics unforeseen by colonial legislation," such as the radical decimation of the Indigenous populations and the phenomenon of racial mixture. The latter created new subjects "not easily categorized by the binary colonial code" who became a seventeenth-century demographic force, exposing the sixteenth-century "political fiction" of the two republics.[47]

The Indigenous subjects of the República de Indios possessed a "special status as Christian vassals of the Crown of Castile" but at the same time were somewhat paradoxically subject to the Crown's "political and socioeconomic subordination."[48] While they were permitted to "maintain internal hierarchies, retain their lands and enjoy relative political autonomy," they were at the same time fundamentally subordinated to the Crown politically and socioeconomically.[49] They were, moreover, designated as "miserable," which implied they lived in a state of grace and required the protection of a paternalistic state.[50] Thus, they were unable to sign contracts or legally dispose of their own land or possessions.[51] The relationship between Crown and Native subject was construed as "contractual and voluntary"—Native towns paid tribute, remained loyal to the king, and in return received the right to "maintain internal hierarchies, retain communal lands and enjoy relative political harmony."[52] The Spanish jurist Juan de Solórzano Pereira (1575–1655) and *oidor* of Lima described the two republics as making up one body of which all limbs are "indispensable in it, and necessary each one in her ministry."[53] Osorio claims that implicit here is the question of the "hierarchical order of viceregal estates and cities" in which the Republic of Indians "was there to serve the Spanish Republic," and Cuzco, where many Native subjects lived, was subordinate to Lima, the theoretically European city.[54]

As members of the Republic of Spaniards, albeit without any of the privileges, the Inquisition surveilled and punished Africans and their descendants in Lima and Mexico City. Most frequently, they were brought before the Inquisition and charged with moral and religious transgressions such as bigamy and blasphemy. In particular, they tended to be charged and punished "for renouncing God or the Virgin or making other blasphemous remarks that the clergy viewed as an expression of ingratitude toward the divine."[55] A great paradox attended the inclusion of Blacks in the jurisdiction of the Holy Office because the Crown did not consider them "long-standing Christians or more trustworthy converts than the Native people." Rather, they existed in an ill-defined limbo as members of the Republic of Spaniards with less clearly defined rights than the Native population.[56] Although it seems as though the Crown never made a formal proclamation regarding the purity of blood of Africans and their descendants, their blood was indeed considered impure. As Martínez details, the concept of *limpieza de sangre* was transported to Spain's American colonies, where it was reformulated to fit new societal realities that included "the survival of native communities and part of the pre-Hispanic nobility, the importance of the conversion project to Spanish colonialism and to Castile's titles to the Americas, the introduction of significant numbers of African slaves into the region, the rapid rise of a population of mixed ancestry, the influx of poor Spaniards seeking to better their lot if not to ennoble themselves, and the establishment of a transatlantic economy based largely on racialized labor forces."[57] Purity of blood was at the heart of this theoretically protected status for Indigenous peoples and for the Spaniards, who placed themselves above all others. To formalize what Spaniards perceived as their superiority in every way, they "designated themselves gente de razón"— those who were uniquely qualified to make rational decisions and were, moreover, "marked by their Christian faith."[58] Indigenous people were, in contrast, only Christian neophytes and "tender plants in the faith" who lacked the "trappings of civilization that Europeans most valued."[59] As the sixteenth century became the seventeenth, the Crown was faced with the reality of a surging number of mixed-race subjects who "were not easily characterized by the binary code" of Spanish or Indigenous.[60] Persons of mixed race, or *castas*, were originally considered not indigenous and therefore, by default, Spanish. Later, however, they were "subject to many of the same types of restrictions that had been applied to indigenous subjects with few of the protections."[61]

Part of the separation between the two republics entailed the theoretical removal of Native peoples from the jurisdiction of the Inquisition and the creation of a special body in New Spain called the Provisorato de Indias, which functioned in a similar manner to the Inquisition but with less autonomy.[62] It is not completely clear why the Crown created this new body in lieu of the Inquisition. One potential reason was fear that overzealous friars might engage in extreme punitive behavior with the Native neophytes, such as that exhibited by Diego de Landa, first bishop of Yucatán, in whose 1562 idolatry trials 4,500 Maya were tortured and 150 died.[63] However, the Provisorato's remit was the same as that of the Inquisition in that it oversaw moral and religious issues including heterodoxy. Moreover, as Martínez clarifies, the Inquisition itself continued to investigate Native affairs, paganism, and idolatry. In her study of baroque Lima, Osorio re-creates the scene of a rare public auto-da-fé held by the Extirpación de Idolatrías—a body that existed only in the Viceroyalty of Peru—in which an Indigenous man, Hernando de Paucar, was burned along with "idols and ornaments" in front of thousands of Andean spectators who had gathered there from far and wide to witness and learn from the punishment.[64]

Africans and their descendants, however, could mobilize the strictures of the Inquisition to try to protect themselves from the often-violent abuses of their masters. Archival research has shown that enslaved Black people "renounced God and His saints while being beaten to provoke the intervention of the Inquisition as a way to be freed, at least momentarily, from the harsh working conditions they endured."[65] This employment of strategic blasphemy by enslaved people could force the aggressor to stop the abuse through fear of which repercussions may ensue should the Inquisition investigate; the Holy Office could jail the enslaved person during a blasphemy trial at the owner's expense or force them to sell the enslaved person, for example.[66] Enslaved people were aware that the Inquisition believed that those who blasphemed while being whipped or otherwise abused could not be held responsible.[67] Enslaved victims of violence often declared that they had been forced to blaspheme as a result of their masters' actions and, in so doing, lost their souls.[68] Invoking the doctrine of salvation, they claimed their salvation was in jeopardy if they were obliged to continue in bondage to their abuser. In addition, sometimes the Inquisition would compel their master to sell them for that reason. As Villa-Flores explains, "Claiming a Christian identity allowed bondsmen to draw the attention of the Holy Office and thus obtaining the protection that judicial courts rarely granted."[69]

Living and Working in the Baroque City

Not only were laws created that divided colonial subjects into two symbolic polities or republics; viceregal authorities also attempted to order urban space according to racial groups. Both Lima and Mexico City, while radically different in their origins and their geography, were similarly organized and ordered with laws that segregated them along racial lines. These laws were formulated shortly after the conquest and created specific spaces for each population group. The very center of the city, the *traza*, was theoretically reserved only for the Spanish, but reality looked very different in urban areas: "The makeshift huts of the poor could be found in city centers and prosperous neighborhoods, tucked into empty lots or on the patios of other buildings."[70] Lima's urban culture was, however, both "fluid and hybrid," and while the central area around the Plaza Mayor was supposedly reserved for Spaniards and other areas of the city designated for Indigenous and Black people and other *castas*, the reality was quite different, as it was in Mexico City.[71] Osorio found evidence from as early as 1613 of what had once been considered "distinct ethnic groups" living and coexisting in shared buildings and dwellings all over the city.[72] Swelling the population numbers and ethnic composition of Lima residents in the latter half of the seventeenth century was rural-urban migration as well as Indians who came to the city on a temporary basis to pay tribute to Spanish *encomenderos*.[73] The cities of Lima and Mexico City attempted to forestall and control mingling through a variety of mechanisms that sought to reinforce hierarchies and mark difference between racial groups. For example, as Emma Mannarelli tells us, different groups received different punishments for the same exact offense. For throwing garbage in the river, Spaniards paid six pesos, but Blacks received a hundred lashes and Indigenous people sixty lashes in jail.[74] Sumptuary laws were issued to try to prevent *castas* from using the same clothes as Spaniards, with a 1631 edict forbidding mulattas, enslaved or not, from wearing garments made of silk or other fabrics identified with Spaniards, because they in particular were "perceived as dangerous to the social order."[75]

The Catholic Church was particularly interested in having Indigenous peoples living together and apart from other groups for a variety of reasons. The friars charged with their evangelization and subsequent Christian observance and piety feared that, should they mix with other groups, they would lose their Native identity and connection with the friars, and they might become mestizos and wear clothes that did not befit their status. They might, moreover, mix with undesirables—whether *castas* or Spaniards—and pick up bad habits, customs, or clothes that were not their own.[76] However, as the seventeenth century advanced, the authorities evinced less interest in protecting the Natives from the influence of Spaniards and began to focus on the former group's refusal to stay in their designated zones and obey instructions: "Having infiltrated the city, [the Indians] do not want to go to Mass or comply with the Church in their parishes. Nor do they know how to pray, nor wish to be counted [in attendance roles] on Sundays, nor to help in their neighborhoods with the duties and offices."[77]

Complaints such as these reveal that both seventeenth-century Lima and Mexico City possessed fluidity in terms of racial mixture and in possibilities for advancement for minoritized groups. Work and living space eroded these boundaries and brought different racial and social groups together, as did organizations such as confraternities.[78] Ben Vinson describes an urban environment in Mexico City where "skilled and crafty pretenders found entry into professions for which they were never intended."[79] He invokes a disorderly and mobile world where "mulattoes became priests, blacks became silversmiths, and plebeians of various hues became politicians and landowners of renown. Some petty criminals became Native lords."[80] The baroque city could not have existed without the labor of Indigenous, Black, and mixed-race subjects whose contributions ran the gamut from architect to skilled craftsmen to laborer, and they were involved in building ecclesiastical and secular institutions key to the functioning of the city.[81] While the Andean master architect José Kondori has been rightly praised for his contributions to Peruvian baroque architecture, many uncelebrated hands also fashioned those buildings and shaped those baroque cityscapes. Blacks and Indigenous peoples also participated in different facets—official or not—that made these cities into the spectacular centers we know them to have been. Africans and Afro-descendants were also essential to other parts of the colonial economy, working as muleteers guiding beasts of burden as they took goods to markets and other commercial destinations. As enslaved people, "Africans were the vanguard of an increasingly extensive commercial economy that revolved around the commodification of goods and people."[82] This economic dependence did not work out exactly how the Crown had designed it. While enslaved people were brought to the colonies to augment this population, "the trade in slaves actually facilitated the growth of the free colored population."[83] By the end of the sixteenth century, the number of births among free Black women in Mexico City rivaled deaths, leading to the creation of "the earliest and one of the largest free black populations in the New World."[84]

The protected status extended to Indigenous peoples did not exempt them from carrying out labor for the Spanish, and they were subject to working conditions that were sometimes as dreadful as those of their African counterparts. The seventeenth century saw Spanish officials proclaiming protections for Native laborers from Spanish colonizers and obliged owners of mines, textile workshops, and sugar mills to pay the workers a "just *jornal*."[85] Rachel O'Toole interprets this "dedication" on the part of the Crown and its colonial intermediaries to further the idea that their Indigenous vassals were "free from unjust coercion" and thus justify the rectitude of their colonial project. At the same time, their wages allowed them to continue to pay tribute to the Crown that constituted "an essential royal revenue" in the seventeenth century.[86] The preconquest communities they were supposedly allowed to maintain were radically transformed, first by the *encomienda* and then, at the end of the sixteenth century, by the *repartimiento* (most specifically in the mines of New Spain and Potosí) and in the *mita* of the Andes. This forced labor "shaped the transformation of colonial indigenous communities and modified their identities."[87]

Africans and Afro-descendants often worked in the most "dangerous and menial positions" and were often positioned as intermediaries in the workplace between Spaniards and Indians. Consequently, they were perceived as more masculine than Indians who were often feminized partly because of their status as vulnerable citizens.[88] Notwithstanding this imposed hierarchical labor structure, the relationship between Indigenous peoples, African and Afro-descendant peoples, as well as their shared descendants, was highly complex. For O'Toole, these racialized groups were "enemies as well as kin, friends and foes—sometimes simultaneously."[89]

Confraternities and Community Formation

Racialized and marginalized groups in baroque Mexico City and Lima were not permitted to hold official roles in the church from which they might wield authority. While women could live in convents as servants or slaves, they could never become nuns, nor could men become priests or friars. Slaves, free Blacks, and mixed-race subjects, as well as Indigenous peoples and women, were all, however, encouraged to be parishioners and to join *cofradías* (confraternities) or religious sodalities organized around the worship of a particular saint. These often-marginalized subjects availed themselves of membership in these lay organizations to "increase their personal status in urban society."[90] While Black confraternities had existed in Spain, they became more significant in the New World given the presence of a "rapidly expanding enslaved population, eager Catholic missionaries, and a more flexible and ambiguous social milieu than that offered by Old World cities."[91] African and Afro-descendant and Indigenous participation in confraternities allows us to see how the "viceregal church successfully drew in a wide range of society."[92] They were particularly central to community formation, social welfare, and well-being in

Black communities because, unlike Indigenous subjects, "people of African descent did not have ancient geographic and communal links to where they lived, nor did they often have multigenerational lineage ties with the people they knew in New Spain."[93]

In a marked difference to other communal spaces accessible to people of African descent, such as "bathhouses, bars selling pulque, gambling houses and brothels," confraternities provided a "legal, Catholic, and customary way for people to socialize" during Catholic holidays, festivals, member funerals, and other occasions.[94] While African and Afro-descendant confraternities were often poor, they did require that members possess some funds, and thus, most evidence of these organizations places them in sizable towns and cities where Blacks and mulattos earned wages.[95] Poverty could also be strategic, as Nicole von Germeten shows in the case of the Confraternity of the Rosario in Valladolid (now Morelia, Mexico), whose members petitioned the bishop to allow them to collect alms outside the city owing to their lack of means.[96] Confraternities employed the monies to help their members who underwent financial difficulties and represented the only social welfare organizations accessible to people of African descent.[97] Sick members would be visited by their *cofrades*, and the latter would help with funeral costs and accompany the body to the church.[98] O'Toole emphasizes that membership in a confraternity cannot be viewed as solely "opportunistic" for the African or Afro-descendant man who participated as a member in Peru; rather, it can also be understood as "an expression of an ongoing cultural adaptation across the Atlantic and southward along the Pacific coast" that combined "diasporic expressions with the possibilities offered by Catholic institutions."[99] Moreover, they helped create a way for African and Afro-descendant subjects to create a "sense of identity within the restrictive social structure of New Spain" and to forge a collective identity through religious observance.[100]

For Indigenous members of confraternities, these organizations became one of the "underpinnings" of their new identity as *indios*.[101] This did not necessarily constitute an erasure of all precontact identity, however, because membership in an Indigenous confraternity allowed them to "erect boundaries between themselves and non-Indians" and symbols of the Andean past such as Inca ancestors became "integral" to this new collective identity."[102] While the community formation the confraternities fostered took place under the auspices of Christianity, Indigenous members nonetheless viewed these organizations as their own.[103] In 1619, there were forty-six confraternities in the valley of Lima: eighteen for Spaniards, thirteen for Indians, and fifteen for Blacks and mulattoes.[104] The confraternities also allowed Indigenous musicians to participate in public life. The Jesuit Colegio de San Pablo trained and supported groups of musicians who played at festivals both within and outside the college.[105] Geoffrey Baker agrees with Paul Charney, detailing that Indigenous people in Peru enthusiastically adopted confraternities and their ceremonies. He ventures that some of their popularity might have come from points of contact between the confraternity and its rituals and some preconquest practices. He remarks on the similarities between the *ayullu*—"the basic unit of Indigenous society," which was organized around the veneration of a specific *huaca* or deity—and the confraternity.[106]

Witchcraft and Other Heterodox Practices: Knowledge Production and Minoritized Subjects

While confraternities permitted Black and Indigenous peoples to engage in community formation through religious participation, magical and healing practices allowed them to exercise specialized knowledge connected to their race and thus wield authority within communities. Leveraging this authority, however, often brought these practitioners into the crosshairs of bodies such as the Inquisition and the Extirpation. One area in which women accrued power through specialized knowledge was female sexual and reproductive practices, and the Extirpation, in particular, took an interest in preventing their use.[107] Osorio explains that records from this body reveal that "abortion practices, sexual encounters, and amorous potions" were particularly scrutinized.[108] These practices were often conceived of by their recipients less as sorcery and more as domestic matters, in that they were deployed to "resolve conflicts among partners" or to "tackle social and emotional problems related to illicit sexual relations, adultery and violence."[109] Osorio also forges a connection between the baroque city of Lima and this use of magic as power. She explains how the testimonies from Extirpation trials make it clear that "plebes could readily recognize and appropriate for their own purposes of 'magic' Lima's urban spaces of power," such as the Plaza Mayor and different important buildings such as churches. She tells the story of Tomasa, an enslaved Black woman who, using coca leaves, conjured the "'seven demons' of the fruit and fish market alleys," as well as those of the street corners on religious procession routes, the sites of triumphal arches, and the street corners adjacent to the Church of Santo Domingo. Osorio describes Tomasa wearing a white cloth over her head in imitation of the *palla* Chabela "while she sprinkled wine on the coca and curtsied to it."[110]

In her important study of the relationship between witchcraft and caste in colonial Mexico, Laura Lewis asserts that the "unsanctioned domain" of magic flipped the taxonomy of caste on its head to privilege the knowledge of Indigenous subjects over Spaniards. Blacks, mestizos, and mulattoes were "reoriented" in this dynamic in their role as intermediaries, attaching themselves to Indians "in a bid to undermine Spaniards."[111] Joan Bristol offers a similar analysis, claiming that Afro-descendants employed magic "to create alternate definitions of authority that diverged from those of the Crown and Spanish elites."[112] As Osorio points out, some scholars have placed racial dynamics at the heart of this practice of love magic and other folk rituals. She cites Elinor Burkett, who claimed that "urban women in seventeenth-century Peru were manipulated by the criteria and needs of a dominant class of white males, who continually frustrated their aspiration with regulations and social practices," as well as Irene Silverblatt, who argues that "rural Andean women rejected Spanish colonialism by taking a political decision to preserve and defend their preconquest culture, largely by taking refuge in the far reaches of the Andes."[113] Osorio, for her part, believes that the practices were "urban and rural, Andean, African and European" and that, furthermore, they mixed "official" and "plebeian" discourses and knowledges to create "a complex process of transculturation" in baroque Lima.[114] We can also extend Osorio's analysis to articulate something that she hints at but does not state explicitly—that the complex hierarchies of race and ethnicity seem to break down when subjects wielded the power of folk practices and "magic." In her examination of Afro-descendant ritual practices, Bristol cites the case of a Spanish *alguacil* who gladly accepted the treatments of a mulatta woman, "a person who would have been considered far inferior to him in terms of calidad, gender, wealth, and power."[115] Bristol attributes this apparent dissolving of hierarchy in the context of "routine" utilization by Spaniards (and others) of ritual cures and folk medicine purveyed by Indigenous or Afro-Mexican curanderos or perhaps "magic" to a desire on the part of these marginalized subjects to assume control over their own lives.[116] Their mobilizing of knowledge to hitherto forbidden authority did not mean they wished to "encroach on Spanish authority and definitions of honor-status rooted in ideas about *limpieza de sangre*, wealth and inherited position"; rather, they wanted to improve the circumstances of their living conditions.[117] However, there were dangers in this transgressive mobilization of authority for Africans and Afro-Hispanics, and Bristol recounts stories of Spaniards who, desiring to reinstate the racial hierarchy, would invoke the power of the Inquisition.[118] In addition, Bristol makes a strong case for the influence of West and West Central African practices on colonial divination and folk medicine alongside Indigenous and some European influences.[119] She also explains that while these practices became hybridized, as Osorio too claims, African and Indigenous beliefs responded to a more capacious understanding of the supernatural world in which "ancestors, spirits and deities behaved in good and bad ways and caused both health and illness depending on how they were treated."[120] Spaniards, of course, subscribed to a more Manichaean view of religious ideology in which demonic forces promoted evil and the saints always strove to bring good into the world. African and Indigenous views of a less dichotomous society often led them into trouble with bodies such as the Inquisition and the Extirpation, who saw these ill-defined boundaries as indications of demonic pacts. Fluidity existed around the definition of witchcraft versus healing, for example, and this definition was often left to the discretion of individual Inquisitors or officials.[121] However, "authority and calidad" were important elements that helped shape the way society at large defined witches and witchcraft, with the non-Spanish population reliant on these remedies because of lack of access to a licensed physician and because academic medical knowledge was "limited" to those with funds or contacts.[122] Native and Afro-descendant peoples were perceived to be "more in tune with the natural world," and their remedies often addressed social problems that "Spanish medicine could not or would not treat."[123] Bristol also notes that, while some practitioners were male, most curers and their clients were women.[124] Just as women of all castes employed curers to procure love magic to place men under their control and create a "world in reverse," enslaved people also utilized magic as clients to try to assert control over their owners and thus over aspects of their lives.[125] Bristol explains that the magic employed in both situations was very similar, if not the same.[126] These types of spells involved putting substances such as powders in their owners' food. She offers the example from 1626 of a slave named Dominga in Tepeaca who bought powders from Native American curers and put them in her owner's chocolate.[127] She notes that in many of these cases, enslaved people were not looking for revenge over their owners but were searching for security, something that proved elusive to them. She stresses, as other historians like Bennett have, that servitude did not define these subjects, who "had skills and relationships outside the realm of work," but that "relationships with their owners and other presumed social superiors played an important role in shaping the contours of their lives."[128]

Indigenous Intellectuals

The type of activities I have referenced can be classified as the production of pragmatic knowledge, defined as something "acquired and expressed through habitus and performance" and then "mobilized and put into action."[129] Indigenous intellectuals, however, also engaged in what Ramos and Yannakakis identify as ideological knowledge—"knowledge in its discursive forms, more widely recognizable as intellectual production."[130] These scholars assert that Indigenous intellectuals "produced and made use of both forms simultaneously" to "make colonial society viable" for them and their communities.[131] They describe the different knowledge production strategies Native people employed to survive the challenges of Spanish colonial rule, strategies that involved "mutual loans, thefts, struggles, and negotiations over knowledge."[132] It is also important to recognize that these intellectual survival techniques often took place in the form of writing, something Indigenous peoples had not practiced in their intellectual and administrative systems before the Spanish conquest. Writing became important and strategic for both these intellectuals and their communities, who were "forced to adapt the directive and organizational roles that existed in their societies prior to the conquest."[133] Those who refused to do so and were caught engaging in preconquest practices were punished or forced underground.[134] Those who proved able to adapt became more socially mobile and worked as "scribes, notaries, legal agents and interpreters."[135] These colonial functionaries, whom Ramos and Yannakakis deem intellectuals, produced administrative and legal documents such as wills, bills of sale, and records of Indigenous municipalities—what Ramos and Yannakakis call "the grist for colonial rule."[136] While these records produce "colonial knowledge" and offer an example of the "legitimization of colonial rule," they also represent the presence of an "archive of indigenous ideas, initiatives and interpretations."[137]

This cadre of scribes also attests to how Indigenous males became educated in the colonial system in both Mexico and Peru. The educational focus of Spanish authorities for Indigenous peoples fell on the elites for whom missionaries founded a network of *colegios* that taught them Christian doctrine, Latin, and Castilian.[138] The most famous example in Lima is the royal boarding school, the Colegio del Príncipe, founded in 1618 by the Jesuits who planned "to mold a select cadre of hereditary chiefs [*curacas*] who teach and personify orthodox Christian values" to resistant Native communities.[139] John Charles, however, recounts that the college's students and graduates did not always conform to the institution's principles and "used their knowledge of Spanish values and legal principles" in ways that did not always "serve colonizing agendas."[140] In her study of Indigenous intellectuals in colonial Peru, Alcira Dueñas also demonstrates how Indigenous scribes strategically employed their Western education in "literacy, rhetoric, Latin, and political theology" along with their "experiential knowledge as subordinated colonial subjects" to construct "critical views of the colonial order" and "empower their own political agendas, reformulating the religious philosophical tenets they learned as part of their education."[141]

Other educational opportunities for Indigenous males came from networks of priests and within Native communities themselves via priests' Native assistants (*fiscales*), Indigenous scribes (*escribanos*), and legal agents (*apoderados*).[142] What is important to note is that pre-Hispanic community and social structure often determined colonial organizations. The decentralized Mesoamerican pre-Hispanic ethnic polities "enjoyed a tradition of political semiautonomy," which then led to a colonial organization of semiautonomous municipalities or *pueblos de indios* that were headed by *cabildos,* which in turn were staffed by Native scribes.[143] In contrast, the Viceroyalty of Peru was built upon the vestiges of a more centralized Inca Empire whose "record keeping and more sparse urbanization provided a different framework."[144]

Conclusion

The baroque urban centers of Mexico City and Lima ostensibly stood as glittering examples of Spanish imperial power in the Americas. Underpinning these spectacular cities was the subjugation of the Native populations as well as the bondage of enslaved peoples forcibly brought from Africa, the marginalization of their descendants, and a burgeoning population of the descendants of both groups. These populations built and sustained these cities in large part, but the Spanish authorities and their creole representatives strove to ensure they did not ascend the social hierarchy. However, while in theory, urban spaces and the institutions that inhabited them supported this exclusion, in practice, marginalized and racialized subjects found multiple ways to develop identities independent of the labor they carried out and their servitude and to live as social actors within these cities.

NOTES

1. Stephanie Merrim, *The Spectacular City, Mexico, and Colonial Hispanic Literary Culture* (Austin: University of Texas Press, 2010), 150.
2. Nora E. Jaffary, *False Mystics: Deviant Orthodoxy in Colonial Mexico* (Lincoln: University of Nebraska Press, 2004), 42. As José Antonio Mazzotti points out: "'criollo' was a Hispanization of the Portuguese 'crioulo,' which originally referred to the offspring of Africans born in the New World. In time, within the Spanish possessions in the Americas, 'criollo' referred to the white descendants of Spaniards born in the New World. 'Criollos' considered themselves to be culturally Europeans, but emotionally their allegiance was to the land or patria where they were born." José Antonio Mazzotti, "*Criollismo*, Creole, and Creolité," in *Critical Terms in Caribbean and Latin American Thought: Historical and Institutional Trajectories*, ed. Yolanda Martínez-San Miguel, Ben Sifuentes-Jauregui, and Marisa Belausteguigoitia (New York: Palgrave Macmillan, 2018), 88.
3. Jaffary, *False Mystics*, 42.
4. Jaffary, *False Mystics*, 42.
5. César Salgado, "Hybridity in New World Baroque Theory," *Journal of American Folklore* 112, no. 445 (1999): 317.
6. Salgado, "Hybridity," 323. As Salgado tells us, Lezama never explicitly defines what he means by "plutonism" but that could be described as "a destructive cosmogonical form of energy that emanates from some primal and volcanic 'big bang' violence" (323).
7. Merrim, *The Spectacular City*, 147, 147–148.
8. Merrim, *The Spectacular City*, 148.
9. Merrim, *The Spectacular City*, 148.
10. Barbara E. Mundy, *The Death of Aztec Tenochtitlan, the Life of Mexico City* (Austin: University of Texas Press, 2015), 3.
11. Herman L. Bennett, *Colonial Blackness: A History of Afro-Mexico* (Bloomington: Indiana University Press, 2009), 5.
12. Ben Vinson, *Before Mestizaje: The Frontiers of Race and Caste in Colonial Mexico* (New York: Cambridge University Press, 2017), 6.
13. Vinson, *Before Mestizaje*, 6.
14. Bennett, *Colonial Blackness*, 18.
15. Proctor, qtd. in Bennett, *Colonial Blackness*, 18.
16. Tamara Walker, "Slavery in Peru," *Oxford Bibliographies*, https://www.oxfordbibliographies.com/display/document/obo-9780199766581/obo-9780199766581-0154.xml; Frederick Bowser, *The African Slave in Colonial Peru, 1524–1650* (Stanford, CA: Stanford University Press, 1974), ix.
17. Bowser, *The African Slave in Colonial Peru*, 55.
18. Joseph E. Harris, *Global Dimensions of the African Diaspora* (Washington, DC: Howard University Press, 1993), 167.
19. Bennett, *Colonial Blackness*, 5.
20. Emily A. Engel, "Locating an American Capital in the Early Modern World," in *A Companion to Early Modern Lima*, ed. Emily A. Engel (Leiden: Brill, 2019), 3.

21. Adine Gavazzi, *Lima: Memoria prehispánica de la traza urbana* (Lima: Apus Graph Ediciones, 2014).
22. Karen Graubart, "'So color de una cofradía': Catholic Confraternities and the Development of Afro-Peruvian Ethnicities in Early Colonial Peru," *Slavery and Abolition* 33, no. 1 (2012): 46. As Graubart details, there is "rough parity" between the growth of Spaniards and Blacks from the 1550s onward, although the documentation is sparse (46).
23. Bennett, *Colonial Blackness*, 1.
24. Bennett, *Colonial Blackness*, 1.
25. Bennett, *Colonial Blackness*, 10, 12.
26. Bennett, *Colonial Blackness*, 9.
27. Bennett, *Colonial Blackness*, 11.
28. Bennett, *Colonial Blackness*, 11.
29. Bennett, *Colonial Blackness*, 11.
30. Bennett, *Colonial Blackness*, 11.
31. Rachel O'Toole, "As Historical Subjects: The African Diaspora in Colonial Latin American History," *History Compass* 11, no. 12 (2013): 1094.
32. O'Toole, "As Historical Subjects," 1094.
33. Bennett, *Colonial Blackness*, 4.
34. Bennett, *Colonial Blackness*, 2.
35. Bennett, *Colonial Blackness*, 11.
36. María Emma Mannarelli, *Private Passions and Public Sins: Men and Women in Seventeenth-Century Lima*, trans. Sidney Evans and Meredith D. Dodge (Albuquerque: University of New Mexico Press, 2007), 120.
37. Bennet, *Colonial Blackness*, 212.
38. Mónica Díaz, "Introduction: Indio Identities in Colonial Spanish America," in *To Be Indio in Colonial Spanish America*, ed. Mónica Díaz (Albuquerque: University of New Mexico Press, 2017), 21. For further information on the construction and use of the term "indio," see Marisa Belausteguigoitia, "From *Indigenismo* to *Zapatismo*: Scenarios of Construction of the Indigenous Subject," in *Critical Terms in Caribbean and Latin American Thought*, ed. Yolanda Martínez-San Miguel, Ben Sifuentes-Jauregui, and Marisa Belausteguigoitia (New York: Palgrave Macmillan, 2018).
39. Díaz, "Introduction," 4.
40. Díaz, "Introduction," 21.
41. Díaz, "Introduction," 21.
42. Díaz, "Introduction," 4.
43. While she focuses on the eighteenth century, which goes beyond the scope of this essay, Tamara J. Walker's study on the intersection of dress and race in Peru demonstrates how enslaved and freed people of African descent used clothing as a means of seizing and expressing different forms of agency and subjectivity. Although owners of enslaved people often outfitted them in a way that sought to demonstrate the owners' social status, Afro-descendant peoples also used clothing as a way of fashioning the self. As Walker writes, "Although we cannot know what was in the hearts and minds of the slaves whose limited access to literacy left their thoughts and feelings about their bodies largely unrecorded, many did take actions that demonstrated just how strong was their own commitment to elegant self-presentation. They had their own ways and reasons to acquire elegant dress. In addition to outfitting themselves in finery, they

provided clothing to social intimates as well. For these men and women, clothing was a key tool with which they laid claim to their humanity and challenged the limits of their condition." Tamara J. Walker, *Exquisite Slaves: Exquisite Slaves: Race, Clothing, and Status in Colonial Lima* (Cambridge: Cambridge University Press, 2017), 16.

44. Vinson explains that the system was "based loosely on the social principles of late medieval Spain where society was organized into an estate system according to hereditary landlord/serf relationships, and borrowing the social stratification underlying the corporate arrangement of Spanish cities, the dual republic was the Spanish attempt to transplant the hierarchies of the Old World onto the racial landscape of the Americas. Indians were to become almost akin to the serfs of Europe, while whiteness stood as a marker of noble status." *Before Mestizaje*, 3.
45. Vinson, *Before Mestizaje*, 2.
46. Vinson, *Before Mestizaje*, 5.
47. Anna More, *Baroque Sovereignty: Carlos de Sigüenza y Góngora and the Creole Archive of Colonial Mexico* (Philadelphia: University of Pennsylvania Press, 2012), 30.
48. María Elena Martínez, *Genealogical Fictions: Limpieza de Sangre, Religion, and Gender in Colonial Mexico* (Stanford, CA: Stanford University Press, 2008), 92.
49. Martínez, *Genealogical Fictions*, 92.
50. Martínez, *Genealogical Fictions*, 103.
51. Martínez, *Genealogical Fictions*, 103.
52. Martínez, *Genealogical Fictions*, 92.
53. Qtd. in Osorio, *Inventing Lima*, 43.
54. Osorio, *Inventing Lima*, 44.
55. Martínez, *Genealogical Fictions*, 220.
56. Martínez, *Genealogical Fictions*, 221.
57. Martínez, *Genealogical Fictions*, 2.
58. Vinson, *Before Mestizaje*, 2–3.
59. Martínez, *Genealogical Fictions*, 103; Vinson, *Before Mestizaje*, 3.
60. More, *Baroque*, 30.
61. More, *Baroque*, 31. The *casta* paintings of the eighteenth century—popular paintings that depicted racial hierarchy and race mixing through fictive family groups—show one facet of how complex questions of race and racial mixing were addressed, principally by elites and dominant social groups. Speaking of the phenomenon in New Spain, Ilona Katzew explains that the motive for their creation and commissioning "can be placed within European concepts of the exotic and the impetus to classify." Ilona Katzew, *Casta Painting: Images of Race in Eighteenth-century Mexico* (New Haven: Yale University Press, 2004), 1. The paintings also speak to what she calls "a special concern with the construction of a particular self-image" and that, of course, this "vision of reality . . . should not be taken at face value but should be analyzed in terms of how identity was formed within the colonial arena." Katzew, 1. Walker discusses the differences between New Spanish *casta* painting and the Peruvian iteration, focusing on topics including chronological variations and differences in how these paintings were commissioned. In Walker's study, her main interest is what she terms "the Peruvian paintings' message about the relationship between clothing, color, and status, particularly in light of their intended audience." Walker, *Exquisite Slaves*, 16.
62. Martínez, *Genealogical Fictions*, 102.

63. Martínez, *Genealogical Fictions*, 102.
64. Martínez, *Genealogical Fictions*, 121–22.
65. Javier Villa-Flores, "Voices from a Living Hell: Slavery, Death, and Salvation in a Mexican Obraje," in *Local Religion in Colonial Mexico*, ed. Martin Nesvig (Albuquerque: University of New Mexico Press, 2006), 236.
66. Villa-Flores, "Voices," 236.
67. Villa-Flores, "Voices," 237.
68. Villa-Flores, "Voices," 236.
69. Villa-Flores, "Voices," 237.
70. On the *traza*, see More, *Baroque Sovereignty*, 164. On the reality in urban areas, see Joan Cameron Bristol, *Christians, Blasphemers, and Witches: Afro-Mexican Ritual Practice in the Seventeenth Century* (Albuquerque: University of New Mexico Press, 2007), 3.
71. Osorio describes how the Reducción de Santiago del Cercado was reserved for Indians and that San Lázaro, across the Rimac River, was for Blacks and mixed-race *castas*. *Inventing Lima*, 24.
72. Osorio, *Inventing Lima*, 24.
73. Mannarelli, *Private Passions*, 22.
74. Mannarelli, *Private Passions*, 32.
75. Mannarelli, *Private Passions*, 32.
76. More, *Baroque Sovereignty*, 166.
77. As cited in More, *Baroque Sovereignty*, 165.
78. Bristol, *Christians, Blasphemers, and Witches*, 2–3.
79. Vinson, *Before Mestizaje*, 2.
80. Vinson, *Before Mestizaje*, 2.
81. O'Toole, "As Historical Subjects," 1094.
82. Bennet, *Colonial Blackness*, 4.
83. Bennet, *Colonial Blackness*, 5.
84. Bennet, *Colonial Blackness*, 5.
85. Rachel O'Toole, *Bound Lives: Africans, Indians, and the Making of Race in Colonial Peru* (Pittsburgh, PA: University of Pittsburgh Press, 2012), 20.
86. O'Toole, *Bound Lives*, 20.
87. Díaz, "Introduction," 25.
88. O'Toole, "As Historical Subjects," 1098.
89. O'Toole, *Bound Lives*, 3.
90. Nicole von Germeten, "Routes to Respectability: Confraternities and Men of African Descent in New Spain," in *Local Religion in Colonial Mexico*, ed. Martin Nesvig (University of New Mexico Press, 2006), 216.
91. Graubart, "'So color de una cofradía,'" 48.
92. Germeten, "Routes to Respectability," 216.
93. Germeten, "Routes to Respectability," 217.
94. Germeten, "Routes to Respectability," 216.
95. Germeten, "Routes to Respectability," 217.
96. Germeten, "Routes to Respectability," 225.
97. Germeten, "Routes to Respectability," 217.
98. Bristol, *Christians, Blasphemers, and Witches*, 105.
99. O'Toole, *Bound Lives*, 58.

100. Bristol, *Christians, Blasphemers, and Witches*, 107.
101. Paul Charney, "A Sense of Belonging: Colonial Indian Cofradias and Ethnicity in the Valley of Lima, Peru," *The Americas* 54, no. 3 (1998): 381.
102. Charney, "A Sense of Belonging," 381–82.
103. Charney, "A Sense of Belonging," 382.
104. Charney, "A Sense of Belonging," 385.
105. Geoffrey Baker, *Imposing Harmony: Music and Society in Colonial Cuzco* (Durham, NC: Duke University Press, 2008), 145.
106. Baker, *Imposing Harmony*, 210.
107. Osorio, *Inventing Lima*, 125.
108. Osorio, *Inventing Lima*, 126.
109. Osorio, *Inventing Lima*, 127.
110. Osorio, *Inventing Lima*, 130.
111. Laura Lewis, *Hall of Mirrors: Power, Witchcraft, and Caste in Colonial Mexico* (Durham, NC: Duke University Press, 2003), 6.
112. Bristol, *Christians, Blasphemers, and Witches*, 165.
113. Osorio, *Inventing Lima*, 132.
114. Osorio, *Inventing Lima*, 132.
115. Bristol, *Christians, Blasphemers, and Witches*, 150.
116. Bristol, *Christians, Blasphemers, and Witches*, 188.
117. Bristol, *Christians, Blasphemers, and Witches*, 188.
118. Bristol, *Christians, Blasphemers, and Witches*, 151.
119. Bristol, *Christians, Blasphemers, and Witches*, 153–54.
120. Bristol, *Christians, Blasphemers, and Witches*, 159.
121. Bristol, *Christians, Blasphemers, and Witches*, 162.
122. Bristol, *Christians, Blasphemers, and Witches*, 162.
123. Bristol, *Christians, Blasphemers, and Witches*, 164.
124. Bristol, *Christians, Blasphemers, and Witches*, 167. Referencing the work of Naomi Quesada, Bristol asserts that "male and female clients had different goals. Men hoped to fulfill their desires for erotic adventures and prove their masculinity, while women tried to create security, using magic to recall straying partners and improve abusive situations" (167).
125. Behar, as cited in in Bristol, *Christians, Blasphemers, and Witches*, 166, 168.
126. Bristol, *Christians, Blasphemers, and Witches*, 169.
127. Bristol, *Christians, Blasphemers, and Witches*, 169.
128. Bristol, *Christians, Blasphemers, and Witches*, 170.
129. Gabriela Ramos and Yanna Yannakakis, *Indigenous Intellectuals: Knowledge, Power, and Colonial Culture in Mexico and the Andes* (Durham, NC: Duke University Press, 2014), 2.
130. Ramos and Yannakakis, *Indigenous Intellectuals*, 1.
131. Ramos and Yannakakis, *Indigenous Intellectuals*, 1.
132. Ramos and Yannakakis, *Indigenous Intellectuals*, 3.
133. Ramos and Yannakakis, *Indigenous Intellectuals*, 7.
134. Ramos and Yannakakis, *Indigenous Intellectuals*, 7.
135. Ramos and Yannakakis, *Indigenous Intellectuals*, 7.
136. Ramos and Yannakakis, *Indigenous Intellectuals*, 7.

137. Ramos and Yannakakis, *Indigenous Intellectuals*, 8.
138. Ramos and Yannakakis, *Indigenous Intellectuals*, 2.
139. John Charles, "Trained by Jesuits: Indigenous Letrados in Seventeenth-Century Mexico," in *Indigenous Intellectuals: Knowledge, Power, and Colonial Culture in Mexico and the Andes*, ed. Gabriela Ramos and Yanna Yannakakis (Durham, NC: Duke University Press, 2014), 61. As Leslie Bethell points out, in many ways Lima's seventeenth-century Colegio del Príncipe set out to emulate the previous century's New Spanish Colegio de Santa Cruz del Tlatelolco, which provided the model for the humanistic education of noble male Indigenous students. Leslie Bethell, *Colonial Spanish America* (Cambridge: Cambridge University Press,1987).
140. Charles, "Trained by Jesuits," 62.
141. Alcira Duenas, *Indians and Mestizos in the "Lettered City": Reshaping Justice, Social Hierarchy, and Political Culture in Colonial Peru* (Boulder: University Press of Colorado, 2010), 34.
142. Ramos and Yannakakis, *Indigenous Intellectuals*, 9.
143. Ramos and Yannakakis, *Indigenous Intellectuals*, 10.
144. Ramos and Yannakakis, *Indigenous Intellectuals*, 16.

BIBLIOGRAPHY

Baker, Geoffrey. *Imposing Harmony: Music and Society in Colonial Cuzco*. Durham, NC: Duke University Press, 2008.

Belausteguigoitia, Marisa. "From *Indigenismo* to *Zapatismo*: Scenarios of Construction of the Indigenous Subject." In *Critical Terms in Caribbean and Latin American Thought: Historical and Institutional Trajectories*, edited by Yolanda Martínez-San Miguel, Ben Sifuentes-Jauregui, and Marisa Belausteguigoitia, 23–36. New York: Palgrave Macmillan, 2018.

Bennett, Herman L. *Colonial Blackness: A History of Afro-Mexico*. Bloomington: Indiana University Press, 2009.

Bethell, Leslie. *Colonial Spanish America*. Cambridge: Cambridge University Press, 1987.

Bowser, Frederick. *The African Slave in Colonial Peru, 1524–1650*. Stanford, CA: Stanford University Press, 1974.

Bristol, Joan Cameron. *Christians, Blasphemers, and Witches: Afro-Mexican Ritual Practice in the Seventeenth Century*. Albuquerque: University of New Mexico Press, 2007.

Charles, John. "Trained by Jesuits: Indigenous *Letrados* in Seventeenth-Century Mexico." In *Indigenous Intellectuals: Knowledge, Power, and Colonial Culture in Mexico and the Andes*, edited by Gabriela Ramos and Yanna Yannakakis, 60–78. Durham, NC: Duke University Press, 2014.

Charney, Paul. "A Sense of Belonging: Colonial Indian Cofradias and Ethnicity in the Valley of Lima, Peru." *The Americas* 54, no. 3 (1998): 379–407.

Díaz, Mónica. "Introduction: *Indio* Identities in Colonial Spanish America." In *To Be Indio in Colonial Spanish America*, edited by Mónica Díaz, 1–30. Albuquerque: University of New Mexico Press, 2017.

Dueñas, Alcira. *Indians and Mestizos in the "Lettered City": Reshaping Justice, Social Hierarchy, and Political Culture in Colonial Peru*. Boulder: University Press of Colorado, 2010.

Engel, Emily A. "Locating an American Capital in the Early Modern World." In *A Companion to Early Modern Lima*, edited by Emily A. Engel, 1–23. Leiden: Brill, 2019.

Gavazzi, Adine. *Lima: Memoria pre-hispánica de la traza urbana*. Lima: APUS Graph Ediciones, 2014.

Graubart, Karen. "'So color de una cofradía': Catholic Confraternities and the Development of Afro-Peruvian Ethnicities in Early Colonial Peru." *Slavery and Abolition* 33, no. 1 (2012): 43–64.

Harris, Joseph E. *Global Dimensions of the African Diaspora*. Washington, DC: Howard University Press, 1993.

Jaffary, Nora E. *False Mystics: Deviant Orthodoxy in Colonial Mexico*. Lincoln: University of Nebraska Press, 2004.

Katzew, Ilona. *Casta Painting: Images of Race in Eighteenth-Century Mexico*. New Haven, CT: Yale University Press, 2004.

Lewis, Laura. *Hall of Mirrors: Power, Witchcraft, and Caste in Colonial Mexico*. Durham, NC: Duke University Press, 2003.

Mannarelli, María Emma. *Private Passions and Public Sins: Men and Women in Seventeenth-Century Lima*. Translated by Sidney Evans and Meredith D. Dodge. Albuquerque: University of New Mexico Press, 2007.

Martínez, María Elena. *Genealogical Fictions: Limpieza de Sangre, Religion, and Gender in Colonial Mexico*. Stanford, CA: Stanford University Press, 2008.

Mazzotti, José Antonio. "*Criollismo*, Creole, and *Creolité*." In *Critical Terms in Caribbean and Latin American Thought: Historical and Institutional Trajectories*, edited by Yolanda Martínez-San Miguel, Ben Sifuentes-Jauregui, and Marisa Belausteguigoitia, 87–100. New York: Palgrave Macmillan, 2018.

Merrim, Stephanie. *The Spectacular City, Mexico, and Colonial Hispanic Literary Culture*. Austin: University of Texas Press, 2010.

More, Anna. *Baroque Sovereignty: Carlos de Sigüenza y Góngora and the Creole Archive of Colonial Mexico*. Philadelphia: University of Pennsylvania Press, 2012.

Mundy, Barbara E. *The Death of Aztec Tenochtitlan, the Life of Mexico City*. Austin: University of Texas Press, 2015.

Osorio, Alejandra. *Inventing Lima: Baroque Modernity in Peru's South Sea Metropolis*. London: Palgrave Macmillan, 2008.

O'Toole, Rachel. "As Historical Subjects: The African Diaspora in Colonial Latin American History." *History Compass* 11, no. 12 (2013): 1094–1110.

———. *Bound Lives: Africans, Indians, and the Making of Race in Colonial Peru*. Pittsburgh, PA: University of Pittsburgh Press, 2012.

Ramos, Gabriela, and Yanna Yannakakis. *Indigenous Intellectuals: Knowledge, Power, and Colonial Culture in Mexico and the Andes*. Durham, NC: Duke University Press, 2014.

Salgado, César. "Hybridity in New World Baroque Theory." *Journal of American Folklore* 112, no. 445 (1999): 316–331.

Villa-Flores, Javier. "Voices from a Living Hell: Slavery, Death, and Salvation in a Mexican Obraje." In *Local Religion in Colonial Mexico*, edited by Martin Nesvig, 235–258. Albuquerque: University of New Mexico Press, 2006.

Vinson, Ben. *Before Mestizaje: The Frontiers of Race and Caste in Colonial Mexico*. New York: Cambridge University Press, 2017.

von Germeten, Nicole. "Routes to Respectability: Confraternities and Men of African Descent in New Spain." In *Local Religion in Colonial Mexico*, edited by Martin Nesvig, 215–234. University of New Mexico Press, 2006.

Walker, Tamara. "Slavery in Peru." Oxford Bibliographies. https://doi.org/10.1093/OBO/9780199766581-0154.

———. *Exquisite Slaves: Race, Status, and Clothing in Colonial Lima*. Cambridge: Cambridge University Press, 2017.

CHAPTER 3

African Slavery in Latin America

MIGUEL A. VALERIO

Of the more than ten million enslaved Africans who survived the Middle Passage (more than two million perished), over seven million were disembarked in what we call today Latin America (Table 3.1). The first enslaved Africans to arrive in the Americas arrived in Hispaniola in 1501. It was there also that the first slave revolution proved successful, although the tragic aftermath details the price Haiti is still paying for this transgression against the project of modernity. Brazil was the last country in the hemisphere to abolish slavery in 1888, shortly after Spain did the same in its remaining American colonies and 387 years after the first enslaved African arrived on American shores. All this has made the Black experience central to the region's history and culture, yet African slavery is hardly part of the national imaginaries of the region—though recent movements (discussed in chapter 14 of this volume) have brought Latin America's Black debt to the forefront of national debates, especially in Colombia and Brazil, but also in unlikely places like Mexico, Chile, and Argentina. In these two last countries, this has been the aftershock of the devastating 2010 earthquake in Haiti, with many Latin American countries taking in Haitian refugees in its immediate aftermath, which in turn brought old racisms to the forefront of national debates. All of it, the enduring legacy and trauma of slavery in the region.

While this chapter provides only a brief overview of slavery and its ideological underpinning in the region, the other chapters in this volume discuss

TABLE 3.1: Estimates of enslaved Africans disembarked in Latin America, 1501–1875

YEAR	SPANISH AMERICA	BRAZIL	FRENCH AMERICA	TOTAL
1501–1525	4,462	4,914	0	9,376
1526–1550	17,763	17,771	0	35,534
1551–1575	19,720	22,174	50	41,944
1576–1600	42,037	67,879	0	109,916
1601–1625	58,445	214,808	0	273,253
1626–1650	31,421	166,017	1,479	198,917
1651–1675	9,464	209,690	5,456	224,610
1676–1700	4,670	261,523	22,265	288,458
1701–1725	0	421,232	95,357	516,589
1726–1750	0	470,236	216,213	686,449
1751–1775	3,634	476,596	278,479	758,709
1776–1800	5,601	623,298	369,121	998,020
1801–1825	15,1367	1,037,342	117,969	1,306,678
1826–1850	35,4813	1,099,018	58,579	1,512,410
1851–1875	18,1526	7,318	0	188,844
Total	88,4923	5,099,816	1,164,968	7,149,707

Source: Slave Voyages (slavevoyages.org/assessments/estimates), September 28, 2021

the Black experience in Latin America within its broader, multiracial, and multiethnic contexts, from 1492 to the present.

Like the study of African slavery in general, the study of African slavery in Latin America is booming. Pioneers like Frederick P. Bowser, A. J. R. Russell-Wood, Enriqueta Vila Vilar, and Herbert Klein paved the way.[1] Today, David Wheat, David Eltis, and Alex Borucki lead the field with their work on the Slave Voyages database and publications that elucidate that data set.[2] For nineteenth-century Brazil, the work of João José Reis and Sidney Chalhoub are required references.[3] Thanks to this scholarship, we know much more about African slavery in the region than we did twenty years ago. We know, for example, of the complex networks of internal trade within the region.[4] Scholars like Herman L. Bennett, Michelle McKinley, Rachel Sarah O'Toole, Erika Edwards, Chloe Ireton, Sherwin K. Bryant, and Ricardo Raúl Salazar Rey have studied the legal dimension and contestation of bondage in the region.[5]

The trade went through several stages. In the sixteenth century, Iberian monarchs granted personal licenses to individuals to transport a given number of enslaved Africans. In 1580, with the unification of the Iberian crowns under Spanish rule, Philip II granted the monopoly of the trade to Portuguese traders under the asiento system. After the dissolution of the Iberian Union in 1640, French, British, and Dutch traders gradually came into the slave trade in Latin America, and by the eighteenth century, the trade to Latin America was part of the larger network of slave traders. In the Caribbean, Havana and Veracruz were the main ports of entry. In South America, Cartagena dominated. In Brazil, Bahia was succeeded by Rio de Janeiro. In the nineteenth century, Cuba and Brazil mostly engaged in the trade.

In cities like Havana, Mexico City, Puebla, Lima, Cartagena de Indias, and Salvador, Brazil, urban slavery was common. Urban slaves did domestic work or construction or worked in *obrajes* (factories). Most slaves, however, lived in rural areas, working in agriculture, principally in the sugar industry (Brazil, Cuba, and Haiti) and mining (Mexico and Peru). (See Figure 3.1.) Slave labor was intensive, from dawn to dusk, and often from before dawn to late into the night. We find late testaments of Latin American slave labor regimes in the few slave narratives to come from the region, both from Cuban autobiographies (Francisco Manzano's [1797–1854] *Autobiography* [1840] and Esteban Montejo's [1860–1973] *Maroon* [1966]) and the several novels Manzano's *Autobiography* inspired, such as Anselmo Suárez Romero's (1818–78)—who knew Manzano and shared the same mentor, Domingo del Monte—*Francisco* (1838–39, but not published until 1880). These narratives and novels, in particular Suárez Romero's *Francisco*, also detail the cruelties regularly dealt out to enslaved Afro–Latin Americans. *Francisco*, in this sense, is the strongest denunciation of slavery from this period.

Iberian Racial Ideology and African Slavery

Engaged in the trans-Saharan slave trade since the Middle Ages, Iberian racial ideology informed the expansion of the trade. If at first the old theory of *hoste fidei* (enemy of the faith) was used to justify African slavery, it soon gave way to racial theories as enslaved Africans contested the *hoste* theory in Iberian courts.[6] In this section, I discuss the racialization of African slavery. I do so principally through an analysis of chapter 2 of book 1 of the Jesuit missionary Alonso de Sandoval's (Seville, 1576–Cartagena de Indias, 1652) manual for ministering to Blacks, *Naturaleza, policia sagrada y profana, costumbres y*

FIGURE 3.1. *African slaves working in the mines of Peru*. Eighteenth century. Biblioteca Real, Madrid, *Trujillo del Perú*, by Baltasar Jaime Martínez Compañón, 1779–1790, MS II/344, plate 112. Courtesy of Patrimonio Nacional, Madrid, Spain.

ritos, disciplina y catecismo evangélico de todos etíopes (Nature, sacred and profane laws, customs and rites of all Africa, and discipline and catechism for Africans; Seville, 1627), which Sandoval later expanded and published as *De instauranda Aethiopum salute* (On restoring salvation to Africans; Madrid, 1647), the title by which it is better known.

That chapter "De la naturaleza de los etíopes, que comunmente llamamos negros" (On the nature of Africans, whom we commonly call Blacks) is an early articulation of the logic that would become the justification for African slavery across the early modern world. Thus, while Sandoval has been rightly recognized as a strong advocate for enslaved Africans in the seventeenth century, he also articulated and discursively reproduced that world's racialization of African slavery.[7] But Sandoval is not an isolated intellectual in this regard. In "On the nature of Africans," he espouses a theory of Blackness that was becoming commonplace in the Atlantic at that time, thanks, in no small part, to African slavery. Yet, while illustrative of a major trend in the early modern Atlantic, Sandoval's text is notable for the way it embraces this theory of Blackness and a theological basis for African slavery.

At the time Sandoval wrote, the enslavement of sub-Saharan Africans had been rationalized for at least a millennium by several Mediterranean societies as a curse from the Abrahamic God.[8] One theory emerged from a long-standing exegesis of Genesis 9:20–27, which tells the story of the curse Noah placed on his son Ham's descendants. According to the biblical story, one day Noah became inebriated and fell asleep in the nude in his tent. When Ham entered the tent and saw his father naked, he went out and informed his two brothers. The next day, when he awoke from his drunken stupor and heard about what Ham had done, Noah interpreted it as ridicule and cursed Ham's son thus: "Cursed be Canaan! The lowest of slaves shall he be to his brothers" (Gen. 9:25).

While the biblical text does not say anything about Ham or Canaan's skin tone, the connection between slavery and Blackness first developed in the Talmud (fifth century CE). In his study of the curse of Ham, as it has become known in scholarship, David M. Goldenberg points out that ancient Israelites came to see the inhabitants of ancient Nubia (parts of present-day Sudan, Eritrea, and Ethiopia), the Kushites, as Ham's descendants.[9] As Goldenberg notes, Nubia represented the southern end of the known world for ancient Israelites. Thus, the Kushites—depicted as Blacks in ancient Egyptian art—represented the remotest people for ancient Israelites. This association of the Kushites, and by extension, sub-Saharan Africans, with Ham's curse became commonplace in the ancient circum–Red Sea region, entering Islam from its founding in the seventh century.

As James H. Sweet has noted, in the Muslim world this connection first appeared in *Tārīkh al-Rusul wa al-Mulūk* (History of the prophets and kings), by Abū Jáfar Muḥammad ibn Jarīr al-Ṭabarī (839–923 CE). Even though it is by a Persian author, the work is considered by scholars to be the major Arabic historical work of that period. According to al-Ṭabarī, "Ham begot all Blacks and people with crinkly hair. . . . Noah put a curse on Ham, according to which the hair of his descendants would not extend over their ears and they would be enslaved wherever they were encountered."[10]

As Iberians entered the Mediterranean slave trade, partnering with Muslim traders in the late Middle Ages, they adopted this racialized rationalization of slavery, which was well established in Iberian culture by the time the Atlantic slave trade began in the first decade of the sixteenth century. Thus, by the time the Atlantic trade began in earnest (c. 1510), *negro* and *preto* already meant "slave" in Spanish and Portuguese, respectively.

In "On the nature of Africans," Sandoval couples the curse of Ham with the then-emerging theory of Blackness. While both the ancients (e.g., Hippocrates, Herodotus, Aristotle, Strabo, Pliny the Elder) and medieval Christian thinkers (e.g., Augustine, Isidore of Seville, Bernard of Clairvaux, Aquinas) had used the environmental theory—that geography determines personhood—to explain human difference, Sandoval's contemporaries were moving away from it. As Sandoval summarized it: "The Philosophers say that the reason why Africans are Black is because of the heat on the surface of the body, which burns and blackens their skin, because the lands where they live are violently hit by the sun, and therefore, very hot. They arrive at this conclusion from experience, seeing among all men around the world as many skin tones as the climates where they live."[11] Like his contemporaries, Sandoval was not convinced by this theory. In this shift, we can see how imperial expansion had unsettled Europeans' previous understanding of human variety—although belief in geographical determinism reemerged in the eighteenth and nineteenth centuries.[12] But what led Sandoval and his contemporaries to doubt the environmental theory was the fact that "Blacks" in Europe had Black children and "whites" in Africa had white children. Sandoval was also intrigued by the fact that African women had "white" children. These children were in fact albinos, but albinism was a mystery to Sandoval's generation.[13] Yet Sandoval does not accept the French barber-surgeon Ambroise Paré's (1510–1590) explanation for albinism, namely that, in Sandoval's words, "all is caused by a strong [maternal] imagination, which imprints in matter an idea of the thing imagined."[14] To which Sandoval responds: "Whence, although I judge all these opinions to have some foundation, I presume that the cause for this wonder [i.e., albinism among Africans] is another, for if it were caused by the imagination or the clime, Spaniards living in Africa, married with Spanish women, would have Black children, and likewise, Blacks living in Spain would have white children, which is not the case. Therefore, this must either proceed from God's will or some intrinsic quality in this people."[15] Where geography had been understood as the efficient cause of African Blackness, parentage became that cause. Sandoval would develop a theory of Blackness in which both epidermis and slavery (Ham's curse) are hereditary. Thus, Sandoval's answer to his own hypothesis—whether Blackness was the result of God's will or of an intrinsic quality in Africans—is that it is both: "The black skin of Africans not only came from the curse Noah put on his son Ham but also is an *innate and intrinsic attribute* of how God created them, which was extreme heat, so that the sons engendered were left this color, as a sign that they descend from a man who mocked his father, to punish his daring. This is supported by Saint Ambrose, who says that Ham means *calidus* or *calor*, hot or heat itself."[16]

Sandoval, however, was not the first Iberian intellectual to put Blackness in such terms. In his 1603 *Historia general de la Yndia Oriental* (General history of the East Indies), Antonio San Román, a fellow Jesuit, expressed the same idea. Africans, contended San Román, were black *ad intrinsecus*.[17] Sandoval most likely had access to San Román's *Historia*, either at the Jesuit school in Cartagena or in Seville, while he prepared *Naturaleza*. Perhaps Sandoval was expanding on San Román's conception of Blackness.

Moreover, the English chronicler George Best (d. 1584) had arrived at a similar conclusion in 1578, through observations similar to those of Sandoval: "I my selfe have seene an Ethiopian as blacke as a cole brought into England, who taking a faire English woman to wife, begat a sonne in al respects as blacke as the father was, although England were his native country, and an English woman his mother: whereby it seemeth this blacknes proceedeth rather of some infection of that man, which was so strong, that neither the nature of the Clime, neither the good complexion of the mother concurring, coulde any thing alter, and therefore, we cannot impute it to the nature of Clime."[18] Best's text illustrates how this understanding of Blackness was becoming commonplace in the Atlantic. It is interesting, however, how he conceives its immutability and heredity as an infectious disease, foreshadowing later conceptions of Blackness.

What is unique about Sandoval's theory, however, is the role theology plays in it. While the other articulations of the early modern theory of Blackness cited here do not employ Ham's curse, Sandoval conjoins this emerging notion of Blackness with theology so that slavery remains part of the equation. This is noteworthy because, in chapter 18 of book 1 of *Naturaleza*,

Sandoval affirms that "at the beginning the Lord our God did not people the Earth with masters and slaves . . . until, as time went on and men grew in malice, they began to tyrannize others' liberty."[19] This, in turn, is intriguing, because while Sandoval does not mention slavery in his theory of Blackness, when he takes up the question of whether African slavery is just or unjust in chapter 17 of book 1, he evades answering the question himself by reproducing a letter from a fellow Jesuit in Angola. Sandoval had written to the letter's author, Father Luis Brandon, asking whether African slaves were or not "bien avidos" (justly procured). Father Brandon answers Sandoval that he should have no "scruples" about African slavery, not only because church authorities had not condemned it but also, and principally, because it was Africans who enslaved Africans. Therefore, African slaves are "bien avidos." Sandoval devotes the rest of the chapter to his own examples that underscore Father Brandon's argument. Thus, African slavery is blamed on Africans rather than Europeans. Recalling Sandoval's theory of Blackness, then, slavery is seen as part of Africans' *marca* (mark) and *pena* (punishment) for their biblical forebear's transgression. From the perspective of Father Brandon's argument, they have been condemned by God to enslave each other.

Crucially for Sandoval, bringing salvation to Africans justified their enslavement: "And to lose so many souls that are taken from Africa, for some are not ill gotten, without knowing which, does not seem a great service to God for so few are the ill-gotten ones, and those that are saved many and properly enslaved."[20] Sandoval's position underscores, as Thomas Holt has argued, that in early modernity, race worked through religion; the reward of "knowing Christ" justified African slavery even if African slaves were not "bien avidos" (justly procured).[21]

After Sandoval, this understanding of Blackness and slavery would become commonplace, not only in the Iberian world but in the Atlantic in general.[22] In his 1649 *Mission evangelica al reyno de Congo* (Evangelizing Mission to the Congo), for example, the Aragonese erudite José Pellicer i Tovar, who, like Best, San Román, and Sandoval, never traveled to Africa, echoed the latter three's words: "That nation is not Black because of the sun's extreme heat as some have thought for, as we said above, the climate is temperate and the heat very moderate. Their Blackness proceeds properly from nature and an intrinsic quality; this can be seen by the fact that the children of Black parents born in Spain are Black."[23] What resonates in this conception of Blackness is the role of heredity, which also has its foundation in ancient thought.[24] This theorization of Blackness as intrinsic to the person solved the challenges posed to the environmental theory by the increased (forced and voluntary) circulation of humans in early modernity.

But Iberian racial thinking is not the only side of the story of Blackness in Latin America. Afro-descendants naturally conceived of and presented themselves as racially different. Chloe Ireton has shown how Blacks in the Iberian world were able to claim Old Christian blood.[25] Elsewhere, Ireton has shown how Africans challenged their enslavement in Iberian courts, contending that they were not barbarians and, therefore, not enslavable.[26] Moreover, scholars such as Herman L. Bennett, R. Douglas Cope, Rachel S. O'Toole, and José Ramón Jouvé Martín have demonstrated how Afro-descendants sought to present themselves as America-born free creoles before colonial authorities.[27] So while Iberian thinkers saw Blacks as "the quintessential foreign element that, like 'Jewishness,' could not be fully assimilated into Spanish colonial society," as María Elena Martínez observed, Blacks defined themselves racially as Spaniards did, that is, as creole subjects.[28] This was central to Black creoles' identity, as they claimed to have been raised in the true faith amid their Spanish and white creole counterparts, to whose commonwealth they also belonged. Thus, as these scholars have shown, Afro–Latin Americans, too, played with colonial racial categories, using them to their advantage when possible.

Resistance

It was also in Latin America that the first slave revolt was recorded on Christmas Eve, 1521, in Santo Domingo. Thus, resistance to slavery was part of the slave experience from early on. Flight to remote areas proved a successful means of resistance. Maroons founded free communities in far-flung places. Some of the communities proved so successful that their successor communities are still in the same areas, like Palenque de San Basilio in Colombia, the Congos of Panama, the Yungas in Bolivia, and Guerrero, Mexico. Unpopulated Latin American spaces also proved fertile ground for Maroons fleeing other empires, like the Garifuna of Honduras.

Some legendary Maroon communities defeated European forces in battle, such as the Palmaristas of Pernambuco, Brazil, the Yangas of Veracruz, Mexico, and the Bayanos of Panama. The Bayanos' resistance forced the Spanish king to negotiate a peace. Yanga achieved the same result nearly seventy years later. Yet none of these communities proved as lasting as those in remote territories that confounded European armies. For in the end, they were all defeated and destroyed by European forces. Nonetheless, such resistance set the precedent for the Haitian Revolution, whose leaders learned from the maroon past. And because Blacks formed a large part of colonial militias, they played a huge role in the wars for independence.

Black Motherhood in the Age of Slavery

The subject of Black motherhood in the age of slavery has been mainly studied through the lens of slavery, whether it is looking at enslaved Black women as breeders or as wet nurses for white children. The most recent and significant studies are gathered in *Motherhood, Childlessness and the Care of Children in Atlantic Slave Societies*, edited by Camillia Cowling, Maria Machado, Diana Paton, and Emily West.[29] While most of the essays in the volume discuss Black motherhood vis-à-vis slavery, its part 4 contains four essays that deal with Black motherhood of Black children. Yet even these essays focus on Black motherhood from the perspective of slavery. Nonetheless, the volume allows us to conclude that Black motherhood in the age of slavery was twofold: of Black children and of white children.

An interesting passage from early colonial Mexico offers a counterpoint to this narrative. It appears in an account of a festival held in Mexico City in 1539. After describing a mock hunt staged by Indigenous actors, the author tells us that the hunt "was nothing compared to the performance of horseback riders made up of men and women who were there with their king and queen, and all on horses, they were more than fifty, wearing great riches of gold and precious stones and pearls and silver; and then they went against the savages [in battle] and they had another hunt, and it was something to be seen the diversity of their faces, of the masks they were wearing, and how the Black women breastfed their little children [*y cómo las negras daban de mamar a sus negritos*] and how they paid homage to the queen."[30]

Not only is this one of the earliest mentions of Black women breastfeeding their own children in a European language; it is also one of the few to do so, for both textual and visual references to Black women breastfeeding would be mostly as wet nurses for white infants. The scholarship, therefore, has paid far more attention to that phenomenon than to Black women breastfeeding their own newborns. We have here, then, precious evidence about how Black women cared for their own offspring. The casual way in which Díaz del Castillo says it speaks to the quotidian nature of Black women breastfeeding their children. It reminds us that this is what came first, before Black wet nurses for white babies, so that when this was taken away from black mothers, the trauma we know they still suffer began.

What I find most important about Díaz del Castillo's phrase is how it marks breastfeeding as a site of kinship for Mexico's Black community at the time. If we extend this idea to the rest of the region and the following centuries, we can see how Black motherhood functioned as a site of kinship for Black communities throughout the slavery era and afterward in Latin America. Language like this and images in nineteenth-century travelogues, especially from Brazil, invite us to expand our understanding of Black motherhood during the age of slavery in Latin America.

Abolition

From the arrival of the first Europeans, Latin America had a free Black population, especially in the cities. Iberian laws accorded slaves certain rights and protections, though more in theory than in practice. Enslaved Africans theoretically had rights to Sunday rest, to marriage, from abuse, and to buy their freedom. Throughout the colonial period, enslaved Afro–Latin Americans brought successful suits on the basis of these rights.[31] Slaves could ask to be sold to another owner if they could prove their owner was abusive. They could also sue to keep the family unit together when their owner threatened to sell a member. When the civil courts proved useless for these ends, some slaves used blasphemy to renegotiate their circumstances.[32] Finally, the children of free and freed women were born free.

When the French National Assembly adopted the Declaration of the Rights of Man, the Haitian question was debated. While it did not result in total abolition, it led to the ban of the trade. The success of the Haitian Revolution brought about the first lasting abolition in the hemisphere. As the colonies rose against Spain, the promise of abolition in exchange for militia service was used as a strategy to attract Black troops. The Spanish side also used this strategy. But when the colonies won the wars of independence, freedom was not always forthcoming. Abolition was achieved only slowly as the Afro–Latin Americans who had fought to win independence pressured the new republics to deliver on their promise (Table 3.2). While that promise was fulfilled for older generations, many were born free through free womb laws. New scholarship has shown how Afro–Latin Americans were the protagonists of their own abolition through daily engagement with and contestation of their society and its norms.[33]

TABLE 3.2: Abolition of the African slave trade and of slavery in Latin America, 1810–1888
Source: Reid Andrews, *Afro–Latin America, 1800–2000*, 57. Haiti added.

COUNTRY	SLAVE TRADE	FREE WOMB LAW	FINAL ABOLITION
Haiti	1793	—	1804
Dominican Republic	1822	—	1822
Chile	1811	1811	1823
Central America	1824	—	1824
Mexico	1824	—	1824
Uruguay	1825 (1838)	1825	1842
Ecuador	1821	1821	1851
Colombia	1821	1821	1852
Argentina	1813 (1838)	1813	1853
Peru	1821	1821	1854
Venezuela	1821	1821	1854
Bolivia	1840	1831	1861
Paraguay	1842	1842	1869
Puerto Rico	1820, 1835 (1842)	1870	1873
Cuba	1820, 1835 (1866)	1870	1886
Brazil	1830, 1850 (1852)	1871	1888

Brazil's bloodless independence meant that the question of slavery was not taken up at this juncture. The question of freedom would be tied to the republican movement instead, and neither would come until after six decades of activism. Like Frederick Douglass in the United States, Luiz Gama, a former slave who was the first Black to attend São Paulo's prestigious law school, fought for abolition in Brazil, though he did not live to see it. Slaves in Cuba and Puerto Rico would remain at Spain's mercy. The First Spanish Republic (1873–74) abolished slavery in Puerto Rico, but it remained in Cuba.

As in the United States, other means of exclusion were found after abolition. In most places, Afro–Latin Americans were erased from the national imaginary. In Brazil and elsewhere, antivagrancy laws landed many Afro-Brazilians in jail. Slavery was gone but racism held ground, as the chapters in this volume attest.

Differences between slavery in Latin America and the United States and elsewhere have led to myths that slavery in Latin America was less cruel, starting with Hegel. While in Latin America, enslaved Africans were legal persons, rather than chattel, in theory, slavery was no less cruel. Accounts of slavery's cruelties in the region abound. Additionally, Afro–Latin Americans were often falsely accused of plots and arrested, tortured, made to render false confessions, and executed, with their remains displayed in cities or towns' gates.

NOTES

1. Frederick P. Bowser, *The African Slave in Colonial Peru, 1524–1650* (Stanford, CA: Stanford University Press, 1974); A. J. R. Russell-Wood, *The Black Man in Slavery and Freedom in Colonial Brazil* (Oxford, UK: St. Martin's Press, 1982); Enriqueta Vila Vilar, *Hispanoamérica y el comercio de esclavos* (Seville, Spain: Escuela de Estudios Hispano-Americanos, 1977); Herbert S. Klein and Ben Vinson, *African Slavery in Latin America and the Caribbean* (New York: Oxford University Press, 2007); Herbert S. Klein and Francisco V. Luna, *Slavery in Brazil* (Cambridge: Cambridge University Press, 2010).
2. Alex Borucki, David Eltis, and David Wheat, eds., *From the Galleons to the Highlands: Slave Trade Routes in the Spanish Americas* (Albuquerque: University of New Mexico Press, 2020).
3. João José Reis, *Slave Rebellion in Brazil: The Muslim Uprising of 1835 in Bahia* (Baltimore: Johns Hopkins University Press, 1995); Sidney Chalhoub, *A Força da escravidão: Ilegalidade e costume no Brasil oitocentista* (São Paulo: Companhia das Letras, 2012).
4. Alex Borucki, *From Shipmates to Soldiers: Emerging Black Identities in the Río de la Plata* (Albuquerque: University of New Mexico Press, 2015); Pablo Miguel Sierra Silva, *Urban Slavery in Colonial Mexico: Puebla De Los Ángeles, 1531–1706* (Cambridge: Cambridge University Press, 2019).
5. Michelle A. McKinley, *Fractional Freedoms: Slavery, Intimacy, and Legal Mobilization in Colonial Lima, 1600–1700* (Cambridge: Cambridge University Press, 2016); Rachel S. O'Toole, *Bound Lives: Africans, Indians, and the Making of Race in Colonial Peru* (Pittsburgh, PA: University of Pittsburgh Press, 2012); Erika Edwards, *Hiding in Plain Sight: Black Women, the Law, and the Making of a White Argentine Republic* (Tuscaloosa: University of Alabama Press, 2020); Ricardo Raúl Salazar Rey, *Mastering the Law: Slavery and Freedom in the Legal Ecology of the Spanish Empire* (Tuscaloosa: University of Alabama Press, 2020).
6. Chloe Ireton, "Black Africans' Freedom Litigation Suits to Define Just War and Just Slavery in the Early Spanish Empire," *Renaissance Quarterly* 73, no. 4 (2020): 1277–1319.
7. See Margaret M. Olsen, *Slavery and Salvation in Colonial Cartagena de Indias* (Gainesville: University Press of Florida, 2004).
8. James H. Sweet, "The Iberian Roots of American Racist Thought," *William and Mary Quarterly* 54, no. 1 (1997): 143–166.
9. David M. Goldenberg, *The Curse of Ham: Race and Slavery in Early Judaism, Christianity, and Islam* (Princeton, NJ: Princeton University Press, 2004), 17–40.
10. Quoted in Sweet, "The Iberian," 148.
11. Alonso de Sandoval, *Naturaleza, policia sagrada y profana, costumbres y ritos, disciplina y catecismo evangélico de todos etiopes* (Seville, Spain: Francisco de Lira, 1627), 73.

12. See Robert Bernasconi and Tommy L. Lott, eds., *The Idea of Race* (Indianapolis: Hackett, 2000); Emmanuel C. Eze, ed., *Race and the Enlightenment: A Reader* (Oxford, UK: Blackwell, 2009).
13. See Ilona Katzew, "White or Black? Albinism and Spotted Blacks in the Eighteenth-Century Atlantic World," in *Envisioning Others: Race, Color, and the Visual in Iberia and Latin America*, ed. Pamela A. Patton (Leiden: Brill, 2016).
14. Sandoval, *Naturaleza*, 73.
15. Sandoval, *Naturaleza*, 74.
16. Sandoval, *Naturaleza*, 74.
17. Antonio Feros, *Speaking of Spain: The Evolution of Race and Nation in the Hispanic World* (Cambridge, MA: Harvard University Press, 2012), 135.
18. Quoted in Kim F. Hall, *Things of Darkness: Economies of Race and Gender in Early Modern England* (Ithaca, NY: Cornell University Press, 1995), 11.
19. Sandoval, *Naturaleza*, 149.
20. Sandoval, *Naturaleza*, 144.
21. Thomas Holt, *The Problem of Race in the 21st Century* (Cambridge, MA: Harvard University Press, 2002), 1–24.
22. See Colin Kidd, *The Forging of Races: Race and Scripture in the Protestant Atlantic World, 1600-2000* (Cambridge: Cambridge University Press, 2006).
23. José Pellicer i Tovar, *Mission evangelica al Reyno del Congo por la Serafica Religión de los Capuchinos* (Madrid: Domingo Garcia i Morrás, 1649), fols. 57v-58r.
24. Benjamin H. Isaac, *The Invention of Racism in Classical Antiquity* (Princeton, NJ: Princeton University Press, 2006), 55-168.
25. Chloe Ireton, "'They Are Blacks of the Caste of Black Christians': Old Christian Black Blood in the Sixteenth- and Early Seventeenth-Century Iberian Atlantic," *Hispanic American Historical Review* 97, no. 4 (2017): 579-612.
26. Ireton, "Black Africans' Freedom Litigation."
27. R. Douglas Cope, *The Limits of Racial Domination: Plebeian Society in Colonial Mexico City, 1660-1720* (Madison: University of Wisconsin Press, 1994); José Ramón Jouvé Martín, *Esclavos de la ciudad letrada: Esclavitud, escritura y colonialismo en Lima (1650-1700)* (Lima: IEP, 2005).
28. María E. Martínez, "The Black Blood of New Spain: Limpieza de Sangre, Racial Violence, and Gendered Power in Early Colonial Mexico," *William and Mary Quarterly* 61, no. 3 (2004): 515.
29. Camillia Cowling et al., eds., *Motherhood, Childlessness and the Care of Children in Atlantic Slave Societies* (London: Routledge, 2020).
30. Bernal Díaz del Castillo, *Historia verdadera de la conquista de la Nueva España (manuscrito "Guatemala")*, 1575, ed. José Antonio Barbón Rodríguez (Mexico City: Colegio de México and UNAM, 2005), 755.
31. Herman L. Bennett, *Africans in Colonial Mexico: Absolutism, Christianity, and Afro-Creole Consciousness, 1570-1640* (Bloomington: Indiana University Press, 2003); McKinley, *Fractional Freedoms*.
32. Javier Villa-Flores, *Dangerous Speech: A Social History of Blasphemy in Colonial Mexico* (Tucson: University of Arizona Press, 2006), 127-147.
33. Angela Alonso, *The Last Abolition: The Brazilian Antislavery Movement, 1868-1888* (Cambridge: Cambridge University Press, 2021); Adriana Chira, *Patchwork Freedoms: Law, Slavery, and Race beyond Cuba's Plantations* (Cambridge: Cambridge University Press, 2022).

BIBLIOGRAPHY

Alonso, Angela. *The Last Abolition: The Brazilian Antislavery Movement, 1868–1888.* Cambridge: Cambridge University Press, 2021.

Andrews, George R. *Afro-Latin America, 1800–2000.* Oxford: Oxford University Press, 2004.

Bennett, Herman L. *Africans in Colonial Mexico: Absolutism, Christianity, and Afro-creole Consciousness, 1570–1640.* Bloomington: Indiana University Press, 2003.

Bernasconi, Robert, and Tommy L. Lott, eds. *The Idea of Race.* Indianapolis: Hackett, 2000.

Borucki, Alex. *From Shipmates to Soldiers: Emerging Black Identities in the Río de la Plata.* Albuquerque: University of New Mexico Press, 2015.

Borucki, Alex, David Eltis, and David Wheat, eds. *From the Galleons to the Highlands: Slave Trade Routes in the Spanish Americas.* Albuquerque: University of New Mexico Press, 2020.

Bowser, Frederick P. *The African Slave in Colonial Peru, 1524–1650.* Stanford, CA: Stanford University Press, 1974.

Bryant, Sherwin K. *Rivers of Gold, Lives of Bondage: Governing through Slavery in Colonial Quito.* Chapel Hill: University of North Carolina Press, 2014.

Chalhoub, Sidney. *A força da escravidão: Ilegalidade e costume no Brasil oitocentista.* São Paulo: Companhia das Letras, 2012.

Chira, Adriana. *Patchwork Freedoms: Law, Slavery, and Race beyond Cuba's Plantations.* Cambridge: Cambridge University Press, 2022.

Cope, R. Douglas. *The Limits of Racial Domination: Plebeian Society in Colonial Mexico City, 1660–1720.* Madison: University of Wisconsin Press, 1994.

Cowling, Camillia, et al., eds. *Motherhood, Childlessness and the Care of Children in Atlantic Slave Societies.* London: Routledge, 2020.

Díaz del Castillo, Bernal. *Historia verdadera de la conquista de la Nueva España (manuscrito "Guatemala"), 1575,* edited by José Antonio Barbón Rodríguez. Mexico City: Colegio de México and UNAM, 2005.

Edwards, Erika. *Hiding in Plain Sight: Black Women, the Law, and the Making of a White Argentine Republic.* Tuscaloosa: University of Alabama Press, 2020.

Eze, Emmanuel C., ed. *Race and the Enlightenment: A Reader.* Oxford, UK: Blackwell, 2009.

Feros, Antonio. *Speaking of Spain: The Evolution of Race and Nation in the Hispanic World.* Cambridge, MA: Harvard University Press, 2012.

Goldenberg, David M. *The Curse of Ham: Race and Slavery in Early Judaism, Christianity, and Islam.* Princeton, NJ: Princeton University Press, 2004.

Hall, Kim F. *Things of Darkness: Economies of Race and Gender in Early Modern England.* Ithaca, NY: Cornell University Press, 1995.

Holt, Thomas. *The Problem of Race in the 21st Century.* Cambridge, MA: Harvard University Press, 2002.

Ireton, Chloe. "Black Africans' Freedom Litigation Suits to Define Just War and Just Slavery in the Early Spanish Empire." *Renaissance Quarterly* 73, no. 4 (2020): 1277–1319.

———. "'They Are Blacks of the Caste of Black Christians': Old Christian Black Blood in the Sixteenth- and Early Seventeenth-Century Iberian Atlantic." *Hispanic American Historical Review* 97, no. 4 (2017): 579–612.

Isaac, Benjamin H. *The Invention of Racism in Classical Antiquity*. Princeton, NJ: Princeton University Press, 2006.

Jouvé Martín, José Ramón. *Esclavos de la ciudad letrada: Esclavitud, escritura y colonialismo en Lima (1650-1700)*. Lima: IEP, 2005.

Katzew, Ilona. "White or Black? Albinism and Spotted Blacks in the Eighteenth-Century Atlantic World." In *Envisioning Others: Race, Color, and the Visual in Iberia and Latin America*, edited by Pamela A. Patton, 142-186. Leiden: Brill, 2016.

Kidd, Colin. *The Forging of Races: Race and Scripture in the Protestant Atlantic World, 1600-2000*. Cambridge: Cambridge University Press, 2006.

Klein, Herbert S., and Ben Vinson. *African Slavery in Latin America and the Caribbean*. New York: Oxford University Press, 2007.

Klein, Herbert S., and Francisco V. Luna. *Slavery in Brazil*. Cambridge: Cambridge University Press, 2010.

Martínez, María E. "The Black Blood of New Spain: Limpieza De Sangre, Racial Violence, and Gendered Power in Early Colonial Mexico." *William and Mary Quarterly* 61, no. 3 (2004): 479-520.

McKinley, Michelle A. *Fractional Freedoms: Slavery, Intimacy, and Legal Mobilization in Colonial Lima, 1600-1700*. Cambridge: Cambridge University Press, 2016.

Olsen, Margaret M. *Slavery and Salvation in Colonial Cartagena de Indias*. Gainesville: University Press of Florida, 2004.

O'Toole, Rachel S. *Bound Lives: Africans, Indians, and the Making of Race in Colonial Peru*. Pittsburgh, PA: University of Pittsburgh Press, 2012.

Pellicer i Tovar, José. *Mission evangelica al Reyno del Congo por la Serafica Religión de los Capuchinos*. Madrid: Domingo Garcia i Morrás, 1649.

Reis, João José. *Slave Rebellion in Brazil: The Muslim Uprising of 1835 in Bahia*. Baltimore: Johns Hopkins University Press, 1995.

Russell-Wood, A. J. R. *The Black Man in Slavery and Freedom in Colonial Brazil*. Oxford, UK: St. Martin's Press, 1982.

Salazar Rey, Ricardo Raúl. *Mastering the Law: Slavery and Freedom in the Legal Ecology of the Spanish Empire*. Tuscaloosa: University of Alabama Press, 2020.

Sandoval, Alonso de. *De instauranda Aethiopum salute: El mundo de la esclavitud negra en América*, 1627, edited by Ángel Valtierra. Bogotá: Empresa Nacional, 1956.

———. *De instauranda Aethiopum salute: Historia de Aethiopia, naturaleza, policia sagrada y profana, costumbres y ritos, disciplina y catecismo evangélico de todos aetíopes, conque se restaura la salud de sus almas*. Vol. 1. Madrid: Alonso de Paredes, 1647.

———. *Naturaleza, policia sagrada y profana, costumbres y ritos, disciplina y catecismo evangélico de todos etiopes*. Seville, Spain: Francisco de Lira, 1627.

———. *Un tratado sobre la esclavitud*, 1627, edited by Enriqueta Vila Vilar. Madrid: Alianza, 1987.

Sierra Silva, Pablo Miguel. *Urban Slavery in Colonial Mexico: Puebla de Los Ángeles, 1531-1706*. Cambridge: Cambridge University Press, 2019.

Sweet, James H. "The Iberian Roots of American Racist Thought." *William and Mary Quarterly* 54, no. 1 (1997): 143-166.

Vila Vilar, Enriqueta. *Hispanoamérica y el comercio de esclavos*. Seville, Spain: Escuela de Estudios Hispano-Americanos, 1977.

Villa-Flores, Javier. *Dangerous Speech: A Social History of Blasphemy in Colonial Mexico*. Tucson: University of Arizona Press, 2006.

CHAPTER 4

Race in Eighteenth-Century Spanish America

MARISELLE MELÉNDEZ

> Todo para indicar que, mediante el ejercicio de la triple ley, llegaremos en América, antes que en parte alguna del globo, a la creación de una raza hecha con el tesoro de todas las anteriores, la raza final, la raza cósmica.
>
> VASCONCELOS, *La raza cósmica*

In 1925, the Mexican intellectual José Vasconcelos proposed his own theory of a fifth race that he called "raza cósmica" to attack social Darwinism theories centered on the racial superiority of certain groups over others. Vasconcelos envisioned a race for Spanish America angled in the fusion of diverse racial groups to form a universal race guided by the principles of the material, the intellectual, and the spiritual.[1] His theory was quite controversial because, to form a new universal race, he consequently ignored and erased the particularities of each racial group. His notion of race was guided by the idea that all races in Spanish America would fuse—or, as he stated, "confuse"—into a new one, achieving in the process a state of perfection. For Vasconcelos, this process of forming "a raza nueva" was not new. He argued that, since colonial times, Spaniards had already created new races when they mixed themselves with Indigenous and Black people, giving birth to what is known as mestizaje.[2] What is clear from this theorization of race is the categorization of people in the colonial past and the miscegenation among groups that was viewed as the foundation and initial stage for thinking about race in the future. Then and now, this need to look at the past remains the same when it comes to formulating the history of race in the Americas.

In *Blood Boundaries: The Limits of Religious and Racial Exclusion in Early Modern Latin America*, Stuart B. Schwartz states that "there may be no topic in early Latin American history that has generated more interest and debate than the issue of race and racial identity—including that identity's characteristics, terminology, effects, history, and hierarchies."[3] This debate among historians and literary scholars is anchored on those who believe that using the concept of race, especially in its connection to racial discrimination, is anachronistic and others who believe that the discriminatory practices associated with the concept of race allow the concept of race to be applied with connotations it has acquired since the nineteenth century.[4] Daniel Nemser, in his article "Race and Domination in Colonial Latin American Studies," proposes an approach to the study of race in colonial Latin America "that centers not on the meaning of race but on processes of racialization and techniques of domination."[5] For Nemser, it is more productive to "place the category of domination at the center" of analyses of racialization because, for him, race is material in nature.[6] In his view, this would allow critics to understand the results that domination techniques had over subaltern subjects in the colonial period.

As enticing as this approach is, it is still relevant to engage with the history of the word *raza* in the context of colonial Latin America, not uniquely through the angle of domination, but with the use of the word based on the definitions that circulated up to the eighteenth century, which related to other important concepts and new scientific approaches to human nature that had developed at the time. For this reason, scholars, including myself, when using the concept of race, tend to offer the definition followed at the time, which in fact allowed certain flexibility, especially if employed along with the concepts of *casta* (caste) and *calidad* (quality), which were used alongside *raza* when referring or classifying the population that inhabited the American continent. Nevertheless, as Robert C. Schwaller argues, after the sixteenth century, both concepts of *casta* and *calidad* had undergone "a process of racialization" to conceive of difference as an inherited natural quality.[7] Indeed, Schwartz has offered a compromised solution to approach the issue of race by stating that, besides accepting "the argument that aspects of purity of blood restrictions and the beliefs of the inheritability of cultural and moral characteristics have a similarity to modern racism," it is important to also consider that "the system of social organization and hierarchy of early modern Spain, Portugal, and their empires importantly incorporated concepts such as nobility, honor, legitimacy of birth, occupation, education, and accomplishment in ways that were quite unlike more modern forms of racial thinking."[8] Schwartz's critical approach to racial thinking best captures how race was viewed, especially in the eighteenth century, and allows us to consider the politics of racial exclusion when discussing race.[9]

Nevertheless, most scholars working on race in the eighteenth century use the concept in a very general way, following the contemporary notion of race more closely.[10] However, to better comprehend how the concept of race was understood and utilized in the eighteenth century in the Spanish American context, one must go back to the definitions that circulated at the time. This chapter discusses how the concept of race was understood, defined, and problematized in the eighteenth century. It offers first a panoramic view of the interpretation of race as a concept at the time, and it follows with concrete examples of eighteenth-century documentation in which the concept of race is interpreted and subsequently theorized.

The Concept of Race in Eighteenth-Century Spanish America

In the first definition found in *Diccionario de autoridades*, compiled between 1726 and 1739, the Spanish word *raza* was defined as follows:

> Casta o calidad del origen o linaje. Hablando de los hombres, se toma mui regularmente en mala parte. Es del Latino *Radix*. Latín. *Genus. Stirps. Etiam generis macula, vel ignominia.* DEFINIC. DE CALATR. tit. 6. cap. 1. Ordenamos y mandamos que ninguna persona, de qualquiera calidad y condición que fuere, sea recibida a la dicha Orden, ni se le dé el Hábito, sino fuere Hijodalgo, al fuero de España, de partes de padre y madre, y de avuelos de entrambas partes, y de legítimo matrimonio nacido, y que no le toque raza de Judio, Moro, Herege, ni Villano. MARIAN. Hist. Esp. lib. 22. cap. 1. No de otra manera que los sembrados y animales, la raza de los hombres, y casta, con la propiedad del Cielo y de la tierra, sobre todo con el tiempo se muda y se embastarda.[11]

This definition derived from the one included in *Tesoro de la lengua castellana o española* by Sebastián de Covarrubias Horozco, which was printed in 1611. In that earlier dictionary, race was defined on the one hand as referring to a caste of horses, but it added: "En los linajes. Se toma en mala parte, como tener alguna raza de moro o judío."[12] Race was also used to refer to the "calidad de otras cosas," including type of textiles, as first noted by Covarrubias and repeated in *Diccionario de autoridades* in 1737. Quality (*calidad*) and caste (*casta*) were still the guiding principles of the concept of *raza* in the eighteenth century. These earlier definitions clearly emphasized the negative connotations of the word by associating it with groups perceived as lacking purity of blood and who did not adhere to Christianity.[13] As Schwartz indicates, "Particularly troubling was the late Iberian medieval idea that culture and rejection of Christian attitudes could be genealogically transmitted."[14] In this sense, religion was an added component to the word, as it was the association with categorization by types. It was also important to be able to identify groups and to determine the quality of people, which had to be done through the act of seeing. Appearance played a crucial role in categorizing others in the eighteenth century, when Enlightenment ideas centered heavily on practices of taxonomy.

In the case of colonial Spanish America, racial and ethnic demographics played an important role in how the concept of race was developed. In the eighteenth century, urban population growth, especially when it came to the presence of enslaved Blacks, free Blacks, and Afro-descendants, was at its highest. Since the first arrival of enslaved Africans to the Americas in the sixteenth century and continuing to the eighteenth century, it is estimated that "ten to eleven million people forcibly migrated to the Americas from Africa."[15] The increase in the enslaved population in the eighteenth century coincided with Spain's commercial goal of establishing a sugar culture in its Caribbean possessions, including Cuba, Puerto Rico, Santo Domingo, and Venezuela.[16]

Royal decrees in the period allowed colonial officials to expand the availability to purchase enslaved Blacks from French Caribbean colonies to Rio de Janeiro and Salvador da Bahia. In fact, in 1789, Charles IV authorized what was referred to as "the beginning of the 'free' slave trade," which allowed any Spanish citizen to "go in his own vessel to any port and obtain as many Blacks as he desired," except from any nation at war with Spain.[17] For example, in the more peripheral Viceroyalty of the Río de la Plata, between 1777 and 1812, as Alex Borucki adds, seventy thousand African slaves arrived in the region mainly from Rio de Janeiro and Salvador da Bahia.[18] In the case of Lima, the capital of the Viceroyalty of Peru, it was estimated that, already at the beginning of the eighteenth century, half the population was Black and of African descent.[19] Finally, in the case of Mexico, the capital of the Viceroyalty of New Spain, out of the hundred thousand people who inhabited the city, 35–40 percent belonged to the Black, mulatto, and mestizo population.[20] The racial and ethnic constitution of the American population made it impossible to talk about taxonomic categorizations without thinking about the highly visible presence of Blacks in the Spanish colonies.

Carl Linnaeus (1707–1778), with the development of his binomial nomenclature and emphasis on taxonomic categorization, established a new classification among human groups. In his famous 1740 *Systema Naturae*, Linnaeus proposed a classificatory division of groups as follows: "white Europeans, red American Indians, Black Africans and brown Asians."[21] Remarkably, his classification still reverberates in our society today. To this classification he later added three other groups—wild men, pygmies, and giants—which, as not related to color, demonstrated, in Outram's words, "the tentative and unstable character of Enlightenment attempts to classify the human race."[22] For Outram, when it comes to race, Enlightenment thinkers were unable to conclusively offer definitive answers on how best to categorize human groups. It is obvious that discourses about race at the time were constructed from a Eurocentric point of view that viewed continents such as America and Africa as underdeveloped and still in need of civilization. Categorizations were added to facilitate the management of populations that were indeed quite diverse. For this reason, as Outram points out, "the nature of humanity itself" kept being a point of contention in the eighteenth century.[23] One can find clear examples of this tendency in newspapers such as the *Mercurio Peruano* (1790–1795) when referring to marginalized groups. For example, in an article published in June 1791 titled "Idea de las congregaciones públicas de los *Negros Bozales*," the editors of the newspaper denounced the inhumane way enslaved Blacks were treated in the haciendas: "Estos desgraciados, hijos del Omnipotente, hermanos nuestros por la incontrastable genealogía de Adan, dotados de una Anima inmortal como la nuestra, compartícipes de la preciosisima sangre de Jesu-Christo, de su Redencion, y de la Bienaventuranza celestial: estos Negros, se hallan en nuestras negociaciones reducidos a un nivel de un fardo de mercancías, y se tratan a veces peor que los jumentos en aquellas mismas Chacras, que ellos riegan con sus sudores."[24]

The editors departed from a religious perspective to underscore the landowners' total disregard for enslaved Blacks to the extent that their treatment equaled the same reserved for donkeys. Slaves' masters saw them as material goods and consequently disregarded their humanity. In this case, the editors made clear that they would never disregard the human aspects of these groups they referred to as *castas* and *naciones*.²⁵ In fact, they began their discussion by clearly stating, "Nuestra voluntad y nuestra razon, vinculadas por un mismo principio, han contemplado siempre a la *Humanidad* como inseparable de la caridad evangélica."²⁶ For the Peruvian editors, reason and religion worked compatibly to characterize Black enslaved populations. This is not to say that, in the context of the article, the editors perceived the Black population as different and prone to "inclinaciones y defectos," especially when engaging in such cultural practices as the ones conducted in their brotherhoods.²⁷ If religion and cultural habits were the initial indicators in the early definition of race, what we also see in the eighteenth century is the incorporation of discussions about the humanity of those sectors of the population who, because of their race, were treated as inferior.

Ilona Katzew summarizes how the colonial elite used the word *race* at the time. She observes that they "identified race with a distinct set of inherited physical traits, but in reality, the perception of economic position and social standing carried as much weight in the overall identification of a person as did appearance."²⁸ Katzew adds that "'putative' or 'reputational' race could often account for one's overall identity as much as somatic characteristics."²⁹ I would like to argue, however, that in the eighteenth century, color and appearance became indeed more relevant when categorizing the racial nature of non-European groups. Furthermore, the phenotypical aspect of the concept became more prevalent and more anchored on what Gillian Rose refers to as scopic regime, which refers to "the ways in which both what is seen and how it is seen are culturally constructed."³⁰ In fact, the whole phenomenon of *casta* painting in the eighteenth century attests to this. As Katzew also notes, the genre managed to guarantee that each race occupied a "social niche assigned by nature" and that there was always a possibility "of improving one's blood through the right pattern of mixing."³¹ This coincides with Pamela A. Patton's argument that "throughout the Ibero-American world, visual and material culture constituted a premier medium—perhaps *the* premier medium—by which such evolving notions of race could be explored and expressed."³² When it came to *casta* categorizations, the racial traits assigned to the Black population underlined their view in society as barbarous and inferior and in fact closer to animals. *Mulato* was derived from "mule"; *lobo* (wolf); *coyote* referred to the offspring of African and Indians; and *zambo* (knock-kneed) and used to refer to the mix of Africans and Indigenous people—all were terms used to denote inferiority. In the case of the African enslaved population, as Katzew reminds us, they were regarded as objects or "material possessions."³³

These stereotypical views had a profound impact on how Europe spoke about the inhabitants of the Americas.

Eighteenth-century travel books and historiographical accounts that emerged after scientific expeditions by Europeans in the Americas began to include many visual illustrations to depict the American people as well as the fauna and flora. In addition, along with the *casta* painting, we find works such as *Trujillo del Perú* by Baltasar Martínez de Compañón, which visually classified and depicted Trujillo's population on the basis of categories such as "Spaniards," "Indians," "Mestizos," "Mulattoes," "Zambos," and "Blacks." Martínez de Compañón decided to record a complete history of the province of Trujillo, Peru, from six years of observations of the inhabitants, including their cultural practices, customs, fashion, and occupation. The nine-volume series of watercolor illustrations commissioned from local artists exemplified how visuality served to reinforce the idea that racial classifications were clearly in place to help facilitate the understanding of difference to better manage the population. The collection of twenty *casta* paintings ordered by Manuel Amat y Junyet, the viceroy of Peru from 1761–1776, and sent to King Charles III in 1770 to be part of the Gabinete de Historia Natural, also reflected the presence of Afro-descendants in the capital city, similar to the *casta* paintings pertaining to Mexico. However, it was in the many voices of enslaved Africans, free Blacks, and people of African descent who took to the ecclesiastical and secular tribunals where we can find abundant cases of these individuals making use of the legal system to claim justice, although many times, they appeared also accused of crimes.

Maribel Arrelucea Barrantes reminds us that slaves went to the Ecclesiastical Tribunal because they found that it gave them an advantage over the civil court. She argues that, "unlike the secular courts, the ecclesiastical courts offered them an unusual equality with the free population" because "they were all considered children of God with souls."[34] Tamara J. Walker also offers a compelling reason that taking these court cases into consideration is so important to understanding enslaved societies in colonial Spanish America. Referring to the case of colonial Peru in particular, she states that, in the absence of slave narratives, the "questions notaries posed to claimants, alleged perpetrators, and witnesses in criminal cases yield answers that, while at times paraphrased, provide a rare first-person accounting of slaves' occupations, living situations, marital status, family composition, and personal relationships."[35] Therefore, it is important to remember, as court cases demonstrate, that enslaved Africans, free Blacks, and Afro-descendants were not passive individuals simply accepting subordination; they were active agents who knew how to use the legal platforms to claim justice. Their visibility in society made it impossible to theorize about race in eighteenth-century Spanish America without taking them into consideration. In addition, their interactions with the rest of society influenced the manner in which race was thought of as an idea in the eighteenth century.[36]

The theorization of America, both in Europe and in the Americas, also had a major impact on how the concept of race evolved beyond its original association with lineage. The American continent and its people were being conceptualized in multiple centers and margins on both sides of the Atlantic, including Lima, Cuzco, Mexico City, Paris, Valencia, Madrid, London, and Faenza. At the core of those conceptualizations, we find the phenomenon of race. In fact, racial theorizations contributed to defining the character not only of Spanish Americans but also of Europeans themselves. At a time when other Europeans read Spain through its relationship to the Americas as an incompetent nation, and when the Americas were observed and categorized through the European lens as places of unreason, Spanish American authors responded to their detractors by creating their own enlightening view and epistemologies of their own lands and populations. Color, physical condition, lifestyle, religion, and social status became some of the many markers in which race was thought of in eighteenth-century Spanish America as part of these discussions. They in fact contributed to further underscore the theorization of race based on skin color and physiognomy, along with the concomitant prejudices attached to it.[37]

Race in Primary Sources

In eighteenth-century Spanish America, race as a discursive category and as a way of thinking was articulated within the famous ideological precepts of the Enlightenment, such as order, progress, utility, and reason. However, the idea of society's progress, as John Robertson has noted, was not solely centered on "material improvement" but also on a "concern to investigate the structure and manners of societies at the various stages of their development, to trace and explain the historical process as passage from 'barbarism' to 'refinement' or 'civilisation.'"[38] Spanish American thinkers were quite aware of these circulating ideas, as I will discuss. In the context of Spain and Spanish America, the Enlightenment ideas were fostered by the Bourbon regime, which pursued "public happiness and material betterment" as two important goals alongside prosperity and population growth.[39] Population policy guided the bulk of the Bourbons' political and economic agendas.[40] Nevertheless, in the period known as the Age of Reason, it is important to be aware that, as Chris Philo argues, this was also an age in which the construction of unreason became a common enterprise.[41] It is at the intersections of reason and unreason that thinking about race became a productive tool of inquiry in the eighteenth century.

To better understand this process, I offer some examples of eighteenth-century primary works that focus on racial identity or marginalized groups as a venue to theorize about race. My discussion is also framed within the context of the racial politics of church and state that dominated colonial society at the time in which racial categorization worked to control and order the local population. It is important to understand, as María Elisa Velázquez argues, that the definition of race in the eighteenth century went through a second process of transformation caused by the increase of the slave trade at the time and the arguments that emerged to justify it.[42] New pseudoscientific arguments centered on the negative results of physical difference, and these influenced how race was applied at the time.[43] It is through the discursive construction of the body, especially Black and Indigenous bodies, where ideas of inferiority, backwardness, and natural difference became fertile grounds to speak about race.

For example, a common way to use the word *raza* as a discursive tool of categorization based on physical attributes can be found in Antonio de Ulloa's (1716–1795) renowned work *Noticias americanas* (1772).[44] In a section of his book, he stated:

> En la raza la de Indios se distinguen menos las diferencias que en las otras: como por exemplo, entre los Negros hay unos belfos de nariz aplanada, y ojos cargados de carne, que comunmente se llaman *Getudos*, y en lugar de cabellos tienen lana. Otros, cuyo color es tan negro como el de aquellos, y las facciones son semejantes á los Blancos, particularmente en boca, nariz, y ojos, y el cabello es lácio, aunque grueso; hay algunos colorados, y otros de color claro, tirando al de los Mulatos. En los Indios se percibe poco la diferencia del color, y aunque en las facciones varían bastante, las que son propias de la raza son sensibles en todo; como es, la frente muy pequeña

y poblada de cabello hasta las extremidades, ó la medianía de las cejas, los ojos pequeños, la nariz.[45]

This passage clearly illustrates how intellectuals at the time viewed the phenomenon of race in its association with physiognomy and pigmentation. Although race is used as a category here, Ulloa also identified these groups based on a visual identification of the body that aimed to produce empirical knowledge of the Black population in relationship to other racial groups. Ulloa theorizes race through the act of visuality. Ruth Hill's recent article on Ulloa's *Noticias americanas* places the text within "the Enlightenment scientific and historiographical genre known as *theories of the Earth*," where his theory of racial differentiation of the Native American population (we must add Black population as well) is grounded in environmental facts or what Hill calls "georacial" theory.[46] Hill adds that, for Ulloa, race "was a cluster of somatic and cultural characteristics produced by variation—the normal course of nature—over time."[47] What is clear from the passage cited earlier is that the application of the concept of race also supposed a material homogeneity among groups in this class, both Blacks and Indigenous communities.

Descriptions such as Ulloa's underscore an emphasis on physical traits and on color that added to the stereotypes used to refer despitefully to marginalized sectors of the population. These stereotypes have had lasting repercussions in Latin America and the way in which Afro-descendants are viewed and treated by political institutions and upper sectors of the population today. This degree of negative racialization is best exemplified by Esteban Terralla y Landa's (1750–1805) racial theorization of Lima in *Lima por dentro y fuera* (1797), wherein he described the city as a world upside down. Racial pigmentation was used to depict the city and its population, and in this portrait, Blacks were associated with waste, lust, dirt, fetidness, and danger. The author asked the reader to be mindful when interacting with those who did not look obviously Black, especially mulatto and Indigenous women, because, "investigando el natal, la estirpe y el nacimiento, / o hay pasas en la cabeza o chicha en los pies corriendo."[48] Physical traits were considered key to determining the racial nature of the individual. This inclination to see race as intertwined with color is part of what Luis Ernesto Valencia Angulo refers to as "lo negro" as a discursive form. He argues that this discourse is the result of "una serie de teorías y prácticas prejuiciosas y racistas desde donde se buscó describir, dominar y controlar a los africanos y a sus descendientes diaspóricos."[49]

In Mexico, Francisco Javier Clavigero (1731–1787) would engage with

European intellectuals such as Cornelius de Pauw (1739–1799), Georges-Louis Leclerc, Comte de Buffon (1707–1788), and the Scottish historian William Robertson (1721–1793) to question their views of the racial nature of the inhabitants of the Americas. He was very critical of De Pauw's term *raza de hombres equívocos* to refer to the supposed backwardness of the American population. In his *Historia antigua de México* (1780), Clavigero quoted De Pauw's description of this classification of race, full of negative connotations and stereotypes about the inhabitants of the Americas. Clavigero explained: "Al principio —dice— no fueron reputados por hombres los americanos, sino más bien sátiros o monos grandes que podían matarse sin remordimiento o reprensión. Al fin, por añadir lo ridículo a las calamidades de aquellos tiempos, un Papa hizo una bula original, en la cual declaró que, deseando fundar obispados en las provincias más ricas de América, le agradó a él y al Espíritu Santo reconocer por verdaderos hombres a los americanos; y así sin esta decisión de un italiano, los habitantes del Nuevo Mundo serían aún, a los ojos de los fieles, una raza de hombres equívocos."[50]

Clavigero found it troublesome that the diverse population of the American continent was collapsed into a single racial category of *hombres equívocos* to justify ideas of inferiority. According to Clavigero, De Pauw depicted Americans, and particularly the Indigenous population, as "hombres que apenas se diferenciaban de las bestias," with signs of degeneration that could be detected in the color of their skin, their hard scalp and lack of facial hair, their inability to remember, their weakness of will, their laziness, and their inclination to moral vices.[51] For the Mexican Jesuit, this label was insufficient and did not capture the complexities of the native Indigenous people or of the Americans in general. It is important to note that for Clavigero, the population of Mexico and the Americas was divided into four groups: native Indigenous people, or "americanos propios," as he called them; a group of Europeans, Asians, and Africans who migrated to the Americas; the descendants of Europeans, Asians, and Africans born in the Americas, referred to as *criollos*; and mixed races, or as he called them "razas mezcladas."[52] On that last group he added that the Spaniards referred to them as *castas* ("llamadas por los españoles castas").[53] One can notice that the concept of race in his view conveyed more properly the mixing of different population groups, also suggesting that the *casta* concept was in use only by the Spaniards. For him, racial mixing was not encapsulated anymore under the rubric of *casta* but under the word *raza*.

In his prologue, Clavigero made clear that by only digging into the history produced on the American continent, Europeans like De Pauw could be corrected. Clavigero also connected the negative impact that the classification of people based on misinformed categorizations of race had when describing the native population of the Americas. To this, he added, "La pasión y los prejuicios en unos autores y la falta de conocimiento o de reflexión en otros, les han hecho emplear diversos colores de los que debieran."[54] For the Mexican scholar, racial characterizations had to be grounded in local sources dating back to the codices to speak truthfully about that racial nature of the Indigenous people.[55] The true history of Mexico and its original people, as well as of the Americas in general, would prove wrong to those who believed that American people could be categorized only as "raza de hombres equívocos."

The Enlightenment was key in resurrecting ideas of environmental determinism that added to the notion of America's backwardness that Clavigero debated. These ideas consequently expanded discussions about race.[56] Charles-Louis de Secondat Baron de Montesquieu (1689–1755) argued that weather in general and changes in temperature had a major impact on the physical state of the human body, and the physical state had an impact on the mental state of the individuals and society in general.[57] The location of the individual determined how the environment affected human reason. It was Buffon who made a direct connection between the impact of the environment and race. As Charles Withers argues, Buffon "distinguished between 'degenerating' and 'isolated' species" on the basis of the degree of geographical variation between humans.[58] In his view, heat was associated with Blackness, Blackness with degeneracy, and degeneracy with Africa and the Americas.[59] In the case of the American continent, Buffon concluded, "Besides, a thousand other circumstances concur in showing that the Continent of America in general ought to be regarded as new land, in which Nature has not had time to acquire all her powers, nor to exhibit them by a numerous population."[60]

Spanish American creoles disputed these beliefs, but the stereotypes that fed the ideas caused a major uproar among Spanish American intellectuals. Ideas that circulated because of this set the fuel for racial Darwinism in the next century. At a time when progress and order were two of the major tenets of the Enlightenment, race worked for Europeans as a political tool to classify the American continent and its people as backward and lacking reason.[61] As a result of these notions, eighteenth-century Spanish historiography became a "reconstruction of self-identity," as Jorge Cañizares-Esguerra argues.[62] In the case of Spanish American authors, this reconstruction centered on the critique of "Eurocentric epistemology" that offered "alternative narratives to those developed in Europe; ones in which Amerindians and Creoles did not appear as degenerate and effete."⁶³ Within these efforts, the categorization of the concept of race served Clavigero and others as a critical venue for reading America and its inhabitants from the other side of the Atlantic with the experience and authority that living there brought to them. However, what many of these intellectuals failed to do was consider people of African descent born in the Americas as Americans. When it came to their assumptions on race, they felt trapped by their own prejudices against the Black population, whom they saw as inferior to the native Indigenous population.

For example, in 1792, Francisco Eugenio de Santa Cruz y Espejo, editor of the newspaper *Primicias de la Cultura de Quito*, published a letter to the editor written by Pedro Lucas Larrea, a Jesuit exiled in Italy.⁶⁴ In the letter, Lucas Larrea stated that he was part of a group of Jesuits translating into Italian *Historia del Reino de Quito*, which was written by his compatriot Don Juan de Velasco. Referring to the European philosophers that both Espejo and Velasco cited in their works, Larrea added, "los hemos leído acá con horror, por las enormes imposturas, falsedades y denigrantísimos dibujos de toda la América, y los Americanos; principalmente el maligno y fanático Prusiano Monsieur Pauw, que dice tantas bestialidades de los Americanos. Contra todos estos han escrito admirablemente Don Francisco Xavier Clavijero, en su excelente Historia de México; un Chileno Molina, en la Historia de Chile; y nuestro Don Juan de Velasco en la citada de Quito."⁶⁵ The comments reiterated the need to read America and its population from a locus of enunciation grounded on local knowledge. In fact, Juan de Velasco, in his *Historia del Reino de Quito en la América Meridional* (1789) took the opportunity, as Clavigero did, to respond to debate about the nature of Spanish American people and their racial nature. The Creole Jesuit responded to the dominant corpus of historiographical works from Enlightenment Europe that focused on the alleged degenerate nature and inhabitants of the Americas. His discussion offered a good example to understand how the phenomenon of race was amplified in the eighteenth century to focus also on intellectual reason.

In the section on natural history, Velasco set out his first attack on De Pauw's theoretical posture that climate determined the character and culture of a society and influenced its level of progress and civilization. De Pauw stated, "La gran humedad de la atmósfera, la prodigiosa cantidad de aguas estancadas, los vapores nocivos, los fluidos corruptos, y la calidad viciada de las plantas y animales, son responsables por la debilidad de la complexión de los habitantes, la aversión que sienten hacia el trabajo, y su incapacitación general para desarrollarse, lo que ha prevenido que los Americanos pudieran salir de su etapa salvaje."[66] For Velasco, it was ridiculous to claim, as De Pauw did, that climate caused the degeneration of everything found in America. He claimed that if this were true, "luego todas las cosas del Nuevo Mundo se han degradado y degenerado en Europa" because of the climate, which would have meant, by De Pauw's theory, that Europe and its inhabitants were also degenerate.[67] Velasco added a critical perspectivism to the Eurocentric view that circulated at the time about the inhabitants of the Americas by stating that the classification of people based on climatic theories lacked substantial validity. To demonstrate his point, Velasco focused on another contentious argument that circulated at the time when describing the racial nature of inhabitants of the Americas, which was their supposed irrational character.

On this issue, Velasco took the opportunity to directly attack William Robertson and his work *History of America* (1777). Velasco's critique of Robertson focused on the historian's claims about the irrational nature of the New World's inhabitants. Velasco began his diatribe by pointing out that Robertson and other philosophers claimed that "no tuvo la América Reino racional" [America did not have a national kingdom].[68] Robertson argued that, as a result of the climate, the people in America had been unable to reach a state of perfection and remained stuck in an inferior animal state, deprived of emotion and reason. Velasco added that, according to Robertson, "lo que entre las naciones cultas se llama razonamiento o investigación especulativa, es totalmente desconocido en este estado bruto de su sociedad, y nunca se convierte en la ocupación o pasatiempo de sus facultades humanas . . . Como un mero animal, lo que está al frente de sus ojos es lo que le interesa o afecta; mientras lo que está fuera del alcance de la vista o en la distancia le causa poca impresión."[69] Such comments, Velasco argued, were based entirely on the writings of De Pauw and Buffon without ever questioning their veracity. Velasco, in turn, provided a list of examples from the Kingdom of Quito to demonstrate that Americans, including Indigenous people, were notable for their rational capacity. He stated that if one were to make a list of all the illustrious and intelligent families of the Kingdom, it would fill "una biblioteca dos veces grande."[70] If in some cases an American did not possess certain knowledge, it was due to lack of instruction, and not because he did not have the capacity to understand. Thus, nor was it right for Robertson to establish a correlation between the moral character of Indigenous people and their physical composition. Velasco contended that this was an erroneous way to classify people. For him, the racial character of the American inhabitants was not a fixed racial category determined purely by the environment and anchored on physical and rational attributes. It was time for European philosophers and scientists to broaden their narrowed racial classification and instead anchor their arguments in the specificities of the diverse regions and populations that composed the vast American continent.

In his effort to discredit Robertson's claims, Velasco offered an alternative approach to thinking about the racial nature of the inhabitants. First, he established that climate did not cause physical imperfection, which in turn did not cause moral imperfection. This was evident from the diversity of people throughout the continent and the fact that they did not show such imperfections. According to Velasco, the fact that America had such varied climates made it impossible to come to an absolute conclusion about whether all its inhabitants were perfect or imperfect. Second, Velasco argued that it was dangerous to take a specific characteristic and apply it to everyone equally without differentiation or exception, because, as he emphasized, "hay mucha y muy notable diversidad y por eso mucha y muy notable injusticia en igualarlos y confundirlos a todos."[71] Therefore, Robertson was committing a serious error in conceptualizing the American inhabitants solely on the basis of the ideas that were circulating in Europe and not on what he would have learned if he had visited the American territories and thoroughly investigated its people, fauna, and flora. Robertson's failure to visit and observe firsthand the continents and people was the cause of his ignorance. Finally, Velasco argued, "es horror y es injusticia, querer hacer propios y característicos de los americanos aquellos defectos, que son comunes y generales a todo el mundo, derivados en todas partes de las mismas causas."[72] Velasco emphasized that for history to be truthful, it must be free of generalizations that confuse the parts with the whole. Classifications and categorizations suffer from a narrow view of things, people, and nature, as they are all the result of specific and individual agendas. It was important, then, to witness, observe, study, and understand the differences that existed between diverse territories and populations. For Velasco, there were three vital actions a writer had to follow when writing about America and its inhabitants. First, it was imperative to conduct in situ physical observations of the space and its inhabitants. Second, it was important to have knowledge of the native language of the inhabitants to understand people's culture more fully. Finally, it was crucial to go through the experience of living among Americans to understand their cultural habits. Only after following these three steps would one understand the difficulty of categorizing people according to certain nomenclatures that did not apply to their reality. Again, his approach brought an important perspectivism that was crucial to discussions of the racial nature of the American population, which put European thinkers' belief into question that the fixed racial categorizations invented in Europe could apply universally.

Conclusion

In her study of race and its legacy in antiquity, Denise Eileen McCoskey offers a great definition of race that aptly applies to the different dimensions of the word as employed in the eighteenth century. McCoskey, referring to antiquity and its aftermath, argues that race "does not derive passively from human anatomy, but it is dependent on social intervention, on the formulation of theories that designate the surface of the human body as the primary vehicle of race and also determine *which* physical features 'matter' in determining racial groups."[73] It is the body upon which race is acted that contributes to the construction of a theoretical and cultural apparatus aimed at categorizing human difference. More importantly, it is social intervention that highly determines the way the concept is utilized, which therefore endows it with that perspectivism that Velasco mentioned. Race and its associations with the concepts of *casta* and *calidad* evolved from the European needs "to identify exteriorize, manipulate, and dominate unfamiliar peoples" to "the persistent delineation of the racial Other in somatic, spatial or regulatory terms that resided firmly in the appearance, locations, and behaviors of the visible human body" along with emphasis on skin color and intellectual capacity.[74] This definition aligns well with the history of the concept of race in late-colonial Latin America as demonstrated by the ways race was used in dictionaries and historiographical and literary accounts.

The nineteenth century is considered the period in which the concept of race as we know it today emerged. In this understanding of race, the main objective was to determine racial classifications and distinctions based on biological justifications anchored in ideas of evolution and natural selection developed by Charles Darwin (1809–1882).[75] The idea that some races were superior to others was the culmination of a long history of obsessive desire to classify difference that went through a transformation in the eighteenth century with the emergence of scientific ideas centered on geographic and environmental approaches that Spanish American intellectuals had to put into question. As Magali M. Carrera has noted, discussions of races beyond the scope of lineage did take place in the eighteenth century when Immanuel

Kant in 1764 used "the term 'race' in the sense of biologically or physically distinct categories of human beings."[76]

In a very recent book, edited by Henry Louis Gates Jr. and Andrew S. Curran, *Who's Black and Why? A Hidden Chapter from Eighteenth-Century Invention of Race* (2022), the editors discussed the submissions presented to a contest hosted by the Bordeaux Royal Academy of Sciences in 1739, which asked for essays on the search for a scientific understanding of the concept of race in the context of what it meant to be Black.[77] Specifically, contestants were to address "the physical cause of Negro's color, the quality of [the Negro's] hair, and the degeneration of both [Negro hair and skin]."[78] Submissions received engaged with these topics from different theoretical angles, including biblical and from the fields of anatomy, natural history, and climatology. What this competition showed was the fact that, for French academicians and, I must add, other Europeans at the time, the color black had become synonymous with "human bondage" and "was a metonym for Africans" and "for slavery and the trans-Atlantic slave trade."[79] Gates and Curran called attention to the fact that, by 1741, when the academy was supposed to have received the submissions, "62,485 African captive men, women, and children are estimated to have boarded ships in chains along the long west coast of Africa, destined for plantations in Brazil, Central America, the Caribbean, and North America."[80] In fact, as the authors add, by the end of the eighteenth century, a total of 4.5 million Africans had been forced to the Americas. Important to consider as well was the role of the port city of Bordeaux as a busy merchant city with ties to exports to and imports from the French Caribbean colonies and ties to slave trading expeditions.

I agree with Gates and Curran's argument that discussions about race in the eighteenth century did not occur in a vacuum. As was the case of colonial Spanish America, racial miscegenation, African forced migration, and the visible presence of a very racially diverse population native to the continent played an important role in how the concept of race was thought and rethought as an idea. The use of the concept in the eighteenth century thus demonstrates its changeable nature, especially as appearance guided by visual recognition constituted a factor also in how people were going to be recognized or classified.[81] "How do you look or appear to look" was still in place at the time, albeit prone to misunderstandings. It is crucial that we look at the discussion that took place in Spanish America in the eighteenth century as part of the history of ideas about race that were increasingly popular at the time in Europe. On both sides of the Atlantic, race as a practice of classification always confronted the challenges that difference, diversity, and transformations carried within. In the eighteenth century, race as a concept and as an idea resisted universal applications in the Americas because race was and remains a social construction prone to subjective interpretations.

NOTES

1. José Vasconcelos, *La raza cósmica: Misión de la raza iberoamericana* (Barcelona: Tipografía Cosmos, 1949), 25.
2. Vasconcelos, *La raza cósmica*, 12.
3. Stuart B. Schwartz, *Blood Boundaries: The Limits of Religious and Racial Exclusion in early Modern Latin America* (Waltham, MA: Brandeis University Press, 2020), 5.
4. For a succinct and enlightened summary of these two tendencies among scholars whose work focuses on of colonial Latin America, see Miguel Valerio's introduction to his *Sovereign Joy: Afro-Mexican Kings and Queens* (Cambridge: Cambridge University Press, 2022). I thank Miguel for allowing me to read and cite his manuscript.
5. Daniel Nemser, "Race and Domination in Colonial Latin American Studies," in *The Routledge Hispanic Studies Companion to Colonial Latin America and the Caribbean (1492–1898)*, ed. Yolanda Martínez San Miguel and Santa Arias (London: Routledge, 2021), 49.
6. Nemser, "Race and Domination," 45. Nemser adds that "race is an effect rather than a cause," and for this reason, domination serves as critical angle for examining the processes through which colonial authorities tried to rule over marginalized groups or what he refers to as racialization (44). In his *Infrastructures of Race: Concentration and Biopolitics in Colonial Mexico* (Austin: University of Texas Press, 2017), Nemser contends that "the emphasis on the fluidity of identity in colonial Latin America has resulted at times in a tendency to downplay the structural character of race" (9). He also adds, "By privileging descriptions of difference and highlighting what could be called the micropolitics of race, such as the elements individuals looked to as signs of identity or the practices they adopted as tools of self-fashioning, some scholars lose track of domination" (9).
7. Robert C. Schwaller, *Géneros de Gente in Early Colonial Mexico: Defining Racial Difference* (Norman: University of Oklahoma Press, 2016), 6. For a more recent examination of how "medieval Iberian notions of difference" evolved from *género de gentes* (style of people) into the concepts of *casta* and *calidad*, see Schwaller's book as well. For a crucial study on how the racial ideology of *casta* in colonial times (especially Mexico) was ingrained into assumptions pertaining to purity of blood, see María Elena Martínez's *Genealogical Fictions: Limpieza de Sangre, Religion, and Gender in Colonial Mexico* (Stanford, CA: Stanford University Press, 2008).
8. Schwaller, *Géneros de Gente*, 8–9.
9. For an outstanding discussion of the policies of exclusion and discrimination as it pertains to race as a category, see Schwartz, *Blood Boundaries*.
10. A good illustration of how race is used in very general terms by some scholars is found in the important volume edited by Walter D. Mignolo and Arturo Escobar, *Globalization and the Decolonial Option* (London: Routledge, 2010), in which the concept of race is cited many times. Aníbal Quijano devotes a brief section of to "'race' and coloniality of power," in his chapter "Coloniality and Modernity/Rationality" (25). Despite saying that "coloniality of power was conceived together with America and Western Europe, and

with the social category of 'race' as the key element of the social classification of colonized and colonizers," there is no definition or critical engagement with the concept itself. Quijano, "Coloniality and Modernity/Rationality," 25. Instead, the words *race* and *racial* appear always in quotation marks and used as referring to social identities within a system of racial classification.

11. *Diccionario de autoridades*, facs. ed. (Madrid: Editorial Gredos, 1990), 3:500. The dictionary's original title was *Diccionario e la lengua castellana en que se explica el verdadero sentido de las voces, su naturaleza y calidad, con las phrases o modos de hablar, y otras cosas convenientes al uso de la lengua*. I follow the original orthography.
12. Sebastián de Covarrubias Horozco, *Tesoro de la lengua castellana o española* (Madrid: Iberoamericana: 2006), 1395.
13. In the fifteenth century, Spain had established the proof of *pureza de sangre* (purity of blood), which, as José Piedra describes it, "involved a trial of faith, race, and national origin, depending on the issue in doubt." "Literary Whiteness and Afro-Hispanic Difference," in *The Bounds of Race: Perspectives on Hegemony and Resistance*, ed. Dominick LaCapra (Ithaca, NY: Cornell University Press, 1991), 286. Individuals in question had to proof their purity in what was called an auto-da-fé (286).
14. Schwartz, *Blood Boundaries*, 7.
15. Roquinaldo Ferreira and Tatiana Seijas, "The Slave Trade to Latin America: A Historiographical Assessment," in *Afro–Latin American Studies: An Introduction*, ed. Alejandro de la Fuente and George Reid Andrews (Cambridge: Cambridge University Press, 2018), 28, who also provide an in-depth discussion of how the slave trade functioned in the Spanish colonies. See also chapter two in Leslie B. Rout's *The African Experience in Spanish America* (Princeton, NJ: Markus Wiener Publishers, 2011).
16. Rout, *The African Experience*, 60.
17. Rout, *The African Experience*, 60.
18. Alex Borucki, *From Shipmates to Soldiers: Emerging Black Identities in the Río de la Plata* (Albuquerque: University of New Mexico Press, 2015), 2.
19. Peter Flindell Klarén, *Peru: Society and Nationhood in the Andes* (New York: Oxford University Press, 2000), 100.
20. María Elisa Velázquez, *Mujeres de origen africano en la capital novohispana, siglos XVII y XVIII* (Mexico City: Universidad Nacional Autónoma de México, 2006), 19.
21. Dorinda Outram, *The Enlightenment* (Cambridge: Cambridge University Press, 2006), 56.
22. Outram, *The Enlightenment*, 56.
23. Outram, *The Enlightenment*, 55. This issue was central as well in the famous sixteenth-century debate between Bartolomé de las Casas (1484-1566) and Juan Ginés de Sepúlveda (1494-1573) on the nature of the Indigenous people, wherein Las Casas saw Indigenous people as humans by nature and Sepúlveda conceived of them as slaves by nature.
24. "Ideas de las congregaciones públicas de los negros bozales," *Mercurio Peruano* 2, no. 48 (1791): 113. Quote from *Mercurio Peruano* follows original orthography. There is no author listed in the article.
25. *Mercurio Peruano*, no. 48 (Lima, 1791), 113.
26. *Mercurio Peruano*, no. 48 (Lima, 1791), 112-113.
27. *Mercurio Peruano*, no. 49 (Lima, 1791), 125. For an in-depth discussion of this newspaper article centered on gender and social deviance, see Meléndez, "*Patria, Criollos,* and Blacks: Imagining the Nation in the *Mercurio peruano,*" *Colonial Latin American Review* 15, no. 2 (2006): 207-227.

28. Ilona Katzew, *Casta Painting: Images of Race in Eighteenth-Century Mexico* (New Haven, CT: Yale University Press, 2004), 45. Katzew adds that the concept of *calidad* epitomizes "the combination of economic, social, cultural, and racial factors that defined an individual" (45). *Calidad* is part of the racial profile of a person.
29. Katzew, *Casta Painting*, 45.
30. Gillian Rose, *Visual Methodologies* (London: Sage, 2001), 6.
31. Katzew, *Casta Painting*, 51.
32. Pamela Patton, "Introduction: Race, Color, and the Visual in Iberia and Latin America," in *Envisioning Others: Race, Color, and the Visual in Iberia and Latin America*, ed. Pamela Patton (Leiden: Brill, 2016), 7.
33. Katzew, *Casta Painting*, 40.
34. Maribel Arrelucea Barrantes, "Slavery, Writing, and Female Resistance: Black Women Litigants in Lima's Tribunals of the 1780s" in *Afro-Latino Voices: Narratives from the Early Modern Ibero-Atlantic World, 1550–1812*, ed. Kathryn Joy McKnight and Leo J. Garofalo (Indianapolis: Hackett Publishing, 2009), 286.
35. Tamara J. Walker, *Exquisite Slaves: Race, Clothing, and Status in Colonial Lima* (New York: Cambridge University Press, 2017), 7.
36. For more on the different ways enslaved Africans and other Black sectors of the population used the ecclesiastical and civil courts to defend themselves, consult the very important edition of *Afro-Latino Voices: Narratives from the Early Modern Ibero-Atlantic World, 1550–1812*, ed. Kathryn Joy McKnight and Leo J. Garofalo (Indianapolis: Hackett Publishing, 2009). When it comes to "the ways urban social relations expanded opportunities for black agency," see the collection of essays in Jorge Cañizares Esguerra, Matt Childs, and James Sidbury, *The Black Urban Atlantic in the Age of Slave Trade* (Philadelphia: University of Pennsylvania Press, 2013), 16, particularly the third section. On the topic of the Black population in colonial Mexico, see the important contribution of Gonzalo Aguirre Beltrán's *La población negra de México: Estudio etnohistórico* (Mexico City: Fondo de Cultura Económica, 1990) and Herman L. Bennett's *Colonial Blackness: A History of Afro-Mexico* (Bloomington: Indiana University Press, 2009). For a more succinct history, see Matthew Restall and Kris Lane's *Latin America in Colonial Times* (Cambridge: Cambridge University Press, 2011), esp. chap. 9.
37. By "theorization of race," I refer to the act of producing knowledge. I follow Pierre Bourdieu's view of theory, which he sees as engaged in the production of knowledge. For him, theory, and especially scientific theory, "emerges as a program of perception and action." Pierre Bourdieu and Loïc J. D. Wacquant, *An Invitation to Reflexive Sociology* (Chicago: University of Chicago Press, 1992), 161. He adds that theory "is a temporary construct which takes shape for and by empirical work" (161). By "empirical," he refers to observation as a phenomenon and what observations are trying to capture.
38. John Robertson, *The Case for the Enlightenment: Scotland and Naples 1680–1760* (Cambridge: Cambridge University Press, 2006), 29. Robertson argues that there are two other main lines of inquiry in the Enlightenment. The first has to do with the importance of "good argumentation" to reach "Reasoned conclusions" (28). The second line of inquiry has to do with the "material betterment" or the "subject of political economy . . . who goals were the wealth of nations (in the plural) and the improvement of the condition of all of society members" (29).
39. Gabriel B. Paquette, *Enlightenment, Governance, and Reform in Spain and its Empire, 1759–1808* (New York: Palgrave Macmillan, 2011), 8–9.

40. Paquette, *Enlightenment*, 98.
41. Chris Philo, "Edinburgh, Enlightenment, and the Geographies of Unreason," in *Geography and Enlightenment*, ed. David N. Livingstone and Charles W. J. Withers (Chicago: Chicago University Press, 1999), 373.
42. Velázquez, *Mujeres de origen africano*, 53.
43. Velázquez, *Mujeres de origen africano*, 54.
44. *Noticias americanas* was published first in 1772 under the title, *Noticias americanas. Entretenimientos physicos-historicos sobre la América Meridional, y la Septentrional Oriental: Comparación general de los territorios, climas y producciones en las tres especies vegetal, animal y mineral; con una relación particular de los Indios de aquellos paises, sus costumbres y usos, de las petrificaciones de cuerpos marinos y de las Antigüedades*. It was printed in Madrid. I quote from the 1792 edition and maintain original orthography.
45. Antonio de Ulloa, *Noticias americanas* (Madrid: Imprenta Real, 1792), 252.
46. Ruth Hill, "The Georacial Past in the New World Present: Antonio de Ulloa's Noticias Americanas," in *The Routledge Companion to the Hispanic Enlightenment*, ed. Elizabeth Franklin Lewis, Mónica Bolufer Peruga, and Catherine M. Jaffe (London: Routledge, 2020), 31.
47. Hill, "The Georacial Past," 34. For the impact of Ulloa's *Noticias americanas* on nineteenth-century ideas on geology, archeology, and paleontology in figures such as Domingo F. Sarmiento, see Hill, who argues that Ulloa falls into the same "biological essentialism and cultural essentialism" that we see in nineteenth-century scholars, when he concludes that Indigenous people are all the same (36).
48. Esteban Terralla y Landa, *Lima por dentro y fuera* (1798; rpt., Exeter, UK: University of Exeter Press, 1978), 45.
49. Luis Ernesto Valencia Angulo, *Negro y afro: La invención de dos formas discursivas* (Cali: Editorial Universidad Icesi, 2019), 27. Valencia Angulo argued that "lo negro como invención discursiva" dates to antiquity, where the color white was perceived as symbol of goodness, purity, sacredness, wisdom, and power, while the color Black was associated with "la manifestación del mal, del pecado, de lo vil, lo impuro, lo débil" (40). On this topic, see also Ildefonso Gutiérrez Azopardo's *La población negra en América* (Santa Fe de Bogotá: Editorial El Búho, 2000).
50. Francisco Javier Clavigero, *Historia antigua de México* (Mexico City: Editorial Porrúa, 1945), 4:247.
51. Clavigero, *Historia antigua*, 4:11.
52. Clavigero, *Historia antigua*, 4:219.
53. Clavigero, *Historia antigua*, 4:219.
54. Clavigero, *Historia antigua*, 1:165.
55. To learn more about what Clavigero had to say on the character of the Indigenous people, see book 1, chapter 17, "Carácter de los mexicanos y demas naciones de Anahuac." *Historia antigua*, 1:165.
56. Important to note is that environmental determinism dates to classical times and became popular during the eighteenth century because the theories "offered an explanation of the material and intellectual progress experienced by European countries over the previous two centuries. Denise Eileen McCoskey, *Race: Antiquity & Its Legacy* (London: I. B. Tauris, 2012), 169.
57. Charles W. J. Withers, *Placing the Enlightenment: Thinking Geographically about the Age of Reason* (Chicago: University of Chicago Press, 2007), 140.

58. Withers, *Placing the Enlightenment*, 145.
59. Withers, *Placing the Enlightenment*, 145.
60. Georges Louis Leclerc Buffon, *Buffon's Natural History, Containing a Theory of the Earth, a General History of Man, of the Brute Creation, and of Vegetables* (London: J. S. Barr, 1792), 105.
61. For an in-depth discussion of how the Enlightenment was read in eighteenth-century Spanish America, see Mariselle Meléndez and Karen Stolley, "Introduction: Enlightenments in Ibero-America," *Colonial Latin American Review* 24, no. 1 (2015): 1–16.
62. Jorge Cañizares Esguerra, *How to Write the History of the New World: Histories, Epistemologies, and Identities in the Eighteenth-Century Atlantic World* (Stanford, CA: Stanford University Press, 2001), 3.
63. Cañizares Esguerra, *How to Write*, 4. For a detailed discussion of the Eurocentric views of Spanish America as developed by Buffon, De Pauw, and Raynal, among others, see Cañizares Esguerra's chapter 1 in *How to Write*.
64. The newspaper *Primicias de la Cultura de Quito* was first published on January 5, 1792, with the endorsement and permission of the Superior Government in 1791. Unfortunately, only seven issues were published. The newspaper ceased to exist in March of the same year, likely due to a combination of economic problems and political persecution.
65. Eugenio Santa Cruz y Espejo, *Primicias de la cultura de Quito* (Quito: Publicaciones del Archivo Municipal, 1947), 25.
66. Quoted in Juan de Velasco, *Historia del Reyno de Quito en la América Meridional* (Quito: Editora El Comercio, 1946), 28–29.
67. Velasco, *Historia del Reyno de Quito*, 1:16.
68. Velasco, *Historia del Reyno de Quito*, 1:175.
69. Velasco, *Historia del Reyno de Quito*, 2:85.
70. Velasco, *Historia del Reyno de Quito*, 1:263.
71. Velasco, *Historia del Reyno de Quito*, 1:247.
72. Velasco, *Historia del Reyno de Quito*, 1:247–248.
73. McCoskey, *Race*, 2. McCoskey also argues that race as it was used up to the nineteenth century was "the product of popular beliefs about human differences" (3).
74. Patton, "Introduction," 5.
75. F. Carl Walton and Stephen Maynard Caliendo, "Origins of the Concept of Race," in *The Routledge Companion to Race and Ethnicity*, ed. Stephen M. Caliendo and Charlton D. McIlwain (London: Routledge, 2011), 4.
76. Magali M. Carrera, *Imagining Identity in New Spain: Race, Lineage and the Colonial Body in Portraiture and Casta Painting* (Austin: University of Texas Press, 2003), 11. Carrera adds that Kant "promoted the idea of an unchanging inner essence within human beings that became attached to the meaning of race" (11).
77. Henry Louis Gates Jr. and Andrew S. Curran, eds., *Who's Black and Why? A Hidden Chapter from the Eighteenth-Century Invention of Race* (Cambridge, MA: Harvard University Press, 2022). The questions that preoccupied the academy and that submissions to the contest needed to address were "Who is Black? And Why?" and "What did being Black signify?," Who's Black and Why? (ix).
78. Gates and Curran, *Who's Black and Why?*, ix.
79. Gates and Curran, *Who's Black and Why?*, x. Regarding color, Gates and Curran add that the color black also was used as a signifier associated with geographical names that contained "etymological roots of the word 'black'" such as Guinea, Niger, Nigritia, among

others (x). For both authors, the "most telling example" when it came to this association was the word *Ethiopia*, derived from the Greek "*aitho* (I burn) and *ops* (face)," a word subsequently used to refer to the entire sub-Saharan portion of the African continent.
80. Gates and Curran, *Who's Black and Why?*, x.
81. As José Antonio Mazzotti indicates, in some cases "the appearance of whiteness" was enough to merit status to some. "Race, Ethnicity and Nationhood in the Formation of Criollismo in Spanish America," in *The Routledge Hispanic Studies Companion to Colonial Latin America and the Caribbean (1492–1898)*, ed. Yolanda Martínez San Miguel and Santa Arias (London: Routledge, 2021), 90.

BIBLIOGRAPHY

Aguirre Beltrán, Gonzalo. *La población negra de México: Estudio etnohistórico*. Mexico City: Fondo de Cultura Económica, 1990.

Arrelucea Barrantes, Maribel. "Slavery, Writing, and Female Resistance: Black Women Litigants in Lima's Tribunals of the 1780s." In *Afro-Latino Voices: Narratives from the Early Modern Ibero-Atlantic World, 1550–1812*, edited by Kathryn Joy McKnight and Leo J. Garofalo, 285–301. Indianapolis: Hackett Publishing, 2009.

Bennett, Herman L. *Colonial Blackness: A History of Afro-Mexico*. Bloomington: Indiana University Press, 2009.

Borucki, Alex. *From Shipmates to Soldiers: Emerging Black Identities in the Río de la Plata*. Albuquerque: University of New Mexico Press, 2015.

Bourdieu, Pierre, and Loïc J. D. Wacquant. *An Invitation to Reflexive Sociology*. Chicago: University of Chicago Press, 1992.

Buffon, Georges-Louis Leclerc. *Buffon's Natural History, Containing a Theory of the Earth, a General History of Man, of the Brute Creation, and of Vegetables*. London: J. S. Barr, 1792.

Cañizares-Esguerra, Jorge. *How to Write the History of the New World: Histories, Epistemologies, and Identities in the Eighteenth-Century Atlantic World*. Stanford, CA: Stanford University Press, 2001.

Cañizares-Esguerra, Jorge, Matt Childs, and James Sidbury. *The Black Urban Atlantic in the Age of Slave Trade*. Philadelphia: University of Pennsylvania Press, 2013.

Carrera, Magali M. *Imagining Identity in New Spain: Race, Lineage and the Colonial Body in Portraiture and Casta Painting*. Austin: University of Texas Press, 2003.

Clavigero, Francisco Javier. *Historia Antigua de México*. Mexico City: Editorial Porrúa, 1945.

Covarrubias Horozco, Sebastián de. *Tesoro de la lengua castellana o española*. Madrid: Iberoamericana, 2006.

Diccionario de autoridades. 1737. Facsimile ed. Madrid: Editorial Gredos, 1990.

Ferreira, Roquinaldo and Tatiana Seijas. "The Slave Trade to Latin America: A Historiographical Assessment." In *Afro-Latin American Studies: An Introduction*, edited by Alejandro de la Fuente and George Reid Andrews, 27–51. Cambridge: Cambridge University Press, 2018.

Gates, Henry Louis, Jr., and Andrew S. Curran, eds. *Who's Black and Why? A Hidden Chapter from the Eighteenth-Century Invention of Race*. Cambridge, MA: Harvard University Press, 2022.

Gutiérrez Azopardo, Ildefonso. *La población negra en América*. Bogotá: Editorial El Búho, 2000.

Hill, Ruth. "The Georacial Past in the New World Present: Antonio de Ulloa's *Noticias americanas*." In *The Routledge Companion to the Hispanic Enlightenment*, edited by Elizabeth Franklin Lewis, Mónica Bolufer Peruga, and Catherine M. Jaffe, 30–42. London: Routledge, 2020.

"Ideas de las Congregaciones Públicas de los *Negros Bozales*." *Mercurio Peruano* (Biblioteca Nacional del Perú) 2, no. 48 (1791): 112–113.

Katzew, Ilona. *Casta Painting: Images of race in Eighteenth-century Mexico*. New Haven, CT: Yale University Press, 2004.

Klarén, Peter Flindell. *Peru. Society and Nationhood in the Andes*. New York: Oxford University Press, 2000.

Martínez, María Elena. *Genealogical Fictions: Limpieza de sangre, Religion, and Gender in Colonial Mexico*. Stanford, CA: Stanford University Press, 2008.

Mazzotti, José Antonio. "Race, Ethnicity and Nationhood in the Formation of *Criollismo* in Spanish America." In *The Routledge Hispanic Studies Companion to Colonial Latin America and the Caribbean (1492–1898)*, edited by Yolanda Martínez San Miguel and Santa Arias, 85–98. London: Routledge, 2021.

McCoskey, Denise Eileen. *Race: Antiquity & Its Legacy*. London: I. B. Tauris, 2012.

McKnight, Kathryn Joy, and Leo J. Garofalo, eds. *Afro-Latino Voices: Narratives from the Early Modern Ibero-Atlantic World, 1550–1812*. Indianapolis: Hackett Publishing, 2009.

Meléndez, Mariselle. "*Patria, Criollos,* and Blacks: Imagining the Nation in the *Mercurio Peruano*, 1791–1795." *Colonial Latin American Review* 15, no. 2 (2006): 207–227.

Meléndez, Mariselle, and Karen Stolley. "Introduction: Enlightenments in Ibero-America." *Colonial Latin American Review* 24, no. 1 (2015): 1–16.

Nemser, Daniel. *Infrastructures of Race: Concentration and Biopolitics in Colonial Mexico*. Austin: University of Texas Press, 2017.

———. "Race and Domination in Colonial Latin American Studies." In *The Routledge Hispanic Studies Companion to Colonial Latin America and the Caribbean (1492–1898)*, edited by Yolanda Martínez San Miguel and Santa Arias, 43–56. London: Routledge, 2021.

Outram, Dorinda. *The Enlightenment*. Cambridge: Cambridge University Press, 2006.

Paquette, Gabriel B. *Enlightenment, Governance, and Reform in Spain and its Empire, 1759–1808*. New York: Palgrave Macmillan, 2011.

Patton, Pamela. "Introduction: Race, Color, and the Visual in Iberia and Latin America." In *Envisioning Others: Race, Color, and the Visual in Iberia and Latin America*, edited by Pamela Patton, 1–17. Leiden: Brill, 2016.

Philo, Chris. "Edinburgh, Enlightenment, and the Geographies of Unreason." In *Geography and Enlightenment*, edited by David N. Livingstone and Charles W. J. Withers, 372–395. Chicago: Chicago University Press, 1999.

Piedra, José. "Literary Whiteness and Afro-Hispanic Difference." In *The Bounds of Race: Perspectives on Hegemony and Resistance*, edited by Dominick LaCapra, 278–310. Ithaca: Cornell University Press, 1991.

Quijano, Aníbal. "Coloniality and Modernity/Rationality." In *Globalization and the Decolonial Option*, edited by Walter D. Mignolo and Arturo Escobar, 22–32. London: Routledge, 2010.

Restall, Matthew, and Kris Lane. *Latin America in Colonial Times*. Cambridge: Cambridge University Press, 2011.

Robertson, John. *The Case for the Enlightenment: Scotland and Naples 1680–1760*. Cambridge: Cambridge University Press, 2006.

Rose, Gillian. *Visual Methodologies*. London: Sage, 2001.

Rout, Leslie B. *The African Experience in Spanish America*. Princeton, NJ: Markus Wiener Publishers, 2011.

Santa Cruz y Espejo, Eugenio. *Primicias de la Cultura de Quito*. Facs. ed. 1791–1792. Quito: Publicaciones del Archivo Municipal, 1947.

Schwaller, Robert C. *Géneros de Gente in Early Colonial Mexico: Defining Racial Difference*. Norman: University of Oklahoma Press, 2016.

Schwartz, Stuart B. *Blood Boundaries: The Limits of Religious and Racial Exclusion in Early Modern Latin America*. Waltham, MA: Brandeis University Press, 2020.

Terralla y Landa, Esteban. *Lima por dentro y fuera*. Exeter, UK: University of Exeter Press, 1978.

Ulloa, Antonio de. *Noticias americanas*. 1772. Madrid: Imprenta Real, 1792.

Valencia Angulo, Luis Ernesto. *Negro y afro: La invención de dos formas discursivas*. Cali, Colombia: Editorial Universidad Icesi, 2019.

Valerio, Miguel A. *Sovereign Joy: Afro-Mexican Kings and Queens, 1539–1640*. Cambridge: Cambridge University Press, 2022.

Vasconcelos, José. *La raza cósmica: Misión de la raza iberoamericana*. Barcelona: Tipografía Cosmos, 1949.

Velasco, Juan de. *Historia del Reyno de Quito en la América Meridional*. 1789. Quito: Editora El Comercio, 1946.

Velázquez, María Elisa. *Mujeres de origen africano en la capital novohispana, siglos XVII y XVIII*. Mexico City: Universidad Nacional Autónoma de México, 2006.

Walker, Tamara J. *Exquisite Slaves: Race, Clothing, and Status in Colonial Lima*. New York: Cambridge University Press, 2017.

Walton, F. Carl, and Stephen Maynard Caliendo. "Origins of the Concept of Race." In *The Routledge Companion to Race and Ethnicity*, edited by Stephen M. Caliendo and Charlton D. McIlwain, 3–11. London: Routledge, 2011.

Withers, Charles W. J. *Placing the Enlightenment: Thinking Geographically about the Age of Reason*. Chicago: University of Chicago Press, 2007.

PART 2

RACE AND NATION

CHAPTER 5

Genealogies of *Blanquitud/ Branquitude*

From Critical Race Theory to Critical Whiteness Studies

RUTH HILL

In both academic and nonacademic discourses on whiteness in the Americas, the semantic slipperiness of *blanquitud/branquitude* and *blanquedad/branquedade* (rendered equally as whiteness in English) and *blanqueamiento/branqueamento* (whitening) is daunting. I survey here critical trends and theorists, highlighting the beginnings and developments of *blanquitud/branquitude* in multiple fields. I also hint at the relevance of critical renderings of *blanquitud/ branquitude* to the world outside of academia, a topic ripe for exploration. As well, I elaborate on the religious dimensions of *europeo* and *blanco/branco* in the sixteenth and seventeenth centuries, for the sexually reproductive unions between different human kinds (*castas, generaciones, linajes*) posed significant challenges to the metaphysical and epistemological underpinnings of nature in Roman Catholic contexts. I connect the problem of "kinding and unkinding"—of racial becoming, in short—to the matrices of *blanqueamiento/branqueamento/blanchiment/whitening* that emerged throughout the Americas at the turn of the eighteenth century. In doing so, I bring to the fore signal achievements and blind spots of conceptual models of *blanquitud/branquitude*.

Critical Race Theory and Critical Whiteness Studies

The unwitting founder of critical whiteness studies was James Baldwin. Whiteness in this critical sense is synonymous with cultural power—ownership of the legal, economic, and political structures or systems. It is in this sense that the founders of critical race theory (CRT) at US law schools defined and elaborated whiteness at the same time that they underscored other now-common racial concepts such as intersectionality and antiessentialism. Beginning in the early 1980s, under the moniker of critical legal studies, Derek Bell, Kimberlé Crenshaw, Patricia Hill, Richard Delgado, and others began to interrogate the legal, economic, and political institutions that secured white hegemony, or whiteness, in the United States. In 1990, in "Whiteness as Property," the legal scholar Patricia Hill integrated capital, colonial society, and whiteness into a cornerstone of subsequent CRT interventions and critical whiteness studies. What is more, Hill essayed what critical whiteness studies in and/or about Latin America and/or Latinx America have not yet envisioned by insisting that we take into account not only African slaves and freed persons but also Native Americans, or first peoples, in relationship to whiteness as an asset or wealth builder.

From 1990 on, critical theory on race, especially on whiteness, issuing from the social sciences and the humanities, continued to fold in work done by CRT colleagues, although luminaries such as Toni Morrison, Valerie Babb, Grace Hale, bell hooks, Cornel West, Ruth Frankenberg, David T. Goldberg, Matthew Frye Jacobson, Matthew Pratt Guterl, and David Roediger treaded more closely in the footsteps of Baldwin's model of whiteness as a construct built from economic, political, and social power, and feeding into the same, as theorized by CRT scholars after Baldwin.[1] It is in this Baldwinian sense and its CRT conceptual refinement that not only law schools but also education schools in the United States, Australia, Great Britain, and Canada continue to study whiteness.

Moreover, in the social sciences, including those undertaken under the umbrella of Latinx studies and gender and sexuality studies, CRT is more relevant than ever, thanks in no small part to the Black Lives Matter movement and to unwitting conservatives who, though ignorant of the distinction between CRT and critical theory on race, and of the fundamental concepts of both, direct web traffic at breakneck speed to CRT sites and articles on CRT posted on social media and Academia.edu. Essays and monographs by many historians and sociologists of *blanquitud* or *branquitude* in different Spanish- or

Portuguese-speaking locales have benefited from the economic heavy lifting done by the CRT movement. In Peru, for instance, juridical pluralism, equality in education, and numerous other manifestations of CRT's impact outside of the United States are being given a critical space that integrates practice-based research and theory.[2] In Brazil, CRT has been impactful, implicitly or explicitly: the meteoric ascent of critical whiteness studies in Brazil has pulled together law schools, education schools, and colleges of arts and sciences. An appreciable impetus—and achievement—of CRT in Brazil has been the racial segment of Brazil's affirmative action program (Sistema de Cotas). Still, the centrality of whiteness to Brazilian society has been scrutinized since the 1950s, and there has been a veritable boom in Brazilian university courses and dissertations on whiteness and racial inequality in Brazil in the early 2000s.[3]

Blanquitud/Branquitude

Lélia González's shadow justifiably looms large over repudiations of *branquitude*, anti-Blackness, and gender inequality through her modelings of an Afro-Brazilian consciousness (*pretoguês*) and an Afro–Latin American identity (*amefricanidade*) rooted in a transnational feminist consciousness.[4] Maria Aparecida da Silva Bento, Maria de Jesus Silveira, and Simone Gibram Nogueira spearhead workshops, courses, and conferences that continue to produce historical, literary, and practice-based perspectives.[5] Bento, in particular, has shaped an entire generation of scholarship by coining the concept of narcissist compacts of racism (*pactos narcísicos no racismo*).[6] She associates "White raciality" (*racialidade branca*) with such tacit or explicit compacts between whites to hire, vote for, and otherwise privilege people who look, talk, and act like they do.[7]

Young Afro-Brazilian scholars and activists such as Silvio Almeida and Raymond Jonathan manifest the integration of CRT-influenced studies on race and critical studies on *branquitude* that integrate Brazilian and US Black feminisms. Almeida's study of institutional racism was explicitly derived from *Black Power* (1967) by the sociologist Charles Hamilton and the activist Kwame Ture (formerly Stokely Carmichael).[8] Activists, poets, and scholars of gender and sexuality studies continue to expand their works and readerships on topics ranging from the intersectionality of class and race in feminism and transfeminism to *branquitude, negritude*, and *colorismo* (colorism). Traditional and social media, from news sites to GQ, no less than performance arts and television and film, disseminate scholarship and interviews with cultural figures on *branquitude* in Brazil to a degree that is unimaginable for most in the United States and Spanish-speaking Americas. The impact of CRT and *branquitude* studies is manifest in the cultural controversies that unfold in the public sphere.

In March 2020, for example, Rede Globo announced that it was planning a lavish series based on the life of Marielle Franco, sidestepping Black professionals from the film and television industry beyond a handful of actors. Franco, long a thorn in the side of Rio's government and elites, was ambushed and shot thirteen times in 2018. Her murder remains unsolved. Throngs of Afro-Brazilian activists, scholars, musicians, directors, screenwriters, and crews responded to the news in a public letter of protest, which lambasted *branquitude*: "It is revolting to see, once again, how *branquitude* wraps its appropriation of the image of a Black, lesbian, from-the-favela woman, mother, daughter, sister, and wife, in good intentions." Further, their "letter of repudiation" recalls Franco's summary of her experiences with the local government in Rio, before concluding, "This is the *modus operandi* of *branquitude*: to appropriate, as if everything belonged to it—our bodies, our subjectivity, our history. It is a disaster; it is violent and racist." Raymundo Jonathan explicitly invokes James Baldwin's assertion that white is not a race but a metaphor for power. Jonathan is the 2018 founder of the Black festival Wakanda in Madureira, an annual gathering for storytelling, theatrical and musical performances, and guided educational tours of Rio de Janeiro, which receives widespread media attention.[9] Therefore, *branquitude* is not race but humanity, for holders of (white) power who are not self-aware.[10] Here, Jonathan's activism implicitly reflects the scholarly distinction between racist white and antiracist white.[11]

In Spanish-language contexts, the research programs of Aníbal Quijano and Bolívar Echeverría implicitly intersect at several points with CRT and critical whiteness studies in the United States. Both, in different ways, make capitalism, modernity, and the Americas ontologically interdependent. Quijano's work crisscrosses with critical whiteness studies.[12] It is arguably less historical than theoretical: for instance, when he assumes that until the era of the European invasions and "conquests" of the Americas, phenotype (which he largely reduces to color) had not serviced coloniality. He astutely observes that "European" and "white" were overlapping categories, yet he ignores the field of critical whiteness studies devoted to *white, blanco, branco,* and *blanquitud* in the Americas.

The word *blanquitud* can lend itself to misunderstandings. On the one hand, *negritud/negritude* is, and always has been, a consciousness-raising, self-affirming movement for those who identify as *Black/negro*. *Blanquitud* intends to capture a defining and paradoxical characteristic that the CRT movement conceptualizes as whiteness as property or whiteness as power: its striving for invisibility, for "nonrace" status. Early Spanish-language attempts to grapple with whiteness in colonial contexts of the Spanish and Portuguese Americas often translated it as *lo blanco, blancura,* or *blanquedad* and explicitly conveyed the theoretical influence of critical whiteness studies conducted in English.[13] The recent AfroLatinx Voices series, organized at the University of California, Berkeley, has brought together scholars of race, many of whom specifically research *blanquitud* and/or *branquitude* in Latin America, the Caribbean, and Latinx America. Their research presentations and dialogues are readily accessible to the public through social media.[14] The 2020 launch of *Journal of Hispanic & Lusophone Whiteness Studies* proves that critical concepts of whiteness in Iberian contexts have varied and have been practiced in asynchronous and geographically divergent contexts. J. M. Pérsanch, the founding editor, has been studying *blanquitud/branquitude* for decades, and his introduction to the field of critical whiteness studies in Latin American contexts is required reading.

Bolívar Echeverría's understanding of *blanquitud* does not engage with that critical literature on whiteness in Spanish and Portuguese. In both the essay "'Imágenes de blanquitud'" and the posthumously published *Modernidad y blanquitud*, Echeverría examines the relationships between capital, modernity, and *blanquitud*, of which the latter concept overlaps with what *whiteness* meant for Baldwin beginning in 1960 and for the CRT movement since the early 1980s.[15] Echeverría's *blanquitud* differs insofar as he throws open the theoretical door to de facto whites—that is, people of color who walk, talk, act, and live like the enfranchised whites who present their culture as the norm. Thus, *blanquitud* is distinct from *blanquedad* or *blancura*: it has been at the service of capitalism since the Western European invasions and colonizations in Africa, Asia, and the Americas. It is, unequivocally for Echeverría, the paradigmatic example of what Toni Morrison liked to call "the serviceability of race." (But see Carlos Fregoso, who does not neatly distinguish *blanquedad, blancura,* and *blanquitud*. And see Valero, who explicitly recurs to Echeverría's *blanquitud* concept while making it synonymous with *blanquedad*.)[16]

Echeverría's "Imágenes de 'blanquitud'" starts off by signaling his recourse to Max Weber as a jumping-off point. Weber's tying together of ethnicity, religion, and modern capitalism echoed the so-called degenerationists from the second half of the nineteenth century who debated not only the end of the so-called white race but also the ballyhooed distinction (since Tocqueville and Chévalier) between the Latin and Anglo-Saxon "races."[17] They too subscribed, to varying degrees, to the interlocking of modern capitalism, Puritanism, and the Anglo-Saxon white race/ethnicity, as Weber was to configure it in *The Protestant Ethic and the Spirit of Capitalism* (1904). That triumvirate translates to *blanquitud*. Unlike *blanquedad*, *blanquitud* also permits non-whites to act, talk, dress, and gesture like whites in order to participate in the privileges of *blanquitud*.

Moreover, Echeverría's turn to Weber happened amid the enunciation and publication of significant models of Latin American modernity (or modernities) that did not give prominence to neo-Marxist thought, much less to Weber's brand of it, and did not intensely focus on race. These critical models illuminated the nineteenth century and its connections to the contemporary period. It is not by chance, then, that Echeverría's understanding of modernity and race and their interdependence is so productive for studying the amalgams of race and modernity in the nineteenth through twenty-first centuries.

Echeverría's influence is especially felt and variegated in his adopted home, Mexico.[18] As well, his *blanquitud* model informs countless studies on Caribbean cultures, Argentina, Chile, the United States, and other multilingual and multicultural societies.[19] (For brevity's sake, I mention only a few recent studies in which critical concepts and bibliographies are inclusive of important earlier efforts.) Echeverría's *blanquitud* is invoked for a variety of purposes and across different geographies and fields, including sociology, psychology, literary history, anthropology, political science, and history, as well as in feminism and gender and sexuality studies in Latin America and institutional Latin Americanism outside of Latin America. A few provocative theories meld *blanquitud* with frameworks other than modernity.[20]

BRANCOS AND CROWN DISPENSATIONS

It seems obvious that *blanquitud/branquitude* turns on legal and social whiteness in order to exercise economic, political, and cultural hegemony. It is not so clear, however, why or how *blanco/branco* became a vexed category in the sixteenth century, nor do we know much about *blanqueamiento/branqueamento* in the eighteenth century. Up to the early 2000s, scholars discussed *blanqueamiento* or *branqueamento* primarily in two contexts: the nationalist drives to encourage Western European immigration to Latin America from the mid-nineteenth century onward and the eugenics campaigns that began in some

Latin American countries at the end of the nineteenth century. My purview here is strictly the conceptualization of *blanqueamiento/branqueamento/blanchiment/whitening* in colonial contexts, for excellent books on human kinds and mixed kinds (*castas, géneros, generaciones, calidades*) continue to be published, but no critical monograph exists on the topic at hand.

As Baldwin reminded us in 1961, the one-drop rule, or hypodescent law, did not exist in the United States until the second decade of the twentieth century. He argued that the twin concepts of white and Black were ontologized when the British and the Spanish crossed the Atlantic with their African slaves in tow. Both categories remained interdependent and proved themselves flexible in the face of immigration in the nineteenth century. From 1959 forward, Baldwin insisted on the cognitive, legal, and social interdependence of both human kinds or categories: "It has escaped everybody's notice that it [hypodescent mythology] doesn't go back as far as the Civil War; it doesn't go back any further than 1900. Those laws that we are trying to overthrow in this country now [1961] are not much older than I am. [William] Faulkner says they are folkways, and one would think they came from Rome. But they came out of Southern legislatures just before the First World War. And they are no older than that."[21]

This passage tells us two things of relevance to conceptualizing *blanco/branco* and *blanqueamiento/branqueamento*. One, most Confederate "heritage" monuments—which were capitalized and built during the very same period—were icons conveying a *new* racial order, a false racial consciousness in the United States, one that denied the historical fact of racial hybridity. That false racial consciousness is unwittingly continued by scholars who propagate the US racial purity–Latin America racial hybridity paradigm, many times with the false consciousness of having sloughed off their false racial consciousness. Two, comparative monographs are urgently needed, not the least because white/*blanco/branco* never was and never is self-evident. This is a problem not only for current scholarship in critical whiteness studies (whether derived from Echeverría's *blanquitud* concept or not) and in antiracist pedagogy and activism but also for CRT itself.

It is now well known that the merchandise that traveled from Acapulco to European ports passed through Manila, and vice versa, and that some of the items were slaves (*piezas*) from Asia. Not only did religious men and Crown bureaucrats in Brazil communicate with their brothers in other new worlds such as Goa; the colonies in Portuguese Asia and America were interconnected through commerce, slavery, and race.[22] The commercial and cultural relations between Goa and Bahia were extensive.[23] Already in the sixteenth century, religious men decried the Portuguese slavers for kidnapping or buying persons from Japan, China, Calcutta, Cambodia, and Burma to transport to Brazil.[24] Until the 1660s, in fact, Portuguese men were encouraged to form households with women in Goa, either descendants of Indigenous peoples in Asia or Africans, whether enslaved, freed, or free. Indeed, the Portuguese Crown decreed that all such marriages were to be treated equally before the law and that government posts were open to all males from such households, regardless of descent and rank.[25] Colonial interconnectedness was an inescapable fact of life that is underestimated in theoretical discussions of *blanco/branco* and *blanqueamiento/branqueamento*.

Just as striking, the original peoples and their descendants in the Portuguese African colonies, as well as *mulatos* born to Portuguese Crypto-Jews and Catholics involved in the transatlantic slave trade, were called *brancos*, or *brancos da terra*, if they were of a high rank due to commerce, agriculture, and military or religious service.[26] Several non-Europeans successfully petitioned the Portuguese Crown in the seventeenth and eighteenth centuries to become knights (which required not only a high rank, or *condição*, but also *limpeza de sangue*) and hold Crown and church positions in the colonies.[27]

Similarly, archival research on marriages in Buenos Aires confirms the usage of *moreno*, *color moreno*, and *pardo* as color terms for free Black males who, in the seventeenth and eighteenth centuries, owned large plantations or small farms and slaves with whom they often had children. Such individuals commanded respect because they legally secured dispensations and privileges out of reach for enslaved and destitute mixed kinds: they were *vecinos* (landowning settlers, not just residents).[28] Most of the discussions of such *morenos* and *pardos* in Argentina and Uruguay appear in scholarship devoted to postabolition and/or nineteenth-century *blanqueamiento*.[29] Still, the quantitative and qualitative work on marriage and mixed kinds in Argentina and Uruguay is a treasure trove.[30]

All this is congruent with Echeverría's emphasis on access to capital and exercise of the same as being constitutive of *blanquitud*. Rank mattered within the fabric of eighteenth-century *blanquitud/branquitude*. There were abundant connections and conduits between Portuguese-, English-, and Spanish-speaking colonial settlers on this score. The quick and well-documented examples are of first peoples by origin but Spaniards or Portuguese by law and society: the descendants of pre-Columbian nobles or royalty in Spanish America and descendants of pre-Spanish nobles or royalty in Spanish Asia.[31] Similarly, chiefs and founders of First Nations in the eighteenth-century United States were not at all treated like common Indigenous persons.

Religious purity, rank, and kind constituted a *blanco/branco* concept that was more diffuse and sinuous than Echeverría's *blanquitud*. The European colonial legal recognition of nobles and royals and their descendants reflected power structures that predated European invasion and usurpation of worlds and peoples beginning in the fifteenth century. I refer to the pre-European past, before *First Nations* needed to be used to distinguish between colonized and colonizer. Pre-European holders and exercisers of capital, including slave labor, predated, but were not eliminated by, the European *blanquitud/branquitude*. Power before, during, and after European modernity came to town, so to speak, with guns blazing, consisted of many capital structures and practices that were not European—were not at all *blancos/brancos*—and cannot be dismissed as premodern or otherwise "not modern."

Further still, religion mattered. Bio-moral structures and strictures of Roman Catholicism compel us to think expansively about *blanquitud/branquitude*. Of note, coinciding with the currents of CRT and US-influenced *branquitude* studies in Brazil is the determined focus in universities to train graduate students to seek out the unpublished lives of unenslaved persons with non-European ancestry who seized on religious and Crown laws and case histories to secure their privileges and duties as *brancos*. Brazilian historians and literary historians have combed through archives and discovered files of cases in which applicants to religious orders, confraternities, and Crown posts petitioned the Portuguese Crown to pardon their "color defect."

In the late seventeenth century and first half of the eighteenth century, complaints to the King's Council of the Overseas Dominions about the occupation of posts by *mamelucos, mestiços (sensu lato),* and *mulatos* issued from Minas Gerais and Rio Grande do Norte in Brazil to São Tomé, Angola, and Cabo Verde. In 1725, the council made explicit to the governor and captain-general of Minas Gerais that *mulatos* or *pardos* within four degrees or generations of their full-blooded African ancestor were not to be appointed to Crown posts or positions of honor in order to prevent such persons without *limpeza de sangue* from bringing dishonor (*infamia*) upon the same.[32] In Pernambuco, Brazil, several priests with some African ancestry legally appealed to King João V (1689–1750) of Portugal, arguing that "*pardos*, or, rather, *mulatos*" could not be excluded from membership in the St. Peter's of the Clergy Confraternity.[33] In an attempt to stem this litigious tide, the confraternity reacted in 1730 by revising its 1713 bylaws to stipulate that no one of the *pardo* kind ("casta parda"), up to and including the fourth generation, would be admitted.[34] Free persons with some African ancestry were fighting the same legal battles for access in Maranhão.[35]

Numerous royal and papal filings for dispensations of "color defect" or "irregularity"—for possessing African descent in a higher degree than the fifth—and illegitimacy have been analyzed by scholars, which confirms one well-trodden route to social ascent for *pardos* in the Luso-Brazilian world who aspired to enter religious orders, hold civil posts, or inherit fortunes from aristocratic fathers. The scholarship on such legal quagmires, which stretched into the early nineteenth century, is extensive, archival, and theoretically sound.[36] There are superb explanations of the bureaucratic mechanism as well as microhistories.[37]

Moreover, even published literature drags us once again into the *branco/ blanco* quicksand in the guise of Portugal's royal pharmacist and King Joao V's personal physician, Cristovão Vaz Carapinho. In a 1738 letter, published in Lisbon as an epilogue to the vita of a Black emperor and saint, Doctor Carapinho fixed *branco* at the fifth degree: "Since, when the trunk is mixed, and one of the progenitors in the descent line is always a White, the fifth-degree descendant comes to be legitimately White, as is attested in Civil and Canon Law."[38] Doctor Carapinho assumed that *branco* and *preto* were legal givens. But given the contested privileges of *brancos* that *mulatos*, *pardos*, and other mixed kinds were petitioning for, many times successfully, it is puzzling to read his causal reference to civil and canon laws. Had the 1726 royal decree for the Portuguese new worlds been or become a Crown law that applied throughout the Portuguese Empire whenever nonreligious, or "civil," posts were won or appointed? Crown laws upheld canon law in almost all matters of faith. Which edicts, briefs, and other papal mandates of canon law was he referencing?

Racial Probabilism

Canon law and its exegetes created conundrums around *branco*—and, for us today, around *branqueamento* and *branquitude*. On the one hand, religious purity statutes—that is, the canon law that barred applicants who were within the fourth degree of a "tinted," or defective, ancestor (viz., a Jew, Moor, slave, heretic, or illegitimate)—repurposed the consanguinity statute for European marriage (no marriage between blood relatives within four degrees, or generations, of the shared progenitor). Still, military orders, religious orders, confraternities, and colleges required only papal approval to make their pertinent general statute, or constitution, stricter than the four-degrees statute rooted in the Roman Catholic canon on consanguinity. On the other hand, the Roman Catholic legal rights for neophytes in the Spanish and Portuguese Indies (Privilegios Índicos) was the canon law that Roman Catholic European emperors upheld. The most relevant right enjoyed by neophytes was marriage dispensation: they were entitled to a Catholic marriage even if the prospective bride and groom were blood relatives within three degrees. Remarkably, popes granted marriage dispensations to all Catholic converts in new worlds, in the plural: that is, to the first peoples and their descendants in the (Roman Catholic) colonial settlements in Africa, Asia, and the Americas.

But moral theology was born in 1600, and with it probabilism, and the neophyte concept expanded into a global cacophony of "probable opinions" over kind and mixed kinds of humans, a controversy that pulled in religious purity statutes, Crown law, Roman law, and medieval canon laws. Probabilism in the field of moral theology argued that in individual cases of conscience not admitting of moral certitude, Catholics could safely follow an opinion established by reason and a single grave authority, even if it was not the more or most probable of opinions. Its fundamental contributions to economics, law, natural sciences, and ethics are well known, as is the fact that probabilism was an epistemology and a methodology—a way of knowing and a way of reasoning that privileged the individual case and its context—that is, local praxis. Probabilism had its roots in medieval and renaissance nominalism, which exercised an enormous influence on theology and other fields of study in sixteenth-century Iberia. The epistemological and metaphysical core of nominalism—and of probabilism, later—was that all moral (i.e., human) existence consists of particular situations: *europeo*, for instance, was not a category, not a universal, any more than mestizo was. The same was true of kinds linked legally and socially to religious purity, paganism, and heresy. Like critical legal studies and critical race theory, probabilism—and what I call racial probabilism—privileged life narratives (or storytelling), intersectionality, and antiessentialism.

When pontiffs made explicit in their briefs and bulls that "*mixtim progeniti* [mixedly engendered], whom they call *Mestizos*" also enjoyed the Portuguese and Spanish Indies marriage dispensation, interpretations (or "probable opinions") issued from theologians, moral theologians, bishops, cardinals, and historians, in Seville and Madrid, as well as in Quito, Lima, Charcas, Bogotá, Manila, Goa, Bahia, Rio de Janeiro, Angola, and other new worlds. The centuries-long flurry of opinions about the semantic scope of the papal phrase "*mixtim progeniti* [mixedly engendered], whom they call *Mestizos*" was the first ever global debate over human mixed kinds. I limit myself to a handful of opinions from a dispute that stretched into the late eighteenth century and seeped into the written and visual cultures of *blanqueamiento/branqueamento*. It thoroughly complicates contemporary concepts of *blanco/branco* and *blanquitud*.

That a person of half-Spanish and half-African descent was a neophyte, or non-European, for the Indies marriage exemption but a European for fasting purposes is mind-boggling today. However, racial probabilism's protracted disputes over the border between mestizo and *español* are on vivid display in the Spanish cardinal Juan Lugo's handbook for theologians and moral theologians.[39] Lugo was a superb example of a nominalist theologian and canonist with nominalist leanings that he brought to bear on understandings of human mixed kinds. He reminded his readers that wine mixed with a slight amount of water, though not pure, was nonetheless wine, according to moral reasoning (as opposed to reasoning in fields such as mathematics). Both pure wine and the slightly diluted wine were morally considered equivalent for the validity of the holy sacrament. Analogically, the pure Indian who was mixed with no Spanish blood whatsoever could not morally be different from the Indian in whom a small amount of Spanish blood was mixed: each was, completely and unconditionally, Indian.

Lugo next turned to the most ancient and quotidian example of hybridity (and bastardy) in brutes: the mule, *qua* mule, was a compound object (50 percent horse, 50 percent ass), irreducible to its primary elements; so, too, the mestizo (50 percent Spanish, 50 percent Indian). Thus, the mestizo invoked by popes for the Indies marriage exemption had to have at least 50 percent non-Spanish blood. He folded the person with 25 percent (*cuarterón/a*) into the *español* category, or kind, by asserting that the offspring of a mule and a mare reverts to the horse kind, not to the mule kind, "so much that . . . he is morally considered a horse." By the same logic, the person with only 25 percent of Spanish blood was an Indian: "So, if, on the contrary, a she-ass [a *mestiza*, or half-Spanish and half-Indian female] conceives with a mule [an Indian male], the offspring returns to the nature and kind of the ass, and he is morally considered an ass, although he differs a little something from other asses." For the Indies marriage dispensation, the child who was 75 percent Indian was, indeed, eligible.

In 1668, Bishop Peña Montenegro of Quito argued for the inclusion of mulattoes in the kind he called *transmarinos* (literally, "transoceanics," derived from the adjective *transmarinos*, or "overseas"). In fact, his opinion sharply differed from Cardinal Lugo's: the bishop included African *cuarterones* and *puchuelos* as well as Indian *cuarterones* and *puchuelos* in his interpretation of the papal phrase *mixtim progeniti*:

> With mulattoes, who are children of a Negress and a Spaniard, the dispensation is understood to include, just as we have said in the previous questions, *cuarterones* and *puchuelas* only, and not all of the descendants. The reason is because in this admixture of Negress and Spaniard, one half of what they have of *transmarinos*, whom the privilege concerns, is lost with each passing generation, and so it is no surprise that within a few generations they come to have so little of transoceanites and so much of Europeans that they are no longer held to be *transmarinos*, that [amount] which they have left not being considerable; although beyond the third degree it is something for physics and metaphysics, that portion of Indian or African comes to shrink so much, from the moral perspective and according to popular opinion, that it is of no significance whatsoever, for *in his rebus moralibus, parum pro nihilo reputatur*, as the Philosopher [Aristotle] says, or as the Jurists say, *Parum, & nihil equiparantur, & parva, non sunt in consideratione*.[40]

His handbook for missionaries and priests was republished numerous times by the nineteenth century.

The very same year, however, the Peruvian canonist and theologian Avendaño issued his opinion in *Thesaurus Indicus*.[41] Wine mixed with a slight amount of water is absolutely said to be wine, but not if they are in equal mixture. By the same reasoning, the offspring of a European father and an Indian mother (or vice versa) was a true mixture of the two kinds: mestizo. A mestizo is not a Spaniard but a composite kind in which elements of the original Spanish and Indian bloods have been extinguished or lost in equal measure, so that the mestizo is neither wine nor water, neither Spaniard nor Indian. What we call hot water, Avendaño argued, is that which has more heat than cold. By analogy, *mixtim progeniti* known as *cuarterones* and *puchuelos* had much more Spanish blood than Indian blood, so they were Spaniards.

Opinions about who was a mestizo for ordination purposes and for the Indies marriage dispensation often intersected. Mixed persons with less than half of non-European lineage litigated memberships, educational access, and political appointments on the legal principle that one cannot enjoy only the burdens and not the privileges of a status. If the Indies marriage law forbade all mixed kinds with less than half non-European blood from enjoying the papal marriage dispensation, as many canonists argued, it was a logical and legal fallacy to forbid them from enjoying the privileges that the European kind held.

The pushback was forceful: numerous orders, confraternities, and town councils demanded that no one who was within four degrees, or generations, of a non-European forebearer be considered. Antonio González de Acuña (1620–1682), a native of Lima, was the first bishop of Caracas in 1670 and became archbishop of Charcas (today La Paz, Bolivia) in 1673. Some years later, he issued edicts regarding the ordination of mixed persons. González de Acuña banned from orders all who had a canonical impediment, including mixed descendants within four degrees of Africans and Indians.[42] But that was just his opinion; it did not halt other interpretations and ordinations.

Not even royal and papal edicts resolved the legal and social reality of one and the same person belonging to two different kinds, or categories, depending on the context. One opinion or edict undid the other. At the turn of the eighteenth century, papal briefs and edicts circulated throughout the Iberian new worlds (and were recirculated in royal decrees), which embraced Cardinal Lugo and Avendaño's shared mestizo concept—that any kind with less than 50 percent of non-European lineage was no longer mestizo. This canon law evolution did not, however, slam the door on litigation of the overlapping religious purity statutes and mestizo concepts.

In fact, it threw open the door in at least two ways. One, it triggered an explosion of *blanqueamiento/branqueamento* schemes in different locales that persons with varying amounts of non-European ancestry could invoke as custom, a bulwark of Roman Catholic and Iberian legal systems. Two, persons who had been pushed out of the mestizo category, after the papal rejection of more capacious mestizo concepts (the bishop of Quito's, for instance), could wield the legal sword of equity.

Blanqueamiento/Branqueamento for Unenslaved Persons

The *blanqueamiento/branqueamento* formulas that emerged—in paint or in ink—at the turn of the eighteenth century reflected how interlocking canon law frameworks that limited access to church and Crown posts and that benefited non-European couples who wished to marry had become increasingly labyrinthine in the seventeenth century. Such formulas allowed individuals with access to Spanish or Portuguese literacy a pathway to legally petitioning for the different sets of duties and privileges that corresponded to different kinds. In theoretical terms, the birth of formal *blanqueamiento/branqueamento* charts and the visual culture of the same might change the way scholars approach later concepts of *blanqueamiento/branqueamento*. More immediately, they of course encourage us to rethink theoretical models of *blanquitud/branquitude*.

For instance, the individual with one-quarter Black lineage could be denominated *cuarterón, negro cuarterón, tercerón*, or *morisco* in the paintings and drawings of human kinds (*castas, generaciones, linajes*). Ordinal nouns such as *tercerones* and *cuarterones* frequently correlated with blood quanta in *blanqueamiento* matrices. Still, in many other equations, the same nominals instead denoted generation, or degree, of distance from a non-European progenitor. Thousands of such schemes exist from Asia, Africa, and the Americas, but only a handful of examples is necessary for us to confirm the heterogeneity of nomenclature, categorization, and structuring of written representations of *blanqueamiento/branqueamento*. A smattering of equations from the Caribbean suggests a variety of structuring matrices that have prompted scholarly exasperation. According to José Gumilla's 1745 *blanqueamiento* table for Black persons in the Orinoco region:

I. De Europeo, y Negra,
sale *Mulata* . . . . | *Dos quartos de cada parte.*
II. De Europeo, y Mulata,
sale *Quarterona* . . . . . . | *Quarta parte de Mulata.*
III. De Europeo, y Quarterona,
sale *Ochavona* . . | *Octava parte de Mulata.*
IV. De Europeo, y *Ochavona*
sale *Puchuela* . . . | *Blanca totalmente.*

Raúl Alfredo Linares cites Gumilla's nomenclature and definition of *mulato, cuarterón, ochavón*, and *puchuelo* (or *blanco/español*) as the very same that he encountered in his archival research for Buenos Aires in the mid-eighteenth century.[43] This fact radically confirms that the counterintuitive is a powerful tool, as metaphysical as it is epistemological, when we confront *blanqueamiento/branqueamento* in Spanish-speaking South America. The same scholar clarifies that *pardo* was used as a color designation rather than as a kind: "'parda como ochavona próxima a españolizarse,'" roughly, "brown like an *ochavona* who is on the verge of becoming a Spaniard."[44]

In Antonio de Ulloa's coeval scheme for Cartagena, where Gumilla lived and taught for decades, there were four kinds mediating between *negro* and *blanco*: *mulato*, or second-degree descendant of a Black person; *tercerón*, or third-degree descendant; *cuarterón*, or fourth-degree descendant; and *quinterón*, or fifth-degree descendant. The latter had an African blood quantum of one-sixteenth (or 6.25 percent) and was a *puchuela*, or "totally White," for Gumilla. While Ulloa admitted that *quinterones* were indistinguishable from Whites, he recorded that one more degree of distance from the Black progenitor was required for *blanqueamiento*: with an African blood quantum of one-thirty-second (3.125 percent), the offspring of a Spaniard and a *quinterón/a* was a *blanco*.

In 1762–1763, the *hacendado* Luis José Peguero from Baní used a generational scheme for inhabitants on the island of Santo Domingo in which the blood quanta matched the ordinal adjectives: for example, *mulato cuarterón* and *indio cuarterón* each had 25 percent non-European lineage. "If the Spaniard sexually reproduces with a *cuarterona* of either of the two aforementioned kinds [*mestizo, mulato*], their produced ones are called *Puchuela[s]*, or semi-whites [*semiblancos*]."[45] There was an important difference in the quanta themselves, of course: Peguero labeled the Indian or Black African with one-eighth a *puchuela*, or "semi-White," whereas Gumilla defined that blood quantum as belonging to an *ochavón/a*. Moreover, Gumilla's *puchuela* was a "totally white person" who had one-sixteenth African ancestry.[46] Notwithstanding their divergent nomenclature, Gumilla and Peguero agreed on the blood quantum required for non-Europeans to lose their kind (African or native) and become Whites: one-sixteenth (or 6.25 percent).

The 1789 Spanish royal edict known as the Código Negro Carolino (Black Code of the Spanish Bourbon Charles IV) explicitly proposed to regulate slavery. Modeled after the French Bourbon Louis XIV's Code Noir for Saint-Domingue (1685; expanded in 1704 and in 1723 to French colonies in South America), it had a considerable gestation period, 1768–1789, during the second wave of Spanish Bourbon reforms. Law 1 reveals the *blanqueamiento* degrees and nomenclature for free people with African ancestry who had children with Spaniards over successive generations.[47] *Mulatos* constituted the first generation (50 percent Black); *pardos* constituted the second generation (25 percent black); *tercerones* (one-eighth Black), the third generation; *cuarterones* (one-sixteenth Black), the fourth generation; mestizos (one-thirty-second Black), the fifth generation; and, finally, the children of mestizos, with only one-sixty-fourth Black lineage, the sixth generation. This generation, finally, was held to be Whites.

By the Código Negro's account, there is a hybridization of structuring matrices. Ordinal nouns such as *tercerones* and *cuarterones* do not correlate with the blood quanta; rather, they refer to generation or degree. The category *pardo* signified the second-generation person with 25 percent African lineage, and slipped in between *mulatos* (the first generation of Black mixed kind) and *tercerones*, or the third generation. (The *pardo* category rarely appeared in *blanqueamiento* equations because its function within the legal and social structures of Iberian colonial settlements varied widely.) In my earlier examples, 25 percent of non-European lineage constituted a *cuarterón* (in blood quanta schemes such as Gumilla's and Peguero's) or a *tercerón* (in the generic degree scheme). Even mestizo made an appearance here as a fifth-generation descendant, with one-thirty-second African lineage. The children of a mestizo and a White (i.e., persons with one-sixty-fourth African lineage) were Whites.

It has been observed that *blanqueamiento* schemes in *casta* portraiture were far less stringent for *indios* than for *negros* in Mexico. The same was true of written sequences in Spanish Asia (the Philippines were under the jurisdiction of the Viceroy of New Spain) and Portuguese Asia. Something similar, but not identical, appeared in Gumilla's *blanqueamiento* sequence for *indios*, which further complicates our redaction of hard-and-fast rules for *blanqueamiento* as well as theoretical understandings of *blanquitud*. At first, his itinerary for *indios* is identical to the one for *negros*, that is, *blanqueamiento* in four steps, or degrees: *mestiza* > *cuarterona* > *ochavona* > *blanca* or *puchuela*.[48] But a caveat proves that eighteenth-century blanqueamiento equations grew out of the bio-moral grammar and vocabulary of the *mixtim progeniti*, or mestizo, debates:

> It should be noted that this chart follows the old standard which was used to determine which of those groups could be included in the term *neophyte* (that is, *newly-converted*), so that missionary fathers could according to their privileges dispense with certain degrees of kinship and relationship in order to marry them morally and legally. But by the new bull of Pope Clement XI it is declared that *neophytes* must be understood to mean "Indians" and "*mestizos*" only, thus Indian quadroons and octoroons are deemed, and must be accounted for as, Whites.[49]

Gumilla's explicit intent in the foregoing passage was not to define neophytes for marriage dispensation; he promised readers to debunk the urban legend that Blacks could not whiten by charting precisely their *blanqueamiento*. Thus, when he turned away from this *blanqueamiento* scheme, he signaled the successive series of sexual reproductive couplings, or "marriages," between Whites and persons with African lineage: "Finally, let it be written in stone that the Mulata whitens by the same degrees/steps that the Mestiza whitens, in the fourth generation, in the following sequence of marriages." This rhetorical sleight of hand was also epistemological and metaphysical: beneath, behind, above, and below the *blanco* concept were the controversies over the concepts neophyte and mestizo.

In the eighteenth century, popes were not the only ones issuing edicts that shaped concepts of kinds, mixed kinds, and *blanqueamiento* schemes and at once gave plaintiffs legal mechanisms for litigating *blancura*. The final critical engagement with *blanqueamiento* is the Spanish Crown's selling of color dispensations, which officially began with the royal decree of 1795. However, twenty-six filings have been discovered and analyzed, the earliest from 1760, in which applicants were purchasing the pardon for either a *quinterón* defect or a *pardo* defect. Such a certificate for purchase (*gracia al sacar*) allowed applicants or their descendants to be ordained, or to hold the respectable title of don, or to marry someone who was of a higher station. The charge was higher for the second, which has puzzled even the foremost authority on the topic, for whom *pardo* signified less African ancestry than *quinterón*.[50] However, if the Crown's *quinterón* concept operated by degrees (fifth-degree descendant), rather than by blood quantum (one-fifth), the defect to be pardoned was one-sixteenth or less of Black ancestry (*quinterón* by degrees), not one-fifth Black ancestry (*quinterón* by blood quantum). The cases were mostly from the Orinoco region. If—and this is a big *if*—the Crown's *blanqueamiento* pattern was structured by degrees, like Ulloa's, the *quinterón* who applied for a royal dispensation was seeking to legally and socially erase the one-sixteenth of African ancestry in order to become a white (one-thirty-second).

I turn now to an archival case of *pardos* that backs up this hypothesis and might radically alter how we read the *gracias al sacar* bestowal of *blancura* or *blanquedad,* which was similar to the color dispensation in Brazil from many decades earlier. It is a case well known to scholars.[51] In 1774, officials of a *pardo* battalion in Caracas complained to the Crown that their appointed superior had too much Indian and African ancestry to be considered a *pardo*. In doing so, they laid bare the degrees of *blanqueamiento* for free people with African lineage who wished to become *pardos*. Mulattoes (50 percent) were Black in the second degree, being descended from a wholly Black parent and a wholly White parent. *Tercerones*, the offspring of a mulatto and a white, were Black in the third degree (one-fourth Black). *Cuarterones* (one-eighth Black) embodied

Blackness in the fourth degree, being the children of a *terceron/a* and a white person. *Quinterones* born to a *cuarterón/a* and a white person were Black in the fifth degree, possessing one-sixteenth African ancestry. The skin color and facial features of *quinterones*, argued officials of the *pardo* battalion, were indistinguishable from those of whites. Here we are reminded of Ulloa's 1748 *blanqueamiento* scheme for Cartagena, although he still demanded one more degree of distance for the white-looking *quinterón* to become a white (one-thirty-second African ancestry).

This legal complaint to the Crown also drew a stark contrast between the *pardo* and the *mulato* in this particular battalion. The *pardo*'s lineage never strayed from the path to whiteness. The *mulato*'s lineage went the other way. The categorical *mulato* had, in fact, a lineage that had not whitened successively; he had in him some mixture of mulatto and Black ("la mezcla de mulato y negro"), they explained to Crown officials, or some mixture of mulatto and Black with Indian. The battalion of *pardos* asserted that authorities in the Kingdom of New Granada customarily refused to admit anyone but *pardos* into the battalion of *pardos*; they recognized as a *pardo* the child born to a *terceron* parent (one-quarter Black) and a *cuarterón* (one-eighth Black) parent and the child born to a *terceron* parent (one-quarter Black) and a *quinterón* (one-sixteenth) parent, for these kinds were approximating whiteness rather than Blackness.[52] To put a finer point on it: in the first scenario, the *pardo* had three-sixteenths Black or Black-Indian blood; in the second, he had five-thirty-seconds, or two-and-a-half-sixteenths. Any Black-*mulato* admixture or Black-*mulato*-Indian admixture greater than three-sixteenths qualified the candidate as an ineligible *mulato*. If the Spanish Crown used for the 1795 royal decree the *pardo* concept and the *quinterón* concept (which was the same as Ulloa's for Cartagena) as they were laid out earlier, it is clear that the two types of dispensations, or *gracias*, had different prices that corresponded to the degrees of Blackness that required royal forgiveness. The *pardo* had less African ancestry than the *quinterón* had; that is why the latter dispensation cost more in the 1795 decree. It remains an open-ended debate, however, not in the least because canon law disputes around the usage of *mixtim progeniti* ("mixedly engendered kinds") and the usage of *limpieza de sangre* intersected. Thus, the archival files under different rubrics (religious purity, marriage, ordination, purchases of royal dispensations—*gracias al sacar*—for color defects) must be studied in tandem. For the time being, however, what we have to work with is an abundance of excellent archival studies that cover different segments of this topic.[53]

In Buenos Aires during the first half of the eighteenth century, the archives yield numerous marriages between *pardos* or *morenos* (i.e., free persons) and slaves, and some of the latter belonged to *pardos*. It is not hard to imagine why, several decades later, such a *pardo* who belonged to the *vecino* class might file for a Crown pardon of his "defective color"—the respectable title of don might be within reach. What we do not know, of course, is how many such petitions there were in the Spanish world before and after the 1795 formalization of this royal color dispensation. Twinam has exhaustively analyzed Cuban, Panamanian, Venezuelan, and other precedents for the 1795 codification, but to date no one has considered that the Portuguese Crown's mechanism for *defeito da cor*—the so-called *dispensa da cor*—might have been a predecessor to the Spanish colonial cases and the Spanish Crown's 1795 decree to sell legal relief to *pardos* and *quinterones*.

Conclusion

In the 1960s, Baldwin vehemently denied that impoverished whites in the US South participated more than marginally in whiteness. In fact, he pitied them because they did not know that they had more in common with impoverished Blacks than they had with whites. In the 1860s, Domingo F. Sarmiento had written of them casually, and in English, as "white trash." Centuries earlier, the waters of whiteness were even rougher to wade through, and they had many estuaries. The structuring and the measuring of eighteenth-century *blanqueamiento/branqueamento* schemes were as confounding as the matrices and metrics of neophyteness for probabilists in the seventeenth and eighteenth centuries. Deciding who was *blanco*, like deciding who was a neophyte, was a matter of human opinion and could achieve no more than moral certitude. It was radically contingent. What began as canon law disputes about religious purity and neophytes in the colonies opened the door, in the eighteenth century, for economically successful, non-Spanish/non-Portuguese individuals who were not legally neophytes—mixed kinds with less than 50 percent African and/or Indian (American or Asian)—to assert the equity principle: one cannot shoulder the legal and social burdens of a law without holding the rights or privileges of the same.

Unlike *blanquedad*, *blanquitud* admitted non-whites who could act, talk, dress, and gesture like whites, according to Echeverría. But just how wealthy and respectable did persons with some non-Spanish or non-Portuguese lineage—excluding here the descendants of precolonial nobles or royals—have to be to gain admission to *blanquitud* as he framed it? And where are we to put those descendants of precolonial nobles or royals from First Nations who became noble Spaniards or noble Portuguese by royal fiat? How can we square contemporary concepts of *blanquitud/branquitude* with the Spanish/Portuguese colonial plebs who had no power, who were homeless or in jail, or who worked alongside slaves in the homes or fields of wealthy landowners of various kinds and higher ranks? What do we do with "una blancura muy ordinaria," that is, the downtrodden or unseemly individual of white ancestry who did not "act white," as Echeverría stipulated for membership in *blanquitud*? In the sixteenth through eighteenth centuries, *blanco/branco* and *blanqueamiento/ branqueamento* were both more resilient and more porous than many theoretical articulations of *blanquitud/branquitude* to date have postulated.

NOTES

1. Valerie Babb, *Whiteness Visible: The Meaning of Whiteness in American Literature and Culture* (New York: New York University Press, 1998); Grace Elizabeth Hale, *Making Whiteness: The Culture of Segregation in the South, 1890–1940* (New York: Pantheon, 1998).
2. Marianella Ledesma Narváez, *Justicia e interculturalidad: Análisis y pensamiento plural en América y Europa* (Lima: Centro de Estudios Constitucionales, 2018).
3. Lourenço da Conceição Cardoso, *O branco "invisível": Um estudo sobre a emergência da branquitude nas pesquisas sobre as relações raciais no Brasil (Período: 1957–2007)* (PhD diss., Universidade de Coimbra, 2008); Lourenço da Conceição Cardoso, "Retrato do branco racista e anti-racista," *Reflexão e Ação* 18, no. 1 (2010): 46–70.
4. Lélia González, *Por um feminismo latino-afro-americano* (Rio de Janeiro: Zahar, 2019).
5. Maria Aparecida da Silva Bento, Maria de Jesus Silveira, and Simone Gibram Nogueira, eds., *Identidade, branquitude e negritude: Contribuções para a psicologia no Brasil: Novos ensaios, relatos de experiência e de pesquisa* (São Paulo: Centro de Estudos das Relações de Trabalho e Desigualdades/Casa do Psicólogo, 2014).
6. Bento, Maria Aparecida da Silva, "Pactos narcísicos no racismo: Branquitude e poder nas organizações empresariais e no poder público" (PhD diss., Universidade de São Paulo, 2002).
7. Maria Aparecida da Silva Bento, *Cidadania em preto e branco* (São Paulo: Editora Ática, 2010).
8. Silvio Almeida, *Racismo estrutural* (São Paulo: Pólen Livros, 2019).
9. Silvia Nascimento, "Wakanda in Madureira: 'O que a colonização separou, Wakanda quer juntar.'" *Mundo Negro* 7 (November 2019).
10. Jonathan quoted in Leonardo Ávila Teixeira, "O que é branquitude." *GQ Globo* 7 (April 2021).
11. Cardoso, "O branco."
12. Aníbal Quijano, "Las paradojas de la colonialidad/modernidad/eurocentrada," *Hueso Húmero* 53 (2009): 30–59; Aníbal Quijano, "Colonialidad del poder, eurocentrismo y América Latina," in *La colonialidad del saber: Eurocentrismo y ciencias sociales*, ed. Edgardo Lander (Buenos Aires: CLACSO, 1992).

13. See María Teresa Garzón Martínez and Eli Bartra, "El lugar de lo blanco: Cartografía de una pregunta," *Veredas: Revista del Pensamiento Sociológico* 13 (2012): 83–104.
14. University of California, Berkeley, Center for Latin American Studies, "No Longer a Racial Democracy: Critical Whiteness in Latin America and the Caribbean," YouTube video, April 28, 2021.
15. Bolívar Echeverría, "Imágenes de la 'blanquitud,'" in *Sociedades icónicas: Historia, ideología y cultura en la imagen*, ed. Diego Lizarazo Arias, Bolívar Echeverría, and Pablo Lazo Briones (Mexico City: Siglo XXI, 2007); Bolívar Echeverría, *Modernidad y blanquitud* (Mexico City: Ediciones Era, 2010).
16. Gisela Carlos Fregoso, "Blanquedad, blanquitud y blanqueamiento," YouTube video, August 12, 2019; Perla Valero, "El devenir-blanco del mundo: Debates Sur-Norte sobre la blanquitud desde Latinoamérica," *Latin American and Caribbean Ethnic Studies*, July 2021.
17. Max Weber, *The Protestant Ethic and the Spirit of Capitalism*, trans. Talcott Parsons (London: Routledge, 1992).
18. See Elena Iturriaga, *Las élites de la ciudad blanca: Discursos racistas sobre la otredad* (Mérida: UNAM and Centro Peninsular en Humanidades y Ciencias Sociales, 2016); Federico Navarrete, "La blanquitud y la blancura, cumbre del racismo mexicano," *Revista de la Universidad de México, Dossier: Racismo* (2020): 7–12; Pablo Caraballo, "El cuerpo utópico de los gais. Masculinidad, blanquitud y deseo en Tijuana." *Estudios Sociológicos* 39, no. 116 (2021): 533–559.
19. On Caribbean cultures, see Jeannette del Carmen Tineo Durán, "Cruzar el charco: Fantasías prometidas de la blanquitud," *MIGRAZINE*, January 2019; Darío Hernán Vásquez-Padilla and Castriela Esther Hernández-Reyes, "Interrogando la gramática racial de la blanquitud: Hacia una analítica del blanqueamiento en el orden racial colombiano," *Latin American Research Review* 55, no. 1 (2020): 65–80; Peter Wade, *Degrees of Mixture, Degrees of Freedom* (Durham, NC: Duke University Press, 2017). On Argentina, see Lea Geler, "African Descent and Whiteness in Buenos Aires: Impossible Mestizajes in the White Capital City," in *Rethinking Race in Modern Argentina*, ed. Paulina L. Alberto and Eduardo Elena (Cambridge: Cambridge University Press, 2016); Gustavo R. Cruz, "Indigenismo y branquitud en el orden racista de la nación," *Revista Intersticios de la Política y la Cultura* 6, no. 12 (2017): 5–30; George Reid Andrews, "Epilogue: Whiteness and Its Discontents," in *Rethinking Race in Modern Argentina*, ed. Paulina L. Alberto and Eduardo Elena (Cambridge: Cambridge University Press, 2016). On Chile, see Andre Webb and Sarah Radcliffe, "La blanquitud en liceos segregados: El racismo institucional en el Sur de Chile," *Antropologías del Sur* 4, no. 7 (2017): 19–38. On the United States, see Mauricio Sánchez Menchero, "Entre blanquitud y negritud: Los procesos identitarios en los ministriles (Estados Unidos, 1840–1930)." *Inter Disciplina* 9, no. 23 (2021); Valero, "El devenir." On other multicultural societies, see Angela Dixon and Edward Telles, "Skin Color and Colorism: Global Research, Concepts, and Measurement," *Annual Review of Sociology* 43 (2017) 405–424.
20. Laura Catelli, *Arqueología del mestizaje: Colonialismo y racialización* (Temuco, Chile: UFRO and CLACSO, 2020).
21. James Baldwin, *Nationalism Colonialism and the United States: One Minute to Twelve* (New York: Liberation Committee for Africa, 1961), 12.
22. Charles Boxer, *Race Relations in the Colonial Portuguese Empire* (London: Oxford University Press, 1963); Sanjay Subrahmanyam, *O império asiático português* (Lisbon: Difel, 1996).

23. Jorge Lúzio Matos Silva, "Sagrado marfim: O império português na Índia e as relações intracoloniais Goa e Bahia, século XVII" (PhD diss., Pontifícia Universidade Católica de São Paulo, 2011).
24. Fernando Rodrigues Montes D'Oca, "Tráfico de escravos e consciência moral: O pensamento antiescravista de Epifânio de Morains," *Revista de Filosofia* 46 (2017): 130–172; Patricia Souza de Faria, "O Pai dos Cristãos e as populações escravas em Goa: Zelo e controle dos cativos convertidos (séculos XVI e XVII)," *História* 39 (2020): 1–30.
25. Ângela Barreto Xavier, *A invenção de Goa: Poder imperial e conversões culturais nos séculos XVI e XVII* (Lisbon: Imprensa de Ciências Sociais, 2008); Ângela Barreto Xavier and Cristina Nogueira da Silva, *O governo dos outros: Poder e diferença no império português* (Lisbon: Imprensa de Ciências Sociais, 2016).
26. Arlindo Manuel Cardeira, "Formação de uma cidade afro-atlântica: Luanda no século XVII," *Revista Tempo, Espaço, Linguagem* 5, no. 3 (2014): 1–39; João Manuel Vaz Monteiro de Figueirôa Rêgo and Fernanda Olival, "Cor da pele, distinções e cargos: Portugal e espaços atlânticos portugueses (séculos XVI a XVIII)," *Tempo* 16, no. 30 (2011): 115–145; Iva Maria Cabral, *A primeira elite colonial atlântica: Dos "homens honrados brancos" de Santiago à "nobreza da terra," finais do século XV–início do século XVII* (Cabo Verde: Pedro Cardoso Livraria, 2015).
27. Ronald Raminelli, *Nobrezas do Novo Mundo: Brasil e ultramar hispânico, séculos XVII e XVIII* (Rio de Janeiro: Editora FGV, 2016).
28. See archival documents in Carlos Alberto Méndez Paz, "Catálogo de informaciones de nobleza, limpieza de sangre y otras calidades." *Revista del Centro de Estudios Genealógicos de Buenos Aires* 1 (1979).
29. See the introduction and bibliography in Alex Borucki, *De compañeros de barco a camaradas de armas: Identidades negras en el Río de la Plata 1760–1860* (Buenos Aires: Prometeo, 2017).
30. See Raúl Alfredo Linares, "Problemas metodológicos en el abordaje genealógico de familias 'diversas,'" in *Mestizaje, sangre y matrimonio en territorios de la actual Argentina y Uruguay, siglos XVII–XX*, ed. Nora Siegrist and Mónica Ghirardi (Buenos Aires: Universidad Nacional de Córdoba, 2008); Miguel Á. Rosal, "Africanos y afrodescendientes en Buenos Aires (1740–1749): Esbozo de un estudio sobre fuentes inéditas y publicadas," *Estudios Históricos*, no. 19 (2018): 1–45.
31. Luis Ángel Sánchez Gómez, *Las principalías indígenas y la administración española en Filipinas* (Madrid: Universidad Complutense, 1991); Patricio Hidalgo Nuchera, *Encomienda, tributo y trabajo en Filipinas (1570–1608)* (Madrid: Universidad Autónoma de Madrid, 1995); Jusep M. Fradera, *Filipinas, la colonia más peculiar: La hacienda pública en la definición de la política colonial, 1762–1868* (Madrid: CSIC, 1999).
32. Conselho Ultramarino, "Parecer do Conselho Ultramarino para que não possa ser eleito vereador ou juiz ordinário homem que seja mulato até quarto grau ou que não for casado com mulher branca."
33. "Requerimento dos clérigos pardos do Bispado de Pernambuco, ao rei [D. João V], pedindo o cumprimento das ordens reais e da Santa Sé para que possam ser admitidos, pois a irmandade de São Pedro dos Clérigos do Recife, contrariando o compromisso, impediu a entrada de sacerdotes pardos ou mulatos."
34. Andrea Simone Barreto Dias, "Festa, poder e protesta: Os incômodos da cor parda em Pernambuco (décadas de 1730 e 1740)," *XXV Simpósio Nacional de História*, Fortaleza, 12–17

July 2009; Janaína Santos Bezerra, "Pardos na cor & impuros no sangue: Etnia, sociabilidades e lutas por inclusão social no espaço urbano pernambucano do século XVIII" (M.A. thesis, Universidade Federal Rural de Pernambuco, 2010); Maria Lemke Loiola, "Defeito o acidente? Mulatos e pardos na produção da hierarquia social em Goiás colonial," Conference paper, 2010.

35. Katy Dayane Araujo Soares, "'Alguma coisa de mulato' ou 'algum sangue da terra': As ordenações sacerdotais no Bispado do Maranhão (1738-1747)," in *Anais do IV Encontro Internacional de História Colonial*, vol. 3, ed. Rafael Chambouleyron and Karl-Heinz Arenz (Belem: ACAÍ, 2014).
36. Daniel Precioso, *Legítimos Vassalos: Pardos livres e forros na Vila Rica colonial (1750-1803)* (São Paulo: Editora UNESP, 2011); João Manuel Vaz Monteiro de Figueirôa Rêgo, "'A honra alheia por um fio': Os estatutos de limpeza de sangue no espaço de expressão Ibérica (sécs. XVI-XVIII)" (PhD diss., Universidade do Minho, 2009); João Manuel Vaz Monteiro de Figueirôa Rêgo and Fernanda Olival, "Cor da pele, distinções e cargos: Portugal e espaços atlânticos portugueses (séculos XVI a XVIII)," *Tempo* 16, no. 30 (2011): 115-145; Mariane Alves Simões, "A Câmara de Vila do Carmo e seus juízes ordinários (1711-1731)" (M.A. thesis, Universidade Federal de Juiz de Fora, 2015).
37. Anderson José Machado de Oliveira, "Dispensa da cor e clero nativo: Poder eclesiástico e sociedade católica na América Portuguesa (1671-1822)" in *Anais do IV Encontro Internacional de História Colonial*, ed. Rafael Chambouleyron and Karl-Heinz Arenz (Belém: Editora Açaí, 2014), vol. 3; Raimundo Agnelo Soares Pessoa, "Comentário: Mulatos ou pardos?" in *Mulatos na sociedade colonial* (O Arquivo Nacional e a História Luso-Brasileira); Loiola, "Defeito"; Ronald Raminelli, "Impedimentos da cor: Mulatos no Brasil e em Portugal, 1640-1750," *Vária História* 28, no. 48 (2012): 699-723; Ronald Raminelli, "Matias Vidal de Negreiros: Mulato entre a norma reinol e as práticas ultramarinas," *Vária História* 32, no. 60 (2016): 699-730.
38. Christovão Vaz Carapinho, "Carta apologética en defensa da cor preta do Emperador São Elesbão, escrita ao author da sua história pelo Doutor Christovão Vaz Carapinho, Médico da Sua Magestade," in *Os dous Atlantes da Ethiopia*, ed. Joseph Pereira de Santa Anna (Lisbon: Antonio Pedrozo Galram, 1735-1738), vol. 2.
39. Juan de Lugo, *Responsorum moralium* (Lugduni: 1651).
40. Alonso de la Peña Montenegro, *Itinerario para párrocos de indios, su oficio y obligaciones* (Madrid: 1668), 404.
41. Diego de Avendaño, *Thesaurus Indicus, seu generalis instructor pro regimine conscientiae in iis quaead Indias spectant* (Antwerp: Jacob Mersium, 1668), vol. 1.
42. Francisco Javier Hernáez, *Colección de bulas, breves y otros documentos relativos a la Iglesia de América y Filipinas* (Vaduz: Kraus Reprint, 1964), 1:95-96; Juan B. Olaechea Labayen, "Aspectos del derecho indiano y el mestizaje en el siglo XVII," *Anuaria Historia del Derecho Español* 47 (1977): 499-521.
43. Linares, "Problemas," 176.
44. Linares, "Problemas," 177.
45. Luis José Peguero, *Historia de la conquista de la isla española de Santo Domingo [Manuscrito]: Traducida de la Historia General de las Indias, escrita por Antonio de Herrera, y de otros autores que han escrito sobre el particular, 1762-63* (Biblioteca Nacional de España, MSS 1479 and 1480), 1:274-275.

46. Peguero, *Historia*, 1:274-275.
47. Manuel Lucena Salmoral, *Los códigos negros de la América Española* (Alcalá: Ediciones UNESCO Universidad de Alcalá, 1996), 202.
48. Joseph Gumilla, *El Orinoco ilustrado y defendido: Historia natural, civil y geográphica de este gran río y de sus caudalosas vertientes*, vol. 1 (Madrid: Manuel Fernández, 1745), 5, 86.
49. Gumilla, *El Orinoco*, I, 5, 85
50. Ann Twinam, *Purchasing Whiteness: Pardos, Mulattos, and the Quest for Social Mobility in the Spanish Indies* (Stanford, CA: Stanford University Press, 2015), 10, 48.
51. Santos Rudolfo Cortés, *El régimen de las "Gracias al Sacar" en Venezuela durante el Período Hispánico* (Caracas: Academia Nacional de la Historia, 1978), vol. 2; Twinam, *Whiteness*.
52. Twinam, *Whiteness*, 45-46.
53. Twinam, *Whiteness*; Zully Chacón M., "La aristocracia del color: La desigualdad de castas," *Boletín de la Academia Nacional de la Historia* 93, no. 371 (2010): 83-126; Diana Sosa Cárdenas, *Los pardos: Caracas en las postrimerías de la colonia* (Caracas: Universidad Católica Andrés Bello, 2010); Carole Leal Curiel, "La querella por una alfombra: La cuestión del buen orden de la república. Valencia, Venezuela, finales del siglo XVIII," *Revista Historia y Memoria*, no. 9 (2014): 163-187.

BIBLIOGRAPHY

Almeida, Silvio. *Racismo estrutural*. São Paulo: Pólen Livros, 2019.

Andrews, George Reid. "Epilogue: Whiteness and Its Discontents." In *Rethinking Race in Modern Argentina*, edited by Paulina L. Alberto and Eduardo Elena, 318-326. Cambridge: Cambridge University Press, 2016.

Avendaño, Diego de. *Thesaurus Indicus, seu generalis instructor pro regimine conscientiae in iis quaead Indias spectant*. Vol. 1. Antwerp: Jacob Mersium, 1668.

Babb, Valerie. *Whiteness Visible: The Meaning of Whiteness in American Literature and Culture*. New York: New York University Press, 1998.

Baldwin, James. *Nationalism Colonialism and the United States: One Minute to Twelve*. New York: Liberation Committee for Africa, 1961.

Bento, Maria Aparecida da Silva. *Cidadania em preto e branco*. São Paulo: Editora Ática, 2010.

———. "Pactos narcísicos no racismo: Branquitude e poder nas organizações empresariais e no poder público." PhD diss., Universidade de São Paulo, 2002.

Bento, Maria Aparecida da Silva, Maria de Jesus Silveira, and Simone Gibram Nogueira, eds. *Identidade, branquitude e negritude: Contribuições para a psicologia no Brasil: Novos ensaios, relatos de experiência e de pesquisa*. São Paulo: Centro de Estudos das Relações de Trabalho e Desigualdades/Casa do Psicólogo, 2014.

Bezerra, Janaína Santos. "Pardos na cor & impuros no sangue: Etnia, sociabilidades e lutas por inclusão social no espaço urbano pernambucano do século XVIII." M.A. thesis, Universidade Federal Rural de Pernambuco, 2010.

Borucki, Alex. *De compañeros de barco a camaradas de armas: Identidades negras en el Río de la Plata 1760-1860*. Buenos Aires: Prometeo, 2017.

Boxer, Charles. *Race Relations in the Colonial Portuguese Empire.* London: Oxford University Press, 1963.

Cabral, Iva Maria. *A primeira elite colonial atlântica: Dos "homens honrados brancos" de Santiago à "nobreza da terra," finais do século XV–início do século XVII.* Cabo Verde: Pedro Cardoso Livraria, 2015.

Caraballo, Pablo. "El cuerpo utópico de los gais: Masculinidad, blanquitud y deseo en Tijuana." *Estudios Sociológicos* 39, no. 116 (2021): 533–559.

Carapinho, Christovão Vaz. "Carta Apologética en defensa da cor preta do Emperador São Elesbão, Escrita ao Author da sua História pelo Doutor Christovão Vaz Carapinho, Médico da Sua Magestade." In *Os Dous Atlantes da Ethiopia,* ed. Joseph Pereira de Santa Anna, 2:209–218. Lisbon: Antonio Pedrozo Galram, 1735–1738.

Cardeira, Arlindo Manuel. "Formação de uma cidade afro-atlântica: Luanda no século XVII." *Revista Tempo, Espaço, Linguagem* 5, no. 3 (2014): 1–39.

Cardoso, Lourenço da Conceição. "O branco 'invisível': Um estudo sobre a emergência da branquitude nas pesquisas sobre as relações raciais no Brasil (Período: 1957–2007)." PhD diss., Universidade de Coimbra, 2008.

———. "Retrato do branco racista e anti-racista." *Reflexão e Ação* 18, no. 1 (2010): 46–70.

Carlos Fregoso, Gisela. "Blanquedad, blanquitud y blanqueamiento." YouTube video, 12 August 2019, https://www.youtube.com/watch?v=0uru7iKBzqc.

Carmen Tineo Durán, Jeannette del. "Cruzar el charco: Fantasías prometidas de la blanquitud." *MIGRAZINE,* January 2019.

Catelli, Laura. *Arqueología del mestizaje: Colonialismo y racialización.* Temuco: UFRO/CLACSO, 2020.

Chacón M., Zully. "La aristocracia del color: La desigualdad de castas." *Boletín de la Academia Nacional de la Historia* 93, no. 371 (2010): 83–126.

Conselho Ultramarino. "Parecer do Conselho Ultramarino para que não possa ser eleito vereador ou juiz ordinário homem que seja mulato até quarto grau ou que não for casado com mulher branca."

Cortés, Santos Rudolfo. *El régimen de las "Gracias al Sacar" en Venezuela durante el Período Hispánico.* Vol. 2. Caracas: Academia Nacional de la Historia, 1978.

Cruz, Gustavo R. "Indigenismo y branquitud en el orden racista de la nación." *Revista Intersticios de la Política y la Cultura* 6, no. 12 (2017): 5–30. https://revistas.unc.edu.ar/index.php/intersticios/article/view/18759.

Dias, Andrea Simone Barreto. "Festa, poder e protesta: Os incômodos da cor parda em Pernambuco (décadas de 1730 e 1740)." *XXV Simpósio Nacional de História,* 12–17 July 2009, Fortaleza, Brazil.

Dixon, Angela, and Edward Telles. "Skin Color and Colorism: Global Research, Concepts, and Measurement." *Annual Review of Sociology* 43 (2017) 405–424.

D'Oca, Fernando Rodrigues Montes. "Tráfico de escravos e consciência moral: O pensamento antiescravista de Epifânio de Morains." *Dissertatio: Revista de Filosofia* 46 (2017): 130–172.

Echeverría, Bolívar. "Imágenes de la 'blanquitud.'" In *Sociedades icónicas: Historia, ideología y cultura en la imagen*, edited by Diego Lizarazo Arias, Bolívar Echeverría, and Pablo Lazo Briones, 57–86. Mexico City: Siglo XXI, 2007.

———. *Modernidad y blanquitud*. Mexico City: Ediciones Era, 2010.

Faria, Patricia Souza de. "O Pai dos Cristãos e as populações escravas em Goa: Zelo e controle dos cativos convertidos (séculos XVI e XVII)." *História* 39 (2020): 1–30.

Fradera, Jusep M. *Filipinas, la colonia más peculiar: La hacienda pública en la definición de la política colonial, 1762–1868*. Madrid: CSIC, 1999.

Garzón Martínez, María Teresa, and Eli Bartra. "El lugar de lo blanco: Cartografía de una pregunta." *Veredas: Revista del Pensamiento Sociológico* 13 (2012): 83–104.

Geler, Lea. "African Descent and Whiteness in Buenos Aires: Impossible *Mestizajes* in the White Capital City." In *Rethinking Race in Modern Argentina*, edited by Paulina L. Alberto and Eduardo Elena, 213–240. Cambridge: Cambridge University Press, 2016.

González, Lélia. *Por um feminismo latino-afro-americano*. Rio de Janeiro: Zahar, 2019.

Gumilla, Joseph. *El Orinoco ilustrado y defendido: Historia natural, civil y geográphica de este gran Río y de sus caudalosas vertientes*, 2nd rev. and exp. ed. 2 vols. Madrid: Manuel Fernández, 1745.

Hale, Grace Elizabeth. *Making Whiteness: The Culture of Segregation in the South, 1890–1940*. New York: Pantheon, 1998.

Hernáez, Francisco Javier. *Colección de Bulas, Breves y otros documentos relativos a la Iglesia de América y Filipinas*. Vol. 1. Vaduz: Kraus Reprint, 1964.

Hidalgo Nuchera, Patricio. *Encomienda, tributo y trabajo en Filipinas (1570–1608)*. Madrid: Universidad Autónoma de Madrid, 1995.

Iturriaga, Elena. *Las élites de la ciudad blanca: Discursos racistas sobre la otredad*. Mérida, Mexico: UNAM/Centro Peninsular en Humanidades y Ciencias Sociales, 2016.

Leal Curiel, Carole. "La querella por una alfombra: La cuestión del buen orden de la república. Valencia, Venezuela, finales del siglo XVIII." *Revista Historia y Memoria*, no. 9 (2014): 163–187.

Ledesma Narváez, Marianella. *Justicia e interculturalidad: Análisis y pensamiento plural en América y Europa*. Lima: Centro de Estudios Constitucionales, 2018.

Linares, Raúl Alfredo. "Problemas metodológicos en el abordaje genealógico de familias 'diversas.'" In *Mestizaje, sangre y matrimonio en territorios de la actual Argentina y Uruguay, siglos XVII–XX*, edited by Nora Siegrist and Mónica Ghirardi, 173–196. Buenos Aires: Universidad Nacional de Córdoba, 2008.

Loiola, Maria Lemke. "Defeito o acidente? Mulatos e pardos na produção da hierarquia social em Goiás colonial." Conference paper, 2010.

Lucena Salmoral, Manuel. *Los códigos negros de la América Española*. Alcalá de Henares: Ediciones UNESCO Universidad de Alcalá, 1996.

Lugo, Juan de. *Responsorum moralium*. Lugduni: 1651.

Matos Silva, Jorge Lúzio. "Sagrado marfim: O Império Português na Índia e as relações intracoloniais Goa e Bahia, século XVII." PhD diss., Pontifícia Universidade Católica de São Paulo, 2011.

Méndez Paz, Carlos Alberto. "Catálogo de informaciones de nobleza, limpieza de sangre y otras calidades." *Revista del Centro de Estudios Genealógicos de Buenos Aires* 1 (1979).

Nascimento, Silvia. "Wakanda in Madureira: 'O que a colonização separou, Wakanda quer juntar.'" *Mundo Negro* 7 (November 2019).

Navarrete, Federico. "La blanquitud y la blancura, cumbre del racismo mexicano." *Revista de la Universidad de México*, Dossier: Racismo (2020): 7-12.

Olaechea Labayen, Juan B. "Aspectos del derecho indiano y el mestizaje en el siglo XVII." *Anuaria Historia del Derecho Español* 47 (1977): 499-521.

Oliveira, Anderson José Machado de. "Dispensa da cor e clero nativo: Poder eclesiástico e sociedade católica na América Portuguesa (1671-1822)." In *Dimensões do catolicismo portugués*, vol. 3 of *Anais do IV Encontro Internacional de História Colonial*, edited by Rafael Chambouleyron and Karl-Heinz Arenz, 15-28. Belém: Editora Açaí, 2014.

Peguero, Luis José. *Historia de la conquista de la isla española de Santo Domingo [Manuscrito]: Traducida de la Historia General de las Indias, escrita por Antonio de Herrera, y de otros autores que han escrito sobre el particular*, 1762-63, 2 vols. Biblioteca Nacional de España, MSS 1479 and 1480.

Peña Montenegro, Alonso de la. *Itinerario para párrocos de indios, su oficio y obligaciones.* Madrid: 1668.

Pessoa, Raimundo Agnelo Soares. "Comentário: Mulatos ou pardos?" *Mulatos na sociedade colonial*. O Arquivo Nacional e a História Luso-Brasileira. https://historialuso.an.gov.br/index.php?option=com_content&view=article&id=5118&Itemid=371.

Precioso, Daniel. *Legítimos vassalos: Pardos livres e forros na Vila Rica colonial (1750-1803).* São Paulo: Editora UNESP, 2011.

Quijano, Aníbal. "Colonialidad del poder, eurocentrismo y América Latina." In *La colonialidad del saber: Eurocentrismo y ciencias sociales*, edited by Edgardo Lander, 201-246. Buenos Aires: CLACSO, 1992.

———. "Las paradojas de la colonialidad/modernidad/eurocentrada." *Hueso Húmero* 53 (2009): 30-59.

Raminelli, Ronald. "Impedimentos da cor: Mulatos no Brasil e em Portugal, 1640-1750." *Vária História* 28, no. 48 (2012): 699-723.

———. "Matias Vidal de Negreiros: Mulato entre a norma reinol e as práticas ultramarinas." *Vária História* 32, no. 60 (2016): 699-730.

———. *Nobrezas do Novo Mundo: Brasil e ultramar hispânico, séculos XVII e XVIII.* Rio de Janeiro: Editora FGV, 2016.

Rêgo, João Manuel Vaz Monteiro de Figueirôa. *"A honra alheia por um fio": Os estatutos de limpeza de sangue no espaço de expressão Ibérica (sécs. XVI-XVIII).* PhD diss., Universidade do Minho, 2009.

Rêgo, João Manuel Vaz Monteiro de Figueirôa, and Fernanda Olival. "Cor da pele, distinções e cargos: Portugal e espaços atlânticos portugueses (séculos XVI a XVIII)." *Tempo* 16, no. 30 (2011): 115-145.

"Requerimento dos clérigos pardos do Bispado de Pernambuco, ao rei [D. João V], pedindo o cumprimento das ordens reais e da Santa Sé para que possam ser admitidos, pois a irmandade de São Pedro dos Clérigos do Recife, contrariando o compromisso, impediu a entrada de sacerdotes pardos ou mulatos." Pernambuco, 1742. Cax. 57, doc. 4943, Lisbon, Portugal, Arquivo Histórico Ultramarino, Pernambuco.

Rosal, Miguel Á. "Africanos y afrodescendientes en Buenos Aires (1740–1749): Esbozo de un estudio sobre fuentes inéditas y publicadas." *Estudios Históricos*, no. 19 (2018): 1–45.

Sánchez Gómez, Luis Ángel. *Las principalías indígenas y la administración española en Filipinas*. Madrid: Universidad Complutense, 1991.

Sánchez Menchero, Mauricio. "Entre blanquitud y negritud: Los procesos identitarios en los ministriles (Estados Unidos, 1840–1930)." *Inter Disciplina* 9, no. 23 (2021).

Simões, Mariane Alves. "A Câmara de Vila do Carmo e seus juízes ordinários (1711–1731)." M.A. thesis, Universidade Federal de Juiz de Fora, 2015.

Soares, Katy Dayane Araujo. "'Alguma coisa de mulato' ou 'algum sangue da terra': As ordenações sacerdotais no Bispado do Maranhão (1738–1747)." In *Anais do IV Encontro Internacional de História Colonial*, ed. Rafael Chambouleyron and Karl-Heinz Arenz, 3:215–229. Belem: ACAÍ, 2014.

Sosa Cárdenas, Diana. *Los pardos: Caracas en las postrimerías de la colonia*. Caracas: Universidad Católica Andrés Bello, 2010.

Subrahmanyam, Sanjay. *O império asiático português*. Lisbon: Difel, 1996.

Teixeira, Leonardo Ávila. "O que é branquitude." *GQ Globo* 7 (April 2021). https://gq.globo.com/Lifestyle/Poder/noticia/2021/04/o-que-e-branquitude.html.

Twinam, Ann. *Purchasing Whiteness: Pardos, Mulattos, and the Quest for Social Mobility in the Spanish Indies*. Stanford, CA: Stanford University Press, 2015.

University of California, Berkeley, Center for Latin American Studies. "No Longer a Racial Democracy: Critical Whiteness in Latin America and the Caribbean." YouTube video, 28 April 2021. https://www.youtube.com/watch?v=NF-HzXbAyzo.

Valero, Perla. "El devenir-blanco del mundo: Debates Sur-Norte sobre la blanquitud desde Latinoamérica," *Latin American and Caribbean Ethnic Studies* 18, no. 2 (2023): 217–226.

Vásquez-Padilla, Darío Hernán, and Castriela Esther Hernández-Reyes. "Interrogando la gramática racial de la blanquitud: Hacia una analítica del blanqueamiento en el orden racial colombiano." *Latin American Research Review* 55, no. 1 (2020): 65–80.

Wade, Peter. *Degrees of Mixture, Degrees of Freedom*. Durham, NC: Duke University Press, 2017.

Webb, Andre, and Sarah Radcliffe. "La blanquitud en liceos segregados: El racismo institucional en el Sur de Chile." *Antropologías del Sur* 4, no. 7 (2017): 19–38.

Weber, Max. *The Protestant Ethic and the Spirit of Capitalism*. 1930. Translated by Talcott Parsons. London: Routledge, 1992.

Xavier, Ângela Barreto. *A invenção de Goa: Poder imperial e conversões culturais nos séculos XVI e XVII*. Lisbon: Imprensa de Ciências Sociais, 2008.

Xavier, Ângela Barreto, and Cristina Nogueira da Silva. *O governo dos outros: Poder e diferença no Império português*. Lisbon: Imprensa de Ciências Sociais, 2016.

CHAPTER 6

Indigenous Populations and Nation-Building Projects on the Central American Isthmus (1810–1930)

PATRICIA ARROYO CALDERÓN AND
MARTA ELENA CASAÚS ARZÚ

In this chapter, we review the history of ethnic difference in Central America from the first days of independence to the 1930s. The complexity of the enterprise becomes evident if we consider that the Central American isthmus, though only half a million square miles and with a little more than forty million inhabitants, is divided into seven nation-states with high levels of ethnic, linguistic, and cultural heterogeneity. From the highlands of Guatemala, mostly peopled by different Maya groups, to the many Black and Afro-Indigenous communities of the coasts of Honduras, Nicaragua, Costa Rica, and Panama, the histories of "race" and "ethnicity" in the region are intricate and diverse.[1]

To these sociohistorical entanglements we must add the thorny issue of working with concepts so overloaded as race, ethnicity, and racial/ethnic difference. Postcolonial thinkers like Aníbal Quijano have explored the inextricable connection between the genesis of the concept of race and the colonial enterprise. The colonization of the Americas marked the moment when certain phenotypical, linguistic, and cultural differences were naturalized as the basis for hierarchical relations between dominant Europeans and subjugated Amerindian and Black groups. In this sense, "race" is nothing more than an imaginary construct linked to the exercise of power. "Racializing" practices and racism in turn permeated every sphere of society, including labor relations, politics, and culture. Following this logic, the end of the colonial period and the emergence of independent nation-states simply altered the forms of racialization and the composition of racialized social groups. As the Kaqchikel historian Edgar Esquit has noted, the modern nation-state characteristically turns to one group to define it as racially and culturally superior—in the case of Guatemala, it was the group self-defined as "white" and Ladino, traits through which it justified its dominance over Indigenous, Black, and other groups defined as "different" and "inferior."[2]

This conception of race insists on its arbitrary—though historically overdetermined—nature. Also, this notion of race highlights its instrumental links to hierarchical power structures and unequal social relations, and coexists with other notions, such as ethnic group and ethnicity, that allow us to study the roles "difference" plays in the articulation of individual subjectivities and collective identities. In general terms, the concept of ethnicity alludes to the notion that a shared ancestry, language, values, and cultural repertoire—among other factors—play a substantial role at the moment of setting boundaries among social groups, as well as when articulating a sense of belonging. On the other hand, it is important to note that the markers considered relevant to establish those "ethnic differences" are flexible and have historically mutated. Finally, it is important not to forget the instrumental dimension that ethnicity acquires in struggles for political and cultural hegemony, especially when we think about multilingual and multicultural contexts that, like the Central American region, have historically been characterized by inequality.

For the purpose of this chapter, we have decided to work with the category of "ethnicity," as we consider that it is crucial to understand how the processes of racialization were produced on the Central American isthmus, as well as understanding the local histories within which the concept of race was elaborated and reelaborated. The category of "ethnicity" will allow us, on one the hand, to pay attention to the vectors of economic, political, social, military, ideological, and other forms of power through which structures of inequality were instituted among certain groups due to phenotypical, language, and cultural differences; historically, these forms of power manifested in diverse forms of pillage, exploitation, exclusion, racism, discrimination, ethnocide, and genocide. On the other hand, the category of "ethnicity" will allow us to attend to the multiple ways in which subaltern (or historically subjugated) groups have formed their subjectivities and imagined and put into practice alternative forms of economic, political, and social organization from the colonial period to the present.[3] The notion of ethnicity, therefore, will allow us to attend to ways in which power has instrumentalized certain traits of Central America's populations to impose structures of inequality that have historically privileged those social groups that emphasize their European ancestry (e.g., Spaniards, Criollos, Whites, Mestizos, Ladinos) at the expense of other social groups strongly racialized (e.g., Amerindians, Blacks, Afro-Indigenous, castas). At the same time, the concept of ethnicity will help us attend to ways in which these racialized and historically subjugated collectives have resisted, contested, or negotiated such power formations, creatively and dynamically configuring and reconfiguring their ethnic identities in the process. We seek, therefore, to position ourselves between the dynamics of top-down racialization and bottom-up constitution, reconstitution, and activation of ethnic identities in the region. No doubt, the correlation of forces between these two poles varied a great deal between the end of the colonial period and the 1930s. It is precisely the fluctuation between these two forces that we propose to detail in this chapter.

From Independence to Exclusionary National Imaginaries

As in other parts of the continent, the colonization of the Central American isthmus begun by Pedro de Alvarado in 1524 brought about the imposition of a system of domination whose main objective was the appropriation of natural resources (e.g., gold, silver, land), material goods (through the encomienda system of Indian tribute), and labor force (through institutions like personal service, forced labor, and slavery). The impact of this process on the Indigenous populations was incalculable. Beyond the human loss, the colonization of Central America forcibly displaced numerous ethnic groups, destroyed many communities, and attempted to eradicate every material and immaterial trace of Amerindians' worldviews and cultures. Nonetheless, this traumatic process did not entail the disappearance of the cultural, social, or identity matrices of native Central Americans, simply their transformation and creative adaptation to the new circumstances of colonial society.[4]

In this manner, when the crisis of sovereignty caused by Napoleon's invasion of the Iberian Peninsula in 1810 hit the Central American isthmus, local Indigenous communities joined the mobilizations that shook the region between 1810 and 1821. In general terms, historians have only marginally taken up the role of Indigenous peoples in the process of independence and see them as mere continuations of the "Indian revolts" that dotted the colonial period.[5] Nevertheless, in the past years, scholars like Aaron Pollack or Gladys Tzul Tzul have dedicated themselves to highlighting the profound political dimensions of Indigenous revolts in Guatemala's highlands. Thus, Pollack has traced a series of important mobilizations—such as the revolts of Patzicía (1811), Momostenango (1811–1812 and 1820), Santa Catarina Ixtahuacán (1813–1814), and Totonicapán (1813 and 1820)—led by Maya communities who were well aware of the events and reforms that were shaking up Europe and the Spanish American colonies. For her part, the K'iche' intellectual Gladys Tzul Tzul has unearthed the history of the participation of Indigenous women in the great rebellion of Totonicapán during the summer of 1820, when Atanasio Tzul and Lucas Aguilar defended their autonomy from the Spanish Crown.[6] Despite recent revisionist readings that underscore the importance of the mobilization of Indigenous communities in the process of independence, on the second centenary of independence of the region, the governments of the isthmus have proposed commemorations that erase the agency of Indigenous and Black peoples, recognizing only the leadership of Criollo *próceres* (forefathers) and ignoring the continuity of elements from the colonial period during the republican era. Consequently, many Maya leaders in Guatemala have opposed and mobilized against these events, especially against the government's use of the ruins of Iximché—the capital of the Kaqchikel Kingdom (1470–1527)—for the inauguration of the bicentennial festivities. Likewise, large sectors of the populace have opposed the celebrations, rallying around the hashtag #200NadaQueCelebrar (#200NothingToCelebrate). In a similar fashion, the Guatemalan media has hosted a lively debate between Indigenous and Ladino intellectuals, where various authors have qualified the festivities as "Criollo commemorations," "colonial deliria," "bicentenariadas" (bicentenary nonsense) or "bicentenary of the Criollo, racist, and misogynist motherland."[7]

In any case, what is clear is that the dissolution of the colonial order brought about a long process of reorganization of identities and ethno-racial relations in Central America. Thus, the new republican governments did not only have to deal with continual territorial disputes, resolve challenges to the sovereignty and legitimacy of political power, and look for the ideal system of government in the region, but they also had to dismantle the socioracial hierarchies developed during the colonial regime.[8] In general terms, we can affirm that—from the 1820s onward—the different Central American territories abolished the *casta* system, converting the great variety of subjects of the Spanish monarchy into republican "citizens." Through political and administrative measures like the abolition of slavery, the elimination of "Indian towns" and Indigenous municipalities, and the abolition of Indian tribute, the intellectual elite of the early nineteenth century—heavily influenced by Enlightenment ideas and utilitarian philosophy—aspired to homogenize Central America's populations, at least from the juridical and political point of view. In practice, these legal and institutional transformations were received differently by different sectors of society. On the one hand, a great deal of Blacks, mulattoes, Indigenous, and *castas* perceived the new republican order as an opportunity for upward social mobility. On the other hand, these transformations had little real impact on Black and Indigenous communities removed from the region's new centers of power. Finally, the abolition of structures like Indian towns and special mayoralties was opposed by some Indigenous elites who saw their position as intermediaries, as well as their source of authority within their communities, in peril.

The best example of this resistance to the early projects of liberal governments is possibly Guatemala. In 1839, a military rebellion led by the Ladino caudillo Rafael Carrera did not only end the project of political unification of the isthmus through the dissolution of the federation of the United Provinces of Central America; some of the first measures adopted by his conservative dictatorship amounted to reinstating the division between the República de Indios (Indian commonwealth) and the República de Españoles (Spanish commonwealth). Carrera also reinstated the Leyes de Indias (Laws of the Indies), Indigenous magistrates and governors, and, finally, the Indigenous justice and mayoralty systems abolished by the federation.[9] The fact that the Indigenous elites of the highlands—especially the K'iche' elite of Quetzaltenango—emerged as key allies of Carrera suggests that this influential sector of the population did not perceive great advantages in the new abstract declarations of equality, liberty, and fraternity promulgated by Central American liberals during these early years.[10]

Notwithstanding, the most radical changes for the Indigenous communities of the isthmus did not come until the last quarter of the nineteenth century, with the liberal reforms that—as in other Latin American contexts—would bring with them a series of economic, political, and cultural transformations of great magnitude.[11] In the Central American case, the emergence of new elites connected to the coffee industry—a product that substantially increased in value at the turn of the century—in the 1860s and 1870s precipitated a series of accelerated processes of land privatization. The institutions most affected by these processes of privatization were, on the one hand, the Catholic Church, and on the other, the Indigenous communities whose communal lands, for the most part, would pass into private hands. Although not all Indigenous communities were affected to the same extent, the commodification and concentration of a great deal of the isthmus's arable lands entailed—in general terms—the impoverishment, proletarianization, and submission of a great part of the Indigenous population to new relations of dominance within haciendas whose owners and administrators were, for the most part, mestizos or Ladinos or foreigners.[12]

The last decades of the nineteenth century brought about, parallel to the already-described structural transformations, new processes of expansion and consolidation of state institutions in the region. If we consider that the basis of the material sustenance of the isthmus's political elite during this period was the production and commercialization of coffee, it should not surprise us that legislative reforms, the expansion of bureaucracy, the building of infrastructure, technological innovation, and the distribution of state resources were guided toward oiling an agro-exporting system whose running depended on an abundantly available Indigenous labor force. Between the 1870s and 1930s, a good portion of the legislative activity in the five Central American republics was oriented toward ensuring enough "Indian hands" for the coffee fields—as well as for public and private infrastructure projects—through several initiatives, like the promulgation of mandatory labor and anti-idleness laws, the requirement of work certifications, and the informal acknowledgment of forced labor in exchange for cash advancements or accumulated debts.[13]

This assault against the material conditions that had guaranteed for centuries the existence and the social reproduction of the isthmus's Indigenous peoples was received with divergent attitudes. In some cases, as Greg Grandin has shown in his study of Quetzaltenango's K'iche' elites, these transformations meant adjustments and adaptations that would modify the internal structures and power relations in Indigenous communities. In other cases (the most frequent), they unleashed distinct forms of resistance, both at the micro and macro levels. Among the most frequent forms of individual resistance was the practice of workhands to escape from one hacienda to another, especially when they were beholden to a hacienda for debt repayment. Another was to run away from gangs of forced laborers working on highways and railways, a tendency that increased during the planting and harvesting of corn. Yet another was providing false names to foremen and gang leaders to later evade capture. Finally, another was to send their minor children to fulfill their forced labor obligations, or even to attack hacienda administrators and owners who were considered particularly abusive.[14] Additionally, during the last decades of the nineteenth century and the first of the twentieth, there were a series of Indigenous and peasant revolts all along the isthmus, of which we may note that of Matagalpa (Nicaragua) in 1881, the Tule—or Dule—rebellion (Panama) in 1925, or the more than forty-five Indigenous revolts in the western provinces of El Salvador (the region where the country's coffee production was concentrated) that culminated in the insurrection of January 1932, led by Nahua-Pipil farmhands.[15]

This strong increase of social conflict in the rural areas of the isthmus manifested itself as ethnic fractures among Indigenous and mestizos or Ladinos, generating a series of material and symbolic consequences of great relevance not only for the turn of the century but also for the coming decades of the twentieth century. In the first place, Indigenous workers' daily resistances to being forcibly or semiforcibly integrated into the coffee production industry (and into the plantations that produced cotton, sugarcane, and bananas for export), along with the eventual attacks against administrators, landowners, and/or the mestizo or Ladino population, contributed to reinforcing the local elites' imaginaries about the "barbarism" of the Indigenous populations and to justify an increase in general violence on the part of the state. As several scholars have shown in the Guatemalan case, new technologies, like the telegraph, and army troops were used in peacetime to shut down strikes and suppress local revolts. These devices were also used to ensure a stable labor force and to capture runaway workers—to the extent that some historians describe Guatemala at the end of the nineteenth century as an "order-and-hacienda" (*orden-finca*) nation-state.[16] In the case of El Salvador, as Patricia Alvarenga has studied, the creation of the police and the National Guard were directly linked to maintaining a productive order in the coffee-growing zones. Thus, we can affirm that it was precisely during this period that a strong semantic association between "Indian" and "(poor) peasant" was established. This is also the moment when the basis for an authoritarian state took hold in the region—a state model that would privilege repressive violence when dealing with the demands of civil society, especially the Indigenous populations.[17]

In second place, these discourses about "barbarism" reinforced the postures that insisted on a supposed inherent "backwardness" and "primitivism" of Indigenous peoples. This discourse, which was already present in the last decades of the colonial period, contributed to the creation of a hefty visual and textual corpus about the so-called Indian problem. In fact, similar to what happened in other Latin American contexts, the last decades of the nineteenth century saw the increased pervasiveness of European racialist doctrines, in particular through the writings of thinkers like Arthur de Gobineau, Herbert Spencer, Gustave Le Bon, and Hippolyte Taine.[18] On the one hand, the political elites of the Central American nations—since the dawn of the nineteenth century—had begun to idealize the Amerindian past, appropriating its mythical figures, symbols, and material vestiges to construct a narrative that emphasized a supposed continuity between the grandeur of preinvasion cultures and the Criollo-republican nation-building project.[19] On the other hand, elite discourses and practices in relation to contemporary Indigenous populations hardened as the century progressed, in what Marta Elena Casaús Arzú and Teresa García Giráldez have called a transition from a model of "civic citizenship" to one of "civilized citizenship."

Even so, the conception of race during this period was not stable, nor were Central American national imaginaries homogeneously constructed.[20] It is important to note that the majority of liberal intellectuals considered that the Indigenous populations had suffered a process of "degeneration" from the arrival of Europeans. Some of them, like the Guatemalan Antonio Batres Jáuregui, blamed such regression on three centuries of colonial rule and a series of "bad habits" acquired by the natives that made them incompatible with the nations' objectives of civilization and progress. The solutions proposed to this supposedly antimodern and antiproductive condition included proposals for miscegenation and "Ladinization." These proposals implied the abolition of Indigenous communities—as fundamental structures of ethnic affiliation—and the expansion of a public education system that would aggressively promote acculturation.[21] To these culturalist conceptions about the "Indian race" were added other biological ones (including eugenics at the beginning of the twentieth century) that considered Indigenous peoples "irredeemable" and proposed the need to "whiten" the nation through public policies that encouraged European immigration and that controlled the capacity and rate of reproduction among Indigenous peoples.[22]

We would like to dwell on these whitening projects, which were particularly powerful in Costa Rica and Guatemala. In the Costa Rican case, the myth of the "white, homogeneous, civilized nation" was widespread at the dawn of the twentieth century among local intellectuals, but it was also circulated beyond the isthmus as part of a transnational imaginary composed of narratives by European and North American travelers, ethnographic expositions, and photographs taken by foreigners. The myth of a "white" Costa Rica spread efficiently despite the fact that late-colonial censuses registered most of the population as mestizo, in spite of the presence of numerous Indigenous communities (e.g., Cabecares, Bribri, Ngäbes), and finally, regardless of the large presence of Black peoples on the Caribbean coast, especially in Limón. The success of this "imaginary of whiteness" was facilitated by two initiatives supported by Costa Rican authorities and intellectual elites. In the first place, between the 1880s and 1930s, local thinkers took the characteristics of the population of the Central Valley and applied them to the rest of the territory until these traits came to be seen as the dominant traits of the "Costa Rican nation." Already since the beginning of the twentieth century, writers like Felipe Molina Bedoya proposed that the Central Valley had been colonized by Spaniards from Galicia with phenotypical traits typical of "whites"; this explained why Costa Ricans stood out for their "progress" and "civilization." This imaginary of whiteness—with its inherent erasure of Indigenous and Black peoples—deepened even more during the first decades of the twentieth century, when it was taken up by intellectuals linked to the progressive wings of unionism and anti-imperialism. This was the case of Joaquín García Monge, founder of the influential magazine *Repertorio Americano* and one of the main writers who contributed to the formation of the national imaginary during this period.[23] In the second place, Costa Rican authorities supported the formation of this imaginary of whiteness by minimizing the presence of Indigenous, Black, and mestizo peoples in national censuses, as well as implementing what Lara Putnam has defined as eugenicist immigration policies starting in 1897, that barred *negros* (Blacks) and *chinos* (Asians) from entering the country.[24]

In Guatemala, despite the fact that most of the population is Indigenous, the elites of the period—highly influenced by Spencerian positivism, degeneration theories, and eugenicist doctrines—also opted for a model of a "white nation" and "whiteness." In particular, the members of the group known as the Generation of 1920 would embrace the idea that miscegenation would lead to a degeneration of the species, as they believed that blood mixtures harmed fertility, adulterated racial traits, and led to "backward" mixed races.[25] Among the members of this generation, the future Nobel laureate Miguel Ángel Asturias stands out thanks to the thesis he wrote to obtain his law degree, "El problema social del indio" ("The Social Problem of the Indian,"

1923), which is basically a eugenicist treatise. According to Asturias—and in opposition to the opinion of most of his contemporaries—the "degeneration" of Guatemala's Indigenous peoples was caused by several economic and social factors, above all, their historical isolation and their lack of mixture with more vigorous races.[26] Hence the solution that Asturias proposed for the formation of a homogeneous nation and "to destroy the malady" that impeded Guatemala's progress: to encourage European immigration—concretely from Switzerland, Belgium, Holland, Württemberg, and the Tyrol—until a sizable majority of purely "white" population was achieved.[27] Although Guatemalan authorities never adopted Asturias's concrete ideas, they did follow the eugenicist immigration policies legislated by other Central American countries, like Costa Rica (1897), Honduras (1929), and El Salvador (1933). In 1936, the dictator Jorge Ubico prohibited the entry of members of the "yellow race" and the "Black race" to Guatemala, as well as of "gypsies" and migrants from a long list of Eastern European, South Asian, and North African countries.

We conclude this chapter by turning to the Salvadoran case, where thousands of Nahua-Pipiles were massacred during the 1930s in the country's western provinces. As various scholars have shown, degenerationist, racialist, and eugenicist doctrines also had a great impact in El Salvador. Intellectuals like David J. Guzmán, Francisco Galindo, and Darío González defended these ideas, which in turn shaped a series of legislative measures designed to achieve "social hygiene" and adopted by successive liberal governments starting in the 1870s. Thus, throughout this period, a succession of policies was implemented with the goal of attracting "white" European immigrants while also correcting the supposed degenerate character of certain sectors of the population, including "alcoholics," "prostitutes," "criminals and delinquents," and the "ill," who were classified as "dangerous groups."[28]

At the same time, as we have already noted, the accelerated process of concentrating land to stimulate coffee production increased social conflicts precisely in the regions with the largest Indigenous populations. Whereas this tension flared up in fragmented forms of resistance at the turn of the century, by the 1920s, the western provinces of Ahuachapán, Santa Ana, and Sonsonate became the setting of an unprecedented wave of mobilizations among local peasants, most of whom were Nahua-Pipil farmhands who would end up joining the Salvadoran Communist Party (Partido Comunista de El Salvador, founded in 1930) and its associated union, Socorro Rojo (Red Aid).[29] The social discontent in the western provinces blew up in mid-January 1932 and took the form of a great revolt led by prominent communists like Farabundo

Martí and Miguel Mármol, but also by Indigenous leaders like Feliciano Ama and Francisco Sánchez.[30] Although the insurrection lasted only three days and led to the death of twenty civilians and thirty soldiers, this revolt immediately reactivated the Criollo imaginaries about the "dangerousness" and "barbarism" of Pipiles and set in motion an unprecedented repression that would last more than two months and claim somewhere between ten thousand and thirty thousand Indigenous peasants.[31]

This traumatic event—known simply as La Matanza (the Massacre)—provoked an authentic "scar" in the collective memory of Salvadorans, with consequences that can still be felt today.[32] In the first place, as a consequence of the repression and persecution against Indigenous peoples in the western provinces, many Pipiles abandoned their native language (Nahuat or Nawat), as well as other ethnic markers, such as the men's shirts and pants made of white cotton, or the women's multicolor skirts. In the second place, the massacre came to underpin common narratives about the "mestizo" nature of the El Salvador population; these narratives had been taking shape since the late 1800s through immigration policies and the manipulation of census data, among other practices, but would consolidate their hegemony only after the ethnocide and the genocide of the Nahua-Pipiles. Finally, La Matanza came to exemplify a model that became more and more frequent in the region after the 1950s: the equation of "Indigenous" and "communists," and "Indigenous" and the "enemy within."

Conclusion

In this chapter, we have summarized the profound transformations that Indigenous peoples in Central America experienced between independence and the 1930s. As we have seen, if the colonization of the isthmus by Spanish Crown officials brought with it blood and destruction, as well as the fragmentation and forced displacement of the Indigenous communities of the region, Indigenous peoples—from the sixteenth century—were able to creatively adapt, reconstruct, and reactivate their ethnic identities. Taking advantage of the relative autonomy that "Indian towns" gave them and the relative inaccessibility of their territories, Central America's native population re-created forms of governance, administration, production, and spirituality that in some cases were kept intact until the last decades of the nineteenth century.

Notwithstanding, between the 1870s and 1930s, there was a seismic change in the region. The liberal reforms marked the start of a continued assault on the material existence of the native peoples of the region by the political and economic elites. These new liberal elites focused on the privatization of communal lands; on transforming Indigenous peoples into forced laborers; on consolidating new state institutions designed to administer, control, and repress Indigenous resistance; and on inserting the isthmus's nations into international markets as exporters of agricultural products, all with the objective of setting Central American nations on the path of "order," "civilization," and "progress." At the same time, the region's intellectual elites developed divergent national imaginaries, oscillating between projects that emphasized the region's mestizoness and models that strived for whiteness. Despite their differences, they all shared the vocation of "building the nation" by eliminating the isthmus's Indigenous, Black, and Afro-Indigenous populations both at the symbolic (through political assimilation, erasure through census, and ethnocide) and material (through genocidal practices) levels.

NOTES

1. Before the arrival of Europeans, the Central American isthmus was unequally populated and organized into different imperial and chiefdom structures, with the most populous areas concentrated in Mayan city-states. During the colonial period, most of the isthmus was under the authority of the Captaincy General of Guatemala, which included regions that are today part of Mexico, such as Chiapas and the Soconusco. Depending on the region, the demographic impact of the slave trade was more or less noteworthy; in turn, the geographic areas where free Blacks settled also varied, as did the nature of interethnic relations between Black and Indigenous populations. The policies of Indigenous assimilation promoted by colonial authorities were more or less successful according to the strength of precolonial social structures and the autonomy different native groups were guaranteed. In contrast, Belize was a British colony until 1973 and presents characteristics beyond the scope of this chapter. During the period of independence, the isthmus was divided into five republics (Panama, whose territory formed part of Colombia, would not acquire its independence until 1903) that would undergo several federalization attempts in the 1820s, 1880s, and 1920s. Each of those states pushed national imaginaries and nation-building projects that required to different degrees the elimination, assimilation, or neutralization (through educational or eugenicist policies, promotion of European immigration, and so on) of Indigenous and Black populations. Considering this territorial and demographic complexity, as well as the divergences in national models, this chapter privileges the study of the ethno-racial dynamics related to the Indigenous peoples of the region, leaving aside analysis of historical processes that have affected the Black populations, as well as the complex processes of articulation of mestizos' and Ladinos' hybrid identities.
2. Edgar Esquit, *La superación del indígena: La política de la modernización entre las élites indígenas de Comalapa, siglo XX* (Guatemala City: Instituto de Estudios Interétnicos, USAC, 2010).

3. Other alternative models of political organization during this period include the Miskito Kingdom in the Caribbean coast of today's Nicaragua, dating to the end of the seventeenth century, the brief experiment with Indigenous sovereignty inaugurated by the K'iche' revolt of Totonicapán in 1820, and the continuity of Indigenous mayoralties.
4. The territorial, economic, and administrative segregation of different sectors of the population constituted the organizational basis of the Captaincy General of Guatemala. This form of population control grouped Indigenous peoples into "Indian towns" and facilitated—from the sixteenth century—the beginning of a series of important processes of ethnic reconstitution. Among them, we can mention the recovery of certain forms of communal organization (e.g., the resurrection of precolonial Maya lineage systems), the establishment of a political and administrative system proper to the "Indian commonwealth" (governors and judges of town councils, separate courts, and other municipal Indigenous offices), and the incrustation of native cosmologies in the new liturgies imposed by Christianity (e.g., confraternities, religious mayoralties). In the case of Guatemala, the separation between the Indian and Spanish commonwealths survived past the fall of the Spanish Empire, until the 1870s. Severo Martínez Peláez, *La patria del criollo: Ensayo de interpretación de la realidad colonial guatemalteca* (Mexico City: Fondo de Cultura Económica, 1998), 499–501.
5. For a general notion of the processes of independence in Central America, see Jordana Dym, *From Sovereign Villages to National States: City, State, and Federation in Central America, 1759–1839* (Albuquerque: University of New Mexico Press, 2006). For a detailed account of the close to sixty "Indian revolts" that erupted in Central America during the late colonial period, see Severo Martínez Peláez, *Motines de indios: La violencia colonial en Centroamérica y Chiapas* (Guatemala City: F&G Editores, 2011).
6. According to Pollack's research on the revolts of Patzicía and Totonicapán, the "revolts" (*motines*) in the Captaincy General after 1810—the year when the Spanish Cortes were convened in Cádiz as a result of the power void caused by the French invasion of the Iberian Peninsula and the subsequent abdication of Charles IV—were caused by two main reasons. In the first place, many of these mobilizations were intended to reject the payment of the "Indian tribute," which, after being abolished by the Cortes in 1811, was still being collected in many communities that were increasingly restless as a result of the contradictory news that arrived from Spain. The second reason for these Indigenous mobilizations was exactly the opposite: the demand to return to the old colonial "Indian tribute" system in the face of the new taxes that Indigenous subjects, legally transformed into "citizens," would be forced to pay according to the Constitution of 1812. Gladys Tzul Tzul's work on the Indigenous uprising of Chuimeq'ena' (Totonicapán) aligns with a new current that insists on retelling Guatemalan and Central American history from the perspective of Indigenous peoples. "Felipa Tzoc, Josefa Tacam, María Tipaz y María Hernández. Las mujeres a 201 años del juicio criminal contra el común de Chuime'q'ena," *Agencia Ocote*, March 7, 2021. Tzul Tzul focuses on recovering the lives of four Indigenous women ignored by the traditional, Criollo-centric, and androcentric historiography of the independence period (Felipa Tzoc, Josefa Tacam, María Tipaz, and María Hernández).
7. Some public intellectuals who have participated in this debate include human rights defender Iduvina Hernández, K'iche' political leader Rigoberto Quemé, Marco Alberto Carrera, and Kaqchikel columnist Sandra Xinico Batz.
8. Among other problems, we can note the territorial dispute with Mexico (to which the

Central American provinces were annexed in 1822 and from which they broke off in 1823) about the sovereignty of Chiapas and the Soconusco, or the perpetual tension between unionist currents (in favor of the unification of all the territories that had made up the Captaincy General of Guatemala) and the separatist tendencies of the five provinces.

9. Besides dissolving that first federation, Carrera's successful revolt ended the secessionist experiment of the State of Los Altos, which had declared independence in 1838. Carrera's partial "return" to colonial laws and practices extended to the end of his administration in 1866. Practically all of Carrera's measures were abolished by the liberal reform of 1871, with the exception of Indigenous mayoralties. Indigenous mayoralties progressively declined in numbers and power in the late 1800s, except in Chichicastenango and Sololá, where they never disappeared. For a complete history of Indigenous mayoralties in Guatemala, see Carlos Fredy Ochoa, *Alcaldías indígenas: Diez años después de su reconocimiento por el estado* (Guatemala City: Asociación de Investigación y Estudios Sociales, 2013), 1:16–25.

10. For an in-depth study of the existing ties between Quetzaltenango's K'iche' elites and Carrera, see Greg Grandin, *The Blood of Guatemala: A History of Race and Nation* (Durham, NC: Duke University Press, 2000), 82–109.

11. The earliest of these liberal reforms or "liberal revolutions" came about in Costa Rica in 1870, followed by Guatemala in 1871; the latest would come about in Nicaragua in 1893, although that country's structural transformations began before this date. In general terms, the liberal reforms entailed the separation of the states' institutions from the church, the appropriation of ecclesiastical assets, the expansion of bureaucracy and administrative apparatuses, and the creation of public school systems, among other measures. For the purposes of this chapter, the most transcendental reform was the dissolution of Indigenous communities (which happened in a rapid fashion in El Salvador in 1881, and more slowly in the case of Nicaragua) and the privatization of a good part of their communal lands.

12. While the cultivation of coffee was concentrated in the foothills of the isthmus, large sugar and cotton plantations proliferated on the coasts (too warm for coffee), and beginning in the 1890s, US companies started to invest in large banana plantations in Honduras, Guatemala, and Costa Rica. At the same time, the Central American republics began to encourage the immigration of European farmers; in many cases this included offering large swaths of land, especially to German immigrants. These transformations had a profound impact on the Indigenous communities of the region, although scholars still debate its specific nature. Some, like Greg Grandin, talk about dynamics of "proletarianization"; others, like Jeffrey Gould, contend that the transformations generated divisions, factionalism, and new forms of stratification in the communities. Gould, *To Die in this Way: Nicaraguan Indians and the Myth of Mestizaje, 1880–1965* (Durham, NC: Duke University Press, 1998).

13. The phrase "Indian hands" (*brazos indígenas*) is nearly ubiquitous in the documentation of the period and eloquently reflects the extent to which "Indian" and "agricultural work" were associated in the minds of the political elites. As the cited laws and practices show, a great deal of that agricultural labor was forced.

14. For a study of some of these forms of resistance during the construction of the Los Altos Railway—designed to connect Guatemala City and Quetzaltenango—between 1911 and 1930, see Grandin, *The Blood*, 174–182. For a detailed study of resistance strategies in west-

ern El Salvador—mostly Nahua-Pipil—between 1880 and 1932, see Ana Patricia Alvarenga Venutolo, *Cultura y ética de la violencia: El Salvador, 1880–1932* (San José: EDUCA, 1996).
15. For a study of the implications of the Matagalpa revolt, see Gould, *To Die in This Way*. For a study of the Kuna/Guna people's conflict with the Panamanian state that culminated in the Dule revolt of 1925, see James Howe, *A People Who Would Not Kneel: Panama, the United States, and the San Blas Kuna* (Washington, DC: Smithsonian Institution Press, 1998). We return to the 1932 massacre later in this this chapter.
16. This influential term was coined by Sergio Tischler Visquerra in *Guatemala, 1944: Crisis y revolución. Ocaso y quiebre de una forma estatal* (Guatemala City: USAC; Puebla, Mexico: Benemérita Universidad Autónoma de Puebla, 1998), where, among other things, he traced the origin of the oligarchic liberal state. There, Tischler situates the origin of the authoritarian and antidemocratic forms of governance developed in twentieth-century Guatemala in the informal institution of the hacienda.
17. As we analyze in our other chapter in this volume, the association between "Indigenous" and "peasant" became fundamental in the 1960s and 1970s, especially with the revitalization of popular mobilizations and the emergence of revolutionary movements in the region. However, we cannot neglect to note that parallel to the establishment of the authoritarian basis of the state, there emerged antiauthoritarian currents that led to important historical events, especially in the 1920s and 1930s. We do not have space here to discuss these currents in depth; suffice it to say that they were prompted by social movements like unionism, anti-imperialism, socialism, agrarianism, and feminism. In general terms, these movements aimed to create a more democratic state, more inclusive national imaginaries, and greater participation and economic opportunities for social sectors traditionally excluded (especially peasants, Indigenous peoples, workers, and women). Despite the strength of the movements, none was able to challenge the hegemony of the exclusionary models we analyze in the remainder of the chapter, nor did they manage to consolidate more democratic institutional models.
18. The countries where these European theorists of the "inequality of races" had the greatest influence were Guatemala and Costa Rica. For an analysis of these thinkers' profound impact in Guatemala, see Marta Elena Casaús Arzú, "La representación del otro en las élites intelectuales europeas y latinoamericanas: Un siglo de pensamiento racialista, 1830–1930," *Iberoamericana: Nordic Journal of Latin American and Caribbean Studies* 40, nos. 1–2 (2010): 13–44. For Costa Rica, see Steven Palmer, "Racismo intelectual en Costa Rica y Guatemala, 1870–1920," *Mesoamérica* 17, no. 31 (1996): 99–121; Ronald Soto Quirós, "Imaginando una nación de raza blanca en Costa Rica: 1821–1914," *Amerique Latine Histoire et Mémoire*, no. 15 (2008).
19. The renewed interest in the precolonial past was initiated when European and North American travelers began to show interest in Maya ruins. Among them, the most relevant may be John Lloyd Stephens, who—according to Ileana Rodríguez, *Hombres de empresa, saber y poder en Centroamérica. Identidades regionales / Modernidades periféricas* (Managua: IHNCA, 2011), 71–101—started the practice of giving primacy to "the Mayan" as the most distinctive and valued element of the precolonial period. This primacy, logical in Guatemala's case, would then extend to territories where the Maya population was marginal—or practically nonexistent—before colonization. We find examples of this "Mayanification" of the precolonial past in Honduras, where the ruins of Copán would occupy a privileged space in the construction of the national imaginary. See Darío Euraque, *Conversaciones históricas con el mestizaje y la identidad nacional en Honduras* (San Pedro Sula,

Honduras: Centro Editorial, 2004); Marvin Barahona, *Pueblos indígenas, estado y memoria colectiva en Honduras* (Tegucigalpa: Editorial Guaymuras, 2009). This also happened in Nicaragua, where, despite the lack of archeological ruins, a similar process took place. See Gould, *To Die*, 196–197. It is important to note that this interest in precolonial ruins led to the state appropriation of material vestiges and other Indigenous cultural elements, especially through the creation of public and private museums. This tendency to appropriate material and symbolic elements pertaining to Indigenous cultures for state purposes persists to this day at the core of the region's tourism industry. For a study of the creation of private museums in Guatemala, see Casaús Arzú, "Museo Nacional y museos privados en Guatemala: Patrimonio y patrimonialización. Un siglo de intentos y frustraciones," *Estudios Digital*, no. 6 (2015): 1–32. For a study of how these nineteenth-century logics continued to weigh on the reconfigurations of museums in El Salvador after the 1992 Peace Accords that ended the civil war there, see Robin Maria DeLugan, *Reimagining National Belonging: Post-Civil War El Salvador in a Global Context* (Tucson: University of Arizona Press, 2012).

20. There are strong discrepancies between the interpretation of the formation of national imaginaries we present here and the position of researchers like Darío Euraque, Jeffrey Gould, Charles R. Hale, and Arturo Taracena, who defend that there existed successful models of "mestizo nation" and feasible national imaginaries based on the ideas of mestizaje. There are also interesting debates about the degree of importance that theories explicitly opposed to the notion of racial inequality—like Hindu-influenced spiritual currents and theosophy, which had many followers in the 1910s—achieved in the region. For alternative interpretations to ours, see Euraque, Gould, and Hale, eds., *Memorias del mestizaje: Cultura política en Centroamérica de 1920 al presente* (Guatemala City: CIRMA, 2005); Taracena, *Etnicidad, nación y estado*.

21. Some of the intellectuals who defended these positions included the anthropologist, philologist, and historian Antonio Batres Jáuregui and the pedagogue, journalist, and writer Vicenta Laparra de la Cerda. These "culturalist" interpretations of ethno-racial difference never disappeared from the Central American intellectual milieu and reemerged in the 1950s thanks to the introduction of functionalist anthropology by US scholars.

22. It is important to note that some Indigenous sectors also embraced these biological interpretations of racial difference to push their own imaginaries about the place Mayas should have in the nation. As Greg Grandin has studied, the K'iche' elites of Quetzaltenango developed their own racial discourse in the late 1800s, emphasizing the idea that the distinctive element that separated Ladinos from Indigenous peoples was "blood" instead of cultural markers like language and clothing. *The Blood*, 130–158. In this fashion, K'iche' elites were able to continue to claim their roles as intermediaries and "representatives of the Indigenous race" vis-à-vis the state at the same time they adopted all the signs of "civilization" and "respectability" required in bourgeois contexts by the turn of the century.

23. On the erasure of Indigenous populations in the Costa Rican national model, see Soto Quirós, "Imaginando," in *Mestizaje, indígenas e identidad nacional en Centroamérica: De la colonia a las repúblicas liberales*, ed. Ronald Soto Quirós y David Díaz Arias (San José: FLACSO, 2007), 40–79; Palmer, "Racismo." On the erasure of Black peoples on the Caribbean coast of Costa Rica, see Lowell Gudmundson, "Black into White in Nineteenth-Century Spanish America: Afro-American Assimilation in Argentina and Costa Rica," *Slavery & Abolition* 5, no. 1 (1984): 34–49, who has studied this same tendency in all of Central America in his most recent works.

24. These "eugenicist" immigration policies were not exclusive to Costa Rica. In the case of El Salvador, the Immigration Law (Ley de Migración) of 1933 banned the entry of persons from China, Mongolia, the Malay Peninsula, the Arabian Peninsula, Lebanon, Palestine, Syria, and Turkey, as well as Blacks and "Hungarians" (a local term for Romani people). At the same time, many Afro-Salvadorans who lived in border towns were expelled to Guatemala and Honduras. See Jorge E. Cuéllar. "Elimination / Deracination: Colonial Terror, La Matanza, and the 1930s Race Laws in El Salvador," *American Indian Culture and Research Journal* 42, no. 2 (2018): 48. In the case of Nicaragua, from 1881 onward, censuses were fundamental to creating the myth of a "mestizo nation." See Gould, *To Die*, 16-19. These strategies were also used in Honduras, in conjunction with a series of immigration policies that opposed the arrival of Black peoples; the policies culminated in 1929 with the passage of a law that prohibited the entry of Blacks as well as Palestinians. According to Suyapa Portillo's research, this generated many conflicts with the hiring policies of the banana companies on the northern coast, which greatly depended on the availability of Black workers from the English-speaking Caribbean.

25. Some of the most important members of this generation include Miguel Ángel Asturias, Epaminondas Quintana, Federico Mora, and Carlos Samayoa Chinchilla. The most comprehensive study of the ideological intricacies of this group is Marta Elena Casaús Arzú and Teresa García Giráldez, *Las redes intelectuales centroamericanas: Un siglo de imaginarios nacionales (1820-1920)* (Guatemala City: F&G Editores, 2005).

26. Among the other causes of "degeneration" mentioned by Asturias were malnutrition, poor hygiene, excessive work, early marriages, illnesses, and alcoholism. "Sociología guatemalteca: El problema social del indio" (bachelor's thesis [licenciatura], Universidad de San Carlos de Guatemala, 1923), 33-38.

27. In his thesis, Asturias also discusses a series of measures "to delay the degeneration of the Guatemalan social group comprised of the Indigenous race" (*El problema*, 56), which included the prohibition of premature weddings, better nutrition, the reduction of the workday to eight hours, education, and encouraging hygiene and miscegenation. Note that Asturias considered these approaches only as "delaying measures" and in no way "solutions" to the so-called Indian problem.

28. See Carlos Gregorio López Bernal, *Tradiciones inventadas y discursos nacionalistas: El imaginario nacional de la época liberal en El Salvador, 1876-1932* (San Salvador: Editorial Imprenta Universitaria, 2007); Mario Daniel Oliva Mancia, "Ciudadanía e higienismo social en El Salvador, 1880-1932" (PhD diss., Universidad Centroamericana "José Simeón Cañas," 2011). Both scholars have studied in depth the influence of hygienist physicians in the configuration of the public sphere in El Salvador since the presidency of Rafael Zaldívar, who governed between 1876 and 1885 and was a doctor himself.

29. Conflicts caused by the regime of land ownership and by poor labor conditions multiplied exponentially between 1880 and 1932 in the mentioned provinces, only to become even more acute in the 1920s—especially after the 1929 stock market crash, which provoked the plummeting of coffee prices in international markets and unleashed an unprecedented wave of violence in the region. Among the more immediate political causes for the 1932 revolt, we can mention the fraud in the municipal elections of late 1931, as well as Maximiliano Hernández Martínez's coup of December 1931. On January 22, 1932, thousands of peasants armed with machetes, farming tools, and some pistols, attacked the barracks of Juayúa, Izalco, Nahuizalco, Tacuba, and Teotepeque. Gould

and Lauria-Santiago, *To Rise in Darkness: Revolution, Repression, and Memory in El Salvador, 1920–1932* (Durham, NC: Duke University Press, 2008), and the documentary *1932: Cicatriz de la Memoria* (San Salvador: Museo de la Palabra y la Imagen, 2005), https://www.youtube.com/watch?v=mLZTTxddCZg&t=33s, explore the role of the PCS and Socorro Rojo in the insurrection.

30. There is an important disagreement in Salvadoran historiography about the leaders of the revolt: some authors emphasize the role of Indigenous activists; others contend that the Communist Party and Socorro Rojo had a greater part, sometimes even suggesting that Indigenous participants were "manipulated" by these entities. For an analysis of this debate, see Virginia Q. Tilley, *Seeing Indians: A Study of Race, Nation, and Power in El Salvador* (Albuquerque: University of New Mexico Press, 2005), 137–168.

31. There is also a lack of agreement about the total number of people killed between January and March 1932; the manner in which the repression was carried out (including the presence of mass graves throughout the region and the absence of official documents, among other things) explains the extreme fluctuation of the figures. However, what is clear is that the insurrection and the subsequent repression were interpreted from the start from an ethno-racial perspective. On the one hand, there are witness accounts from Ladino peasants expressing the general belief that the revolt was something in which only "the natives" or "the more Indian" had participated. See *1932: Cicatriz de la Memoria*. On the other hand, a good deal of the repression was carried out by irregular militias recruited among the Ladino population of the affected municipalities, who for months dedicated themselves to "hunt" and summarily execute Indigenous men and women with the support of the authorities. The viciousness of these voluntary militias was of such magnitude that Virginia Tilley qualifies the events in the months after January 1932 as a true "racial war." *Seeing Indians*, 156–164. Finally, there are many accounts by military leaders, missionaries, and landowners in which one can find explicit calls to exterminate the region's Indigenous population "from the root up," like the US had exterminated Native Americans. Tilley, *Seeing Indians*, 162–163.

32. We take the phrase *cicatriz de la memoria* (memory scar) from the eponymous documentary directed by Jeffrey Gould and Carlos Henríquez Consalvi. Besides the consequences we detail in the main text, "La Matanza" generated an atmosphere of terror and a culture of silence that led many survivors not to share their experiences—neither in public nor in the intimacy of the family—until after the end of the civil war in El Salvador (1980–1992), when they were already of advanced age.

BIBLIOGRAPHY

Alvarenga Venutolo, Ana Patricia. *Cultura y ética de la violencia: El Salvador, 1880–1932*. San José: EDUCA, 1996.

Asturias, Miguel Ángel. "Sociología guatemalteca: El problema social del indio." Bachelor's thesis (*licenciatura*), Universidad de San Carlos de Guatemala, 1923.

Barahona, Marvin. *Pueblos indígenas, estado y memoria colectiva en Honduras*. Tegucigalpa: Editorial Guaymuras, 2009.

Casaús Arzú, Marta Elena. "Museo Nacional y museos privados en Guatemala: Patrimonio y patrimonialización: Un siglo de intentos y frustraciones." *Estudios Digital*, no. 6 (2015): 1–32.

Casaús Arzú, Marta Elena. "La representación del otro en las élites intelectuales europeas y latinoamericanas: Un siglo de pensamiento racialista, 1830-1930." *Iberoamericana: Nordic Journal of Latin American and Caribbean Studies* 40, nos. 1-2 (2010): 13-44.

Casaús Arzú, Marta Elena, and Teresa García Giráldez. *Las redes intelectuales centroamericanas: Un siglo de imaginarios nacionales (1820-1920)*. Guatemala City: F&G Editores, 2005.

Cuéllar, Jorge E. "Elimination/Deracination: Colonial Terror, La Matanza, and the 1930s Race Laws in El Salvador." *American Indian Culture and Research Journal* 42, no. 2 (2018): 39-56.

DeLugan, Robin Maria. *Reimagining National Belonging: Post-Civil War El Salvador in a Global Context*. Tucson: University of Arizona Press, 2012.

Dym, Jordana. *From Sovereign Villages to National States: City, State, and Federation in Central America, 1759-1839*. Albuquerque: University of New Mexico Press, 2006.

Esquit, Edgar. *La superación del indígena: La política de la modernización entre las élites indígenas de Comalapa, siglo XX*. Guatemala City: Instituto de Estudios Interétnicos (USAC), 2010.

Euraque, Darío. *Conversaciones históricas con el mestizaje y la identidad nacional en Honduras*. San Pedro Sula, Honduras: Centro Editorial, 2004.

Euraque, Darío, Jeffrey Gould, and Charles R. Hale, eds. *Memorias del mestizaje: Cultura política en Centroamérica de 1920 al presente*. Guatemala City: CIRMA, 2005.

Gould, Jeffrey. *To Die in this Way: Nicaraguan Indians and the Myth of Mestizaje, 1880-1965*. Durham, NC: Duke University Press, 1998.

Gould, Jeffrey, and Carlos Henríquez Consalvi, dirs. *1932: Cicatriz de la memoria*. San Salvador: Museo de la Palabra y la Imagen, 2005.

Gould, Jeffrey, and Aldo Lauria-Santiago. *To Rise in Darkness: Revolution, Repression, and Memory in El Salvador, 1920-1932*. Durham, NC: Duke University Press, 2008.

Grandin, Greg. *The Blood of Guatemala: A History of Race and Nation*. Durham, NC: Duke University Press, 2000.

Gudmundson, Lowell. "Black into White in Nineteenth-Century Spanish America: Afro-American Assimilation in Argentina and Costa Rica." *Slavery & Abolition* 5, no.1 (1984): 34-49.

Howe, James. *A People Who Would Not Kneel: Panama, the United States, and the San Blas Kuna*. Washington, DC: Smithsonian Institution Press, 1998.

López Bernal, Carlos Gregorio. *Tradiciones inventadas y discursos nacionalistas: El imaginario nacional de la época liberal en El Salvador, 1876-1932*. San Salvador: Editorial Imprenta Universitaria, 2007.

Martínez Peláez, Severo. *Motines de indios: La violencia colonial en Centroamérica y Chiapas*. Guatemala City: F&G Editores, 2011.

———. *La patria del criollo: Ensayo de interpretación de la realidad colonial guatemalteca*. Mexico City: Fondo de Cultura Económica, 1998.

Ochoa, Carlos Fredy. *Alcaldías indígenas: Diez años después de su reconocimiento por el estado*. Vol. 1. Guatemala City: Asociación de Investigación y Estudios Sociales, 2013.

Oliva Mancia, Mario Daniel. "Ciudadanía e higienismo social en El Salvador, 1880–1932." PhD diss., Universidad Centroamericana "José Simeón Cañas," 2011.

Palmer, Steven. "Racismo intelectual en Costa Rica y Guatemala, 1870–1920." *Mesoamérica* 17, no. 31 (1996): 99–121.

Pollack, Aaron. "Protesta en Patzicía: Los pueblos de indios y la 'vacatio regis' en el Reino de Guatemala." *Revista de Indias* 78, no. 272 (2018): 147–173.

———. "Totonicapán, 1820: One of the Tips of the Iceberg?" In *Independence in Central America and Chiapas, 1770–1823*, edited by Aaron Pollack, 158–187. Norman: University of Oklahoma Press, 2019.

Portillo Villeda, Suyapa. *Roots of Resistance: A Story of Gender, Race, and Labor on the North Coast of Honduras*. Austin: University of Texas Press, 2021.

Putnam, Lara. *The Company They Kept: Migrants and the Politics of Gender in Caribbean Costa Rica, 1870–1960*. Chapel Hill: University of North Carolina Press, 2002.

Rodríguez, Ileana. *Hombres de empresa, saber y poder en Centroamérica. Identidades regionales / Modernidades periféricas*. Managua: IHNCA, 2011.

Soto Quirós, Ronald. "Imaginando una nación de raza blanca en Costa Rica: 1821–1914." *Amerique Latine Histoire et Mémoire*, no. 15 (2008). http://journals.openedition.org/alhim/2930.

Soto Quirós, Ronald, and David Díaz Arias. *Mestizaje, indígenas e identidad nacional en Centroamérica: De la colonia a las repúblicas liberales*. San José: FLACSO, 2007.

Tilley, Virginia Q. *Seeing Indians: A Study of Race, Nation, and Power in El Salvador*. Albuquerque: University of New Mexico Press, 2005.

Taracena, Aruro. *Etnicidad, nación y estado en Guatemala*. Tomo 1. Antigua: CIRMA, 2002.

Tischler Visquerra, Sergio. *Guatemala, 1944: Crisis y revolución. Ocaso y quiebre de una forma estatal*. Guatemala City: USAC; Puebla, Mexico: Benemérita Universidad Autónoma de Puebla, 1998.

Tzul Tzul, Gladys. "Felipa Tzoc, Josefa Tacam, María Tipaz y María Hernández: Las mujeres a 201 años del juicio criminal contra el común de Chuime'q'ena." *Agencia Ocote*, March 7, 2021, https://www.agenciaocote.com/blog/2021/03/07/las-mujeres-a-201-anos-del-juicio-criminal-contra-el-comun-de-chuimeqena/.

CHAPTER 7

Reconsidering the "Racial Other"

Nation Building, Citizenship, and Interracial Alliances in Latin America and the Caribbean

JORGE DANIEL VÁSQUEZ[1]

After the decline of European empires in Latin America, both the state and nation were built in a simultaneous process. The new governments, inspired by the European model of the nation-state, were faced with divisions in their populations between diverse national and cultural identities that challenged the legitimacy, stability, and popular support for the construction of the new nation-states.[2] Thus, in the wake of the revolutions and movements for independence, the successful creation of a nation became the basis of legitimacy for the new republics.

According to López-Alves, the special relationship between state and nation, as well as creating a national identity, are original Latin American contributions to modernity. Therefore, throughout the nineteenth and early twentieth centuries, the new republics had to attach an in-the-making nation to an in-the-making state. Latin America's new ruling elites asserted their power in the name of change and novelty and defined the nation in terms of a promising future to capture the support of a very heterogeneous population.

The ideals around "the future of the nation" were fundamental to creating a national imagination that incorporated both republican expressions of government (parties, elections) and expressions of the imaginary of Indigenous, Afro-descendant peoples. This incorporation, however, did not prevent the reinscription of racial discrimination in the emerging states' legal codes or social relations in general.

What is crucial for the analysis here is that there are two competing projects in this process of nation building: on the one hand, the ruling elites' move to make exclusion or subordination a condition of the incorporation of Indigenous and Afro-descendant communities in their project, and on the other hand, these communities' struggle to impose their imaginaries of modernity on the construction of the national community. In comparison, the ruling elites constructed the "racial other" as essentially different and therefore distant from modernity, whereas the Indigenous and Afro-descendant communities constructed political strategies to confront the move toward exclusion that sought to condemn them to continue in slavery, in forced paid and unpaid labor, or on the verge of extermination.

The phrase "racial other" already speaks of a certain degree of recognition. Any degree of recognition implies a relationship, but it is the matter of power that reveals the relationship's terms. I contend that the category "racial other" includes the articulation between difference and inequality in the sense that, for Mabel Moraña, emerges from the work of José Carlos Mariátegui (1894–1930). Thus, while the continuity of the subsidiary labor of global capital accumulation to which the Indigenous and Afro-descendant populations in Latin America were subjected speaks of the economic and political inequality on which the privileges, hierarchies, and exclusions of the oligarchic project are based, *difference* implies "the delimitation of a concrete historical and political position that is ethically situated in relation to networks of power and the political and ideological alternatives of a given era."[3]

Latin American nations, multiracial and multiethnic, were built amid bonds that translated colonial relations while at the same time confounding states whose authorities saw the masses as a threat, yet could not escape from contending with their demands.[4] The continuity of such a confrontation, between an elitist will to exclude and the struggle for the extension of citizenship on nondiscriminatory terms, characterizes the national community's permanent construction in Latin America.

Thus, the conflict revolving around the connections between nation, citizenship, and race is at the heart of forming the nascent republics and their continuation into the twentieth century. Following Torres Santana, this conflict can also be considered the concrete expression of the two paths that republicanism has taken in Latin America: democratic and antidemocratic. The latter consists of recognizing as citizens only those who possess "freedom and autonomy" by the fact of owning property and thus excluding non–property owners (who were called "nationals") from political life. On the other hand, democratic republicanism "attacks oligarchies wherever they come from: from within republicanism, from liberalism, or from any political program that builds monopolies of power."[5] The colonial legacy and its continuity through the racial division of labor in Latin America cause those unfree to be considered in turn as "racial others." It is here that the dispute between two republicanisms is, in a certain sense, the same dispute between two nation models.

I propose this construction of racial others based on how both models of the nation mentioned earlier are manifested. In either case, nations are multiracial in their composition, but it is necessary to think mainly about their political configuration as opposed to merely their demographic composition. It is the political configuration that determines whether the place of the "racial other" is established on the basis of differences that seek a racial hierarchy or as a matter of difference between life and death.

This chapter considers events from the nineteenth and early twentieth centuries up until the mid-twentieth century. In this sense, I extend López-Alves's argument to demonstrate how "racial others" continued to use political, legal, and cultural instruments to reject notions of exclusionary citizenship that went beyond the first two decades of the twentieth century. I am also interested in demonstrating how interracial alliances were part of the development of these strategies and, at the same time, one of the particularities of the production of modernity in Latin America.

The struggle of interracial coalitions indicates that the nation's project is not closed but is a constant conflict production. Under such conditions, state violence is the despotic expression of the will to exclude. In other words, its necropolitical derivation. In turn, these coalitions show how political agendas are necessary to seek control of institutions, reforms, or political power to aim at the equality of the unfree. Thus, the struggles of the "racial others" have been crucial in shaping the nation-state, or, in other words, nation building is a work that the racial others, through the strategies and resources at their disposal, have historically undertaken.

A Historical Sociology of Interracial Alliances

This chapter addresses the formation of nations in Latin America in the period opened by the Haitian Revolution in 1804 and up to the national-popular governments in the first half of the twentieth century. I argue that it is possible to locate the confrontation between the two nation models by looking at this period in Latin American history. This perspective allows us to address the production of interracial alliances as a strategy to counteract the pretension of building nation-states through exclusionary citizenship.

I call "interracial alliances" the building process of collectives integrated by Black, Indigenous, mulatto, mestizo, or white people for political purposes. These alliances are contingent and circumscribed in the power relations structured since colonialism. Nevertheless, in the dispute for nonexclusionary citizenship, these strategic alliances contribute significantly to the nation's construction, demanding the expansion of citizenship in terms of equality.

This perspective allows us to go beyond the analysis focused on mestizaje as an ideology of domination in Latin America or on the condition of ambiguity that traverses the mestizo subject. Moreover, this perspective emphasizes a different reading in which the "racial others" appear essentially opposed to the project of state or national community construction by privileging an identity discourse. Just to be clear, mestizaje did function politically as a discourse of domination. Nevertheless, the complexity of the Nation in Latin America requires consideration of the agency of the "racial others." In the end, following Mariátegui, the concern is about thinking on the processes of formation of social identities "not by relying on essentialism but instead through the materiality produced by experience and social consciousness."[6]

As we shall see, interracial coalitions are an expression of the production of social consciousness. This definition does not mean that social class divisions were absent in these coalitions. On the contrary, interracial alliances were conflicting and contradictory. Nor were they perennial. However, their value is not episodic, but structural in the construction of states and nations because, as Coronel says, historical conflicts over citizenship contribute to an accumulation of historical struggles renewed in periods of crisis.[7]

I draw on historiographical work on the formation of the nation in Latin America and the Caribbean to argue how the "racial others," through alliances, reframed the political conflict around citizenship. To this end, I combine into three groups secondary sources about seven countries in the region that allow us to glimpse at least three elements of the configuration of such a conflict: the political ideals and interests that allow the formation of interracial alliances, the ways in which the debate on race forces the extension of the conception of citizenship, and the conditions that cause the weakening or dissolution of interracial alliances.

The first refers to the struggle against slavery in response to how the political or colonial elites, white or Creole, implemented slave systems on the island of Hispaniola, in Cuba, and in Colombia in the nineteenth century. The second refers to the articulation between Indigenous people (mainly peasants) and mestizos (predominantly urban dwellers) in Bolivia and Ecuador. The third discusses how the authoritarianism employed in building an exclusionary nation model led to genocidal violence against "racial others" in Guatemala and the Dominican Republic in the first half of the twentieth century. In both cases, violence was part of modernization.

In each of the cases analyzed, it is not possible to encapsulate the totality of the nation-building processes within the historical moments on which I focus in this work. An attempt at such a circumscription would lead us to reductionistic analyses and to the misguided notion that the production of the "racial other" can be defined as quintessentially democratic, oligarchic, popular, or authoritarian. On the contrary, the cases analyzed from the nineteenth and twentieth centuries are chosen to demonstrate the Latin American and Caribbean dynamism in terms of nation building, the dispute over citizenship, and the contributions of interracial alliances.

Antiracism, Republicanism, and the Struggle for Equality in Haiti, Cuba, and Colombia

In his major work *Black Jacobins*, C. L. R. James highlighted the material and existential conditions of the antislavery, antiracist, and anticapitalist revolution in the French colony of Saint-Domingue. Haiti occupied a central place of accumulation by slavery for France and was pivotal in adjusting imperial forces between England, Spain, France, and the United States' nascent empires.

For James, analysis of the Haitian Revolution (1791–1804) involves considering the forces of slave insurrections, the systems of negotiation between actors and political authorities, the imperialist reaction, and the military achievements led by the ex-slave Toussaint-Louverture. Thus, the period of the Haitian Revolution includes the appropriation of the ideals of liberty and equality, especially in light of the Jacobin decree formally abolishing slavery in 1794, Toussaint-Louverture's control over the island of Hispaniola in 1801, the French invasion in 1802 to reinstate slavery, and the seal of independence achieved by the ex-slave army in 1804. Despite the contradictions in this process, the unconditional abolition of slavery and political autonomy from the empire were always ineluctable. The Black slaves' active role in confronting their exploitation and subjugation conditions implied their articulation as an army in liberation wars.

Two elements are fundamental in the formation of the Haitian republic in the framework of nation building. The first has to do with the fundamental and universal form of the revolutionary struggles that include interracial coalitions in the set integrated by revolutionary masses, middle-class sectors, and economic power groups. James says:

> In April 1792, not yet three years after the fall of the Bastille, the white Patriots in Port-au-Prince were being besieged by a composite army of royalist commandants, white planters, brown-skinned Mulattoes, and black slaves, none of them constrained but all for the time being free and equal partners. No doubt most of the rich were only awaiting the restoration of "order" to put the slaves back in their places again, but the mere fact of the revolutionary association and the temporary equality meant that the old spell was broken and things would never be the same again.[8]

In his analysis of *Black Jacobins*, Nesbitt highlights the leading role of the colonized masses and the coalitions necessary to defeat the great exploiters. It is fundamental that coalitions between Black people and mulattoes meant transcending the class differences between these two groups, as did the integration of white planters from the beginning of the Haitian Revolution's uprisings.[9]

The second element is how the Haitian Revolution constituted a countermodernity.[10] For Grüner, the Haitian Revolution, by questioning the structure of colonialism in terms of race and class, constitutes the historical event without which there would be no possibility of an actual revolution of universal scope. Thus, Article 14 of the constitution of the nascent republic of Haiti, "all Haitians would henceforth be known as 'blacks,'" declares that the revolution is "no longer only political, it was also (inseparably) social and ethnocultural or racial."[11]

Consequently, the Haitian Revolution created a reality that broke with the liberal-modern continuum by embarking on republican state-building projects with a narrative of emancipation that contested the contradictorily universalist but exclusionary version embodied by the French Republic. Probably the most significant lesson of the universalism of the Haitian Revolution is that, on the foundation of a society of equals "achieving freedom and Independence, color was made no bar to political participation."[12]

In other scenarios, the formation of nation-states involved the decisive intervention of Afro-descendant populations during the independence process. Such is the case of the Cuban independence process, as well as that of Afro-Colombians during the civil wars between conservatives and liberals in the nineteenth century. In Colombia's case, Sanders analyzes how interracial alliances allowed subaltern groups to achieve social and political rights in the nation's formation.

The Afro-Colombian populations of the southwestern region negotiated their access to citizenship in a political-military alliance with the liberal party between 1840 and 1870, leading to the mobilization of interracial armies. Liberal antislavery ideals and public manumission ceremonies by some supporters of the liberal party led Afro-descendants to align themselves with a political option to abolish slavery.

Faced with the conservative will to deny free Afro-Colombians the right to cultivate their own land, the Afro-Colombians militarily ensured the triumph of the Liberal Party, which was already in power. The defeat of the conservatives in 1851 meant the abolition of slavery. In turn, Afro-Colombians' mobilization allowed the Liberal Party to hold power long enough to influence Afro-Colombian populations' inclusion in the construction of the national community and several social conquests.

Afro-Colombians, who had been liberated as part of this alliance, while not enfranchised, played a critical role in the popularity of the Liberal Party among the working class. Sanders demonstrates how, through the Liberal Party, Afro-Colombians not only created their own political current (taking the name "popular liberals") but also were irreplaceable in the party's dynamism and electoral success in the popular electorate.[13] By appropriating participatory structures such as "democratic societies," the popular liberals pressured their allies to support a radical discourse on land rights. One of the most active democratic societies of the popular liberals was the Palmira Democratic Society. In 1868, it pushed before the national government for the right to use the land against landowners' prohibitions on the collection of firewood and the occupation of the margins of large estates.

Both the Liberal Party and Afro-Colombians depended on this alliance to remain in power. However, the alliance was severely weakened when the liberal elites refused to distribute land equitably and guarantee the right of Afro-descendants to property, which led to the conservatives regaining power. Despite the setbacks in social conquests sought by the conservatives, the political and interracial alliance allowed the nation to see that "politics was not only a contest between factions of elite gentlemen whose clients followed them mindlessly but also a space that subalterns could appropriate and reframe, even given their limited means."[14]

Besides, the intervention of people of African descent in their respective nations' formations involved the controversy around racial democracy. The myth of racial democracy, specially formulated in Brazil and popularized by the sociologist Gilberto Freyre, holds that Brazil's racial mixing would have created a society with equal opportunities for white and Black people. The myth of racial democracy was rightly criticized for its elitist origin, functioning as an immobilizer of the Afro-Brazilian population and overlapping the racist violence against the Black population in Brazil.

The case of Cuba is different from Brazil's situation and allows us to problematize the exclusionary model of the nation and its conflictual relationship with the myth of racial democracy. In Cuba, slavery abolition and racial equality were part of the nationalist rhetoric at independence.[15] On the strength of colonial control, Cuban independence could not have been achieved without an interracial alliance. The Cuban army was composed of whites, mulattoes, and Cubans in a nationalist project that, in the first republic of 1901, inspired the founding myth of the "racial fraternity."

In his analysis of the myth of racial democracy in Cuba, de la Fuente states that this case exemplifies "the capacity of subordinate groups to appropriate and manipulate the nation-state's cultural project to their own advantage."[16] Afro-Cubans reappropriated the nation's foundational myth based on racial democracy as a political instrument to legitimize their participation and inclusion in society. While white elites manipulated José Martí's discourse to accuse Afro-Cubans of being "racist" when they demanded racial equality, Afro-Cubans "presented Martí's racially fraternal republic a goal to be fulfilled, rather than an achievement."[17] This appropriation allowed Afro-Cubans to demand equality in social, political, and economic life. In particular, Afro-Cubans challenged the narrative that Black freedom was a product of white generosity and emphasized the republic as a product of their creation and that the racially equal Nation should become a reality.

This political strategy does not mean that, effectively, Afro-Cubans achieved the historical production of a racially fraternal society, but it does mean that there are two forces or two projects conflicted in the center of the formation of the nation: a national project of exclusionary citizenship versus a national project that derives its legitimacy from an inclusive approach to citizenship.

Even when the United States significantly influenced the new republic's administration (between 1899 and 1902), Cuban nationalism functioned as a brake, slowing the propagation of scientific racism from the Global North. In fact, in the 1901 Constituent Assembly, Afro-Cubans' participation in the shaping of the nation was enough to defeat the United States' interest in denying universal suffrage to the illiterate (and consequently excluding the majority of Afro-Cubans). With the right to vote, Afro-Cubans gained an important influence in the country's political life in the following decades, even though racist discourses, especially against Afro-Cuban political organizations, were not extinguished. In this sense, the most relevant case was the massacre of the members of the Independent Party of Color in 1912. This popular party legitimately pursued the political representation of the Black population and the improvement of Cubans' living conditions. The party was accused of being racist, was legally prohibited by a constitutional amendment, and its leaders and members were massacred by the Cuban government.[18] Once again, the manipulation of Martí's rhetoric in Cuban elites' hands served to continue racial inequality. Nevertheless, Afro-Cubans continued to dispute what the nation should mean in the following decades and made it a central issue in the process that led to the 1940 constitution.[19]

The three cases respond to the formation of alliances inspired by ideals of equality, were ways of extending the concept of citizenship to counteract an exclusionary spirit, and note the challenges that limited the ultimate efficacy of these historical alliances.

In Colombia, the formation of interracial alliances found its limits when free Black people demanded a structural reform guaranteeing land ownership. Among the elite liberals, there was a conception of equality between races in social and political terms, but not in economic terms, while the popular liberals considered this a fundamental factor in constituting themselves as actual citizens. In Cuba, the manipulation of the white elites' national discourse made it possible to accuse the most visible political organization of the Black republicans of being "racist" and to incite homicidal violence against the Independent Party of Color.

In turn, the three cases allow us to understand how the ideals of equality in Latin America affected the construction of the national community, not exclusively as a concession of power within the elites' hegemony but as a process of political struggle.

In Haiti, the revolutionary struggle implied the appropriation of the ideals of liberty and equality, which, because of the antislavery bent, broke with the abstract discourse around the republic. That is to say, the production of justice with equality necessarily implied the condemnation of racism as a mechanism of justification of accumulation by exploitation but also by annihilation. In Colombia, the fusion between difference and inequality was on the conservatives' ideological side; however, the alliance between liberal politicians and Afro-Caucanos allowed for an original popular version of liberalism. In Cuba, Black people disputed with whites the strategic use of the myth of racial fraternity, revealing two national projects in dispute. Although in Haiti, the leadership of the ex-slaves in the armies stands out, in all cases, the emancipatory mobilizations of a large part of the Black population translated into valid resources for the nation's attempt to constitute itself in democratic terms. Within the framework of this dispute, "the racial others," even from strategic alliances, read the nation as their own project and citizenship as their conquest.

Indigenous, Peasant, and Mestizo Political Articulations in Bolivia and Ecuador

In Bolivia and Ecuador, the two models of nationhood were disputed in the first half of the twentieth century. Understanding this dispute requires going beyond the dualistic perspective that separates Indigenous and non-Indigenous protest in these two Andean countries.

In the 1920s, Bolivia's Indigenous communities saw their leaders establish alliances with the workers' radical forces. These alliances represented a shift from the nineteenth century in which the Indigenous allied with fragments of the liberal and republican elite to contest control of the state. Such a shift mainly came from a selective use of law to counter the colonial legacy and the use of mobilization to claim their land rights from a discourse of equality.[20]

This background is fundamental concerning Bolivian national life's most significant milestone in the twentieth century. In 1952, the National Revolutionary Movement (Movimiento Nacionalista Revolucionario, MNR) carried out a coup against the military government presided by Hugo Ballivián and initiated the "National Revolution." The analysis of interracial alliances goes beyond the thesis that reduces Indigenous groups' role to adherence to mining unions or leftist organizations. On the contrary, the interracial uprisings nurtured an accumulation of subaltern sectors' struggles in the history of the democratic struggle for social, economic, and political justice. Other examples of these alliances date back at least to the late 1920s when the urban group Túpac Amaru collaborated with rural Indigenous people or urban activists who collaborated with workers in the hacienda strikes of 1939.

In her historiographical work, Gotkowitz argues that the 1947 strikes and revolutions carried out by interracial and cross-class articulations that were woven in opposition to the populist government of Gualberto Villarroel (1943–1946) were fundamental to the 1952 revolution.

It was during the Villarroel government that, in 1944, the abolition of forced labor was decreed, and the Indigenous Aymara leader Francisco Chipana and the Indigenous Quechua leader Dionisio Miranda presided over the Bolivian Indigenous Congress in 1945. The most significant value is perhaps the democratizing effect of expanding the debate on citizenship, despite the indigenist and paternalistic policies of the Villarroel government. The Indigenous people denounced the state's desire to ignore them as political actors and made interpretations of the law abolishing forced labor, which broadened the government's reforms and nourished the first proposals for agrarian reform in 1953.

The uprisings in haciendas and communities in Cochabamba, Chuquisaca, Tarija, Oruro, and La Paz between January and June 1947 denounced the illegal practices through which the rural population was being kept under domination. Although slavery in Bolivia was formally abolished in 1880, in the mid-twentieth century, the Indigenous people demanded "the end of slavery," and with it an end to the humiliation and hierarchies imposed by landowners. Thus, they integrated demands for land rights and tenure, formal schooling, unionization, and Indigenous local government in their discourse.

The Indigenous uprisings in the rural areas of Apoyapa and Tapacarí were integrated with strikes and mobilizations in La Paz and Cochabamba. Some members of the police and local authorities even collaborated with the uprisings.[21]

The interracial struggles rejected the restriction of citizenship rights to the urban sector's inhabitants and condemned the exploitation of Indigenous peoples and the peasantry. Racist arguments about the characteristics of rural dwellers, mostly Indigenous, show how the construction of the "racial other" led to an exclusionary model of nationhood throughout the twentieth century. Such racism was challenged by the vindication of the Indigenous identities. The vindication of ethnic identities did not suppose a denial of their identities as political subjects.[22]

The centralization of taxes and land dispossession by the oligarchic castes against the peasantry and the Indigenous were causes for articulating the popular subjects with the Bolivian Revolution. However, MNR's policies of guaranteeing land tenure to a fraction of the peasantry and army sectors provoked the weakening of the national-popular project and the conditions for a military-peasant pact.

At the time of the MNR-led Bolivian Revolution (1952–1964), the alliances that developed between the left, the labor movement, the Indigenous movement, and the peasantry could not sustain the revolution. The lack of structural tools to guarantee material conditions for popular sectors was accompanied by the orthodox left's instrumentalism.[23] Therefore, the MNR articulated the national anti-imperialist desire, the peasantry, and the ruling class, taking away the capacity of power and action within the leftist movements.

In the northern Andes, in March 1935, the Ecuadorian and communist militant Joaquín Gallegos Lara (1909–1947) signed four pages in which he describes the meeting that took place on May 1, 1934, at the Casa del Obrero in Quito in which the Indigenous leader Ambrosio Lasso (1902–1970) was present. Gallegos Lara, a mestizo writer from the coastal region, penned the memoir while Lasso was imprisoned due to his political activity in the latifundios (i.e., *huasipungos*) in the Central Highlands region.

Gallegos Lara's testimony occurs within the configuration of the political scene in Ecuador that opens from the general strike on November 15, 1922, and intensified in 1934 and the decade after. This period was marked by a series of strikes and uprisings throughout the country. The 1922 strike unleashed the repression ordered by President José Tamayo, in which the army caused the deaths of approximately three hundred workers in Guayaquil. The years 1934, 1935, and 1936 were crucial in social movements that integrated Indigenous and urban workers. In 1944, the communist and socialist parties and part of the army proclaimed the so-called Glorious Revolution against the fraud committed by the Liberal Party.

For Valeria Coronel, the period from the Independence wars to the social crisis of the 1930s is marked by the political articulation of subaltern subjects in forming national identity. In this period, a national-popular articulation of subordinate populations was built through a national alliance between peasant Indigenous organizations against the landed elites, with the support of the Communist Party and legal assistance from the socialists.

The participation and redistribution strategies demanded by the Indigenous and their political inclusion in national life were part of nation-building processes during these decades. For example, institutions such as the Ministerio de Bienestar Social y Trabajo were significant spaces for dialogue between Indigenous peasants and the state regarding land expropriation and labor conflicts.[24]

In 1933, the Socialist Party referred to "the Indian problem," appealing to the recognition of economic, social, political, and cultural aspects of Indigenous population. Three years later, the party declared that it would fight "in favor of the Indian and the *montubio* against their subjection to the inhuman exploitation of the semi-feudal regime that persists in the countryside."[25] In 1938, the socialist congress declared that "the indigenous race" should "receive economic aid from the State and cultural attention for their complete liberation."[26]

The discourse of the Communist Party, led by Ricardo Paredes, differed from that of the Socialist Party by emphasizing the double character of Indigenous exploitation: racial oppression (from the prejudice of the "inferior race") and economic oppression. Communists addressed the ethno-economic nature of the Andean region and the different formations of class consciousness. From the Conference of Indigenous Leaders in 1935, communist activists integrated into their political discourse "the presence of oppressed indigenous nationalities in Ecuador."[27]

Peasants' struggles for land access were deeply politicizing and won them the support of a significant part of the national army. In sum, the 1930s saw the formation of a left-wing popular movement under whose pressure the racial boundaries of citizenship were negotiated.[28]

As in Bolivia's national revolution in 1952, the Ecuadorian Glorious Revolution was preceded by an accumulation of Indigenous and interracial struggles that disputed the nation model and contributed to the formation of social identities incorporating consciousness around citizenship.

However, during the constituent process that followed the revolution (1944–1945), the working classes' interests were betrayed by their representatives. Except for the communist Ricardo Paredes, as the representative elected by the Indigenous organizations, the assembly members (mostly members of the mestizo elite) had a paternalist and assimilationist vision that contradicted Indigenous participation in the Glorious Revolution. Indeed, analysis of the assembly's debates attests to the subordinate populations' weak power and the strong influence of the traditional elites. From both the right and the left, many assembly members were reluctant to extend citizenship and voting rights to illiterate and marginalized populations, such as the urban working poor, Indigenous peoples, and women. Indigenous people were even considered a risk to national unity by the assembly.

For Becker, the constitutional outcome of 1945 was mainly due to the failure of the leftist organizations' strategy of backing the populist leader Velasco Ibarra to assume the presidency after the 1944 revolution.[29] Betraying the leftist bases that supported him, Velasco Ibarra banned the Communist Party, repealed the new 1945 constitution, and reinstated the 1906 constitution guaranteeing the continuity of the latifundia.

In both Bolivia and Ecuador, nation building included the struggle against the exclusion of racial others from alliances with leftist political sectors. These interracial alliances were vital in the popular use of rights for demands for control over capital and racial justice. Among the political ideals that allowed the formation of such alliances was the goal of building a legal base that would break the continuity of colonial forms of exploitation at the cultural and material levels.

The model of the nation based on exclusive citizenship was restored in accordance with the vision of the ruling classes, which came after the revolutions in both countries. In Bolivia, the modernization project promoted by the MNR went backward in the discourse of national sovereignty; in Ecuador, the National Assembly that succeeded the 1944 revolution did not incorporate the racial content into the nation model pursued until the moment of its repeal in 1945. Nevertheless, these two cases show that the character of a national project cannot be taken for granted but is always subject to the contest between the will of elites (whether paternalistic or despotically exclusive) and resistance from "racial others" whose struggles also influence the construction of states.

Production and Annihilation of the Racial Other during Dictatorships in the Dominican Republic and Guatemala

During the dictatorship of Rafael Leonidas Trujillo (1930–1938), the Dominican Republic's state configuration included economic modernization and the formation of state institutions within structural reforms. Given that in the 1930s, the state had not come to control the border zone between the Dominican Republic and Haiti, daily social life was crossed not by national differences (between Haitians and Dominicans) but by family ties, friendship, and commercial exchanges.

In his analysis of the origins of despotism, the historian Richard Turits demonstrates how Trujillo became an anti-Haitian racist, partly as a measure to legitimize his ability to control the territory under his command, as well as to generate a nation. In October 1937, General Rafael Leonidas Trujillo ordered his army to kill all Haitians who lived on the Dominican Republic's northwestern boundary, which bordered Haiti.

Before the Trujillato, the border between these two countries was not delimited, and Dominicans and Haitians lived in a porous zone between different cultures in which national or racial boundaries did not demarcate their system of relations. Cultures and ethnicities were rather multiple and intermingled. Thus, for the genocidal army, coming from outside, it was not easy to differentiate who was Haitian and who was not. They confronted questions about what was to be done with the Haitians whose families had lived several generations in the Dominican Republic? What about those who were children of Haitians and Dominicans? Were they Haitians or not?

The army used the pronunciation of Spanish words as a supposed test to decide who was Haitian. In the testimonies collected by Turits, words such as *perejil* (parsley) or *tijera* (scissors) showed the ability to pronounce the *r* in Spanish, and so their mispronunciation was a sign of Haitian identity. The same is true in its opposite. Before an army guard, it was not necessary to show a birth certificate while you could pronounce *perejil*. The pronunciation was "a false proof," "a mock confirmation," or as Achille Mbembe states, the performance of "a phantasmagoria" that transformed Haitians into "foreigners," as well as people of African origin were transformed into "blacks."[30]

Around fifteen thousand ethnic Haitians were slaughtered by "machete" in the Haiti–Dominican Republic border region.[31] This fact was critical because the policies of establishing the border between Haiti and the Dominican Republic became an articulating axis of the national construction process furthered by the Trujillato.

Pro-Trujillo intellectuals produced discursive resources emphasizing the need to rescue the nation's sovereignty from other invaders through the values of patriotic identity, which made possible the emergence of discriminatory and racist practices concerning Haitians. At the same time that this racist ideology was being further institutionalized, a modernizing agenda initiated in 1934 expanded, creating a sector of Dominican landowning peasants. Thus, the peasantry lost its autonomy and became the social base of support for the authoritarian regime.[32]

The Haitian massacre produced ethnic and cultural estrangement between Dominicans and Haiti's inhabitants, whereby civilians and the military force exercised the right to defend and purge the nation of foreign invaders during the dictatorship.

Thus, racism played a decisive role in the reconfiguration of the pattern of accumulation among the power groups in the Dominican Republic and the modernization of the productive structures, forcing peasants to leave free breeding and cultivation, to work under the economic conditions of the dictatorship, and to become accomplices in violent practices. Racism was not a cause but a product of the nationalist aim of authoritarian and exclusionary citizenship.

Different from the Dominican Republic, in Guatemala, during the nineteenth century, the Maya-Quiché communities and their elites were recognized within the oligarchic state's elitist project. The Indigenous mythology's strength made it impossible to ignore the Maya, so they tried to include their aristocracies in the landed republic.

During the 1920s and 1930s, there was a turn around the Indigenous problem and the nation's problem. Although during the 1920s, the intellectuals who addressed the Indigenous issue were inspired by the civilizing ideal of nineteenth-century liberalism (i.e., "the Indigenous must be civilized"), they were also under the influence of positivist racism, which ranged from eugenic theories to assimilationist proposals.[33] However, in the 1930s, the Indigenous question ceased to be linked to the nation's discourses and strengthened policies aimed at "improving the race" by banning Indigenous people's reproduction or promoting their direct annihilation.

For Casaús, during the 1930s, journalists and intellectuals circulated racist discourses that considered the Indian as "incapable of regenerating himself" and therefore an obstacle to development. One of the exemplary cases of this discourse is the racist writer, journalist, and politician Carlos S. Chinchilla, whose statements about the impossibility of "the Indian coming out of his lethargy" permeated the long public discourse of the twentieth century.[34] At the foundation of the twentieth-century Guatemalan state, racism made the white elites' leadership and exploitation of Indigenous labor viable during the thirteen-year dictatorship under General Jorge Ubico.[35]

Debates on the social and political history of nation-state formation in Guatemala also involve the complexity resulting from the struggle to generate equations between popular actors with a democratic discourse of citizenship that, in different episodes, challenged "the nation without Indians." For example, the connection between Maya-Quiché Indigenous communities and socialist parties in the 1920s and 1930s generated an identity between the middle-class left and the Indigenous communities that negotiated the agrarian reform in 1952 under Arbenz's government (1951–1954).

The struggle for agrarian reform is part of an accumulation of several decades of political struggles. The pacts of Indigenous social movements (*q'echíes*) and leftist movements in the 1920s, 1930s, and 1940s were significant in disputes around nation building. However, the US-orchestrated coup d'état against Arbenz was the culmination of the ten-year open process of the Guatemalan Revolution that began with the overthrow of Ubico's thirteen-year dictatorship in 1944.

Greg Grandin's analysis of the political work of Indigenous leader José Ángel Icó (1875–1950) and his nephew Alfredo Cucul shows how peasant struggles focused on creating alternative networks of rural power from 1920 to 1954.

The Indigenous people's struggle pursued land rights and the elimination of forced labor. While Icó led a large demonstration to the capital city in 1946, in 1952, Cucul was selected to address an assembly of the Guatemalan Workers' Party in demand for agrarian reform. For opponents of the reform, such as the Catholic Church, the proactivity of Indigenous peoples' protagonist role was considered "a sin of democracy." Cucul's approach was based on the interracial and interclass alliances between Ladinos and Indigenous people that had given rise to a structure of 185 unions in different areas of the country.[36]

The two most significant social conquests of the revolution, the Labor Code of 1947, which abolished all existing vagrancy laws, and the Agrarian Reform of 1952, were the cornerstones for breaking paternalistic ties with the executive or local officials. Also, the discourse of the Indigenous leaders speaks of the broadening of citizenship, since "Cucul's political engagement with a wider world remained rooted in community. He spoke in Q'eqchi,' and his words were broadcast throughout the country."[37]

Although the collaboration of the Ladinos was due to a mixture of "idealism, nationalism, opportunism, and resentment of the power wielded by large *finqueros*," highlighting the interracial alliances is essential to see how nation building and state reform were disputed in Guatemala from the organization of popular actors of different racial status.[38] These organizations were activated from parties such as the Partido Guatemalteco del Trabajo (Guatemalan Labor Party) and from diverse "insurgent" appeals.

However, this process would not last long due to internal pressures and the US intervention in 1954. The Agrarian Reform could hardly be consummated, and with its fall, the former rural powers claimed their land back and organized the counterinsurgency. The National Anticommunist Committee was created, and the violent repression that sought to restore the already-lost old power relations began.

An escalation of violence from the *finqueros* (landowners), with the state's help, quickly taken over by the counterrevolutionaries organized in committees and with the local authorities, attacked the communists through the manipulation of criminal law and unleashed persecution. New technologies and ideologies brought from the United States were necessary to curb the radicalization of the platforms and strategies promoted among leftist groups. The US intervention in Guatemala in 1954 consolidated the racist-authoritarian roots and stifled attempts at social organization, resulting in the annihilation of political militants and the massacre of approximately two hundred thousand Guatemalans, mostly Indigenous, between 1960 and 1996.

Indeed, the literature we have chosen for both cases emphasizes the authoritarian drift of modernization projects that involved genocidal violence against racial others. In the case of Guatemala, this also included mestizo leftist militants. This historiography highlights how dominant elites might use state violence to consolidate exclusionary models of nationhood.

Both cases allow us to see the place of race in an authoritarian and selective integration of the groups that led to the nation's formation. In the so-called Haitian massacre in the Dominican Republic in 1937, the peasants were incorporated through authoritarianism and racism. In Guatemala, this authoritarian integration was made from the production of a civil war. In both the Dominican Republic and Guatemala, important intellectual sectors contributed to forming a racist imaginary based on positivist and eugenic assumptions exploited by the dictatorships.

On the border between the Dominican Republic and Haiti there were forms of ethnic interaction without hierarchy, but in Guatemala, the interactions between Indigenous and mestizos were forged in the heat of political struggle. Although the politics of US intervention in Guatemala slowed the connection between democracy, interracial alliances, and leftist organizations, the memory of these connections speaks to the political tradition of organizing in pursuit of nonexclusionary citizenship.

The critique of serfdom and the possibilities of effective citizenship for Indigenous people with the collective land use were part of the dispute over the form the nation should take. For the interracial coalitions in Guatemala, citizenship meant a guarantee of protection for discriminated groups that would have to come through not only economic reform but also the consolidation of collective rights.

Conclusion

Unlike in Europe, national identity in Latin America and the Caribbean was not built on a glorious past or common historical roots, or on the idea of Manifest Destiny, as in the United States. On the contrary, in Latin America, there was an open conception of the future and a dispute over the nation's model.

To understand the nation's formation in Latin America and the Caribbean, I have framed the production of racial others within the political conflictivity provoked by two competing conceptions of the nation. This article's two models encompass various dimensions of the political processes through which "racial others" and their alliances fought for just social relations and resisted racial or economic subordination.

Among the dimensions encompassed by these models is the appropriation of republican and liberal ideals in antislavery and antiracist struggles, the popular use of the law against the reproduction of various forms of serfdom, the legitimate occupation of institutions of political representation, the demand for collective rights to the use of land, and the end of racial discrimination in social life. Nevertheless, we also find national projects that pursued the racialization of rights, the racist manipulation of republican ideals, the instrumentalization of the political participation of racial others, the refusal to guarantee the ownership of land by racial others, the production of narratives as ideological justifications for genocidal violence, and the intervention of local and international powers to halt democratization processes through genocidal violence. However, this confrontation shows that, contrary to elites' colonial notion of culture, for interracial alliances, overcoming the racist matrix depends on reconfiguring the nation's political terrain.

The sociological approach to the history of interactions between ethnic or racial groups consists of accounting for the political ideals and interests that enable interracial alliances, how racial others contest the exclusionary notion of citizenship, and the legitimate or violent limitations of such alliances within the political arena. These three elements are critical both for the study of other historical moments in the seven cases discussed in this chapter and other scenarios in Latin America and the Caribbean.

NOTES

1. I am grateful to Liliam Fiallo, Germán Chiriboga, and Aaron Yates for their comments. All translations from Spanish are mine.
2. Fernando López-Alves, "Los caminos de la modernidad: Comparando a Europa y Estados Unidos con América Latina," *América Latina Hoy*, no. 57 (2011): 51–77.
3. Mabel Moraña, *Philosophy and Criticism in Latin America: From Mariátegui to Sloterdijk* (Amherst, NY: Cambria, 2020), 53.
4. Carlos Sempat Assadourian, "Modos de producción, capitalismo y subdesarrollo en América Latina," in *Modos de producción en América Latina*, ed. José Aricó (Buenos Aires: Siglo XXI, 1974); López-Alves, "Los caminos de la modernidad."
5. Aylinn Torres Santana, "Signos y realizaciones republicanas en América Latina: Líneas gruesas para el diálogo con los populismos," in *A contracorriente: Materiales para una lectura renovada del populismo*, ed. Luciana Cadahia, Valeria Coronel, and Franklin Ramírez (La Paz: Vicepresidencia del Estado Plurinacional de Bolivia, 2018), 47.
6. Moraña, *Philosophy and Criticism*, 53. See José Carlos Mariátegui, *Seven Interpretive Essays on Peruvian Reality*, trans. Marjory Urquidi (1928, preprint: Austin: University of Texas Press, 1971).
7. Jorge Daniel Vásquez and Bernardo Villegas, "Populismo y ciclos de conflictividad política en el Ecuador: Una entrevista con Valeria Coronel," *Theorein: Revista de Ciencias Sociales* 4, no. 1 (2019): 19.
8. C. L. R. James, *The Black Jacobins* (New York: Vintage Books, 1989), 109–110.
9. Nick Nesbitt, "Fragments of a Universal History: Global Capital, Mass Revolution, and the Idea of Equality," in *The Black Jacobins Reader*, ed. Charles Forsdick and Christian Høgsbjerg (Durham, NC: Duke University Press, 2017).
10. Eduardo Grüner, *The Haitian Revolution. Slavery, Capitalism, and Counter-modernity* (Cambridge, UK: Polity, 2020).
11. Grüner, *The Haitian Revolution*, 181.
12. Gurminder Bhambra, "On the Haitian Revolution and the Society of Equals," *Theory, Culture & Society* 32, no. 7–8 (2015): 268.
13. James Sanders, "Citizens of a Free People: Popular Liberalism and Race in Nineteenth-Century Southwestern Colombia," *Hispanic American Historical Review* 84, no. 2 (2004): 308–309.
14. Sanders, "Citizens of a Free People," 313.
15. Ada Ferrer, *Insurgent Cuba: Race, Nation, and Revolution, 1868–1898* (Chapel Hill: University of North Carolina Press, 1999).
16. Alejandro de la Fuente, "Myths of Racial Democracy: Cuba, 1900–1912," *Latin American Research Review* 34, no. 3 (1999): 42.
17. Fuente, "Myths of Racial Democracy," 52.
18. Tomás Fernández Robaina, *El negro en Cuba, 1902–1958* (Havana: Ciencias Sociales, 1990), 46–103.
19. Julio César Guanche, "La Constitución de 1940: Una reinterpretación," *Cuban Studies*, no. 45 (2017): 66–88.
20. Laura Gotkowitz, *A Revolution for Our Rights* (Durham, NC: Duke University Press, 2007); Forrest Hylton and Sinclair Thomson, *Revolutionary Horizons: Past and Present in Bolivian Politics* (London: Verso, 2007), 47–61.
21. Gotkowitz, *A Revolution*, 260.

22. Hylton and Thomson, *Revolutionary Horizons*, 62-72.
23. Kevin F. Young, "Alianzas revolucionarias del siglo XX en Bolivia: Entre la coalición y la ruptura," *Fuentes* 11, no. 49 (2017): 6-18.
24. Valeria Coronel, "Orígenes de una democracia corporativa: Estrategias para la ciudadanización del campesinado indígena, partidos políticos y reforma territorial en Ecuador (1925-1944)," in *Historia social urbana: Espacios y flujos*, ed. Eduardo Kingman (Quito: FLACSO, 2009).
25. Marc Becker, "Indigenous Nationalities in Ecuadorian Marxist Thought," *A Contracorriente* 5, no. 2 (2008): 43.
26. Becker, "Indigenous Nationalities," 43.
27. Becker, "Indigenous Nationalities," 45.
28. Valeria Coronel, "The Ecuadorian Left during Global Crisis: Republican Democracy, Class Struggle and State Formation (1919-1946)," in *Words of Power, the Power of Words: The Twentieth-Century Communist Discourse in International Perspective*, ed. Giulia Bassi (Trieste, Italy: EUT Edizioni Università di Trieste, 2019).
29. Marc Becker, "State Building and Ethnic Discourse in Ecuador's 1944-1945 Asamblea Constituyente," in *Highland Indians and the State in Modern Ecuador*, ed. Kim Clark and Marc Becker (Pittsburgh, PA: University of Pittsburgh Press, 2007).
30. Richard Turits, "A World Destroyed, a Nation Imposed: The 1937 Haitian Massacre in the Dominican Republic," *Hispanic American Historical Review* 82, no. 3 (2002): 617; Achille Mbembe, *Critique of Black Reason* (Durham, NC: Duke University Press, 2017), 39.
31. Turits, "A World Destroyed," 590.
32. Richard Turits, "Fundamentos del despotismo: Los campesinos, los intelectuales y el Régimen de Trujillo," in *Retrospectiva y perspectiva del pensamiento político dominicano*, ed. Rafael Núñez (Santo Domingo: Dirección de Información, Prensa y Publicidad de la Presidencia, 2005).
33. Marta Elena Casaús, *Genocidio: La máxima expresión del racismo en Guatemala. Una interpretación histórica y una reflexión* (Guatemala City: F&G Editores, 2008), 36.
34. Casaús, *Genocidio*, 39.
35. Casaús, *Genocidio*, 41-2.
36. Greg Grandin, *The Last Colonial Massacre: Latin America in the Cold War* (Chicago: University of Chicago Press, 2011).
37. Grandin, *The Last Colonial Massacre*, 57.
38. Grandin, *The Last Colonial Massacre*, 55.

BIBLIOGRAPHY

Assadourian, Carlos Sempat. "Modos de producción, capitalismo y subdesarrollo en América Latina." In *Modos de Producción en América Latina*, edited by José Aricó, 47-81. Buenos Aires: Siglo XXI, 1974.

Becker, Marc. "Indigenous Nationalities in Ecuadorian Marxist Thought." *A Contracorriente* 5, no. 2 (2008): 1-46.

———. "State Building and Ethnic Discourse in Ecuador's 1944-1945 Asamblea Constituyente." In *Highland Indians and the State in Modern Ecuador*, edited by Kim Clark and Marc Becker, 105-119. Pittsburgh, PA: University of Pittsburg Press, 2007.

Bhambra, Gurminder. "On the Haitian Revolution and the Society of Equals." *Theory, Culture & Society* 32, nos. 7-8 (2015): 267-274.

Casaús, Marta Elena. *Genocidio: La máxima expresión del racismo en Guatemala. Una interpretación histórica y una reflexión*. Guatemala City: F&G Editores, 2008.

Coronel, Valeria. "The Ecuadorian Left during Global Crisis: Republican Democracy, Class Struggle and State Formation (1919-1946)." In *Words of Power, the Power of Words: The Twentieth-Century Communist Discourse in International Perspective*, edited by Giulia Bassi, 315-337. Trieste, Italy: EUT Edizioni Università di Trieste, 2019.

———. "Orígenes de una democracia corporativa: Estrategias para la ciudadanización del campesinado indígena, partidos políticos y reforma territorial en Ecuador (1925-1944)." In *Historia social urbana: Espacios y flujos*, edited by Eduardo Kingman, 323-364. Quito: FLACSO, 2009.

de la Fuente, Alejandro. "Myths of Racial Democracy: Cuba, 1900-1912." *Latin American Research Review* 34, no. 3 (1999): 39-73.

Fernández Robaina, Tomás. *El negro en Cuba, 1902-1958*. Havana: Ciencias Sociales, 1990.

Ferrer, Ada. *Insurgent Cuba: Race, Nation, and Revolution, 1868-1898*. Chapel Hill: University of North Carolina Press, 1999.

Gotkowitz, Laura. *A Revolution for Our Rights*. Durham, NC: Duke University Press, 2007.

Grandin, Greg. *The Last Colonial Massacre: Latin America in the Cold War*. Chicago: University of Chicago Press, 2011.

Grüner, Eduardo. *The Haitian Revolution. Slavery, Capitalism, and Counter-Modernity*. Cambridge, UK: Polity, 2020.

Guanche, Julio César. "La Constitución de 1940: Una reinterpretación." *Cuban Studies*, no. 45 (2017): 66-88.

Hylton, Forrest, and Sinclair Thomson. *Revolutionary Horizons: Past and Present in Bolivian Politics*. London: Verso, 2007.

James, C. L. R. *The Black Jacobins*. New York: Vintage Books, 1989.

López-Alves, Fernando. "Los caminos de la modernidad: Comparando a Europa y Estados Unidos con América Latina." *América Latina Hoy*, no. 57 (2011): 51-77.

Mariátegui, José Carlos. 1928. *Seven Interpretive Essays on Peruvian Reality*. Austin: University of Texas Press, 1971.

Mbembe, Achille. *Critique of Black Reason*. Durham, NC: Duke University Press, 2017.

Moraña, Mabel. *Philosophy and Criticism in Latin America: From Mariátegui to Sloterdijk*. Amherst, NY: Cambria, 2020.

Nesbitt, Nick. "Fragments of a Universal History: Global Capital, Mass Revolution, and the Idea of Equality." In *The Black Jacobins Reader*, edited by Charles Forsdick and Christian Høgsbjerg, 139-161. Durham, NC: Duke University Press, 2017.

Sanders, James. "Citizens of a Free People: Popular Liberalism and Race in Nineteenth-Century Southwestern Colombia." *Hispanic American Historical Review* 84, no. 2 (2004): 277-313.

Torres Santana, Aylinn. "Signos y realizaciones republicanas en América Latina: Líneas gruesas para el diálogo con los populismos." In *A contracorriente: Materiales para una lectura renovada del populismo,* edited by Luciana Cadahia, Valeria Coronel, and Franklin Ramírez, 41-63. La Paz: Vicepresidencia del Estado Plurinacional de Bolivia, 2018.

Turits, Richard. "Fundamentos del despotismo: Los campesinos, los intelectuales y el Régimen de Trujillo." In *Retrospectiva y perspectiva del pensamiento político dominicano,* edited by Rafael Núñez, 60-78. Santo Domingo: Dirección de Información, Prensa y Publicidad de la Presidencia, 2005.

Turits, Richard. "A World Destroyed, a Nation Imposed: The 1937 Haitian Massacre in the Dominican Republic." *Hispanic American Historical Review* 82, no. 3 (2002): 589-635.

Vásquez, Jorge Daniel, and Bernardo Villegas. "Populismo y ciclos de conflictividad política en el Ecuador: Una entrevista con Valeria Coronel." *Theorein: Revista de Ciencias Sociales* 4, no. 1 (2019): 233-253.

Young, Kevin F. "Alianzas revolucionarias del siglo XX en Bolivia: Entre la coalición y la ruptura." *Fuentes* 11, no. 49 (2017): 6-18.

CHAPTER 8

Looking through Layers of Jewishness in Latin America

ARIANA HUBERMAN

To be Jewish is to be at the crossroads of racial and ethnic debates, and while it is not accurate to speak of a Jewish race, for there are Jews of almost every race on the planet, referring to Jews as an ethnicity has also been questioned.[1] This is because of the great diversity that characterizes the group that is the focus of this chapter. And yet Jewish communities worldwide, including in Latin America, have strong identity ties to their ethnic subgroups. Intermarriage and relocation have complicated these categories, but first-generation immigrants and many of their descendants still identify as Ashkenazi Jews from Eastern Europe, Sephardi Jews from North Africa, Turkey, Greece, and the Balkans, as well as Mizrahi Jews from the Middle East (e.g., Iran, Syria, Lebanon). The one thing that Jews tend to share is the feeling of being the Other within. In her famous text *Strangers to Ourselves*, Julia Kristeva traces back the intrinsic element of foreignness inherent in being Jewish to the biblical figure of Ruth the Moabite.[2] Edmond Jabès goes further, proposing that to be Jewish means to keep open the question of difference.[3] For Jews in Latin America, that difference has involved the particularities of the region's historical understanding of race, which is the central thread of this volume.

According to Sandra McGee Deutsch, the issue of race in Latin America includes both cultural and phenotypic characteristics. For example, perceptions of race align with the foundational discourse of civilization (whites) versus barbarism (people of color). She explains that Jews, as ethnic others, confound place of origin (Europe, North of Africa, Middle East) and destination (urban centers versus countryside) with this deeply entrenched binary.[4] In fact, many of them do not belong to either side of the binary: they are not white, but they are not quite racially different, either. The elusiveness of these categories is not unique to Latin American Jews. Still, their experience takes on particular tones in the highly diverse cultural and historical contexts that have affected their experience in the region since the beginning. The hybrid nature of Latin American culture, which consists of Indigenous, Spanish, Christian, Muslim, Asian, African, and the rest of the cultural wealth brought by free migration and forced relocation to the continent, has shaped the Jewish experience and cultural productions of Jews in Latin America.

Their experience is also marked by economic, religious, and cultural disparities. Each migrant has their own set of circumstances and personal journey. This is why it is essential to discuss the historical perception of the Jew as an Other through the lens of intersectionality. Awareness about how social constructions of race and ethnicity, class, religion, gender, and sexual orientation differ according to place of origin, host country, and the changes that have taken place over time is essential to get a sense of the complex history and the great diversity that characterizes this group.

In this chapter, I discuss key moments in the history of Jews in Latin America, highlighting the central role of changing attitudes toward race and ethnicity that have framed their experience. Central to this is the interaction between Jews and non-Jews, including waves of antisemitism and self-segregation, as well as a continuous integration into host countries by participating in politics, education, professions, community organizations, and more. Some of the main themes that are prominent in this group's cultural production include the intergenerational conflicts that resulted from the process of transculturation by the second and third generations. These are evident in their use of language (e.g., Yiddish, Ladino, Haketia, Arabic, German, Hebrew) and divergent attitudes toward religion, tradition, gender, and sexuality.[5] The chapter ends with an introduction to the current bibliography about the Latin American Jews in the United States, Israel, and Canada.

Historical Overview

Our story begins in Sepharad, which is usually remembered by the edict of expulsion of Jews on March 31, 1492.[6] Reyes Col-Telechea proposes that we focus on the positive and collaborative relationship between Christians, Muslims, and Jews that lasted twelve centuries, which allowed for the flourishing of these three cultures.[7] Religious tolerance was at the root of cultural and economic prosperity and collaboration between the three major religious groups.[8] Of particular note is the Renaissance in Al-Andalus during the tenth century. Sadly, the arrival of more fundamentalist leaders in the eleventh century represented the beginning of the end of this fruitful chapter, which culminates with Queen Isabel and King Fernando taking over Granada and unifying Spain under Catholicism. Interestingly, for the Jews of Sepharad, the fifteenth century witnessed both: compulsory conversions and a golden age for Jewish mysticism, as well as Talmudic studies.[9]

Jewish presence in Latin America can be traced back to Columbus's crew, the Spanish Conquest, and colonial times.[10] After the 1492 expulsion edict, Jews were forced to convert to Catholicism or flee to countries such as Portugal, the Netherlands, North Africa (Algeria, Morocco, and Tunisia), Greece, and Turkey. Religious intolerance reached Portugal about five years later, in 1497—so Jews fled, hiding their identity. Even though they were not allowed to migrate to Spanish colonies legally, many went and kept practicing Judaism in hiding, risking being captured and killed. Some of the *cristianos nuevos* (newly converted) were actually crypto-Jews whose descendants kept some Jewish rituals and beliefs over generations. Many confess not actually knowing that some of their family traditions stemmed from Judaism.[11] Crypto-Jews settled in the new urban centers in Peru, Mexico, and Cartagena, and farther south. They eventually integrated with the majority Christian and mestizo population but remained on the margins of colonial society. During the eighteenth century, Curaçao became a hub for Jews to practice openly in the Americas. The Jews of Curaçao, the north of Brazil, and other sea merchants from harbor cities in the Caribbean were originally from the Netherlands, Portugal, and other places where Sephardi Jews had escaped in the fifteenth century. They became a source of financial support for Jewish communities in the United States and elsewhere in the continent. This group is distinct for its preference for rootlessness and transnationalism, which stems from the nature of transatlantic commerce.[12]

Immigration Patterns

Jews became visible in public life in Argentina, Mexico, Peru, and Chile by the second part of the nineteenth century, during urbanization and economic and social development. Several new nations instigated immigration in more or less intentional ways. But Jews did not start arriving in large numbers until World War I with the intensification of pogroms (violent mob attacks by non-Jews) in Eastern Europe. By 1889 there were a few thousand Jews of different origins, languages, and trades living in Latin America, such as Sephardi Jews of Portuguese descent in the Caribbean; Ashkenazi Jews from France, Germany, Switzerland, and England in urban centers across the continent; and Moroccan Sephardim in Amazonian urban centers, attracted there by business related to the extraction of natural rubber (Brazil and Peru). They were heterogeneous regarding religious observance, languages they spoke, and the various levels of assimilation to their countries of origin. Their cultural customs varied greatly, but Sephardi Jews were in the majority.[13] This was the case until the arrival of large contingents of Ashkenazi Jews from Central and Eastern Europe to Latin America between 1889 and 1917. At the beginning of the twentieth century, of the estimated 150,000 Jews who lived in Latin America, the vast majority settled in Argentina, and about 80 percent of them were Ashkenazi.[14]

The Agricultural Dream

One of the most interesting chapters of the history of Jews in Latin America is the one that took place in the countryside.[15] This experiment was conceived as one of the possible answers to save the large populations of Jews suffering violence and extreme poverty in Eastern Europe. One solution was to seek the emigration of Jews to Palestine, today's Israel, following Theodor Herzl's Zionist movement (1897). Another solution was proposed by Baron Maurice de Hirsch, founder of the Jewish Colonization Association, or JCA (1891).[16] They bought lands in Palestine, Turkey, the United States, Argentina, Brazil, and other places in Latin America. The first group of 824 Jews that arrived to work in the countryside came in 1889 on a ship named *Weser*. The group was initially headed to Entre Ríos, Argentina, but their arrival was plagued by a series of misfortunes.[17] In 1889 only about 150,000 Jews had access to agricultural work in Europe. Many of the immigrants who signed up to come through the JCA did not have that opportunity. But they were inspired by the Jewish Enlightenment movement, the Haskalah, which identified working the land, a mitzvah specified in the book of Genesis, with physical, mental, and spiritual health for the Jews of Europe and many others. It represented a way out of the brutal violence of the pogroms in Russia and Eastern Europe. The original plan was to help 3,250,000 Jews to flee Eastern Europe. However, at its highest point, the JCA managed to have only 33,000 people working the land in Argentina, where they had the most success.[18] The organization managed to purchase about 617,000 hectares of land. Immigrants arriving in these agricultural settlements had their travel expenses covered and received between 185 and 370 acres of land, a house with two rooms, a kitchen, a water hole, ten to twenty cows, up to fifty chickens, seeds, working tools, and some money for the first few months. But they had to repay the land and house in low-interest monthly installments. The JCA rules were stringent regarding late payments, and the children of the colonists could not receive loans to buy land. These structural limits to prosperity and growth, as well as the pull of better education in urban centers, prompted the youth to leave, which represented the beginning of the end of the agricultural dream in Argentina.[19] Alberto Gerchunoff's seminal text *The Jewish Gauchos* (1910) is the best-known text of this time period, but there are many others.[20]

Similar but less successful attempts were made in Bolivia and the Dominican Republic. Bolivia received a late contingent of immigrants from Germany and Austria as World War II was breaking, and there were virtually no other options for Jews to flee their countries. The poor Andean nation represented a stopover on the refugees' way to the United States or Argentina.[21] Most of the German and Austrian Jews who arrived in Bolivia were highly assimilated and chose to settle in the main cities. Still, a small group of them tried to work land purchased by the mining entrepreneur Mauricio Hochschild, who had established himself in Bolivia with additional funds from the Refugee Economic Corporation and the Agro-Joint. Between 1940 and 1952, about forty-two families attempted to work the high-altitude, challenging terrain. These lands required Indigenous agricultural techniques that the immigrants lacked. The experiment lasted about six years. The cultural distance between these European immigrants and the local Aymara population of the highlands proved an insurmountable barrier.[22] In *Hotel Bolivia,* Leo Spitzer studies photos taken by members of this Austrian Jewish refugee group portraying Indigenous peoples' customs and daily tasks. He reads these portraits of the exotic "Other" as bringing back a "sense of 'civilized' self, and perhaps confirm a vision of themselves that many of them may have begun to question during their trauma of displacement, a vision of European cultural modernity and progress."[23] These pictures reveal the complicated and uneven gaze between two ethnic Others in Latin America, which I revisit at the end of the chapter.[24]

A similar short-lived attempt at the agricultural dream occurred in the Dominican Republic between 1938 and 1945. Trujillo's government invited Jewish immigrants, among other Europeans, with the goal of "whitening" society. He offered them a banana plantation named Sosúa.[25] Only young single men in optimal physical conditions were admitted to emigrate there, which proved highly shortsighted, especially given the urgency of saving Jews from Nazism.[26] Most of the men who came to Sosúa came from urban centers in Germany and Austria. The land was largely barren, and by comparison with the JCA, they were given many fewer resources: only two hectares of land, a house, two cows, a horse, and working tools. The immigrants were isolated from the rest of society, so integration was impossible. Ultimately, only about eight hundred people worked in Sosúa, even though about three thousand received visas to establish themselves in the Dominican Republic.

Latin America and the Holocaust

Latin American nations' attitudes varied toward Nazism and the Holocaust. Argentina's relationship with Nazi Germany was particularly complex.[27] The Nazi Party established an office in Buenos Aires in the early 30s. In 1937, German schools and other institutions founded an organization to oppose Nazism under the name "the other Germany"[28] Two years later, President Roberto Ortiz dissolved the Nazi Party office in Argentina, but activities continued clandestinely. During those years, Brazil and Argentina openly restricted the quota of Jewish refugees. From 1933 to 1943, only about twenty-four thousand Jews were allowed into Brazil and between thirty-two thousand and thirty-nine thousand in Argentina. During World War II, only Argentina and Chile continued diplomatic relations with Germany until the former declared war under the pressure of the United States in March 1945.[29]

Consolidation of Jewish Communities in Latin America

The Jewish community in Latin America peaked by the mid-twentieth century, with its most significant community of about 450,000 people in Argentina. They expressed their migratory experience and culture through newspapers, theater, radio, and television, first in the languages they brought with them: Yiddish, Arabic, Haketia, and Ladino, but eventually, they started sharing their culture in Spanish. Books were a central tenet of Jewish Latin American culture.[30] Some of the most salient figures are authors Alberto Gerchunoff (Argentina), César Tiempo (Argentina), Moacyr Scliar (Brazil), Germán Rozenmacher (Argentina), Isaac Goldemberg (Perú), Isaac Chocrón (Venezuela), Manuela Fingueret (Argentina), Margo Glantz (Mexico), Isaac Goldemberg (Peru), José Kozer (Cuba), Teresa Porzecanski (Uruguay), Marjorie Agosín (Chile and United States), Tamara Kamenszain (Argentina), Perla Suez (Argentina), Rosita Kalina (Costa Rica), and Angelina Muñiz Huberman (Mexico).[31] But film, music, and theater were also crucial in the production of Latin American Jewish culture.[32] In terms of earning a living, Jews followed a familiar path. Starting at the end of the nineteenth century, newly arrived immigrants from North Africa, the Middle East, and Eastern Europe tended to work as peddlers, selling small household items and fabrics in installments.[33] This was true for Jewish immigrants in most countries in Latin America. But this activity reinforced local anti-Semitic tropes, and it was expected to be temporary and left behind as soon as immigrants could raise enough to own a store or start a small factory.

Other lines of work that Jews gravitated to also reflected the skills they brought with them. In Eastern Europe, a large majority of men and women worked at textile factories, so they worked in small factories. Eventually, many managed to start their own business and hire new arrivals.[34] There were Jewish immigrants with artisanal skills who worked as carpenters, jewelers, and shoemakers, to name a few. And like most immigrants, they hoped their children would have more skilled professions. Many in the second generation became lawyers, accountants, architects, psychologists, dentists, and doctors, while others became part of the bourgeoisie through industry. Many have followed the path of letters and education, becoming teachers, professors, and scholars.

When it comes to focusing on Jewish culture in their daily lives, secular socialist and communist Jews, especially the first generation, were passionate about Yiddishkeit, which they kept vibrant in theaters, libraries, cultural centers, summer camps, sports clubs, and schools. Their passion for Yiddish culture was paralleled only by their desire to integrate into society and to push forward social justice. However, over time, most Jews in Latin America became part of the neoliberal bourgeois lifestyle of the middle and upper middle classes in urban centers. A small percentage became very successful in different areas such as print media, mining, and the garment and construction materials sectors. Another small portion of the community remained under the poverty line, although this group grew exponentially during the economic crisis of Argentine great depression in the early 2000s.[35]

Regarding religious observance, Jewish immigrants to Latin America varied from Orthodox to fully assimilated and everything in between. For many Ashkenazi Jews, a desire for a more secular life was one of the drives to emigrate. However, Sephardi and Mizrahi Jews remained observant and more attached to traditions, especially in Brazil and Mexico.[36] When the various ethnic subgroups started building synagogues, they organized them according to their place of origin to preserve their cultural traditions. The first rabbis to arrive in the nineteenth century were Orthodox, but eventually, the Conservative and Reform movements found their way to Latin America. Rabbi Marshall Meyer of the Conservative movement was a central figure in the revival of Judaism during the 1960s and 1970s, with his approach influenced by liberation theology. Based in Argentina for several decades, he reshaped the continent's Jewish practice by establishing the Seminario Rabínico Latinoamericano. Graduates went on to lead synagogues all over Latin America, from Buenos Aires to Mexico and eventually to New York City.[37] Despite Rabbi Meyer's influence in the 1970s, religious observance dwindled among the younger generations. This was until the arrival of the Chabad movement, which revolutionized the Jewish world, attracting secular Jews back to the fold.[38] The success of this movement in Latin America was received with strong opposition by secular families because of fear of their youth drifting away to Orthodox observance and by Conservative and Reform rabbis who saw their membership dwindling, primarily because of assimilation and intermarriage, but also because of Chabad's appeal due to the surprisingly low stakes they require for Jews to join the community and participate in their events without demanding strict observance, but of course hoping to get Jews to return to tradition.[39]

Latin American Jews and Politics

Politics have also produced fractures in Latin American Jewish communities. The primary division started in the first half of the twentieth century between those who affiliated with synagogues and leading institutions (e.g., AMIA, Asociación Mutual Israelita Argentina), who generally adhered to Zionism, and the minority of nonaffiliated Jews who tended to align with internationalist values. Zionism has long been the glue that holds these communities together.[40] For many years, Israel was more important than ethnic subdivisions and intergenerational conflicts. It was the answer to thousands of years of persecution that many Jews in Latin America and the world had dreamed of, but not everyone was on board. Yet the establishment of the State of Israel in 1948 deepened the fracture between Jews who had brought socialist and communist ideologies from Eastern Europe (many had been active in union organizing there) and the rest of the community, which embraced the return of Jews to their ancestral land (Israel) at the heart of the Zionist movement.[41] The Arab-Israeli conflict and current Israeli politics have added additional tension and divisions throughout the community, especially with some among the younger generations moving away from Zionism.[42] And when it comes to local politics, like everyone else, Jews support different political parties.[43]

Many descendants of left-leaning Jews, and many others, faced the wrath of the junta during the 1970s in Argentina. Some joined Montoneros and other militant groups, others chose not to bear arms but stood up for social justice issues (teachers, students, union leaders, university professors, rabbis, and social workers), and others were in the wrong place at the wrong time. They all suffered human rights abuses during the Dirty War. The number of Jews who were kidnapped, tortured, and killed in the Dirty War is striking. According to a report, about 7 percent of the disappeared were of Jewish descent and almost 16 percent of those who were killed, when Jews accounted for only about 0.8 percent of the population at the time.[44] A similar case took place in Chile and Uruguay.[45] Because most of these young men and women were unaffiliated and most likely not Zionists, the response from the community leadership (DAIA, Delegación de Asociaciones Israelitas Argentinas) was highly problematic, and the organization chose not to intervene in the hopes of protecting the Jewish community and their institutions (e.g., schools, synagogues).[46] Nonetheless, the Israeli embassy helped about five hundred people escape to Israel, many of them thanks to the influential rabbi Marshall Meyer.[47] Among those who he helped escape was Jacobo Timerman, whose seminal text *Prisoner without a Name, Cell without a Number* (1981) describes the "special" treatment given to Jewish detainees in clandestine camps in the context of a neo-Nazi ideology. He writes about torturers holding the infamous *Protocols of the Elders of Sion* as true. His testimony reveals that the junta's desire to destroy the progressive section of the population went further with Jews, who, according to Timerman, they wanted to "eradicate" from society.[48] In 1983, Argentina saw the return of democracy with the election of Raúl Alfonsín. He chose to include a number of Jews in his government, "earning" the antisemitic misnomer of "Sinagoga Radical."[49] Rabbi Marshall Meyer was invited to be part of the CONADEP (Comisión Nacional sobre a Desaparición de Personas), the committee investigating human rights violations during the dictatorship.

Political violence also came from abroad; in the early 1990s, the Jewish community in Argentina was rocked by two fatal bombings that demolished the Israeli embassy in Buenos Aires (1992) and the AMIA community center (1994).[50] The attacks were carried out by Hezbollah with the backing of Iran and Syria and with support from local police.[51] While there was widespread support for the Jewish community in the immediate aftermath of the attacks, with a massive outpour of people claiming "we are all Jews," the sense of security of Jews in Argentina was shattered. Also, serious community rifts in the community resulted from DAIA's leadership's response to government involvement in the corruption that mired the investigation of both terrorist attacks. In 2015, Alberto Nisman, the prosecutor in charge of the AMIA case, was found shot dead in his apartment, and the culprits have not yet been discovered.

Latin American Jews in the World

One of the lesser-known chapters in the history of Latin American Jews is the large percentage of those who have moved to Israel, the United States, Europe, and Canada and continue to identify with their Latin American origin. This is a line of research that is starting to get more attention.[52] The first waves of emigration started around 1948, when Jews from Latin America began to make aliyah.[53] Beyond the strong pull to return to Eretz Israel, practical factors such as financial need have also influenced their decision. The crisis of 2001–2002 in Argentina is a good example: Israel helped facilitate aliyah for six thousand Jews, and many others fled to Miami, Winnipeg, or wherever else they could go to earn a livelihood.

Other factors that play into making aliyah include geographic and political isolation. In a previously published piece, I studied two communities of Jewish mestizos, one in the Amazonian town of Iquitos, Peru, and the other in Cuba.[54] The community in Iquitos is formed by the offspring of Indigenous women and Jewish men from Morocco and several European countries who went to the Amazonian jungle at the end of the turn of the nineteenth century because of the rubber boom.[55] The origin of the Cuban Jewish community follows a closer pattern to Mexico, with a larger Sephardi community and a smaller Ashkenazi one. But the present state of the community is similar to the one in Iquitos because most of the community left the country with the rise of Castro, and the people who stayed behind intermarried. So, the current population is mostly racially and ethnically mixed, except for a few elders.[56] These communities are dwindling rapidly as they seek formal conversion to make aliyah, for a chance for a better life, and to be more connected to larger Jewish communities.[57]

Latin American Jews in the United States have also been the focus of academic interest lately.[58] For example, Laura Limonic studies Jews from Mexico, Venezuela, and Argentina living in Boston and New York.[59] Her research reveals the main factors that inform how Latin American Jews adapt to their life in the United States: class, religious observance, and general attitudes toward Jews in their countries of origin. Some of the difficulties they face in adapting to Jewish communities in the United States have to do with the fact that in Latin America, Jews tend to live together in self-selected neighborhoods. A large proportion belongs to athletic clubs, synagogues, and other Jewish institutions. Many send their children to Jewish schools. For their part, US Jews tend to blend with non-Jews in the suburbs and mainly connect through synagogue affiliations, with few options for nonobservant Jews to feel part of a strong enclave. Jews from Latin America express a sense of loss in the United States for being part of a community that did not depend on religious observance.[60]

Intersectionalities and Intergenerational Conflicts

I started this chapter by highlighting the importance of intersectionalities in understanding the complex threads that weave the Jewish experience in Latin America. Just like for Latin American Jews abroad, Jewish immigrants arriving in Latin America carried with them external factors that affected their transition and their expectations of the New World. External factors, such as religious observance, cultural expectations, whether they came from and arrived in urban or rural settings, violence-related trauma related to place of origin, financial status, and capacity to learn Spanish or Portuguese also stressed intergenerational differences. The second generation inherited their parents' memories and added their own experiences, following similar and new challenges. The main threat to Jewish communities in Latin America was (and in some sense continues to be) intermarriage and assimilation.[61] Over time, the freedom to express non-heteronormative identities, with younger generations embracing queer identities, gender fluidity, and transsexuality, started to question tradition and family structure.[62] However, this was not the first time traditional values had been threatened. At the turn of the nineteenth century, Jewish men got involved in the business of forced prostitution and sex work.[63] Today, attitudes toward gender and sexuality, as well as intermarriage, appear to be more open in the more secular urban centers such as Buenos Aires, Montevideo, and São Paulo, with fewer changes in historically more observant and traditional communities, such as the Jewish communities in Mexico City and Lima.[64]

New Comparative Methodologies

This final section discusses how the field is evolving in regard to the question of Jews, race, and ethnicity. The historians Raanan Rein and Jeffrey Lesser have encouraged researchers of Latin American Jewish studies away from a linear perspective with a focus on Jewish subethnic groups. They believe that studying minority groups from a comparative lens yields more accurate and interesting answers. For example, Lesser studies Jews, Koreans, Arabs, and Japanese in Brazil, and the essays included in *The New Ethnic Studies in Latin America* compare the cultural experiences of Jews and people of Middle Eastern descent to portray the fluidity of ethnic identities as they evolve when interacting with other groups in Chile and Argentina.[65] Claudia Stern compares similarities and tensions between Jews' and Arabs' ascension to middle-class status between 1930 and 1960 in Chile. She discusses the complex dual perception of immigrants as modernizers and less educated (especially for Jews from the Middle East and Arabs). Studies such as these demonstrate that identities are always a work in progress, a continuous dance between ancestry, history, and culture, and that perceptions of Others are always informed by race, class, and attitudes toward immigrants in the host country.

For Latin American Jews, the experience of being Other has fluctuated over time. Historically, Jews have experienced the entire span from being discriminated against, massacred, and/or forcibly exiled from just about every continent in the world to integrating well into society and holding important positions in government, education, and industry. So even though antisemitism has been a constant shadow for Jews everywhere, including in Latin America, Jews also have become part of the social fabric. Still, Jews have had to grapple with the sense of precarious whiteness, of being the Other within, to never be quite safe or fully accepted. In spite of that, a large number of Jews have a place of privilege in the middle and upper middle classes of Latin America. This becomes evident when Jews interact with other minority ethnic groups, racial Others stuck in a chronic lack of access to basic human rights and systemic racism.[66] These instances reveal the layers that contribute to the experience of being in the minority. Race, ethnicity, class, gender, culture, and historical context represent fluctuating factors that are central to the lives of Jews in Latin America and of Latin American Jews abroad, making their experience both distinct and shared.[67] It is my hope that readers will gain a more profound sense of the challenges and growth that result from the migratory experiences of Latin American Jews and their descendants to appreciate a heightened sense of community with immigrants of all origins and personal circumstances today.

NOTES

1. Judah M. Cohen says that US and European Jewish studies focus on "culture" and "identity" when studying different groups of Jewish origin. He questions the validity of thinking of Jews as an ethnic group with multilayered examples of the cultural production of Jews in Latin America and also from Latin American Jews in the United States and Israel. Cohen traces the changing focus of Latin American Jewish studies over time to point at areas of growth that still need to be addressed. "The Ethnic Dilemmas of Latin American Jewry," in *Rethinking Jewish-Latin Americans*, ed. Jeffrey Lesser and Raanan Rein (Albuquerque: University of New Mexico Press, 2008), 266–284.
2. "The insertion of foreignness at the very root of Jewish royalty is somewhat disturbing, and Ruth is not the only foreigner to enter Jewish lineage in the Bible." Julia Kristeva, *Strangers to Ourselves* (New York: Columbia University Press, 1991), 76. She opens up the concept of identity by recognizing the foreign within in psychoanalytical terms and as a collective experience. The unconscious fractures the integrity of the "I" to include "otherness." Kristeva, 181.
3. Edmond Jabès, *Del desierto al libro* (Córdoba, Argentina: Alción Editora, 2001), 42. Erin Graff Zivin enters this dialogue with the concept of wandering signifier to address the problems that arise from representing constructions of Jewish identity from a cultural, ideological, racial, and political perspective. She looks at the figure of the Jew in literature written in Latin American countries, where the majority of ethnic others are of Indigenous and African descent. She proposes that *Jew* "functions as a powerful node onto which a fundamental anxiety toward difference can be projected and performed." *The Wandering Signifier: Rhetoric of Jewishness in the Latin American Imaginary* (Durham, NC: Duke University Press, 2008), 20.
4. Sandra McGee Deutsch explains the particularities of Argentine Jews' precarious iden-

tification with whiteness in connection with local perceptions of their culture and behavior. She studies the complicated self-association of Jews who arrived from the Arab world with Sephardim (originally from Spain) to blend into the local understandings of whiteness. "Insecure Whiteness: Jews between Civilization and Barbarism, 1880s–1940s," in *Rethinking Race in Modern Argentina*, edited by Paulina Alberto and Eduardo Elena. (Cambridge, UK: Cambridge University Press, 2016), 25–52. Jeffrey Lesser studies the problematic connection between Jews and "whiteness" in the context of rising nationalism in Brazil in the 1930s. He links the negative perception of Jews in Brazil with their "insidious non-white race whose racial difference was dangerously invisible." "Imagining Otherness: The Jewish Question in Brazil, 1930–1940," in *Latin America and the Caribbean: Fragments of Memory*, ed. Kristin Ruggiero (Brighton, UK: Sussex Academic Press, 2005), 35.

5. For an innovative study of the complex uses of languages in multiple generations of Jews in this continent, see Evelyn Dean-Olmsted and Susana Skura, "Jewish Latin American Spanish," in *Handbook of Jewish Languages* (Leiden: Brill, 2017), 490–503. The Jewish Argentine artist Mirta Kupferminc has a well-known series of etchings inspired by the Tower of Babel. In the introduction to a 2017 exhibit catalog titled *Traduttore-Tradittore* she writes: "As a daughter of immigrants I was raised as a 'stranger' in my own homeland. Another language was spoken in my home, thus sometimes I felt 'different.' I learned variants of a so-called mother tongue. . . . Transit, exile and diaspora; are not mere historical and geographical situations, but spatial metaphors of human existence. . . . Open existence to a dimension of Otherness. This is what I learned from the story of Babel."

6. Unless otherwise noted, this historical overview relies heavily on Laikin Elkin's seminal book, *The Jews of Latin America*, 3rd ed. (Boulder, CO: Lynne Rienner Publishers, 2014). Some sections are based on the introduction I cowrote with Alejandro Meter: *Memoria y representación: Configuraciones culturales y literarias en el imaginario judío latinoamericano* (Rosario, Argentina: Beatriz Viterbo, 2006).

7. Although for the Jews of Iberia, it was not until the tenth century that their culture reached its full splendor: Angelina Muñiz-Huberman, *La lengua florida* (Mexico City: Fondo de Cultura Económica, 1989), 15. The introduction to this book details the cultural advances of Jews during this period in areas such as religion, linguistics, sciences, and ethics.

8. Reyes Coll-Tellechea, "Remembering Sepharad," in *Memory, Oblivion, and Jewish Culture in Latin America*, ed. Marjorie Agosín (Austin: University of Texas Press, 2005), 3–14.

9. In the end, after twelve hundred years, the most extended period in history when Jews could reside in one place, they were given only three months to prepare to leave. In a curious twist of history, five centuries later, Jews were given three years to reclaim Spanish citizenship. Dalia Kandiyoti and Rina Benmayor, *Sephardi Jews, Citizenship, and Reparation in Historical Context* (New York: Berghahn Books, 2023).

10. Ilan Stavans writes about the case of Luis de Torres, who was born Yosef ben Ha-Levi Haivri. He was mentioned in Columbus's diary. Evidence that he was probably still faithful to his Jewish origins includes that he spoke in Hebrew to Indigenous people in San Salvador, believing that they descended from the Lost Tribes of Israel: "Introduction," in *I Am of the Tribe of Judah: Jewish Poetry from Latin America*, edited by Stephen Sadow (Albuquerque: University of New Mexico Press, 2023).

11. Some examples of contemporary literary works that reflect the life of crypto-Jews in the Americas include Sabina Berman's play *Herejía* (Mexico City: Mexicanos Unidos, 1985)

147–211; Antonio Muñoz Molina, *Sefarad* (Madrid: Alfaguara, 2001).
12. For a window into the life of Jacob Brandon Maduro, a central figure in this group, see Dalia Wassner, "The Port Jew and Nuestra América: Narratives of Collective Responsibility and Belonging," *PaRDeS: Journal of the Association for Jewish Studies in Germany* 28 (2023): 84–99.
13. Laikin Elkin, *The Jews of Latin America*, 50–53. For a history of Sephardic Jews in Argentina, see Adriana Brodsky, *Sephardi, Jewish, Argentine: Community and National Identity, 1880–1960* (Bloomington: Indiana University Press, 2016).
14. Lakin Elkin, *The Jews of Latin America*, 78.
15. Laikin Elkin, *The Jews of Latin America*, 101–124.
16. The word *colonization* that is part of the organization's name is problematic in multiple ways, especially in the context of Jewish and Latin American history. However, *colonia* was the term used at the end of the nineteenth century to refer to agricultural communities (e.g., Jewish, Italian). Silvio Huberman cites "La ley de Tierras y Colonias, dictada por el presidente Nicolás Avellaneda en 1976," in *Los pasajeros del* Weser: *La conmovedora travesía de los primeros inmigrantes judíos a la Argentina* (Buenos Aires: Random House Mondadori, 2014), 21.
17. Silvio Huberman, *Los pasajeros del Weser*, 103–117. The journalist memorializes vividly the difficulties the group encountered upon arrival, including initial complications in settling in lands in the province of Buenos Aires, which forced them to homelessness and resulted in the death of over sixty children due to infectious diseases (101). Dr. Wilhelm Loewenthal, who was involved in checking the conditions on the ground to establish agricultural colonies, found the immigrants stranded and famished in Palacios train station in Santa Fé province. He brought the news to the Ministry of Foreign Affairs and lobbied for the establishment of Moisesville. It was founded with fifty to sixty families. Loewenthal was crucial in founding the Jewish Colonization Association (JCA) with Baron Maurice de Hirsch in 1891. *Los pasajeros del* Weser focuses on the people, including log names of the first group, and it includes personal memories of the birth of the agricultural colonies in Argentina.
18. For an excellent in-depth study that includes the state of the colonies in the twenty-first century, see Iván Cherjovsky, *Recuerdos de Moisés Ville: La colonización agrícola en la memoria colectiva judeo-argentina (1910–2010)* (Buenos Aires: UAI, 2017).
19. The JCA business model to preserve funds for future migrants proved disastrous when it came down to saving the Jews from their terrible living conditions in Eastern Europe. This was primarily because of the strict selection process: Laikin Elkin, *The Jews of Latin America*, 101–113.
20. Among the many literary renditions of the agricultural chapter of Jewish life in Latin America captured in literature and film, very few were written by women. See Rebeca Mactas Alpersohn's *Los judíos de las Acacias* (Buenos Aires: Julio Glassman, 1936), and Nora Glickman's *Hilván de instantes* (Santiago de Chile: RIL, 2015). In terms of film, see Iván Cherjovsky's documentary *The Jerusalem of Argentina* (INCAA, 2017) and María Victoria Menis's *Camera Obscura* (Sophie Dulac Productions, Todo Cine SA, 2008).
21. In his book *Hotel Bolivia*, Leo Spitzer depicts the desperate efforts of Jews to gain paperwork to leave Nazi-occupied Europe and their brief but fascinating life in the Andean nation. *Hotel Bolivia: The Culture of Memory in a Refuge from Nazism* (New York: Hill and Wang, 1998), 3–46.
22. Laikin Elkin, *The Jews of Latin America*, 117–119.

23. Spitzer, *Hotel Bolivia*, 98.
24. Flavio Fiorani poses a similar question in his analysis of US-based Guatemalan author Eduardo Halfon's novel *Mañana nunca lo hablamos*: "El encuentro infantil con la violencia y su marca traumática obran como disparador de preguntas relacionadas a la cuestión del posicionamiento de judíos e indígenas en el conflicto... ¿por qué los judíos de clase empresarial, se consideran como *outsiders* respecto a la guerra civil? ¿es pertinente la equiparación de alteridad judía y alteridad indígena? ¿los judíos guatemaltecos pueden considerarse ladinos?" *Habitar la distancia: Ficciones latinoamericanas sobre el judaísmo* (Rome: Nova Delphi, 2022) 25.
25. This venture was organized by DORSA, which was part of the JOINT (the most prominent Jewish organization that supported Jews in distress worldwide since 1914). Jews in New York, a main source of financial backing for the organization, questioned supporting Sosúa because of Trujillo's highly problematic history of human rights violations. Laikin Elkin, *The Jews of Latin America*, 116.
26. Laikin Elkin, *The Jews of Latin America*, 113–117.
27. For a history of the presence of Nazism in Chile, see Graeme S. Mount, "Chile and the Nazis," in *Memory, Oblivion, and Jewish Culture in Latin America* (Austin: University of Texas Press, 2005), 77–90. See also Rossana Cassigoli, "On Nazi Presence in Chile," *Acta Sociológica* 61 (2013): 157–177.
28. See Germán Friedmann, "La 'otra Alemania' y las identidades judeoalemanas," *Historia Política.com* (2007), https://acontracorriente.chass.ncsu.edu/index.php/acontracorriente/article/view/452.
29. Several Latin American consuls helped Jews gain passage by issuing illegal paperwork. Many are honored in the Righteous among the Nations program, at Yad Vashem in Jerusalem: Haim Avni, "Los países de América Latina y el Holocausto," *Shoá, Enciclopedia del Holocausto* (Jerusalén: Yad Vashem y EDZ Nativ, 2004), 85–94.
30. Alejandro Dujovne offers a peek into this period in his study of the central role of books in the creation of Jewish culture in the city of Buenos Aires. He traces Spanish and Yiddish publishing houses, bookstores, and libraries, as well as newspapers published in the multiple languages of the Jewish community during the first half of the twentieth century to look at the convergence of culture, education, and political perspectives. "Print Culture and Urban Geography: Jewish Bookstores, Libraries and Printers in Buenos Aires, 1910–1960," in *The New Jewish Argentina: Facets of Jewish Experiences in the Southern Cone* (Leiden: Brill, 2013), 81–108.
31. We should also mention Ana María Shua (Argentina), Alicia Borinsky (Argentina/United States), Luisa Futoransky (Argentina), Mario Szichman (Argentina), Diana Raznovich (Argentina), Gloria Gervits (Mexico), Marcelo Birmajer (Argentina), Myriam Moscona (Mexico) Mauricio Rosencof (Uruguay), Tamara Tenenbaum (Argentina), Andrés Neuman (Argentina/Spain), and Sergio Chejfec (Argentina/United States).
32. See Nora Glickman and Gloria Waldman, eds., *Argentine Jewish Theatre: A Critical Anthology* (Lewisburg, PA: Bucknell University Press, 1996); *Evolving Images: Jewish Latin American Cinema*, edited by Nora Glickman and Ariana Huberman (Austin: University of Texas Press, 2017); *Mazal Tov, Amigos! Jews and Popular Music in the Americas*, edited by Amalia Ran and Moshe Morad (Leiden: Brill, 2016).
33. Laikin Elkin explains the internal and external reasons for the attraction of Jewish immigrants to this line of work: literacy, familiarity with commerce in the Old world are some of the internal reasons, and the lack of an effective distribution of goods in the economic

infrastructure in Latin America are some of the external ones. *The Jews of Latin America*, 125-130. This activity is described in detail in two novels, from Peru and Venezuela, respectively: Isaac Goldemberg's *The Fragmented Life of Don Jacobo Lerner* (Hanover, NH: Ediciones Norte, 1976) and Alicia Freilich Segal's *Cláper* (Caracas: Fundarte, 1987).
34. Nadia Zysman studies how the garment industry in Argentina helped the Jewish community to get organized and how Jews influenced the industry at large by modeling new spaces of labor (at home, in workshops, and in factories). She discusses their involvement in the labor movement and in women's entrance into the workforce. Zysman also re-creates the social network that allowed for fast integration of Jews who arrived to the neighborhood of Villa Lynch (Buenos Aires) with previous skills in the textile industry. "Factory, Workshop, and Homework: A Spatial Dimension of Labor Flexibility among Jewish Migrants in the Early Stages of Industrialization in Buenos Aires," in *The New Ethnic Studies in Latin America* (Leiden: Brill, 2017), 16-31.
35. Laikin Elkin, *The Jews of Latin America*, 125-148.
36. For more on the Jewish community in Mexico, see Laikin Elkin, *The Jews of Latin America*, 271-279.
37. Laikin Elkin, *The Jews of Latin America*, 296-297. The congregation B'nai Jeshurun, on the Upper West Side of New York City, was run by Marshall Meyer when he returned to the United states in the mid-1980s with several of his disciples from Argentina. Daniel Fainstein discusses this transformational figure for the Jewish community in Argentina and Latin America and how liberation theology inspired his involvement with human rights during the Dirty War: "Rabbi Marshall T. Meyer as a Transnational Expatriate and Innovative Religious Entrepreneur: From the United States to Argentina and Back," *Contemporary Jewry* 41, no. 4 (2021): 823-841.
38. Chabad tends to be very accepting of the seculars' lack of knowledge of ritual practices, and they don't require membership fees. Given their mandate to rekindle the spark of divinity in every Jew, they welcome secular Jews worldwide to weekly events, from Shabbat meals, to after-hours mingling for young and single professionals, and upbeat events to celebrate the Jewish holidays. This is why they have been so successful in strengthening Jewish identity and the return to observance in various degrees..
39. Laikin Elkin, *The Jews of Latin America*, 164-168.
40. "Zionism is the movement for the self-determination and statehood for the Jewish people in their ancestral homeland, the land of Israel. The vast majority of Jews around the world feel a connection or kinship with Israel, whether or not they explicitly identify as Zionists, and regardless of their opinions on the policies of the Israeli government." Antidefamation League, "Zionism," August 29, 2024, https://www.adl.org/resources/glossary-term/zionism.https://www.adl.org/resources/glossary-term/zionism. For a detailed history of the political forces behind UN Resolution 3379, which has been fueling worldwide antisemitism ever since, see Sidney Liskofsky, "UN Resolution on Zionism," *American Jewish Year Book* (1977): 97-126.
41. Nerina Visacovsky has written two seminal books about progressive Jewish groups in Argentina and their secular Jewish school system that was ahead of their times in Argentina. First is *Argentinos, judíos y camaradas tras la utopía socialista* (Buenos Aires: Editorial Biblos, 2017). The second offers a comparative look at the progressive movements in Jewish communities that thrived from the 1950s to the 1980s across the Americas: Canada, the United States, Mexico, Chile, Uruguay, Brazil, and Argentina: *Cultura judeoprogresista en las Américas* (Buenos Aires: Imago Mundi, 2022). Left-leaning Jews had actu-

ally started arriving at the turn of the twentieth century. Some joined anarchist causes in Argentina and later became part of the republican brigades during the Spanish Civil War. Leonardo Senkman writes about the case of Simón Radowitzky, a Jewish Ukrainian immigrant anarchist living in Argentina who murdered Ramón Falcon, the head of the police responsible for the May Day massacre of 1909 in Buenos Aires. After serving over twenty years in jail, he went on to join the fight of Republicans during the Spanish Civil War: "Simón Radowitzky: Revolution, Exile, and a Wandering Jew Imaginary," in *Jewish Imaginaries of the Spanish Civil War: In Search of Poetic Justice*, ed. Cynthia Gabbay (London: Bloomsbury Publishing, 2022); Roberto Baschetti, *Argentinos. Judíos. Rebeldes. Revolucionarios* (Buenos Aires: Jirones de Mi Vida, 2023). José Moya studies the larger social and historical context of Jews involved in anarchism alongside Italian and Spanish immigrants during the first decade of the twentieth century in "What's in a Stereotype? The Case of Jewish Anarchists in Argentina," in *Rethinking Jewish-Latin Americans*, 55–88.

42. To learn more about the effect the impact of Israeli politics and the Israeli-Palestinian conflict have had on Argentine Jews, see Emmanuel Kahan, *Parte del aire: El conflicto árabe-israelí en la cultura y la política argentina (1967–1982)* (Buenos Aires: Prometeo, 2023).

43. For a study on Argentine Jews and local political affiliations, see *Argentina, Israel, and the Jews: Perón, the Eichmann Capture and After* (Bethesda: University Press of Maryland, 2003).

44. Comisión de Solidaridad con Familiares de Presos y Desaparecidos en la Argentina, *La violación de los derechos humanos de argentinos judíos bajo el regimen militar (1976–1983)* (Buenos Aires: Colección Testimonios, 2006), 15.

45. Valeria Navarro-Rosenblatt discusses the case of young leftist unaffiliated Jews in Chile who tried to make a difference toward social change. Many of them were targeted by the military repression and have not received the scholarly attention that their Argentine counterparts have. "The Untold History: Voices of Non-Affiliated Jews in Chile, 1940–1990," in *The New Ethnic Studies in Latin America*, ed. Ranaan Rein, Stefan Rinke, and Nadia Zysman (Leiden: Brill, 2017), 128–147.

46. For more on this problematic chapter, see Laikin Elkin, *The Jews of Latin America*, 235–238.

47. Laikin Elkin, *The Jews of Latin America*, 233–238. Luis Roniger and Deby Babis document the difficulty these young men and women had adapting to life in Israel. Most ended up leaving to Spain, other countries in Europe, and Latin America. See "Latin American Israelis: The Collective Identity of an Invisible Community," in *Identities in an Era of Globalization and Multiculturalism: Latin America in the Jewish World*, ed. Judith Bokser Liwerant (Leiden: Brill, 2008), 297–320.

48. Jacobo Timerman, *Prisoner without a Name, Cell without a Number* (New York: Vintage, 1982), 66. Alejandro Meter explains the extent to which people involved with the junta (from top-tier military to the torturers) perceived Jews as part of a conspiracy to infiltrate society with subversive motives, and thus echoed the tenets of "final solution" in the way they went about selecting, kidnapping, and torturing Jewish youth: "Barbarie y memoria: El Holocausto y la dictadura en la narrativa argentina de hoy," in *Memoria y representación: Literatura y cultura judía en América Latina* (Rosario, Argentina: Beatriz Viterbo, 2006), 67–68. In fact, the junta's approach to eradicating progressive members of society was strongly influenced by Nazism. Laikin Elkin cites Colonel Camps: "First we will kill the guerrillas. Then we will kill the guerrillas' families. Then we will kill the friends of

their families, and the friends of their friends, so that there will be no one left to remember who the guerrillas were." *The Jews of Latin America*, 234. As a result, the number of dead by the junta was six times the number of militants involved in guerrilla groups. But their plan to eradicate the memory of the disappeared failed miserably. Some of the texts that re-create the connection between the Holocaust and the Dirty War include Manuela Fingueret, *Hija del silencio* (Buenos Aires: Planeta, 1999), Nora Strejilevich, *Una sola muerte numerosa* (Miami: Universidad de Miami, 1997). Edna Aizenberg studies the interrelated history of the Holocaust memorial and the memorial for the disappeared in Montevideo in "Nation and Holocaust Narration: Uruguay's Memorial del Holocausto del Pueblo Judío," in *Rethinking Jewish-Latin Americans*, 207-230. See also Emmanuel Kahan's "Memories That Lie a Little: New Approaches to the Research into the Jewish Experience during the Last Military Dictatorship in Argentina," in *The New Jewish Argentina*, 293-313.
49. A pun on Unión Cívica Radical is the name of Alfonsín's political party.
50. See Beatriz Gurevich, "After the AMIA Bombing: A Critical Analysis of Two Parallel Discourses," in *The Jewish Diaspora in Latin America and the Caribbean: Fragments of Memory*, ed. Kristin Ruggiero (Brighton, UK: Sussex Academic Press, 2005), 86-106.
51. "Hezbollah wields significant power in Lebanon, where it operates as both a Shiite political party and militant group. It opposes Israel and Western powers operating in the Middle East, and it functions as a proxy of Iran, its largest benefactor. The group has faced unprecedented scrutiny from the Lebanese public amid the country's political and economic crisis." Council of Foreign Relations, "What Is Hezbollah," August 29, 2024, https://www.cfr.org/backgrounder/what-hezbollah.
52. See Judit Bokser Liwerant, "Klal Yisrael Today: Unity and Diversity. Reflections on Europe and Latin America in a Globalized World," in *A Road to Nowhere?* (Leiden: Brill, 2013), 299-333.
53. See Roniger and Babis, "Latin American Israelis"; Adriana Brodsky, "Argentine Sephardi Youth: Between Aliyah and Activism, 1960-1970," *Journal of Jewish Identities* 8, no. 2 (2015): 113-135. Ilan Stavans discusses the history and current presence of Latin American Jews in Israel, including their presence in the kibbutz movement, their contributions to Israeli culture, the use of language, and multigenerational differences in terms of connection to Latin America in "Making Aliyah," in *The Seventh Heaven: Travels through Jewish Latin America* (Pittsburgh, PA: University of Pittsburgh Press, 2019) 220-265. See also Adrián Krupnik, "Failed Expectations of Middle-Class Migrants and the Zionist Hegemonic Narrative: Jewish-Argentine Returnees from Israel in the 1960s," *Journal of Israeli History* 40, no. 1 (2022): 187-211.
54. This is a term coined by Ariel Segal in *Jews of the Amazon: Self-Exile in Paradise* (Philadelphia: Jewish Publication Society, 1999), xi
55. Many Jews ended up opening department stores that provided tools and other goods to tap the rubber trees. Segal himself became deeply involved with the community acting as a religious mentor and a representative of the group, his account of their story is personal and compelling. In *Jews of the Amazon*, Segal frames the group's circumstances within the debate of "Who is a Jew?" with a focus on the drift between the Ashkenazi Jews of Lima and the mestizo Jews of Iquitos (97-132). Some of the obstacles mestizo Jews encountered when seeking recognition included the fact that the community originated from Jewish fathers and Indigenous mothers, as well as the religious hybridity of their religious practices (63-96).
56. In terms of numbers, of the ten thousand to twelve thousand Jews who lived in Cuba

before the rise of Castro, about a thousand people identify as Jews in Cuba today. But only roughly twenty-five are Jewish from both mother and father. Those who stayed behind were granted special privileges, like access to kosher beef and Passover goods. They were also allowed to keep their institutions, and the Jewish school was allowed to function until 1975, when the government decided to close it two years after Castro broke relations with Israel after the Six-Day War. Margalit Bejarano, "The Jewish Community of Cuba: Between Continuity and Extinction," *Jewish Political Studies Review* 3, nos. 1–2 (1991): 126–128. The anthropologist Ruth Behar confirms that many people, including Cuban Jews in the United States, were surprised that the community survived. Even US Cubans thought that whoever was left would not be able to practice Judaism under Castro: Ruth Behar, *An Island Called Home: Returning to Jewish Cuba* (New Brunswick, NJ: Rutgers University Press, 2007), 22, 27.

57. Cuban Jews were already connected to US and Canadian Jews who gave them financial support. The case of Iquitos is more complicated because while they have received the support of Argentine and Israeli rabbis to convert to make aliyah, they were also rejected by the conservative Jews from Lima who do not identify with the mestizo Jews of Iquitos.
58. See Margalit Bejarano, "Changing Identities in a Transnational Diaspora: Latin American Jews in Miami," in *Jews and Jewish Identities in Latin America*, ed. Margalit Bejarano, Yaron Harel, Marta F. Topel, and Margalit Yosifon (Boston: Academic Studies Press, 2017), 35–51.
59. Laura Limonic, *Kugel and Frijoles: Latino Jews in the United States* (Detroit: Wayne State University Press, 2019.)
60. Some artistic expressions about Jewish Latinxs in the United States include Adriana Katzew's art (Mexico/United States), Ilan Stavans's literature (Mexico/United States), Eduardo Halfon's literature (Guatemala/United States), and Ruth Behar's documentary and literature (Cuba/United States).
61. See Nora Glickman's "Interfaith Relations between Jews and Gentiles in Argentine and US Cinema," in *Evolving Images: Jewish Latin American Cinema*, ed. Nora Glickman and Ariana Huberman (Austin: University of Texas Press, 2017), 204–224. Intermarriage has played a positive role in the survival of Jewish communities in places like Cuba, and in Iquitos, Perú.
62. Some of the texts that address Latin American Jewish LGBTQ issues include Rawet, Samuel. *Homossexualismo: sexualidade e valor*. Brazil: Olivé Editor, 1970; Isaac Chocrón, *Pájaro de mar por tierra* (Mexico City: Debolsillo, 1972); Alberto Guzik, *Risco de vida* (Porto Alegre: Globo, 1995); Sara Levi Calderón [Sylvia Feldman], *Dos mujeres* (Madrid: Egales, 2014); Diana Raznovich, "De atrás para adelante," *Actos desafiantes* (Lewisburg, PA: Bucknell University Press, 2002); Marcelo Birmajer, *Eso no* (Barcelona: Tusquets, 2003); Angelina Muñiz Huberman, *La burladora de Toledo* (Mexico City: Planeta, 2008). For a discussion of the intersectionality of being part of the LGBTQ community and being Jewish, see Aharoni, Gabriela Jonas, "Another among Others: A Game of Paradoxes and Shifting Notions of Otherness," *Post Script* 38 (2019).
63. For a study of this chapter in Jewish immigration, see Mir Yarfitz, *Impure Migration: Jews and Sex Work in Golden Age Argentina* (New Brunswick, NJ: Rutgers University Press, 2019). This historical phenomenon inspired several pieces of literature, such as Nora Glickman's play *Una tal Raquel*, in Glickman, *Teatro* (Buenos Aires: Nueva Generación, 2000), and Clara Beter's [César Tiempo] *Versos de una . . .* (Buenos Aires: Claridad, 1926). For a

study of literature and film related to this topic, see Amy K. Kaminsky, *The Other/Argentina: Jews, Gender, and Sexuality in the Making of a Modern Nation* (Albany: State University of New York Press, 2021).

64. Of course, there are exceptions to this general statement, especially among the younger generations. For a rare view of the changes taking place in family structures in Lima's Jewish community from the second half of the 1950s to the 2010s, see Romina Yalonetzky, "Just Like Us, but Jewish: Jewishness, Ethnicity, Class Affinity and Transnationality in Lima," *Ethnicities* 19, no. 6 (2019): 1101–1120.
65. Jeffrey Lesser, "How the Jews Became Japanese and Other Stories of Nation and Ethnicity," in *Rethinking Jewish-Latin Americans*, 41–54.
66. These interactions are captured in Gerchunoff's short stories *Los gauchos judíos* (Buenos Aires: Aguilar, 1975) and in the photographs taken by Austrian Jews fleeing the Nazis in the 1940s of Aymara people as portrayed by Spitzer in *Hotel Bolivia*.
67. It is important to avoid the concept of uniqueness connected to social identities because what makes us unique are "our contributions." D. Rios, M. J. Bowling, and J. Harris "Decentering Student 'Uniqueness,'" in *Intersectional Pedagogy: Complicating Identity and Social Justice*, ed. Kim A. Case (New York: Routledge, 2017), 211.

BIBLIOGRAPHY

Aharoni, Gabriela Jonas. "Another among Others: A Game of Paradoxes and Shifting Notions of Otherness." *Post Script* 38 (2019). 59–69.

Aizenberg, Edna. "Nation and Holocaust Narration: Uruguay's Memorial del Holocausto del Pueblo Judío." In *Rethinking Jewish-Latin Americans*, edited by Lesser and Rein, 207-230. Albuquerque: University of New Mexico Press, 2008.

Avni, Haim. "Los países de América Latina y el Holocausto." *Shoá, Enciclopedia del Holocausto Jerusalén. Yad Vashem y EDZ Nativ*, 2004. 85–94.

Baschetti, Roberto. *Argentinos. Judíos. Rebeldes. Revolucionarios*. Buenos Aires: Ed. jirones de mi vida, 2023.

Behar, Ruth. *An Island Called Home: Returning to Jewish Cuba*. New Brunswick, NJ: Rutgers University Press, 2007.

Bejarano, Margalit. "Changing Identities in a Transnational Diaspora: Latin American Jews in Miami." In *Jews and Jewish Identities in Latin America*, 35–51. Boston: Academic Studies Press, 2017.

———. "The Jewish Community of Cuba: between Continuity and Extinction." *Jewish Political Studies Review* 3, nos. 1–2 (Spring 1991). 115–40.

Berman, Sabina. *Herejía: En el nombre de Dios*. Mexico City: Editores Mexicanos Unidos, 1985.

Beter, Clara [César Tiempo]. *Versos de una . . .* Buenos Aires, Editorial Claridad, 1926.

Birmajer, Marcelo. *Eso no*. Barcelona: Tusquets, 2003.

Brodsky, Adriana M. "Argentine Sephardi Youth: Between Aliyah and Activism, 1960–1970." *Journal of Jewish Identities* 8, no. 2 (2015): 113–35.

———. *Sephardi, Jewish, Argentine: Community and National Identity*. Bloomington: Indiana University Press, 2016.

Cassigoli, Rossana. "On Nazi Presence in Chile." *Acta Sociológica* 61 (2013): 157-77.
Cherjovsky, Iván. *The Jerusalem of Argentina*. Argentina: INCAA. 2017. Film.
———. *Recuerdos de Moisés Ville: La colonización agrícola en la memoria colectiva judeo-argentina (1910-2010)*. Buenos Aires: UAI Editorial, 2017.
Chocrón, Isaac. *Pájaro de mar por tierra*. Mexico City: Ed. Debolsillo, 1972. 101-12.
Cohen, Judah M. "The Ethnic Dilemmas of Latin American Jewry." In *Rethinking Jewish-Latin Americans*, edited by Lesser and Rein, 266-84. Albuquerque: University of New Mexico Press, 2008.
Coll-Tellechea, Reyes. "Remembering Sepharad." In *Memory, Oblivion, and Jewish Culture in Latin America*, edited by Marjorie Agosín, 3-14. New York: University of Texas Press, 2005.
Comisión de Solidaridad con Familiares de Presos y Desaparecidos en la Argentina. *La violación de los derechos humanos de argentinos judíos bajo el régimen militar (1976-1983)*. Buenos Aires: Editorial Milá, 2006.
Dean-Olmsted, Evelyn, and Susana Skura. "Jewish Latin American Spanish." In *Handbook of Jewish Languages*, edited by Kahn, Lily, and Aaron D. Rubin. Leiden: Brill, 2017.
Deutsch, Sandra McGee. "Insecure Whiteness: Jews between Civilization and Barbarism, 1880s-1940s." In *Rethinking Race in Modern Argentina*, edited by Paulina Alberto and Eduardo Elena, 25-52. Cambridge: Cambridge University Press, 2016.
Dujovne, Alejandro. "Print Culture and Urban Geography: Jewish Bookstores, Libraries, and Printers in Buenos Aires, 1910-1960." In *The New Jewish Argentina: Facets of Jewish Experiences in the Southern Cone*, edited by Adriana M. Brodsky and Raanan Rein, 81-108. Leiden: Brill, 2013.
Fainstein, Daniel. "Rabbi Marshall T. Meyer as a Transnational Expatriate and Innovative Religious Entrepreneur: From the United States to Argentina and Back." *Contemporary Jewry* 41, no. 4 (2021): 823-841.
Fingueret, Manuela. *Hija del silencio*. Buenos Aires: Planeta, 1999.
Fiorani, Flavio. *Habitar la distancia: Ficciones latinoamericanas sobre el judaísmo*. Rome: Nova Delphi, 2022.
Freilich Segal, Alicia. *Cláper*. Caracas: Fundarte, 1987.
Friedmann, Germán. "La 'otra Alemania' y las identidades judeoalemanas." *HistoriaPolítica.com*, 2007. https://acontracorriente.chass.ncsu.edu/index.php/acontracorriente/article/view/452.
Gabbay, Cynthia, ed. *Jewish Imaginaries of the Spanish Civil War: In Search of Poetic Justice*. New York: Bloomsbury Publishing, 2022.
Gerchunoff, Alberto. *Los gauchos judíos*. Buenos Aires: Aguilar, 1975.
Glickman, Nora. *Hilván de instantes*. Santiago de Chile: RIL Editores, 2015
———. "Interfaith Relations between Jews and Gentiles in Argentine and US Cinema." In *Evolving Images: Jewish Latin American Cinema*, 204-224. Austin: University of Texas Press, 2017.
———. "Una tal Raquel." Buenos Aires: Nueva Generación, 2000.
Glickman, Nora, and Ariana Huberman, eds. *Evolving Images: Jewish Latin American Cinema*. Austin: University of Texas Press, 2017.

Glickman, Nora, and Gloria Waldman, eds. *Argentine Jewish Theatre: A Critical Anthology.* Lewisburg, PA: Bucknell University Press, 1996.

Goldemberg, Isaac. *La vida a plazos de don Jacobo Lerner.* Hanover, NH: Ediciones Norte, 1976.

Graff Zivin, Erin. *The Wandering Signifier: Rhetoric of Jewishness in the Latin American Imaginary.* Durham, NC: Duke University Press, 2008.

Gurevich, Beatriz. "After the AMIA Bombing: A Critical Analysis of Two Parallel Discourses." In *The Jewish Diaspora in Latin America and the Caribbean Fragments of Memory,* edited by Kristin Ruggiero, 86–106. Brighton, UK: Sussex Academic Press, 2005.

Guzik, Alberto. *Risco de vida.* Porto Alegre, Brazil: Editora Globo, 1995.

Halfon, Eduardo. *Mañana nunca lo hablamos.* Valencia, Spain: Pre-Textos, 2011.

Huberman, Ariana, and Alejandro Meter. *Memoria y representación: Literatura y cultura judía en América Latina.* Rosario, Argentina: Beatriz Viterbo Editoras, 2006.

Huberman, Silvio. *Los pasajeros del Weser: La conmovedora travesía de los primeros inmigrantes judíos a la Argentina.* Buenos Aires: Sudamericana, 2014.

Jabès, Edmond. *Del desierto al Libro.* Córdoba, Argentina: Alción Editora, 2001.

Kahan, Emmanuel. *Memories That Lie a Little: Jewish Experiences during the Argentine Dictatorship.* Leiden: Brill, 2019.

———. *Parte del aire: El conflicto árabe-israelí en la cultura y la política argentina (1967–1982).* Buenos Aires: Ed. Prometeo, 2023.

Kaminsky, Amy K. *The Other/Argentina: Jews, Gender, and Sexuality in the Making of a Modern Nation.* Albany: State University of New York Press, 2021.

Kandiyoti, Dalia, and Rina Benmayor, eds. *Reparative Citizenship for Sephardi Descendants: Returning to the Jewish Past in Spain and Portugal.* Vol. 16. New York: Berghahn Books, 2023.

Kristeva, Julia. *Strangers to Ourselves.* New York: Columbia University Press, 1991.

Krupnik, Adrián. "Failed Expectations of Middle-Class Migrants and the Zionist Hegemonic Narrative: Jewish-Argentine Returnees from Israel in the 1960s." *Journal of Israeli History* 40, no. 1 (2022): 187–211.

Kupferminc, Mirta. *Traduttore-tradittore.* The Third Jerusalem Biennale, 2017 exhibit catalog.

Laikin Elkin, Judith. *The Jews of Latin America.* 3rd ed. Boulder, CO: Lynne Rienner Publishers, 2014.

Lesser, Jeffrey, and Raanan Rein. "How the Jews Became Japanese and other stories of Nation and Ethnicity." *Jewish History* 18, no. 1 (2004): 7–17.

———. "Imagining Otherness: The Jewish Question in Brazil, 1930–1940." In Kristin Ruggiero, ed., *The Jewish Diaspora in Latin America and the Caribbean: Fragments of Memory.* Brighton, UK: Sussex Academic Press, 2005.

———, eds. *Rethinking Jewish–Latin Americans.* Albuquerque: University of New Mexico Press, 2008.

Levi Calderón, Sara [Sylvia Feldman]. *Dos mujeres.* Madrid: Egales, 2014.

Limonic, Laura. *Kugel and Frijoles: Latino Jews in the United States.* Detroit: Wayne State University Press, 2019.

Liwerant, Judit Bokser, and Eliezer Ben-Rafael. "Klal Yisrael Today: Unity and Diversity. Reflections on Europe and Latin America in a Globalized World." In *A Road to Nowhere?*, edited by Julius Schoeps and Olaf Glöckner, 299-333. Leiden: Brill, 2013.

Mactas Alpersohn, Rebeca. *Los judíos de Las Acacias*. Buenos Aires: Julio Glassman, 1936.

Menis, María Victoria. *Camera Obscura*. Film. 2008.

Mount, Graeme S. "Chile and the Nazis." In *Memory, Oblivion, and Jewish Culture in Latin America*, edited by Marjorie Agosín, 77-90. Austin: University of Texas Press, 2005.

Moya, José C. "What's in a Stereotype? The Case of Jewish Anarchists in Argentina." In *Rethinking Jewish-Latin Americans*, edited by Lesser and Rein, 55-88. Albuquerque: University of New Mexico Press, 2008.

Muñiz Huberman, Angelina. *La burladora de Toledo*. Mexico City: Planeta, 2008.

Muñoz Molina, Antonio. *Sefarad*. Madrid: Alfaguara, 2001.

Navarro-Rosenblatt, Valeria. "The Untold History: Voices of Non-Affiliated Jews in Chile, 1940-1990." In *The New Ethnic Studies in Latin America*, edited by Rein, Rinke, and Zysman, 128-147. Leiden: Brill, 2017.

Ran, Amalia, and Moshe Morad, eds. *Mazal Tov, Amigos! Jews and Popular Music in the Americas*. Leiden: Brill, 2016.

Rawet, Samuel. *Homossexualismo: Sexualidade e valor*. Brazil: Olivé Editor, 1970.

Raznovich, Diana. *De atrás para adelante: Actos desafiantes*. Lewisburg, PA: Bucknell University Press, 2002.

Rein, Raanan. *Argentina, Israel, and the Jews: Perón, the Eichmann Capture and After*. Bethesda: University Press of Maryland, 2003.

Rein, Raanan, Stefan Rinke, and Nadia Zysman, eds. *The New Ethnic Studies in Latin America*. Leiden: Brill, 2017.

Rios, D., Bowling, M. J., and Harris J. "Decentering Student 'Uniqueness.'" In *Intersectional Pedagogy: Complicating Identity and Social Justice*, edited by Kim A. Case, 194-213. New York: Routledge, 2017.

Roniger, Luis, and Deby Babis. "Latin American Israelis: The Collective Identity of an Invisible Community." In *Identities in an Era of Globalization and Multiculturalism: Latin America in the Jewish World*, edited by Judith Bokser Liwerant, 297-320. Leiden: Brill, 2008.

Ruggiero, Kristin ed. *Latin America and the Caribbean: Fragments of Memory*. Brighton, UK: Sussex Academic Press, 2005.

Sadow, Stephen, ed. *I Am of the Tribe of Judah: Jewish Poetry from Latin America*. Albuquerque: University of New Mexico Press, 2023.

Segal, Ariel. *Jews of the Amazon: Self-Exile in Paradise*. Philadelphia: Jewish Publication Society, 1999.

Senkman, Leonardo. "Simón Radowitzky: Revolution, Exile, and a Wandering Jew Imaginary." In *Jewish Imaginaries of the Spanish Civil War: In Search of Poetic Justice*, edited by Cynthia Gabbay. New York: Bloomsbury Publishing, 2022. 56-75.

Spitzer, Leo. *Hotel Bolivia: The Culture of Memory in a Refuge from Nazism*. New York: Hill and Wang, 1998.

Stavans, Ilan. Introduction to *I Am of the Tribe of Judah: Jewish Poetry from Latin America*, edited by Stephen Sadow. University of New Mexico Press, 2023. 1-22.

Strejilevich, Nora. *Una sola muerte numerosa*. Miami: University of Miami, 1997.

Timerman, Jacobo. *Prisoner Without a Name, Cell Without a Number*. New York: Vintage, 1982

Visacovsky, Nerina. *Argentinos, judíos y camaradas tras la utopía socialista*. Buenos Aires: Editorial Biblos, 2017.

———, ed. *Cultura judeo-progresista en las Américas*. Buenos Aires: Ed. Imago Mundi, 2022.

Wassner, Dalia. "The Port Jew and Nuestra América: Narratives of Collective Responsibility and Belonging." *PaRDeS: Journal of the Association for Jewish Studies in Germany* 28 (2023): 84-99.

Yalonetzky, Romina. "Just Like Us, but Jewish: Jewishness, Ethnicity, Class Affinity and Transnationality in Lima." *Ethnicities* 19, no. 6 (2019): 101-120.

Yarfitz, Mir. *Impure Migration: Jews and Sex Work in Golden Age Argentina*. New Brunswick, NJ: Rutgers University Press, 2019.

Zysman, Nadia. "Factory, Workshop, and Homework: A Spatial Dimension of Labor Flexibility among Jewish Migrants in the Early Stages of Industrialization in Buenos Aires." In *The New Ethnic Studies in Latin America*, edited by Rein, Rinke, and Zysman 16-31. Leiden: Brill, 2017.

CHAPTER 9

Race and Nationalism

Hierarchical Imaginaries, Institutional Racism, and Fantasies about the Mestizo

IVÁN FERNANDO RODRIGO-MENDIZÁBAL
AND MARCEL VELÁZQUEZ CASTRO

Race permeated the development of Latin American nation-states. Under the ideals of liberty, citizenship, republican order, modernity, and civilization, after independence, the new republics cemented their social and political formation under the leadership of two groups: creoles and mestizos. But where were the Indigenous peoples and Afro–Latin Americans in the national projects? Were African slavery and Indian forced labor merely systems of exploitation, or did they create systems of cultural domination and future exclusion from citizenship? If racism functioned as a system of social cognition and domination, how did it commingle with the social hygiene movement and positivism and with the questions of national language and civil progress? Were immigrants from other regions of the planet included in the national narrative? Although in many cases creoles and mestizos made up the politico-military elite that led the independence movement and took an active part in the formation of the new nations, given their social dominance, they also prolonged the symbolic exclusion of Indigenous peoples and Afro–Latin Americans from the national body.

This chapter analyzes the tensions among race, nationalism, and modernity in the history of Bolivia, Ecuador, and Peru, with an emphasis on social processes and cultural discourse. The aim is to understand regional developments and the differences and interactions among these variables (race, nationalism, and modernity) from the second half of the nineteenth century to the first decades of the twentieth century. Anderson's now-classic definition of a nation as "an imagined political community and imagined as both inherently limited and sovereign" has been critiqued by postcolonial theorists.[1] And in the case of Bolivia, Ecuador, and Peru, the idea of nation must be nuanced given the weight of intellectual culture, the printing press, and the press in the nineteenth century, as we are dealing with majority oral, multilingual, and illiterate societies. All in all, it must be recognized that the elite imagined the nation through communicative-literary mechanisms that imitated "the cultural structure and ideology of modern liberal states" and resolved any fissure with romantic "post-epic" exits.[2] But if the communicational social structure and narrative were the unifying factor for those who imagined the nation, it must also be noted that regional determinants, the multiplicity of dominant microformations of national identities, equally truncated Simon Bolivar's vision of one great Latin American nation. Even if the nationalism that emerged from these processes guided the consolidation of the new republics, it also deepened the segregation of Indigenous peoples and other groups.

In this context, from the second half of the nineteenth century, the concept of race emerged thanks to the "scientific racism" in vogue in certain intellectual and political circles. The concept of race, in turn, gave rise to the idea of the mestizo nation. In Peru, Bolivia, and Ecuador, when the national states were already being consolidated and connected to European capitalism and modernity through commerce and export of raw materials like guano, silver, and cacao, racism took hold as the urban creole elites' response to the abolition of slavery, Indigenous tribute, and other institutional forms of segregation in the Andes. Despite the formal legal promise of equality, the cultural construction of racial difference was accentuated and articulated with old colonial forms of domination and exploitation of the working classes. If the nineteenth-century notion of race as a "social construction" served to categorize individuals according to skin color, racial heterogeneity was understood as an obstacle to national consolidation.[3] Paradoxically, at the same time, the word race (raza) was used in a political and ideological vein with "a positive effect in the regions with biological and culture mixture, upholding mixture as something central to the nation."[4] This is the case in the Andean republics, including Colombia.

If we discuss the racism of Latin American nations, it is for the overwhelming presence of the social formations of landed and mestizo elites who were trying to forge a certain national identity and distinguish themselves from those excluded from the national project. In Bolivia, Ecuador, and Peru, there was already a high percentage of Indigenous peoples. As Telles notes, "Latin American society was majority rural and nonwhite until the end of the nineteenth century."[5] Telles cites George R. Andrews, who estimated that in "1800, 18% of Mexicans, 26% of Colombians and Peruvians, and 30% of Brazilians were whites, though it was impossible to distinguish between whites and mestizos."[6] And considering the importation of enslaved Africans, "39% of Colombians were of African descent, while 60% of Mexicans and 63% of Peruvians were indigenous."[7] Moreover, "20% of Colombians were indigenous, while 10% of Mexicans and 6% of Peruvians were Black."[8] Note, then, that these national groups were mainly made up of nonwhites, Indigenous peoples, and Afro-descendants. In Bolivia, the Indigenous population, which was the largest national group, was 27,941 in 1846.[9] For Ecuador, Hassaurek, citing Manuel Villavicencio and his *Geography of the Republic of Ecuador* (1858), states that the white, Euro-descendant population was 601,219, while "pure Indians," 462,400, and Afro-descendants, named "pure negroes," 7,831, the mixtures of Blacks, Indigenous, and Whites, 36,592, and the "savages of the East of Cordillera," 200,000. Thus, Ecuador's total population was 1,308,042. But then Hassaurek states that those numbers are erroneous because the Indigenous population was larger than the white population.[10] For its part, Peru, according to Gootenberg, had 1.5 million inhabitants, of which 66 percent were Indigenous.[11] Despite the high unreliability of nineteenth-century population statistics, we can infer that the century closed with more than 3.5 million inhabitants, the percentage of Indigenous peoples remaining the same, but the Black population declining.

Beyond population changes, Andean countries lived through distinct political processes in the nineteenth century. In Bolivia and Peru, more cities were vying for centrality and more differentiated socioeconomic zones. Peru was more centralist, and the debate about national migration was dominated by Lima. Catholic-conservative intellectualism was stronger in Ecuador. Nonetheless, in the three countries, racism served as the explicit or implicit foundational ideology of social order and exclusionary practices against the Indigenous and Black populations, associated with manual labor, certain regions, and illiteracy. A difference in the Peruvian case, in relation to other Andean nations, is the emergence of racist discourse against Chinese immigrants, who could also be found in other Latin American countries, like Cuba and Mexico, as can be seen in other chapters of this volume.

Sociohistorical Context and Some Milestones

During the period under scrutiny here, in Bolivia, it is worth mentioning Manuel Isidoro Belzu (1848–1855), who was first de facto and then elected president, and José Manuel Pando (1899–1904), leader of the federal revolution, who championed the liberalism of the first decades of the twentieth century. In Ecuador, the liberal José María Urbina (1851–1856) was also first de facto and then elected; Gabriel García Moreno (1860–1865, 1869, 1869–1875), a leader who espoused the idea of a Catholic state, was thrice president, two terms as elected and a brief period as de facto; and Eloy Alfaro (1895–1901, 1906–1911), who led the Ecuadorian radical liberal revolution. In Peru, Ramón Castilla governed for two terms (1845–1851, 1855–1862) and led the formation of a republican nation-state, and Manuel Pardo (1872–1876) was the first civilian president; he believed in a practical republic with a modern vision associated with material progress, which was greatly undone by the War of the Pacific (1879–1883). Pardo's ideals and his Civil Party were influential during the first decades of the twentieth century.

Bolivia and Ecuador already had a convulsive democratic life, tensed by liberals and conservatives, truncated by military coups, and threatened by invasions by neighboring countries led by political exiles. The distinct histories of Bolivia and Ecuador, despite their own vicissitudes during the period under scrutiny here, at the same time end with the fall of liberalism and the assassinations of their most modernizing leaders, Pando and Alfaro. In Peru, for its part, a multitemporal and multispatial society prevailed, dominated by the modernizing philosophy of the political elite and the supremacy of the landed oligarchy and its control over the labor force. In the decade of the 1860s, Juan Bustamante's (1808–1868) role stands out. Bustamante defended Indigenous people and led a revolt in Huancané that exposed the limits of a creole republicanism based on Indigenous labor. Afterward, in the first decades of the twentieth century, the so-called aristocratic republic was instituted. This scheme gave total control of the state to the Civil Party and forged an alliance between the modernizing commercial elite and conservatives, yet managed to guarantee a public space for debate and critique.

In Bolivia, Belzu confronted the ruling elite that clung to power and the landed gentry. He integrated the forces of subaltern formation and Indigenous peoples—who called him "Tata," which means "father" and "lord" in Aymara—along with the army. The support of these three entities allowed him to govern. Although slavery was abolished in the Constitution of 1826, Belzu finally eradicated it in the Constitution of 1851. His antioligarchic position has led certain scholars to see in his administration the establishing of a utopic project designed to favor the subaltern majority.[12]

After Belzu's tenure, racism worsened. Gruner notes that "nineteenth-century discussions about the inclusion of indigenous peoples in national life were a simple illusion, since their participation and citizenship was denied from the start."[13] This means that the presence of Indigenous peoples in Bolivian national reality was always seen as a "problem," although public politics and a different administration wanted to integrate them, albeit without recognizing their citizenship. This problem became evident between 1880 and 1890, when Indigenous clamors about landlessness and other injustices were labeled "rebellions," while at the same time trying to project "the image of a white Bolivian republic with almost no indigenous peoples."[14] To quench the threat of Indigenous rebellions, the Bolivian state made military service compulsory for Indigenous men to "domesticate" them.[15] This did not impede the uprising of Pablo Zárate, known as the "fierce Willka"—a word in ancient Aymara that means "sun" or "person gifted with sacred, supernatural power by the sun"—in 1899, demanding the distribution of land.[16] Pando took advantage of Zárate's revolt to start a revolution, which led to the Federal War of 1899. Pando forged an alliance with Zárate "Willka" and made him a military officer. Later, after helping liberals gain power, Zárate wanted to form a government with Aymaras and Quechuas. This angered the liberal militancy, and Pando had Zárate arrested and dismantled the Indigenous army and their reform project.[17]

In Ecuador, Urbina abolished slavery in 1852 through the Law for the Manumission of Slaves. Recognizing social equality implied also recognizing the citizenship of Indigenous peoples and Blacks, not merely removing the tributes these groups were required to pay. Although abolition was supported by the landed elite of the coast, it was opposed by slave-owning elites in the provinces of Imbabura, Loja, Azuay, and Pichincha, who prevented the enforcement of the manumission law until it was reaffirmed by the National Convention of 1856.[18] Despite this new scenario, precarious labor was not suppressed by subsequent administrations, which showed that the elite controlled the economy and that Blacks and Indigenous peoples lived in extreme poverty.[19] New efforts for equality measures came with Alfaro's radical liberalism. Alfaro came to power thanks to the support of coastal peasants from Manabí and Esmeraldas. His administration tried to integrate Indigenous peoples and Blacks into national life with antidiscrimination legislation, wage regulation, the elimination of tribute and multigenerational labor obligations, and improved access to education. But these measures failed under the pressure of the new merchant and financial bourgeoisie, which demanded cheap labor for their projects.[20] To confront the antiliberalism of the elites after the failure of Alfaro's project, Blacks organized militarily for what was called the War of the Afro-Esmeraldeños, a guerrilla war between 1913 and 1916.[21]

In Peru, Castilla, a decisive actor in the formation of the republican state, abolished slavery in 1854, as well as eliminated Indian tribute, two forms of socioracial domination. Despite this rupture with the colonial past, manual labor continued to be degrading, and the naturalized correlation between physical and menial labor and Black and Indigenous peoples was sustained. Even after abolition, Afro-Peruvians' right to full citizenship was debated. The stigmas of slavery, its association with irrationality and immorality and threat to social order, which had its zenith in the years of independence and the following decades, hindered Afro-Peruvians' integration into national projects. For his part, Juan Bustamante, the traveling, military Puneño, congressman, and prefect of Lima, was a complex figure, part of republican civil service without setting aside his activism as defender of education and Indigenous rights. He denounced military service, menial labor, the plunder of land, and the abuses of the clergy—in sum, the exploitation and exclusion of Indigenous peoples. He founded the Society of Friends of the Indians (Sociedad de Amigos de los Indios). For Tejada, Bustamante's political career was the expression of Andean liberalism: it held as central tenets equality under the law, individual freedom, government protection of the vulnerable, and the inclusion of Indigenous peoples in the national project.[22]

In November 1866, Indigenous peoples in Huancané (Puno) rose up against a law that sought to reestablish Indigenous tributes. The fear sparked by this rebellion brought about harsh military repression. The Indigenous uprisers were portrayed as violent savages. The government feared the looting of the Peruvian Southeast, which never came. Behind this military tactic was a conspiracy against President Mariano Ignacio Prado (ruler between 1865 and 1867 and in 1867, 1867–1868, and 1876–1879) and the Liberal Constitution of 1866, led by conservatives. During this turmoil, there were several confrontations and losses, including the death of Juan Bustamante, who was leading the

Indigenous militias, by military troops loyal to conservatives.[23] This was the first insurrection against a republican order that excluded and oppressed the majority of the population and that ideologically strengthened this oppression through stereotypes and prejudices.

Nationalist Romanticism and the Appropriation of the Image of the Indian

As contradictory as it may seem, despite the prevailing racism, Latin American nations, particularly the Andean ones, knew how to deal ideologically with the national problem and presence of Indigenous, Black, and other peoples by integrating into sociopolitical discourse the idea of racial mixture, mestizaje. The national being was mestizo, a citizen whose mixed ancestry personified the nation. For B. Muratorio, the tendency among Andean nations was an outward racial presentation of countries where Indigenous people were integrated into the national. Thus, elites and mestizos began to elaborate the discourse of an identity anchored on the "ancestral"—but not real, Indian—for the latter meant making the country look backward and uncivilized.[24] Intellectuals who sought to solve the "Indian problem," under Romantic aspirations, lent themselves to this process of discursive integration, equating Indigenous and Black peoples with barbarism and savagery.[25] This was contrasted with an exaltation of the myth of the Inca past, thus fashioning a model of a "precivilization" that was completed and improved by republican mestizo forces, bridging the mythologized Inca past with the republican present.

Romantic thought accentuated the "mestizo nation's" civilized relation not with the Spanish past, but with the Inca one. The return to the ancestral was linked to the landscape, the Andean air, the Andean range, Inca buildings. Langebaek, however, notes that nineteenth-century Latin American Romanticism was conservative. For this Romanticism, there was nothing gratuitous in returning to or claiming "the autochthonous tradition"; "its pretense to return to 'its own history' sought to forge a shield that would defend society from the changes conservatives feared the most: the liberation of society, its modernization and democratization, not to mention the frightful individualism that threatened the national unity."[26] What was being preserved of the past to make the new history and the new nation? For Langebaek, moral values, social structures and customs, "immutable" traces of the mestizo.[27] But the ideological appropriation of the mythical Indian meant having tamed the race and recognizing that it came from an imperial past. According to Cruz

Rodríguez, in Bolivia the result was that the mestizo had been born from "the ideal exchange between creoles and glorious indigenous ancestors," *cholaje* being a "racial degeneration," a weakness that stained the nation and that needed to be eliminated.²⁸ In the Ecuadorian case, above all for the elites who benefited from agricultural exports, "Indians were the 'semiotic peons' of their iconographic interests and to legitimize their economic success. In this process, an image of an Ecuador as a Collective Being began to be constructed. In this system of representation, the image of mestizaje emerged as a 'metanarrative,' constructed in a dialectic process of exclusion of the indigenous Other."²⁹

According to Vaca-Guzmán, Romanticism as a literary and ideological current in Bolivia emerged toward 1840 with the "illness of sentimentalism which moreover is endemic and particular to the Bolivian temperament," and which, in relation to the Indigenous subject, was developed by "spirits more enthusiastic than admiring, blind depots that held it up as a model of patriarchal government."³⁰ Therefore, certain Romantic novels have brave Indigenous heroes subsumed within the new history weaved from mestizo ideology. This is notable in Victorino Rivero's *Amarrá i Espól* (1871), an allegorical novel that, seeking to reproduce Indigenous speech, was presented like this: "In Amrrá you will find the ladies and the girls, the portrait of a faithful wife, in memory of her husband; and youth, the personification of America's destiny, which under Inca rule and other pure Americans, represented by Manco Capac, was blissful, while it was disgraced under Spanish colonialism, recast by Espól."³¹

In Claudio Pinilla's *Guanaiquile* (1882), a revolt in Zongo in 1624 led by the cacique Guanaiquile is reimagined through social Darwinism. José Benito Guzmán's *Leyenda judicial* (1883) and Lindaura Anzoátegui de Campero's *Huallparrimachi* (1894) represent the descendants of Indigenous peoples. *Leyenda judicial* portrays Alejo Calatayud, the leader of an uprising in Cochabamba in 1730, and *Huallparrimachi*, the Indigenous leader Juan Huallparrimachi, a mestizo who was representative of the emancipatory cause because of his "Inca-Spanish" ancestry and because he was a poet and a patriot. Soto observes that in these works there is a "whitening" of ancestral Indians since they are ideologically accepted into Bolivian nationality.³² These representations, all in all, had nothing to do with "the Bolivian state's systemic efforts to eradicate the indigenous community and institute private property," facts that were hidden and ignored by the Bolivian intelligentsia.³³

In Ecuador, García Moreno was the intellectual who preached Romanticism to the nation while he was a student leader at the Central University.[34] Although his Romantic fervor was short-lived, it was quickly taken up by conservatives. This did not prevent García Moreno from fighting for the rights of Indigenous and Black peoples, albeit under the moralizing authority of the Catholic Church. García Moreno, during a senate debate "Protecting the Mulatos of Esmeraldas," said that the nation needed to overcome the colonial mentality that kept Indians in abject poverty, denounced the deception in which they lived, and supported the mulattoes' cause. For all of them, it was difficult to teach and make them know their rights.[35] Outside this reflection, in literature, the Romantic adoption of the Indian is as the "good savage" that lived in the Amazon region of Ecuador. Thus, in José Peralta's *Chumbera, leyenda original* (1876), which tells of an Indigenous uprising in the mining region of Logroño in 1599, the Shuaras—known as wild head cutters—are represented as barbarians, although the Indigenous hero, the young Chumbera, who falls in love with a white woman, is a warrior. Another case is Juan León Mera's novel *Cumandá o un drama entre salvajes* (1879). In this novel, the savage is "as impetuous as water rolling down a mountainside, nothing can contain him."[36] Regarding the indigenous people of the Sierra, contrary to the impetuous warriors, in an essay, Juan Montalvo described Indigenous peoples as "like the ass, he is an ignorant thing.... The soldier takes him to sweep the barracks, the priest to carry the saints on his shoulders in the processions.... This is his cruel condition.... If my pen could cry and I were writing a book entitled 'The Indian,' I would make the world weep."[37]

In Peru, Romanticism flourished between 1850 and 1870. There is no significant novel that clearly expressed the national horizon through love of country and interethnic marriages, as in Sommer's model. Nor is there a Romantic recreation of the Inca world. Nonetheless, there were short stories in newspapers, like Ricardo Palma's "Traditions," which imagined creole-Limeña culture as the center of national identity. In its imaginary there was room for the Hispanic colonial tradition, but not the Indigenous one.[38] Palma represented aspects of the popular sensibility of the urban population, the linguistic hegemony of Spanish, and creole knowledge. This Lima is presented in his work as composed of a Westernized creole elite in permanent interaction with a heterogeneous social subject, popular, and with African elements. Palma contributed to the consolidation of the discourse of mestizaje and in the joyous but conflictive recognition of cultural plurality. On the other hand, different from Palma's social and cultural apotheosis of mestizaje, in literature there were other ways of narrating the national imaginary from a racial point of view, such as Clorinda Matto de Turner's *Tradiciones cuzqueñas* (1884) and *Leyendas y recortes* (1893).[39] For Velázquez Castro, in "most of her 'legends,' Matto de Turner sets her stories in the context of the first years of colonization. Some refer to Andean traditions of the past that were still alive. . . . In various occasions the protagonist is a white conquistador and a beautiful Indian woman, who live an impossible love: their union cannot be replicated socially."[40] This failed nationalist Romanticism sought the tragic idealization of the ancestral Andean population, women in particular. Yet it did not forge a national image that included contemporary Indigenous peoples or their culture, still perceived as part of the backward past.

African Heritage, Linguistic Hygiene, and Xenophobia: Prejudices and Social Ills

In the first decades of independence, slavery—legal, social, and economic—was part of the private life and material experience of Andean cities. This status quo was brought to an end by legislation and public policy in the second half of the nineteenth century. However, other means of control over the lives of Indigenous, Black, and mixed-race peoples and Chinese immigrants survived to the first decades of the twentieth century, above all in hacienda work and domestic service. The body of the worker, made to endure these premodern labor relations, was at the disposal of the landed elite, who not only benefited from the worker's labor but also had full immunity to punish the worker physically and sexually.

Before slavery was outlawed, above all in Lima, there existed a slave market formalized in the public sphere through advertisement of the sale and purchase of male farming slaves and female wet nurses, cooks, and laundresses. After the abolition of slavery, among Andean countries, there was continuity, for such advertisements became solicitation for childcare, domestic work, and the like. Indigenous and Black "workers" were paid ridiculously low wages; that is to say, the same sectors were condemned to physical and domestic labor.[41] In Peru, the Black population was the target of sustained racism after slavery. Blacks settled in farming valleys south of Lima, on the northern coast, and in Lima's poor neighborhoods. They were socially discriminated, perceived as symbols of the ignorant masses, and associated with irrationality and immorality.

As for the Black experience in Ecuador and Colombia, most of the settlements resulted from the colonial regime, particularly in the valleys and coasts. Although manual labor was initially destined for the Indigenous population, haciendas and even religious orders, like the Jesuits, soon replaced them with enslaved Africans, especially in agriculture.[42] In the nineteenth century, following abolition, Afro–Latin Americans formed communities like Chota and Guayaquil and Esmeraldas on the coast, although they remained in servile labor circumstances. It should be noted that, like Indigenous peoples, Blacks were made to take the family names of the families that enslaved them, for there was still a notion that there existed a master-slave relationship by which landed elites and elite classes still considered themselves the owners of Black peoples. Even if there was a race-and-class divide, this did not stop intermingling, something that is denied even to this day out of shame.[43] When the national railroad was begun, during García Moreno's administration, Afro-descendants were "imported" from the English Caribbean and Haiti. These latter were the cause of another mestizaje, bringing about families with English and French last names, which were preferred on the coast.[44] In this context, Jurado Noboa has researched the genealogy of some Ecuadorian presidents.[45] He found that Vicente Ramón Roca (1845–1849)—leader of a revolt that sought to institute liberal policies—was an Afro-mestizo who was ridiculed or avoided by Quito elite classes.[46] Eloy Alfaro's (1895–1901, 1906–1911)—leader of a radical liberal revolution—case was identical. In contrast, Hidalgo and Handelsman have studied the rich oral traditions in the vast and complex Afro-Ecuadorian literature, which surpasses Peru's and Bolivia's Black letters.[47]

As for Afro-Bolivians, it must be said that after independence and decades of laboring in the mines, they settled in the inter-Andean valley of Yungas, whose origins lie in the colony. Until the mid-1800s, Bolivia's Black population was 27,941, and those still enslaved numbered 1,391, although most were employed in agriculture, besides domestic work.[48] Afro-Bolivians celebrated Belzu's abolition of slavery in the Constitution of 1851. Sánchez Canedo notes that Yungas recognized Belzu as "their liberator, presented him the banner of the High Altar of their church, and composed a *saya*—Bolivia's national dance—in his honor."[49] Despite this milestone, Afro-Bolivians were excluded from Bolivian society and labeled as lazy, thieves, and criminals.[50]

Since colonial times, there has been a racial language that is still used against mixed-race individuals. Thus, according to Crespo, in the Bolivian case, the racial idiom imposed the category of *casta*, reflecting the existence and tensions among the country's diverse ethno-racial groups. From this, we get the half-white, half-Indigenous mestizo; the creole born of a white woman and a mestizo man; the half-white, half-Black *mulato*; the *cuarentón* born of a white man and a mulata woman; the *quinquerón* of a white woman and a male *cuarentón*; the white (*blanco*) of a white woman and a male *quinquerón*; the *zambo* from Black and mulata or a Chinese woman; the Black *zambo* (*zambo prieto*) from a Black woman and a *zambo*; the Black (*negro*) from a Black man and a *zamba prieta*.[51] These labels were also used in Peru and Ecuador, with added pejoratives like *ugly, dumb, bowlegged*, and *flat-nosed*.

However, beyond the foregoing labels, the greatest tension has been among mestizos, whites, and *cholos*. *Cholo* was coined as an insult during the colonial era. For example, Arona wrote that *cholaje* "is one of the many castas that infects Peru."[52] *Cholo* often refers to the children of Indigenous individuals and mestizos; in Peru, the label is used for the lower classes, and in Ecuador, for the indigenized mestizo.[53] In Bolivia, it pointed out who was "whitened," that is, the Indian or the indigenized mestizo who tried to dress as European. In any case, a *cholo* was distinguished from an Indian because he was a merchant, owned parcels of land, traded in livestock in local markets, and even had some authority.[54] The immense presence of *cholos* in the Andean world challenged the creole and mestizo elites' nationalist discourse and aggravated racism among the dominant classes. The ruling elite used racial discrimination to keep everyone in their imagined social place.

One form this discourse took was language hygiene. Aymara and Quechua—Quichua in Ecuador—were the object of critique and censure. In 1889, Vaca-Guzmán wrote that if there was anything that survived from Bolivia's Aymara and Quechua cultures, besides their "semi-barbaric" peoples, it was their equally "semi-barbaric languages, organically sterile in the sphere of intellectual creativity."[55] For Vaca-Guzmán, "the Aymara or Quechua Indian does not produce anything and he modulates some phrases to the tune of the *charango*, his rhyme, if it can be called that, only reveals truncated, incomplete, unbearably trivial thoughts."[56] This disdain for Andean languages fed a hygienic philosophy that called for eliminating any traces of Aymara and Quichua from Spanish.

In Peru's case, the country was always imagined as monolingual. Spanish, the language of the elites, silenced the other languages spoken in the country (Quechua, Aymara, and a dozen Amazonian languages). Thus, schools ratified the cultural domination of Spanish, not only as a hegemonic language but also as a civilizing one, which implied the subjugation and contempt of American languages. Linguistic stigma was a form of racial discrimination in Peru. In the nineteenth and twentieth centuries, Blacks, Indians, and Chinese immigrants were constantly mocked for the way they spoke Spanish. The lettered elite loved to publish texts that mocked Andean Spanish or the way Black servants or Chinese immigrants supposedly spoke. This consolidated "proper" Spanish as the only legitimate language and disqualified other linguistic possibilities.

Likewise, from Lima, during the second half of the nineteenth century, an artificial correlation between decency, hygiene, and whiteness on the one hand, and indecency, illness, and Blacks, Indians, and Chinese immigrants on the other, was constructed. Within these cultural markers, we must inscribe the mandate to whiten one's face among Lima's diverse population, principally among women: the poorest with rice water, and those who could afford them, with European creams. Without denying the practical advantages of soap, it is impossible to see its association with colonialism, racism, and hygiene. The politics of admittance to "civilization," through the consumption of Western goods, presupposed that dirty and nonwhite were synonymous, as in Pear's Soap ads, which accompanied the development of British imperialism. Soap became a symbol of modernity, a materialization of the violence of colonialism, and a ratification of explicit racism; it motivated the fantasies of civilization, hygiene, and whiteness among the "brown" social sector. Even medical science and hygienist thought confirmed the triumph of soap. This was how, since the 1850s, a correlation was established between the beautiful, white, and decent. This correlation strengthened the legitimacy of the racial hierarchization of Peru.[57]

Unlike in Ecuador and Bolivia, where such a xenophobic-racist discourse did not take hold, in Peru there was one against Chinese immigrants, whose language, customs, and culture were the target of ferocious racism. Although Peru had several campaigns and legislative projects to promote European immigration, such as the Society for European Immigration (Sociedad de Inmigración Europea), which had an office in every department and was promoted by Pardo, what stands out for its volume was the Chinese immigration between 1850 and 1910. It is estimated that one hundred thousand Chinese nationals settled in Peru during this period. Most of them engaged in agriculture, gathering guano and building railroads in several parts of the country. From the perspective of the menial labor market, Chinese immigrants replaced the formerly enslaved population, as it happened in Cuba, as discussed in another chapter of this volume.

Anti-Chinese racism connected Chinese bodies and social practices with yellow fever, the bubonic plague, and several outbreaks of tuberculosis in

Lima. This was one of the ideological responses, a sociocultural response to an imagined threat, but which was fed by an increase in immigration, new labor relations, overcrowding, and a long history of dehumanizing Asian alterity.

Lima's Chinese population increased in the first decades of the twentieth century with the importation of Asian laborers, promoted by members of the Civil Party, and a sustained migration from rural towns to the city. Between 1903 and 1908, 11,742 workers arrived from China, and 1,000 the following year.[58] This labor force began to create their own places of work and to compete successfully with urban workers, generating a profound rejection and violence from the popular sector against Chinese Limeños. On the other hand, from 1870, the precarious conditions around today's Central Market (Mercado Central) led to poor living conditions, overcrowding, and insalubrity, similar to other popular neighborhoods of Lima, of Indigenous neighborhoods, as well as Black neighborhoods, former slave barracks. Discrimination against Chinese Limeños was "scientifically" strengthened by the diffusion of racialism, an ideological perspective that looked at social and cultural characteristics in terms of race as an essential reality with superior and inferior races. Modern urban epidemics fueled xenophobia and racial discrimination against Chinese Limeños. Limeños' cultural violence against Chinese immigrants at the beginning of the twentieth century was prevalent in political and literary texts and satirical cartoons.[59]

In the context of this verbal violence, of course, was strengthened negative characterization of Chinese Limeños through the language of hygienics: "vicious and abject," "degradation and dirtiness," "immorality and corruption." Likewise, two cultural practices, Chinese immigrants' penchant for games and opium, both considered immoral, were singled out. Chinese Limeños were represented as a threat to the national project. In this context, the magazine *Fray K. Bezón* (1907–1910) condensed racist and social prejudices against Chinese immigrants and distinguished itself by its virulence expressed through its humorous language replete with a carnivalesque and popular vision. Likewise, physical and moral accusations against them formed part of Latin America's modern racist discourse since 1850.[60]

In Peru, the adoption of racialist ideas was documented, and it configured a system of cognition, social domination, and labor exploitation shared by social elites, academic discourse, the press, and the popular sector. This explains the organized attacks against Chinese immigrants and their properties between 1904 and 1909, in which Lima's poor took part in a visible way. After the destruction of Otaiza Alley by Mayor Guillermo Billingurst,

President Augusto Leguía issued a decree that halted Chinese immigration to Peru. Afterward, Leguía signed the Porras-Wu Ting Fang protocol, which allowed Chinese immigration but not of manual laborers seeking to stay.[61]

Italians were the second-largest group of immigrants in Peru. They arrived voluntarily in a sustained way since the 1850s and mainly settled in the port of El Callao and the city of Lima. According to Worrall, thirteen thousand Italians arrived in the first decades of the twentieth century.[62] Unlike Chinese immigrants, Italians easily assimilated to Limeño society thanks to their customs, Romance language, and religion, and through economic activities, bakeries, and bodegas. They were also important in labor activities and associated with ideas of radical republicanism. Unlike with Chinese immigrants, there was no discourse of exclusion, although some insults, such as *gringo bachiche*, did exist, but Peruvian women accepted them as partners in marriage for their European phenotypes.

The "Indian Problem" in the Twentieth Century

The tension of invisibilizing Indigenous peoples—as well as Blacks and Asian immigrants—put on greater display the racist discourse about the "Indian problem." Although this idea dates back to the nineteenth century, it acquired sociopolitical connotations, connected with the idea of a modern nation—the one emerging from capitalist progress and the idea of a more advanced civilization—bourgeois in essence, in the twentieth century.

In Peru, for example, positivists believed in a society ruled by the ideals of civilization and progress, in the manner of European models, where Indigenous and Black groups constituted a threat to the nation, residue from the past. If Palma promoted *criollismo* (nativism), with colonial and Hispanophilic resonances, as the national image, González Prada criticized the oligarchy, seeking to vindicate Indigenous peoples, calling Lima a "purulent nucleus."[63] All in all, the search for a civilization that craved material progress and Western culture entailed a repudiation of Indigenous culture as well as of urban culture with a high Black presence and of far-flung regions, like the Amazonian departments.

The defeat in the War of the Pacific (1879–1884) brought about new social conditions that led to a new approach to the problem of race in Peru. Besides the vindication of the Indian as a brave man that had resisted the Chilean invasion in the Andes, there were lettered figures, like Clorinda Matto, that called for preserving and recognizing Quechua as a central element of national identity.[64] In ideological terms, González Prada was the first to emphatically affirm the relation between Indian and nation in Peru in an 1888 speech: "Creoles and foreigners are not the true Peru; the nation is made up of the masses of Indians on the east side of the Andes. It has been three hundred years since the Indian has been relegated to the lower rungs of civilization, possessing barbaric vices and lacking European virtues. School teachers, it is your job to galvanize the race under the tyranny of the justice of the peace, of the governor and the priest, that stupefying trinity of the Indian."[65]

Unable to avoid a social evolution focus, González Prada could not help but propose education, above all literacy, as a tool of Indigenous liberation and redemption. González Prada shared this historical position about Indigenous peoples, however, for Blacks he had an essentialist and ahistorical vision. For González Prada, Indigenous peoples were the basis for the dreamed nation, but Afro-Peruvians were a colonial residue. The Indian was an ardent enemy of the white man, but the Black was his ally because he was historically and sexually aligned with the oligarchy through slavery. The Indian lives away from the corrupting coast, the Black lives there.[66] In another chapter of this book, José Carlos Mariátegui's indigenist ideas are explored, amplifying my reading of González Prada, incorporating the economic dimension of the "problem of the land."[67] Mariátegui, however, kept the racist outlook about Blacks and Chinese immigrants.[68]

In another ideological current, in Peru, the fin de siècle civicism was formulated under positivism and social Darwinism and saw the Indian race as decadent and weak. However, from the work and experience of certain associations for lawyers, doctors and engineers, certain material conditions and social relations begin to be privileged to explain the behavior and cultural characteristics of certain social groups, such as Indigenous, urban poor, and Blacks. It is in this context that the concept of race and its hierarchy acquired new meanings, for the emancipation of social groups and civilization can be achieved through education, hygiene, and work. Thus, two other Andean countries converge in the tendency to educate Indigenous peoples, which was already being discussed by education policymakers, precisely to address the "Indian problem." This solution to the race problem through education was a form of acculturation since it sought to implicitly silence Andean languages. It must be noted, moreover, that the right to free public education was more an ideal than a reality, for there were not enough schools. However, the emancipatory potential of Spanish education for Indigenous peoples cannot be denied, as the racist phrase attests: "An educated Indian is a lost Indian."

In Peru, a key moment was the Election Act (Ley Electoral) of 1895, which established direct suffrage and made literacy a requirement to vote. For this reason, literacy became a criterion of exclusion from citizenship. Before the act, tax-paying Indians could vote, but the new exclusion lasted for most of the twentieth century. It was only in 1979 that illiterate Peruvians were allowed to vote.

In Ecuador, responding to García Moreno's preoccupation with standardizing Spanish, his minister of war, Francisco Javier Salazar, published *El método productivo de enseñanza primaria aplicado a las escuelas de la república del Ecuador* (The effective method of teaching primary education in the public schools of the Republic of Ecuador, 1869), which was required in all schools. It recommended that in order not to force Indigenous children to speak Spanish, educators should start with their native tongue, Quichua: "The educator dedicated to the honorable task of leading the Indian race to civilization, must begin by instructing children in the Quichua language that they understand and speak."[69] This should be followed by syllabaries and bilingual books for an effective translation.

In a certain way, Salazar's text sought to clean Spanish of Indigenous expressions and words, which had been assimilated into Spanish from the colonial period, with the aim of "civilizing" the Indian. Above all, in the east, in the Amazon region, priests were the ones charged with "educating" and "evangelizing" Indigenous peoples. This endeavor sought to have Indigenous people recognize the authority and sovereignty of the government. For example, in his travelogue, Rafael Cáceres wrote, "If the Indian does not see firmness in authority, he will spend months upon months in their forests, content with his savage ways."[70] In fact, Amazonian peoples were distinguished from those of the highlands. Amazonians were seen as "unfaithful savages" or "savages Indians [that have not yet been converted and] who professed a sort of fetichism."[71]

If clerics warmly embraced the task of educating Indigenous peoples, it was because García Moreno sought to establish a Catholic state in Ecuador. After his death, although they were not in politics, priests were the ones who continued the "civilizing" mission. In his now-classic sociological study *El indio ecuatoriano*, Jaramillo Alvarado argued that all public policies regarding indigenous peoples were pure rhetoric, just as the civilizing missions were a paternalistic solution. What was real, for him, was to return the land, vindicate the Indian, pay him just for his work and, above all, "secure and guarantee his economic situation," that is, give him the full status of citizenship.[72] The one who should be "educated" was truly the boss and the authority. These theses opened the way to a new mentality in Ecuadorian society. In 1925, when liberalism parted from the path set by Alfaro, there was a new turn in national politics with the socialist and modernizing Julian Revolution. The "problem of the Indian" remerged with efforts to dignify the race, although this discourse did not go beyond the rhetorical realm.[73] The same year (1925), another cleric, Ricardo Delgado Campeáns, recalling García Moreno's ideas, proposed that to solve the "Indian problem" and bring Indigenous people's dignity, it was necessary to organize and educate them. Delgado Campeáns even recognized that some Indigenous communities were nations, and as such, they should be looked at differently and not with the disdain with which they were treated.[74] If these ideas had prevailed, a novel like Jorge Icaza's *Huasipungo* (1934), which decried the oppression of Indigenous peoples, would have never been written.[75]

In Bolivia, some clerics took up the education and evangelizing mission, though without official support. Especially in the Highlands (the Altiplano), syllabaries were used to try to teach Indigenous individuals Spanish. Despite its colonialist implications, one of the most fervent educators, Father Carlos Felipe Beltran, complained about the oppression of Indigenous peoples and the need to integrate them into social and economic life.[76] In his *Civilización del indio* (Indian civilization, 1872), he admonished: "Oh beloved Indian! I can finally put this syllabary in your hands. Study and commit to memory the onomatopoeic scale and you will read with the ease of Aymara."[77] Beltrán published at least five textbooks. Unfortunately, in 1879, Moreno, one of the most influential positivists, criticized those books because "indigenous languages, far from helping indigenous people advance, keeps them back. For this reason, Beltrán's books are more praiseworthy than useful. The true advancement of the Bolivian Indian will come from the fusion of the former with the Spanish race, and the submission of indigenous languages to the dominance of Spanish."[78]

Finally, in this context, we must note the work of the Bolivian essayist and novelist Alcides Arguedas, who stated the "Indian problem" clearly. His most pertinent work on the subject is *Pueblo enfermo* (Infirm race), published in 1909. Arguedas dedicates a long chapter to the "ethnic problem." For Arguedas, "the Indian is a savage, as shy as a wild beast, happy with heathen rituals and the cultivation of the sterile earth that without doubt will soon bring an end to their race."[79] Elsewhere he reiterates these ideas: "The indigenous race is irredeemably lost and it is a dead race."[80] And curiously, since he could not make Indigenous peoples disappear with a magic act, he proposed that the Indian must be "adapted" to modern society and given a "solid education" and even "change his conditions."[81]

Conclusion

Racism, a system of cognition and domination, was hegemonic in the Andes from the 1850s onward. It traversed all social sectors, carried colonial resonances, and was strengthened by positivism and social Darwinism. In Peru, Ecuador, and Bolivia, countries with large Indigenous populations, the Europhile creole elites, with a mestizo base, kept the lower sectors of society out public life.

Romantic discourse idealized the Inca past seeking to assimilate the privilege of the original civilizations, connecting them with the demand of the republican creole elites. Education was seen as a way to incorporate Indigenous peoples into modern society while at the same time seeking to erase their culture and language. Slavery and other forms of labor exploitation contributed to racism against Blacks and Amerindians, for they were seen not only as merely laboring bodies but also as alien to the equality of citizenship and civil rights.

The discourse of mestizaje and racist practices have concurred in the history of Peru, Ecuador, and Bolivia. The ideology of mestizaje promoted by intellectual elites since the 1890s and later by the state, was asymmetrical, pigmentocratic, and classist. It was a narrative of collective identity that valued European culture above the Andean, that enthroned whiteness and whitening and pigmentocracy, that associated education with economic capacity. To be a mestizo was to speak correctly in the hegemonic tongue and to disdain Indigenous and Black ancestors but never European ancestors.

Finally, in Peru, European immigration did not take place in the desired volume or conditions. Instead, there was a great Chinese migration for labor that quickly freed itself from the yoke of exploitative labor and managed to make inroads in the cultural and economic life of the country despite the great racial violence it faced.

NOTES

1. Benedict Anderson, *Imagined Communities: Reflections on the Origin and Spread of Nationalism* (London: Verso, 2006), 6; Partha Chatterjee, *Empire and Nation: Selected Essays* (New York: Columbia University Press, 2010), 25-6.
2. José Carlos Mainer, *Historia de la literatura española: El lugar de la literatura española* (Barcelona: Crítica, 2012), 20; Doris Sommer, *Foundational Fictions: The National Romances of Latin America* (Berkeley: University of California Press, 1993), 12.
3. Peter Wade, *Race and Ethnicity in Latin America* (New York: Pluto Press, 1997), 16.
4. Edward Telles, "El proyecto de etnicidad y raza en América Latina (PERLA): Los datos cuantitativos y lo que está en juego," in *Pigmentocracias color, etnicidad y raza en América Latina,* ed. Edward Telles and Regina Martínez Casas, trans. Fatna Lazcano (Mexico City: Fondo de Cultura Económica, 2019), 34.
5. Telles, "El Proyecto de etnicidad," 31.
6. Telles, "El Proyecto de etnicidad," 31.
7. Telles, "El Proyecto de etnicidad," 31-32.
8. Telles, "El Proyecto de etnicidad," 32.
9. Alberto Crespo, *Esclavos negros en Bolivia* (La Paz: Academia Nacional de Ciencias de Bolivia, 1977), 200.
10. Friedrich Hassaurek, *Four Years among Spanish-Americans* (New York: Hurd and Houghton, 1868), 124.
11. Paul Gootenberg, *Población y etnicidad en el Perú republicano (siglo XIX): Algunas revisiones* (Lima: IEP, 1995), 20.
12. Andrey Shchelchkov, *La utopía social conservadora en Bolivia: El gobierno de Manuel Isidoro Belzu 1848-1855* (La Paz: Plural, 2011), 205.
13. Wolf Gruner, "'Los parias de la patria': La discriminación estatal de los indígenas en la República de Bolivia (1825-1952/53)," in *Identidad, ciudadanía y participación popular desde la colonia al siglo XX,* ed. Josefa Salmón and Guillermo Delgado (La Paz: Plural, 2003), 1:184.
14. Gruner, "Los parias de la patria," 185.
15. Gruner, "Los parias de la patria," 186; Brooke Larson, *Indígenas, élites y Estado en la formación de las repúblicas andinas, 1850-1910* (Lima: IEP, Pontificia Universidad Católica del Perú, 2002), 171.
16. Pilar Mendieta Parada, "Por órdenes del Papa Santo de Roma: La 'Proclama de Caracollo' de Pablo Zárate Willka (1899)," *Revista Ciencia y Cultura* 23, no. 42 (2019): 157.
17. Laura Gotkowitz, *A Revolution for Our Rights: Indigenous Struggles for Land and Justice in Bolivia, 1880-1952* (Durham, NC: Duke University Press, 2007), 37-38.
18. Rocío Rueda Novoa, "Desesclavización, manumisión jurídica y defensa del territorio en el norte de Esmeraldas (siglos XVIII-XIX)" *Procesos: Revista Ecuatoriana de Historia,* no. 43 (2016), 17-18.
19. Catalina Ribadeneira Suárez, *El racismo en el Ecuador contemporáneo entre la modernidad y el fundamentalismo étnico: El discurso del otro* (Quito: Abya-Yala, 2001), 54.
20. Diego Iturralde, "Nacionalidades indígenas y Estado nacional en Ecuador," in *Los derechos colectivos: Hacia su efectiva comprensión y protección,* ed. María Paz Avila Ordóñez and María Belén Corredores Ledesma (Quito: Ministerio de Justicia y Derechos Humanos; Alto Comisionado de las Naciones Unidas para los Derechos Humanos, 2009), 109.

21. José Figueroa, *Republicanos negros: Guerras por la igualdad, racismo y relativismo cultural* (Bogotá: Planeta, 2022), 263.
22. Sergio Tejada Galindo, *Tras los pasos de Juan Bustamante: Apuntes biográficos y políticos* (Lima: Construyendo la Nación, 2019), 84–94.
23. Tejada, *Tras los pasos*, 66–72.
24. Muratorio, as cited in Ribadeneira Suárez, *El racismo*, 55.
25. Ribadeneira Suárez, *El racismo*, 56.
26. Carl Henrik Langebaek, "Civilización y barbarie: El indio en la literatura criolla en Colombia y Venezuela después de la independencia," *Revista de Estudios Sociales*, no. 22 (2005): 47.
27. Langebaek, "Civilización y barbarie," 48.
28. Edwin Cruz Rodríguez, "El 'problema indígena' y la construcción de la nación en Bolivia y Ecuador durante el siglo XIX: La perspectiva de las luchas por la hegemonía" *Diálogo Latinoamericanos*, no. 19 (2012): 59.
29. Muratorio as cited in Ribadeneira Suárez, *El racismo*, 55.
30. Santiago Vaca-Guzmán, "Las letras en Bolivia," in *América literaria: Producciones selectas en prosa y verso*, ed. Francisco Lagomaggiore (Buenos Aires: Imprenta de La Nación, 1890), 352, 350.
31. Victorino Rivero, *Amarrá i Espól, novela histórica* (Santa Cruz de la Sierra: Imp. de Cayetano H. Daza, 1871), 3.
32. Juan Pablo Soto Jiménez, "Introducción," in *Ficcionalización de Bolivia: La leyenda / novela del siglo diez i nueve 1847–1896*, ed. Juan Pablo Soto Jiménez y Máximo Pacheco Balanza (Cochabamba, Bolivia: n.p., 2016), 1:32.
33. Soto Jiménez, "Introducción," 52.
34. José Ignacio Burbano, "La revolución romántica y la restauración neoclásica: Estudio preliminar," in *Poetas románticos y neoclásicos: La colonia y la República*, ed. José Ignacio Burbano (Puebla: J. M. Cajica y Secretaría General de la Undécima Conferencia Interamericana de Quito, 1960), 29–30.
35. Gabriel García Moreno, *Escritos y discursos: Escritos oficiales. Recopilados y publicados por la Sociedad de la Juventud Católica de Quito y anotados por su presidente D. Manuel María Pólit* (Quito: Imp. del Clero, 1888), 50–51.
36. Juan León Mera, *Cumandá: O un drama entre salvajes* (Quito: Imp. del Clero, 1879), 108.
37. Juan Montalvo, "Impresiones de un diplomático," *El Espectador* (Paris: Librería Franco-Hispano-Americana, 1888), 206.
38. Ricardo Palma, *Tradiciones y artículos históricos* (Lima: Imp. Torres Aguirre, 1899).
39. Clorinda Matto de Turner, *Leyendas y recortes* (Lima: Imp. La Equitativa, Matto Hermanos Editores, 1893); Clorinda Matto de Turner, *Tradiciones cuzqueñas: Leyendas, biografías y hojas sueltas* (Arequipa: Imp. de La Bolsa, 1884).
40. Marcel Velázquez Castro, "La narrativa breve de Clorinda Matto: De la tradición y leyenda románticas al cuento modernista," *Escritura y Pensamiento* 15, no. 31 (2012): 90–91.
41. Roberto Choque Canqui, "La servidumbre indígena andina de Bolivia," in *El siglo XIX: Bolivia y América Latina*, ed. Rossana Barragán et al. (Lima: Institut Français d'Études Andines, 1997), 475.
42. Rosario Coronel, "Indios y esclavos negros en el valle del Chota colonial," in *El negro en la historia de Ecuador y del sur de Colombia*, ed. Rafael Savoia (Guayaquil: Centro Cultural Afro-Ecuatoriano, Depto. de Pastoral Afro-Ecuatoriano, 2002), 172, 183.
43. Ezio Garay Arellano, "Los negros en Guayaquil en 1850," in *El negro en la historia*, 126.

44. Ezio Garay Arellano, "La élite económica de los negros en Guayaquil de 1792 a 1765," in *El negro en la historia*, 120.
45. Fernando Jurado Noboa, "Presidentes del Ecuador con ancestro africano," in *El negro en la historia*, 156, 160.
46. Jurado Noboa, "Presidentes del Ecuador," 159.
47. Laura Hidalgo, *Décimas esmeraldeñas* (Quito: Libresa, 1995); Michael Handelsman, *Lo afro y la plurinacionalidad: El caso ecuatoriano visto desde su literatura* (Quito: Abya-Yala, 2001).
48. Bogumila Lisocka-Jaegermann, "Los afrodescendientes en los países andinos: El caso de Bolivia," *Revista del CESLA* 1, no. 13 (2010): 324.
49. Walter Sánchez Canedo, "Identidades sonoras de los afrodescendientes de Bolivia," *Traspatios: La transformación del Estado y del campo político en Bolivia, Revista del Centro de Investigaciones CISO*, no. 2 (March 2011): 153.
50. Baldomero Menéndez, *Manual de geografía y estadística del Alto Perú ó Bolivia* (Paris: Librería de Rosa y Bouret, 1860), 121.
51. Crespo, *Esclavos negros*, 39–40.
52. Juan de Arona, *Diccionario de peruanismos: Ensayo filológico* (Lima: Imp. de J. Francisco Solis, 1883), 168.
53. Moisés Sáenz, *Sobre el indio peruano y su incorporación al medio nacional* (Mexico City: Publicaciones de la Secretaría de Educación Pública, 1933), 273.
54. Hassaurek, *Four Years*, 124.
55. Vaca-Guzmán, "Las letras," 350.
56. Vaca-Guzmán, "Las letras," 353.
57. Marcel Velázquez Castro, *Hijos de la peste: Una historia de las epidemias en el Perú* (Lima: Taurus, 2020), 44–45.
58. Humberto Rodríguez Pastor, "La calle del Capón, el callejón Otaiza y el Barrio Chino," in *Mundos interiores: Lima 1850–1950*, ed. Aldo Panfichi and Felipe Portocarrero (Lima: Universidad del Pacífico Centro de Investigación, CIUP, 2004), 417.
59. Velázquez Castro, *Hijos de la peste*, 130.
60. Velázquez Castro, *Hijos de la peste*, 139.
61. Jorge Basadre, *Historia de la República del Perú* (Lima: Editorial Universitaria, 1983), 282.
62. Janet E. Worrall, "Growth and Assimilation of the Italian Colony in Peru: 1860–1914," *Studi Emigrazione (Rome)* 13, no. 41 (1976): 42.
63. Manuel González Prada, *Bajo el oprobio* (Paris: Tipografía de Louis Bellenand et Fils, 1933), 168.
64. Oswaldo Holguín Callo, "El indio valeroso en la literatura de la Posguerra con Chile," in *La república de papel. Política e imaginación social en la prensa peruana del siglo XIX*, ed. Marcel Velázquez Castro (Lima: Fondo Editorial Universidad de Ciencias y Humanidades, 2009), 242.
65. Manuel González Prada, *Pájinas libres* (Paris: Tipografía de Paul Dupont, 1894), 72.
66. Marcel Velázquez Castro, *Las máscaras de la representación: El sujeto esclavista y las rutas del racismo en el Perú (1775–1895)* (Lima: Fondo Editorial de la Universidad Nacional Mayor de San Marcos y el Banco Central de Reserva del Perú, 2005), 260.
67. José Carlos Mariátegui, *7 ensayos de interpretación de la realidad peruana* (Lima: Biblioteca Amauta, 1968), 30–31.
68. Mariátegui, *7 ensayos*, 270–271.
69. Francisco Javier Salazar, *El método productivo de enseñanza primaria aplicado a las escuelas de la república del Ecuador* (Quito: Imp. Nacional por M. Mosquera, 1869), 78–79.

70. Rafael Cáceres, *La provincia oriental de la República del Ecuador: Apuntes de viaje* (Quito: Imprenta de la Universidad, 1892), 45.
71. Juan León Mera, *Catecismo de geografía de la República del Ecuador* (Quito: Imprenta Nacional, 1875), 66, 51.
72. Pío Jaramillo Alvarado, *El indio ecuatoriano: Contribución al estudio de la sociología nacional* (Quito: Imp. y Encuadernación Editorial Quito, 1922), 177.
73. Juan José Paz y Miño Cepeda, *La Revolución Juliana: Nación, ejército y bancocracia* (Quito: Abya-Yala, 2000), 46.
74. Ricardo Delgado Campeáns, *El problema indígena, organización y educación del indio* (Quito: Tip. Editorial Chimborazo, 1925), 4, 5.
75. Jorge Icaza, *Huasipungo* (Quito: Imp. Nacional, 1934).
76. Carlos Felipe Beltran, *Civilización del indio: Silabario con la doctrina cristiana español-quichua* (La Paz: Imprenta Boliviana de C. F. Beltran, 1872).
77. As cited in Gabriel René Moreno, *Biblioteca Boliviana: Catalogo de la seccion de libros i folletos* (Santiago de Chile: Impr. Gutenberg, 1879), 166.
78. Moreno, *Biblioteca Boliviana*, 166–167.
79. Alcides Arguedas, *Pueblo enfermo: Contribución a la psicología de los pueblos hispanoamericanos* (Barcelona: Vda. de Luis Tasso, 1909), 36.
80. Arguedas, *Pueblo enfermo*, 237.
81. Arguedas, *Pueblo enfermo*, 237.

BIBLIOGRAPHY

Anderson, Benedict. *Imagined Communities: Reflections on the Origin and Spread of Nationalism*. London: Verso, 2006.

Anzoátegui de Campero, Lindaura. *Huallparrimachi*. Potosí, Bolivia: Imp. de El Tiempo, 1894.

Arguedas, Alcides. *Pueblo enfermo: Contribución a la psicología de los pueblos hispanoamericanos*. Barcelona: Vda. de Luis Tasso, 1909.

Arona, Juan de. *Diccionario de peruanismos: Ensayo filológico*. Lima: Imp. de J. Francisco Solis, 1883.

Basadre, Jorge. *Historia de la República del Perú*. Lima: Editorial Universitaria, 1983.

Beltran, Carlos Felipe. *Civilización del indio: Silabario con la doctrina cristiana español-quichua*. La Paz: Imprenta Boliviana de C. F. Beltran, 1872.

Burbano, José Ignacio. "La revolución romántica y la restauración neoclásica: Estudio preliminar." In *Poetas románticos y neoclásicos: La colonia y la República*, edited by José Ignacio Burbano, 26:23–55. Puebla, Mexico: J. M. Cajica y Secretaría General de la Undécima Conferencia Interamericana de Quito, 1960.

Cáceres, Rafael. *La provincia oriental de la República del Ecuador: Apuntes de viaje*. Quito: Imprenta de la Universidad, 1892.

Chatterjee, Partha. *Empire and Nation: Selected Essays*. New York: Columbia University Press, 2010.

Choque Canqui, Roberto. "La servidumbre indígena andina de Bolivia." In *El Siglo XIX: Bolivia y América Latina*, edited by Rossana Barragán et al., 475–485. Lima: Institut Français d'Études Andines, 1997.

Coronel, Rosario. "Indios y esclavos negros en el valle del Chota colonial." In *El negro en la historia de Ecuador y del sur de Colombia*, edited by Rafael Savoia, 171-187. Guayaquil: Centro Cultural Afro-Ecuatoriano, Depto. de Pastoral Afro-Ecuatoriano, 2002.

Crespo, Alberto. *Esclavos negros en Bolivia*. La Paz: Academia Nacional de Ciencias de Bolivia, 1977.

Cruz Rodríguez, Edwin. "El 'problema indígena' y la construcción de la nación en Bolivia y Ecuador durante el siglo XIX: La perspectiva de las luchas por la hegemonía." *Diálogo Latinoamericanos*, no. 19 (2012): 33-68.

Delgado Campeáns, Ricardo. *El problema indígena, organización y educación del indio*. Quito: Tip. Editorial Chimborazo, 1925.

Figueroa, José. *Republicanos negros: Guerras por la igualdad, racismo y relativismo cultural*. Bogotá: Planeta, 2022.

Garay Arellano, Ezio. "La élite económica de los negros en Guayaquil de 1792 a 1765." In *El negro en la historia de Ecuador y del sur de Colombia*, edited by Rafael Savoia, 113-121. Guayaquil: Centro Cultural Afro-Ecuatoriano, Depto. de Pastoral Afro-Ecuatoriano, 2002.

———. "Los negros en Guayaquil en 1850." In *El negro en la historia de Ecuador y del sur de Colombia*, edited by Rafael Savoia, 123-133. Guayaquil: Centro Cultural Afro-Ecuatoriano, Depto. de Pastoral Afro-Ecuatoriano, 2002.

García Moreno, Gabriel. *Escritos y discursos: Escritos oficiales. Recopilados y publicados por la Sociedad de la Juventud Católica de Quito y anotados por su presidente D. Manuel María Pólit; precede un prólogo por D. Juan León Mera*. Quito: Imp. del Clero, 1888.

González Prada, Manuel. *Bajo el oprobio*. Paris: Tipografía de Louis Bellenand et Fils, 1933.

———. *Pájinas libres*. Paris: Tipografía de Paul Dupont, 1894.

Gootenberg, Paul. *Población y etnicidad en el Perú republicano (siglo XIX): Algunas revisiones*. Lima: IEP, 1995.

Gotkowitz, Laura. *A Revolution for Our Rights: Indigenous Struggles for Land and Justice in Bolivia, 1880-1952*. Durham, NC: Duke University Press, 2007.

Gruner, Wolf. "'Los parias de la patria': La discriminación estatal de los indígenas en la República de Bolivia (1825-1952/53)." In *Identidad, ciudadanía y participación popular desde la colonia al siglo XX*, edited by Josefa Salmón and Guillermo Delgado, 1:181-190. La Paz: Plural, 2003.

Handelsman, Michael. *Lo afro y la plurinacionalidad: El caso ecuatoriano visto desde su literatura*. Quito: Abya-Yala, 2001.

Hassaurek, Friedrich. *Four Years among Spanish-Americans*. New York: Hurd and Houghton, 1868.

Hidalgo, Laura. *Décimas esmeraldeñas*. Quito: Libresa, 1995.

Holguín Callo, Oswaldo. "El indio valeroso en la literatura de la Posguerra con Chile." In *La república de papel: Política e imaginación social en la prensa peruana del siglo XIX*, edited by Marcel Velázquez Castro, 235-273. Lima: Fondo Editorial Universidad de Ciencias y Humanidades, 2009.

Icaza, Jorge. *Huasipungo*. Quito: Imp. Nacional, 1934.

Iturralde, Diego. "Nacionalidades indígenas y Estado nacional en Ecuador." In *Los derechos colectivos: Hacia su efectiva comprensión y protección*, edited by María Paz Avila

Ordóñez and María Belén Corredores Ledesma, 103–125. Quito: Ministerio de Justicia y Derechos Humanos; Alto Comisionado de las Naciones Unidas para los Derechos Humanos, 2009.

Jaramillo Alvarado, Pío. *El indio ecuatoriano: Contribución al estudio de la sociología nacional*. Quito: Imp. y Encuadernación Editorial Quito, 1922.

Jurado Noboa, Fernando. "Presidentes del Ecuador con ancestro africano." In *El negro en la historia de Ecuador y del sur de Colombia*, edited by Rafael Savoia, 153–169. Guayaquil: Centro Cultural Afro-Ecuatoriano, Depto. de Pastoral Afro-Ecuatoriano, 2002.

Langebaek, Carl Henrik. "Civilización y barbarie: El indio en la literatura criolla en Colombia y Venezuela después de la independencia." *Revista de Estudios Sociales*, no. 22 (2005): 46–57.

Larson, Brooke. *Indígenas, élites y Estado en la formación de las repúblicas andinas, 1850–1910*. Lima: IEP, Pontificia Universidad Católica del Perú, 2002.

Lisocka-Jaegermann, Bogumila. "Los afrodescendientes en los países andinos: El caso de Bolivia." *Revista del CESLA* 1, no. 13 (2010): 317–329.

Mainer, José Carlos. *Historia de la literatura española: El lugar de la literatura española*. Barcelona: Crítica, 2012.

Mariátegui, José Carlos. *7 ensayos de interpretación de la realidad peruana*. Lima: Biblioteca Amauta, 1968.

Matto de Turner, Clorinda. *Leyendas y recortes*. Lima: Imp. La Equitativa, Matto Hermanos Editores, 1893.

———. *Tradiciones cuzqueñas: Leyendas, biografías y hojas sueltas*. Arequipa, Peru: Imp. de La Bolsa, 1884.

Mendieta Parada, Pilar. "Por órdenes del Papa Santo de Roma: La 'Proclama de Caracollo' de Pablo Zárate Willka (1899)." *Revista Ciencia y Cultura* 23, no. 42 (2019): 141–164.

Menéndez, Baldomero. *Manual de geografía y estadística del Alto Perú ó Bolivia*. Paris: Librería de Rosa y Bouret, 1860.

Mera, Juan León. *Catecismo de Geografía de la República del Ecuador*. Quito: Imprenta Nacional, 1875.

———. *Cumandá: O un drama entre salvajes*. Quito: Imp. del Clero, 1879.

Montalvo, Juan. "Impresiones de un diplomático." *El Espectador* 3: 164–212. Paris: Librería Franco-Hispano-Americana, 1888.

Moreno, Gabriel René. *Biblioteca Boliviana: Catalogo de la Seccion de Libros i Folletos*. Santiago de Chile: Impr. Gutenberg, 1879.

Palma, Ricardo. *Tradiciones y artículos históricos*. Lima: Imp. Torres Aguirre, 1899.

Paz y Miño Cepeda, Juan José. *La Revolución Juliana: Nación, ejército y bancocracia*. 2nd ed. Quito: Abya-Yala, 2000.

Peralta, José. *Chumbera, leyenda original*. Cuenca: n.p., 1876.

Pinilla, Claudio. *Guanaiquile*. La Paz: Imp. de la Unión Americana, 1882.

Ribadeneira Suárez, Catalina. *El racismo en el Ecuador contemporáneo entre la modernidad y el fundamentalismo étnico: El discurso del otro*. Quito: Abya-Yala, 2001.

Rivero, Victorino. *Amarrá i Espól, novela histórica*. Imp. de Cayetano H. Daza, 1871.

Rodríguez Pastor, Humberto. "La calle del Capón, el callejón Otaiza y el Barrio Chino." In

Mundos interiores: Lima 1850-1950, edited by Aldo Panfichi and Felipe Portocarrerro, 397-430. Lima: Universidad del Pacífico Centro de Investigación (CIUP), 2004.

Rueda Novoa, Rocío. "Desesclavización, manumisión jurídica y defensa del territorio en el norte de Esmeraldas (siglos XVIII-XIX)." *Procesos: Revista Ecuatoriana de Historia*, no. 43 (2016): 9-35.

Sáenz, Moisés. *Sobre el indio peruano y su incorporación al medio nacional*. Mexico City: Publicaciones de la Secretaría de Educación Pública, 1933.

Salazar, Francisco Javier. *El método productivo de enseñanza primaria aplicado a las escuelas de la república del Ecuador*. Quito: Imp. Nacional por M. Mosquera, 1869.

Sánchez Canedo, Walter. "Identidades sonoras de los afrodescendientes de Bolivia." *Traspatios, La transformación del Estado y del campo político en Bolivia, Revista del Centro de Investigaciones CISO*, no. 2 (March 2011): 145-171.

Sommer, Doris. *Foundational Fictions: The National Romances of Latin America*. Berkeley: University of California Press, 1993.

Soto Jiménez, Juan Pablo. "Introducción." *Ficcionalización de Bolivia: La leyenda / novela del siglo diez i nueve 1847-1896*, edited by Juan Pablo Soto Jiménez y Máximo Pacheco Balanza, 1:9-54. Cochabamba: n.p., 2016.

Tejada Galindo, Sergio. *Tras los pasos de Juan Bustamante: Apuntes biográficos y políticos*. Lima: Construyendo la Nación, 2019.

Telles, Edward. "El proyecto de etnicidad y raza en América Latina (PERLA): Los datos cuantitativos y lo que está en juego." In *Pigmentocracias color, etnicidad y raza en América Latina*, edited by Edward Telles and Regina Martínez Casas, translated by Fatna Lazcano, 13-56. Mexico City: Fondo de Cultura Económica, 2019.

Vaca-Guzmán, Santiago. "Las letras en Bolivia." In *América literaria: Producciones selectas en prosa y verso*, 2nd ed., edited by Francisco Lagomaggiore, 1:349-354. Buenos Aires: Imprenta de La Nación, 1890.

Velázquez Castro, Marcel. *Hijos de la peste: Una historia de las epidemias en el Perú*. Lima: Taurus, 2020.

———. *Las máscaras de la representación: El sujeto esclavista y las rutas del racismo en el Perú (1775-1895)*. Lima: Fondo Editorial de la Universidad Nacional Mayor de San Marcos y el Banco Central de Reserva del Perú, 2005.

———. "La narrativa breve de Clorinda Matto: De la tradición y leyenda románticas al cuento modernista." *Escritura y Pensamiento* 15, no. 31 (2012): 75-103.

Wade, Peter. *Race and Ethnicity in Latin America*. New York: Pluto Press, 1997.

Worrall, Janet E. "Growth and assimilation of the Italian colony in Peru: 1860-1914." *Studi Emigrazione (Rome)* 13, no. 41 (1976): 41-61.

CHAPTER 10

Interethnic Conflict and Sociocultural Contributions of Asian Diasporas in Latin America and the Caribbean

IGNACIO LÓPEZ-CALVO

Because of the limitations of space and the wide nature of both the term *Asian* and the region to be covered, in this chapter I concentrate mostly on Chinese and Japanese immigrations in a few Latin American and Caribbean countries. Beginning in the sixteenth century with the first yearly and then semiannual voyages of the Manila Galleons, which lasted from 1565 through 1815, the importation of both free and unfree, racialized Asian labor to Latin America and the Caribbean has had an undeniable repercussion in the region. This global silver trade brought Filipinos and *Sangleyes* (Sangleys; persons of Chinese and native Filipino mixed ancestry during the Spanish colonial era in the Philippines), either as sailors or enslaved, most of whom were unable to return. As Tatiana Seijas reveals, during the late sixteenth and seventeenth centuries, the numerous South and Southeast Asians who were enslaved and brought to Mexico in the Manila Galleon were initially categorized as "chinos" and then as "Indians": "In time, chinos came to be treated under the law as Indians (the term for all native people of Spain's colonies) and became Indigenous vassals of the Spanish crown after 1672. The implications of this legal change were enormous: as Indians, rather than chinos, they could no longer be held as slaves."[1]

But the first mass migration of Asians to Latin America and the Spanish Caribbean was that of Chinese indentured laborers (referred to with the derogative epithet *coolies* and officially known as *colonos* or settlers) to Spanish Cuba beginning in 1847. Local planters reluctantly resorted to them as they saw a dire need to progressively replace enslaved African labor in their sugarcane plantations due to the 1807 British ban on the Atlantic slave trade (paradoxically, the British would later engage in slavery-like practices during the so-called coolie trade). For several years, however, many of the 150,000 Chinese indentured laborers who landed on the island worked, in semislavery conditions, side by side with enslaved Africans and their descendants in plantations and sugar mills. Among the push factors for the emigration of some seven million Cantonese after the 1830s were the changes in Chinese migration laws to relieve overpopulation, poverty, famine, political instability, European colonialism, and armed conflict, including the Opium Wars (1839–1843, 1856–1860), the Christian-inspired Taiping Rebellion (1850–1864), the Sino-Japanese War (1894–1895), and the Boxer Rebellion (1898–1900), which left millions of people impoverished or dead.

Facing the same difficulties in attracting the desired European labor as their Cuban peers, planters in newly independent Peru also found a temporary solution in Chinese indentured workers. In Mexico, half a century later, much of the Chinese immigration was composed of free entrepreneurs, as also happened in Panama, although there were also Chinese indentured laborers living and working in appalling conditions in henequen plantations in Yucatán and other Mexican states. With time, as Elliott Young suggests, the Chinese became "the model aliens around whom immigration restrictions were developed and the legal category of the alien was built."[2]

Following in the Chinese laborers' footsteps were the Japanese, who, fifty years later, arrived first in Chiapas, Mexico, and then in Peru and Brazil. In this last country, cheap and controlled labor was also needed because of the abolition of African slavery and the refusal of European workers to live and work in the unacceptable conditions offered by coffee planters. Likewise, Chinese internal migration to urban areas in Peru after the end of the War of the Pacific (1879–1883) had left its plantations in need of cheap labor. In Cuba, Peru, Mexico, Brazil, Panama, and other countries, both Chinese and Japanese immigrants would make major contributions to these countries' agricultural development, adding later to many other areas of the economy and culture. Tellingly, the forced departure of the Chinese from Sonora and Sinaloa during the 1930s, of the Japanese from Northwestern Mexico during World

War II, and of Chinese shop owners from Cuba after the Cuban Revolution all had notoriously negative repercussions for the respective local economies.

Chinese Immigration in Cuba

Havana had the first and, for some time, also the most populous Chinatown in Latin America. Although the "coolies" were initially imported using official funding designated for White migration, once they landed in Cuba, they became racialized and poorly treated by planters who were used to slave labor. Their main motivation was not necessarily to lead a transition to free labor but, rather, to preserve the capitalist system that had made Cuba the largest exporter of sugar in the world since Haiti's independence.

On June 3, 1847, the first 207 Chinese contract workers from Amoy (93 of the original passengers died during the 131-day and 13,000-nautical-mile voyage) arrived at the Port of Regla on Havana Bay aboard the Spanish brigantine *Almirante Oquendo*. By the time the so-called coolie trade, or "yellow trade," ended in 1874, some 150,000 immigrants from China (mostly from the southern, coastal province of Guangdong, in the Pearl River Delta) had entered, both legally and illegally, the island, which at the time only had 1.4 million inhabitants (by contrast, the United States at the time, with a population of 38 million, only had 63,000 Chinese immigrants).

While initially the Qing government regarded Chinese emigrants as traitors who did not deserve its protection, only the investigation led by Chinese imperial commissioner Ch'en Lan Pin into enforced recontracting and other abuses committed against indentured workers stopped this regrettable human trade in Cuba and Peru.[3] The high mortality rate in the ships bringing Chinese workers to Cuba and Peru—approximately one-fifth of the recruits died— was a combined result of the crew's cruelty, suicides, and frequent mutinies. As revealed in *The Cuba Commission Report: A Hidden History of the Chinese in Cuba* (1877) by a Chinese imperial commission led by Ch'en Lan Pin, many of these indentured workers were kidnapped or deceived by countrymen (others enrolled as payment for debts or in exchange for opium) who made false promises.[4] Once in the Cuban plantations, the guaranties included in the treaties signed by the Spanish government were mostly ignored.

For eight years, the indentured laborers had to work an average of twelve hours a day in conditions of servitude and for a much lower salary than promised. After the term was over, most had not been able to save enough to return home. Because the Chinese were considered sojourners who were supposed to return the China, and thus not expected to naturalize, they were forced to (or saw no alternative to) recontracting with the same farmers, or else they were imprisoned or sent to do hard labor in a depot. Besides mutiny and suicide (mid-nineteenth-century Cuba had the highest suicide rate in the world),[5] Chinese indentured workers resisted by rebelling in the plantations and fleeing. Once they were finally relieved from their servitude, many found a source of income as street vendors and later opened their own shops in the cities. This gave rise to the first Chinatowns and to the creation of Chinese societies.

Besides the participation of the approximately six thousand *chinos mambises* in the two wars of independence against Spain (1868–1898; some led Chinese battalions as officers in the insurgent army), which the Chinese community in Cuba has often used as evidence of their patriotism and right to belong within the national imaginary, the Chinese have made numerous contributions to Cuban cuisine, art, language, music, literature, and even to the Cuban dialect of Spanish.[6] In the musical field, for example, the Chinese flute has been described as the center of the Cuban orchestra and of Cuban music, and Chinese pentatonic scales have been considered influential to Cuban *danzón*. Other Chinese musical instruments incorporated into Cuban culture are the *cu* drums, played during the lion dance, and the *cajita china* (Chinese little box), a wooden percussion instrument used by *rumba, danzón,* and *son* musicians. Well-known Cuban writers of Chinese descent are Regino Pedroso, José Lezama Lima, Severo Sarduy, and Zoé Valdés; among visual artists, Wifredo Lam and Flora Fong.

Chinese Immigration in Peru

Along with Brazil (though the Chinese migrated much later to this country), Peru boasts the largest population of Chinese ancestry in Latin America (between 15 percent and 17 percent of Peruvians). Beginning in 1849, they were brought as cheap contract labor for the guano fields of the Chincha Islands (where working conditions were the harshest and the suicide rate the highest), the sugarcane and cotton plantations, and, after 1868, for railroad construction. Even more so than in the case of Cuba, the mortality rate during the transoceanic voyage was very high: for example, 109 of the 350 aboard the ship *Lady Montague* perished. In 1856, the Peruvian government admitted that one-third of the "coolies" imported died during the journey. Once in Peru, their chances of survival were even lower. According to Isabelle Lausent-Herrera, "Between 1849 and 1876 nearly half of the Chinese brought into Peru (aged from 9 to 40, rarely older) died from exhaustion, suicide or ill treatment."[7] As happened in Cuba, Peruvian landowners hired Black foremen who often used physical punishment against the Chinese workers, a frequent source of interracial conflict, along with the relationships between Chinese men and Black women. By the time this inhumane "coolie trade" was ended in 1874, after the signing of the Tientsin (Tianjin) Treaty of Friendship and Commerce, approximately 100,000 mostly male, contract laborers had landed in Peru, becoming a major factor in the development of this country's coastal agriculture.

In contrast with the Chinese in Cuba, who resorted to their participation in the Wars of Independence against Spain as a source of ethnic pride, approximately 1,500 Chinese indentured workers in Peru, tired of the abuse they had suffered, sided with the Chilean invading army during the War of the Pacific. In revenge, on January 15, 1881, approximately three hundred Chinese were killed, and Chinese businesses were sacked, even though many others in the community remained loyal to the Peruvian side.

Among the numerous economic and cultural contributions made by the Chinese Peruvian, or *tusán*, community, one of the most remarkable is the *chifa*, or Chinese Peruvian restaurant, whose food has become a central part of Peru's rich culinary tradition.[8] The *tusans*, like the Nikkei, have also made major contributions to Peruvian literature, with writers such as the poet and *indigenista* thinker Pedro Zulen, the novelist and short-story writer Siu Kam Wen, the poets Julia Wong and Sui-Yun, and the chronicle writer Julio Villanueva Chang, founder of the magazine *Etiqueta Negra*.[9]

Chinese Immigration to Mexico

After the initial arrival of some Chinese in Mexico aboard the Manila Galleon, the mass migration began during the 1870s in response to Porfirio Díaz's government's need for cheap labor to build railroads and to colonize sparsely populated areas with rebellious Indigenous populations. Frustrated by his inability to attract European immigrants (part of his "modernization" program consisted of "whitening" the population in the country), Díaz reluctantly accepted the politician Matías Romero's suggestion of recruiting Chinese guest workers, perceived at the time as submissive and hard-working.

This demand for Chinese labor coincided with the timely passing of the 1882 Chinese Exclusion Act in the United States: it has been estimated that approximately 70 percent of Chinese migrants to Mexico between 1895 and 1910 had been previously expelled from the United States. They settled in the developing northern states of Baja California, Sonora, and Chihuahua, often hoping to illegally remigrate to the United States, in what Robert Chao Romero considers the inception of undocumented immigration from Mexico: "The Chinese were the first 'undocumented immigrants' from Mexico, and they created the first organized system of human smuggling from Mexico to the United States."[10]

Formalized Chinese immigration began in 1899 with the signing of the bilateral Treaty of Amity, Commerce, and Navigation, which established diplomatic relations between Mexico and Imperial China. By the 1920s, there were 26,000 Chinese in communities throughout most of the Mexican geography, who moved swiftly from cheap laborers to merchants (reaching a monopoly of grocery and clothing stores in northern Mexico) thanks to their frugality, industriousness, and intraethnic and relative-based work relationships and mutual support: some Chinese entrepreneurs in Mexico sponsored the voyage of Cantonese relatives and others, who accepted low pay while they gained business experience. With time, many learned Spanish, became Catholic, naturalized, adopted Spanish names, and married local women, since there were initially no antimiscegenation laws and very few Chinese women.

Despite their small numbers and their being initially welcome, racism and economic jealousy inspired anti-Chinese associations, who lobbied local and federal governments for discriminatory measures. Beginning in August 1929, the Great Depression increased the hostility against Chinese immigrants, as they became scapegoats for many of the country's social ills: they were accused of bringing diseases, creating unfair competition, and refusing to integrate into Mexican society and to hire Mexican nationals in their businesses. Anti-Chinese hysteria culminated with the deportation of the Chinese and their Mexican families (their Mexican wives, derogatorily called *chineras*, lost their nationality and were legally considered Chinese) from Sonora and Sinaloa in the 1930s, mostly to the United States, whence the US government felt compelled to pay for a second deportation to China. Along with economic boycotts, looting, and racist taxing and legislation, there were several massacres of Chinese, the most notorious of which was the one in Torreón, Coahuila, on May 15, 1911, where Maderista troops, aided by local citizens and using the false excuse that some Chinese were shooting first, brutally murdered 303

Chinese immigrants. This tragic massacre has inspired two excellent, recent works: Julián Herbert's *La casa del dolor ajeno: Crónica de un pequeño genocidio en La Laguna* (The House of the Pain of Others, 2015) and Beatriz Rivas's novel *Jamás, nadie* (Never, Nobody, 2017).[11]

Among several other Mexican writers of Chinese ancestry are the poets Óscar Wong, Sergio Loo, and Roberto Rico Chong, the novelist Roberto Wong, and the poetry and prose writer Selfa Chew. Among performers, one can list Sarahí Lay Trigo and the poet and cabaret artist Dulce Chiang (Ma Dam Chiang), who has followed in Lyn May's footsteps.

Japanese Immigration to Mexico

After the United States, Canada, and Hawaii began passing laws that restricted Japanese immigration in 1908, Latin America became the new destination for those immigrants that the Japanese government advertised as "the whites of Asia."[12] María Elena Ota Mishima, the pioneer of the study of Japanese migrations to Mexico, reveals that most of these immigrants came from Fukuoka Prefecture, on the southwestern island of Kyūshū.[13] Between 1890 and 1901, Ota Mishima adds, most of the nearly 10,000 Japanese immigrants had traveled freely to work in agriculture; during the following decade, however, most migrated under contract. Then, between 1907 and 1924, many arrived as undocumented immigrants, because of the signing of the 1907 Gentlemen's Agreement between Japan and the United States. Mostly qualified immigrants arrived between 1917 and 1928, and between 1921 and 1940, *yobiyose* immigrants were requested to come from Japan to work in Mexico.[14] Finally, between 1951 and 1978, most were technical workers in specialized fields.

While in June 1873, Peru became the first Latin American country to establish diplomatic relations with Japan, and the treaty was signed on unequal terms. Porfirio Díaz's Mexico, in 1888, would become the first country in the world to sign a treaty based on reciprocal treatment with Japan: the Friendship, Commerce, and Navigation Treaty allowed the free circulation of citizens between both countries. As a result, Mexico was also the first Latin American country chosen by Japanese emigrants. The first twenty-eight *colonos* (settlers), financially supported by their government, along with six other immigrants who were not tied to a contract, arrived in Chiapas in 1897 with the goal of growing coffee. They worked on lands located in Escuintla, Chiapas, which had been purchased the previous year by the Japanese government, led by its foreign minister and minister of education, Viscount Enomoto Takeaki. Although this Colonia Enomoto, the first Japanese settlement in Latin America, ended up being an economic failure, thousands of Japanese would later arrive to work not only in agriculture (some purchased land in Mexico without governmental support) but also in fishing and other fields, mostly in Baja California, Sonora, and Mexico City.

Despite all the hardships, the Nikkei community in Mexico suffered comparatively less oppression and persecution than the Chinese. One of the reasons was the international prestige accrued by the Empire of Japan thanks to its recent victory over the Russian Empire in 1905, which led some to believe, particularly during the Mexican Revolution, that the Japanese were natural-born military experts. While several Japanese immigrants were recruited as soldiers and military officers, the Chinese were often persecuted and, in several cases, massacred. Along these lines, Japan's colonial possessions provided these immigrants with attributes of honorary whiteness. Although the Mexican government broke diplomatic ties with Japan in 1941, it refused, unlike several other Latin American countries, to abide by Washington's request to send its Japanese residents to US internment camps to prevent them from becoming spies or from committing acts of sabotage (also to use them in the exchange of prisoners with Japan). Instead, they were relocated away from coastal areas and the US border, at their own expense, mainly in designated areas in Mexico City but also in Guadalajara and other cities.

Among the many contributions of Mexican Nikkeijin to literature and the arts, one can include the beautiful poetry of the Issei (first-generation immigrant) Mitsuko Kasuga (pen name: Akane), the paintings and murals of Luis Nishizawa Flores, and the performance art of Irene Akiko Iida. There are also numerous Nikkei visual artists in Mexico, including Akio Hanafuji, Carmen Harada, Cinthia Miyake, Fumiko Nakashima, and Kenta Torii, as well as singers like Yoshio, Kenji Hiromoto, and Hansae Hirata. The Nikkei Alejandro Ramírez Honda is a renowned puppeteer.

Japanese Immigration in Peru

Peru became the second Latin American country to receive Japanese immigrants when on April 3, 1899, the steamship *Sakura Maru* arrived at the port of Callao with 790 male workers. Despite the "remigration" (for many, it was their first time in their ancestral homeland) of many Japanese Latin Americans to Japan beginning in the late 1980s, Peru still has an estimated 50,000 Nikkei, the second-largest community in Latin America after Brazil's (between 1.2 million and 1.4 million). Most Japanese immigrants were fleeing poverty or military conscription and came from the southern prefectures, including the Ryūkyū Islands (mostly from Okinawa). Encouraged by the Japanese government and emperor to emigrate, they became the cheap labor desperately needed in Peruvian sugarcane plantations after the abolishment of African slavery and the internal urban migration of the Chinese indentured workers whom they were about to replace. Withstanding hunger and mistreatment on the farms, after their contracts were over, some Japanese became owners of large plantations, but most moved to Lima and other coastal cities, where they succeeded as small business owners. Peaking in the 1930s, Japanese immigration to Peru ended by the early 1970s. By then, however, this ethnic community had established an important cultural bridge between Japan and Peru.

Through the *yobiyose* system, some immigrants invited relatives and friends to join them in Peru. This, along with their frequent refusal to intermarry (they would bring "picture brides" from Japan) and the economic jealousy of some Peruvians, led to accusations of refusing to integrate into Peruvian society and to violent attacks, such as the looting of Japanese businesses and homes in Lima in May 1940. But the most egregious Nipponophobic act was the expropriation, kidnapping, and deportation of 1,771 members of the Nikkei community to US internment camps for over two years during World War II. Once the war was over, the Peruvian government accepted the return of Italian and German nationals, but not that of most Japanese deportees. Whereas some were sent to Japan, 364 remained as stateless refugees until they won a legal battle to stay in the United States. As happened in Mexico and Brazil, many Nikkeijin in Peru were forcibly removed from coastal areas for fear that they would provide intelligence assistance for a potential landing of the Imperial Japanese Navy.

Peruvian Nikkeijin became particularly visible after the engineer Alberto Fujimori beat the soon-to-be Nobel laureate and novelist Mario Vargas Llosa in the 1990 presidential elections. Fujimori became the third South American ruler of East Asian descent, after the heads of state Arthur Chung in Guyana and Henk Chin A Sen in Suriname. The Nikkeijin have also made major contributions to Peruvian cuisine, literature (José Watanabe, Augusto Higa, Fernando Iwasaki, Doris Moromisato, Carlos Yushimito), the visual arts (Tilsa Tsuchiya and Venancio Shinki), and music (Angélica Harada, known as "Princesita de Yungay," or Little Princess from Yungay, and César Ychikawa, the vocalist of the band Los Doltons).

Japanese Immigration in Brazil

As in other Latin American and Caribbean countries, after the gradual abolition of African slavery and the failure to attract European workers, Brazil opted for Japanese immigration (after rejecting the option of bringing Chinese laborers) to solve the cheap labor scarcity on labor-intensive coffee plantations. Under the excuse of alleviating overpopulation, the Japanese government actually expected emigration—as part of its imperial expansionism—to extend its political influence abroad, to improve its international image as a modern and altruistic state, to ease social tensions, and to open up markets for Japanese products in Latin America. It also hoped that the emigrants' remittances would improve the country's dire economic situation and that these Nikkei communities would export food and other resources to Japan.

More than 164,000 Japanese immigrants arrived in Brazil between 1917 and 1940, creating, by the 1930s, the second-largest Nikkei community in the world (the largest today, despite the *dekasegi*—temporary worker—"reverse" migration to work in Japanese factories in Japan). By 1935, the Brazilian government, concerned with having a potential fifth column within its national borders, began to introduce immigration quotas. As happened in Peru, Japanese immigrants soon became disappointed with the appalling living and working conditions, and some fled the plantations at night. While in Peru they fled to the cities, in Brazil they stayed in rural areas, mostly in the states of São Paulo and Paraná. Also as in Peru, many Nikkeijin came to own large plantations in Brazil. They also built, at times with the Japanese government's help, their own *núcleos colônias* or immigrant communities, which kept them relatively isolated from the majority of Brazilians. This led them to practice endogamy within their ethnic group. Before the end of World War II and the ensuing devastation of their fatherland, few Japanese were interested in the Portuguese language and Brazilian culture, as they saw themselves as sojourners. This attitude brought about distrust from mainstream society.

After Getúlio Vargas's nationalist Estado Novo dictatorship (1937–1945) began a "Brazilianization" process that outlawed Japanese-language newspapers, books, and radio stations, as well as speaking Japanese in public or teaching it in schools, most of the community became misinformed about the war's developments, as they were not familiar with Portuguese. The hostilities only increased once Brazil joined the Allied forces in 1942, with the implementation of movement restrictions (a safe-conduct pass was required), property confiscation, forced relocation from coastal areas (as happened in Mexico and Peru), and the closing of Japanese associations. In addition, they were not allowed to hold meetings or participate in political activities. Japanese Brazilians resisted by creating clandestine schools and associations, including the powerful, nationalist Shindō Renmei (Subject Path League), one of the first terrorist organizations in the Americas. Founded in the state of São Paulo in 1942, its members refused to believe that Japan had surrendered at the end of World War II and wounded or murdered Japanese immigrants who publicly acknowledged their country's defeat.

Besides the Nikkeijin's significant contribution to the development of agriculture in Brazil, several, including Mário "Japa" and Suely Yumiko Kanayama, are known for their participation in the armed struggle against the dictatorship during the 1970s. Among the numerous artists, the amateur photographer Haruo Ohara left an important record of mid-twentieth-century daily life in the Nikkei agricultural settlements in southeast Brazil. Other Japanese Brazilian artists are Tomie Ohtake, Madalena Hashimoto Cordaro, Erica Kaminishi, and Óscar Oiwa. As to Japanese Brazilian literary production, which is by far the largest in Latin America, among the numerous writers are Oscar Nakasato, Júlio Miyazawa, Ryoki Inoue, Lúcia Hiratsuka, Laura Honda-Hasegawa, and Jorge J. Okubaro. A well-known filmmaker is Tizuka Yamasaki.

Korean Immigration in Mexico

Though at a much smaller scale, Korean immigration was, initially, the third Asian alternative sought by the Mexican government to solve the constant labor shortages caused by planters' unwillingness to pay living wages to Mexican workers. In 1905, the owners of henequen plantations in Progreso, in the Yucatán Peninsula, imported more than a thousand Korean immigrants, who were mistreated, with many of them suffering beatings or imprisonment. After the completion of their four- to five-year contracts, most had to either stay in Mexico or remigrate to Cuba because they had been unable to save enough money to return home. Unlike Chinese and Japanese immigrants, Koreans migrated to Mexico with their entire families, as happened with the Japanese in Brazil. Koreans have traditionally been the Asian group that remigrates more often within the Americas. In this context, during the 1970s, additional South Korean immigrants would migrate from either South Korea or other Latin American countries, such as Argentina and Paraguay. Still a small community, but now concentrated in Mexico City, it reached its peak in 1997 with 19,500 individuals, before shrinking to 14,571 by 2005, and to 11,800 (876 naturalized Mexicans) by 2009. There is currently a Koreatown known as Little Seoul in the Zona Rosa of Mexico City, with restaurants and other businesses opened by recent immigrants. The Association of Korean Residents in Mexico opened a Korean-language weekend school in Mexico City known as the Korean School in Mexico, and since the 1990s, there has also been a Korean-language paper newspaper named *Hanin Diario*.

Korean Immigration in South America

Unlike the Chinese and Japanese, for the most part, Korean immigrants do not intentionally or strategically migrate to Latin American countries as a stepping stone to eventually migrate to the United States. As Chong-Sup Kim and Eunsuk Lee point out:

> Many Koreans who migrated to Latin America already paid considerable costs for their movement to Latin America, with an intention of permanent migration in most of the cases. They learned the language and culture and how to survive in a new society, while struggling to integrate themselves into the society. When they feel they are failing, because of crisis or whatever reasons there might be, they have less motivation to stay in destination. They may choose a new destination where they expect better opportunities but does not involve high costs in relocating, in other words, a country of short distance, using the same language, and most importantly with higher economic growth.[15]

In fact, many Koreans have returned to Latin America from the United States because they preferred the living conditions and standards throughout Latin America to their lives in the United States or South Korea. Specifically, many positively highlight the relative "tranquility" and sense of camaraderie they experience in South American countries (laidback versus cut-throat atmosphere).[16] As stated, Korean immigrants in South America have shown a high propensity to remigrate several times to countries such as the United States, Canada, South Korea, and Mexico, producing a spread-out, regional emigration that Kyeyoung Park has termed "a rhizomatic diaspora." For instance, a significant proportion of the nascent Korean population in Argentina during the 1970s did not arrive directly from Korea but through Paraguay or, in a few cases, Chile.[17]

Among Korean Chilean writers, we have the poet and academic Moisés Park and the playwright Kyoung H. Park.[18]

Empowering the Chinese by Denying Black Accomplishments

In the numerous attempts in Latin American cultural production to empower Chinese immigrants by denying the accomplishments of enslaved Africans and their descendants, we find an antecedent of the model minority myth in the United States. I have studied elsewhere different literary representations of Afro-Asian, interethnic, sociocultural interactions in Latin America and the Caribbean, focusing in particular on the image of the eroticized *china mulata* and on the Black ally who expresses sympathy or even marries the Asian protagonist, falling at times into the "magical negro" category of the abnegated ally whose only role—devoid of full autonomy or agency—in the narrative is to help the Asian protagonist reach his or her life goals.[19]

The iconic figure of the *china mulata* in Cuba is important because, among other things, it problematizes the idea that Chinese immigrants lived in complete isolation from mainstream society. Indeed, marriages between Chinese men and Afro-Cuban women were quite common, as reflected in Cuban literature. Tellingly, the legendary beauty of the sexualized and libidinized *china mulata* is central to works such as Mayra Montero's *Como un mensajero tuyo* (The Messenger, 1998), Zoé Valdés's *Te di la vida entera* (I Gave You All I Had, 1996), Leonardo Padura Fuentes's *La cola de la serpiente* (The Serpent's Tail, 2001), and Antonio José Ponte's short story "A petición de Ochún" (At the Request of Ochún, 1964), included in his collection *Cuentos de todas partes del imperio* (Tales from the Cuban Empire, 2000).[20] One finds additional evidence of the cultural hybridity produced by interactions between these two ethnic groups in the figure of the popular (unofficial) saint Sanfancón, a syncretic Chinese orisha that is typically associated with the Catholic saint Santa Bárbara as well as with the orisha Changó in Santería. The existence of Sanfancón, revered not only by the Chinese and their descendants but also often by Blacks in Cuba, proves how Chinese folk religion was deeply influenced by Afro-Cuban religions such as Santeria, Palo Monte, and Abakuá.[21]

Plantation owners feared the powerful effects that the solidarity between Chinese and Blacks could have against the status quo, even though confrontations between both groups were not uncommon. Thus, as Young reveals, "Cuban regulations insisted that overseers were the only ones who could carry out the punishments and that the beatings could never occur within 'sight of the blacks.'"[22] Cuban authorities, who incidentally considered the Chinese a superior race to Africans (though inferior to the White race), perhaps feared an alliance between both groups if they came to realize that they were suffering the same type of abuse and oppression.

In this chapter, however, I focus instead on the animosity and clashes between people of African and Asian descent as represented in Latin American and Caribbean cultural production. Both these alliances and the animosity between Asians and Blacks contribute to challenging the official discourses of mestizaje and *mulataje* that ultimately favored whiteness over Indigenous, Black, or Asian worldviews. David Palumbo-Liu has studied conservative rearticulations of the "yellow peril" and the model minority myth in the United States. As he explains, arguing that "Confucian, traditional Asian values" and post-Confucian entrepreneurship make Asians well suited for success in the US economy, some Caucasian ideologues have resorted to Asian economic success to claim that they are not racists when maintaining that Latinos and Blacks are marked by purported social pathologies and failures: conservatives needed a weapon to use against liberals who were pushing civil rights legislation—they found it in Japanese Americans, whose reputed success showed that urban poverty and violence were not the outcomes of institutional racism, but of constitutional weaknesses in minorities that were only exacerbated by the welfare state. In short, the model minority myth provided the opportunity for conservatives to situate the causes of these problems outside consideration of institutional racism and economic violence: the success of Japanese Americans was used to dispute a structural critique of the US political economy.[23]

I contend that one can find a precedent of this line of thought in Latin American and Caribbean cultural production. As mentioned in the chapter by Iván Fernando Rodrigo-Mendizábal in this volume, early in 1928 the Peruvian Marxist thinker José Carlos Mariátegui, in his *7 ensayos de interpretación de la realidad peruana* (Seven Interpretative Essays on Peruvian Reality), had conflated the contributions (or, in his opinion, lack thereof) of both Blacks and Chinese: "The Chinese and Negro complicate *mestizaje* on the coast. Neither of these two elements has so far contributed either cultural values or progressive energies to the formation of nationality."[24] Indeed, the destinies of these two ethnic groups, as well as the assessment of their contributions to national societies in Latin America and the Caribbean, have often been inextricably linked. After all, the importation of Chinese "coolies" in Cuba and Peru (and later, of Japanese farmworkers in Peru and Brazil) took place, as mentioned, because of the progressive banishing of African enslaved labor due to the 1807 British-induced ban on the Atlantic slave trade (slavery was abolished in Peru in 1854, in Cuba in 1886, and in Brazil in 1888) and the ensuing inability to attract European farm labor. Enslaved Africans and Chinese and Japanese indentured workers share, as a result, a common history of bondage, marronage, and suicide.

Moreover, among the depositions by Chinese indentured workers in Cuba collected in *The Cuba Commission Report*, some denounce the fact that formerly enslaved Africans, who were working as overseers, would often beat and kill them: "I saw a man named A-chi so severely struck on the neck by the Negro overseer that he died in three days."[25] The Chinese respondents also confess to feeling a deep humiliation upon noticing the preferential treatment received by Blacks or upon being punished by enslaved or formerly enslaved foremen. Favoritism toward Blacks, according to Wu Yeh-ch'êng's deposition, was apparent even when Blacks and Chinese joined forces against common oppression by their employers: "Four Negroes in league with certain recently arrived Chinese killed the new administrator. By an outlay of money on the part of our employer, the participation of the Negroes was not mentioned, and the crime was imputed to us."[26] Chinese claimants also lament the fact that Western countries are fighting for the abolition of African slavery while concomitantly allowing the so-called yellow trade. Thus, Jên Shih-chên and two others complain: "We learn that friendly relations now exist between China and the greater powers of the West, and that it is by the efforts of the latter that the traffic in Negro slaves has been suppressed. Why do they not render to us a similar service?"[27] In her introduction to *The Cuba Commission Report*, Denise Helly speculates on the plausible causes of this animosity between Chinese and Blacks: "because they received salaries at all, and because some sought to establish relations with black women, the Chinese became potential objects of jealousy for some male slaves."[28]

Similarly, in the case of Peru, according to Humberto Rodríguez Pastor, formerly enslaved Black foremen often mistreated Chinese indentured workers in Peruvian plantations: "Black foremen with whips frequently controlled Asians, taught them submissiveness, and taught them how to meet their work assignments. These Blacks were also in charge of daily locking them up in barracks; some specialized in chasing runaway Chinese. Blacks and Chinese were rivals who frequently manifested the rivalry."[29] Juan de Arona, in his *La inmigración en el Perú* (Immigration in Peru, 1891), likewise avers, "Blacks, during slavery, had no masters other than White people; Chinese had White and Black people."³⁰ He later adds resentment and religious differences as a reason behind this racial tension:

> On the haciendas and farms, the Chinese were treated, with some exceptions, with more or less intense rigor. The shackles, the platen, the stocks, the whip were not idle, as they say, besides the general mistreatment they received from their immediate foremen, most of whom were men of color and slaves at one time and later manumis. The revengeful viciousness and fierce pleasure with which these manumisses or slaves would brandish on another body the same whip that had so often marked their flesh will be understood. There is no tradition in which a Chinese has found mercy in a man of color. Among the reasons were religious differences, which firmly led the other "colored" people to believe that the Chinese were not "people."³¹

It has also been documented that Chinese indentured workers killed several Black foremen to escape the plantations or simply as revenge for the corporal punishment endured from them. In some cases, Latin American planters would encourage these hostilities between Chinese and Black laborers to prevent interethnic alliances against the plantation owners. Among other tactics, they would pit aggressive Black overseers against Chinese indentured workers or would use enslaved Blacks to repress "coolie rebellions" in the plantations. For this same reason, they would house Blacks and Chinese indentured workers in separate buildings, much to the preference of both ethnic groups.

Rodríguez Pastor mentions a violent brawl between Blacks and Chinese in the Valley of Cañete during the summer of 1881, after a Chinese man flirted with an Afro-Peruvian woman, which was plausibly the last drop after years of animosity between the two groups.³² In a chapter titled "A Criminal Chronology of Peru" and included in his autobiographical novel *Viaje a Ítaca*, the Chinese Peruvian author Siu Kam Wen provides a revised version of this tragic episode that took place during the Chilean occupation: "Lima now occupied, and the country in disorder, the Indian and Black populations of Cañete rise in arms to settle an old score with coolies in the valley. They are out to vindicate a Black woman's beating at the hands of an Oriental during carnival. According to Juan de Arona's conservative estimate, about one thousand coolies are killed in one day."³³ Young elevates the number of Chinese massacred by Black and Mestizo peasants in the Cañete Valley to "at least 1,000 and perhaps as many as 1,700,"[34] which makes it the worst massacre of Chinese in the Americas. He provides different possible motivations behind the atrocity, including xenophobia after the Chinese supported the Chilean invading army, being seen as economic competitors, class tensions (mostly merchants, rather than peasants, were murdered), freeing themselves from debt, or a broader attack to the sugar estates, that is, against Chinese, Whites, and their property.[35] The brutal manner in which they were murdered is also indicative of the deep-seated animosity among the ethnic groups: "The cadavers of the Chinese were strewn around the middle of the stately patio ... which served as a Bacchanalian and cannibalesque desecration for women and boys. The same black women who had shared in the conspiracy gifted by the victims ridiculed the bodies by mutilating them and putting them in their open mouths as a mockery, forming a cigarette out of the bloody and palpitating members that they had amputated. 'Leave this one for me!' shouted the black women fighting over the victims, drunk with blood like the women who had dismembered Pentheus."[36]

Likewise, Gonzalo Paroy Villafuerte has studied the so-called Batallón Cuchara, a group of young, multiethnic citizens of Lima known as *mataperros* (urchins) between 1863 and 1911, whose hobby was to harass the Chinese in town, particularly Chinese street sweepers.[37] In a way, as Paroy Villafuerte explains, Blacks and Whites in Lima were finally united in their common hate of the Chinese. These poor, barefooted Chinese devoted to the low-paying job of sweeping and mopping the streets of Lima starting at midnight had to withstand these vandalic attacks and insults (like *chino macao*), but they also defended themselves with their brooms, and in some cases, successfully. They were often attacked by drunkards and exposed to diseases. According to Paroy Villafuerte, these attacks were particularly common when there were fireworks. After the show, the "Spoon Battalion" would appear in military formation, carrying sticks left over from the fireworks and stones, to attack the Chinese near the Plaza Central in Lima. Apparently, onlookers found it funny, and the local police ignored the attacks.

Yet intermarriage between the two social groups was common: since most of the Chinese who arrived in Cuba and then to Peru were male, many ended up marrying women of African ancestry. As does Chen Pan, the protagonist of the novel *El cazador de monos* (*Monkey Hunting*, 2003) by the Cuban American author Cristina García, after Chinese indentured workers finished their contracts, they would sometimes purchase a Black slave with the goal of freeing and then marrying her.[38] Thinkers such as González Prada mocked the miscegenation between Chinese men and Black women in Peru with humorous poems:

> Here lies Manongo,
> Of pure Latin stock,
> His mother came from the Congo
> And his father was born in China.³⁹

As stated, Latin American defenders of Chinese immigration have recurrently praised Chinese achievements by contrasting them with the perceived underachievement of Blacks. Thus, even though she chastises the implicit racism in the discourse of eugenics, the Peruvian intellectual Dora Mayer (1868–1959), in her study *La China silenciosa y elocuente* (The Silent and Eloquent China, 1924), vehemently defends the Chinese and *tusanes* (Chinese Peruvians) by contrasting what she sees as their many achievements with the purported failures of Afro-Peruvians. In her view, the process of integration into Peruvian mainstream society was smoother for Blacks because, she argues, they completely lost their culture; Chinese indentured workers, by contrast, had a "more authentic civilization," which allowed them to keep their own language and culture but thwarted proper assimilation: "The Black man did not keep his language, never had his own writing system or traditions so esteemed as to appreciate them as a prize of his race. The Chinese man, on the other hand, did not expect all to come from the cultural system to which he was being integrated."⁴⁰

Decades earlier, Juan de Arona, in his *La inmigración en el Perú* (Immigration in Peru, 1891), had also praised the positive qualities of the Chinese (including their cooking abilities, restaurants, hygiene, and overall contributions to Peruvian economy and culture) by contrasting them with what he deemed as the degenerate habits of Afro-Peruvians: "Whereas one can see gangs of men of color going around, yelling up and down main streets, during work hours, and in areas where the upper echelons of society dwell, dirtying the sidewalk with their spittle as they chat about topics that are outside of their understanding, an Asian man strolls along: always carrying something in his hand or hanging from his shoulder, or showing work-related concerns in his face. Whereas the Black carrier asks us with insolence: 'will you give me a four' (40 cents), the Chinaman, solicitous and thankful, carries our load for less."⁴¹

Some Latin American authors and painters of mixed Chinese and African ancestry have expressed their pride in both heritages. This was the case, for instance, of the Cuban painter of Afro-Chinese ancestry Wifredo Lam (1902–1982) and of the Cuban *modernista* and later social poet Regino Pedroso (1896–1983). Thus, in his "auto-bio-prólogo" (auto-bio-prologue) to his poetry collection *Nosotros* (Us), Pedroso, the son of a Black mother and a Chinese father, celebrates his belonging to "the human race," his pigmentation is "black-yellow. (With no other mixture)," and his lack of European ancestry.[42] Along these lines, the Peruvian writer and mathematician Enrique Verástegui (1950–2018) shared Chinese and African blood and, according to his sister Isabel Verástegui in an interview for *China Hoy*, was equally proud of all his ethnic heritages (Cantonese, African, Basque, Andean): "He has several races, he never wanted to show interest for one particular race because he maintained that he had all the races. Then, he, in his poetry, talks about all the races. He was aware that he was a mestizo."[43] Verástegui, in his last column in the journal *Expreso*, where he reviewed Julia Wong's book *Pessoa por Wong*, described his own ethnic heritage thus: "Enrique Verástegui Ah Tao Ko—surname of my maternal grandparents from Guandong, field engineers who came to Peru to provide technology to coastal agriculture."[44] He was the great-grandson of Juan Evangelista Peláez, a man from Guandong who, according to Isabel Verástegui, would always say "My surname was loaned."[45] When Juan received Catholic baptism, he took the surname Peláez from his godfather, and to this day, the Verástegui family does not know the original Cantonese last name. Enrique Verástegui, according to his sister, "stopped using the surname Peláez for a long time to honor that Chinese last name."[46] Juan Evangelista Peláez was one of the 3,000 Cantonese who migrated, starting in the mid-nineteenth century, to the fertile plantations of the Cañete Valley to work in cotton and sugarcane plantations.

By contrast, in his *Apunte histórico de los chinos en Cuba* (Historical Notes on the Chinese in Cuba, 1927), the Afro-Chinese or *chino mulato* Cuban Antonio Chuffat Latour compares what he considers the failures of Afro-Cubans with the cultural integration of the Chinese, their efforts to "civilize themselves," and their refinement, which he compares to that of Caucasians.[47] Euphemistically referring to Blacks as "the other race," Chuffat Latour proceeds to vilify them as a strategy for Chinese empowerment: "While the other race pitifully wasted time in silly things and stupidity, without any aspirations or pretensions to anything."[48] Furthermore, he associates Chinese superior intelligence with the whiteness of their skin: "The intellectualism acquired by the Chinese is the main reason they have surpassed other races in every social order. The Chinese considers himself White, period. His level of intelligence is superior."[49] Like Dora Mayer in Peru, Chuffat Latour claims that, in Cuba, the Chinese were more educated and prepared than Blacks, hence the difference in social achievements. In reality, as is well known, the Chinese were able to maintain their languages and cultures because of the continued immigration patterns and their uninterrupted ties with the sending communities in the homeland. Besides sending letters and remittances, Chinese men occasionally managed to make voyages back to their hometowns, often to marry women or make investments. People of African ancestry, by contrast, were not able to enjoy these exchanges, which contributed to their partial uprootedness and loss of cultural memory.

On the other hand, Chuffat Latour elevates the heroism of the Chinese (the *chinos mambises*) during the Cuban independence wars against Spain by juxtaposing it to what he sees as the underperformance of unarmed Afro-Cubans, who were, in his view, more a nuisance than anything else.[50] Rhetorically camouflaging his own prejudice and racism, he paternalistically justifies these perceived failures by ascribing them to their lack of education and even quotes a poem by a Chinese in Cuba that condemns their enslavement. Therefore, like Dora Mayer's, Chuffat Latour's advocacy for Chinese empowerment is carried out at the expense of Blacks, even though his mother was an African, and throughout the text, he describes himself as an Afro-Cuban. In any case, it would not be too far-fetched to assume that the fact that Chinese merchants sponsored Chuffat Latour's publication influenced his one-sided racial views.

This time resorting to inherited cultural and traditional values rather than education, the Chinese Cuban author Napoleón Seuc offers a similar approach in his essay *La colonia china de Cuba 1930–1960* (The Chinese Colony of Cuba, 1998), but without naming specific races. As evidence, Seuc calls attention to the economic success of the East Asian tigers (Hong Kong, Taiwan, Singapore, and South Korea) as well as to those of overseas Chinese in several Asian countries: "The dissimilitude in economic growth among different peoples and ethnicities in this century makes us think that there are factors of a cultural, traditional and hereditary nature, but not of a genetic one, that provide a margin of advantage for certain races—in the free and competitive world market of modern economy, in the free-trade doctrine of open (not protectionist) societies—over other races and peoples of the Earth."[51]

Overall, as stated, this tactic of misrepresenting the achievements of Afrodescended communities to empower the Chinese community is reminiscent of the Model Minority myth in the United States, which has used the economic success of some Asian communities to justify the discrimination of other ethnic groups, such as the African American and Latinx communities.

Conclusion

Asian immigrants and their descendants in Latin America have made important contributions to the economies and sociocultural lives in their host countries. They have also affected Latin American national identities, as their mere presence challenged the traditional White-Indigenous or White-Black dichotomies of the discourses of mestizaje and *mulataje*, respectively. The ancient cultural heritages brought by Asian diasporas have contributed greatly not only to the region's literature,[52] cuisine, art, language, and music, but also to its aspirations of independence (the case of the *chinos mambises* in Cuba) and its revolutions (Chinese Cubans in the Cuban Revolution and Japanese immigrants in the Mexican Revolution).[53]

Their cultural production often negotiates cultural belonging as well as cultural difference and hybridization, all the while historicizing and rescuing from oblivion their experience as racialized social groups. It likewise reflects the heterogeneity of these communities, challenging the essentialist idea of a static identity and proposing, instead, fluid identities that develop according to the circumstances or evolve from one generation to the next, leaning toward a progressive cultural integration into mainstream national cultures.

Their historical experiences are also quite different, as the levels and types of Sinophobia and Nipponophobia varied from country to country. In fact, the Chinese were the victims of the third-largest genocide in the history of the Americas, after those of the Native Americans and the enslaved Africans, while the Japanese were not subjected to such horrendous levels of mortality. According to Young, approximately 12 percent of enslaved Africans died in transit during the Atlantic slave trade, roughly the same percentage of Cantonese who died during the "yellow trade" while traveling to Latin America (a voyage three times longer than that of the enslaved Africans) between 1847 and 1874.[54] Furthermore, whereas, for the most part, Japanese and Koreans migrated legally, in many cases Chinese immigrants were undocumented and they remigrated—crossing international borders between Mexico, the United States, Canada, and Cuba—without authorization. As Young points out, "Chinese were remarkably successful in evading state controls."[55] And whereas emigration was encouraged by the Japanese government since the

Meiji Restoration, the Qing government in China first prohibited and then discouraged it.

The Chinese, often constructed as aliens and cultural outsiders by the state, were, in fact, the first people in the world to be targeted with immigration restrictions based exclusively on their ethnicity.[56] They began with the 1882 Chinese Exclusion Act in the United States and continued, in the Mexico of the 1920s and 1930s, as a result of the nativist, anti-Chinese campaigns inspired by economic jealousy, eugenicist beliefs, and the prevailing discourse of mestizaje that was supposed to unite the nation.

There were also major differences in the immigrant experiences within the same ethnic group. Thus, most Japanese immigrants in Mexico, despite also being the victims of xenophobia, did not initially endure the stigma associated with being indentured workers, nor were they compelled to flee from plantations owned by local planters who mistreated them, the case in Peru and Brazil. Likewise, whereas indentured Chinese workers in Cuba, Peru, and the Yucatán Peninsula in Mexico were first coerced or swindled in some cases with misrepresentations of what awaited them in the Americas, and then dreadfully mistreated (besides being sold in auction blocks and renamed like slaves, in Peru they were branded in their faces in some cases),[57] other Chinese, such as the ones who left California for Mexico after the Chinese Exclusion Act and, in some cases, then remigrated to Cuba, were for the most part free entrepreneurs who had a less challenging experience. Similarly, the Chinese in Peru could not count on their heroic participation in the wars of independence to demonstrate their patriotism and right to belong within the national project, as the Chinese in Cuba have often done; on the contrary, the fact that some of them supported the invading Chilean army was a stigma that made their cultural integration even more difficult. And subethnic groups, such as Ryukyuans (mostly from Okinawa), were often twice marginalized by feeling rejected by both the local mainstream society and mainland Japanese (Naichijin) immigrants.

There are also commonalities among these ethnic groups, however. For example, besides the fact that all three communities, Chinese, Japanese, and Koreans, at some point experienced indentured servitude in certain countries, both the Chinese and the Japanese were considered a threat to the state at different times throughout their immigrant histories: while the Chinese and their Mexican families were deported from the Mexican states of Sonora and Sinaloa during the early 1930s, purportedly for this very reason, the alienated Japanese were displaced from coastal and border areas, interned, and deported during World War II. Also during this period, after the Japanese invaded Manchuria, creating the puppet state of Manchukuo in 1932, the animosity between the Chinese and Japanese communities in Latin America grew. Thus, in Peru some Chinese reported their Nikkei neighbors to Peruvian and American authorities so that they could be deported to internment camps in the United States and even placed Chinese flags on their businesses to avoid being confused with the Japanese.

Finally, both the Chinese and the Japanese resisted exploitation and oppression. Chinese "coolies" often rebelled in the barracoons, ships, and plantations, or committed suicide at a high rate, which influenced the Cuba Commission sent by the Chinese emperor that ended the "Coolie Trade" in 1874. In turn, the Japanese would flee the plantations and even founded, in the São Paulo of the 1940s, Shindō Renmei, one of the first terrorist organizations in the Americas, whose members refused to believe that Japan had surrendered at the end of World War II and wounded or murdered Japanese immigrants who publicly acknowledged their country's defeat.

NOTES

1. Tatiana Seijas, *Asian Slaves in Colonial Mexico: From Chinos to Indians* (Cambridge: Cambridge University Press, 2014), 1.
2. Elliott Young, *Alien Nation: Chinese Migration in the Americas from the Coolie Era through World War II* (Chapel Hill: University of North Carolina Press, 2014), 10.
3. Including the extension of additional months to the contract because of days missed due to illness or debts accrued in the shop where they were forced to buy, at higher prices, their food, and other needed items.
4. Ch'en Lan Pin, *The Cuba Commission Report: A Hidden History of the Chinese in Cuba*, intro. Denise Helly (Baltimore: Johns Hopkins University Press, 1993).
5. Young, *Alien Nation*, 84.
6. See Beatriz Varela's *Lo chino en el habla cubana* (Chinese Influence in Cuban Spanish) (Miami: Ediciones Universal, 1980).
7. Isabelle Lausent-Herrera, "Tusans and the Changing Chinese Community in Peru," in *Chinese in Latin America and the Caribbean*, ed. Tan Chee-Beng and Walton Look Lai (Leiden: Koninklijke Brill NV, 2010), 143.
8. The term *tusán*, used to refer to Chinese descendants, is used mostly in Peru. The term comes from the Chinese *Tusheng* (local born). The word *chifa* comes from Mandarin *chī fàn*, literally meaning "eat meal." According to Watt Stewart, *chifas* were initially known as *chinganas* or *fondas*. *Chinese Bondage in Peru* (Durham, NC: Duke University Press, 1951), 126. Mariela Balbi has explored the history of the *chifa* in her book *La historia de los chifas en el Perú* (Lima: Universidad de San Martín de Porres, 1999).
9. For an annotated bibliography on literature by Peruvians of Asian descent and academic studies on this cultural production, see my article "Asian-Peruvian Literature," included in *Oxford Bibliographies in Latin American Studies*, ed. Ben Vinson (New York: Oxford

Interethnic Conflict and Sociocultural Contributions 273

University Press, 2012). https://www.oxfordbibliographies.com/display/document/obo-9780199766581/obo-9780199766581-0082.xml, August 29, 2024.
10. Robert Chao Romero, *The Chinese in Mexico, 1882–1940* (Tucson: University of Arizona Press, 2010), 3.
11. For an analysis of Herbert's narration, see Ignacio M. Sánchez Prado's 2017 *"La casa del dolor ajeno* de Julián Herbert: No-ficción, memoria e historicidad en el México contemporáneo," *MLN* 132, no. 2 (2017): 426–440, and my 2019 "Necropolítica, espectrología china e impunidad en *La casa del dolor ajeno* de Julián Herbert," in *Narrativas de lo chino en las Américas y la Península ibérica*, ed. María Montt Strabucchi and Amelia Saiz López (Biblioteca de China Contemporánea. Barcelona: Bellaterra, 2019).
12. Jeffrey Lesser, *A Discontented Diaspora: Japanese Brazilians and the Meanings of Ethnic Militancy, 1960–1980* (Durham, NC: Duke University Press, 2007), 5.
13. María Elena Ota Mishima, *Siete migraciones japonesas en México: 1890–1978* (Mexico City: El Colegio de México, 1985).
14. Literally meaning "to call over," it was a system through which an established Japanese immigrant could request someone living in Japan to come work for him by applying to the Japanese consulate.
15. Chong-Sup Kim and Eunsuk Lee, "Growth and Migration to a Third Country: The Case of Korean Migrants in Latin America," *Journal of International and Area Studies* 23, no. 2 (2016): 78–79.
16. Kyeyoung Park, "A Rhizomatic Diaspora: Transnational Passage and the Sense of Place among Koreans in Latin America," *Urban Anthropology and Studies of Cultural Systems and World Economic Development* 43, no. 4 (2014): 506.
17. Park, "A Rhizomatic Diaspora," 492.
18. For a study of these two Korean Chilean authors and other Chilean authors of Asian descent, see Maria Montt Strabucchi's "Asian Chilean Writing and Film, and Chilean Orientalism," in *A History of Chilean Literature*, ed. Ignacio López-Calvo (Cambridge: Cambridge University Press, 2021).
19. See my article "From Interethnic Alliances to the 'Magical Negro': Afro-Asian Interactions in Asian American Literature," *Humanities* 7, no. 4.110 (2018): 1–10.
20. Mayra Montero, *Como un mensajero tuyo* (Barcelona: Tusquets, 1998). See also *The Messenger*, trans. Edith Grossman (New York, NY: Harper Flamingo, 1999); Zoé Valdés, *Te di la vida entera* (Barcelona: Planeta, 1996); *I Gave You All I Had*, trans. Nadia Benabid (New York: Arcade Publishing, 1999); Leonardo Padura Fuentes, *Adiós Hemingway: La cola de la serpiente* (Havana: Unión, 2001); Antonio José Ponte, "A petición de Ochún," in *Cuentos de todas partes del Imperio* (Anger, France: Éditions Deleatur, 2000); *Tales from the Cuban Empire*, trans. Cola Franzen (San Francisco: City Lights, 2002).
21. For additional information on Sanfancón, see Frank F. Scherer's essay "Sanfancón: Orientalism, Self-Orientalization, and 'Chinese Religion' in Cuba," in *Nation Dance: Religion, Identity, and Cultural Difference in the Caribbean*, ed. Patrick Taylor (Bloomington: Indiana University Press, 2001).
22. Young, *Alien Nation*, 77.
23. David Palumbo-Liu, *Asian American: Historical Crossings of a Racial Frontier* (Stanford, CA: Stanford University Press, 1999), 172.
24. José Carlos Mariátegui, *Seven Interpretative Essays on Peruvian Reality*, trans. Marjory Urquidi (Austin: University of Texas Press, 1971), 279. See also "7 ensayos de interpretación de la realidad peruana," *Mariátegui total*, vol. 1 (Lima: Amauta, 1994).

25. Ch'en Lan Pin, *The Cuba Commission Report*, 105.
26. Ch'en Lan Pin, *The Cuba Commission Report*, 88.
27. Ch'en Lan Pin, *The Cuba Commission Report*, 90.
28. Denise Helly, "Introduction," in *The Cuba Commission Report. A Hidden History of the Chinese in Cuba* by Ch'en Lan Pin (Baltimore: Johns Hopkins University Press, 1993), 20.
29. Humberto Rodríguez Pastor, *Hijos del celeste imperio en el Perú (1850–1990): Migración, agricultura, mentalidad y explotación* (Lima: Sur Casa de Estudios del Socialismo, 2001), 38. "El negro chicotero frecuentemente controló a los asiáticos, les enseñó a someterse, y los instruyó en las formas como debían cumplir sus actividades en el trabajo. Estos negros se encargaron también del diario encierro en el galpón y algunos fueron los especialistas en buscar a los chinos cimarrones. Negros y chinos fueron rivales que frecuentemente exteriorizaron esta rivalidad." All translations are my own unless otherwise indicated.
30. Juan de Arona, *La inmigración en el Perú* (Lima: Universo, 1891), 43. "Los negros en la esclavitud no tuvieron más tiranos que los blancos, los chinos, á los blancos y á los negros."
31. Arona, *La inmigración*, 43. "Los chinos eran tratados en las haciendas y chacras, salvo excepciones, con rigor más o menos intenso. Los grillos, la platina, el cepo, el látigo, no andaban bobos, como se dice, fuera del maltrato general que recibían de sus inmediatos capataces, hombres de color los más, y esclavos en su tiempo y manumisos más tarde. Ya se comprenderá la saña vengativa y el placer feroz con que esos manumisos o esclavos blandirían sobre otro cuerpo el mismo látigo que tantas veces había marcado las carnes de ellos. No hay tradición que un chino haya encontrado piedad en un hombre de color, contribuyendo en mucho las preocupaciones religiosas, que firmemente hacían creer a los otros 'coloreados' que los chinos no eran 'gente.'"
32. Rodríguez Pastor, *Hijos del celeste imperio*, 97.
33. Siu Kam Wen, *Viaje a Ítaca* (Morrisville, NY: Ediciones Diana, 2004), 99. "1881. 16 de enero. Saqueo de Lima. Después de la batalla de Miraflores y con las tropas de ocupación a punto de entrar a Lima, un populacho encabezado por oficiales del ejército en retirada saquea e incendia las tiendas de los chinos, en venganza por la colaboración que miles de culíes de esa nacionalidad prestan al ejército invasor. Según Spenser St. John, el enviado británico en el país, unos 70 chinos son muertos en el curso del saqueo. 1881. Febrero. Saqueos y matanzas en Cañete. Con Lima ocupada y el país en desorden, la población india y negra de Cañete se alza para saldar una vieja cuenta con los culíes chinos que viven y laboran en el valle. El pretexto es el altercado entre uno de los orientales y una morena durante el carnaval. Según el cálculo conservador de Juan de Arona, unos mil culíes son muertos en un día de desmanes desaforados."
34. Young, *Alien Nation*, 79.
35. Young, *Alien Nation*, 78–79.
36. Arona as cited in Young, Alien Nation, 79.
37. Gonzalo Paroy Villafuerte, "El ataque del Batallón Cuchara: Odios y conflicto entre chinos y mataperros en Lima (1863-1911)," *Revista Historia 2.0, Conocimiento Histórico en Clave Digital* 3, no. 5 (2013): 92–102.
38. Cristina García, *Monkey Hunting* (New York: Knopf, 2003). See also *El cazador de monos*, trans. María Eugenia Ciocchini (Barcelona: Emecé, 2003).
39. Manuel González Prada, *Grafitos* (Paris: Tip. de Louis Bellenand et Fils, 1937), app. 9. "Aquí descansa Manongo, / de pura raza latina, / su madre vino del Congo, / y su padre nació en la China."

40. Dora Mayer de Zulen, *La China silenciosa y elocuente* (Lima: Renovación, 1924), 110. "El negro no conservó su idioma, no tuvo nunca escritura propia, ni tradiciones tan amadas que las preciara como un galardón de su raza. El chino, al contrario, no lo esperaba todo de la organización del sistema cultural a que ingresaba."
41. Arona, *La inmigración*, 47-48. "Mientras á los hombres de color se les ve rodar en pelotones vociferando por las mas principales calles, en horas de trabajo, y aún apostados en los mejores centros de la sociedad escogida, ensuciando la acera con su salivación y charloteando de materias extrañas á su condición, el asiático se desliza de largo: llevando siempre algo en la mano ó al hombro, ó en el semblante la preocupación del trabajo. Mientras el negro cargador nos dice insolentemente: 'me dará Ud. un cuatro' (40 cts.) el chino solícito y agradecido nos lleva un bulto por un real."
42. Regino Pedroso, *Nosotros* (Havana: Letras Cubanas, 1984), 9. "Negro-amarilla (Sin otra mezcla)."
43. As cited in Enrique Verástegui, "El aporte tusán al Perú," *Expreso.com*, July 22, 2018. "Tiene varias razas, él nunca quiso mostrar interés por una sola raza porque él consideraba que tenía todas la razas. Entonces él, en su poesía habla de todas las razas. Estaba consciente de que él es un cruzado." Another Afro-Chinese Peruvian author is Mario Choy Novoa, who published short stories in the 1980s such as "Butaca del paraíso" (Seat in Paradise) Premio Copé de Cuento 1979 (Lima: Copé, 1981) and the bilingual "May God Grant You Happiness" / "Dios quiera que seas dichosa," in *From the Threshold / Desde el umbral: Contemporary Peruvian Fiction in Translation*, bilingual ed., ed. Luis A. Ramos-García and Luis Fernando Vidal (Austin: Studia Hispanica Editors, Prickly Pear Press, 1987).
44. Verástegui, "El aporte tusán," n.p. "Enrique Verástegui Ah Tao Ko—apellido de mis abuelos maternos provenientes de Cantón, ingenieros de campo llegados a Perú para tecnificar la agricultura costeña."
45. Verástegui, "El aporte tusán," n.p. "Yo tengo el apellido prestado."
46. Verástegui, "El aporte tusán," n.p. "Dejó de usar el apellido Peláez por mucho tiempo en honor a ese apellido chino."
47. Antonio Chuffat Latour, *Apunte histórico de los chinos en Cuba* (Havana: Molina, 1927); "El refinamiento de la raza blanca," *Apunte histórico*, 15-16; "Civilizarse," *Apunte histórico*, 16.
48. Chuffat Latour, *Apunte histórico*, 16. "Mientras que la otra raza perdía lastimosamente el tiempo en sandeces y boberías, sin aspiraciones ni pretensiones a nada."
49. Chuffat Latour, *Apunte histórico*, 16. "La intelectualidad adquirida por los chinos es el factor principal que ha superado a otras razas en todo el orden social. El chino se considera blanco y basta. La superioridad de inteligencia."
50. Chuffat Latour, *Apunte histórico*, 63.
51. Napoleón Seuc, *La colonia china de Cuba 1930-1960: Antecedentes, memorias y vivencias* (Miami: Ahora Printing, 1998), 172. "La disimilitud en el crecimiento económico de este siglo de pueblos y etnias diferentes nos inclina a pensar que hay factores tradicionales, hereditarios, pero de origen cultural, no genético, que dan cierto margen de ventaja a ciertas razas—en el libre y competitivo mercado mundial de la economía moderna, en el librecambismo de las sociedades abiertas [no proteccionistas]—sobre otras razas y pueblos de la tierra."
52. For more information on literature by Latin Americans of Asian ancestry, see my books *Imaging the Chinese in Cuban Literature and Culture* (Gainesville: University Press of Florida, 2008), *The Affinity of the Eye: Writing Nikkei in Peru* (Tucson: University of Ari-

zona Press, 2013), *Dragons in the Land of the Condor: Writing Tusán in Peru* (Tucson: University of Arizona Press, 2014), *Japanese Brazilian Saudades: Diasporic Identities and Cultural Production* (Louisville: University Press of Colorado, 2019), and *The Mexican Transpacific: Nikkei Writing, Visual Arts, and Performance* (Nashville, TN: Vanderbilt University Press, 2022).

53. For additional information on the role of Chinese Cubans in the Cuban Revolution, see Armando Choy, Gustavo Chui, and Moisés Sío Wong's *Our History Is Still Being Written. The Story of Three Chinese-Cuban Generals in the Cuban Revolution* (New York: Pathfinder, 2005). For more information on the role of the Japanese in the Mexican Revolution, see Jerry García's 2014 *Looking Like the Enemy: Japanese Mexicans, the Mexican State, and US Hegemony, 1897-1945* (Tucson: University of Arizona Press, 2014) and my recent *The Mexican Transpacific*.

54. Young, *Alien Nation*, 30.

55. Young, *Alien Nation*, 3-4.

56. Young, *Alien Nation*, 12.

57. Young, *Alien Nation*, 47.

BIBLIOGRAPHY

Arona, Juan de. *La inmigración en el Perú*. Lima: Universo, 1891.

Balbi, Mariella. *La historia de los chifas en el Perú*. Lima: Universidad de San Martín de Porres, 1999.

Chao Romero, Robert. *The Chinese in Mexico, 1882-1940*. Tucson: University of Arizona Press, 2010.

Ch'en Lan Pin. *The Cuba Commission Report: A Hidden History of the Chinese in Cuba*. Introduction by Denise Helly. Baltimore: Johns Hopkins University Press, 1993.

Choy, Armando, Gustavo Chui, and Moisés Sío Wong. *Our History Is Still Being Written: The Story of Three Chinese-Cuban Generals in the Cuban Revolution*. Edited by Mary-Alice Waters. New York: Pathfinder, 2005.

Choy Novoa, Mario. "Butaca del paraíso." *Premio Copé de Cuento 1979*. Lima: Copé, 1981.

———. "May God Grant You Happiness" / "Dios quiera que seas dichosa." In *From the Threshold / Desde el umbral: Contemporary Peruvian Fiction in Translation*, bilingual ed., edited by Luis A. Ramos-García and Luis Fernando Vidal, 257-262. Austin, TX: Studia Hispanica Editors, Prickly Pear Press, 1987.

Chuffat Latour, Antonio. *Apunte histórico de los chinos en Cuba*. Havana: Molina, 1927.

García, Cristina. *El cazador de monos*. Translated by María Eugenia Ciocchini. Barcelona: Emecé, 2003.

———. *Monkey Hunting*. New York: Knopf, 2003.

García, Jerry. *Looking Like the Enemy: Japanese Mexicans, the Mexican State, and US Hegemony, 1897-1945*. Tucson: University of Arizona Press, 2014.

González Prada, Manuel. *Grafitos*. Paris: Tip. de Louis Bellenand et Fils, 1937.

Helly, Denise. "Introduction." In *The Cuba Commission Report. A Hidden History of the Chinese in Cuba*, by Ch'en Lan Pin, 1-30. Baltimore: Johns Hopkins University Press, 1993.

Kim, Chong-Sup, and Eunsuk Lee. "Growth and Migration to a Third Country: The Case of

Korean Migrants in Latin America." *Journal of International and Area Studies* 23, no. 2 (2016): 77–87.

Lausent-Herrera, Isabelle. "Tusans and the changing Chinese community in Peru." In *Chinese in Latin America and the Caribbean*, edited by Tan Chee-Beng and Walton Look Lai, 143–183. Leiden: Koninklijke Brill NV, 2010.

Lesser, Jeffrey. *A Discontented Diaspora: Japanese Brazilians and the Meanings of Ethnic Militancy, 1960–1980*. Durham, NC: Duke University Press, 2007.

López-Calvo, Ignacio. *The Affinity of the Eye: Writing Nikkei in Peru*. Tucson: University of Arizona Press, 2013.

———. "Asian-Peruvian Literature." In *Oxford Bibliographies in Latin American Studies*, edited by Ben Vinson. New York: Oxford University Press, 2012. https://www.oxfordbibliographies.com/display/document/obo-9780199766581/obo-9780199766581-0082.xml.

———. *Dragons in the Land of the Condor: Writing Tusán in Peru*. Tucson: University of Arizona Press, 2014.

———. "From Interethnic Alliances to the 'Magical Negro': Afro-Asian Interactions in Asian American Literature." *Humanities* 7, no. 4.110 (2018): 1–10.

———. *Imaging the Chinese in Cuban Literature and Culture*. Gainesville: University Press of Florida, 2008.

———. *Japanese Brazilian Saudades: Diasporic Identities and Cultural Production*. Denver: University Press of Colorado, 2019.

———. *The Mexican Transpacific: Nikkei Writing, Visual Arts, and Performance*. Nashville, TN: Vanderbilt University Press, 2022.

———. "Necropolítica, espectrología china e impunidad en La casa del dolor ajeno de Julián Herbert." In *Narrativas de lo chino en las Américas y la Península ibérica*, edited by María Montt Strabucchi and Amelia Saiz López, 55–70. Biblioteca de China Contemporánea. Barcelona: Bellaterra, 2019.

Mariátegui, José Carlos. *Seven Interpretative Essays on Peruvian Reality*. Translated by Marjory Urquidi. Austin: University of Texas Press, 1971.

———. "7 ensayos de interpretación de la realidad peruana." In *Mariátegui total*, vol. 1. Lima: Amauta, 1994.

Mayer de Zulen, Dora. *La China silenciosa y elocuente*. Lima: Renovación, 1924.

Montero, Mayra. *Como un mensajero tuyo*. Barcelona: Tusquets, 1998.

———. *The Messenger*. Translated by Edith Grossman. Harper Flamingo, 1999.

Montt Strabucchi, Maria. "Asian Chilean Writing and Film, and Chilean Orientalism." In *A History of Chilean Literature*, edited by Ignacio López-Calvo, 403–422. Cambridge: Cambridge University Press, 2021.

Ota Mishima, María Elena. *Siete migraciones japonesas en México: 1890–1978*. 1982. Mexico City: El Colegio de México, 1985.

Padura Fuentes, Leonardo. *Adiós Hemingway. La cola de la serpiente*. Havana: Unión, 2001.

Palumbo-Liu, David. *Asian American: Historical Crossings of a Racial Frontier*. Stanford, CA: Stanford University Press, 1999.

Park, Kyeyoung. "A Rhizomatic Diaspora: Transnational Passage and the Sense of Place among Koreans in Latin America." *Urban Anthropology and Studies of Cultural Systems and World Economic Development* 43, no. 4 (2014): 481–517.

Paroy Villafuerte, Gonzalo. "El ataque del Batallón Cuchara: Odios y conflicto entre chinos y mataperros en Lima (1863–1911)." *Revista Historia 2.0, Conocimiento Histórico en Clave Digital* 3, no. 5 (2013): 92–102.

Pedroso, Regino. *Nosotros*. Havana: Letras Cubanas, 1984.

Ponte, Antonio José. "A petición de Ochún." In *Cuentos de todas partes del Imperio*. Angers, France: Éditions Deleatur, 2000.

———. *Tales from the Cuban Empire*. Translated by Cola Franzen. San Francisco: City Lights, 2002.

Rodríguez Pastor, Humberto. *Hijos del celeste imperio en el Perú (1850–1990): Migración, agricultura, mentalidad y explotación*. Lima: Sur Casa de Estudios del Socialismo, 2001.

Sánchez Prado, Ignacio M. "*La casa del dolor ajeno* de Julián Herbert: No-ficción, memoria e historicidad en el México contemporáneo." *MLN* 132, no. 2 (2017): 426–440.

Scherer, Frank F. "Sanfancón: Orientalism, Self-Orientalization, and 'Chinese Religion' in Cuba." In *Nation Dance: Religion, Identity, and Cultural Difference in the Caribbean*, edited by Patrick Taylor, 153–170. Bloomington: Indiana University Press, 2001.

Seijas, Tatiana. *Asian Slaves in Colonial Mexico: From Chinos to Indians*. Cambridge: Cambridge University Press, 2014.

Seuc, Napoleón. *La colonia china de Cuba 1930–1960: Antecedentes, memorias y vivencias*. Miami: Ahora Printing, 1998.

Siu Kam Wen. *Viaje a Ítaca*. Morrisville, NY: Ediciones Diana, 2004.

Stewart, Watt. *Chinese Bondage in Peru*. Durham, NC: Duke University Press, 1951.

Valdés, Zoé. *I Gave You All I Had*. Translated by Nadia Benabid. New York: Arcade Publishing, 1999.

———. *Te di la vida entera*. Barcelona: Planeta, 1996.

Varela, Beatriz. *Lo chino en el habla cubana*. Miami: Ediciones Universal, 1980.

Verástegui, Enrique. "El aporte tusán al Perú." *Expreso.com*, 22 July 2018. https://www.expreso.com.pe/opinion/el-aporte-tusan-al-peru/.

Young, Elliott. *Alien Nation: Chinese Migration in the Americas from the Coolie Era through World War II*. Chapel Hill: University of North Carolina Press, 2014.

CHAPTER 11

Mobilizing Black Culture against Racism
The Negritude Movements in Latin America

CARLOS ALBERTO VALDERRAMA RENTERÍA

During the 1970s, a wave of antisystemic movements shook the world (Arrighi and others),[1] among them the Afro-diasporic struggles and mobilization.[2] Scholars recognize the value and importance of the Black freedom movements in the United States and the African liberation movements on the African continent. However, they discount the presence of Black social movements in Latin America during this time.[3] Both critics and believers of the Latin American countries' racial paradise images agreed that because of the racial ideology of mestizaje, it was almost impossible that a massive Black mobilization could emerge in the region.[4] I argue that analysts' problem is that they measured Afro–Latin American politics through the lens or experience of African Americans in the United States and anticolonization movements on the African continent, and not through Afro-Latinos' own political circumstances. As Paschel suggests, "Movements in those two countries have not only become canonical examples of anti-racist struggle in the social movement literature, but also in the world."[5] Consequently, the Négritude movements in Latin America passed unnoticed in the social movement literature and debates.

Although Paschel's survey of the Black politics in Latin America lists a number of new studies that acknowledge early Black mobilizations and show alternative forms of Black politics during the 1970s in Latin America,[6] an analysis of the trajectory of the negritude movements in the region is still absent. As Feldman states, "It seemed to many outsiders that Black in Spanish Latin America—especially in the Black Pacific—were unaffected by the spirit of negritude that flourished elsewhere."[7] Not surprisingly, scholars do not refer to its existence as a major contributor to Black politics and subjectivity formations in Latin America,[8] and those scholars who studied the movements reduced it to a cultural phenomenon.[9]

Despite that, "we know that the ideological and legal context of Latin American countries was very different from that of apartheid or Jim Crow, and this difference may have necessitated a different kind of response," there is still an African-Americanization of the social and political struggles of Afro-descendants in Latin America that does not permit scholars to appreciate the alternatives posed by the negritude discourses.[10] Some argue that Black politics in Latin America emerged mostly out of African American struggles; as Andrews states it, Black "students and professionals got together in the 1970s and 1980s to create Afro–Latin American organizations similar to those of the civil rights movement in the United States."[11]

In this chapter, I map the field of Black politics that constituted the rise and fall of the negritude movements in Latin America during the 1970s and mid-1980s. I focus on three aspects that describe its trajectories in the region. First, the formation of Black organizations and agendas against racism in countries like Brazil, Colombia, Ecuador, Peru, and Panama. Second, the emergence of transnational spaces of articulations and networks. And third, I point out some of their ambiguities, contributions, and legacies. I argue that despite the racial ideology of mestizaje or racial democracy, people of African descent could form national and international Black counterpublics to mobilize their Black cultural politics and agendas within the framework of negritude to challenge racism in Latin America. I suggest that black counterpublics constituted national and international Black social movements over which later Black urban and ethno-racial movements of the 1980s and 1990s built their politics and campaigns against racism, and in favor of ethno-racial citizenship rights in Latin America, respectively.[12]

Conceptual and Methodological Horizons

If social movements are a "sustained campaign of claim making, using repeated performances that advertise their claim, based on organizations, network, traditions, and solidarities that sustain these activities," I would argue that this definition comes very close to what the trajectory of negritude movements was in Latin America.[13] The negritude movement was a heterogeneous process of Black politics that mobilized racial discourses of negritude to affirm and revalue Black culture and identity for about two decades in Latin America. It began in academic and cultural public spheres, and ended up turning into more social, cultural, and political organizations in countries such as Colombia, Ecuador, Panama, Peru, and Brazil. I affirm that the reasons that the negritude movements passed unnoticed in academia is because they did not involve mass-movement forms of contentions, understood as "arrays of contentious performances that are currently known and available within some set of political actors."[14]

Their movement campaigns—"a sustained challenge to power holders"[15]—did not display a large number of supporters on the streets or in massive public events.[16] Most negritude movements' repertoire of contentions were limited in number and did not involve massive public protests or demonstrations—strikes, blockades, and marches. Instead, they created public spheres such as encounters, *tertulias*, and social and political organizations; folkloric, musical, theater, and academic groups; and conferences and congresses to debate and circulate discourses of Black culture and identity. Although the negritude movements articulated forms of social movement organizations,[17] their main form of organization was the constitution of Black public spheres and counterpublics.[18]

Alongside the logic of numbers, the negritude movements in Latin America did not display a logic of inflicting material damage.[19] In other words, the movements did not use violence as their primary form of protest. In contrast, they performed dialogues, discussions, writings and articles, essays, novels and poems, music and dances in public spheres to challenge racist epistemes that represented and defined Blackness as an inferior racial group. However, the negritude movements could develop the logic of bearing witness, which demonstrates their strong commitment to affirming Black identities, culture, and the African legacies, as well as to making claims of the existence of racism in Latin America.[20]

Because a field is "made up of a set of forces or actors struggling to define and redefine the terms and conditions of the social relations that constitute the limits and the possibilities of the field,"[21] I understand that the terrain in which the negritude movements took form was contested by different actors with diverse agendas and interests.[22] I agree with Laó-Montes and Paschel that Black politics in Latin America cannot be fully comprehended within national borders.[23] There is a degree of permeability from discourses and actors outside of the nation-states. I would say that this is how Black politics is constructed in the African diaspora. It is made up of national and international disputes and solidarities.

Defining the terrain of social and political relations in which Black politics in Latin America took place as a complex field of politics with national and international alignments and conflicts allows me to understand the negritude movements in tensions or in line with other African diaspora antiracist projects. Within this field of politics, negritude discourses coexisted with Black power, Black feminism, *negrismo*, Afro-Americanism, Black Marxism, and anticolonialism discourses, as well as racial ideologies of oppression—mestizaje, racial democracy, Indigenismo, liberalism, and Marxism—that disputed and contested the meaning of Blackness. As Paschel argues, "Fields are not only about contestation over material power but also about the power of representations, who defines the language of the debate and who legitimates categories."[24]

Finally, we cannot forget that this field of politics aligned with antiracist agendas—ethnic and human rights—encouraged by UNESCO.[25] Thus, proponents of the negritude in Latin America mobilized their discourses and public events with the financial support of this international organization. In this sense, three international public events—Congresses of Black Culture of the Americas in Colombia (1977), Panama (1980), and Brazil (1982) and others—transpired with the support of UNESCO. Also, it debunked eugenic theories with new studies, discouraged the use of racial words, and promoted the use of ethnic concepts.[26]

This chapter assumes a critical and relational sociohistorical perspective of the emergence and decline of the negritude movements in Latin America. I draw on qualitative data I collected during my fieldwork in Colombia (2015–2016). I interviewed and met more than sixty Black men and women, former activists of the negritude movements in the country, and I conducted archival research analysis on national and international newspapers, newsletters, and personal documents shared by interviewees.[27] I also draw on specialized literature on Black politics in Latin America to present a complete description of the rise and fall of the negritude movements in Latin America during the 1970s and mid-1980s. Here, I map all forms of Black politics, collective actions, and public spheres that explicitly framed their emergence under the influence of the negritude movements.

The chapter is organized as follows. First, I summarize the racial formation in Latin America. Second, I describe the origin and main characteristics of the negritude movements in the Francophone African diaspora world. Third, I analyze the formation of Black organizations and the public sphere in Colombia, Brazil, Ecuador, Panama, and Peru. I pay special attention to their cultural, social, and political agendas. Then, I present the international space of articulation and end the chapter with some reflections on the ambiguities, contributions, and legacies of the negritude movements.

Racial Formation in Latin America

Race is and is not exclusively about skin color; as Hanchard recognizes, "Race in this regard is not only a marker for phenotypical difference, but of status, class, and political power."[28] Race is an instrument of politics that changes purposefully to rule those defined as racially inferior by structuring social relations of power and by creating cultural representations of racial dominance and superiority-inferiority.[29] In contrast to the United States, racism has not always been overtly explicit or visible in Latin America. Here, a clear-cut distinction between Black and white—a drop of blood—became blurry as a result of racial mixture. However, despite the changing meaning of race or racism in Latin America,[30] there is an enduring or persisting racial episteme—to use Foucault's language—that ends up classifying, treating, and defining Blackness as an inferior racial group or culture. As Wade states, "Only one thing was certain: to be black or Indian was bad, to be white was good."[31]

Quijano explains that this racial episteme started with the coloniality of power, which in Latin America incorporated a caste system of racial classification based on the interpretation of "*limpieza de sangre*, clean blood, supposedly free from the 'taint' of black or Indian (or Jewish or Moorish) blood."[32] "The ranks of the mixed themselves were also strongly heterogeneous, with supposed ancestry and physical appearance powerful signs of status and positions."[33] Thus, in Latin American countries, the blacker one social group is perceived, the more uncivilized, barbaric, and savage that group is defined; in sharp contrast, the whiter one social group is defined, the more civilized and modern it is considered.

This racial episteme regulated the presence and/or inclusion of Afro-descendants in official and public spheres. Take, for instance, Latin American countries' ideals and practices of citizens after achieving independence (1820–1850). Scholars describe how ideal qualities of citizens were literacy, property ownership, and individual autonomy.[34] "Only properly cultured and educated men were deemed to have 'civic virtue,' only they were capable of self-government; and only they accrued equal rights."[35] Thus, Blacks, Indigenous communities, and women were excluded from exercising full citizenship.

During the time of economic industrialization and modernization of the Latin American countries—the late nineteenth century—the eugenics movement emerged in Europe, a pseudoscientific movement aimed at improving whiteness by preserving their genetic purity.[36] Since nonwhites were seen as an innate inferior race, eugenics thought of the Latin American racial mixed populations as a sign of degeneration.[37] For Paschel, this mongrelization meant that Latin American nations were destined for backwardness and subject to neocolonial occupation.[38]

Latin American elites and politicians responded by implementing a Lamarckian notion of eugenics. Lamarck offered a flexible perspective that fit into the Latin American realities and offered "indirect support for the *mestizaje* concept that interracial intimacy between a white person and a black person would allow the resulting child to acquire whiteness and all the positive attributes socially associated with whiteness."[39] In short, elites thought that Blackness would somehow disappear because of the strongest gene of whiteness. While conservative elites proposed bringing European immigrants to Latin American countries with economic benefits and closed national borders to darker racial groups, liberal elites ran hygiene and sanitation campaigns and implemented educational programs.[40] *Blanqueamiento*, or whitening, became a racial mechanism to get rid of Blackness. As Appelbaum and colleagues suggest, "By uplifting their fellow citizens, they insisted, they would improve their national stock and compete with more advanced nations."[41]

Latin American intellectuals and elites adopted an anti-imperialist stance by asserting Latin American mestizaje and rejecting ideas of racial degeneration. Alongside mestizaje emerged *indigenismo*—an intellectual movement that promoted Indian culture, tradition, and legacies in Latin America—as a variant form of mestizaje;[42] intellectuals like Cuban José Martí, Brazilian Gilberto Freyre, and Mexican José Vasconcelos, among others, articulated discourses of mestizaje and *indigenismo* that emphasized the benefits of racial mixing of Latin American societies. "In casting the mestizo as the modern racial ideal . . . intellectuals challenged the prevalent coupling of whiteness with modernity and citizenship."[43]

Despite the racial discriminations and exclusions experienced by people of African descent, later into the twentieth century, these discourses of mestizaje fed elites' thoughts and imageries of Latin American countries as racially democratic societies.[44] These discourses of mestizaje, and racial democracy served Latin American elites to deny the existence of racism in spite of the clear evidence of its reality. As Hernández contends, "Latin American racial denial is deeply embedded within racially hierarchical environments."[45] Because of the prevalent discourses of mestizaje and racial democracy, scholars argue that these racial ideological apparatuses made Afro-Latinos consent and conform to the racial order in Latin America.[46] In what follows, I present how the negritude mobilization occurred in Latin America during the 1970s and mid-1980s.

The Emergence of Negritude and Its Critics

Despite racial ideologies of mestizaje and democracy, and Marxist and right-conservative ideological battles, Afro-descendants in Latin America found their own ideological frameworks or referents in the African diaspora to address racism and define Black culture and identity on their own terms.[47] The negritude discourses were one of them. They emerged in Paris, where former participants attended universities.[48] Aimé Césaire coined the term *negritude* in an article published in *L'Étudiant Noir*: "Since the Antilleans were ashamed of being Negroes, . . . [and] négre, . . . I took the liberty of talking about negritude."[49] This move resignified the meaning of blackness, as Frantz Fanon considers: "This negritude, hurled against the contempt of the white man, has alone proved capable in some sectors of lifting taboos and maledictions."[50]

The negritude is far away from a homogeneous project. In short, it can be said that for Aimé Césaire, negritude means anticolonialism, rebelliousness, and self-affirmation. For León Damas, negritude entails not only a rediscovery of Africa but also "intellectual, cultural, social and political positioning against racism, colonialism and capitalism";[51] and for Léopold Sédar Senghor, negritude was an ontology; a vital force; an essence that derived from African despite the "cultural borrowing" from European.[52] The problem with negritude was its reduced framework to explain the complexity of the problems African descendants face. First, Léopold Sédar Senghor situated the reason in European culture and emotion in African legacies as vital forces that drive and complement each other within a context of cultural borrowings. Well, that was a problematic statement. It deprives African civilization of its own intellectual capacity to reason; and second, negritude became a universalized ideology that pretended to represent diverse forms of racial dominations and

Black consciousness. Thus, proponents of the negritude were strongly criticized for obliterating local, national, and regional experiences of oppression—class, gender, and identity. Indeed, scholars agree that its ideological feature triggered to say goodbye to negritude and, instead, to say hello to and welcome class discourses.[53] Critics expressed that negritude discourse looked subjective and as a problem of one specific racial group—Blacks—in contrast to the more objective and universal condition of class.[54]

The narrative of the negritude that became dominant in academia and Black spheres has been what these critics made.[55] I do not pretend here to deny their arguments and critiques about the negritude discourse and its difficulties in explaining the problems of African descendants in the African diaspora. However, critics constantly missed the insurgent face of negritude.[56] First, we cannot forget that "negritude . . . was a blend of Pan-Africanism, socialism, and psychoanalysis."[57] Thus, negritude represents both politics and social movements. Second, despite their own difficulties and pitfalls, negritude discourses challenged the Western racial episteme of Blackness as a synonym for backwardness and savagery. Negritude claimed back the humanity of African descendants. It recovered and praised African culture, traditions, and civilizations and offered a Black vision of Blackness to challenge racial oppression.[58]

Black Academic and Cultural Public Spheres in the 1940 and 1960s

The peak of the negritude movements occurred during the late 1970s and mid-1980s when the Congress of Black Culture in the Americas took place in Colombia (1977), Panama (1980), and Brazil (1982). Nonetheless, since the early 1940s and 1960s, negritude discourses had appeared in Black cultural and academic spheres in Colombia, Brazil, and Peru. For example, discourses of negritude have an initial reception among Black artists, musicians, and intellectuals. Davis shows how negritude discourses influenced the emergence of Afro-Brazilian Abdías do Nascimento's Teatro Experimental do Negro (TEN) between 1944 and 1961 in Rio de Janeiro. TEN was composed of Afro-Brazilian men and women. They realized several actions to disseminate their constructions of Blackness that were the formation of a Black theater where Afro-Brazilian Quilombos, life, problems, and aspirations of Blacks were discussed. The newspaper *Quilombo* not only acknowledged prominent Afro-Brazilian intellectuals and invited them to debate ideas of racial democracy but also promoted the rights of black women—"Fala Mulher" was a column edited by the journalist María Nascimento—and beauty—two annual beauty pageants, the Tar Baby and the Queen of the Mulatas.

Teatro Experimental do Negro also organized two national congresses: the first National Negro Congress (1950s) and the National Congress of Black Women, to address Black issues of both Black women and men. In politics, TEN supported José Correa Leite, founder of the Association of Black Brazilians and the director of the newspaper *Alvorada*, and Geraldo Campos de Oliveira, director of TEN in São Paulo, for Congress. TEN realized that ballots were also a weapon in the struggle for Black rights. Although TEN never became a mass movement, "masses of black Brazilians, who had never before gathered around issues of race, were attracted to the Brazilian versions of Negritude and Black Soul in the 1960s."[59] Thus, negritude had a profound and lasting effect on other Black intellectuals, artists, and musicians who would follow, creating new groups and cultural organizations. For example, Davis points out Olodum, Ilye Ayê, Muzenza, Negritude Junior, and Cidade Negra.

The Afro-Colombian novelist Arnoldo Palacios participated in the Congress of Black Writers and Artists in Paris, organized by former members of the Présence Africaine (1956). According to his own testimony, he spoke with former founders of the negritude movements and Frantz Fanon.[60] Later, Arnoldo Palacios and the Syrian-Lebanese Tufik Meluk Aluma from Chocó in the Pacific region, who subscribed to the magazine *Présence Africaine*, hosted *tertulias* in Tufik Meluk Aluma's house. The Black intellectual and activist Amilcar Ayala remembers that he, the Black politician Natanael Díaz's son Eduardo Díaz, Arnoldo Palacios, and others "held meetings at the home of Dr. Tufik Meluk Aluma."[61] Former participant Arturo Bobb also remembers, "[With] Tufik Meluk Aluma, we made infinite meetings in his house, over there in the north of Bogotá. He had a very large library . . . after that . . . we were in different activities."[62]

Out of these *tertulias*, the Movimiento Joven Internacional José Prudencio Padilla, Cultura Negra e India, in Colombia emerged in 1973. This youth organization coalesced with African American students who came to study in Bogotá, Colombia, with Fulbright fellowships. Among them was Laurence Prescott, a scholar who has dedicated his life to the study of Black literature in Colombia. He told me that among the African Americans were scholars Marvin Lewis, David Gilliam, and his wife, Bonita Gilliam. Out of these casual encounters, Entendimiento Mutuo emerged. A transnational Black public sphere in which African Americans and Afro-Colombians "discussed in group or individually the ideas of Malcolm X, Martin Luther King

Jr., Frantz Fanon, and others. We learned the names of Diego Luis Córdoba, Natanael Díaz and other Afro-Colombian leaders."[63] Later, in 1975, participants in the Entendimiento Mutuo held the First Week of Black Culture in Colombia held at a public library in Bogotá. Among the Black issues attendants debated were the legacy of Aimé Césaire's negritude, African legacies, and Black cultural identity in Colombia.[64]

The negritude discourses influenced first the siblings Victoria and Nicomedes Santa Cruz's artistic movements in Peru. Feldman affirms that "Nicomedes Santa Cruz was the sole voice of the Peruvian negritude from the late 1950s to the 70s." Also, she states, Nicomedes Santa Cruz "shared much with the international negritude movement a propensity to strategically essentialize people of African descent, identifying and celebrating their common traits and experiences."[65] Thus, using dance, poems, songs, theater plays, and oral tradition—*décimas*—the Santa Cruz siblings not only opened new Black public spheres in Peru but also propagated a positive image of Africa, Black identity, and African legacies. "From then on, everything that they composed [had] a totally folkloric but also negritude looks."[66] Rolando Campos's Perú Negro (1960), Velásquez Zamudio and Juan Tasayco's Melamodernos collectives and Grupo Harlem (1969), respectively, were influenced not only by the African American cultural movements but also by the Santa Cruz siblings' vision of negritude.[67]

The Black field of politics during these times comprised other African diaspora narratives of Blackness, for instance, *negrismo* and Melville Herskovits's African American and Black folkloric studies. Although the line between these perspectives and negritude was very blurred, negritude discourses helped conceive Blackness as a site of Black politics, a form of politics that sought to affirm Blackness and denounce injustice. During the 1970s, the field of politics became more radical with the presence of class, Black power and the decolonization of Africa, and the Caribbean discourses.

The Negritude Movements in the Convulsive 1970s

The field of politics became even more contested, and therefore much more ideologically competitive, during what Andrews termed the *blackening* of the region.[68] As Hanchard states, "Negritude as a belief system was one facet of a wider, insurgent recognition of things African, or of the 'diaspora.'"[69] Thus, the field of politics presented serious discursive disputes not only among negritude, Black power, and anticolonialism movements but also against Marxist followers,[70] as well as authoritarian regimes in Brazil, Colombia, and elsewhere.[71]

Discourses of negritude took hold in a very diffuse way among individuals and collectives in Brazil. It was mostly about an attitude of empowerment rather than a real Black mobilization with a clear politics.[72] Negritude took a supraideological manifestation "focused on an originary return to African 'roots' as the basis of any political or cultural practice. Here Negritude operated as a cornerstone for the edifice of negro definition, the celebration of 'otherness' and differentiation from the West. Its symbolic manifestations were found in the emphasis on wearing west African garb, name changing, the aforementioned donning of Afro hairstyles during the Black Soul period."[73] On the other hand, Hanchard sustains that Afro-Brazilians influenced by the negritude discourses attempted to have African and Afro-Brazilian history teachings in the Brazilian educational system. This shows that negritude became an important catalyst for Afro-Brazilian identity-based politics that influenced upcoming Afro-Brazilian organizations.[74]

Discourses of negritude influenced the emergence of several forms of Black politics with different racial agendas in Colombia. I focus just on three of them that I consider the most relevant: the mestizo negritude led by the well-known Zapata Olivella siblings, especially Manuel Zapata; the liberal negritude led by the politician Valentin Moreno; and the desubjugating Black culture led by the Black sociologist and activist Amir Smith Córdoba. These organizations show how the discourses of negritude moved from a moderate expression of Black politics to more radical and Afrocentric modalities.[75] At the beginning of the 1970s, Manuel Zapata Olivella reopened his Center for the Afro-Colombian Studies and created the Foundation for the Colombian Folkloric Research, as well as his magazine *Letras Nacionales,* in Bogotá. His sister Delia Zapata Olivella created her dance and choreographic "Palenque Foundations," plus multiple folkloric dance groups in Bogotá and Cali. Finally, his younger brother Juan Zapata Olivella opened the Museo de Arte Negro (Black Art Museum) in the Colombian Caribbean. These organizations promoted an agenda of radical and challenging mestizaje. Instead of eliminating any trace of Blackness and discounting racism, the Zapata Olivellas' construction of mestizaje was not "racially innocent."[76] They know Colombia's racial mixture was "the result of power relations expressed in the slavery system, coloniality and racial discriminations against black and indigenous communities."[77] Although very much ambiguous, their mestizo negritude agenda affirmed the physical and cultural presence of Afro-Colombian as a necessary condition for the construction of a national mestizo identity. In 1977, Manuel Zapata Olivella and José Campos Dávila from Peru held the First Congress of Black Culture in the Americas in Cali.

With liberal negritude, the meaning and practice of negritude passed from being an academic and intellectual project (like the mestizo negritude) to being a political project in the strict sense of the term *politic* (political party). The liberal Afro-Colombian politician Valentin Moreno founded first the social organization Consejo Nacional de la Población Negra Colombiana (National Council of the Colombian Black Population) in the city of Cali. This organization held local, regional, and national encounters between 1975 and 1980. This organization promoted debates about Black issues by leading a national social and political process that proclaimed what can be defined as liberal racial justice.[78] They also critiqued Delia and Manuel Zapata Olivella's promotion of Black folklore as a valid form of Black politics because of its reinforcements of racial stereotypes. In the encounter held in Medellín (1977), the Consejo Nacional representatives coalesced with Juan Zapata Olivella to launch a Black political party named Movimiento de Negritudes y Mestizajes (Mestizaje and Negritude Movement) that campaigned for public offices.[79]

Juan Zapata Olivella campaigned for the 1978 presidency of Colombia, and other Black leaders campaigned for local and regional corporations. The Black presidency campaign drew a lot of attention: "It breaks with the negative ideas and attitudes generally conceived and adopted towards the black people of this country and... arouses an unprecedented hopeful enthusiasm among the country's black communities."[80] However, expectations changed drastically when Zapata Olivella decided to annex his presidential candidacy to that of the white liberal candidate Carlos Lleras Restrepo. The Black political disappointment was huge. The Consejo Nacional was doomed. This betrayal basically marked the end of the organization.[81]

Finally, what I call desubjugating Black culture (*des-avasallamiento cultural*) is an academic project led by Centro para la Investigación de la Cultura Negra en Colombia (CICUN). Its idea of negritude meant decolonization and antiracism: "It is the reunion of blacks with their own identity; it is an important and necessary passage that occurs and must be given socially, historically and culturally."[82] This organization not only created a Black press—the journal of *Négritude* and the newspaper *Presencia Negra*—but also produced bibliographical materials about the racial problems and Black intelligentsia in Colombia. There were *Cultura negra y avasallamiento cultural* in 1980, *Visión sociocultural del negro en Colombia* in 1986, and *Vida y obra de Candelario Obeso* in 1984. Finally CICUN organized five annual academic and cultural seminars between 1978 and 1983—Seminarios sobre Formación y Capacitación de Personal Docente en Cultura Negra—to train school teachers on Black culture and history.[83]

The First and Second Congresses of the Black Culture of the Americas inspired the emergence of the Black organization in Ecuador and Panama.[84] In Ecuador, Black professionals, artists, and activists founded Black study, research, and cultural centers devoted to Afro-Ecuadorian aesthetics, history, culture, and Black consciousness-raising. In 1979, Juan García founded the Centro de Estudio Afroecuatorianos. In 1981, Salomón Chalá and a group of friends founded the Movimiento Afroecuatoriano Conciencia, and his brother founded the Centro de Investigación de la Familia Negra in 1983. Previously, Afro-Ecuadorian intellectual Nelson Estupiñán Bass founded the magazine *Meridiano Negro* in 1980, a platform that became "the voice of the negritude" in Ecuador.[85]

In Panama, Black organizations influenced by negritude discourses emerged under the authoritarian regime of Manuel Noriega. The Centro de Estudios Panameño emerged in 1980 to organize several cultural events. For example, it inaugurated the Museo del Hombre Afro-Antillano, performed Afro-Panamanian dance and music in public and national theater, and between 1981 and 1983 held three national congresses on the Black presence in Panama.[86]

Transnational Spaces of Articulations

Both the Afro-Colombian Manuel Zapata Olivella and the Afro-Peruvian Nicomedes Santa Cruz participated in the International Colloquium on Negritude and Latin America in Dakar organized by Léopold Sédar Senghor in 1974. Nicomedes Santa Cruz participated as a speaker. He talked about the negritude in Latin America.[87] Manuel Zapata Olivella returned to Colombia with the purpose of replicating what he learned in Dakar in Latin America. First, he participated as a speaker on negritude at the First Week of Black Culture organized by Entendimiento Mutuo and Movimiento Joven Internacional José Prudencio Padilla in 1975. Second, Manuel Zapata Olivella and Afro-Peruvian José Campos Dávila, founder of the Instituto de Estudios Afro-Peruanos, held the First Congress of Black Culture of the Americas in Cali, Colombia. The Second Congress of Black Culture of the Americas took place in Panama. The Centro de Estudios Panameño organized it in 1980, and Abdias do Nascimento held the Third Congress of Black Culture of the Americas in São Paulo, Brazil, in 1982.

These congresses of Black culture represented the spirit of the Pan-African movements in Latin America, not only a hemispheric effort of people of African descent from everywhere in the African diaspora reflecting on their own Blackness and Black culture—as Manuel Zapata Olivella expressed at the inauguration of the first Congress, "this is a new era for the American Identity," a Blackened American identity that recognizes the sufferings and Black contributions[88]—but also an opportunity to condemn racism and its inseparable relationships with class, slavery, and colonialism. In short, although these Congresses did not become long-lasting networks,[89] they constituted a hemispheric Pan-African call for African and African descendants to unite against racial oppression.[90]

The Congresses of Black Culture of the Americas are important for another reason. Latin American Black women could begin to create transnational spaces of articulation out of the congress dynamics long before the formation of the Red de Mujeres Afrolatinoamericanas y Afrocaribeñas was created in 1992.[91] For the First Congress in Cali, Black women's agendas were marginalized. Their problems were not discussed, although Black women's organizations had already existed in Brazil and the United States.[92] However, some Black and white-mestizo women—among them the Black intellectual and scholar Mara Viveros Viyoga—demanded "to every black man of the world to recognize that the achievement of a renewed world characterized by a more meaningful life for the black family and society in general depend, to a large extent, on black women's liberation from the burden imposed by the double stereotype, which circumscribes their existence to role of sexual and reproductive objects."[93] Although ambiguous, because it reproduces the gender stereotype of the caregiver, the claim condemns "the discrimination ... [to which] the black woman is constantly a victim, not only by the white-mestizo but also by the black himself."[94]

The Second Congress did not include a Black women's agenda either, but Black women attendants managed to include their agendas for the Third Congress held in Brazil. There, Black women discussed and condemned the sterilization campaigns against Black women, as well as physical, psychological, and sexual exploitation and violence; the unequal access to employment, education, health, and salaries; and the disregarded role of women as cornerstones in the accumulation of wealth and the formation of the new American societies.[95] They also demanded the legalization of abortion and reproductive rights and the inclusion of a woman, Esperanza Brown, as a vice president of Third Congress and as international coordinator of the congresses, since these positions were always in the charge of Black men. They also claimed that Black women's issues must not be reduced to a specific table. They must be discussed at every table of the congresses.

The first Conference of Black Women of the Americas was held between July 15 and 25, 1984, in Esmeraldas, Ecuador. This was an autonomous space for Black women "planned during the Third Congress of the Black Culture of the Americas, held in São Paulo."[96] The Centro de Estudios Afro-Ecuatorianos led the organization of the conference with the support of the national office for women of the Ministry of Social Welfare.[97] Delegates came from Ecuador, Brazil, Cuba, Colombia, Costa Rica, and the United States. Among other things, Black women discussed the "triple exploitation of black women, for being a woman, for being a black woman and for being from the working class."[98] I cannot ensure that this meeting was translated into transnational networks sustained over time, but it was a pioneering antecedent of the later transnational scenarios of Black women that emerged in later decades.[99]

Ambiguities, Contributions, and Legacies

This chapter maps the trajectory of negritude movements in Latin America. It shows how the negritude movements developed cultural and academic forms of Black politics—*tertulias* encounters, folkloric and theater groups, study and research centers, and so on. Also, the negritude movements involved social— with a reduced social base—and political forms of Black politics, specifically in the Colombian case. Like their French-speaking counterparts, the negritude movements in Latin America opened transnational spaces such as the Congresses of Black Culture of the Americas. In contrast, the Latin American version of negritude opened transnational spaces for Black women.

The discussions and debates that took place in the congresses reconceptualized the idea of negritude. First, attendants recognized how the dominant white societies manipulated Black African cultural elements as instruments of domination and subjection.[100] Second, negritude is not about "a mass return to the African continent, but it is more about an identification with black culture and the struggle in the various countries where black people are present."[101] Third, they conceived of negritude "as an alternative strategy of participation and rights claiming in Colombia and in other countries that attended to the

Congress."[102] However, we cannot deny its elitist character. It was a movement whose main characteristic was intellectual and academic, with a reduced social agenda. The Ecuadorian case is the exception.

The foregoing is an example of the importance of Black culture and African legacies for Black mobilization in Latin America. Black culture became a site of Black politics. Black identity and culture mobilized the connection between Africa and its cultural legacies with people of African descent in Latin America. Also, negritude discourse provided a framework for Afro-descendants to discuss issues of race and racism in Latin America. Thus, the negritude movements were a Black political mobilization process that prepared and disputed the terrain—racial consciousness—for the arrival of other African diasporic projects such as Cimarronism and the ethno-racial movements of the 1990s.

NOTES

1. Giovanni Arrighi, Terence K. Hopkins, and Immanuel Maurice Wallerstein, *Antisystemic Movements* (London: Verso, 1989). Their politics were based on culture and identity claims inasmuch as their agendas proposed alternative ways of social relations based on their own traditions and symbols, Alberto Melucci, *Acción colectiva, vida cotidiana y democracia* (Mexico City: El Colegio de México, 1999). As Michel-Rolph Trouillot puts it, "Minorities of all kinds . . . voice their cultural claims, not on the basis of explicit theories of culture, but on the name of historical authenticity." "Adieu, Culture: A New Duty Arises," in *Global Transformations: Anthropology and the Modern World* (New York: Palgrave Macmillan, 2003), 10. According to Arrighi et al., *Antisystemic Movements*, and Agustín Laó-Montes, "Mapping the Field of Afro–Latin American Politics: In and out of the Civil Society Agenda," in *Beyond Civil Society: Activism, Participation, and Protest in Latin America*, ed. Sonia E. Alvarez et al. (Durham, NC: Duke University Press, 2017), this was a cycle of protests that constituted a new revolutionary era of social politics—"the new left"—that struggled against the capitalist world system.
2. For instance, Black mobilizations for the liberation of Africa in the African continent; the Black freedom movements in the United States; the Rastafari and funk movements in the Caribbean, England, and Brazil; Black feminism—all showed how democracy and freedom were privileges that only few could enjoy in Western societies. George Reid Andrews, *Afro-latinoamérica, 1800–2000* (Madrid: Iberoamericana Vervuert, 2007); Tanya Katerí Hernández, *Racial Subordination in Latin America: The Role of the State, Customary Law, and the New Civil Rights Response* (Cambridge: Cambridge University Press, 2013); Laó-Montes, "Mapping the Field"; Michael Omi and Howard Winant, *Racial Formation in the United States: From the 1960s to the 1990s* (New York: Routledge, 1994).
3. Anthony W. Marx, *Making Race and Nation a Comparison of South Africa, the United States, and Brazil* (Cambridge: Cambridge University Press, 1998); Omi and Winant, *Racial Formation*; Peter Wade, "The Cultural Politics of Blackness in Colombia," *American Ethnologist* 22, no. 2 (1995): 341–357.
4. Tianna S. Paschel, "Repensando la movilización de los afrodescendientes en América

Latina," in *Estudios afrolatinoamericanos: Una introducción*, ed. Alejandro de la Fuente and George Reid Andrews (Buenos Aires: CLACSO, 2018), 269.
5. Paschel, "Repensando la movilización de los afrodescendientes," 270.
6. Paschel, "Repensando la movilización de los afrodescendientes," 270–271.
7. Heidi Carolyn Feldman, *Ritmos negros del Perú: Reconstruyendo la herencia musical africana* (Lima: Instituto de Etnomusicología, Instituto de Estudios Peruanos, 2009), 85.
8. Andrews, *Afro-latinoamérica*; Laó-Montes, "Mapping the Field"; Omi and Winant, *Racial Formation*; Tianna S. Paschel, *Becoming Black Political Subjects: Movements and Ethno-Racial Rights in Colombia and Brazil* (Princeton, NJ: Princeton University Press, 2016); Paschel, "Repensando la movilización de los afrodescendientes"; Wade, "The Cultural Politics of Blackness"; Howard Winant, *The World Is a Ghetto: Race and Democracy since World War II* (New York: Basic Books, 2001).
9. Darién J. Davis, "Understanding the Black Modernists: The Legacy of Negritude and the Celebration of Blackness in Brazil," in *Negritude: Legacy and Present Relevance*, ed. Isabelle Constant and Kahiudi C. Mabana (Newcastle, UK: Cambridge Scholars, 2009); Feldman, *Ritmos Negros*; Michael Hanchard, *Orpheus and Power: The Movimento Negro of Rio de Janeiro and São Paulo, Brazil, 1945–1988* (Princeton, NJ: Princeton University Press, 1998).
10. Paschel, "Repensando la movilización de los afrodescendientes," 270.
11. Andrews, *Afro-latinoamérica*, 295. See also Carlos Efrén Agudelo, *Multiculturalismo en Colombia: Política, inclusión y exclusión de poblaciones negras* (Medellín: Carreta Editores, Institut de Recherche pour le Développement, Universidad Nacional de Colombia: Instituto Colombiano de Antropología e Historia, 2005); Hanchard, *Orpheus and Power*; Marx, *Making Race and Nation*; Mark Q. Sawyer, *Racial Politics in Post-Revolutionary Cuba* (Cambridge: Cambridge University Press, 2006); Wade, "The Cultural Politics of Blackness."
12. Juliet Hooker, "Indigenous Inclusion/Black Exclusion: Race, Ethnicity and Multicultural Citizenship in Latin America," *Journal of Latin American Studies* 37, no. 2 (2005): 285-310; Laó-Montes, "Mapping the Field"; Paschel, *Becoming Black Political Subjects*.
13. Charles Tilly and Sidney Tarrow, *Contentious Politics* (Boulder, CO: Paradigm Publishers, 2007), 8.
14. Tilly and Tarrow, *Contentious Politics*, 11.
15. Tilly and Tarrow, *Contentious Politics*, 114.
16. Donatella Della Porta and Mario Diani, *Social Movements: An Introduction* (Malden, MA: Blackwell Publishing, 2006), 171.
17. Della Porta and Diani, *Social Movements*, 140.
18. Carlos Alberto Valderrama, "La diferancia cultural negra en Colombia: Contrapúblicos afrocolombianos," *Revista CS*, no. 29 (2019): 209–242.
19. Della Porta and Diani, *Social Movements*, 173.
20. Della Porta and Diani, *Social Movements*, 176.
21. Paschel, *Becoming Black Political Subjects*, 16.
22. Laó-Montes, "Mapping the Field"; Paschel, *Becoming Black Political Subjects*.
23. Laó-Montes, "Mapping the Field"; Paschel, *Becoming Black Political Subjects*.
24. Paschel, *Becoming Black Political Subjects*, 16.
25. Paschel, *Becoming Black Political Subjects*; Peter Wade, *Raza y etnicidad en Latinoamérica* (Quito: Abya-Yala, 2000).
26. Wade, *Raza y etnicidad*; Winant, *The World Is a Ghetto*.
27. Carlos Alberto Valderrama, "The Negritude Movements in Colombia" (PhD diss., University of Massachusetts Amherst, 2018).

28. Hanchard, *Orpheus and Power*, 14.
29. Omi and Winant, *Racial Formation*.
30. Andrews, *Afro-latinoamérica*; Nancy P. Appelbaum et al., eds., "Introduction: Racial Nations," in *Race and Nation in Modern Latin America* (Chapel Hill: University of North Carolina Press, 2003); Hanchard, *Orpheus and Power*; Hernández, *Racial Subordination*; Sawyer, *Racial Politics*; Wade, *Raza y Etnicidad*.
31. Peter Wade, *Blackness and Race Mixture: The Dynamics of Racial Identity in Colombia* (Baltimore: Johns Hopkins University Press, 1993), 9.
32. Aníbal Quijano and Michael Ennis, "Coloniality of Power, Eurocentrism, and Latin America," *Nepantla: Views from South* 1, no. 2 (2000): 533–580.
33. Wade, *Blackness and Race Mixture*, 8–9.
34. Andrews, *Afro-latinoamérica*; Appelbaum et al., "Introduction: Racial Nations"; Hanchard, *Orpheus and Power*; Hernández, *Racial Subordination*; Sawyer, *Racial Politics*; Wade, *Raza y etnicidad*.
35. Appelbaum et al., "Introduction: Racial Nations," 4.
36. Appelbaum et al., "Introduction: Racial Nations"; Hernández, *Racial Subordination*; Paschel, *Becoming Black Political Subjects*.
37. Appelbaum et al., "Introduction: Racial Nations"; Marisol de la Cadena, *Indigenous Mestizos: The Politics of Race and Culture in Cuzco, Peru, 1919–1991* (Durham, NC: Duke University Press, 2000); Paschel, *Becoming Black Political Subjects*; Wade, *Raza y etnicidad*.
38. Paschel, *Becoming Black Political Subjects*.
39. Hernández, *Racial Subordination*, 21–22.
40. Andrews, *Afro-latinoamérica*; Appelbaum et al., "Introduction: Racial Nations"; Hernández, *Racial Subordination*; Paschel, *Becoming Black Political Subjects*.
41. Appelbaum et al., "Introduction: Racial Nations," 6.
42. Appelbaum et al., "Introduction: Racial Nations"; Cadena, *Indigenous Mestizos*; Wade, *Blackness and Race Mixture*.
43. Appelbaum et al., "Introduction: Racial Nations," 7.
44. Paulina Alberto and Jesse Hoffnung-Garskof. "'Democracia Racial' e Inclusión Racial," in *Estudios afrolatinoamericanos: Una introducción*, ed. Alejandro de la Fuente and George Reid Andrews (Buenos Aires: CLACSO, 2018); Appelbaum et al., "Introduction: Racial Nations"; Hanchard, *Orpheus and Power*; Paschel, *Becoming Black Political Subjects*; Wade, *Blackness and Race*.
45. Hernández, *Racial Subordination*, 6.
46. Paschel, "Repensando la movilización de los afrodescendientes." Between the 1970s and mid-1980s, combined factors or mechanisms operated ambiguously against and in favor of the rise and fall of the negritude movements in Latin America. Given the limited space here, I only mention them: the rise and fall of the authoritarian regimes and dictatorships in Latin America; the radicalization of class discourses and struggles and anti-Marxist discourses in the context of the Cold War, Cuban Revolution, and Marxist-Leninist guerrilla groups; the international environment against racial violence (Nazism) and scientific racism (eugenics), followed by the removal of race-related and promotion of ethnic-related languages and studies by UNESCO and others. See Valderrama, *Negritude Movements*. Paradoxically, UNESCO and national states promoted ethnic and cultural rather than racial differences due to the terrible effects of the Holocaust. Winant, *The World Is a Ghetto*, 35. Thus, mestizaje became even an stronger ideology against racism while deepening the official denial of racism in Latin America. It was the circulation of

African diaspora racial projects and discourses that led people of African descent in Latin America to critique and demystify these racial ideologies.

47. Some of them were the Haitian Revolution, negrism, the Pan African Congress, Garveyism, the New Negro Movement, the Harlem Renaissance, the Negritude movement, Afro-Cubanism, the independence of African countries, the civil rights movement, Malcolm X, Martin Luther King Jr., the Black Panther Party, the Rastafari movement, hip-hop, and salsa, among others. These Afro-diasporic cultural and political experiences are somehow connected and mutually influenced by each other. They are, in some cases, parallel phenomena. See Laó-Montes, "Mapping the Field"; Reiland Rabaka, *The Negritude Movement: W. E. B. Du Bois, Leon Damas, Aimé Césaire, Léopold Senghor, Frantz Fanon, and the Evolution of an Insurgent Idea* (Lanham, MD: Lexington Books, 2015); Ronald W. Walters, *Pan Africanism in the African Diaspora: An Analysis of Modern Afrocentric Political Movements* (Detroit: Wayne State University Press, 1993).
48. There were Étienne Léro, Jules Monnerot, René Menil, Aimé Césaire, León Damas, Léonard Sainville, Aristide Maugée, the Achille brothers, Sajous of Cayes from Martinique, Guadeloupe, Guyana, and Haiti; later they were joined by African students Léopold Sédar Senghor, Osmane Sosé, and Birado Diop, from Senegal.
49. As cited in Rene Depestre, "Hello and Goodbye to Negritude," in *Africa in Latin America: Essays on History, Culture, and Socialization*, ed. Manuel Moreno Fraginals and Leonor Blum (New York: Holmes & Meier, 1984), 268.
50. Frantz Fanon, *The Wretched of the Earth*, trans. Richard Philcox, intro. Jean-Paul Sartre and Homi K. Bhabha (New York: Grove Press, 2004), 151.
51. As cited in Rabaka, *The Negritude Movement*, 107.
52. Rabaka, *The Negritude Movement*, 117.
53. Depestre, "Hello and Goodbye."
54. Depestre, "Hello and Goodbye"; Fanon, *The Wretched*; Rabaka, *The Negritude Movement*.
55. Depestre, "Hello and Goodbye"; Hanchard, *Party/Politics*; Walters, *Pan Africanism*.
56. Rabaka, *The Negritude Movement*; Carlos Alberto Valderrama Rentería, "La política cultural de la negritud en Latinoamérica: Debates del Primer Congreso de la Cultura Negra de las Américas, Cali, Colombia, 1977," *Journal of Latin American and Caribbean Anthropology* 26, no. 1 (2021): 104–123.
57. Hanchard, *Orpheus and Power*, 182n28.
58. Rabaka, *The Negritude Movement*; Valderrama, "La diferancia cultural negra."
59. Hanchard, *Orpheus and Power*, 111.
60. Arnoldo Palacios, personal interview, February 15, 2015.
61. Amilcar Ayala, personal interview, March 20, 2015.
62. Arturo Bobb, Skype interview, April 15, 2015.
63. Laurence Prescott, email interview, June 1, 2016.
64. Valderrama, *Negritude Movements*, 185.
65. Feldman, *Ritmos negros*, 84.
66. Feldman, *Ritmos negros*, 105.
67. Néstor Valdivia Vargas, *Las organizaciones de la población afrodescendiente en el Perú: Discursos de identidad y demandas de reconocimiento* (Lima: GRADE Grupo de Análisis para el Desarrollo, 2013); Feldman, *Ritmos negros*.
68. Andrews, *Afro-latinoamérica*, 297.
69. Hanchard, *Orpheus and Power*, 116.
70. Indeed, for some Black Marxists, negritude was dead. See Samuel D. Anderson, "'Negritude

Is Dead': Performing the African Revolution at the First Pan-African Cultural Festival (Algiers, 1969)," in *The First World Festival of Negro Arts, Dakar 1966: Contexts and Legacies*, ed. David Murphy (Liverpool, UK: Liverpool University Press, 2016).
71. Andrews, *Afro-latinoamérica*.
72. Hanchard, *Orpheus and Power*, 116.
73. Hanchard, *Orpheus and Power*, 120–121.
74. Davis, "Understanding the Black Modernists"; Hanchard, *Orpheus and Power*.
75. Valderrama, *Negritude Movements*.
76. Hernández, *Racial Subordination*, 9.
77. Valderrama, *Negritude Movements*, 170.
78. Michael C. Dawson, *Black Visions: The Roots of Contemporary African-American Political Ideologies* (Chicago: University of Chicago Press, 2001).
79. Valderrama, *Negritude Movements*, 240
80. M. Wabgou, Jaime Arocha Rodríguez, A. J. Salgado Cassiani, and J. A Carabalí Ospina. *Movimiento Social Afrocolombiano, Negro, Raizal y Palenquero: El largo camino hacia la construcción de espacios comunes y alianzas estratégicas para la incidencia política en Colombia* (Bogotá: Universidad Nacional de Colombia, 2012), 109.
81. Valderrama, *Negritude Movements*.
82. Valderrama, *Negritude Movements*, 274.
83. Valderrama, *Negritude Movements*.
84. Jhon Antón Sánchez, *El proceso organizativo afroecuatoriano, 1979–2009* (Quito: FLACSO, 2011), 98; Gerardo Maloney, "Introducción: Segundo Congreso de cultura negras de las Americas," in *Congresos de cultura negra de las Américas*, ed. Cuadernos Negros Americanos (Ecuador: Centro Cultural Afro-Ecuatoriano, 1989), 53.
85. Antón Sánchez, *El proceso organizativo afroecuatoriano*, 99.
86. Maloney, "Introducción," 53.
87. Feldman, *Ritmos negros*, 142.
88. Valderrama Rentería, "La política cultural."
89. Paschel, "Repensando la movilización de los afrodescendientes," 297.
90. Valderrama Rentería, "La política cultural."
91. Ochy Curiel, "La Red de Mujeres Afrolatinoamericanas y Afrocaribeñas: Un intento de acción política transnacional atacado por la institucionalización," CEPI Working Paper No. 1, 2006.
92. Hanchard, *Orpheus and Power*; Paschel, *Becoming Black Political Subjects*.
93. Valderrama Rentería, "La política cultural."
94. Valderrama Rentería, "La política cultural."
95. Cuadernos Negros Americanos, *Congresos de cultura negra de las Américas* (Guayaquil, Ecuador: Centro Cultural Afro-Ecuatoriano, 1989).
96. Palenque, "Palenque: Boletín informativo afro-ecuatoriano" (Guayaquil, Ecuador: Centro Cultural Afroecuatoriano, 1985), 3.
97. Palenque, "Palenque."
98. Palenque, "Palenque," 3.
99. Paschel, "Repensando la movilización de los afrodescendientes."
100. Comisión Etnia Negra y Mestizaje, "Etnia negra y mestizaje," in *Primer Congreso de la Cultura Negra de las Américas, Cali, Colombia: Actas*, ed. Fundación Colombiana de Investigaciones Folclóricas (Bogotá: UNESCO, Fundación Colombiana de Investigaciones Folclóricas, ECOE, 1988), 147.

101. Comisión Etnia Negra y Mestizaje, "Etnia negra y mestizaje," 147.
102. Comisión Etnia Negra y Mestizaje, "Etnia negra y mestizaje," 147.

BIBLIOGRAPHY

Agudelo, Carlos Efrén. *Multiculturalismo en Colombia: Política, inclusión y exclusión de poblaciones negras.* Medellín: Carreta Editores, Institut de Recherche pour le Dévelopment, Universidad Nacional de Colombia: Instituto Colombiano de Antropología e Historia, 2005.

Alberto, Paulina, and Jesse Hoffnung-Garskof. "'Democracia racial' e inclusión racial." In *Estudios afrolatinoamericanos: Una introducción*, edited by Alejandro de la Fuente and George Reid Andrews, 317–378. Buenos Aires: CLACSO, 2018.

Anderson, Samuel D. "'Negritude Is Dead': Performing the African Revolution at the First Pan-African Cultural Festival (Algiers, 1969)." In *The First World Festival of Negro Arts, Dakar 1966: Contexts and Legacies*, edited by David Murphy, 143–160. Liverpool, UK: Liverpool University Press, 2016.

Andrews, George Reid. *Afro-latinoamérica, 1800–2000*. Madrid: Iberoamericana Vervuert, 2007.

Antón Sánchez, Jhon. *El proceso organizativo afroecuatoriano, 1979–2009*. Quito: FLACSO, 2011.

Appelbaum, Nancy P., Anne S. Macpherson, and Karin Alejandra Rosemblatt, eds. "Introduction: Racial Nations." In *Race and Nation in Modern Latin America*, 2–31. Chapel Hill: University of North Carolina Press, 2003.

Arrighi, Giovanni, Terence K. Hopkins, and Immanuel Maurice Wallerstein. *Antisystemic Movements*. London: Verso, 1989.

Cadena, Marisol de la. *Indigenous Mestizos: The Politics of Race and Culture in Cuzco, Peru, 1919–1991*. Durham, NC: Duke University Press, 2000.

Comisión Etnia Negra y Mestizaje. "Etnia negra y mestizaje." In *Primer Congreso de la Cultura Negra de las Américas, Cali, Colombia: Actas*, edited by Fundación Colombiana de Investigaciones Folclóricas. Bogotá: UNESCO, Fundación Colombiana de Investigaciones Folclóricas, ECOE, 1988.

Cuadernos Negros Americanos. *Congresos de cultura negra de las Américas*. Guayaquil: Centro Cultural Afro-Ecuatoriano, 1989.

Curiel, Ochy. "La Red de Mujeres Afrolatinoamericanas y Afrocaribeñas: Un intento de acción política transnacional atacado por la institucionalización." CEPI Working Paper 1, 2006. http://interamericanos.itam.mx/working_papers/01OCHY.pdf.

Davis, Darién J. "Understanding the Black Modernists: The Legacy of Negritude and the Celebration of Blackness in Brazil." In *Negritude: Legacy and Present Relevance*, edited by Isabelle Constant and Kahiudi C. Mabana, 277–291. Newcastle, UK: Cambridge Scholars, 2009.

Dawson, Michael C. *Black Visions: The Roots of Contemporary African-American Political Ideologies*. Chicago: University of Chicago Press, 2001.

Della Porta, Donatella, and Mario Diani. *Social Movements: An Introduction*. 2nd ed. Malden, MA: Blackwell Publishing, 2006.

Depestre, Rene. "Hello and Goodbye to Negritude." In *Africa in Latin America: Essays on History, Culture, and Socialization*, edited by Manuel Moreno Fraginals and Leonor Blum, 251–272. New York: Holmes & Meier, 1984.

Fanon, Frantz. *The Wretched of the Earth*. Translated by Richard Philcox. Introduced by Jean-Paul Sartre and Homi K. Bhabha. New York: Grove Press, 2004.

Feldman, Heidi Carolyn. *Ritmos negros del Perú: Reconstruyendo la herencia musical africana*. Lima: Instituto de Etnomusicología, Instituto de Estudios Peruanos, 2009.

Hanchard, Michael. *Orpheus and Power: The Movimento Negro of Rio de Janeiro and São Paulo, Brazil, 1945–1988*. Princeton, NJ: Princeton University Press, 1998.

———. *Party/Politics: Horizons in Black Political Thought*. Oxford: Oxford University Press, 2006.

Hernández, Tanya Katerí. *Racial Subordination in Latin America: The Role of the State, Customary Law, and the New Civil Rights Response*. Cambridge: Cambridge University Press, 2013.

Hooker, Juliet. "Indigenous Inclusion/Black Exclusion: Race, Ethnicity and Multicultural Citizenship in Latin America." *Journal of Latin American Studies* 37, no. 2 (2005): 285–310.

Laó-Montes, Agustín. "Mapping the Field of Afro–Latin American Politics: In and out of the Civil Society Agenda." In *Beyond Civil Society: Activism, Participation, and Protest in Latin America*, edited by Sonia E. Alvarez, Jeffrey W. Rubin, Millie Thayer, Gianpaolo Baiocchi, Agustín Laó-Montes, Arturo Escobar, 103–121. Durham, NC: Duke University Press, 2017.

Maloney, Gerardo. "Introducción: Segundo Congreso de cultura negras de las Americas." In *Congresos de cultura negra de las Américas*, edited by Cuadernos Negros Americanos, 49–56. Ecuador: Centro Cultural Afro-Ecuatoriano, 1989.

Marx, Anthony W. *Making Race and Nation a Comparison of South Africa, the United States, and Brazil*. Cambridge: Cambridge University Press, 1998.

Melucci, Alberto. *Acción colectiva, vida cotidiana y democracia*. Mexico City: El Colegio de México, 1999.

Omi, Michael, and Howard Winant. *Racial Formation in the United States: From the 1960s to the 1990s*. 2nd ed. New York: Routledge, 1994.

Palenque. *Palenque: Boletín informativo afro-ecuatoriano*. Guayaquil: Centro Cultural Afroecuatoriano, 1985.

Paschel, Tianna S. *Becoming Black Political Subjects: Movements and Ethno-Racial Rights in Colombia and Brazil*. Princeton, NJ: Princeton University Press, 2016.

———. "Repensando la movilización de los afrodescendientes en América Latina." In *Estudios afrolatinoamericanos: Una introducción*, edited by Alejandro de la Fuente and George Reid Andrews, 269–316. Buenos Aires: CLACSO, 2018.

Quijano, Aníbal, & Michael Ennis. "Coloniality of Power, Eurocentrism, and Latin America." *Nepantla: Views from South* 1, no. 2 (2000): 533–580.

Rabaka, Reiland. *The Negritude Movement: W. E. B. Du Bois, Leon Damas, Aimé Césaire, Léopold Senghor, Frantz Fanon, and the Evolution of an Insurgent Idea*. Lanham, MD: Lexington Books, 2015.

Sawyer, Mark Q. *Racial Politics in Post-Revolutionary Cuba*. Cambridge: Cambridge University Press, 2006.

Tilly, Charles, and Sidney Tarrow. *Contentious Politics*. Boulder, CO: Paradigm Publishers, 2007.

Trouillot, Michel-Rolph. "Adieu, Culture: A New Duty Arises." In *Global Transformations: Anthropology and the Modern World*, 97–116. New York: Palgrave Macmillan, 2003.

Valderrama, Carlos Alberto. "La diferancia cultural negra en Colombia: Contrapúblicos afrocolombianos." *Revista CS*, no. 29 (2019): 209–242.

———. "The Negritude Movements in Colombia." PhD diss., University of Massachusetts Amherst, 2018.

Valderrama Rentería, Carlos Alberto. "La política cultural de la negritud en Latinoamérica: Debates del Primer Congreso de la Cultura Negra de las Américas, Cali, Colombia, 1977." *Journal of Latin American and Caribbean Anthropology* 26, no. 1 (2021): 104–123.

Valdivia Vargas, Néstor. *Las organizaciones de la población afrodescendiente en el Perú: Discursos de identidad y demandas de reconocimiento*. Lima: GRADE Grupo de Análisis para el Desarrollo, 2013.

Wabgou, M., Jaime Arocha Rodríguez, A. J. Salgado Cassiani, and J. A Carabalí Ospina. *Movimiento Social Afrocolombiano, Negro, Raizal y Palenquero: El largo camino hacia la construcción de espacios comunes y alianzas estratégicas para la incidencia política en Colombia*. Bogotá: Universidad Nacional de Colombia, Sede Bogotá, Facultad de Derecho, Ciencias Políticas y Sociales, Instituto Unidad de Investigaciones Jurídico-Sociales Gerardo Molina, 2012.

Wade, Peter. *Blackness and Race Mixture: The Dynamics of Racial Identity in Colombia*. Baltimore: Johns Hopkins University Press, 1993.

———. "The Cultural Politics of Blackness in Colombia." *American Ethnologist* 22, no. 2 (1995): 341–357.

———. *Raza y etnicidad en Latinoamérica*. Quito: Abya-Yala, 2000.

Walters, Ronald W. *Pan Africanism in the African Diaspora: An Analysis of Modern Afrocentric Political Movements*. Detroit: Wayne State University Press, 1993.

Winant, Howard. *The World Is a Ghetto: Race and Democracy since World War II*. New York: Basic Books, 2001.

CHAPTER 12

Beyond Binaries

Genealogies of Mestizaje and Mulataje in Améfrica Ladina

AGUSTÍN LAÓ-MONTES

This chapter will attempt to achieve three entwined goals: First, to construct a genealogy of the multiple meanings and different political-epistemic values of distinct discourses of mestizaje, locating them in time and space within the historical universe we now call Latin America in four world-historical moments, focusing on the emergence of "Mestiza/o" and "Mulatto/a" as categories of ethnic-racial classification/stratification and their implications for the patterning of social power and national imaginaries in the region.[1] Second, to articulate an analysis of regimes of pigmentocracy and ideologies of colorism in Latin America and the Hispanic Caribbean, paying special attention to the grammars of *mulataje* and their significance in the configuration of constellations of class, ethnic-racial, and gender and sexual power. And third, to analyze the complex and contradictory roles of discourses of mestizaje and *mulataje* in the patterning and reproduction of the modern/colonial matrix of power and knowledge as it takes shape in the region.

Theorizing Mestizajes: Archaeologies and Genealogies

The task of theorizing "mestizaje" as a category is complex and even deceptive, given its *longue durée* historicity, its controversial range of meanings, and its ambiguous set of political and epistemic values.[2] In light of this political-epistemic ambiguity and historical complexity, and against the commonsense current of reducing mestizaje to ethnic-racial "miscegenation" and cultural "hybridity," I pursue an archaeo-genealogical method to explore not only its multiple meanings and values, but more so, its historical conditions of possibility, terms and types of discourse, strategies and effects of power, and associated forms of subjectivity.[3]

In that pursuit, I converge with Laura Catelli's elaboration of an archaeology of mestizaje for "excavating and unearthing the strategies, practices, and discourses deployed in the context of colonial relations of power and domination" that produced "the conditions of possibility for the emergence of the concept of mestizaje," to counter "the scientific and culturalist discourses about mestizaje since the middle of 19th and the beginnings of the 20th century,"[4] thus developing a genealogy of mestizaje "different from that which conceive it as a process of configuration of a new biological, social, cultural, and ethnic group."[5] Catelli argues that "until now practically delinked from its sine qua non condition, namely, the ethno-racial and heterosexual relations of force and war in which it occurred . . . the concept of mestizaje lacks its profound analytical and critical potential."[6] She contends that there are "few critical engagements systematizing its analysis in the archaeo-genealogical terms proposed" to account for the "discursive transfers and semantic displacements, since the colonial discourses of caste, from naturalism to biological anthropology, to biopolitics and the cultural narratives of the nation, all within the frame of coloniality." In short, Catelli analyses "mestizaje as an instrument and discursive effect of biopower in the context of coloniality," instituted as a "strategy of conquest moved within the axes of sexuality and race," up to the "persistence in the present of the social, economic, subjective and imaginary effects produced by mestizaje."[7] Thus, through an archaeo-genealogical method, she pursues the potential of mestizaje as a category that could be "a fundamental critical axis for the interpretation of our complex and diverse pasts and presents."[8]

This approach entails elaborating on analytics of mestizaje to reveal its historical permutations, epistemic foundations, and power constellations. On that note, some key questions are as follows: What kind of category is mestizaje? What are its ethical-political and epistemic values, located in time and space? How and when did mestizaje discourses come to be? How have its contested meanings and effects of power as a discursive formation historically changed? Why and how are discourses of mestizaje mediated and composed by ethnic-racial, gender, and sexual dimensions of social power and cultural expression? On that point, I contend that mestizaje should be conceptualized as social process, discursive formation, and historical category.

Catelli's distinction between "carnal mestizaje" and mestizaje as ideology or discourse encompasses this threefold unpacking of its status as a category. As a social process, mestizaje tends to be understood simply as ethnic-racial mixing, not only in lay knowledge but also in intellectual and governmental discourses. Beyond common sense, in a critical mode, Catelli characterizes carnal mestizaje as a "political strategy of alliance" that served as a resource of conquest in early colonial times through the "giving or taking by force of women" as a vehicle of power that "refocus[es] through gender, relations of war and domination, broadening and complexifying the field of analysis and exercise of colonial power."[9] She highlights how this substratum of violence in carnal mestizaje has constituted a "war of races" since the colonial period, representing an "entanglement of the axis of gender, race, and sexuality in the formation of what we can call, extending the Foucauldian field of inquiry, the technologies of coloniality."[10] More than simply sexual intercourse of people from different ethnic-racial designations, as a major resource of patriarchal power, carnal mestizaje a keystone in establishing the order of domination that Maria Lugones named as a modern/colonial gender system.

In this vein, Silvia Rivera Cusicanqui writes about mestizaje "of blood" as a "structural" and "political" phenomenon that "determines social relations" from the locus of family, lineage, and sexuality, and has done so since the early moment of conquest and colonization."[11] Likewise, Catelli proposes "rethinking mestizaje as a strategy applied to women, on the first place over the bodies of indigenous women in contact situations, as a real and effective practice of colonial domination."[12] Hence, mestizaje, as a construct to signify historical processes that articulate gender, sexuality, and ethnic-racial mediations of power, culture and the self, within the modern/colonial matrix we call coloniality, constitutes a truly intersectional critical category.[13]

As our genealogy will show, mestizaje became a discursive formation between the nineteenth and twentieth centuries that marked the transition from caste classifications to discourses of mestizaje as dominant terrains of racial and cultural identification. Mestizaje becomes a key category in the contested terrain that configures the terms of discourses of civilization, culture, and race that began to define Latin America as a world region (*patria grande*) composed of a plurality of nation-states (*patria chica*). Marisol de la Cadena captures the centrality and complexity of such a process when she argues that, "as a discursive formation with the generative potential of affirming or denying the construction of the nation, mestizaje is best defined as a political dialogue—stratified and open—articulated by a dense intertextual web which included literary and scientific writings, artistic and political events, murals and paintings, museums and state policies, etc."[14] We will develop such arguments about mestizaje as discursive formation and as a key category in the founding ideologies of Latin Americanism and its corresponding nationalisms later in this chapter.

One of the main challenges in theorizing mestizaje as a category of historical analysis and critique is its extreme elasticity, its excessive range of significations that tend to translate into political and epistemic ambiguities. In a comprehensive study of what she calls "the cult mestizaje," Marilyn Grace Miller discusses "the semantic jungle that mestizaje represents in Latin America."[15] She contends that given its historical duration, regional reach, and political and epistemic significance, "mestizaje can be used as a lens through which to read the complexities and contradictions of Latin American social and literary history at both the regional and the local levels," while observing that "such an enterprise is extremely illuminating, even when summarizing the multitudinous effects of mestizaje as a racial discourse is ultimately impossible."[16] On that note, Miller argues there is a theoretical problem, stating, "due to overuse, the term mestizaje now suffered from *epistemological poverty and inherent conceptual obliqueness.*"[17] Again, the archaeo-genealogical method we pursue here, as a strategy of decolonial critique, is a potent critical praxis to grapple with the challenges of addressing mestizaje as social process, historical category, and discursive formation.

An important indicator of the ambiguity of mestizaje is its normative valuations. There is a history of binary oppositions between good and bad mestizaje. This polemic character can be traced to the very emergence of the figure of the mestizo/a in the early modern and colonial period. Miller reads that contradiction in the very character of Doña Marina (also known as Malintzin and La Malinche), the Indigenous woman "given" as wife to Hernán Cortés. "La Malinche is either the face of disaster, La Chingada, or a pillar of resistance and survival, the womb of cultural annihilation, or the fertile ground of cultural diplomacy. This duality seems inescapable, so that at times mestizaje's 'rise' and 'fall' appear to occur simultaneously" writes Miller.[18] On that point, she also refers to Osvaldo Guayasamin's differentiation of mestizaje as "cultural resistance" and "cultural devastation," as well as Florencia Mallon's distinction between "official mestizaje" and "mestizaje of resistance."[19] Similarly, Lourdes Martínez-Echazábal describes mestizaje as a "double-edged sword" that can imply "backwardness and barbarism" or "civilization and progress," and argues that "pessimistic" and "optimistic" postures of mestizaje as an "amalgamation of races" share objectives of whitening.[20]

In counterpoint to the ideologies of mestizaje that became hegemonic in the 1920s, which were "generally considered antiracist, anti-imperial, and more inclusive of a greater portion of Latin America's diverse citizenry in political and cultural engagements,"[21] scholars such as Antonio Cornejo Polar consider "the concept of mestizaje . . . as offering harmonic images of what obviously is fragmented and belligerent, proposing figurations that deeply are only pertinent to those for whom it is convenient to imagine our societies as smooth and non-conflictive spaces of conviviality."[22] Cornejo Polar characterizes mestizaje as a "desire for an impossible harmony."[23] In a similar note, Rivera Cusicanqui contends that "mestizaje is a political concept that had intended to produce a homogeneous identity but keeps occult and reinforce the exclusions and segregations of caste society."[24] Likewise, mestizaje discourses are a main target of critique of contemporary Black and Indigenous movements in Latin America and the Caribbean. This chapter is inscribed within these critical engagements, at the same time aiming to articulate and explore tensions and ambiguities within and between different formulations of mestizaje as a historical category and as a discursive formation.

Subjects of Mestizaje: Figures of Mestiza/o and Mulatta/o

Arguably, the mestiza/o is a historical figure who came to be before the rise of mestizaje discourses in the late nineteenth and early twentieth centuries. According to Covarrubias, the noun *mestizo* was first used to name an animal "engendered by diverse species of animals, from the verb '*mesceo*,' which is, for mixing," explaining that it "comes from the Latin *miscēre* (to mix)."[25] Covarrubias also states that, more than signifying the "offspring of Spaniards in the Indies," *mestizo* "carr[ies] on the meaning of bastard illegitimate mixture, that is to say, bad caste."[26] Catelli observes that "the term mestiza appears early (1531) [in the Americas] in the testament of Pedro de Vadillo, an inhabitant of La Española."[27] In this line, Marisol de la Cadena indicates that "in Medieval Spain, Christians who prefer to ally with Muslims against King Rodrigo (rejecting the cleanliness of blood guaranteed by loyalty to the crown) were labeled as *mistos*."[28] Adding that conceived as "promiscuous mixers, agitators of the social hierarchies authorized by the Christian King, mestizos were seeing as 'loss souls or God,' [and as] *perros mestizos.*"[29] Such negative connotations of the early figure of the mestizo were developed in contrast to the term *castizo*, which signified chastity, cleanliness, purity, and moral rightness. In counterpoint, the signifier *mestizo* is a derivative "from the Latin *merece*, which is associated with moving, unsettling, [and] mixing for agitation."[30]

The identification of certain subjects as mestiza/o in early modernity was the product of an extension and transition from the Iberian contact zone, where the first racial discourses were conceived with criteria of "blood purity" (or lack thereof),[31] against the bedrock of Christianity, to the transatlantic contact zone wherein processes of conquest, colonization, and slavery were the foundation for the emergence of modern/colonial racial formations and racist regimes. José Buscaglia contends that "the association between mestizo and bastard results from the translation and racialization of Iberic terms to the New World in the conquest period."[32] Likewise, Ben Vinson noticed that "a new attitude toward racial mixture began to emerge gradually between the 1540s and 1570s [when] the term mestizo began appearing with more frequency, becoming virtually synonymous with illegitimacy."[33] Nonetheless, such negative normative valuations of mestiza/o subjects in early modernity were more expressions of imperial discourse than expressions of mestizo consciousness as demonstrated by a classic counterpoint of the meanings of mestizaje in Guaman Poma vis-à-vis Garcilaso de la Vega.

The Inca Garcilaso de la Vega, often presented as an early expression of mestizo consciousness, affirmed positively such identity as a liminal location that allowed him to juggle between the best of a variety of historical worlds. He wrote: "To us the offspring of Spaniard and Indians they call mestizos to say that we are mixed of both nations, it was imposed by the first Spaniards who had kids with Indian women, and given that it was imposed by our parents and because of its signification, I call it myself with full mouth, and am honored with it."[34] A counterpoint can be found in Guaman Poma de Ayala's critique of mestizaje and mestizo subjects from the standpoint of ethnic purity and Indigenous aristocratic integrity. On that note, Guaman Poma affirms, "The principal chiefs who married their daughters with mixed Indians, lose their dignity and preeminence as principal chiefs in this kingdom ... the man who married with a mixed Indian is mestizo, as well as his offspring."[35]

This counterpoint reveals contradictions and ambiguities in mestizo consciousness that will remain as a constant in mestizo discourses as well as in representations of mestizo subjects. In that vein, scholars write about "the variety of connotations and dialogisms of the colonial category mestizo, highlighting its semantic instability,"[36] arguing that "the figure of the mestizo in its long duration concentrate a range of gazes which go from the celebratory, as in the Inca Garcilaso de la Vega, to the most visceral contempt as in the case of Domingo Faustino Sarmiento."[37] Indeed, in the case of Sarmiento, we see another tension in the representation of the subjects of mestizaje, between mestizos understood as miscegenation of "Europeans" with "Indians," and mulattoes as hybrids of "Whites" with "Blacks." Paradoxically, Sarmiento, a main architect of a highly influential racist ideology, championing a binary opposition of "civilization" and "barbarism," between Western modern white (European and Euro-descendant) civilized culture and its atavistic traditional others ("Blacks," "Indians," "Peasants"), saw mestizos as part of the "problem" to be solved in order to achieve modernity and progress, whereas he represented mulattoes positively. Sarmiento represented mestizos as subjects who "resulted in a homogeneous totality that is distinguished by its love of idleness and industrial incapacity,"[38] in contrast to mulattoes, whom he characterized as "a race inclined towards civilization, endowed with talent and with the finest aspirations of progress."[39] Arguably, such apparent contradiction in Sarmiento's argument, given his advocacy "to exterminate savages," his insistence that solving so-called Indian and Negro "problems" by means of extermination were necessary to achieve "progress," as well as his evaluation of mestizaje as disturbance of the purity of the "Caucasian race," was the result of at least two reasons: the perception that a few Blacks were not a real threat in Argentina, and his association of mulattoes with urban spaces that were taken as the locus of modernity and civilization.

The figure of the mulatta/o can also be traced to the long sixteenth century.[40] Covarrubias defines mulatto as "the offspring of Black women and White men, or viceversa [sic]: and as an extraordinary mix that was compared to the nature of the mule."[41] In her now-classic study, Lourdes Martínez-Echazábal elaborates a historical analysis of the category of *mulatez* as "a signifier of the position of the mulatto in the material and symbolic order" to "unveil the mechanisms which make possible mulatez as a sign/signifier of difference, as a vital element in the intellectual and political rhetoric, and aesthetic creation of those Hispanic-speaking countries Fernando Ortiz called Afroamerica."[42] On that note, she argues that "American *mulataje* emerged in the context of slavery from the sexual relation, largely forced, between White masters and enslaved women," adding such patriarchal practices continued "later with rape of White women in contexts of rebellion, relations of Mistresses and enslaved men, concubinages of poor Europeans (peasants, urban subaltern sectors) with Black and Mulatto women, etc."[43] This reveals the figure of the mulatta/o as an offspring of carnal mestizaje. In that same tune, Catelli contends that her interpretation of caste paintings demonstrates that "mestizaje and mulataje come from a common process of racialization, and that in the 18th century there was a creole discourse of mulatez," while arguing that analyses that "center on the body of the mulatta are an excellent point of departure for a comparison with the discourse of mestizaje which function in the opposite direction, given that they erase indigenous women and the mestiza from the memory of the nation."[44] This counterpoint of mestizo and mulatto women provides clues to understand the differential articulations of race and gender in the historical path from carnal mestizaje and to the emergence of discourses of mestizaje in the nineteenth century, as we will see.

The figure of the mulatto/a is the principal subject of mestizaje in places of predominance of Afro-descendants such as Brazil and Cuba. Marilyn Grace Miller affirms that *mulatez* is "a particularly Caribbean response to the cult of mestizaje," and hence in such spaces "the race problem is the problem of the mulatto."[45] On that note, *mulataje* can be described as the main mode of mestizaje in *Our Afroamerica*,[46] where the ambiguities ascribed to mestizo subjects point toward the creation of a middle social-racial strata, namely mulatta/o, in a context of pigmentocracy and anti-Black racism. Such contradictory social-racial location, product of "an intermediate class and caste position," implies "an image of the mulatto as superior to the Black subject but inferior to Whites, an ambivalent and contradictory being who oscillates but doesn't belong to either of the two worlds," and also entails a "polysemy attributed to the mulatez" that leads to stereotypical binaries such as "tragic mulatto" versus "enlightened mulatto."[47] In this vein, the figure of the mulatta/o became a primary source of racial signification from caste paintings in the eighteenth century to the literature of *mulataje* in the nineteenth and twentieth centuries, as we discuss later in this chapter. Hence, in the historically specific (local, regional, global) racial order of things, mulattoes occupy a plurality of subject positions from being enslaved to being overseers, from artisans and skilled workers who became political vanguard and radical working-class intellectuals to architects of relatively conservative Black elite middle strata and political classes.

In this light, Carl Degler formulated the argument about what he called a "mulatto escape hatch" in reference to mulataje as a sort of strategy to escape from the rigors of anti-Black racism and form a racial middle strata, especially in Brazil.[48] Such an argument has been amply debated, and scholars have demonstrated that even though pigmentocracy is a meaningful factor in social inequalities and racial discrimination, Black and Mulatto subjects suffer from shared racial oppression, from a subaltern position in the distribution of power, wealth, and recognition.[49] In fact, the differentiation of mulatto as a separate category vis-à-vis Black is a matter of debate not only in scholarship but also, and even more, in Black social movements and the public sphere in general.

For instance, in Cuba the "Societies of Color" were organized since the late nineteenth century to reunite "Blacks" and "Mulattoes" in a broad national movement against racism, and for Black collective empowerment within the struggle against Spanish colonialism.[50] In the last part of the twentieth century in Brazil and Colombia, "Black" ("Negro" in Spanish and Portuguese) became a political identity to group together Afro-descendants of a variety of phenotypes and coloration in Black social movements.[51] Nevertheless, while in Brazil, *pardo* (the equivalent of mulatto) is a relevant racial category, in Colombia (any of its regions), the regimes of pigmentocracy had not produced a fleshed-out semiosis of *mulataje* where mulatta/o is a separate category.[52]

The rest of the chapter is dedicated to drawing a script for a genealogy of mestizaje and *mulataje* in Latin America and the Spanish-speaking Caribbean. Before performing such move, I briefly discuss two arguments in exchange with Marisol de la Cadena. The first is related to the significance of making a theoretical and political distinction between mestizo discourses coined by mulatta/o and mestiza/o subjects themselves and mestizaje as a discursive formation with its technologies of power/knowledge and modes of subjection and subjectivation,[53] an argument I elaborate later. Here, de la Cadena claims that she wants to "rescue mestizos from mestizaje ... [in order] to challenge the conceptual politics (and political activism) that, in a simplistic fashion, following a transitional teleology, purify mestizos to outside of indigeneity."[54] In this way, de la Cadena contends that "mestizos can't be contained by the notion of empirical hybrids [because] they evoke a conceptual hybridity epistemologically inscribed in the very notion of mestizo a conceptual hybrid [that] houses social taxonomies derived from different forms of consciousness and regimes of knowledge [corresponding to] a classificatory order expressed through ideas of civilization and progress articulated trough notions such as race, class, culture, sexuality, ethnicity, geography, and education."[55] I highlight two aspects of this proposition: first is the embeddedness of mestizo subjects and mestizaje discourses in historical constellations of power, culture, and knowledge, which shape their character as racialized subjects and discourses, at the same time that they indicate a complexity that transcends mere racial definitions. The other point is a critique of binary oppositions between "Mestizos" and "Indians" that we can extend to dichotomies between "Blacks" and "Mulattoes," which imply looking into historical definitions within more complex continuums (articulations, convergences and divergences) between those ethnic-racial categories. On that subject, de la Cadena coined the concept of Indigenous-Mestizos to analyze the historical fluidity of articulations between "Mestizo" and "Indigenous" identities in Cuzco.[56]

In that vein—and this is the second point with which we close this section—de la Cadena contends that "as WEB Du Bois explained the case of double consciousness for Afro-Americans in the United States, indigenous intellectuals think from inside and outside European and Indigenous forms of knowledge."[57] On that note, I argue for a Mestiza/o double consciousness to conceptualize the contradictory social-racial locations of mestiza/o and mulatta/o subjects, positioned in between "Black" and "White" and/or at the crossroads of "Whiteness-Creoleness" and "Indigeneity," which imply a multiplicity of possibilities in such a "third space," as we will see.

From Early Modern Racial Discourses to the Rise and Fall of the Caste System

The terms *mestizo/a* and *mulatta/o* to signify a particular type of human subject emerged in the historical transition from an Iberian contact zone of unequal exchanges and uneven developments between classes, genders, peoples, and cultures, to the transatlantic contact zone between the nascent continents of the Americas, Africa, and Europe that was the axis of the *longue durée* process of conquest and colonization by rising European transterritorial empires, establishment of the institution of chattel slavery, with a brutal initiative to reshape geography, memory, formations of knowledge, cultural praxis, and modes of subjectivity, that configured over time a modern-colonial capitalist world system.[58] The emergence of racial discourse was a principal tenet of this sea change that, by the nineteenth century, had articulated the world itself as a historical universe. Quijano argues that racial classification became the *diferentia specifica* that distinguished the modern-colonial matrix he baptized as the coloniality of power.[59] Arguably, racial discourse and racial stratifications emerged in the late medieval or early modern Iberian Peninsula with genealogical and religious evaluations of "pureza de sangre" (lack or endowment of "blood purity"), that distinguished "Christians" from "Moors" and "Jews" as separate "races" or "castes."[60] Such proto-racial distinctions served as basis for the new categories created in the context of colonization, servitude, and slavery, such as "Indio" and "Negro," that eventually founded the evolution from "Christian" to "European" and to "White."

The expressions *mestiza/a* and *mulatta/o*, as we said, were coined in this historical universe and grew as categories of ranking within the racial discourses of colonialism, slavery, and early modern transatlantic capitalism. The scholarship demonstrates continuities and changes from cultural-religious racial rankings effected through hierarchies of "blood purity" in the Iberian Peninsula to racial classifications/stratifications such as "indio" and "negro" created in the context of modern colonialism and slavery.[61] The most salient distinction is between Iberian proto-racial rankings based on cultural-religious difference that classified "Moors" and "Jews" as lacking "blood purity" in relation to "Christians" who were evaluated as "pure" and "chaste." This quality of chastity, which in Spanish translates to *casto*, also relates to the noun *castizo*, which means being "Castilian" (from the territory of "Castilla"). In early modern significations, *castizo* also connoted being "chaste," in opposition to *mestizo*, associated with impurity, immorality, and bad conduct. This schema served as filo-semantic historical background for the caste system that became the main discursive and legal framework for the rise of racial discourses and classifications in Iberian America in the sixteenth through eighteenth centuries.

A key question to analyze the meanings of mestizaje in the early modern period is, What roles did it play in the conquest and colonization and how did it relate to slavery? Rivera Cusicanqui's view of "blood mestizaje" as the "practice of raping and hoarding women by Spanish landlords, priests and soldiers"—which reveals how the "invading society had access to a double service: women's labor force [as well as] sexual service, so eloquently denounced by Waman Poma, that condemned indigenous women to give birth to 'mesticillos' despised both by Spanish and Indigenous societies"[62]—is pertinent to answer such questions. Likewise, Catelli conceptualizes carnal mestizaje as a "strategy of domination," a power device exercised through the "war of races," which serves as a resource of conquest and colonization.[63] In the context of chattel slavery, miscegenation was largely the product of the sexual abuse (rape, labor, reproduction to produce enslaved children) of enslaved women and, to a minor extent, of enslaved males, animalized as stallions, and/or as pleasure providers for mistresses. In that fashion, sexualities of the enslaved served as resources of domination and dehumanization that enacted their racialization as lesser beings. The term *mulatta/o* was initially used in the Americas in reference to the offspring of such utterly violent (physically and epistemically) relations of domination. The zoological analogy that engendered the signifier *mulatta/o* as a derivative from "mule" expresses racist identifications of Black bodies with animals.

Casta constructs (more labels and images than categories) are the main referents we have of such processes of carnal mestizaje. In principle, caste classifications constituted a schema of social-racial ranking that expressed forms of otherness defined against the bedrock of "Europeanness" and "Christianness" that defined the nascent "White" Western subject.[64] On that note, mestiza/o (mixture of "White" and "Indian") and mulatta/o (miscegenation of "Black" and "White") constituted key categories of racial otherness in the colonial order of things. In view of the vastly diverse mixture of bodies and cultures through processes of colonization that created the Americas, caste hierarchies and labels were coined and informed legal codes for regulation of sexuality and marriages and lineage, social status, cultural recognition, and political power. "Caste" became a racial mark to label impure bodies and inadequate cultures produced by forbidden racial-sexual intercourses. In legal terms, it shaped a strict nomenclature of exclusions (sex, marriage, property, public authority), but in actual social practice, it was looser and messier.

As Ben Vinson demonstrates in his historical analysis of caste, "in spite of the Spanish empire's craving for fixed identities, the truth is that there was great fluidity and racial mixture was key source of social mobility."[65] He also argues that the "fundamental concepts, ideological frameworks, and principles that undergirded what has become known as the Spanish colonial caste system (were influenced by) astrology and early modern science that . . . ingrained [the] mythos of white supremacy. Anchored in considerations of religious purity, *limpieza de sangre* . . . [with] a lineage-based taxonomy to trace genealogical change over time."[66] On that note, caste rankings express fundamental features of processes of racialization and power asymmetry in Latin America's colonial period in vital realms of social life, like sexuality, government, access to property, and wealth.[67] Nonetheless, "casta increasingly manifested itself to be an unstable idea. The more it was used, the more its explanatory power seemed to slip."[68] Here, Vinson shows how "rarer castes" such as *lobo*, *zorro*, and *zambo* were less submitted to regulation and revealed the fluidity and stability of caste classifications.[69]

An argument to emphasize in this genealogy is what Vinson defines as the path "from Castizaje to Mestizaje." He defines "*castizaje* [as the] process by which casta groups shifted, transformed, moved, and intermingled with each other," arguing that as "a stage along the route of mestizaje . . . castizaje was effectively protomestizaje . . . mestizaje in the making."[70] Vinson is not arguing for a teleology that leads to mestizaje ideology, but rather historicizing how castizaje forged the conditions of possibility for the rise of mestizaje discourses in nineteenth and twentieth centuries. Counterpointing them as representing two distinct historical moments with their respective racial projects, he contends that while *casta* rankings were products of imperial discourse, mestizaje was a staple of nationalist projects. On that note, he claims that while "casta attempted to demarcate and accentuate differences between people, in the hope of bringing a stronger social order[, m]estizaje placed greater emphasis on commonality and hybridity to engineer order and unity."[71] I contend that these distinctions account for caste constructs being more fluid and unstable than racial rankings that correspond to mestizaje, even though racial categories are, generally speaking, ambiguous, polyvalent, historically contingent, and multiply mediated. "Caste" and "race" are highly intersectional (or imbricated) categories, mediated by power relations of class, gender, sexuality, and other factors, and configured by criteria such as quality and good conduct (or lack thereof). For instance, castes of *mulataje*, like mulattoes and *zambos*, were considered of "color quebrado" (broken color), an irreducible limit for social-racial mobility.

Caste paintings that flourished, especially in Peru and Mexico between the sixteenth and eighteenth centuries, are a prime source to analyze racial formations in colonial Latin America. They represent caste nomenclatures through scenes that highlight images of different castes, spelling out their names and imaging racial hierarchies. In her analysis of the relation between caste paintings, colonial racial imaginaries in the eighteenth century, and the formation of a creole racial imaginary, Catelli shows how "caste painting is a key instance of 18th century creole consciousness, manifest in the dispute between Creoles and Peninsulars, and in prejudices against castes of Blacks and Indians."[72] On that note, caste paintings embody, enact, and constitute the regimes of visuality that configure racial imaginaries and racial signification in colonial Latin America.[73] However, scholars argue that caste paintings neither constituted a representation of the complexity and fluidity of racial labeling nor represented a coherent system of racial categories.[74] From presentist perspectives, caste paintings are often described as "scenes of mestizaje," but as Catelli contends, that "becomes anachronic, given that the term mestizaje is a neologism of the nineteenth century, as miscegenation."[75] In the same line of thought, she argues that in caste paintings, "the carnal mestizaje of the conquest is transcribed visually and verbally through scenes of patriarchal domesticity organized by caste hierarchies," wherein they "suggest a link between creole discursivity and the production of visuality related to a mestizaje distinct from nationalist, but from our archaeological focus represents a key antecedent."[76] But caste paintings came to an end, along with the fall of caste laws, with the rise of independence in the early nineteenth century.

Emerging Discourses of Mestizaje and the Invention of Latin America

The anticolonial struggles that forged former Iberian America into a world region composed by independent nation-states resulted in regional reconfigurations of geopolitics, governmentalities, economies, cultural production, racial projects, and conceptions of the self. The liberal ideologies that guided new formations of nation-state abolished caste legislations, evaluated as atavistic obstacles to modern citizenship. In this context, mestizaje emerged as a key category in the contested terrain of national and regional self-definitions. In the nationalist discourses of the incipient countries, mestizaje tended to be taken in negative ways, as symptomatic of the "Indian problem" and "Black problem" to be "solved" with strategies of whitening by means of promoting European immigrations, by annihilating *indios*, *negros*, mestizos, and mulattoes through social and ethnic cleansing (war, emigrations) and/or "improving races" with miscegenation with "better races."[77]

The meanings of mestizaje in the contested terrain of racial projects that defined nascent nations and region oscillate between seeing it as part of the racial problem impeding modernization and progress, as expressed in Bunge's assertion that "the mestizo is an unfortunate fact [causing] to impair Spanish lineage," as claimed by Martínez-Echezábal,[78] and seeing it vis-à-vis the advocacy of mestizaje as a defining feature of the region (*patria grande*) and its nations (*patria chica*) by foundational figures of Latin Americanism such as Simón Bolívar and José Martí. Bolívar used the title "Racial Harmony in the Mixed Society of the New World" for a draft of his famous "Letter to Jamaica,"[79] a key text in the conception of the region as an ethnic-racial mixture of cultures of European, Amerindian, and African descent. Nonetheless, such positive valuation of mestizaje would not gain prominence until the fin de siècle invention of Latin America from the nineteenth to the twentieth century. José Martí coined the phrase "Our Mestizo America" in a world-historical juncture in which we highlight a global crisis, the Spanish-Cuban-American-Filipino War, and the invention of Latin America.[80] In the now-canonical essay "Our America," Martí shifted the discourse of the *indio* and *negro* as problem, to be reimagined as constituents of a regional civilization based on ethnic-racial harmony.[81] On that beat, Martí writes about "our mestiza America" and asserts that "there can be no racial hate, because there are no races."[82]

Arguably, Martí was the most critical decolonial intellectual-activist at the very moment of the invention of Latin America. His critique of Occidentalism, his identification with subaltern sectors (Blacks, Indigenous, "the poor of the earth") pointing toward an early radical populism, and his principled antiracist posture represent a radical strand of anticolonial thought and politics in nineteenth-century Latin America and the Caribbean, which Martí shared with figures such as Antonio Maceo in Cuba, Ramon Emeterio Betances in Puerto Rico, and Antenor Firmin in Haiti.[83] Their antiracist search for racial harmony to build national and regional community contrasts with a genealogy of hegemonic Latin Americanism that had been named as "arielismo,"[84] in light of the influence of Uruguayan Jose Enrique Rodó's essay *Ariel*, wherein Latin America appears as heir to Western Civilization's aesthetic and humanistic moral superiority vis-à-vis the United States, represented as the Anglo-Saxon utilitarian hemispheric other, identified as "Caliban."[85]

This kind of elite anti-imperialism, where Latin America is conceived as heir of Hellenic aesthetics and ethics and as new locus of Western modernity vis-à-vis the American empire, and against the "barbaric" threats of internal others (Indigenous, Blacks, peasants, workers), continued the tradition of racist discourse championed by Sarmiento, who understood mestizaje as "an impediment to Latin America's well-being and psychological balance."[86] This thread of discourse and politics constituted a lineage of Latin American racism in which mestizaje was seen as a sort of contamination of racial purity and a threat to the fraternity of whiteness.[87] Such tradition, deeply entrenched in hegemonic ideologies of region, race, and nation, was largely framed within the terms of scientific racism, positivism, social Darwinism, and eugenics of the nineteenth century, where mestizaje was signified as synonymous with racial miscegenation, mixed race, and hybridity. Among the architects of this nineteenth-century Latin American racial project, we highlight intellectuals like Alcides Argueda who argued that Bolivia's sickness was caused by mestizos who he called "inferior, lazy, and indolent elements" and praised "Hitler call to attention to the danger of miscegenation of peoples," as well as the Argentinian José Ingenieros, who classified mestizos as members of "inferior races" who should not mix with "superior races."[88] In this vein, where mestizaje becomes a key category in Latin American racism,[89] we can also include arguments such as Juan Antonio Saco's, advocating against slavery based on a "fear of the Africanization of Cuba" and defending mestizaje between White males and "colored women" as a means of white recolonization through "improving the race."[90] Arguably, both postures on mestizaje, "pessimistic" and "optimistic," had common objectives of "whitening based on positivistic logics" as an epistemic premise of so-called scientific racism.[91]

In Brazil, *mestiçagem* was also reconfigured in the period as a category of racial discourse. In the late nineteenth century, Raymundo Nina Rodrigues, a light mulatto medical doctor, pioneered Brazilian anthropology and a national tradition of eugenics. Standing from racial hierarchies of the era of scientific racism, Rodrigues advocated for racial hygiene against racial mixing that he saw as a foundation of moral degeneracy, insanity, and criminality.[92] This negative evaluation of *mestiçagem* contrasted with a long history of the idea of Brazil as a "showcase of racial mixing." In 1888, the French traveler Gustave Aimard wrote of Brazil as a "festival of colors," celebrating its "blending of races," while in the early twentieth century, Sílvio Romero called it a "country of mixed blood," proudly claiming "we are mestizos if not in our blood at least in our soul."[93] Such a celebratory gaze of Brazilian *mestiçagem*, which for a long time even seduced critical Black intellectuals like W. E. B. Du Bois, was one of the principal sources of "mulatto fictions" of racial harmony that were one of the principal paths for the emergence of mestizaje (in Portuguese, *mestiçagem*) as a discursive formation in the first two decades of the twentieth century.

The Rise of Mestizaje/Mestiçagem as Hegemonic Discourse of Race, Region, and Nation

In 1945, Salvador de Maradiaga argued that "the truly representative class and type of the Indies was the man of mixed blood—mestizo or mulatto . . . the soul of the Indies is, then, in its essence, a mestizo soul."[94] How did we get to this point in which it became common sense to many that "mestizaje and Latin Americanness are indissoluble terms"?[95] How did the positive valuation of mestizaje predominate to the extent that it came to define a hegemonic discursive formation? The turn from the nineteenth to the twentieth century marked a hemispheric dialectic of identity and difference with the emergence of the US empire as key world player vis-à-vis the invention of Latin America as a world region, framed as a civilizational and racial distinction between "Anglos" and "Latins." Such a geopolitical and ideological turn, along with the critiques of scientific racism by intellectual and political currents in the social sciences led by Franz Boas's rejection of the very notion of race in favor of ethnicity, linked to the emergence of anticolonial and Pan-African movements,[96] framed the epistemic and political conditions of possibility for the rise of "the cult of mestizaje."[97] As stated earlier, through the nineteenth century, key figures such as Simón Bolívar and José Martí positively defined mestizaje as a foundational feature of region and nation.

By the 1920s, the move to make mestizaje a defining ethnic-racial category of region and nation began to be dominant in Latin America.[98] An epistemic-political current championed by intellectuals such as José Vasconcelos in Mexico, Gilberto Freyre in Brazil, and Fernando Ortiz in Cuba led a transformation of racial projects and ideologies of identity and culture, in which Latin American nations and the region itself were defined in terms of racial and cultural mestizaje. This led to the constitution of mestizaje as hegemonic ideology of race, nation, and region, turning into common sense their conception as "Our Mestizo America."

The Latin American public intellectual and statesman with whom the rise of mestizaje discourses is mostly associated is Mexican José Vasconcelos. His *The Cosmic Race* is the most discussed text representing "the cult of mestizaje."[99] Its publication around the same time that Vasconcelos was Mexico's minister of education and traveled throughout Latin America gave great projection and political salience to the book. Its main argument is that mestizaje in Latin America engendered a "cosmic race" that he defines as a "synthetical race, the integral race, made up of the genius and the blood of all peoples and for that reason, more capable of true brotherhood and of a truly universal vision."[100] The subtitle, *Mission of the Ibero-American Race*, spells out Vasconcelos's project of vindicating Latin America as the locus of the most advanced civilization on Earth as the product of its mestizaje, resignified as a foundation of civilizational progress. To that end, he aimed to argue against claims, from Europe and the United States, but also by Latin American White Creole elites, that mestizos and mulattoes were inferior races. In that vein, Juliet Hooker contends, "Vasconcelos's '*mestizofilia*, that is *mestizaje* as thoroughly desirable,' directly challenged the dominant view, derived from scientific racism, that mixed-race populations were inferior."[101] Thus, Vasconcelos championed a process of consolidation of mestizaje as a discursive formation that constituted a new hegemonic racial project.

Nonetheless, there are meaningful tensions in Vasconcelos's discourses and politics that we should explore minimally in this chapter. The first refers to the anticolonial and anti-imperialist vein in Vasconcelos's mestizophilia. Vasconcelos pursues Rodó's anti-imperialist lineage based on a binary between the ugly gringo and an aestheticized Latin American subject. He conceived the cosmic race as a fusion but also as a project grounded on the cultural (aesthetic, ethnic, spiritual) features of Latin American civilization. Such mestizo futurism was framed in opposition to US imperial domination and the disdain scientific racism had of Latin American nations as "mongrels" and as embodying the "Latin" heritage of the "Black Legend."[102] On that note, Hooker contends that "Vasconcelos's enormously influential conception of Latin American mestizaje as an anti-colonial ideology developed in response to US imperialism."[103] However, in the same beat she argues that "the trope of Latin America's racial advantage vis-à-vis the US thus emerges at a specific historical moment and serves a certain anti-colonial function for Latin American elites, yet one of its more problematic consequences is the way in which it tends to elide racism in the region in order to assert Latin America's superior racial politics in comparison to the USA."[104] On that note, Vasconcelos's mestizaje futurism serves as a device to obscure Latin American racism and continues the elite anti-imperialist tradition represented by "arielismo."[105]

The second element is an inquiry into the racial reasoning and racial politics embedded in Vasconcelos's arguments and actions. *The Cosmic Race* starts with the slogan "Spirit will speak through my race," expressing Vasconcelos's "aesthetic eugenics" and view of mestizaje as producing a "fifth race" as ground and horizon for cultural and spiritual excellence.[106] There is an antiracist nucleus in his argument, in his critique of "the ideology of white supremacy and superiority in Europe and the United States,"[107] and his defense of mestizaje as a process of ethnic-racial and cultural democratization. At the same time, he advocates for mixing among "proximate races, in affinity with Bunge and Saco, wherein 'inferior races' will ascend until achieving the synthesis of the fifth race or cosmic race,"[108] an Occidentalist argument, built from criteria of whiteness as hierarchical measure, that reveals a racist thread in Vasconcelos.

This led critics, past and present, to argue that his project was "profoundly racist [because] his cosmic mestizaje is simply an ideological façade to promote Hispanic-Christianity superiority as racial redeeming of humanity."[109] Nonetheless, I concur with Hooker that "internal contradictions in the text" reveal both antiracist and racist currents in *The Cosmic Race*.[110] We will see later how these tensions offer space for different appropriations of Vasconcelos's racial reasoning and racial politics, and of mestizaje discourses in general.[111] But more than just contradictions in Vasconcelos, such tensions reveal contradictions inherent to mestizo discourse and the pitfalls of a racial reasoning that celebrates ethnic-racial mixture while keeping racial hierarchy intact.

In Brazil, the most renowned intellectual of *mestiçagem* was Gilberto Freyre whose *Casa-Grande e Senzala* (1933; in English, *The Masters and the Slaves*) is now the principal referent for what came to be known as Brazilians' ideology of racial democracy.[112] The book fleshed out Freyre's argument that *mestiçagem*, a product of sexual encounters, primarily between White males and Black/Mulatto women, should be celebrated as a defining trait of Brazilian culture, as a source of its peculiar sensuality, creativity, and flexibility. As put by Miller, "in a gesture very similar to . . . Vasconcelos' elaboration of the idea of the 'cosmic race,' Freyre shifted the focus from miscegenation as racial mixture, from hybridity as a pathology, to *mestiçagem* as productive of a rich, multi-accented culture."[113] But Freyre's celebratory narrative understood *mestiçagem* as ethnic-racial transculturation, without accounting for the modes of domination that shaped the practices of racial/patriarchal violence that constitute processes of mestizaje.[114]

Freyre pursued a tradition in which *mestiçagem* was positively portrayed as emblematic of the rich cultural diversity and openness of Brazil, expressed since the aesthetic vanguards of the early twentieth century by writers such as Mário de Andrade and Oswald de Andrade who defended a "mestiço paradigm, which extolled cultural and racial hybridity as the foundation for a unified national identity."[115] Such lineage was picked up by Jorge Amado, who in his novels elevated the figure of the mulatta as incarnating an esthesis of sensuality as representative of Brazilianness.[116]

The poetics of *mulatez* was largely a Caribbean movement that emerged in the 1930s along with the Negritude movement. Three Antillean poets, Nicolás Guillén (Cuba), Luis Pales Matos (Puerto Rico), and Manuel del Cabral (Dominican Republic), are mostly associated with a poetics of *mulatez*.[117] Guillén's book *Songoro Consongo*, subtitled *Mulatto Poem*, can be read as a manifesto of mulatto aesthetics. In the introduction, he claims that his "mulatto verses" can be "repugnant to many people, because they deal with matters of blacks and of the community" but they "are formed . . . of the same elements which are present in the ethnic composition of Cuba" because "we are all of a rather uncertain background" and given that "the African injection is so deep in this land . . . I believe that we won't have a well-developed Creole poetry if we forget the black. The black—in my judgment—provides essential ingredients in our cocktail."[118] Against the current of framing mestizaje and *mulataje* within hierarchies of whiteness, Guillén affirms his mulatto identity as a way of vindicating the values of Blackness within an antiracist discourse.[119]

Guillén's critics claim that his mulatto poetics expressed a particular discourse of mestizaje that emphasized and promoted racial harmony, thus hiding racial oppression and struggles. Vera Kutzinski contends that Guillén's poetics of *mulatez* is sustained by an ideology that "en-gendered and de-racialized" Cuba, "thus reinforcing, rather than dismantling, existing social hierarchies."[120] Miller argues that "mulatez is generally enunciated from the position of the male writer, and, historically, the mulatta has been represented as the focus of colonial desire and aggression in the Caribbean,"[121] agreeing with Kutzinski's contention that "Guillén's conception of a racial (or raceless) utopia in '*Balada de los dos Abuelos*' is predicated on the erasure of a black woman . . . in whose violated body the two races actually met."[122] These tensions in Guillén's mulatto poetics reveal paradoxes in mestizaje itself, as the contradiction between recognizing Blackness and denying the centrality of racism. Such sprains and strife reflect epistemic hybridizations and political negotiations in discourses of *mulatez*. On that note, Ríos Ávila argues that "the hybridity of mulatto culture, far from resolving itself in a fusion without any residue of a third race, is staged as a struggle, as an internal tension."[123]

In this vein, Guillén's *mulataje*, articulated in his notion of "color cubano" to signify Cuban nationality, is a key note within a Cuban tradition of mestizaje pioneered by José Martí and Antonio Maceo, and continued by leading intellectuals such as Fernando Ortiz, Alejo Carpentier, and Roberto Fernández Retamar. Reading race in Ortiz is particularly polemic in light of the counterpoint between the utterly racist argument in his *Los negros brujos* (1906) and his explicitly antiracist writings, a turning point being his *Cuban Counterpoint* (1940), where he coined the concept of transculturation.[124] Ortiz became a founding figure of Afro-Cuban studies, with pathbreaking archival and ethnographic research on aesthetics, music, religion, history, politics, and social policy. Following Martí's tradition, Ortiz sustained that rejecting the very notion of race was a premise for combating racism. In *Cuban Counterpoint*, transculturation became a key category for explaining sociohistorical conflicts and convergences (geopolitical, ethnic-racial, economic, cultural, territorial), through which the terrain of Cuban nationhood is forged. Ortiz conceptualized such processes as an *ajiaco* (a rich and diverse stew) a concept-metaphor that signifies his analysis of mestizaje and *mulataje*. His counterpoints of the power mediations (imperial, class, racial) that constitute *cubanía* bring a critical content to Ortiz's discourse of mestizaje, including an analysis of the historical-structural substratum for his culturalist analysis of race and nation in Cuba based on a teleology of racial harmony.[125]

The wave of antisystem movements that catalyzed a world crisis from 1955 to 1975 engendered a critical Latin Americanism in which mestizaje discourses elevated subaltern sectors as representative of region and nations. In that vein, Fernández Retamar envisioned mestizaje from the standpoint of the Cuban Revolution as refashioning the character of Caliban as a concept-metaphor representing the peasants, workers, Indigenous, Blacks, and students who compose "Latin American people" as a revolutionary subject and main source of regional cultures. Fernández Retamar celebrated Martí's maxim of "Our America Mestiza," and pursued Vasconcelos's rationale that Latin America is "a case unique to the entire planet: a vast zone for which mestizaje is not an accident but rather the essence, the central line,"[126] while his radical populism departed from prior elite discourse and politics. Nonetheless, such a sort of radical mestizaje, which became common sense in the critical Latin Americanism of the 1960s, was still premised on an anti-imperialist episteme wherein the United States was seen as a racist empire based on a racist dichotomy of "White" over "Black," in contrast to Latin America, a mestizo continent where race was secondary to class and racism was at best a minor problem.

The historical conditions of possibility (political and epistemic) for the fall of mestizaje as hegemonic discourse were framed by the crisis of the sixties and restructuration that since the 1980s forged neoliberalism as the dominant rationality (economic, political, cultural) of the new era of capitalist globalization. The rise of Black and Indigenous movements in the 1980s that claimed their own voices to be heard in self-representation of their "ancestrality" and advocated for "interculturality" as means of deep historical transformations catalyzed constitutional changes that by the late 1980s declared countries across the region as multicultural, multiethnic, and even plurinational, against the rhetoric of harmony and fusion of mestizaje discourses. In the intellectual realm, the postmodern-postcolonial moment marked an epistemic critique of grand narratives of modernity, identity, development, and progress, thus challenging nationalist ideologies such as mestizaje as a master discourse of regional and national culture and self.

Reinventions and Critiques of Mestizaje in Late Capitalist Modernity and Coloniality

The so-called Washington Consensus took a turn toward "multicultural neoliberalism" in the 1990s in response to a rising crisis and to claims for representation and redistribution from Black and Indigenous movements. Such a shift implied a change in dominant racial projects from monoculturalist mestizaje discourses to multiculturalist diversity. By the same token, postmodernist and postcolonial critiques promoted ontologies of difference and revalued hybridity as a category to conceptualize the entangled, ambiguous, unstable, contested, and changing character of subjects and cultures. On that note, intellectuals such as Homi Bhabha, Néstor García Canclini, and Stuart Hall signified hybridity as a category of critical analysis.

García Canclini has been criticized for his culturalist analysis wherein hybridity as cultural fluidity in globalized circuits is disengaged from racism and lacks critique of neoliberal racial and patriarchal capitalism. Ella Shohat argues that the concept of hybridity hides power relations because it builds upon a logic of articulation that undermines analysis of domination and resistance. Similarly, Gayatri Spivak contends that a postcolonial model of hybridity, such as Homi Bhabha's, lacks substantive analysis of class and gender, and is so "macrological that it cannot account for the micrological texture of power."[127] In counterpoint, Catelli concurs with Bhabha's signification of hybridity not as fusion, but as "radical heterogeneity, discontinuity, radical transformation of forms,"[128] which nurtures the "third space [which] is not synonymous with synthesis, but consists in an interstice of conflict and ambivalence with structural and political reverberations . . . a space of power we could call the mestizo effect."[129] On this note, hybridization is analogous to Glissant's creolization as a "process of containment" that is deeply framed in the "history of slavery, racial terror and sub-alternate survival in the Caribbean (that involves an addition of) conflicts, traumas, ruptures and the violences of uprooting" and "is unpredictable, produces no synthesis and is a continuous, fluent and contradictory process."[130] Additionally, Hall's notion of hybridity, understood as a category of creolization, is a hallmark of his argument of "new ethnicities" in "global postmodern" constellations of power, grounded in a critical analysis of neoliberal racial capitalism.[131]

Mestizaje as ideology, category, and metaphor has been revisited in US Latinx studies and politics. The early Chicano movement use of the slogan "Que viva la raza" to vindicate a mestizo "bronze race" also vindicated Vasconcelos for antiracist politics and ethnic-racial self- affirmation. The recycling of mestizaje in Latinx discourse and movements has been connected to "different racial projects" from "cultural and racial vindication" in the Chicano movement, to support "color blindness where mestizaje is equated with destruction of race" in strands of Latinx political thought, as argued by Juliet Hooker.[132] She observes that "many Latino political theorists" suffer from conceptions of race and mestizaje in Latin America that ignore that "American ideas about race were developed in direct conversation with US empire[,] and US racial politics" are "at odds with contemporary racial politics in the region," and that Latin American "ideologies of mestizaje were . . . utilized by conservative elites to . . . defend the region's standing in light of scientific racism, legitimize their rule over racially diverse populations, and obscure the reality of racism in their countries."[133] Such contradictions in travels and translations of mestizaje in "Our America," south and north of the Rio Grande, which express tensions and contradiction of mestizaje discourses, are deeply revealed and worked out in Gloria Anzaldúa's "new mestiza."

Anzaldúa, in her *Borderlands/La Frontera*, claims that to "adopt the subject position of the 'new mestiza' requires developing a tolerance for contradictions, a tolerance for ambiguity" and argues that "She learns to juggle cultures. She has a plural personality, she operates in a pluralistic mode."[134] Asserting that "the spirit will speak through the woman of my race," Anzaldúa genders Vasconcelos's maxim that opens *The Cosmic Race*.[135] In such a move of recycling and reinvention of mestizaje discourse, Anzaldúa signifies the US-Mexico border as a liminal space that reveals the plurality (class, gender, sexuality) of hybrid subjects and enables "a new mestiza consciousness of the borderlands," often taken as definitional of a subject of radical change.[136] In a gesture of mestizo futurism, she writes, "in a few centuries, the future will belong to the mestiza."[137] But as Hooker argues, "Anzaldúa 'queers' mestizaje by highlighting queer, female Chicanas as the pre-eminent US Latino subject [which] provides a corrective to the heteronormativity of most mestizo futurisms . . . yet her repurposing of mestizaje in the service of a feminist Chicana/Latina political project depended on a selective reading of Vasconcelos that reified the myth that Latin American mixture equaled racial egalitarianism

[that] precluded the articulation of a full feminist critique of the patriarchal gender politics of mestizaje."[138]

In turn, Miller asserts that "few readers have realized how radically Anzaldúa had to revise (or misread) Vasconcelos to suit her theoretical argument" given that Vasconcelos denounces *pochismo*, "a hybrid Mexican-US cultural phenomenon and important antecedent to Chicano aesthetics."[139] From another angle, Josefina Saldaña argues that, "in our Chicano reappropriation of the biologized terms of mestizaje and indigenismo, we recuperate the Indian from the ancestral past instead of recognizing contemporary indigenous peoples."[140] These critical engagements with Anzaldúa's mestizaje, while recognizing its critical edge, show the pitfalls and paradoxes inherent to mestizaje discourse.[141]

The end of mestizaje as hegemonic discourse of nation, race, and region in Latin America has two principal sources, the riss of movements of Afro-descendants and of Indigenous in the 1990s, which concurred with debates in critical Latin Americanism that emerged in the same context of crisis of Western capitalist civilization. Intellectual-activists from Afro–Latin American and Indigenous movements critique mestizaje discourse as silencing their voices, devaluing their histories, and hiding racism through ideologies of racial democracy, thus contributing to the reproduction of ethnic-racial oppression. This critical analysis of mestizaje is now common sense in the political cultures of Black and Indigenous movements across the continent. Similarly, scholars such as Antonio Cornejo Polar characterize mestizaje discourse as "the discourse of impossible harmony,"[142] while anticolonial or decolonial intellectuals challenge the very "idea of Latin America" as an offspring of ideological contests of White Creole elites, between those looking to solve "Indian" and "Negro" as "problems," and others who defend mestizaje as the defining feature of the regional civilization which serves as "our" path to whiteness vis-à-vis the American empire.[143] Such arguments, tailored in subaltern perspective, aim to value "Black" and "Indigenous" histories and epistemes, to unsettle and redefine the continent from locations of colonial difference.[144] In counterpoint, mestizaje as category is reconceptualized in Latin American cultural studies as a key feature of Latin America's postmodern condition. For Nelly Richard, hybridization signifies the processes of "appropriation-reconversion" characteristic of translocal circuits of cultural exchange that embody "the role of racial-cultural mestizaje and other forms of transculturation in the formation of Latin America."[145] Latin American modernist Marxisms revisited mestizaje as in the valorization of cultural mestizaje as a constitutive element of the baroque ethos that defines Latin American modernity in Bolívar Echeverría.[146]

A strand of scholarship in the Anglo academy aims to recast mestizaje as a critical category of social and historical research. A number of social scientists revisited mestizaje calling for "more nuanced analyses," acknowledging the role of dominant mestizaje ideologies in reproducing inequalities and discrimination while arguing that actual practices of mestizaje express processes of cultural and ethnic-racial exchange through which subjects negotiate identity, culture, and social power. On that note, such scholars "considered the ways in which mestizaje can be used as a tool of self-empowerment by racially marginalized populations and as a conceptual basis for elites to adopt antiracist perspectives."[147] Peter Wade asserts that "mestizaje is a space of struggle and contest," whereas Edward Teller and Stan Bailey argue that "an embrace of mestizaje does not erase existing racial hierarchies."[148] This "rethinking mestizaje" scholarship had produced nuanced investigations of key themes such as cultural production, inequalities, and everyday processes of identification. Nonetheless, critics had raised two sets of issues: on the one hand, a theoretical challenge to a methodological nationalism that tends to understand racial distinctions of the United States and Latin America as a binary between a white-nonwhite dichotomy in the United States vis-à-vis a complex ethnic-racial continuum in Latin America;[149] and on the other, questioning the political implications of embracing mestizaje. Here, Tanya Hernández argues for a "thicker account of race in the US," accounting for a plurality of systems of racial classification that will show a "greater number of points of similarity would be elucidated across the regions," implying that "a more nuanced view of the US racial context would better assist Latin American racial justice movements [to] confront any potential retrograde co-optations of the reconsiderations of mestizaje."[150] Hence, she concludes that, unwittingly, "the emerging literature reconsidering mestizaje may be drawn in to extol the presumed exceptionalism of mestizaje and undermine the racial justice challenge to the exclusionary aspects of racial democracy mestizaje."[151]

A matter of debate in the racial politics of mestizaje relates to the character and implications of pigmentocracy and colorism. I distinguish pigmentocracy, defined as social-racial stratifications based on skin color, from colorism, understood as political distinctions based on color. Color hierarchies are a key component of the epidermic dimensions of racism, especially of anti-Black racism. On that note, pigmentocracy informs societal practices of racial exclusion as well as discrimination among "people of color." In turn, colorism is a kind of racial politics that tends to reduce racialization and racism to color hierarchies. But the "color line" is not simply defined by tones of skin color; rather, it is a historically configured set of criteria (phenotypical, cultural, social) to make ethnic-racial differentiations that are not fixed categories but fluid processes.[152] In this line, a key question is, How do we locate bodies labeled as mulatta/o in racial stratifications and racial politics? From one angle, mulatta/o subjects can be seen as occupying contradictory social-racial locations, as in their diverse roles as enslaved, overseers, and even slave owners during chattel slavery. From another perspective, insofar as mulattoes are racialized subjects, submitted to the violences of anti-Black racism, as shown in the systematic rape of mulatto women in slave scenes and their ongoing reduction to objects of white desire in the "afterlives of slavery." There have been two main historical responses to such tensions in *mulatez*: the first is coalition building between darker and lighter bodies reunited with categories such as "Black" and "Colored," as in the Independent Party of Color (Cuba) and the NAACP (United States) in the early twentieth century, and the Movimento Negro Unificado in 1970s Brazil;[153] the counterpoint is colorism, which tries to establish sharp distinctions between "Blacks" and "Mulattoes" as racial categories and political subjectivities.

A classic example of colorism is the debates between Booker T. Washington and Marcus Garvey, who claimed they were authentic Blacks vis-à-vis W. E. B. Du Bois, who they rejected as a privileged mulatto. Du Bois rebutted colorism as analytically equivocal given that the color line is a complex historical process and product beyond pigmentocracy, and politically dangerous because it fractures Black coalitions. Colorism had risen in current debates among Black feminists in Brazil and Colombia, especially within a new generation in which lighter-skinned women had been questioned for having "privileges" that allowed them to "occupy Black women spaces." In counterpoint, Black feminists like Sueli Carneiro contend that such colorism undermines political unity among Black women of lighter and darker skins, forged in struggles against racism and sexism.[154] Along the same lines, decolonial Black feminists such as Ochy Curiel argue that facing a modern and colonial matrix of power configured by imbrications (class, gender, race, sexuality) requires understanding and combating all these entangled modes of oppression and building bridges from the standpoint of "multiple radical subjects" fighting for pluriversal decolonization and liberation. In this light, pigmentocracy is a necessary but insufficient criterion to analyze ethnic-racial formations, and colorism a problematic premise for racial politics.

Manuel Zapata Olivella utters a decolonial radical proposition from the position of critical mulatto discourse. In the title of his autobiographical book ¡Levántate mulato! Por mi raza hablará el espíritu, Zapata Olivella radicalizes Vasconcelos's maxim "Spirit will speak through my race" with a call and gesture of self-affirmation, "Stand up, Mulatto."[155] He writes, "Am I really a traitor to my race? A slippery zambo? A mulatto sellout? Or simply an American mestizo who seeks to defend the identity of his oppressed bloods?"[156] On that point, Zapata Olivella enacts a critical strand of mulatto discourse that articulates a radical politics of mestizaje, anticolonial and antiracist, embodying a plural subject engaged in multiple solidarities—Africana, Indigenous, popular. On that note, Zapata establishes a critical distance from "racial democracy mestizaje discourses" while identifying with "Negritude" and framing his epistemic and political project within an Afro-diasporic (not a nationalist) framework.[157] Zapata Olivella's politics and poetics of *mulatez*,[158] standing from an Afro-Indigenous (*zambo*) from Colombia's Caribbean, plural-subject position, expresses a not just a double but a multiple mulatto consciousness, a crossroads subaltern location,[159] which in some determinate iterations becomes a foundation for a decolonial radical mestizaje.

In summary, this chapter has shown the polyvalence of mestizaje and *mulataje* as social-historical processes constitutive of and mediated by the modern-colonial matrix we conceptualize as the coloniality of power and knowledge, as a category of analysis that, insofar as it embodies key power relations, contains an inherent contradiction for being either a device of domination and/or a resource of critique, as a discursive formation and ideological arena in which dominant discourses of nation-race-region has been dilucidated and debated, and as a terrain of racial politics where political-cultural subjectivities, geopolitics, and historical projects engage in contests. The ambiguity and contradictory character of the racial politics of mestizaje and *mulatez* are seen in counterpointing their distinct political meanings in Colombia, Cuba, and the Dominican Republic. While Afro-Colombian social movements associate mestizaje with white dominance and label Creole elites as "blanco-mestizas," in Cuba, mulattoes are positively identified as mestiza/o, and in the Dominican Republic, the Octubre Mulato in the late 1980s was a stepping stone to self-affirmation of African ancestry and Blackness that led to the celebration of the foundational conference of the Network of Afro–Latin American and Caribbean Women in 1992 in the context of the campaign against the five hundred years of the conquest.

Our archaeo-genealogical analysis demonstrated, in tune with Catelli, that "carnal mestizaje" served as a colonial strategy of power, whereas hegemonic discourses of mestizaje continued the biopolitics of coloniality power and knowledge by means of postcolonial nationalist ideologies and practices. From another angle of vision, Hooker argues, ideologies of mestizaje have always been contested, precisely because they were produced in the midst of social conflicts and political upheavals, and as Wade contends, "mestizaje and its components are always subjected to the hierarchies of political and economic power and to hierarchies of racism,"[160] at the same time that discourses of mestizaje and mestizaje itself as a category are constitutive of constellations of power (at local, national, and regional scales) and in this way are constitutive of patterns of domination and practices of resistance and self-affirmation. On that point, mestizaje can constitute a "third space," beyond binaries, with the potential to unsettle the category of race itself. Hence, our mapping of the ambiguities, aporias, contradictions, and contested values of mestizaje and mulataje as critical categories. In light of such political ubiquity and epistemic messiness, we are doomed to continue being seduced by the puzzles of mestizaje.

NOTES

1. I am using the category of *Amefrica Ladina,* coined by the Afro-Brazilian feminist Lélia Gonzalez, "A categoria político cultural de Amefricanidade," *Tempo Brasileiro,* nos. 92–93 (1988): 69–82, as a move to unsettle categorical monological significations of the region, by means of recognizing the largely invisible presence of what I call "Our Afroamerica," for more complex and contradictory genealogy of the historical universe we call Latin America. This kind of political-epistemic move entails the creation and deployment of categories such as "Amefrica Ladina" and "Abiayala" ("the big land of all of us" in Kuna language), created by intellectual-activists of movements of Afro-descendants and Indigenous peoples, to elaborate "post-Occidentalist, non-imperial geo-historical categories," as argued by Fernando Coronil, "Mas allá del occidentalismo: Hacia categorias geo-historicas no-imperialistas," in *Teorías sin disciplina: Latinoamericanismo, poscolonialidad y globalización del debate,* ed. Santiago Castro-Gómez and Eduardo Mendieta (Mexico City: Editorial Miguel Ángel Porrúa, 1998).
2. In this chapter, I use the word *mestizaje* (in Spanish), because it is a signifier of a polyvalent category (historical, cultural, philosophical) coined in the Romance languages, and even more so in the Iberian world, whose complexity is not translatable by equivalent words in English such as *miscegenation* and *hybridity,* as we will see.
3. I use this kind of method, building from Foucault, but at the same time departing from his Eurocentric perspective, and elaborating the methodology from a decolonial position, in Agustín Laó-Montes and Arlene Dávila, *Mambo Montage: The Latinization of New York* (New York: Columbia University Press, 2001); Agustín Laó-Montes, *Contrapunteos diaspóricos: Cartografías políticas de nuestra Afroamerica* (Bogotá: Universidad Externado de Colombia, 2020).

4. Laura Catelli, *Arqueología del mestizaje: Colonialismo y racialización* (Temuco, Chile: UFRO UP & CLACSO, 2020), 64, 140, 254, respectively. All the translations of Catelli's work are mine.
5. Catelli, *Arqueología del mestizaje*, 38.
6. Catelli, *Arqueología del mestizaje*, 38.
7. Catelli, *Arqueología del mestizaje*, 39. Through her book titled *Arqueología del mestizaje* (Archaeology of Mestizaje), Catelli builds an argument about mestizaje, rigorously and creatively elaborating Foucault's analytics of power while transcending his Eurocentric and Occidentalist limitations, thus constructing her own decolonial or postcolonial mode of critique. In this light, Catelli conceptualized mestizaje as a historical trajectory of discursive formations with power and knowledge effects with their corresponding modes of subjection and subjectivation.
8. Catelli, *Arqueología del mestizaje*, 39.
9. Catelli, *Arqueología del mestizaje*, 31.
10. Catelli invokes Foucault's concept-metaphor of war of races to analyze the violence embedded in sexual and racial intercourse since the colonial times until neocolonial continuities in the present and how dominant discourses of mestizaje tend to obscure such violences. As mentioned, Catelli turns Foucauldian analytics into a resource for decolonial and postcolonial critique, overcoming Foucault's shortcomings. See Catelli, *Arqueología del mestizaje*, 132.
11. Silvia Rivera Cusicanqui, *Violencias (re)encubiertas en Bolivia* (La Paz: Mirada Salvaje, 2010), 65.
12. Catelli, *Arqueología del mestizaje*, 39.
13. I use the concept of intersectionality in the radical and critical sense of Patricia Hill Collins to signify the multiple mediations of power within a "matrix of domination" that constitute formations of culture, knowledge, politics, and the self. See Patricia Hill Collins, *Intersectionality as Critical Theory* (Durham, NC: Duke University Press, 2019).
14. Marisol de la Cadena, ed., *Formaciones de indianidad: Articulaciones raciales, mestizaje y nación en America Latina* (Bogotá: Editorial Envion, 2007), 99. All translations to Marisol de la Cadena's quotes are mine.
15. Marilyn Grace Miller, *Rise and Fall of the Cosmic Race: The Cult of Mestizaje in Latin America* (Austin: University of Texas Press, 2004), 6.
16. Miller, *Rise and Fall of the Cosmic Race*, 3.
17. Miller, *Rise and Fall of the Cosmic Race*, 3. The phrase with italics represents Miller's quote of De Grandis and Bernd.
18. Miller, *Rise and Fall of the Cosmic Race*, 23.
19. Miller, *Rise and Fall of the Cosmic Race*, 24.
20. Lourdes Martínez-Echazábal, *Para una semiótica de la mulatez* (Madrid: J. Porrúa Turanzas, 1990), 34. All translations from Lourdes Martínez-Echazábal's *Para una semiótica de la mulatez* are mine.
21. Miller, *Rise and Fall of the Cosmic Race*, 3.
22. Antonio Cornejo-Polar, "El discurso de la armonía imposible (El Inca Garcilaso de la Vega: Discurso y recepción social)," *Revista de Crítica Literaria Latinoamericana* 19, no. 38 (1993): 75. Translations from Cornejo-Polar are mine.
23. Cornejo-Polar, "El discurso de la armonía imposible," 75.
24. Rivera Cusicanqui, *Violencias (re)encubiertas*, 67.

25. Sebastián de Covarrubias Orozco, *Tesoro de la lengua castellana o española* (Madrid: Luis Sanchez, 1611); Catelli, *Arqueología del mestizaje*, 170.
26. Catelli, *Arqueología del mestizaje*, 170.
27. Catelli, *Arqueología del mestizaje*, 224.
28. Cadena, *Formaciones de indianidad*, 89.
29. Cadena, *Formaciones de indianidad*, 89.
30. Cadena, *Formaciones de indianidad*, 91.
31. For the emergence of racial classifications and stratification in the context of late medieval and early modern Iberian Peninsula wherein the biological or naturalistic metaphor of "blood purity" as based on Christian Catholic faith vis-à- vis "Moor" and "Jewish" consider "infidels" and "impure," and how this evolved into the first racial discourses, see, e.g., Max S. Hering Torres, "Colores de piel: Una revisión histórica de larga duración," in *Debates sobre ciudadanía y políticas raciales en las Américas negras*, ed. Claudia Mosquera-Rosero-Labbé et al. (Bogotá: Universidad Nacional de Colombia-Universidad del Valle, 2010); Max S. Hering Torres, *Rassismus in der Vormoderne: Die "Reinheit des Blutes" im Spanien der Frühen Neuzeit* (Frankfurt: Campus Verlag GmbH, 2006); María Elena Martínez, *Genealogical Fictions: Limpieza de Sangre, Religion, and Gender in Colonial Mexico* (Stanford, CA: Stanford University Press, 2008); Max S. Hering Torres, María Elena Martínez, and David Nirenberg, eds., *Race and Blood in the Iberian World* (Zurich: LIT Verlag, 2012).
32. José F. Buscaglia-Salgado, *Undoing Empire: Race and Nation in the Mulatto Caribbean* (Minneapolis: University of Minnesota Press, 2003), 3.
33. Ben Vinson, *Before Mestizaje: The Frontiers of Race and Caste in Colonial Mexico* (Cambridge: Cambridge University Press, 2017), 12.
34. "A los hijos de español y de india o de indio y española nos llaman mestizos por decir que somos mezclados de ambas naciones, fue impuesto por los primeros españoles que tuvieron hijos en indias y por ser nombre impuesto por nuestros padres y por su significación me lo llamo yo a boca llena, y me honro con él." *Cuzco, 1609* (de la Vega 1991, 627), as cited in Cadena, *Formaciones de Indianidad*, 89. The translation is mine. There is a vast literature and considerable debate on the character and implications of the positive mestizaje discourse of El Inca Garcilaso de la Vega. An assessment of such discussions transcends the scope of this chapter.
35. Cadena, *Formaciones de indianidad*, 90. "Los caciques principales que cazaren a sus hijas con yndios mitayos pierden las honrras y primenencia del cacique principal en este rreyno. [. . .] El hombre, casándose con una mitaya India es mestizo sus hijos y sus descendientes. Ayacucho, 1615" (Poma de Ayala 1980, 734), as cited in Cadena, *Formaciones de indianidad*, 90.
36. Cadena, *Formaciones de indianidad*, 88.
37. Catelli, *Arqueología del mestizaje*, 46.
38. Domingo F. Sarmiento, *Facundo: Or, Civilization and Barbarism* (1845; New York: Penguin Classics, 1998), 43.
39. Martínez-Echazábal, *Para una semiótica de la mulatez*, 43.
40. I am using the concept of the long sixteenth century following the path of Fernand Braudel, who analyzes centuries not in simple chronological fashion but as long periods within the lifetime of capitalist modernity, which represent the *longue durée* structures of historical capitalism. In this definition, the long sixteenth century represents the period

circa 1450 to 1650. See Fernand Braudel, *Civilization and Capitalism, 15th–18th Century*, vol. 3, *The Perspective of the World* (Berkeley: University of California Press, 1992); Braudel, *The Mediterranean and the Mediterranean World in the Age of Philip II*, vol. 1 (Berkeley: University of California Press, 1996).

41. Catelli, *Arqueología del mestizaje*, 226.
42. Martínez-Echazábal, *Para una semiótica de la mulatez*, 5.
43. Martínez-Echazábal, *Para una semiótica de la mulatez*, 6.
44. Catelli, *Arqueología del mestizaje*, 229.
45. Miller, *Rise and Fall of the Cosmic Race*, 47.
46. I coined the concept "Our Afroamerica" as a geo-historical category to signify the Afro-Latinx/American universe from the Patagonia to North America. See Laó-Montes, *Contrapunteos diaspóricos*.
47. Martínez-Echazábal, *Para una semiótica de la mulatez*, 9.
48. Carl Degler, *Neither Black nor White: Slavery and Race Relations in Brazil and the United States* (New York, NY: Macmillan, 1971), 3.
49. One of the latest interventions demonstrating shared social inequalities and racial discrimination of subjects and bodies differentially labeled as "Black" and "Mulatto" (or mixed race) is Tanya K. Hernández *Multiracials and Civil Rights: Mixed-Race Stories of Discrimination* (New York: New York University Press, 2018). The body of literature on the subject in Brazil is broad. See, e.g., Marcelo Paixão, *500 anos de solidão: Ensaios sobre as desigualdades raciais no Brasil* (Curitiba, Brazil: Appris, 2013.); Marcelo Paixão, *A lenda da modernidade encantada: Por uma crítica ao pensamento social brasileiro sobre relações raciais e projeto de Estado-nação* (Curitiba, Brazil: Editora CRV, 2014); Edward Telles, *Race in Another America: The Significance of Skin Color in Brazil* (Princeton, NJ: Princeton University Press, 2006).
50. See Aline Helg, *Our Rightful Share: The Afro-Cuban Struggle for Equality 1886–1912* (Chapel Hill: University of North Carolina Press, 1995); Oilda Hevia Lanier, *El directorio central de las sociedades negras de Cuba (1884–1894)* (Havana: Editorial Ciencias Sociales, 1996).
51. The very term *mulatta/o* is constantly submitted to critique in activist and academic spaces given its origins as a zoological classification, its colonial character, and its implication for hierarchical distinctions among people of African descent. For comparisons of Black movements in Brazil and Colombia, see Tianna Paschel, *Becoming Black Political Subjects: Movements and Ethno-Racial Rights in Colombia and Brazil* (Princeton, NJ: Princeton University Press, 2016); Agustín Laó-Montes, "Caribbean Borderlands and Travelling Theories: Imperial Frontier, Translocal Nations, Federation of Diasporas, Planetary Archipelago," in *Liquid Borders: Migration as Resistance*, ed. Mabel Moraña (Abingdon, UK: Routledge, 2020).
52. It is important to observe that "pardos" were an important category in the nineteenth century, in the territory that today is the Caribbean coast of Colombia. As demonstrated in a revisionist historiography, "pardos" were among the leadership of the struggle that produced the first independence of Colombia with the establishment of the Independent Republic of Cartagena in 1812. See Aline Helg, *Liberty and Equality in Caribbean Colombia 1770–1835* (Chapel Hill: University of North Carolina Press, 2004); Marixa Lasso, *Myths of Harmony: Race and Republicanism during the Age of Revolution, Colombia, 1795–1831* (Pittsburgh, PA: University of Pittsburgh Press, 2007); Alfonso Múnera, *El Fracaso de la Nación* (Bogotá: Crítica, 2000).

53. Several intellectuals, including Étienne Balibar, Partha Chatterjee, and Michel Foucault, distinguish two moments in processes of subject formation: *subjection*, which refers to how constellations of power and regimes of truth facilitate the configuration of subjects by subjugating bodies and cultures within determinate orders of domination, and *subjectivation*, which signifies processes of self-affirmation by means of resistances, struggles, and collective actions through which bodies become historical subjects. See Laó-Montes and Dávila, Mambo Montage; Laó-Montes, *Contrapunteos diaspóricos*.
54. Cadena, *Formaciones de indianidad*, 86.
55. Cadena, *Formaciones de indianidad*, 86.
56. See Marisol de la Cadena, *Indigenous Mestizos: The Politics of Race and Culture in Cuzco, Peru, 1919–1991* (Durham, NC: Duke University Press, 2000), in which through long-term historical and ethnographic research, she unsettles both "Indigenous" and "Mestizo" as categories that are ambivalent and polyvalent. Their significations and articulations are embedded in constellations of power, regimes of knowledge, ideologies, and struggles, which shape their contested terrains of meanings and their effects of power.
57. Cadena, *Formaciones de indianidad*, 112.
58. I am extending the concept of contact zone, coined by Mary Louise Pratt to conceptualize processes of transculturation that occur in the context of US imperial domination (political-economic and geopolitical), but also of aesthetic, gnoseological, political, and cultural exchange of all sorts (of elites and also of subaltern sectors) that occur within such historical universes. See Agustín Laó-Montes, "Reconfigurations of Empire in a World-Hegemonic Transition: The 1898 Spanish-Cuban-American-Filipino War," in *Revisiting the Colonial Question in Latin America*, ed. Mabel Moraña and Carlos A. Jáuregui (Madrid: Iberoamericana Editorial Vervuert, 2008); Buscaglia-Salgado, *Undoing Empire*. The division of the world in continents is a product of modern and colonial imagination, see Christian Grataloup, *L'invention des continents* (Paris: Larousse, 2009). There is a vast body of scholarship that conceptualizes processes of globalization that constituted a modern colonial capitalist world system. See especially Janet Abu-Lughod, *Before European Hegemony: The World System A.D. 1250–1350* (New York: Oxford University Press, 1991); Braudel, *The Mediterranean*; Enrique Dussel, *1492: El encubrimiento del otro: Hacia el origen del "mito de la modernidad": Conferencias de Frankfurt, octubre de 1992* (Bogotá: Antropos, 1992); Enrique Dussel, *The Underside of Modernity* (Atlantic Highlands, NJ: Humanities Press, 1996); Aníbal Quijano, *Modernidad, identidad y utopía en América Latina* (Lima: Sociedad y Política Ediciones, 1988); Michel-Rolph Trouillot, *Global Transformations: Anthropology and the Modern World* (New York: Palgrave Macmillan, 2004); Immanuel Wallerstein, *The Essential Wallerstein* (New York: New Press, 2000).
59. Aníbal Quijano, "Colonialidad del poder y clasificacion social," *Journal of World Systems Research* 11, no. 2 (2000): 342–386.
60. Quijano, "Colonialidad del Poder," 374. There is considerable debate about the historical timing of the emergence of racial discourse, as well as racial classifications and stratifications. Some, like Cheikh Anta Diop, argue that anti-Black racism is prior to modernity and the product of an ancient slave trade between the Maghreb and sub-Saharan Africa. *The African Origin of Civilization: Myth or Reality* (Chicago: Chicago Review Press, 1989). Others contend that racialization is an offspring of the eighteenth-century European Enlightenment and nineteenth-century scientific racism. I argue that racial discourses, and racial classifications or stratifications, are principal pillars of the configuration of

the modern colonial world system in the long sixteenth century, particularly determined by modern colonialism and chattel slavery, building from proto-racial discourses of the Iberian Peninsula. For arguments along these lines, see, e.g., Martínez, *Genealogical Fictions*; Quijano, "Colonialidad del Poder"; Wallerstein, *The Essential Wallerstein*.

61. See, e.g., Javier Irigoyen Garcia, *Moors Dressed as Moors: Clothing, Social Distinction and Ethnicity in Early Modern Iberia* (Toronto: University of Toronto Press, 2017).
62. Rivera Cusicanqui, *Violencias (re)encubiertas*, 72.
63. Catelli, *Arqueología del mestizaje*, 86. As stated, Catelli developed Foucault's analytics of power as a methodological resource of decolonial critique and, in that endeavor, elaborates an analysis of mestizaje as a device (the Spanish *dispositivo* corresponds more to the category) of racial-patriarchal power, characterized by fierce violent practices (corporal, sexual, symbolic) on and against the bodies of racialized and sexualized others that she conceptualizes by extending the meanings of Foucault's notion of war of races.
64. We still need to produce a comparative genealogy of discourses of whiteness accounting for its differential conception in Occidentalist imperial discourse. Analyses tend to concentrate on English and French empires since the eighteenth century. However, we can already see the category "Blanco" in texts such as Juan Latino's letter to King Carlos III in the sixteenth century. In her analysis of caste paintings, Catelli contends that "the identity imagined by Creole elites was relational, White and pure, not mestiza." *Arqueología del mestizaje*, 207.
65. Vinson, *Before Mestizaje*, 16.
66. Vinson, *Before Mestizaje*, 53.
67. The dictionary of the Real Academia Española (1726) defined *raza* as "the caste or quality of one's lineage." Vinson argues there was "great definitional overlap between *raza* and *casta* from the fifteenth century . . . both terms had emerged from ruminations over lineage, nature, and breeding, with a particular emphasis on purity." *Before Mestizaje*, 58.
68. Vinson, *Before Mestizaje*, 54.
69. Indeed, what he call "rarer cases" are the less representative ones, such as *lobo* and *zorro*, while *zambo* (a combination of Black and Indian) was more common. Catelli, *Arqueología del mestizaje*, argues that "the caste system, a legal system of socioracial hierarchies created by Spanish law and colonial elite in response to the growth of the mestizo population" and adds that "one of the traits of Creole identity appears to be configured by resistance to mixture with people from another race or of less quality." Even though I agree with the thrust of her argument, I take issue with the characterization of caste rankings as a system given its extreme variability and resistance to codification. *Arqueología del mestizaje*, 205. In this vein, de la Cadena argues that "colonial policies concerning purity were not totally intolerant mixture as we supposed today . . . not all individuals that 'we' call 'mixed' were label mestizos. They could be considered Spaniards, Creoles, and also Incas until the 18th century." *Formaciones de indianidad*, 89.
70. Vinson, *Before Mestizaje*, 63.
71. Vinson, *Before Mestizaje*, 61.
72. Catelli, *Arqueología del mestizaje*, 218.
73. The concept of regimes of visuality or visual regimes to conceptualize how racial formations (imaginaries, discourses, classifications or stratifications) are largely configured by historically determinate modes of educating the gaze, a key dimension of processes of racialization that I define as a perverse pedagogy of the eye. See Deborah Poole, *Vision, Race, and Modernity: A Visual Economy of the Andean Image World* (Princeton, NJ: Princeton University Press, 1997), Laó-Montes, *Contrapunteos diaspóricos*.

74. See, e.g., Catelli, *Arqueología del mestizaje*; Martínez-Echazábal, *Para una semiótica de la mulatez*; Lourdes Martínez-Echazábal, "Mestizaje and the Discourse of National/Cultural Identity in Latin America, 1845–1959," *Latin American Perspectives* 25, no. 3 (1998): 21–42; Miller, *Rise and Fall of the Cosmic Race*; Vinson, *Before Mestizaje*.
75. Catelli, *Arqueología del mestizaje*, 31.
76. Here, there are two apparently antithetic arguments about mestizaje: on the one hand, the idea that racial miscegenation produced "mongrels" of inferior racial stock and human character, and on the other hand, a view of mixture with "better races" as a path to "racial improving" founded on a Lamarckian genetic rationales, according to which predominance of "superior races" triumph over time.
77. Catelli, *Arqueología del mestizaje*, 221.
78. Martínez-Echazábal, *Para una semiótica de la mulatez*, 32.
79. Bolívar, as cited in Miller, *Rise and Fall of the Cosmic Race*.
80. The very idea of Latin America is a product of the late nineteenth century, mediated by three main historical events: first, a civilizational-racial imperial ideology that distinguished "Anglos" and "Latins" in the context of the struggle for world hegemony between the British and French empires; second, a disenchantment with admiration of US empire by Creole elites in power in the nascent nations of Ibero-America, especially after the 1846–1848 Mexican-American War in which the United States acquired around half of Mexico's national territory; and the 1898 Spanish-Cuban-American-Filipino War, when the American Empire became a principal player in world geopolitics and turned the Caribbean to a "backyard" in its imperial discourse and geopolitics. Such a world-historical moment was overdetermined by the world crisis (1873–1898). See, e.g., Fernando Coronil, *The Fernando Coronil Reader* (Durham, NC: Duke University Press, 2019); Coronil, "Mas allá del occidentalismo"; Gilbert Joseph, Catherine LeGrand, and Ricardo Donato Salvatore, eds., *Close Encounters of Empire: Writing the Cultural History of US-Latin American Relations* (Durham, NC: Duke University Press, 1998); Laó-Montes and Dávila, *Mambo Montage*; Laó-Montes, "Reconfigurations of Empire"; Walter Mignolo, *The Idea of Latin America* (Malden, MA: Blackwell, 2006).
81. See, e.g., Laó-Montes, "Reconfigurations of Empire." As Martínez-Echazábal argues in "Mestizaje and the Discourse of National/Cultural Identity," in "Our America," Martí made a radical move in trying to transcend the dichotomy of civilization versus barbarism, which set up the terms of racial discourse and shaped discussions about race and nation across the region throughout the nineteenth century.
82. José Martí, *Nuestra América* (1893, reprint: Guadalajara, Mexico: Universidad de Guadalajara, 2002). The political and epistemic character and values of such a move by Martí which can be considered a foundation of Latin American discourses of racial harmony are matter of great debate, given the deeply anticolonial and antiracist nature of his ideology and politics, in contrast to most mestizaje discourses.
83. In fact, when Martí was found dead after his fall in Dos Pinos, Cuba, a copy of Firmin's book *On the Equality of Human Races*, partly written as a rebuttal of Gobineau, was found on his briefcase. I develop the argument of Martí's critique of Occidentalism and his decolonial political-epistemic positioning and perspective through a contrapuntal reading of his "Our America" and Rodó's "Ariel," in Laó-Montes, "Reconfigurations of Empire."
84. Betances and Firmin launched proposals for pan-Caribbean regional federations, whereas Martí and Puerto Rican Eugenio Maria de Hostos advocated for Bolívar's project of Latin American unity based on discourses of mestizaje.
85. "Ariel" is the character in Shakespeare's drama *The Tempest* who represents Western ratio-

nality and its intelligentsia, in contrast to "Caliban," another character in the play who represented the "barbarian" other.
86. Sarmiento, *Facundo*, 3.
87. In the emerging Latin American continent and its nation-states, proving "whiteness" was particularly important to Creole elites whose belonging to the fraternity of whiteness was questioned by European and US elites who evaluated them as nonwhite or less white precisely because of perceived miscegenation and/or with civilizational-racial discourses like the Black legend that ascribed hierarchical distinction among European heritages.
88. Arguedas and Ingenieros, as cited in Martínez-Echazábal, "Mestizaje and the Discourse of National/Cultural Identity," 27.
89. Here racism is conceptualized as one of the main regimes of domination (along with capitalism, patriarchy, and imperialism) in the modern-colonial matrix of power that configures the modern-colonial capitalist world system. In this sense, racism signifies the structures, imaginaries, and practices that configure and enact racial domination and discrimination as key components of social, economic, political, and cultural power in capitalist modernity. I develop this argument in Lao-Montes, *Contrapunteos diaspóricos*.
90. Martínez-Echazábal, *Para una semiótica de la mulatez*, 35.
91. See Martínez-Echazábal, "Mestizaje and the Discourse of National/Cultural Identity."
92. Rodrigues used the methodology of "craniometry," elaborated by the Italian physician Cesare Lombroso (1835–1909), as a principal device of positivist criminology as a discipline in the rising social sciences. It informed emerging social policies of racial hygiene, against conventional notions of crime and punishment as natural. Rodrigues was highly influential in Brazilian social science and social policy.
93. As cited in Miller, *Rise and Fall of the Cosmic Race*, 96.
94. As cited in Miller, *Rise and Fall of the Cosmic Race*, 3.
95. Agustín Basave Benítez, *México mestizo: Análisis del nacionalismo mexicano en torno a la mestizofilia de Andrés Molina Enríquez* (Mexico City: Fondo de Cultura Económica, 1992), as cited in Miller, *Rise and Fall of the Cosmic Race*, 28.
96. Boasian critiques of "race" as a fictive category that was the product of the philosophical racism of the Enlightenment and the scientific racism shaped by nineteenth-century positivism, social Darwinism, and eugenics, became influential in early twentieth century social sciences (especially anthropology), and became connected with rising anticolonial and Pan-Africanism movements, as expressed in the 1900 First Pan-African Conference in London, the 1911 Universal Race Congress in London, and the 1916 Easter Rising in Ireland.
97. Some key conceptualizations of the rise of mestizaje as hegemonic discourses (nationalist and regional) in early twentieth-century Latin America are Martínez-Echazábal, *Para una semiótica de la mulatez*; Cadena, *Formaciones de indianidad*; Miller, *Rise and Fall of the Cosmic Race*; Catelli, *Arqueología del mestizaje*.
98. I use the term *ethnic-racial* to conceptualize the entanglement of phenotypical and cultural components of racial identifications and stratifications, which corresponds to a theorization of "race," "ethnicity," and "culture" as intertwined categories of collective belonging and social hierarchy. See, e.g., Stuart Hall, *The Fateful Triangle: Race, Ethnicity, Nation*, W. E. B. DuBois Lectures (Cambridge, MA: Harvard University Press, 2017); Laó-Montes and Dávila, *Mambo Montage*; Laó-Montes, *Contrapunteos diaspóricos*; Floya Anthias and Nira Yuval-Davis, *Racialized Boundaries: Race, Nation, Gender, Colour and Class and the Anti-Racist Struggle* (London: Routledge, 1993).

99. José Vasconcelos, *La raza cósmica, misión de la raza iberoamericana* (Madrid: Agencia Mundial de Librería, 1925).
100. Vasconcelos, *La raza cósmica*, 17.
101. Juliet Hooker, *Theorizing Race in the Americas: Douglass, Sarmiento, Du Bois, and Vasconcelos* (New York: Oxford University Press, 2016), 156.
102. A classic exposition of miscegenation as producing degenerate beings labeled as "mongrels" is Alfred P. Schultz, *Race or Mongrel* (Boston: Page, 1908). For the "Black Legend" as an Anglo (British and US) imperial discourse against the Spanish empire and its legacies, see Maria DeGuzman, *Spain's Long Shadow: The Black Legend, Off-Whiteness, and Anglo-American Empire* (Minneapolis: University of Minnesota Press, 2005).
103. Hooker, *Theorizing Race*, 160.
104. Hooker, *Theorizing Race*, 162.
105. Hooker, *Theorizing Race*, 162.
106. Vasconcelos, *La raza cósmica*, 3. Vasconcelos critiqued eugenics insofar as it articulated a negative analysis of racial mixing but did not criticize eugenics per se. This is clearly revealed with his characterization of his racial reasoning as "esthetics eugenics" and in his advocacy of mestizaje between "proximate races" guided by whiteness as criterion of superiority as the ideal scenario for miscegenation, for which he gave Argentina as best example.
107. Miller, *Rise and Fall of the Cosmic Race*, 43.
108. Martínez-Echazábal, "Mestizaje and the Discourse of National/Cultural Identity." In the same vein, Miller demonstrates that, for Vasconcelos, "the lower types of the species will be absorbed by the superior type," thus pursuing the racist reasoning of scientific racism as expressed in Latin American intellectuals like Bunge and Saco. *Rise and Fall of the Cosmic Race*, 32. For example: "In this manner . . . the Black could be redeemed, and step by step, by voluntary extinction, the uglier stocks will give way to the more handsome. . . . The Indian, by grafting onto the related race, would take the jump of millions of years . . . and in a few decades of aesthetic eugenics, the Black may disappear, together with the types that a free instinct of beauty may go on signaling as fundamentally recessive and undeserving, for that reason, of perpetuation" (35).
109. Uruguay Cortazzo González, "El mulato cósmico: Relectura del mestizaje en Manuel Zapata Olivella," *Literatura y Autoritarismo*, no. 19 (2017): 22. As put by Rubén Ríos Ávila, "the cosmic race is another name for Hispanism, its mestizo name," as cited in Miller, *Rise and Fall of the Cosmic Race*, 36.
110. Hooker, *Theorizing Race*, 160. Hooker's thorough critical reading of Vasconcelos show how in later works, such as *Indología: Una interpretación de la cultura ibero-americana* (Barcelona: Agencia Mundial de Librería, 1926) and *Bolivarismo y monroísmo: Temas iberoamericanos* (Santiago de Chile: Ediciones Ercilla, 1934), "Vasconcelos formulated a more radical critique of Latin American elites' aspirations to whiteness . . . *Indología* contains passages that recognize black and indigenous contributions to Latin American identity, while *Bolivarismo y Monroísmo* directly addresses racial discrimination against Latinos during the nadir era of US race relations." In turn, Miller argues that, almost immediately after the publication of *The Cosmic Race*, Vasconcelos began to backtrack and lose faith in the notion of Latin America as providentially mestizo, for which she offers a quote from the 1948 edition of *The Cosmic Race*, where Vasconcelos writes, "it remains to be seen whether the unlimited and inevitable mixture is a favorable factor to the increment of culture or if, to the contrary, it will produce a decadence . . . of worldwide proportions," *Rise and Fall of the Cosmic Race*, 41.

111. Vasconcelos's mestizaje became a key referent in Latin American nationalist ideologies and regionalism in the early twentieth century until the emergence of critical discourses vindicating ancestrality and interculturality forged by Indigenous and Black movements since the 1970s and 1980s, and the coming of neoliberal multiculturalism as a discursive formation informing emerging racial projects and ideologies of collective identification. But given that nationalist ideologies and racial projects are contested fields of power and signification, Vasconcelos-type mestizaje always faced criticisms and competing discourses, for instance as those which continued to define "Blacks" and "Indians" as a "problem," and hence "Mestizos" and "Mulattoes" as irremediable "inferior races."

112. Gilberto Freyre, *Casa-grande e senzala: Formação da família brasileira sob o regime da economia patriarcal* (São Paolo: Livraria José Olympio Editora, 1933). For the English version, see Gilberto Freyre, *The Masters and the Slaves: A Study in the Development of Brazilian Civilization*, trans. Samuel Putnam (New York: Alfred A. Knopf, 1964). Freyre himself did not use the category of "racial democracy," but his whole argument created the political and epistemic conditions for it to become a principal ideologeme in Brazilian intellectual and governmental racial discourse that became "common sense" and a foundation for a considerable "racial hegemony" until challenges from Afro-Brazilian social movements and antiracist discourses began to undermine it in the 1980s.

113. Miller, *Rise and Fall of the Cosmic Race*, 97.

114. Freyre's defense of *mestiçagem* as an argument to celebrate an alleged condition of racial democracy in Brazil, represented as a sort of racial paradise, became one of the principal targets of Afro-Brazilian social movements and antiracist intellectuals. A landmark in such history of critique that unsettled the hegemony of the ideology of racial democracy are two interventions in the 1950s: on the one hand, from Black intellectuals like Abdias do Nascimento, who argued that racial democracy was a powerful myth that reproduced Brazilian racism by denying racial oppression exercised in the rape of enslaved Black women in the era of slavery, as well as in racial discrimination and police violence in the contemporary period, to rather argue that Afro-Brazilians suffer from a history of genocide; and on the other hand, from a research project sponsored by UNESCO in which intellectuals from the nascent Brazilian sociology like Florestan Fernandes demonstrated the persistence of class and racial inequalities in Brazil, thus influencing the character and course of Brazilian social science.

115. As cited in Miller, *Rise and Fall of the Cosmic Race*, 104.

116. Amado, a principal exponent of the poetics of *mulatez* in Brazil, identified *mulataje* as a principal expression of Brazilian *mestiçagem* that was best achieved on his native territory of Salvador, Bahia, which he understood as a mulatto land. His most renowned novel in this vein is *Tenda dos milagres* (São Paolo: Record, 2001), *Tent of Miracles*, published in 1969, trans. Barbara Shelby (New York: Alfred A. Knopf, 1971). Amado sustained a friendship with W. E. B. Du Bois that, arguably, was an important source for Du Bois's "mulatto fictions." See Hooker, *Theorizing Race*. Juliana Góes, "Brazil in Du Bois: Challenges to Build a Trans-American Pan-Africanism," in *Du Bois on Latin America and the Caribbean: Trans-American Pan-Africanism and Global Sociology*, ed. Juliana Góes et al. (Albany: State University of New York Press, 2023), demonstrates how Du Bois changed his view of Brazil as a racial democracy since the 1940s when, as part of his radicalization toward a Marxist and anti-imperialist posture, he began to critique racism in Brazilian society.

117. See Buscaglia-Salgado, *Undoing Empire*; Vera M. Kutzinski, *Sugar's Secrets: Race and the Erotics of Cuban Nationalism* (Charlottesville: University Press of Virginia, 1993); Martínez-Echazábal, *Para una semiótica de la mulatez*; Rubén Ríos Ávila, *La raza cómica: Del sujeto en Puerto Rico* (San Juan: Ediciones Callejón, 2002). Miller described *mulatez* as "a particularly Caribbean response to the cult of mestizaje" and argues "an exploration of mulatez thus provides an opportunity to question the specific place of the Caribbean within the complex rhetorical matrix of Latin American mestizaje." *Rise and Fall of the Cosmic Race*, 47.
118. Nicolás Guillén, *Songoro Consongo: Poema mulato* (Biblioteca Americana, 1931), 3.
119. The space and scope of this chapter do not allow for a minimal discussion on the politics of *mulatez*. However, it is germane to say that Pales Matos, who was neither Black nor mulatto, did not identify his poetics that way, at the same time that he affirmed a poetics of *mulatez* as representative of Caribbean cultures (as in his poem *Mulata antilla*), against the Puerto Rican and Latin American racism that pervaded intellectual and public discourse. Pales's racial gaze and racial politics are a matter of debates that express inherent tensions in discourses of *mulatez*.
120. As cited in Miller, *Rise and Fall of the Cosmic Race*, 46.
121. As cited in Miller, *Rise and Fall of the Cosmic Race*, 46.
122. The centrality of the figure of mulatto women in discourses of *mulatez* in the Americas is a key theme that has been a matter of many historiographical, ethnographic, and cultural studies. A landmark is the account of the French traveler Médéric Moreau de Saint-Méry, who wrote in the eighteenth century that "the mulatto is a priestess of the goddess Venus, whose entire being only exists to give herself to love, with a fire so fiery that it is extinguished only with death," articulating a long tradition of representing her as a binary between the "seductive and tragic mulatta." *A Civilization That Perished: The Last Years of White Colonial Rule in Haiti* (1797; Lanham, MD: University Press of America, 1985).
123. Ríos Ávila, as cited in Miller, *Rise and Fall of the Cosmic Race*, 65.
124. Fernando Ortiz, *Contrapunteo cubano del tabaco y azúcar* (Havana: Editorial de Ciencias Sociales, 1983). For the English version, see Fernando Ortiz, *Cuban Counterpoint: Tobacco and Sugar*, trans. Harriet de Onís (Durham, NC: Duke University Press, 1995). Fernando Ortiz, *Hampa Afro-cubana: Los negros brujos: Apuntes para un estudio de etnología criminal* (Madrid: Librería de Fernando Fé, 1906), pursued Lombrosian craniometry (as did Nina Rodrigues) to study "criminality" of "Afro-Cuban" urban marginal dwellers, especially members of the Abakuá religion. In counterpoint, Jesús Guanche Pérez and José Antonio Matos Arévalo edited a volume of Ortiz's writings on "race and racism," in which they argue that Ortiz opposed the very notion of race and was antiracist since the early twentieth century. *Fernando Ortiz Contra la raza y los racismos* (Havana: Editorial Nuevo Milenio, 2013). Other scholars stress what they read as ruptures from an early twentieth-century racist reasoning took a turn into pro-Black antiracist perspective that guided most of his production. Yet another interpretation argued that changes in Ortiz scholarship and epistemic-political postures did not account for a complete rupture from his biased positions.
125. Martínez-Echazábal contends, "As a cultural paradigm, 'Cuban color' co-existed with the 1928 anthropophagia movement in Brazil (another culturalist paradigm) and the paradigm I refer to as mestizaje-as-transculturation, articulated by Gilberto Freyre in *The Mansions and the Shanties* in 1936 and theorized four years later by Ortiz (1940)," thus

showing a common thread in mestizaje discourse as a staple of culturalist nationalism. "Mestizaje and the Discourse of National/Cultural Identity," 35-36.
126. José Martí, *Nuestra América*, critical ed. (1891; Guadalajara, Mexico: Universidad de Guadalajara, 2002), 15.
127. As cited in Miller, *Rise and Fall of the Cosmic Race*, 105.
128. Homi Bhabha, *The Location of Culture* (London: Routledge, 1994), 13, calls such forms of hybridization processes "interstitial hybridity" as such "uneasy" and "restless."
129. Catelli, *Arqueología del mestizaje*, 153. Catelli turns the concept of "third space" into a category of decolonial critique, arguing it "make[s] visible the political effects the interstitial position of mestizos as subjects of discourse and agents of colonial cultural difference [as] mestizo offspring formed part of reconfiguration of power relations, reopening interstitial third spaces in the war of races called conquest" which continued through different means and discourses until now.
130. This correspondence between a critical hybridity and creolization is also argued by Young and Catelli. However, the very concept of hybridity tends to be based on a notion of cultures and ethnic-racial categories as coherent wholes vis-à-vis their understanding as fields of relations that are by definition complex, contradictory, contested, and changing. Édouard Glissant differentiates his argument for "creolization" and "archipelago thinking" from discourses of mestizaje which tend toward essentialism, fusion, and lacking analysis of domination. See *Poetics of Relation* (Ann Arbor: University of Michigan Press, 1997); "Creolization in the Making of the Americas," *Caribbean Quarterly* 54, nos. 1-2 (2008): 81-89.
131. Hall influences a Black British tradition of critical race theory that pursues his postcolonial reconceptualization of hybridity to elaborate theories and politics of the African diaspora as a fluid and plural, yet interconnected, web of aesthetic, cultural, epistemic, and political exchanges constituting a translocal field Gilroy calls the "Black Atlantic." Paul Gilroy, *The Black Atlantic: Modernity and Double Consciousness* (Cambridge, MA: Harvard University Press, 1993).
132. Juliet Hooker, "Hybrid Subjectivities, Latin American Mestizaje, and Latino Political Thought on Race," *Politics, Groups, and Identities* 2, no. 2 (2014): 1.
133. Hooker, "Hybrid Subjectivities," 3. In another study, *Theorizing Race*, Hooker developed a methodology for "theorizing race in the Americas" through transnational juxtapositions, against the methodological nationalism of the conventional comparative method. In this vein, Hooker contends that, "if mestizaje in Latin America did not function as a form of racial egalitarianism, then mestizaje as such is not inherently anti-racist [and hence] Latino political theorists in the USA who adopt benevolent accounts of mestizaje stand in sharp contrast to the strong criticisms of such narratives by increasingly vocal contemporary indigenous and black movements in Latin America, which tend to argue that theories of harmonious mestizaje have served to legitimize racial hierarchy and discrimination in the region." "Hybrid Subjectivities," 197.
134. Gloria Anzaldúa, *Borderland-La Frontera: The New Mestiza* (San Francisco: Aunt Lute Books, 1987), 79.
135. Anzaldúa writes, "Por la mujer de mi raza hablará el espíritu," referring to Vasconcelos's "Por mi raza hablará el espíritu." *Borderland*, 79.
136. Anzaldúa's "new mestiza" as a foundation for radical political identities has been a matter of much debate, especially within feminisms of "Women of Color" and "Third World Women."
137. Anzaldúa, *Borderland*, 83.

138. Hooker, *Hybrid Subjectivities*, 7.
139. Miller, *Rise and Fall of the Cosmic Race*, 37. Miller makes an interesting reading of Guillermo Gómez-Peña's postmodern and postcolonial, critical, and ironic resignifications of mestizaje in the context of globalization where deterritorialization and the rise of postnationalist hybridizations (e.g., humorously named *Chicariricuas*, a mix of Puerto Rican mulatto/a and Chicano mestizo/a), constitute the border as a global condition, setting the stage for a transnational "subversive mestizaje" wherein "Latino cultural production becomes the new, quintessential site of mestizaje, epitomized in the performance-based genres practiced by Gómez-Peña and Sifuentes." *Rise and Fall of the Cosmic Race*, 141-149.
140. Saldaña, as cited in Catelli, *Arqueología del mestizaje*, 258. The erasure of indigenous voices in mestizaje discourses and particularly in Chicano and Latinx accounts represents an important line of critique.
141. Making a decolonial move in the discussion, Catelli contends that "to compare the mestizajes of Anzaldúa and Vasconcelos . . . makes visible the subjective, discursive, and imaginary effects of the strategy of mestizaje in distinct scenarios, in the long duration of coloniality." *Arqueología del mestizaje*, 152-153.
142. Cornejo-Polar, "El discurso de la armonía imposible," 1.
143. See Mignolo, *The Idea of Latin America*; Laó-Montes and Dávila, *Mambo Montage*; Laó-Montes "Reconfigurations of Empire."
144. There are numerous debates between (and within) political-epistemic positionings and perspectives we can call as anticolonial, decolonial, postcolonial, and subalternist. See, e.g., John Beverley, *Subalternity and Representation. Arguments in Cultural Theory* (Durham, NC: Duke University Press, 1999); Silvia Rivera Cusicanqui *Ch'ixinakax utxiwa: Una reflexión sobre prácticas y discursos descolonizadores* (Buenos Aires: Tinta Limón, 2010); Santiago Castro-Gómez, *El tonto y los canallas: Notas para un republicanismo transmoderno* (Bogotá: Pontificia Universidad Católica, 2019); Agustín Laó-Montes and Jorge Daniel Vásquez, "Crítica decolonial de la filosofía y doble crítica en clave de Sur," in *Sujeto, decolonización, transmodernidad: Debates filosóficos latinoamericanos*, ed. Mabel Moraña (Madrid: Iberoamericana Editorial Vervuert, 2018).
145. Nelly Richard, "The Latin American Problematic of Theoretical-Cultural Transference: Postmodern Appropriations and Counter-appropriations," *South Atlantic Quarterly* 92, no. 3 (1993): 453. The argument of "appropriation-reconversion" to analyze transcultural bridges became a common staple of Latin American cultural studies, as can be seen in figures such as Néstor García Canclini and George Yúdice.
146. Latin American Marxisms have a long and complex history with discourses of mestizaje, as can be observed in Mariátegui's ambiguous reception of Vasconcelos: "no one has imagined the future of America with so much ambition or with such vehement hope as José Vasconcelos." Quote in Miller, *Rise and Fall of the Cosmic Race*, 28.
147. Tanya K. Hernández, "Envisioning the United States in the Latin American Myth of Racial Democracy Mestizaje," *Latin American and Caribbean Ethnic Studies* 11, no. 2 (2016): 199.
148. As cited in Hernández, "Envisioning the United States," 200.
149. Against the methodological nationalism that is common sense in comparative analyses of "race" and racism in the Americas, that tends to be framed in terms of a dichotomy between homogenized conceptions of racial formations in Latin American vis-à-vis the United States, we should cultivate rigorous historical investigations to research processes of ethnic-racial formation and racist regimes at local and national scales,

while identifying and analyzing regional patterns (historical and structural) of racial domination and racial politics. In fact, processes of racialization and racist regimes have not only national, but also translocal and transnational dimensions, as shown in the workings of forms of racialization ascribed to Latin America in the United States, which Bonilla-Silva calls the Latin Americanization of US racial relations. Such a line of research is represented by scholars such as Tanya K. Hernández, *Racial Subordination in Latin America: The Role of the State, Customary Law, and the New Civil Rights Response* (Cambridge: Cambridge University Press, 2014); Hooke, *Theorizing Race*; Laó-Montes, *Contrapunteos diaspóricos*.

150. Hernández, "Envisioning the United States," 200.
151. Hernández, "Envisioning the United States," 201. Hernández provides important examples, such as the fierce debate over the establishment of affirmative action in Brazilian universities between advocates in the Black movement in coalition with antiracist intellectuals developing critical race studies and Africana studies vis-à-vis a coalition of social actors from across the political spectrum (from right to left), who actively opposed affirmative action, many of them arguing that it was an import from US racial politics without applicability in Brazil.
152. Du Bois coined the category of "the color line" as a concept-metaphor to signify racial formations and racist regimes in the modern world that he conceived as a racialized modernity. As a signifier of "race," the "color line" was defined by color and configured by a matrix of power that includes global capitalism, white imperialism, racial states, and racialized exploitation of labor, which framed a global color line, a divide between "the darkest peoples of the world" in "Africa, Asia, Oceania" who live "behind a veil," and the hearts of Whiteness in Europe and people of European descent. W. E. B. Du Bois, *The Souls of Black Folk*, edited by Brent Hayes Edwards (New York, NY: Oxford University Press, 2009).
153. The hegemonic narrative within Black movements in Brazil is to unite "Pretos" (Blacks) and "Pardos" (Mulattoes) within the unifying category of "Negro." Scholarship in social science also demonstrates that "pretos" and "pardos" tend to share conditions of socioeconomic inequality and relative lack of political power. See, e.g., Paixão, *500 anos de solidão*; Paixão, *A lenda da modernidade encantada*; Telles, *Race in Another America*.
154. In fact, Black feminists such as Sueli Carneiro and Edna Roland were the first to coin the signifier "Afrodescendant" in the late 1980s as a political identity to group people of African descent not only of different skin colors but also of a diversity of locations (e.g., generational, territorial, class, gender, nationality) in the same political identity. However, the term *afrodescendiente* is more commonly used in Afro–Latin American regional politics than in Brazil, where "Negro" is the most widely used self-descriptor of the Black movement.
155. Manuel Zapata Olivella, *¡Levántate mulato! Por mi raza hablará el espíritu* (Bogotá: Rei Andes, 1990). In English, the title is "Stand-Up Mulatto: Spirit Will Speak through My Race."
156. Zapata Olivella, *¡Levantate mulato!*, 1.
157. For Afro-diasporic epistemic and political perspectives to understand and act upon the modern colonial world, against pervasive nationalism (methodological and political), see, e.g., Brent Hayes Edwards, *The Practice of Diaspora: Literature, Translation, and the Rise of Black Internationalism* (Cambridge, MA: Harvard University Press, 2003); Gilroy, *The Black Atlantic*; Agustín Laó-Montes, "Decolonial Moves: Trans-locating Afri-

can Diaspora Spaces," *Cultural Studies* 21, nos. 2–3 (2007): 309–338; Lorand J. Matory, *Black Atlantic Religion: Tradition, Transnationalism, and Matriarchy in Afro-Brazilian Candomblé* (Princeton, NJ: Princeton University Press, 2005).
158. I used the term *mulatez* though this chapter, following Martínez-Echazábal's historical "semiotics of mulatez," *Para una semiótica de la mulatez*. I also find useful Cortazzo González's concept of *mulatismo*, which he uses "to differentiate from the nationalist ideology of mestizaje proposed by White authors. Mulatismo, in my view, implies a critique of racial oppression in favor of ethnic liberation, which goes through destructuring epistemic colonialism. . . . Mulatismo hence, as a critical mestizaje, against positions that defend the existence of racial peace, a pacific mestizaje which mask[s] the reality of discrimination that will prolong Eurocentric Creole power" Cortazzo González, "El mulato cósmico."
159. For a conceptualization of the Caribbean as a crossroads of modernity—on the one hand, a colonial laboratory of imperial designs and capitalist development, and on the other hand, a creative ground for modernities of liberation and alternatives to modernity—see Laó-Montes, "Caribbean Borderlands."
160. Hooker, *Hybrid Subjectivities*, 13.

BIBLIOGRAPHY

Abu-Lughod, Janet. *Before European Hegemony: The World System A.D. 1250–1350*. New York: Oxford University Press, 1991.

Amado, Jorge. *Tenda dos milagres*. 1969. São Paolo: Record, 2001.

———. *Tent of Miracles*. Translated by Barbara Shelby. New York: Alfred A. Knopf, 1971.

Anthias, Floya, and Nira Yuval-Davis. *Racialized Boundaries: Race, Nation, Gender, Colour and Class and the Anti-Racist Struggle*. London: Routledge, 1993.

Anzaldúa, Gloria. *Borderland-La Frontera: The New Mestiza*. San Francisco: Aunt Lute Books, 1987.

Beverley, John. *Subalternity and Representation: Arguments in Cultural Theory*. Durham, NC: Duke University Press, 1999.

Bhabha, Homi. *The Location of Culture*. London: Routledge, 1994.

Braudel, Fernand. *Civilization and Capitalism, 15th-18th Century*. Vol. 3, *The Perspective of the World*. Berkeley: University of California Press, 1992.

———. *The Mediterranean and the Mediterranean World in the Age of Philip II*. Vol. 1. Berkeley: University of California Press, 1996.

Buscaglia-Salgado, José F. *Undoing Empire: Race and Nation in the Mulatto Caribbean*. Minneapolis: University of Minnesota Press, 2003.

Cadena, Marisol de la, ed. *Formaciones de indianidad: Articulaciones raciales, mestizaje y nación en América Latina*. Bogotá: Editorial Envion, 2007.

Cadena, Marisol de la. *Indigenous Mestizos: The Politics of Race and Culture in Cuzco, Peru, 1919–1991*. Durham, NC: Duke University Press, 2000.

Castro-Gómez, Santiago. *El tonto y los canallas: Notas para un republicanismo transmoderno*. Bogotá: Pontificia Universidad Católica, 2019.

Catelli, Laura. *Arqueología del mestizaje: Colonialismo y racialización*. Temuco: UFRO UP & CLACSO, 2020.

Cornejo Polar, Antonio. "El discurso de la armonía imposible (El Inca Garcilaso de la Vega: Discurso y recepción social)." *Revista de Crítica Literaria Latinoamericana* 19, no. 38 (1993): 73–80.

Coronil, Fernando. *The Fernando Coronil Reader*. Durham, NC: Duke University Press, 2019.

———. "Mas allá del occidentalismo: Hacia categorias geo-historicas no-imperialistas." In *Teorías sin disciplina: Latinoamericanismo, poscolonialidad y globalización del debate*, edited by Santiago Castro-Gómez and Eduardo Mendieta. Mexico City: Editorial Miguel Ángel Porrúa, 1998.

Cortazzo González, Uruguay. "El mulato cósmico: Relectura del mestizaje en Manuel Zapata Olivella." *Literatura y Autoritarismo*, no. 19 (2017): 19–28.

Covarrubias Orozco, Sebastián de. *Tesoro de la lengua castellana o española*. Madrid: Luis Sanchez, 1611.

Degler, Carl. *Neither Black nor White: Slavery and Race Relations in Brazil and the United States*. New York: Macmillan, 1971.

DeGuzman, Maria. *Spain's Long Shadow: The Black Legend, Off-Whiteness, and Anglo-American Empire*. Minneapolis: University of Minnesota Press, 2005.

Diop, Cheikh Anta. *The African Origin of Civilization: Myth or Reality*. Chicago: Chicago Review Press, 1989.

Du Bois, W. E. B. *The Souls of Black Folk*. Edited by Brent Hayes Edward. New York: Oxford University Press, 2009.

Dussel, Enrique. *1492: El encubrimiento del otro: Hacia el origen del "mito de la modernidad": Conferencias de Frankfurt, Octubre de 1992*. Bogotá: Antropos, 1992.

———. *The Underside of Modernity: Apel, Ricoeur, Rorty, Taylor and the Philosophy of Liberation*, trans. Eduardo Mendieta. Atlantic Highlands, NJ: Humanities Press, 1996.

Edwards, Brent Hayes. *The Practice of Diaspora: Literature, Translation, and the Rise of Black Internationalism*. Cambridge, MA: Harvard University Press, 2003.

Freyre, Gilberto. *Casa-grande e senzala: Formação da família brasileira sob o regime da economia patriarcal*. São Paolo: Livraria José Olympio Editora, 1933.

———. *The Masters and the Slaves: A Study in the Development of Brazilian Civilization*. Translated by Samuel Putnam. New York: Alfred A. Knopf, 1964.

Gilroy, Paul. *The Black Atlantic: Modernity and Double Consciousness*. Cambridge, MA: Harvard University Press, 1993.

Glissant, Édouard. "Creolization in the Making of the Americas." *Caribbean Quarterly* 54, nos. 1–2 (2008): 81–89.

———. *Poetics of Relation*. Ann Arbor: University of Michigan Press, 1997.

Góes, Juliana. "Brazil in Du Bois: Challenges to Build a Trans-American Pan-Africanism." In *Du Bois on Latin America and the Caribbean: Trans-American Pan-Africanism and Global Sociology*, edited by Juliana Góes et al. Albany: State University of New York Press, 2023.

Gonzalez, Lélia. "A categoria político cultural de Amefricanidade." *Tempo Brasileiro*, nos. 92–93 (1988): 69–82.

Grataloup, Christian. *L'invention des continents*. Paris: Larousse, 2009.

Guanche Pérez, Jesús, and José Antonio Matos Arévalo, eds. *Fernando Ortiz contra la raza y los racismos*. Havana: Editorial Nuevo Milenio, 2013.

Guillén, Nicolás. *Songoro Consongo: Poema mulato.* Havana: Biblioteca Americana, 1931.

Hall, Stuart. *The Fateful Triangle: Race, Ethnicity, Nation.* W. E. B. Du Bois Lectures. Cambridge, MA: Harvard University Press, 2017.

Helg, Aline. *Liberty and Equality in Caribbean Colombia 1770–1835.* Chapel Hill: University of North Carolina Press, 2004.

———. *Our Rightful Share: The Afro-Cuban Struggle for Equality 1886–1912.* Chapel Hill: University of North Carolina Press, 1995.

Hering Torres, Max S. "Colores de piel: Una revisión histórica de larga duración." In *Debates sobre ciudadanía y políticas raciales en las Américas Negras,* edited by Claudia Mosquera-Rosero-Labbé et al., 113–160. Bogotá: Universidad Nacional de Colombia and Universidad del Valle, 2010.

———. *Rassismus in der Vormoderne: Die "Reinheit des Blutes" im Spanien der Frühen Neuzeit.* Frankfurt: Campus Verlag, 2006.

Hering Torres, Max S., María Elena Martínez, and David Nirenberg, eds. *Race and Blood in the Iberian World.* Zurich: LIT Verlag, 2012.

Hernández, Tanya K. "Envisioning the United States in the Latin American Myth of Racial Democracy Mestizaje." *Latin American and Caribbean Ethnic Studies* 11, no. 2 (2016): 189–205.

———. *Multiracials and Civil Rights: Mixed-Race Stories of Discrimination.* New York: New York University Press, 2018.

———. *Racial Subordination in Latin America. The Role of the State, Customary Law, and the New Civil Rights Response.* Cambridge: Cambridge University Press, 2014.

Hevia Lanier, Oilda. *El directorio central de las sociedades negras de Cuba (1884–1894).* Havana: Editorial Ciencias Sociales, 1996.

Hill Collins, Patricia. *Intersectionality as Critical Theory.* Durham, NC: Duke University Press, 2019.

Hooker, Juliet. "Hybrid Subjectivities, Latin American Mestizaje, and Latino Political Thought on Race." *Politics, Groups, and Identities* 2, no. 2 (2014): 188–201.

———. *Theorizing Race in the Americas: Douglass, Sarmiento, Du Bois, and Vasconcelos.* New York: Oxford University Press, 2016.

Joseph, Gilbert, Catherine LeGrand, Ricardo Donato Salvatore, eds. *Close Encounters of Empire: Writing the Cultural History of US-Latin American Relations.* Durham, NC: Duke University Press, 1998.

Kutzinski, Vera M. *Sugar's Secrets: Race and the Erotics of Cuban Nationalism.* Charlottesville: University Press of Virginia, 1993.

Laó-Montes, Agustín. "Caribbean Borderlands and Travelling Theories: Imperial Frontier, Translocal Nations, Federation of Diasporas, Planetary Archipelago." In *Liquid Borders: Migration as Resistance,* edited by Mabel Moraña. Abingdon, UK: Routledge, 2020.

———. *Contrapunteos diaspóricos: Cartografías políticas de nuestra Afroamerica.* Bogotá: Universidad Externado de Colombia, 2020.

———. "Decolonial Moves: Trans-locating African Diaspora Spaces." *Cultural Studies* 21, no. 2–3 (2007): 309–338.

———. "Reconfigurations of Empire in a World-Hegemonic Transition: The 1898 Spanish-

Cuban-American-Filipino War." In *Revisiting the Colonial Question in Latin America*, edited by Mabel Moraña and Carlos A. Jáuregui. Madrid: Iberoamericana Editorial Vervuert, 2008.

Laó-Montes, Agustín, and Arlene Dávila, eds. *Mambo Montage: The Latinization of New York*. New York: Columbia University Press, 2001.

Laó-Montes, Agustín, and Jorge Daniel Vásquez. "Crítica decolonial de la filosofía y doble crítica en clave de Sur." In *Sujeto, decolonización, transmodernidad: Debates filosóficos latinoamericanos*, edited by Mabel Moraña. Madrid: Iberoamericana Editorial Vervuert, 2018.

Lasso, Marixa. *Myths of Harmony: Race and Republicanism during the Age of Revolution, Colombia, 1795–1831*. Pittsburgh, PA: University of Pittsburgh Press, 2007.

Martí, José. *Nuestra América*. 1891. Critical ed. Guadalajara, Mexico: Universidad de Guadalajara, 2002.

Martínez, María Elena. *Genealogical Fictions: Limpieza de Sangre, Religion, and Gender in Colonial Mexico*. Stanford, CA: Stanford University Press, 2008.

Martínez-Echazábal, Lourdes. "Mestizaje and the Discourse of National/Cultural Identity in Latin America, 1845–1959." *Latin American Perspectives* 25, no. 3 (1998): 21–42.

———. *Para una semiótica de la mulatez*. Madrid: J. Porrúa Turanzas, 1990.

Matory, Lorand J. *Black Atlantic Religion: Tradition, Transnationalism, and Matriarchy in Afro-Brazilian Candomblé*. Princeton, NJ: Princeton University Press, 2005.

Médéric Moreau de Saint-Méry. *A Civilization That Perished: The Last Years of White Colonial Rule in Haiti*. Lanham, MD: University Press of America, 1985.

Mignolo, Walter. *The Idea of Latin America*. Malden, MA: Blackwell, 2006.

Miller, Marilyn Grace. *Rise and Fall of the Cosmic Race: The Cult of Mestizaje in Latin America*. Austin: University of Texas Press, 2004.

Múnera, Alfonso. *El fracaso de la nación*. Bogotá: Crítica, 2000.

Ortiz, Fernando. *Cuban Counterpoint: Tobacco and Sugar*. Translated by Harriet de Onís. Durham, NC: Duke University Press, 1995.

———. *Contrapunteo cubano del tabaco y azúcar*. 1940. Havana: Editorial de Ciencias Sociales, 1983.

———. *Hampa afro-cubana: Los negros brujos: Apuntes para un estudio de etnología criminal*. Madrid: Librería de Fernando Fé, 1906.

Paixão, Marcelo. *500 anos de solidão: Ensaios sobre as desigualdades raciais no Brasil*. Curitiba: Appris, 2013.

———. *A lenda da modernidade encantada: Por uma critica ao pensamento social brasileiro sobre relações raciais e projeto de Estado-nação*. Curitiba, Brazil: Editora CRV, 2014.

Paschel, Tianna. *Becoming Black Political Subjects: Movements and Ethno-Racial Rights in Colombia and Brazil*. Princeton, NJ: Princeton University Press, 2016.

Poole, Deborah. *Vision, Race, and Modernity: A Visual Economy of the Andean Image World*. Princeton, NJ: Princeton University Press, 1997.

Quijano, Aníbal. "Colonialidad del poder y clasificación social." *Journal of World Systems Research* 11, no. 2 (2000): 342–386.

———. *Modernidad, identidad y utopía en América Latina*. Lima: Sociedad y Política Ediciones, 1988.

Richard, Nelly. "The Latin American Problematic of Theoretical-Cultural Transference: Postmodern Appropriations and Counter-appropriations." *South Atlantic Quarterly* 92, no. 3 (1993): 453–459.

Ríos Ávila, Rubén. *La raza cómica del sujeto en Puerto Rico*. San Juan: Ediciones Callejón, 2002.

Rivera Cusicanqui, Silvia. *Ch'ixinakax utxiwa: Una reflexión sobre prácticas y discursos descolonizadores*. Buenos Aires: Tinta Limón, 2010.

———. *Violencias (re)encubiertas en Bolivia*. La Paz: Mirada Salvaje, 2010.

Sarmiento, Domingo F. *Facundo: Or, Civilization and Barbarism*. 1845. New York: Penguin Classics.

Schultz, Alfred P. *Race or Mongrel*. Boston: Page, 1908.

Telles, Edward. *Race in Another America: The Significance of Skin Color in Brazil*. Princeton, NJ: Princeton University Press, 2006.

Trouillot, Michel-Rolph. *Global Transformations: Anthropology and the Modern World*. New York: Palgrave Macmillan, 2004.

Vasconcelos, José. *Bolivarismo y monroísmo: Temas iberoamericanos*. Santiago de Chile: Ediciones Ercilla, 1937.

———. *Indología: Una interpretación de la cultura ibero-americana*. Barcelona: Agencia Mundial de Librería, 1926.

———. *La raza cósmica, misión de la raza iberoamericana*. Madrid: Agencia Mundial de Librería, 1925.

Vinson, Ben, III. *Before Mestizaje: The Frontiers of Race and Caste in Colonial Mexico*. Cambridge: Cambridge University Press, 2017.

Wallerstein, Immanuel. *The Essential Wallerstein*. New York: New Press, 2000.

Zapata Olivella, Manuel. *¡Levántate mulato! Por mi raza hablará el espíritu*. Bogotá: Rei Andes, 1990.

CHAPTER 13

Genealogy of Indigenist Translations

From Colonized Methodologies to Indigenous Self-Determination in Peru, Twentieth and Twenty-First Centuries

CHRISTIAN ELGUERA

Indigenism on Trial

In his seminal work *La narrativa indigenista peruana*, Tomás Escajadillo argues that a genuine indigenist work relies not only on a social vindication but also on "enough proximity" to the represented world.[1] In dialogue with this author, I propose that my concept of indigenist translation articulates a variety of dissimilar authors that have one essential indigenist characteristic in common.[2] From aesthetical to social perspectives, indigenist translators manifest the desire to speak for the Other, the ambition to create a representation on Indigenous realities according to the political and literary projects of non-Indigenous intellectuals. In *Siete ensayos de interpretación de la realidad peruana* (*Seven Interpretive Essays on Peruvian Reality*, 1928), José Carlos Mariátegui, one of the foremost Peruvian politicians and founder of the Peruvian Socialist Party, described the transition from non-Indigenous to Indigenous literatures.[3] In his essay "Proceso de la literatura," Mariátegui discussed the works of indigenists who decided to represent Andean realities, landscapes, and characters in their oeuvres. In a noteworthy paragraph, he pointed out that "Indigenist literature cannot give us a strictly authentic version of the Indian, for it must idealize and stylize him. Nor can it give us his soul. It is still a mestizo literature and as such is called indigenist rather than indigenous."[4] In the following decades after Mariátegui, mestizo and creole intellectuals employed Western categories to understand the Andes rather than promote the sovereignty of Indigenous subjects. In this regard, my conception of Indigenism is not limited to one specific historical period or cultural practice. Politicians from conservative or revolutionary positions, literati, social scientists, and terrorist groups forged an Indigenist "system that belongs to Western cultural conventions."[5] From 1900 to the present day, this system produced stereotypes, prejudices, and misrepresentations about Andean cultures, or a colonial genealogy of indigenist translations.[6]

Susan Bassnett notes that "the study and practice of translation is inevitably an exploration of power relationships within textual practice that reflect power structures within the wider cultural context."[7] Therefore, this chapter presents a genealogy of indigenist translations, that is to say, the acts of translating indigeneity from national, multicultural, and neoliberal assumptions. As these translations penetrate every crevice of political and academic debates about Peruvian Indianness and Mestizaje, we must explain how they authorize social hierarchies and practices of racialization. Indigenist writers or politicians translated Indigenous cultures for non-Indigenous audiences following precepts and ideologies from their own realities. In other words, mestizo and creole intellectuals understood or interpreted Andean lives according to colonial methodologies. As a result, Indigenous people became objects of research. As Linda Tuhiwai Smith notes: "The objects of research do not have a voice and do not contribute to research or science. In fact, the logic of the argument would suggest that it is impossible, ridiculous even, to suggest that the object of research can contribute to anything."[8] In the process of translation, the original Indigenous culture lost its sovereignty. As a result, the "translated Indian" repeats the ethnocentric script proposed by the indigenist translator. As a tool of colonial methodologies, indigenist discourses could be understood also as ethnocentric translations that "achieves a systematic negation of the strangeness [Indianness]."[9] Therefore, the Indigenism studied in this chapter expresses "a style that facilitates the textualization of other cultures, that encourages the construction of diagrammatic answers to complex cultural questions."[10] This diagrammatic project consists of the "domestication" of foreign ways of living. Following Burton Raffel's ideas, we can perceive that indigenist translators "enter [a] territory controlled by custom and habit (that is, culture), rather than by mere lexica."[11] Custom and habit refer to what Talad Asad calls "ways of living," or to Indigenous ontological, epistemic, and political practices that intellectuals and politicians translate to control or domesticate radical alterities. Thus, indigenism refers "not to linguistic matter per se, but to [Indigenous] 'modes of thought' that are embodied in such matter."[12] My understanding of Indigenism as a cultural translation that perpetuates colonial relationships relies on the anthropological works of Marisol de la Cadena and Eduardo Viveiros de Castro. On the one hand, de la Cadena understands translation as a process that connects and separates multiple ontological and epistemic practices. On the other hand, de Castro conceives translation as an interpretation "of the 'native's' practical and discursive concepts into the terms of anthropology's conceptual apparatus."[13]

Indigenist translators explained to national and international readers what it is to be Indigenous, how they think, feel and live, and highlighted hierarchies and distances between non-Natives and the others. As the historian Rebecca Earle suggests, Mexican and Peruvian indigenists supported the project of a mestizo nation to underscore the foreignness and remoteness of Native peoples in the twentieth century.[14] Mestizaje sought to control radical differences, promoting a national propaganda of Aztec and Inca symbols. In this way, the indigenist project reflects what Chakrabarty calls historicism or a lineal history that divides between the Indigenous past and the desired modernization.[15] Mariátegui, in dialogue with other Peruvian intellectuals like Manuel González Prada and Luis E. Valcárcel, translated Indigenous culture as the starting point of the future country. Peru would have to be communist, but taking into account its Native ancestry. With regard to this Inca evocation, Peruvian indigenists manifested an essentialist viewpoint about indigeneity, ignoring historical differences between pre-Hispanic Incas and coetaneous peasants.[16]

In his book *The Impure Imagination* (2006), Joshua Lund explores how Mexican intellectuals reinvented the notion of mestizaje as a symbol of unity in opposition to the negative perspectives of European thinkers about fusion or hybridity. Lund suggests that José Vasconcelos in *La raza cósmica* (1925) and *Indología* (1926) epitomizes a positive conception of mestizaje to consolidate a unified Mexican nation in which cultural differences converge in one identity or one race.[17] In this light, mestizaje became the principal characteristic of nationalization, a national symbol that distinguished Mexico from other countries. In his next publication, *The Mestizo State*, Lund highlights that such a conception of race is insufficient and he prefers to recognize the materiality of racial struggles.[18] In this vein, he states that race is "the concept around which the actual political battle over land resources comes to light and is rendered narrative. Racialization is the aesthetic mode for the representation of this battle."[19] Lund's statement is crucial because of its rereading of race and mestizaje. In conclusion, the mestizo is more than a mixed person or the symbol of a mixed nation; she/he is a kind of settler who tries to conquer Indigenous lands and impose national sovereignty according to racial discourses. In this light, I contend that intercultural translation was a central resource to impose mestizo's authority over Native territories and identities.

Indigenist translators do not promote interruptions or defiance to the projects of mestizo/creole nations. If "a good translation is one that allows the alien concepts to deform and subvert the translator's conceptual toolbox," then Indigenism just had satisfied the frameworks and expectations of non-Indigenous intellectuals and politicians about Native peoples.[20] Indigenists produce their own Indians, promoting a petrified cultural body. In this regard, Enrique López Albújar wrote in "Como habla la coca": "The Indian, without knowing it, is a Schopenhaurenist" fixing an identity to colonized peoples.[21] Indigenism legitimized a project of colonialism that sought to define Native ways of living. Considering this hegemony, it is important to remember with Frantz Fanon that "the immobility to which the colonized subject is condemned can be challenged only if he decides to put an end to the history of colonization."[22] When the colonized subject speaks for themselves, we enter the complexities of self-translation and self-determination. In recent years, Native activists and writers have rewritten the legacy of literary and governmental Indigenism. Their decolonial task is not easy, given the hegemony of indigenist modes of knowing.[23] In this vein, it is plausible to formulate this question: is it possible to imagine Indigenous histories and identities beyond the commands of the mestizo-creole intelligentsia?

Race, Exoticism, and Cultural Translation

In Peru, between the end of 1800 and the first years of the twentieth century, two young and prominent scholars proposed cultural translations of Indigenous people marked by a racial thought. On the one hand, Clemente Palma in his bachelor thesis *El porvenir de las razas en el Perú* (1897) argued that the Indian was "stupid, because of the weakness of his personality and rational inactivity."[24] Indeed, Palma noted that "the Indian never tries to make contact with the elements of superman's progress."[25] On the other hand, José de la Riva Agüero y Osma highlighted in *Carácter de la literatura del Perú independiente* (1905): "The Indian is resentful; he detests the white man and the mestizo with all his energy ... In his mind, in a parallel fashion to the slaves, the Indian accumulates mortal and eternal aversions."[26] In another paragraph, the academic considers that the real problem was not the Indian, but the geography in which he resides. The Andean highlands were a truculent and sordid scenery according to Riva Agüero's perspective. He affirms: "In the Andes there is something diabolic and bewitched."[27] After reading both texts, the reader could ask: what was the contact between Palma, Riva Agüero, and Andean peoples? It is worth remembering the notion of intimacy proposed by Spivak as follows: "Translation is the most intimate act of reading."[28] The reading of Palma and Riva Agüero relied on racial preconceptions that accentuated distances between their intellectual group and inferior native cultures.[29]

In the first decades of the twentieth century, indigenist translators annulled the presence of real Indians and, simultaneously, recognized the value of ancestral traditions, namely the Inca legacy. For example, José Santos Chocano, a well-known poet in the Peruvian fin de siècle literature, wrote many poems focused on Andean customs. Chocano dedicates his poetry collection *Alma América* (1906) to the Spanish king. The poet explains to Alfonso XIII: "There is in my verses nothing but warmth and vitality: / The Andes transmit the life to my stanzas."[30] In the famous poem "Blason," the author acknowledges the Indigenous heritage in his own body. However, the lyric speaker feels an admiration for the Inca civilization, ignoring the economic and social realities of contemporary Native subjects. "Blason" must be read as advocacy for a mestizaje that reduces and controls indigeneity as we can see in this line: "When I am Inca, I give my tribute to the Sun."[31] In other moments, Chocano declares the superiority of Spain over Indigenous cultures, remarking that "the Andes are silvery, but the Spaniard Lion is made with gold," "The blood is Spanish, but the beat is Inca."[32] In comparison to the evident racism of Palma and Riva Agüero, Chocano expresses a type of violence characterized by the exoticization and cultural appropriation of Andean societies. However, in both cases, these indigenist translators forged a figure that Alcida Rita Ramos has called "the virtual Indian" to understand how the Brazilian government had controlled the life and identities of Indigenous peoples.[33]

Enrique López Albújar, another contemporary of Palma, Riva Agüero, and Chocano, published a short-story collection called *Cuentos andinos* (1920).

In texts such as "Los tres jircas," "Cómo habla la coca," and "El brindis de los yayas," López Albújar transforms Quechua ontologies and epistemologies into exotic or primitive habits. Rather than create a cultural dialogue between lettered audiences and Indigenous subjects, the narrator prefers to remark on the inferiority and otherness of highlanders. In addition, the author deliberately translates Quechua pluriverses into fictional worlds. Therefore, the interaction between the *jircas*, or mountains, became something absurd or impossible in the anthropocentric discourse of Western culture endorsed by the writer. This tendency to use Indigenous knowledge as a literary trope was also repeated by younger generations. In "El alfarero," Abraham Valdelomar converted Indigenous world-making practices into magic or malefic rituals.[34] In another narration, "El camino hacia el sol," Valdelomar translates the Inca Empire as an Arcadian geography in which everything is perfect and beautiful. His indigenist translation could be seen as the fictionalization of Native ancestral knowledge, perpetuating the unreality and exotism of Indigenous worlds.

Translating the Andes from a Revolutionary Viewpoint

Notwithstanding the intellectual efforts to essentialize or idealize Andean culture, we can identify numerous Indigenous rebellions in southern Peru. The Rumi Maqui rebellion in 1915, for example, demonstrated to Lima audiences that native subjects existed beyond indigenist translations, that is to say, beyond passivity, stupidity, inferiority, and exoticization.[35] During the decades of 1920 and 1930, a new cohort of intellectuals denounced colonial violence against Andean peoples on haciendas. Authors such as Pedro Zulen, Dora Mayer, José Carlos Mariátegui, and Gamaliel Churata conceived of the hacienda regime as a feudal practice that impeded the development of the country. As an example of the inhuman conditions of labor in Peruvian haciendas—principally in the North and in the Andes—I want to mention the testimony of Juan H. Pévez, a peasant leader from Ica on the coast. Pévez's testimony tells of exploitation the during the 1920s in a coastal city. For Pévez, the hacienda was "an small state into the Peruvian large state," referring with these words to the power of *hacendados* to control and exterminate peasant lives.[36] In this light, magazines such as *Amauta, El Boletín Titikaka, La Sierra,* and *Chirapu* considered that Andean realities were a fundamental resource for imagining a new nation.[37] A variety of writers depicted the violence on haciendas and the everyday practices of highlanders, creating networks between rural realities and urban audiences. The worry of these intellectuals about the role of Indians in the country implies the production of another kind of indigenist translation. It demanded social and economic justice in the Andes. However, this *indigenismo* also imposed foreign categories over Indigenous realities. In early essays, in particular *Tempestad en los Andes* (1927), Luis E. Valcárcel articulates what could be called a philanthropic translation of Indigenous lives. With pompous style, Valcárcel idealizes Inca legacies to demonstrate that the Andes were the pillar of the nation. Reflecting on the identity of the country, Valcárcel proposes that Indianness was the epitome of authenticity or nationalism. Indeed, the author connects Andean uprisings with the communist doctrine of that period. We can read in a famous statement that "the indigenous proletariat waits for Lenin." In this light, I contend that *Tempestad* perceived Indigenous and peasant populations through the lens of mestizo expectations. Valcárcel traces a program of rebellions to confront the hegemony of latifundistas and *gamonales* in Andean communities. This point reveals his interest in vindicating underrepresented collectives. Nonetheless, the author never looks at the projects of Native subjects themselves. The indigenist translator produces a script that must be performed by the others. To be sure, this generation of indigenists assumed that this script was the most appropriate to resolve the social stratification in Andean communities.[38]

José Carlos Mariátegui, who wrote the prologue to *Tempestad*, promptly reoriented Valcárcel's ideas in his own oeuvre. Thus, in the mid-1920s, we can observe a transition from philanthropic to revolutionary translations that will determine the representations of Andean people in the next decades. Influenced by Louis Baudin's thesis on the socialism of the Incas, Mariátegui argued that Soviet socialism was a logical model to implement in Peru. For Mariátegui, land issues were crucial in the configuration of the peasant agency. Nevertheless, for him, the political horizon of peasantry would be their insertion into socialist regimes of power. Socialism's agents envisioned the peasantry as representative of a productive force in favor of a revolutionary economy. Certainly, Mariátegui did not hope for a mechanical imposition or translational circuit from one reality to another. In fact, he insisted Peruvian socialism was "neither imitation nor copy" of the Russian political system.[39] However, Mariátegui developed an intimate relation between socialism and Indigenous cultures in his conceptions of Peruvian identity and progress.[40] In other words, he preferred to build a socialist nation rather than recognize existing Indigenous political and ontological practices.[41]

The dilemma of indigenist translators between 1920 and 1930 was between imposing their own sociopolitical interests or attempting to understand ancestral ways of knowledge and politics in Andean societies. For example, the category of "El nuevo indio" coined by Uriel García illustrates the distance between *indigenismo* and Native experiences in Andean geographies. García translated Indians following doctrines of national mestizaje and discourses of cultural essentialization, in particular about the role of Indigenous women as symbols of pure indigeneity.[42] By contrast, Gamaliel Churata was one of the authors who most probably tried to understand Indigenous cultures from a Native viewpoint. In parallel with his political activity, Churata wrote poems and literary pieces as an advance of his seminal novel *El pez de oro*.[43] Because of familial and economic difficulties, he never published the book until 1957. Without a doubt, *El pez de oro* mirrors the desires of mestizo intellectuals to understand Indigenous realities from a cultural perspective.[44] However, in contrast to *Tempestad* and Mariátegui's writings, the text also signals an attempt to make visible the multiple ontologies that constitute Indigenous territories such as the worlds of the dog Thumos and the powerful beings of Lake Titicaca.[45]

César Vallejo's works also illustrate the intricacies of the indigenist translation. In "Literature on Trial," José Carlos Mariátegui recognizes that Vallejo's poetry, in particular *Los heraldos negros* (1919), reveals an Indigenous sensitivity. For Mariátegui, poems such as "Idilio muerto" and "Ausente" manifest the nostalgia and pessimism of the Indian population. However, Vallejo's translation is more complex than the supposed melancholy suggested by Mariátegui and other intellectuals during this period (e.g., Luis Alberto Sánchez). For example, in his novel *Fabla salvaje* (1923), Vallejo translates a pathological aesthetic to an Andean village. The protagonist of this narration, Balta, seems the hero of a gothic novel rather than an Andean commoner. In a subsequent novel, *Hacia el reino de los Sciris* (concluded in 1927), Vallejo remarks on the warlike attitude of the Inca society.[46] As an intercultural translator, we can see Vallejo investigated the practices, rites and traditions of this Indigenous empire. In contrast with Valdelomar's exoticism, Vallejo tries to be a faithful translator who re-creates the historical conquest of the Incas over the Sciris and the Chachapoyas. In subsequent years, Vallejo's act of translating oscillates between the imperial past and the present resistances of the Andean populace. For example, *El tungsteno* (1931) is an impressive novel that defies several injustices against the townspeople of La Oroya, one of the most important mining centers in those years. Here, the communist ideology impregnates the resolutions of Vallejo as a translator, who highlights the sociopolitical struggles of the Andean workers against capitalist corporations. The last of Vallejo's narrative work, the play *La piedra cansada* (concluded in 1937), fuses Inca history and socialist standpoints. This dramatic piece comprises the political, literary, and cultural interest of Vallejo as an indigenist translator. In *La piedra cansada*, the Inca systems represent a hierarchical society in which the Indians are valuable only for their workforce to construct temples. Topor, one of the workers, became an Inca after playing a salient role in the war against the *kobras*.[47] Here, Vallejo is a translator who edits and transforms an original text (the Inca world) according to his ideological and literary viewpoints. First, Topor's coronation as Inca mirrors a communist perspective about a society in which there are no social hierarchies. Second, the *kobras* are fictitious people invented by the author to create a climate of adventure and suspense. By the same token, Vallejo conceives Topor not as an Indigenous warrior, but as a mortified character who kills the princess Oruya and resigns as Inca to live a mortified destiny.

José Maria Arguedas: Mestizaje, Peasants Uprisings, and Ontological Translations

After the discussions of the 1920s and 1930s, the decades of 1950 and 1960 constituted a crucial moment in the production of indigenist translations. If Ciro Alegría epitomized the social engagement of *indigenismo* in novels such as *Los perros hambrientos* and *El mundo es ancho y ajeno*, the literary and anthropological work of José Maria Arguedas offers a glimpse of the complexities, contradictions, and changes of Andean peoples in parallel with the rise of the Peruvian social sciences.[48] Throughout the 1950s, Arguedas argued that the mestizo was the most representative figure of the Andes due to centuries of cultural exchange between Quechua and Western cultures. He expressed this idea in his most famous novel, *Los ríos profundos* (*Deep Rivers*).[49] At a formal level, the writing of this novel reflects the regional variety of Andean Spanish in Peru. Meanwhile, in reference to the content, the protagonist, Ernesto, is a young mestizo who maintains solidarity with oppressed Quechua people, such as the *chicheras* or *colonos*.[50] The narrator's language and Ernesto's behavior demonstrate how Arguedas, in dialogue with *indigenismo*, favored the role of the mestizo mediator over other characters in the Peruvian Andes. According to the Kichwa scholar Armando Muyolema, *indigenismo* comprises a mestizo strategy to annul or control Indigenous voices.[51] For instance, a national project of miscegenation addresses Arguedas's attention to Quechua in the 1950s.[52] The mestizo nation recognizes a specific type of indigeneity that evokes the notion of *indio permitido*, that is to say, the Indian as "a reified, postcard image of the Indigenous culture while preserving the unquestioned cultural hegemony of the mestizo and creole elites in the daily fabric of social life."[53]

By contrast, in the Quechua poems *Tupac Amaru Kamaq Taytanchisman* (1962), *Todas las sangres* (1964) and *El zorro de arriba y el zorro de abajo* (1971), Arguedas reformulated his conception of Indianness.[54] The numerous peasant uprisings between 1950 and 1960 were a pivotal factor in Arguedas's turn.[55] In a letter to John Murra, Arguedas recognized the influence of Andean resistances in his 1962 Quechua poem. After a long period of oppression, the peasants claimed the land as a way to confront the hegemonic power of latifundism in the region. This regime of power signified the humiliation and subjugation of Indigenous and peasant bodies. If latifundism was a dominant economic model in Cusco, we can observe the progress of the mining industry in Cerro de Pasco, headed by the Cerro de Pasco Corporation. Mining also involves the territorial expansion of colonizers to the end of reinforcing the financial development of the country. This colonial situation motivated the peasant insurgency, which consisted of invasions or seizures. Faced with this situation, the Peruvian government claimed sovereignty over Indigenous and peasant territories as a way to protect latifundism, mining, and national security.[56]

Peasants organized rebellions in cooperation with leftist allies such as Hugo Blanco and Hector Bejar. Notwithstanding these alliances, the Peruvian left ignored the peasants' territorial assumptions. Considering that many leftist leaders and *guerrilleros* "remained separated from the peasantry by an immense cultural and linguistic barrier which they never were able to surmount," Quechua practices of politics and territoriality lost their importance.[57] In her research about the fight of Mariano Turpo, Marisol de la Cadena explains how peasant leaders, and notably their ways of relating to nonhuman agents or Earth beings, were fully ignored by leftist programs. Mariano Turpo, like many other Runa (Quechua) peasant figures, was an impossible existence to Western political thought. Leftists never took the interaction among humans and nonhumans seriously, considering it a "superstition," "a delusion," and a "remnant of the past."[58] By contrast, in *Tupac Amaru Kamaq Taytanchisman*, "La agonía de Rasu Ñiti," and *Todas las sangres*, Arguedas depicted the connections between Indigenous ontologies, epistemologies, and political agency.[59] In this vein, he foregrounds the role of nonhuman beings such as the Wamani (Mountain God) and the Amaru (Serpent God) in Indigenous social mobilizations.

Arguedas also considered that Andean subjects preserved their systems of knowledge and political organizations despite the process of migration to coastal cities. With regard to migration, Arguedas debated with members of the so-called Peruvian Generation of the 1950s, such as Luis Felipe Angell, Luis Jaime Cisneros, Julio Ramón Ribeyro, and Sebastián Salazar Bondy.[60] Such intellectuals advocated for a stereotypical translation of Andean migrants as victimized, acculturated, or alienated subjects. Unlike these representations, Arguedas conceived of migration as an opportunity to reinvigorate and disseminate Andean values around urban contexts. In *Tupac Amaru Kamaq Taytanchisman*, the reader can perceive an idealized perspective regarding forced displacement. However, it is important to note that this utopian translation sought to confront the discourses of assimilation and the destruction of ancestral practices. In 1965, in the famous roundtable about *Todas las sangres*, Arguedas and several renowned social scientists discussed two ways of translating Andean realities. On the one hand, Jorge Bravo Bresani, Henri Favre, and Aníbal Quijano proposed a translation according to which Indigenous traditions will disappear as a result of national progress and the process of *cholaje*.[61] On the other hand, Arguedas produced translations that emphasized the continuity of Quechua ontologies and epistemologies. To the social scientists, Arguedas's fictional work represented an unreal and old Andean culture in contrast to the modernization of the country.

In 1959, Arguedas started his translation of the Huarochirí manuscript from Quechua to Spanish.[62] Arguedas's first reaction to the manuscript was astonishment and fascination because of the cosmological world portrayed and the Quechua variation employed.[63] Arguedas, I contend, learned two considerable aspects from the Huarochirí world to write his last narrative project. First, the memory of powerful nonhuman beings (e.g., huacas, foxes) in the Peruvian coast—a place assumed to be without Native roots. Second, the variety of dialects in the same Indigenous language family. Regarding this point, it must be clear that the linguist Alfredo Torero helped Arguedas in the last and most strenuous stage of his translation in 1966. To be sure, the letters between Arguedas and Murra inform us about the struggles of Arguedas to translate this text, in particular the so-called supplements 1 and 2.[64] In fact, Arguedas's facet as translator was crucial to change his initial project of writing a monograph about Chimbote and to envisage the narrative universe of *El zorro de arriba y el zorro de abajo*. Therefore, I suggest reading this narration as an effort to transfer the cosmogonic and linguistic dimensions of an Indigenous text from the sixteenth century to the port city of Chimbote in the 1960s.

Arguedas identified in his posthumous novel how an accelerated process of industrialization devastated the lives of Quechua migrants in Chimbote. But he also perceived the continuation of Indigenous practices beyond capitalism and acculturation. For example, Chimbote is also populated by powerful nonhuman beings such as the fox Don Diego who revitalizes the sick bodies of Andean subjects. In contrast to translations that envisage an unstoppable modernization of the Andes, Arguedas imagines another translational perspective, namely ontological translation.[65] In other words, he described how Quechua peoples continued with their own political organizations, relationships with nonhuman entities, and sacred standpoints of territoriality into urban geographies at national and international scales without refusing Western cultural practices.

The Translator Juan Velasco Alvarado

On October 3, 1968, General Juan Velasco Alvarado led a coup against the Peruvian president Fernando Belaúnde Terry, inaugurating the Revolutionary Government of the Peruvian Armed Forces. This process impacted the political life of the country, promoting many laws such as educational reform and the nationalization of petroleum. The most significant policy instituted by Velasco's tenure was the Law by Decree 17716 for Agrarian Reform, issued on June 24, 1969.[66] The government implemented and executed this law following its plan to promote radical social change. However, rather than promote Indigenous sovereignties, Velasco's cultural translations focused on peasants as productive land laborers recognized by the nation-state. Velasco's Agrarian Reform consisted of the expropriation of haciendas in favor of the peasants who worked them. As we saw in preceding sections, the hacienda was a necropolitical space administered by *gamonales*, or landlords. As we saw in Pévez's testimony, the nefarious activities of *gamonales* were widespread across numerous haciendas until the 1969 Agrarian Reform. Therefore, Velasco successfully concluded a regime of colonial violence and promoted a vindication of the peasant Indigenous populace based on land rights. The military regime conferred land property to the hacienda workers to foster agricultural production according to national projects of modernization. With this goal in mind, the regime created state-administered syndicates that introduced the peasantry into an industrial economy. The syndicate meant the transformation of traditional communities into productive organizations under the control of the government. It is important to note that the agrarian reform truly benefited only one specific sector of the peasantry. For example, the former hacienda workers, who integrated into the national syndicate system, received more loans and portions of land for cultivating than the colonos or simple *comuneros* from adjacent communities.[67]

Translating rural populations into productive workers was possible thanks to efforts of the Sistema Nacional de Apoyo a la Movilización Social (National System of Support for Social Mobilization, SIN AMOS). SIN AMOS (lit., "without masters") disseminated the nationalist ideology of the state and imposed its power around the country, co-opting new partisans and sympathizers. SIN AMOS mirrored the project of cultural translation addressed by the armed forces. It is not a coincidence that it has been called the *aplanadora*, or the leveler, in allusion to its radical campaign of indoctrination, ignoring other political position taking. According to Heilman, SIN AMOS controlled and organized the "peasant participation in the agrarian reform."[68] Considering that the Peruvian military repressed guerrillas led by communist leaders and peasants, the 1969 Agrarian Reform tried to prevent new revolts in the Andes, highlighting the military's ability "to handle peasant uprisings."[69] Indeed, the revolutionary government issued Decree Law 19400, which sought to replace peasant organizations in favor of national agrarian leagues and federations. Considering these official translations, the Confederación Campesina del Perú (Peruvian Peasant Confederation, CCP) and its general secretary, Manuel Llamohja, criticized Velasco's policies, underlining the authoritative nature of their reforms. Llamohja wrote furious manifestos against agrarian decrees, calling for "a true agrarian reform of antifeudal and antiimperialist character."[70] Likewise, he demanded that militaries "make 'reforms' in their respective countries with the aim of calming the masses who fight for land and their liberation from the clutches of capital exploitation."[71] According to this leader, the agrarian reform law was promulgated to quash peasant struggles for land, introducing union organizing to control violence and disorganization. In fact, in syndicates, "the representatives of the landowners and the State outnumber[ed] the representatives of the campesinos."[72] In this way, only the state had the authority to administer peasant territories. Llamohja also refused to accept the military rule of compensation, the so-called agrarian debt, based on the peasant's obligation to economically indemnify the expropriated landlords. According to this rule, "comuneros must help pay for the expropriation of the hacienda from its former owners even though they will not get direct use of the land."[73]

However, Andean peasants also reelaborated Velasco's laws to meet their needs. Saturnino Huillca, for example, adopted Velasco's translation to obtain specific benefits for his community in Cusco. Unlike Llamohja, Huillca became an icon of the success of the Agrarian Reform, publishing a testimony in which he declared his profound admiration for Velasco. In the book *Huillca: Habla un campesino peruano*, published by Hugo Neira, he affirms: "Juan Velasco Alvarado is a man that raises a hope in our hearts."[74] Moreover, Huillca was engaged in the implementation of syndicates, declaring: "It will be a good institution to all the peasants. It has an important value."[75] Huillca's case exemplifies how the government used an intensive system of propagandizing to reinforce the hegemony of Velasco's indigenist translations. As many scholars have discussed, visuality was a fundamental fulcrum to legitimize the 1969 Agrarian Reform. The Peruvian artist Jesús Durand was responsible for the aesthetic of these designs, called *pop achorado*, or insolent pop. The meaning of such insolence refers to the representation of peasants as people with energy and pride in their indigeneity. According to Durand, his interest was to portray peasants beyond the stereotypes of subalternity. Nonetheless, this kind of representation exoticized minorities according to military rule. As Bourque and Palmer signal, "one consequence of the government's initiatives has been to reduce the peasantry alternatives for national political influence," assuming "the integration of the rural sectors into national life."[76] In other words, Velasco's visual propaganda is an example of a colonial translation that engulfed peasant Indigenous subjects into military stereotypes. Translated as a unified group and reduced in its political autonomy, the peasant Indigenous population became a symbol of the revolution addressed by the armed forces.

Paternalist Translations: Alan García in the Rimanakuys

During Alan García's tenure (1985–1990), peasants became passive receptors of government economic proposals. In his first national message, García identified himself as the savior of Peru's subaltern subjects. He manifested this paternalism as follows: "From this day, if anyone has been told by the comuneros and unemployed, the State will speak to our history in their name, in search of justice and the wealth."[77] Such a scene evokes the notion of a ventriloquist, as it was labeled by the Ecuadorian scholar Andrés Guerrero. According to Guerrero, "The ventriloquist performs a trans-scriptural act: he pursues a strategy of representation" in which the Indian becomes "an absence" into the semantic fields of liberal states.[78] The indigenist translator as a ventriloquist never perceives the peasants' demands but only a national representation, or at worst a genealogy of mistranslations. García's principal concern—compared to Velasco's, for example—was to transform the peasant economy rather than promote social justice in Andean communities. In his presidential speeches, he envisaged the "translated Indian" as the sturdy pillar of national economic development.[79] In his article "The Consolidation of Alan García's Government in Peru" (1987), John Crabtree observes that García "established a variety of new aid programs, including Direct Assistance to Communities, the Micro-Regional Development Fund, new subsidies to agricultural producers and a greatly increased volume of loans at concessional rates through the Banco Agrario."[80] Within these programs and institutions, national officers completely controlled peasant activities. García recognized the urgency in helping peasants, but only under the terms of his absolute dominion. In this way, he reduced or ignored the agency of social movements and popular participation. One of his national speeches exemplifies this situation. García promised to confront the importation of food or what he called, underlining a nationalist ideology, the colonization of food. He affirmed that the state should promote the consumption of local products. Such a project reflected the contradictory facets of the García's tenure. On the one hand, he vindicated rural business in the name of nationalism, and on the other hand, peasants had no political participation in their government.

Indeed, García criticized the agrarian reform declared by Velasco. Unlike Velasco, García fomented an agrarian movement that consisted of increasing the production of peasant lands, recognizing the role of the peasantry as an active force. He tried to transform agriculture into a fulcrum with which to stabilize the national economy. For this reason, he oriented various projects and decrees to maximize land production, provide aid credits and loans, and promote the selling of seeds and fertilizers. According to García, the development of a peasant economy signified a symbol of democracy, nationalism, and an anti-imperial politic. García showed an optimistic tone about the success of his agrarian policies until 1989. In that year, he admitted the calamitous problems of the rural economy, declaring his admiration for peasant survival in a context of economic crisis and internal warfare. In his annual speech of 1989, García forged an ideal representation of the Peruvian peasantry as follows: "The Minister [of Agriculture], who is a man who works the land, said to us, we have to trust in the rural work and its beliefs. It does not depend on bank credit but on peasant talent."[81] Following García's ideas, the peasant became a hero who resisted the crisis with bravery. Possessing a peculiar gift ("the peasant talent"), he does not care about financial aid and continues his activities in favor of the nation. Once again, peasants exist only as serfs of the Peruvian state.

During 1986, García held meetings with peasant and Indigenous leaders. Such gatherings were known as *rimanakuys* (from the Quechua verb *rimay*, "to speak"). This could have represented a great opportunity to encourage intercultural and symmetrical dialogues between the nation-state and the peasantry. Nevertheless, the *rimanakuys* only reproduced a multicultural translation of indigeneity. In opposition to the traditional politics of the country, García presented himself as a vindicator of the poorest—of the people without power. However, in García's speech we can perceive an inclination toward translating and controlling peasant voices. Affirming his superiority as chief of state, García considered that peasants could not speak. Therefore, his government must represent rural demands, translating their experiences according to a paternalist viewpoint. As Devine Guzmán has observed, the *rimanakuys* forged an image of peasantry based on the fictional characters of *El mundo es ancho y ajeno* (*Broad and Alien Is the World*, 1941).[82] García identifies real peasants like Rosendo Maqui, the protagonist of Alegría's novel. This comparison was a strategy for controlling an unknown reality. This simple anecdote exemplifies how national authorities mistranslated peasant realities, ignoring their factual claims and necessities. Indeed, the public dialogues of *rimanakuys* reiterated colonial hierarchies between peasants and the state. Apparently, such meetings sought to establish a symmetric relation "president to president." However, García represented peasants as isolated figures and victims without any agency. Echoing Fabian's work about otherness, I consider that the problem with García's speeches lies in classifying who is rational and who is primitive.[83] García reinforces power hierarchies between the president's contemporary world, his skills in translating Andean realities, and the temporal distance of peasants, without resources to transmit their own viewpoints.

The Internal Armed Conflict: Translating the Andes as Ruined Geographies

Cynthia McClintock explains that peasant disappointment in the face of failed government policies produced the rise of terrorism. She notes: "They [the peasants] had hoped the Marxist parties and the new democratic government would improve their lot, only to see their situation worsen. Some peasants were thus ready to listen to the appeals of Sendero Luminoso."[84] Between Velasco's and García's governments, the Peruvian Communist Party Shining Path started its armed fight against the Peruvian nation-state. According to Abimael Guzmán, the leader of Shining Path, the reason for the violence was a desire for the liberation of peasantry after years of oppression in a feudal country. To be sure, Shining Path supported peasant claims in its first years, considering that "the peasantry, particularly the poor peasant, was the closest ally of this group."[85] Nevertheless, members of Shining Path perceived themselves as a different ethnic group from peasant and Indigenous subjects. As a movement largely constituted by Ayacucho mestizos of the middle class without ties to peasantry or Native communities, Shining Path translated rural populations into bodies to be sacrificed in the name of national revolution. Thanks to Gustavo Gorriti's observation, we can understand how terrorists classified peasants' lives and territories: "As the Shining Path document directly noted: 'To strike!, the key is to raze. And to raze means leave nothing behind.'"[86] It is important to note that "to strike" underscores the consequences of terrorist violence. To conquer native bodies and geographies, *senderistas* imposed vexation and torture on Native bodies. As Anne Lambright reminds us, terrorists obligated peasants to kill their own animals as a form of repression.[87] But Shining Path was not the only menace to Andean populations. The Peruvian Armed Forces were responsible for numerous crimes against peasants. In the name of national security, soldiers killed, raped, and tortured Native people. In 1986, Alberto Flores Galindo denounced how the military contributed to the destruction of Andean societies.[88] Between 1980 and 1988, almost 2,477 peasants died. Such a number of corpses expresses two profound dilemmas. On the one hand, the Peruvian nation-state and terrorist groups translated peasants into insignificant lives or bodies to be annihilated. On the other, national authorities ignored the dramatic realities of Andean areas for decades, especially in peasant and Indigenous territories, which facilitated the rise of terrorist ideology. McClintock notes that during the years of the Velasco agrarian reform: "Political authorities virtually absented themselves from the more remote highlands regions."[89] Thus, the extermination of peasants during the internal war was made possible because the state never heard peasant Indigenous claims beyond national rhetoric or indigenist translations. In light of these events, Rodrigo Montoya's declaration in 1987 was reasonable: "The [Quechua] world is condemned to disappear if it continues under the current cultural domination."[90]

From Neoliberalism to the Struggles for Indigenous Self-Determination

Between 1990 and 2000, Alberto Fujimori's government promoted numerous neoliberal policies in Peru. In this regard, Fujimori implemented numerous assistance programs to legitimize his power over underrepresented populations. In rural areas, for example, national representatives created the National Nutritional Assistance Programme (Programa Nacional de Asistencia Alimentaria, PRONAA) to foster dependent relationships between peasant women and the government.[91] Furthermore, Fujimori supported extractivist economies, particularly in mining areas such as Cajamarca.[92] Indeed, Fujimori's policies produced a neoliberal thinking throughout the country, reducing any possibility of social resistance. In this context, Peru was an exception in the Andean region. In Bolivia and Ecuador, Indigenous collectives reinforced their empowerment in the national public sphere during the 1990s. In Brazil, the Indigenous movement confronted the government's efforts to ignore their constitutional rights through the so-called law of *marco temporal*, a bureaucratic strategy to reduce the sovereignty of Native peoples over their territories. Also in 1990, in Chile, politicians toughened the Law of National Security to reduce Mapuche protests. These countries exhibit a historical tradition of Indigenous resistance in contrast with the passivity or the minimal Native participation in the Peruvian political field. In the preceding section, I mentioned the tensions between the peasant collectives and the national state. However, the goal of peasant leaders such as Andrés Luna Vargas and Hugo Blanco was to promote a communist revolution beyond the traditions, epistemologies, and ontologies of rural subjects. Here it is important to compare the Peruvian case with the genealogy of Indigenous empowerment in Bolivia. In *Earth Politics*, Waskar Ari researches the Alcaldes Mayores Particulares, a group organized by Aymara politicians such as Gregorio Titiriku, José Toribio Medina, Meliton Gallardo, and Andrés Jach'aqullu. Between 1921 and 1951, these activists "brought the Aymara gods, such as the Pachamama and the Achachilas, back into the discussion in order to reach a broader audience."[93] After the Bolivian National Revolution of 1952, the Aymara activists continued with their critiques against the doctrines of mestizaje and nationalism. In this venue, the work of Fausto Reinaga and his hope for an Aymara political empowerment were fundamental to the birth of the Katarista movement in the 1970s.[94]

In Peru, by contrast, for many years mestizos or non-Indigenous politicians spoke in the name of the so-called subalterns, imposing their own scripts as unquestionable national models. In the two most recent decades, however, we can perceive Indigenous leadership in organizations such as the National Confederation of Peruvian Communities Affected by Mining (CONACAMI) and the Interethnic Association of the Peruvian Amazon (AIDESEP). To reinforce their demands, CONACAMI and AIDESEP have cemented ties with international environmental movements. The connection between indigeneity and political ecology has been an important strategy to make visible the detrimental consequences of neoliberal extractivism in Indigenous geographies. In this regard, we can identify a tendency for defending territorial rights in dialogue with ecological agendas. Terms such as *ecoterritorial conflicts* and *environmental conflicts* allow us to understand the claims of Native peoples in extractivist zones such as Conga, Tía María, and Las Bambas, to mention a few cases.[95] In addition, another notable change in recent years regarding Indigenous movements in Peru is the leadership of Native women such as Ruth Buendía (Ashaninka), Teresita Antazú (Yanesha), Elsa Merma, and Máxima Acuña.

Finally, it is important to mention the rise of Indigenous literatures, in particular Quechua poetry.[96] This is a tendency in connection with other Native literary traditions across Abiayala. These works confront the colonialism of Latin American lettered cities and governments. In Brazil, the Macuxi author Jaider Esbell challenges a national narrative proposed by the modernist Mario de Andrade.[97] In accordance with Esbell, de Andrade distorts the traditions of his Macuxi people, converting a powerful deity such as Makunaima into a comical character portrayed in the novel *Macunaíma: O herói sem nenhum caráter* (1929). The Macuxi intellectual recovers what was usurped or mistranslated by the Brazilian writer. Mapuche women writers such as Mariela Fuentealba Millaguir and Daniela Catrileo confront the Chilean oppressive colonial regime that has destroyed the Wallmapu and their people for centuries.[98] The current expressions of Indigenous writing in Abiayala reflect a will for self-determination and sovereignty in political and cultural scales. Native authors conceive of their works as vehicles for demanding territorial rights and social and racial justices in contexts of brutal colonization. In the Peruvian Quechua context, the works of Lily Flores, Eduardo Ninamango, Dida Aguirre, Gloria Cáceres, and Washington Córdova Huamán signify the act of translating Andean realities from the perspectives of writers in Quechua.[99] Aguirre and Córdova Huamán, for example, underscore the role of nonhuman entities such as mountains and animals in the political resistances of Quechua people. Both authors have translated their cultures beyond the indigenist literary repertoire of exoticism, romanticism, and multiculturalism. Highlighting the connections between Quechua ontologies, epistemologies, and politics, Aguirre and Córdova Huamán invite us to understand a world of many worlds in which nonhuman beings are not literary tropes but political agents that promote new routes of decolonization. If indigenist translations have perpetuated a variety of colonial hierarchies, contemporary Indigenous intellectuals are translating their own cultures to confront these power relations.[100] In this way, they defy colonial expectations of reading about Andean worlds and Native subjects.

Conclusion

In this chapter, I have attempted to present a summary of what I call indigenist translation and Indigenous self-translations during the twentieth and twenty-first centuries. My principal aim is to show how mestizo/*criollo* or non-Indigenous writers, intellectuals, and politicians created a particular representation of Indigenous peasant societies through a process of intercultural translation. In this regard, representatives of Peruvian literature, social sciences, and political life translated Andean cultures according to their own agendas or disciplines, ignoring or misrepresenting the ways of life of these real people. In this regard, I traced this genealogy to confront this "research of the origin," that is to say, the discourse that Indigenous peoples exist only as the primordial seed of Latin American countries. My notion of indigenist translations engages in dialogue with other categories such as the "indio permitido" or "virtual Indian." In all these cases, authorities and intellectuals transform Native experiences into discourses aligned with national ideologies of revolution or modernity. It is important to note that Indigenous peasant societies interact with modern and international spheres in dialogue with their own traditions. Therefore, indigenist translations express a colonial methodology that employs national or modern paradigms to attempt to understand Native societies. Consequently, indigeneity became a discourse produced by non-Indigenous subjects. Nonetheless, in recent years we have been able to perceive how Indigenous intellectuals and activists are producing their own knowledge according to their viewpoints and political agendas. The transition from indigenist translation to Indigenous self-determination invites me to formulate two questions to decolonize our conceptions about indigeneity in Peru. First, why was *indigenismo* a predominant tendency in Peru until recent decades? I posit that it was provoked by a hegemonic discourse of mestizaje that justified the acculturation of Native differences. By contrast, Mapuches, Aymaras, and Kichwas employ the notion of Indigenous nationalities to confront the project of only one Latin American nation-state. At the same time, these native movements refuse the discourse of neoliberal multiculturalism that seeks to include minorities and subsequently reduce their empowerment. In Peru, the fight for Indigenous sovereignty is pending because the discourses of nationalism and multiculturalism have eroded the possibilities of radical self-determination. As a result, Indigenous demands do not have a leading role in the Peruvian public spheres. Regarding this invisible or limited agency, I want to pose my last question: how can we create new perspectives and methodologies to comprehend Andean realities beyond *Indigenismo*? For example, Indigenous painters, writers, and scholars such as Rember Yahuarcani (Shipibo), Dina Ananco (Awajun Wampis), and Óscar Huamán Águila (Quechua), respectively, are translating their realities to a wider audience beyond exoticism or Romanticism. In Peruvian academia, we need to problematize indigenist frameworks to propose decolonial methodologies. Returning to Mariátegui, it is time to reinforce the empowerment of Indigenous voices; it is time to confront governmental multiculturalism, mestizo cultural appropriations, and to put the colonial genealogy of *indigenismo* on an unflinching trial.

NOTES

1. Luis Alberto Sánchez identifies important differences between the "indigenist novel" characterized by a social orientation and the "Indianism" that represents indigenous subjects as mere ornaments. *Proceso y contenido de la novela hispano-americana* (Madrid: Editorial Gredos, 1953), 544–545.
2. Tomás Escajadillo establishes differences between romantic, exotic, and sociopolitical indigenism. In this venue, he distinguishes the social novels of Ciro Alegría from the modernist short stories of Ventura García Calderón. The author also proposes the category of "neo-indigenismo" in reference to a narrative style that reconceptualizes indigenist tropes in connection with other aesthetics such as *realismo mágico*. *La narrativa indigenista peruana* (Lima: Amaru Editores, 1994).
3. José Carlos Mariátegui, *Seven Interpretive Essays on Peruvian Reality*, trans. Marjory Urquidi (Austin: University of Texas Press, 1971).
4. Mariátegui, *Seven Interpretive Essays*, 274.
5. Antonio Cornejo Polar, *La "trilogía novelística clásica" de Ciro Alegría* (Lima: Latinoamericana Editores, 2004), 117.
6. My notion of indigenist translation is based on the concept of Andeanism proposed by Orin Starn, "Missing the Revolution: Anthropologists and the War in Peru," *Cultural Anthropology* 6, no. 1 (1991): 63–91. According to Starn, anthropologists preferred to analyze rituals rather than focus on the social circumstances of peasant communities that

Genealogy of Indigenist Translations   369

motivated the rise of the terrorist group Shining Path (64). Social scientists created their own translation of Andean societies focused on ancestral practices and ignored the socioeconomic realities of those societies between the 1960s and 1970s.

7. Susan Bassnett, "The Meek or the Mighty: Reappraising the Role of Translator," in *Translation, Power, Subversion*, ed. Román Álvarez and M. Carmen-África Vidal (Clevedon, UK: Multilingual Matters, 1996), 21.
8. Linda Tuhiwai Smith, *Decolonizing Methodologies: Research and Indigenous People* (London: Zed Books, University of Otago Press, 2012), 64.
9. Antoine Berman, *The Experience of the Foreign: Culture and Translation in Romantic Germany* (Albany, NY: SUNY Press, 1992), 5.
10. Talal Asad, "The Concept of Cultural Translation in British Social Anthropology," in *Writing Culture: The Poetics and Politics of Ethnography*, ed. James Clifford and George Marcus (Berkeley: University of California Press, 1996), 164.
11. Burton Raffel, *The Art of Translating Prose* (University Park: Pennsylvania State University Press, 1994), 25.
12. Asad, "The Concept of Cultural Translation," 142. From a conservative and literary perspective, Harish Trivedi proposed a harsh critique to the notion of cultural translation, noting that advocates of the category are not translators properly, and they speak in the same language about other cultures (i.e. Spanish or English). "Translating Culture vs. Cultural Translation," in *In Translation: Reflections, Refractions, Transformations*, ed. Paul St.-Pierre and Prafulla C. Kar (Amsterdam: John Benjamins, 2007), 285.
13. Eduardo Viveiros de Castro, "Perspectival Anthropology and the Method of Controlled Equivocation," *Tipití: Journal of the Society for the Anthropology of Lowland South America* 2, no. 1 (2004): 4–5.
14. Rebecca Earle, *The Return of the Native: Indians and Myth-Making in Spanish America, 1810–1930* (Durham, NC: Duke University Press, 2007).
15. Dipesh Chakrabarty, *Provincializing Europe: Postcolonial Thought and Historical Difference* (Princeton, NJ: Princeton University Press, 2009).
16. In his memoirs, Valcárcel notes: "There was a general desire to know the Peruvian Indians around the world. The mere mention of Peru provoked in the Europeans this idea: 'the country of the Incas.'" *Memorias* (Lima: IEP, 1981), 308. In one of his public discourses in 1986, the former president Alan García refers to peasants as "descendants of the Incas."
17. Joshua Lund, *The Impure Imagination: Toward a Critical Hybridity in Latin American Writing* (Minneapolis: University of Minnesota Press, 2006), 111.
18. Joshua Lund, *The Mestizo State: Reading Race in Modern Mexico* (Minneapolis: University of Minnesota Press, 2012), x.
19. Lund, *The Mestizo State*, xv.
20. de Castro, "Perspectival Anthropology," 5.
21. Enrique López Albújar, *Cuentos andinos: Vida y costumbres indígenas* (Impr. Lux de E. L. Castro, 1924), 266.
22. Frantz Fanon, *The Wretched of the Earth*, trans. Richard Philcox, intro. Jean-Paul Sartre and Homi K. Bhabha (New York: Grove Press, 2004), 15.
23. Regarding how colonizers have interpreted Indigenous cultures, Audra Simpson points out: "Knowing and representing people within those places requires more than military might; it required the methods and modalities of knowing—in particular, categorization, ethnological comparison, linguistic translation, and ethnography." *Mohawk Interruptus: Political Life across the Borders of Settler States* (Durham, NC: Duke University Press,

2014), 95.
24. Clemente Palma, *El porvenir de las razas en el Perú* (Lima: Solar, Revista de filosofía iberoamericana, 2007), 14.
25. Palma, *El porvenir de las razas*, 15.
26. José de la Riva Agüero y Osma, *Carácter de la literatura del Perú independiente* (Lima: Fondo Editorial PUCP, 1962), 190.
27. Riva Agüero y Osma, *Carácter de la literatura*, 190.
28. Gayatri C. Spivak, "The Politics of Translation," in *Outside in the Teaching Machine* (New York: Routledge, 2009), 205.
29. Motivated by European racial thought, many Latin American intellectuals translated Indigenous collectives as obstacles to the progress and the whitening of their countries. This was not a unique characteristic of Peruvian writers and academics. In Brazil, we can find a similar disdain regarding Black populations. See Christian Elguera, "Antiracist Spatial Narratives in Daniel Munduruku's Crônicas de São Paulo: Indigenous Place-Names and Migration in the Paulista Capital City," in *Poetics of Race in Latin America*, ed. Mabel Moraña (London: Anthem Press, 2022).
30. José Santos Chocano, *Alma América: Poemas indo-españoles* (Madrid: Librería de la Viuda de C. Bouret, 1906), VI.
31. Chocano, *Alma América*, 35.
32. Chocano, *Alma América*, 35.
33. Alcida Rita Ramos, *Indigenism: Ethnic Politics in Brazil* (Madison: University of Wisconsin Press, 1988).
34. Abraham Valdelomar, *Los hijos del sol* (Lima: Municipalidad de Lima, 2021). Notwithstanding his struggles with Palma, Riva Agüero, Chocano, and López Albújar, Abraham Valdelomar reiterated colonial depictions of Indigenous realities. In this venue, Escajadillo's classification ignores how colonialism permeates even the works of the most engaged writers with Native habits.
35. Regarding the Ecuadorian indigenist Jorge Icaza, Marc Becker observes: "Icaza's portrayal of passive and powerless Indians is ironic because as he penned Huasipungo [novel published in 1934], Indigenous peoples were staging a sustained systematic critique of Ecuador's political economy," *Indians and Leftists in the Making of Ecuador's Modern Indigenous Movements* (Durham, NC: Duke University Press, 2008), 50.
36. Juan H. Pévez, *Memorias de un viejo luchador campesino* (Lima: Illa-Tarea, 1983). In May 1920, Pévez proposed: "Eliminar los elementos de tortura que usaban cuando no realizaban los trabajos de la hacienda a satisfacción de los patrones. Los hacendados contaban con elementos de tortura como el cepo, la barra, el tortor y otros elementos terribles aparte de palos, látigos" (119).
37. See Ulises Juan Zevallos-Aguilar, "Editorial Titikaka Puno (1926–1930): La producción editorial en el Perú," *Mitologías Hoy* 21 (2020): 50–51; Alex Hurtado, "La resemantización del vanguardismo en Chirapu," *Escritura y Pensamiento* 20, no. 40 (2021): 39–41.
38. In this regard, they expressed their disagreement with other intellectuals such as Dora Mayer, who co-founded the Pro-Indigenous Association with Pedro Zulen. Mariátegui, for example, considered that Mayer represented an acquiescent position in the face of gamonalist atrocities on haciendas.
39. José Carlos Mariátegui, "Aniversario y balance," *Amauta*, no. 17 (1928): 3.
40. Authors have analyzed the contradiction between Mariátegui's conception of Indianness in Peru and his national project, such as Jorge Coronado, *The Andes Imagined: Indi-*

genismo, Society and Modernity (Pittsburgh, PA: University of Pittsburgh Press, 2009), 43–44, and Armando Muyolema, "De la 'cuestión indígena' a lo 'indígena' como cuestionamiento: Hacia una crítica del latinoamericanismo, el indigenismo, y el mestiz(o)aje," in *Convergencia de tiempos: Estudios subalternos/contextos latinoamericanos, estado, cultura, subalternidad*, ed. Ileana Rodríguez (Amsterdam: Rodopi, 2001), 342. Certainly, as Mabel Moraña argues, this Peruvian thinker denounced colonialism in Latin America. "Mariátegui en los nuevos debates: Emancipación, (in)dependencia y 'colonialismo supérstite' en América Latina," in *José Carlos Mariátegui y los estudios latinoamericanos*, ed. Mabel Moraña and Guido Podestá (Pittsburgh, PA: Instituto Internacional de Literatura Iberoamericana, 2009), 66. Nonetheless, he also proposed a nation characterized by the superiority of Western ideologies over local assumptions. We can perceive this hierarchy in the following passage: "The experience of the Orient . . . has proved to us that even after a long period of collapse, an autochthonous society can rapidly find its own way to modern civilization and translate into its own tongue the lessons of the West." Mariátegui, *Seven Interpretive Essays*, 283.

41. This position taking has spawned numerous disagreements between communists and Indians that have lasted into the present. Even Hugo Blanco, who developed an intimate collaboration with peasant movements, had the principal aim of victory of a leftist revolution.
42. Marisol de la Cadena, *Indigenous Mestizos: The Politics of Race and Culture in Cuzco, Peru, 1919-1991* (Durham, NC: Duke University Press, 2000), 202.
43. Gamaliel Churata, *El pez de oro* (Madrid: Cátedra, 2012). According to the correspondence between Mariátegui and Eudocio Ravines, Churata was a principal figure in the organization of the Peruvian Socialist Party in Puno.
44. Mabel Moraña, *Churata postcolonial* (Lima: Centro de Estudios Literarios Antonio Cornejo Polar, 2015), 216.
45. Unfortunately, Peruvian readers ignored this publication, and Churata had no followers until the mid-1990s. *El pez de oro* exemplifies a crucial problem of Peruvian literature focused on Indigenous realities. It is well to remember that the most notable representatives of this literary corpus are non-Indigenous writers. In most cases, they write in Spanish, and despite their proximity to Andean or Amazonian cultures, the reader can perceive a distortion and manipulation of ancestral practices. Therefore, Churata represents the skills and limits of non-Native intellectuals to translate Quechua and Aymara systems of knowledge and political practices.
46. César Vallejo, *Narrativa completa* (Lima: Ediciones Copé, 2012), 172–173.
47. César Vallejo, *Teatro completo* (Lima: Fondo Editorial PUCP, 1979), 2:200–221.
48. Marisol de la Cadena, "The Production of Other Knowledges and Its Tensions: From Andeanist Anthropology to Interculturalidad?" *Journal of the World Anthropology Network*, no. 1 (2005): 21–22.
49. José María Arguedas, *Los ríos profundos* (Buenos Aires: Losada, 1958).
50. *Chicheras* refers to the group of women who sell *chicha de jora*, a beverage in the Andes. Meanwhile, *colonos* designate peasants who work on haciendas. It is the most denigrative position even among other Indigenous groups.
51. Muyolema, "De la 'cuestión indígena,'" 332.
52. Antonio Cornejo Polar, "Condición migrante e intertextualidad multicultural: El caso de Arguedas," *Revista de Crítica Literaria Latinoamericana* 21, no. 42 (1995): 101–109; Estelle Tarica, *The Inner Life of Mestizo Nationalism* (Minneapolis: University of Minnesota Press,

2008). Arguedas also advocated for mestizaje in ethnographic essays such as "Evolución de las comunidades indígenas: El valle del Mantaro y la ciudad de Huancayo" (1957) and "Estudio etnográfico de la feria de Huancayo" (1957).

53. Silvia Rivera Cusicanqui, "Colonialism and Ethnic Resistance in Bolivia: A View from the Coca Markets," in *Empire and Dissent: The United States and Latin America*, ed. Fred Rosen (Durham, NC: Duke University Press, 2008), 143.

54. José María Arguedas, *Tupac Amaru Kamaq Taytanchisman* (Lima: Ediciones Salqantay, 1962); José María Arguedas, *El zorro de arriba y el zorro de abajo* (Buenos Aires: Losada, 1971).

55. Mabel Moraña, *Arguedas/Vargas Llosa: Dilemas y ensamblajes* (Madrid: Iberoamericana; Frankfurt: Vervuert, 2013), 139.

56. The most violent repression occurred between 1960 and 1962, specifically in the localities of Rancas and Yanahuanca in Cerro de Pasco. The massacres of Rancas (1960) and Yanahuaca (1962) are fundamental episodes in comprehending the nature of Tupac Amaru Kamaq Taytanchisman.

57. Leon G. Campbell, "The Historiography of the Peruvian Guerrilla Movement, 1960–1965," *Latin American Research Review* 8, no. 1 (1973): 46.

58. Marisol de la Cadena, *Earth Beings: Ecologies of Practice across Andean Worlds* (Durham, NC: Duke University Press, 2015): 98.

59. Christian Elguera, "El Wamani es Wamani: La lógica relacional no-humana en La agonía de Rasu-Ñiti de José María Arguedas," *Revista Communitas* 5, no. 10 (2021): 38.

60. Christian Elguera, "Ontological Migrations in José María Arguedas's Tupac Amaru Kamaq Taytanchisman: The Triumph of Runa Migrants against the Colonial Violence in Lima," *Diálogo* 23, no. 2 (2020): 126–127.

61. Tara Daly, *Beyond Human: Vital Materialisms in the Andean Avant-Gardes* (New Brunswick, NJ: Rutgers University Press, 2019), 96; Priscilla Archibald, *Imagining Modernity in the Andes* (Lewisburg, PA: Bucknell University Press, 2011), 79. In the roundtable about *Todas las sangres* (June 23, 1965), Jorge Bravo Bresani invited Aníbal Quijano to participate in the conversation with Arguedas. In the first edition that transcribes this roundtable, *¿He vivido en vano? Mesa redonda sobre todas las sangres, 23 de junio de 1965* (Lima: Instituto de Estudios Peruanos, 1985), we can read Quijano's intervention. In one passage, he declares: "the Indian leadership does not exist in the current peasant movement. It is only an exception that appears as an isolated moment. The Indian leader is in a process of cholificación already" (60).

62. José María Arguedas, *Las cartas de Arguedas* (Lima: Fondo Editorial PUCP, 1996), 22.

63. *Dioses y hombres de Huarochirí*, trans. José María Arguedas (Lima: Museo Nacional de Historia; Instituto de Estudios Peruanos, 1966).

64. Arguedas, *Las cartas*, 133.

65. Elguera, "Ontological Migrations."

66. Juan Velasco Alvarado, "Mensaje a la nación con motivo de la promulgación de la ley de la reforma agraria," in *Velasco: La voz de la revolución* (Lima: Ediciones Peisa, 1972). Some years prior, in 1962, the Peruvian Junta Militar outlined a project for agrarian reform in response to the peasant struggles headed by the Trotskyist leader Hugo Blanco in La Convención and Lares (Cusco). Furthermore, in his second year as head of state, in 1964, Fernando Belaúnde Terry approved Law 15037 or the Law of Agrarian Reform.

67. Cynthia McClintock notes: "Although the Peruvian Reform thus hurt hacendados severely, it helped only some 10 or 15 percent of the nation's peasantry, namely those

on the large coastal and highland haciendas." *Peasant Cooperatives and Political Change in Peru* (Princeton, NJ: Princeton University Press, 1981), 62–63.
68. Heilman, "Through Fire and Blood," 151.
69. Susan Bourque and David Scott Palmer, "Transforming the Rural Sector: Government Policy and Peasant Response," in *The Peruvian Experiment: Continuity and Change Under Military Rule*, ed. Abraham F. Lowenthal (Princeton, NJ: Princeton University Press, 1975).
70. As cited in Jaymie Patricia Heilman, "Through Fire and Blood: The Peruvian Peasant Confederation and the Velasco Regime," in *The Peculiar Revolution: Rethinking the Peruvian Experiment under Military Rule*, ed. Carlos Aguirre and Paulo Drinot (Austin: University of Texas Press, 2017), 152.
71. As cited in Heilman, "Through Fire and Blood," 152.
72. Manuel Llamohja, *Now Peru Is Mine: The Life and Times of a Campesino Activist* (Durham, NC: Duke University Press, 2006), 134.
73. Bourque and Palmer, "Transforming the Rural Sector," 188.
74. Saturnino Huillca, *Huillca: Habla un campesino peruano* (Havana: Casa de las Américas, 1970), 109.
75. Huillca, *Huillca*, 117. Finally, Huillca participated in *Kuntur Wachana*, a movie directed by Federico García Hurtado that translated peasantry from the perspective of the revolutionary government. This case exemplifies how the Velasco regime sought to edit and control the history of peasant insurgency. However, it is also important to recognize the agency of Huillca to get power in a context of political changes. Regarding how peasant leaders negotiated with Western cultural practices, de la Cadena notes, "Individuals like Mariano Turpo from Lauramarca, and Saturnino Huillca, who had been political leaders since the early 1930s and were still active in the 1970s was a path to empowerment." *Indigenous Mestizos*, 192.
76. Bourque and Palmer, "Transforming the Rural Sector," 186, 192.
77. Alan García Pérez, "Mensaje del presidente constitucional del Perú," 28 July 1989 (Congreso de la República), 9.
78. Andrés Guerrero, "The Construction of a Ventriloquist's Image: Liberal Discourse and the 'Miserable Indian Race' in Late 19th-Century Ecuador," *Journal of Latin American Studies* 29, no. 3 (1997): 590.
79. José Luis Rénique, *La batalla por Puno: Conflicto agrario y nación en los Andes peruanos* (Lima: La Siniestra Ensayos, 2016), 327.
80. John Crabtree, *Peru under García: An Opportunity Lost* (London: Palgrave, 1992), 813.
81. García Pérez, "Mensaje del presidente constitucional," 15.
82. Tracy Devine Guzmán, "Rimanakuy '86 and Other Fictions of National Dialogue in Peru," *Latin Americanist* 51, no. 1 (2009): 89.
83. Johannes Fabian, *Time and the Other: How Anthropology Makes Its Object* (New York: Columbia University Press, 2002), 75.
84. Cynthia McClintock, "Why Peasants Rebel: The Case of Peru's Sendero Luminoso," *World Politics* 37, no. 1 (Oct. 1984): 81.
85. Carlos Iván Degregori, *El surgimiento de Sendero Luminoso: Ayacucho 1969–1979* (Lima: IEP, 2009): 26.
86. Gustavo Gorriti, *The Shining Path: A History of the Millenarian War in Peru* (Chapel Hill: University of North Carolina Press, 1999): 188.
87. Anne Lambright, *Andean Truths: Transitional Justice, Ethnicity, and Cultural Production in*

Post-Shining Path Peru (Liverpool: Liverpool University Press, 2016): 146.
88. Alberto Flores Galindo, In Search of an Inca: Identity and Utopia in the Andes (Cambridge: Cambridge University Press, 2010): 378.
89. McClintock, "Why Peasants Rebel," 79.
90. Rodrigo Montoya, La cultura quechua hoy (Lima: Hueso Húmero Ediciones, 1987): 16.
91. Patricia Oliart, "Indigenous Women's Organizations and the Political Discourses of Indigenous Rights and Gender Equity in Peru," Latin American and Caribbean Ethnic Studies 3, no. 3 (2008): 301.
92. Jeffrey Bury, "Livelihoods, Mining and Peasant Protests in the Peruvian Andes," Journal of Latin American Geography 1, no. 1 (2002): 5–6.
93. Waskar Ari, Earth Politics: Religion, Decolonization, and Bolivia's Indigenous Intellectuals (Durham, NC: Duke University Press, 2014), 3.
94. Fausto Reinaga, Manifiesto del Partido Indio de Bolivia (La Paz: Ediciones PIB, 1970).
95. Rocío Silva Santisteban, Mujeres y conflictos ecoterritoriales: Impactos, estrategias, resistencias (Madrid, SP: Asociación de Investigación y Especialización sobre Temas Iberoamericanos, 2017), 43–44; Eduardo Gudynas, "Conflictos y extractivismos: Conceptos, contenidos y dinámicas," Decursos, Revista Ciencias Sociales, no. 27-28 (2014): 87.
96. Regarding the current production of Quechua literature, I recommend Gonzalo Espino, Narrativa quechua contemporánea (Lima: Pakarina Ediciones, 2019); Ulises Juan Zevallos-Aguilar, "Poesía quechua peruana y antiextractivismo," Diálogo 22, no. 1 (2019): 73–86; Alison Krögel, Musuq illa: Poética del harawi en runasimi (Lima: Pakarina Ediciones, 2021).
97. Jaider Esbell, "Makunaima, o meu avô em mim!" Iluminuras 19, no. 46 (2018): 12–39.
98. Ruth Mariela Fuentealba Millaguir, Cherrufe: La bola de fuego (Valdivia, Chile: CONADI, 2008); Daniela Catrileo, "El desamparo," Revista Casa de las Américas, no. 300 (2020): 43–47.
99. Dida Aguirre, Jarawi (Lima: Universidad Nacional Federico Villarreal, 2000).
100. Susan Bassnett and Harish Trivedi, Post-colonial Translation: Theory and Practice (London: Routledge, 1998), 5; John Milton and Paul Bandia, Agents of Translation (Amsterdam: John Benjamins, 2009), 1–2; Maria Tymoczko and Edwin Gentzler, eds., Translation and Power (Amherst: University of Massachusetts Press, 2002), xxviii.

BIBLIOGRAPHY

Aguirre, Dida. *Jarawi*. Lima: Universidad Nacional Federico Villarreal, 2000.

Archibald, Priscilla. *Imagining Modernity in the Andes*. Lewisburg, PA: Bucknell University Press, 2011.

Arguedas, José María. *Las cartas de Arguedas*. Lima: Fondo Editorial PUCP, 1996.

———. *Los ríos profundos*. Buenos Aires: Losada, 1958.

———. *Tupac Amaru Kamaq Taytanchisman*. Lima: Ediciones Salqantay, 1962.

———. *El zorro de arriba y el zorro de abajo*. Buenos Aires: Losada, 1971.

Arguedas, José María, Jorge Bravo Bresani, Alberto Escobar, Henri Fevre, José Matos Mar, José Miguel Oviedo, Aníbal Quijano, and Sebastián Salazar Bondy. *He vivido en vano? Mesa Redonda sobre Todas las Sangres, 23 de junio de 1965*. Lima: Instituto de Estudios Peruanos, 1985.

Ari, Waskar. *Earth Politics: Religion, Decolonization, and Bolivia's Indigenous Intellectuals*. Durham, NC: Duke University Press, 2014.

Asad, Talal. "The Concept of Cultural Translation in British Social Anthropology." In *Writing Culture: The Poetics and Politics of Ethnography*, edited by James Clifford and George Marcus, 141–164. Berkeley: University of California Press, 1996.

Bassnett, Susan. "The Meek or the Mighty: Reappraising the Role of Translator." In *Translation, Power, Subversion*, edited by Román Álvarez and M. Carmen-África Vidal, 10–24. Clevedon, UK: Multilingual Matters, 1996.

Bassnett, Susan, and Harish Trivedi. *Post-Colonial Translation: Theory and Practice*. London: Routledge, 1998.

Becker, Marc. *Indians and Leftists in the Making of Ecuador's Modern Indigenous Movements*. Durham, NC: Duke University Press, 2008.

Berman, Antoine. *The Experience of the Foreign: Culture and Translation in Romantic Germany*. Albany: SUNY Press, 1992.

Bourque, Susan, and David Scott Palmer. "Transforming the Rural Sector: Government Policy and Peasant Response." In *The Peruvian Experiment: Continuity and Change under Military Rule*, edited by Abraham F. Lowenthal, 179–219. Princeton, NJ: Princeton University Press, 1975.

Bury, Jeffrey. "Livelihoods, Mining and Peasant Protests in the Peruvian Andes." *Journal of Latin American Geography* 1, no. 1 (2002): 3–16.

Cadena, Marisol de la. *Earth Beings: Ecologies of Practice across Andean Worlds*. Durham, NC: Duke University Press, 2015.

———. *Indigenous Mestizos: The Politics of Race and Culture in Cuzco, Peru, 1919–1991*. Durham, NC: Duke University Press, 2000.

———. "The Production of Other Knowledges and Its Tensions: From Andeanist Anthropology to Interculturalidad?" *Journal of the World Anthropology Network*, no. 1 (2005): 13–33.

Campbell, Leon G. "The Historiography of the Peruvian Guerrilla Movement, 1960–1965." *Latin American Research Review* 8, no. 1 (1973): 45–70.

Castro, Eduardo Viveiros de. "Perspectival Anthropology and the Method of Controlled Equivocation." *Tipití: Journal of the Society for the Anthropology of Lowland South America* 2, no. 1 (2004): 3–22.

Catrileo, Daniela. "El desamparo." *Revista Casa de las Américas*, no. 300 (2020): 43–47.

Chakrabarty, Dipesh. *Provincializing Europe: Postcolonial Thought and Historical Difference*. Princeton, NJ: Princeton University Press, 2009.

Chocano, José Santos. *Alma América: Poemas indo-españoles*. Madrid: Librería de la Viuda de C. Bouret, 1906.

Churata, Gamaliel. *El pez de oro*. Madrid: Cátedra, 2012.

Cornejo Polar, Antonio. "Condición migrante e intertextualidad multicultural: El caso de Arguedas." *Revista de Crítica Literaria Latinoamericana* 21, no. 42 (1995): 101–109.

———. *La "trilogía novelística clásica" de Ciro Alegría*. Lima: Latinoamericana Editores, 2004.

Coronado, Jorge. *The Andes Imagined: Indigenismo, Society and Modernity*. Pittsburgh, PA: University of Pittsburgh Press, 2009.

Crabtree, John. *Peru under García: An Opportunity Lost*. London: Palgrave, 1992.

Daly, Tara. *Beyond Human: Vital Materialisms in the Andean Avant-Gardes*. Lewisburg, PA: Rutgers University Press, 2019.

Degregori, Carlos Iván. *El surgimiento de Sendero Luminoso: Ayacucho 1969-1979*. Lima: IEP, 2009.

Dioses y hombres de Huarochirí. Translated by José María Arguedas. Lima: Museo Nacional de Historia; Instituto de Estudios Peruanos, 1966.

Earle, Rebecca. *The Return of the Native: Indians and Myth-Making in Spanish America, 1810-1930*. Durham, NC: Duke University Press, 2007.

Elguera, Christian. "Antiracist Spatial Narratives in Daniel Munduruku's Crônicas de São Paulo: Indigenous Place-Names and Migration in the Paulista Capital City." In *Poetics of Race in Latin America*, edited by Mabel Moraña, 185-200. London: Anthem Press, 2022.

———. "Ontological Migrations in José María Arguedas's Tupac Amaru Kamaq Taytanchisman: The Triumph of Runa Migrants Against the Colonial Violence in Lima." *Diálogo* 23, no. 2 (2020): 119-132.

———. "El Wamani es Wamani: La lógica relacional no-humana en La agonía de Rasu-Ñiti de José María Arguedas." *Revista Communitas* 5, no. 10 (2021): 27-42.

Esbell, Jaider. "Makunaima, o meu avô em mim!" *Iluminuras* 19, no. 46 (2018): 12-39.

Escajadillo, Tomás. *La narrativa indigenista peruana*. Lima: Amaru Editores, 1994.

Espino, Gonzalo. *Narrativa Quechua Contemporánea*. Lima: Pakarina Ediciones, 2019.

Fabian, Johannes. *Time and the Other: How Anthropology Makes Its Object*. New York: Columbia University Press, 2002.

Fanon, Frantz. *The Wretched of the Earth*. Translated by Richard Philcox. Introduced by Jean-Paul Sartre and Homi K. Bhabha. New York: Grove Press, 2004.

Flores Galindo, Alberto. *In Search of an Inca: Identity and Utopia in the Andes*. Cambridge: Cambridge University Press, 2010.

Fuentealba Millaguir, Ruth Mariela. *Cherrufe: La bola de fuego*. Valdivia, Chile: CONADI, 2008.

García, Uriel. *El nuevo indio*. 1930. Lima: Editorial Universo, 1973.

García Pérez, Alan. "Mensaje del presidente constitucional del Perú," 28 July 1989. Congreso de la República.

Gorriti, Gustavo. *The Shining Path: A History of the Millenarian War in Peru*. Chapel Hill: University of North Carolina Press, 1999.

Guerrero, Andrés. "The Construction of a Ventriloquist's Image: Liberal Discourse and the 'Miserable Indian Race' in Late 19th-Century Ecuador." *Journal of Latin American Studies* 29, no. 3 (1997): 555-590.

Gudynas, Eduardo. "Conflictos y extractivismos: Conceptos, contenidos y dinámicas." *Decursos, Revista Ciencias Sociales*, nos. 27-28 (2014): 79-115.

Guzmán, Tracy Devine. "Rimanakuy'86 and Other Fictions of National Dialogue in Peru." *Latin Americanist* 51, no. 1 (2009): 75-97.

Heilman, Jaymie Patricia. "Through Fire and Blood: The Peruvian Peasant Confederation and the Velasco Regime." In *The Peculiar Revolution: Rethinking the Peruvian Experiment under Military Rule*, edited by Carlos Aguirre and Paulo Drinot, 149-170. Austin: University of Texas Press, 2017.

Huillca, Saturnino. *Huillca: Habla un Campesino Peruano*. Havana: Casa de las Américas, 1970.

Hurtado, Alex. "La resemantización del vanguardismo en Chirapu." *Escritura y Pensamiento* 20, no. 40 (2021): 35–50.

Krögel, Alison. *Musuq Illa: Poética del Harawi en Runasimi*. Lima: Pakarina Ediciones, 2021.

Lambright, Anne. *Andean Truths: Transitional Justice, Ethnicity, and Cultural Production in Post-Shining Path Peru*. Liverpool, UK: Liverpool University Press, 2016.

Llamohja, Manuel. *Now Peru Is Mine: The Life and Times of a Campesino Activist*. Durham, NC: Duke University Press, 2006.

López Albújar, Enrique. *Cuentos andinos: Vida y costumbres indígenas*. Lima: Impr. "Lux" de E. L. Castro, 1924.

Lund, Joshua. *The Impure Imagination: Toward a Critical Hybridity in Latin American Writing*. Minneapolis: University of Minnesota Press, 2006.

———. *The Mestizo State: Reading Race in Modern Mexico*. Minneapolis: University of Minnesota Press, 2012.

Mariátegui, José Carlos. "Aniversario y balance." *Amauta*, no. 17 (1928): 1–3.

———. *Seven Interpretive Essays on Peruvian Reality*. Translated by Marjory Urquidi. Austin: University of Texas Press, 1971.

McClintock, Cynthia. *Peasant Cooperatives and Political Change in Peru*. Princeton, NJ: Princeton University Press, 1981.

———. "Why Peasants Rebel: The Case of Peru's Sendero Luminoso." *World Politics* 37, no. 1 (October 1984): 48–84.

Milton, John, and Paul Bandia. *Agents of Translation*. Amsterdam: John Benjamins, 2009.

Montoya, Rodrigo. *La cultura quechua hoy*. Lima: Hueso Húmero Ediciones, 1987.

Moraña, Mabel. *Arguedas/Vargas Llosa: Dilemas y ensamblajes*. Madrid: Iberoamericana; Frankfurt: Vervuert, 2013.

———. *Churata postcolonial*. Lima: Centro de Estudios Literarios Antonio Cornejo Polar, 2015.

———. "Mariátegui en los nuevos debates: Emancipación, (in)dependencia y 'colonialismo supérstite' en América Latina." In *José Carlos Mariátegui y los estudios latinoamericanos*, edited by Mabel Moraña and Guido Podestá, 41–96. Pittsburgh, PA: Instituto Internacional de Literatura Iberoamericana, 2009.

Muyolema, Armando. "De la 'cuestión indígena' a lo 'indígena' como cuestionamiento: Hacia una crítica del latinoamericanismo, el indigenismo, y el mestiz(o)aje." In *Convergencia de tiempos: Estudios subalternos/contextos latinoamericanos, estado, cultura, subalternidad*, edited by Ileana Rodríguez, 327–364. Amsterdam: Rodopi, 2001.

Oliart, Patricia. "Indigenous Women's Organizations and the Political Discourses of Indigenous Rights and Gender Equity in Peru." *Latin American and Caribbean Ethnic Studies* 3, no. 3 (2008): 291–308.

Palma, Clemente. *El porvenir de las razas en el Perú*. 1897. Lima: Solar, Revista de Filosofía Iberoamericana, 2007.

Pévez, Juan H. *Memorias de un viejo luchador campesino*. Lima: Illa-Tarea, 1983.

Raffel, Burton. *The Art of Translating Prose*. University Park: Pennsylvania State University Press, 1994.

Ramos, Alcida Rita. *Indigenism: Ethnic Politics in Brazil.* Madison: University of Wisconsin Press, 1988.

Reinaga, Fausto. *Manifiesto del Partido Indio de Bolivia.* La Paz: Ediciones PIB, 1970.

Rénique, José Luis. *La batalla por Puno: Conflicto agrario y nación en los Andes peruanos.* Lima: La Siniestra Ensayos, 2016.

Riva Agüero y Osma, José de la. *Carácter de la literatura del Perú independiente.* Lima: Fondo Editorial PUCP, 1962.

Rivera Cusicanqui, Silvia. "Colonialism and Ethnic Resistance in Bolivia: A View from the Coca Markets." In *Empire and Dissent: The United States and Latin America,* edited by Fred Rosen, 137–161. Durham, NC: Duke University Press, 2008.

Sánchez, Luis Alberto. *Proceso y contenido de la novela hispano-americana.* Madrid: Editorial Gredos, 1953.

Silva Santisteban, Rocío. *Mujeres y conflictos ecoterritoriales: Impactos, estrategias, resistencias.* Madrid: Asociación de Investigación y Especialización sobre Temas Iberoamericanos, 2017.

Simpson, Audra. *Mohawk Interruptus: Political Life across the Borders of Settler States.* Durham, NC: Duke University Press, 2014.

Smith, Linda Tuhiwai. *Decolonizing Methodologies: Research and Indigenous People.* London: Zed Books, University of Otago Press, 2012.

Spivak, Gayatri C. "The Politics of Translation." In *Outside in the Teaching Machine,* 200–225. New York: Routledge, 2009.

Starn, Orin. "Missing the Revolution: Anthropologists and the War in Peru." *Cultural Anthropology* 6, no. 1 (1991): 63–91.

Tarica, Estelle. *The Inner Life of Mestizo Nationalism.* Minneapolis: University of Minnesota Press, 2008.

Trivedi, Harish. "Translating Culture vs. Cultural Translation." In *In Translation: Reflections, Refractions, Transformations,* edited by Paul St-Pierre and Prafulla C. Kar, 277–287. Amsterdam: John Benjamins, 2007.

Tymoczko, Maria, and Edwin Gentzler, eds. *Translation and Power.* Amherst: University of Massachusetts Press, 2002.

Valcárcel, Luis E. *Memorias.* Lima: IEP, 1981.

———. *Tempestad en los Andes.* Lima: Editorial Universo, 1972.

Valdelomar, Abraham. *Los hijos del sol.* 1921. Lima: Municipalidad de Lima, 2021.

Vallejo, César. *Narrativa completa.* Lima: Ediciones Copé, 2012.

———. *Teatro completo.* Vol. 2. Lima: Fondo Editorial PUCP, 1979.

Velasco Alvarado, Juan. "Mensaje a la nación con motivo de la promulgación de la ley de la reforma agraria." In *Velasco: La voz de la revolución.* Lima: Ediciones Peisa, 1972.

Zevallos-Aguilar, Ulises Juan. "Editorial Titikaka Puno (1926–1930). La producción editorial en el Perú." *Mitologías Hoy* 21 (2020): 46–58.

———. "Poesía quechua peruana y antiextractivismo entre 2009–2012." *Diálogo* 22, no. 1 (2019): 73–86.

CHAPTER 14

On Democratic Imaginaries in a Discriminatory Society

The Colonial Foundations of Racialization and Land Struggles in Contemporary Brazil

TRACY DEVINE GUZMÁN

> Vocês olham para terra indígena e chamam
> de 'terra improdutiva.'
> Nós chamamos isso de vida.[1]
> SONIA GUAJAJARA, to the Commission
> on Human Rights and Legislative Participation
> of the Brazilian Senate. April 11, 2019

Brazil's 2010 census data revealed that the majority of Brazilians did not self-identify as white. Of the 190,755,799 people queried that year, 14,517,961 self-identified as Black (*preto*); 82,277,333 as "brown" or mixed-race (*pardo*); 2,084,288 as "yellow" (*amarelo*); 817,963 as Indigenous (*indígena*); and 6,608 as "other" (*outro*). These numbers signified a 1.51 percent increase in Black Brazilians, a 4.23 percent increase in "brown" Brazilians, a .59 percent increase in Asian Brazilians,[2] and a stable Indigenous population compared to the previous count in 2000.[3] While the COVID-19 pandemic postponed the 2020 census to 2022, other social indicators revealed that the upward trajectory in nonwhite self-identification continued despite the contentious and racialized politics of the Bolsonaro administration.[4] This trend invigorated both popular and academic debate over the efficacy and fairness of differentiated citizenship rights as established by the 1988 Constitution, as well as by the trajectory of affirmative action initiatives that culminated in the 2010 Estatuto da Igualdade Racial (Statute for Racial Equity).[5] In a context of ongoing, virulent racism, these laws and policies helped foster greater opportunities and well-being for some Black and Indigenous Brazilians with regard to higher education, civil service, land tenure, housing, health care, and access to credit, for example.[6] At the same time, they have heightened social tensions and deepened political divisions among an infinitely diverse, deeply miscegenated national population whose racialization in public and private discourses and spaces varies radically over time and across a vast territory while also depending—historically speaking—far more on phenotype, culture, and class than on biology or genetics.

Tracing this ambiguous, constantly shifting demographic scenario from its colonial roots to the neocolonial present, this chapter examines some of the interwoven legal, political, social, and cultural processes through which Brazil's "white" minority came to control not only most of the country's power structures but also its preferred modes of imagining itself—collectively appropriating Black and Indigenous cultural products, imagery, and ideas as decidedly Brazilian, *mestiço*, and thus their own while at the same time relegating Black and Indigenous people to social invisibility or political irrelevance. In light of the enduring tendency in Brazilian society for what Giorgio Agamben called "inclusion by exclusion,"[7] I argue that the upward trajectory in official self-identification with Blackness and Indigeneity points not only to the long-standing mobilization of Indigenous and Afro-descended Brazilians for social justice but also to a fundamental demand for presence as heterogeneous, racialized subjects within the country's racist, homogenizing, purportedly democratizing national imaginary. This perennial struggle for representation—in terms of speaking for and maintaining a physical presence—powerfully informs the ways dominant Brazilian society has conceptualized its governance, history, and cultural production, and perhaps most crucially in a twenty-first century context, its territory. As Sonia Guajajara points out in the epigraph to this chapter, relations with land are, for many Brazilians, a racialized experience.

What's in a Name? On Unstable Identifications and Contested Resources

A well-known household survey of 82,577 Brazilians conducted by the Instituto Brasileiro de Geografia e Estatística (Brazilian Institute of Geography and Statistics, IBGE) in 1976 elicited 135 distinct responses to an open-ended question posed by researchers: "What color are you?" For decades thereafter, scholars and teachers of Brazil cited this social experiment as a testament to the socially constructed, sometimes arbitrary nature of racialized identification and categories across the country, noting particularly the 130 terms that interviewees invented and expressed to indicate that they were identifiable to themselves and others as something other than "just" *branco, preto, pardo,* or *amarelo* (the four official color categories used for the national census at the time).[8] Among the more unanticipated and notable examples, for example, were *azul* (blue), *lilás* (lilac), and *roxa* (purplish).[9]

For those trying to make sense of the country's racial landscape, the takeaway from this celebrated poll was (at least) threefold: First, that the official census categories for naming and identifying "race" were too limited and thus sorely inadequate for navigating or characterizing the complex realities of racialized identity and identification as they were lived. Second, that the exercise of self-identification, as opposed to the then-customary procedure of having one's "racial character" chosen by a census official from a predetermined set of options, revealed categories and categorizations completely unanticipated by those involved in the science of demographic data collection.[10] And third, that Brazil's oft-commented and oft-studied racial composition—broadly categorized as *mestiçagem*, or miscegenation—had resulted in a complex and oftentimes contradictory demographic configuration whose terminology alone would complicate any meaningful initiative to address structural racism, discrimination, or the underrepresentation of Black and Indigenous people in positions of social, political, and economic power.

Toward the end of the twentieth century and during the first decade of the twenty-first, for example, proponents of affirmative action measures to address inequity in education and public-sector employment were increasingly subjected to accusations of "importing" racial categories (and with them, racism) from the United States in their attempt to solve social problems that were uniquely Brazilian. The anthropologist Carlos Borges, for example, has asserted regularly on the popular *Nação Mestiça* website that admissions policies enacted through Brazil's higher educational quota system during the first decade of the twenty-first century are akin to *mestiçofobia*, or fear of mixed-race peoples.[11] *Mestiçofobia*, he concludes, is a form of racism (and this phrase— *mestiçofobia é racismo,* "mestizophobia is racism"—is the motto of the Nação Mestiça collective). Borges puts it thus: "O sistema de cotas . . . não irá jamais corrigir as desigualdades sociais no Brasil; irá sim fomentar a desigualdade étnica pela destruição dos mestiços, que foram paradigmas de uma raça brasileira por vários séculos" (The quota system will never correct social inequities in Brazil but will instead foment ethnic inequity by destroying the *mestiços* who were the paradigm of a Brazilian race for various centuries).[12]

For Borges and like-minded proponents of the Nação Mestiça message, affirmative action policies resembling those implemented in countries like the United States, where historically, legal frameworks and social mobility for minority communities and "mixed-race" peoples have been highly structured and regulated,[13] are not only misguided for the comparatively amorphous Brazilian context, but in fact, they argue, "anti-Brazilian." A deeply divisive matter across Brazil, so-called *discriminação positiva* (positive discrimination) has faced long-standing opposition that has only intensified during the divisive age of *bolsonarismo*, sparking resentment with regard to diverse forms of institutional access as well as the distribution and protection of valuable resources—particularly, contested lands.

This latter question has been tremendously detrimental not only for Indigenous peoples but also for *Quilombolas*—the name given historically to residents of *quilombos* (in some regions, *mocambos*), or the colonial-era communities of Africans who escaped or were freed from enslavement beginning in the late sixteenth century; and in a modern-day context, a self-designation used by some of their descendants.[14] Amid ongoing, intense debate regarding land distribution, occupation, and ownership across the country, and with the ultimate effect of pitting groups of economically marginalized peoples against one another, hindering the demarcation and titling of traditional territories for Native communities and *Quilombolas* (in keeping with the 1988 Constitution), was one of Bolsonaro's most popular campaign promises—and one that he, his administration, and their supporters worked hard to keep.[15]

This contention points to an obvious and yet highly problematic and consequential paradox in dominant society, which manages to celebrate and promote Black and Indigenous peoples and communities in the past, but not in the present, when, per dominant thinking, they ought to divest themselves of just enough difference to slip into a national(ist), all-encompassing, *mestiço* paradigm.[16] While the seventeenth-century Quilombo dos Palmares lives large in Brazil's popular imaginary as a symbol of self-determination for resisting Portuguese rule for over a century in the Capitania de Pernambuco, for example, ongoing *Quilombola* claims to contested territory in the twenty-first century are subject to widespread debate and even ridicule. Every November 20, five states and over a thousand cities across the country commemorate the Dia da Consciência Negra (Day of Black Consciousness) to mark the 1695 death of Palmares's most famous freedom fighter, Zumbi, while rampant police brutality targeting Black Brazilians has persisted into the first decades of the twenty-first century.[17] The 2018 death of well-known Rio de Janeiro city councilwoman Marielle Franco sparked outrage across Brazil and the world, but not enough to determine who ordered her assassination by a retired police officer.[18] Impunity for those who perpetuate quotidian violence against Black Brazilians continues rampant in rural as well as urban settings, and in 2019, 77 percent of all murder victims nationwide were Black.[19]

Of course, spatial and territorial integrity is essential to the health, safety, material viability, and overall well-being of all marginalized communities. Already in a precarious state and confronting uneven levels of state protection under Workers' Party rule, those who had advocated for constitutional land rights and associated material interests between 2003 and 2016 faced new and grave setbacks under Bolsonaro. After the outset of his administration in 2019, funding and staffing for many of the institutional bodies attending to the interests of these communities—the Fundação Cultural Palmares, the Fundação Nacional do Índio (FUNAI), and the Instituto Nacional de Colonização e Reforma Agraria (INCRA), for example—were cut drastically, making an already slow and labyrinthine process of land recognition and protection even slower and more convoluted.[20] As of late 2021, a total of 200 *quilombos* (out of thousands) received title (52 from the federal government and 148 from a state government), and only three *Quilombola* land petitions were processed and finalized after Bolsonaro took office.[21]

At the same time, while violent and deadly incursions into Indigenous territories and other forms of devastation skyrocketed across Brazil after Bolsonaro took office, FUNAI reneged institutionally on its responsibility for protecting Native peoples from a wide variety of outside interests, limiting its intervention to lands that had already been approved formally for demarcation while that lengthy process was ongoing.[22] What is more, the Bolsonaro administration placed the legal processes by which demarcation and titling for traditional Black and Indigenous communities occur under the authority of the Ministry of Agriculture, Livestock, and Food Supply—an entity dominated by agribusiness, powerful land interests, and the so-called "ruralist" lobby, all of which posit the constitutionally sanctioned territorial protection of minority communities as a zero-sum game whose potential consequences run counter to their narrow geopolitical interests and, above all, their bottom line.[23]

A perpetual complaint of these interests, which have repeatedly sought to pit the needs and well-being of Indigenous peoples and *Quilombolas* against those of other communities who remain underrepresented in the halls of power, is that respecting people's constitutional rights to ancestral territory concentrates too much land in the hands of too few people.[24] In a context of limited resources and even more limited access to the means necessary to acquire them, granting title or legal occupation in recognition of differentiated citizenship rights triggers fear among big landholders and antipathy among those who are unlikely to ever own land, often leading to bitter accusations of "reverse racism," racial hucksterism, or some combination thereof.[25] Critics resent, for example, the fact that 13.8 percent of national territory has been protected and reserved officially as Indigenous lands while less than 0.5 percent of the national population is Indigenous, often questioning the legitimacy and "authenticity" of Native self-identification, or attributing Indigenous activism and self-defense to the intervention of meddling anthropologists or international nongovernmental organization workers who don't know their proper place and are probably spying for the communists anyway.[26]

While Article 67 of the 1988 Constitution stipulated that traditional Indigenous lands would be demarcated within five years of the document's promulgation, upward of eight hundred Indigenous territories still await demarcation more than two decades into the twenty-first century. Unlawful and violent incursions by a variety of resource pirates into demarcated Native lands—as well as those communities stuck somewhere within the tangled bureaucracy of demarcation—spiked drastically after 2019, encouraged by lack of oversight, inconsistent law enforcement, the gutting of existing protection mechanisms, and the overtly anti-Indigenous rhetoric of the executive and his proxies.[27] Furthermore, in light of a precedent-setting Supreme Court case between the Institute for the Environment of Santa Catarina, FUNAI, and the Xokleng Laklãnõ Indigenous people regarding a disputed Indigenous Territory (IT) in Santa Catarina, all pending demarcations across the country faced the significant threat of never being realized—a result that would pose a national, regional, and global environmental threat.[28]

With regard to land protection for traditional, rural Afro-descendant communities, in comparison, only between 0.1 percent and 0.2 percent of national territory was dedicated to protected *remanescentes de quilombos* as of late 2021,[29] despite the fact that up to sixteen million *Quilombolas* resided across Brazil—approximately 7.5 percent of the overall national population.[30] Similar to the current situation of traditional Indigenous lands, *quilombos* are protected in theory by the 1988 Constitution, whose Title X, Article 68, states: "Aos remanescentes das comunidades de quilombos que estejam ocupando suas terras, é reconhecida a propriedade definitiva, devendo o Estado emitir-lhes títulos respectivos" (Permanent ownership shall be recognized for the descendants of the colonial maroon communities who are in occupation of their lands, and the state shall grant them the respective title deeds).[31] In practice, however, the majority of *quilombos* remain not only unprotected and without title, but entirely unrecognized. While the lack of coordination among municipal, state, and federal governments makes it difficult to quantify the situation of *Quilombola* territories in precise or standardized terms, a compendium of state and scholarly sources attests to the facts that, as of 2021, between 1,500 and 1,700 certified *quilombos* remained under study for government titling but lacked the official documentation necessary for the process to move forward.[32] Lack of funding and chronic understaffing also means that thousands of other *quilombos* have not even been certified.

Because, as the anthropologist Jan French concluded in her 2009 study of *Quilombola* and Indigenous identity formation in the Brazilian Northeast, "there is no social justice without redistributive justice,"[33] the traditional holders of power—including power as it manifests in diverse ways through territory—have had little incentive to support or recognize newly rearticulated identities that are tied to any valuable resource, and particularly not to land occupation or ownership. In fact, scholars from the PUC-Rio Climate Policy Initiative concluded in a 2016 study of impediments to agrarian reform that 38 percent of all national territory was held privately, and most of those lands were dedicated to agricultural use. On the other hand, the combined total of all Indigenous lands, all *quilombos*, and all urban areas across Brazil comprised only 14.5 percent of national territory.[34] "At the current pace [of entitlement]," they determined, "it may take INCRA more than 900 years to issue land titles to all the communities that have already been officially recognized."[35]

These data point to some of the myriad ways the "coloniality of power" manifests through land tenure onto a map of twenty-first-century Brazil.[36] Through continued economic, political, and social marginalization, on the one hand, and on the other hand, the powerful presence and enduring fetishization of racial "mixture" (or the so-called *raça brasileira*, or Brazilian race) in many aspects of private and public life, Black and Indigenous peoples have been perpetually excluded not only from the physical spaces that they have the constitutional right to occupy but also from the Brazilian community imagined as national.[37] The desire for, and celebration of, miscegenation and the ongoing institutionalization of racialized discrimination not only live side by side, but in fact go hand in hand, as the undying lore of racial democracy is an uninterrupted expression of Brazil's unique and foundational "racial contract," or as Charles Mills put it, "the differential privileging of . . . whites as a group with respect to . . . nonwhites as a group; the exploitation of their bodies, land, and resources, and the denial of equal socioeconomic opportunities to them."[38]

State Formation as Violence

> Eu tenho certeza de que nós fizemos um
> país bonito. . . . Nós somos melhores,
> porque [somos] lavados em sangue negro,
> em sangue índio, melhorado, tropical. . . .
> Nós somos Roma.
>
> — DARCY RIBEIRO[39]

In 1996, the prolific and controversial anthropologist, ethnographer, politician, educator, and novelist Darcy Ribeiro made the above reflection in response to a query about the meaning of his life's work: to understand, explain, and help make a good life for *o povo brasileiro* (the Brazilian people)— also the name of his best-known book. A provocative figure in life and death, Ribeiro made many enemies over the course of a long and diverse career, in part due to his unwavering, virulent critique of what he labeled Brazil's "dominant class," whom he characterized as "canalhas," "finos," and "educados" (fine, polite, educated scoundrels) who "needed to be hung."[40] Like many leftist intellectuals, he fled Brazil after the 1964 military coup and would not return until 1976, finally receiving amnesty in 1980. During the twelve years he spent exiled in Uruguay, Chile, and Peru, Ribeiro dedicated time to advising progressive administrations; to university teaching and institutional reform; to writing novels; and most importantly, to trying to understand Brazil and its place in the Americas and the world. The extended period away from home enabled him to conceptualize and articulate more succinctly the preoccupation that had inspired his writing for decades: "Por que o Brasil ainda não deu certo?" (Why hasn't Brazil turned out right yet?).[41]

In over a dozen books, thousands of pages, and several decades, Ribeiro addressed the question from overlapping disciplinary and methodological angles—through lenses of social science, creative writing, educational theory, and autobiographical reflection, for example. In practical terms, he dedicated decades to advocacy and policy work across the country—as an ethnographer in the Amazon, a university administrator in Brasília, and a vice governor and federal senator in his adopted state of Rio de Janeiro. While this multifaceted intellectual and personal perspective makes his work notable among the best-known theorists of Brazil, he is also remembered for his self-proclaimed "failures" to achieve his most consequential goals: to "save the Indians of Brazil," to make quality education accessible to all Brazilian children, and to carry out a successful agrarian reform.[42] Not coincidentally, each of these failures stemmed from the explanation he developed in the aftermath of the dictatorship regarding Brazil's collective inability to *dar certo*, or to turn out right: a situation of internal colonialism whereby an impoverished majority lived and died under the thumb of a small and powerful elite. As he put it: "Não há, nunca houve, aqui um povo livre, regendo seu destino na busca de sua própria prosperidade. O que houve e o que há é uma massa de trabalhadores explorada, humilhada e ofendida por uma minoria dominante, espantosamente eficaz na formulação e manutenção de seu próprio projeto de prosperidade, sempre pronta a esmagar qualquer ameaça de reforma da ordem social vigente" (There is not, and never has been, a free people here, governing its destiny in search of its own prosperity. What there was, and what there is, is a mass of exploited workers, humiliated and offended by a dominant minority that is amazingly efficient in formulating and maintaining its own project of prosperity, always ready to crush any threat of reform of the prevailing social order).[43]

Missing from this brief articulation of Ribeiro's argument is any overt consideration of race or ethnicity or how those factors impact the power struggles that lie at the heart of his conceptualization of the country and its social and political problems. This gap does not, of course, represent a failure on behalf of the author to understand that race and ethnicity are fundamental concepts for explaining the formation of Brazilian society and the lived experiences of Brazilian people (or people living inside Brazilian borders). Indeed, the anthropologist-novelist-politician wrote prolifically on those topics for decades. It does, however, point to a widely shared sense, also present in much of Brazil's canonical intellectual tradition, that despite the genocidal violence of state formation as reflected in the epigraph to this section, race and ethnicity are somehow secondary to other explanatory factors and can be reasonably subsumed into other kinds of social categorization, such as class, cultural practice, and regional identities.

Brazilianness as Antiracist Racism

This whitewashed conviction has formed and informed widespread notions about the stratification of Brazilian society along something other than racial lines since the first half of the twentieth century, when Brazilian intellectuals who shared Ribeiro's dedication to their national project worked to chip away at the pessimistic prognoses that generations of influential Europeans had offered for their mostly nonwhite country, beginning in the colonial period, moving through independence, and into the final decades of Empire. In the long shadow of travelers, scientists, artists, and diplomats who had preached mixing as degeneration, and helped to convince governing elites—including Dom Pedro II himself—that *branqueamento* (whitening) was the best, and perhaps only path forward for the country, well-known Brazilian scholars, writers, and public officials labored to right their sinking ship by supplanting the racist theories of the Mortons, Gobineaus, and Agassizes of the world with new, regenerative, more creative, and more hopeful conceptualizations of *mestiçagem*.[44] Like their contemporaries across Latin America who endeavored to conceptualize racial and cultural "mixing" as a potential benefit to society rather than an inevitable burden,[45] many of Ribeiro's intellectual ancestors revisited the Black and Indigenous presence in Brazil with optimistic pragmatism, railing against the scientific racism of polygenist craniologists and others of their ilk who had condemned their country (and continent) to failure or even disappearance. "O que se sabe das diferenças da estructura entre os craneos de brancos e negros não permite generalizações," quipped Gilberto Freyre in 1933. "Já houve quem observasse o facto de que alguns homens notáveis teem sido indivíduos de craneo pequeno e authenticos idiotas, donos de cabeças enormes" (What is known about the differences in structure between the skulls of whites and Blacks does not allow for generalizations. Some have already observed the fact that some remarkable men have been small-skulled individuals [and others], authentic idiots with huge heads).[46]

In his best-known work, *Casa-grande e senzala* (The Masters and the Slaves, 1933) Freyre would elaborate this simultaneous defense of Brazil and critique of the country's detractors, famously claiming that all Brazilians were at least little Black, irrespective of whether they knew or acknowledged it: "Todo brasileiro, mesmo o alvo, de cabello louro, traz na alma, quando não na alma e no corpo . . . a sombra, ou pelo menos a pinta, do negro" (Every Brazilian, even the very white one with blond hair, carries in his soul, when not in his soul and body... the shadow, or at least the trace, of the Negro).[47] Regardless of its visually perceptible nature, then, the ubiquitous African influence on Brazil was for Freyre a source of strength and pride: "Os escravos vindos das áreas de cultura negra mais adiantada formam um elemento activo, creador, e quasi que se pode accrescentar nobre na colonização do Brasil; degradados apenas pela sua condição de escravos,... desempenharam uma função civilizadora. Foram a mão direita da formação brasileira; os portugueses e os índios, a mão esquerda" (The slaves coming from the areas of more advanced Black culture formed an active, creative, and one might add, noble element in the colonization of Brazil; degraded only by their condition as slaves, ... they played a civilizing function. They were the right hand of Brazilian formation; the Portuguese and the Indians, the left).[48]

In Freyre's influential thinking, this "civilizing" influence permeated all aspects of everyday life, from spirituality, cultural practice, and cuisine to child raising, language use, and a variety of interpersonal communications. Not as readily notable as Africanness, and in his view, less sophisticated, Brazil's Indigenous inheritance was also of great import for understanding the country and its people, especially in assessing its particular contribution to humanity alongside its hemispheric neighbors. As he put it: "O Brasil é dos paizes americanos onde mais tem se salvo da cultura e dos valores nativos. O imperialismo português... se desde o primeiro contacto com a cultura indígena, feriu-a de morte, não foi para abatel-a de repente, com a mesma fúria dos ingleses na America do Norte. Deu-lhe tempo de perpetuar-se em varias sobrevivencias uteis" (Brazil is one of the American countries where most of the Native culture and values have been saved. Portuguese imperialism... if from the first contact with the Indigenous culture, mortally wounded it, it was not to kill it suddenly, with the same fury of the English in North America. It allowed time to perpetuate itself through various useful forms of survival).[49] A counterpoint to the formidable social legacy of European racism and the power of the Brazilian intellectual class and political leaders who in the early twentieth century adopted it for themselves, the interpretation of Freyre and like-minded thinkers was for its day not only progressive but also revolutionary. Countering the eugenicist discourses of earlier generations who had sought to dilute the presence of Black and Native peoples in national society and culture, and getting in a dig at the racists in North America, Freyre's take on the complex racial and cultural makeup of the country made it possible, at least in theory, for all Brazilians to be the inheritors and beneficiaries of the country's African and Indigenous influence—whether in blood, in spirit, or both—without necessarily revealing any phenotypical trace thereof. It was to that framing of the past in national thought—ultimately, an appropriation of Black and Indigenous suffering by a general population who had not shared the same historical experience—that Ribeiro would appeal half a century later with his conceptualization of Brazil as a "new Rome."

Three years after the publication of *Casa-grande*, the historian Sérgio Buarque de Holanda added his best-known work to this intellectual tradition with a celebrated study of what he called *Raízes do Brasil* (Roots of Brazil).[50] Like Freyre, who penned the introduction to his book, Buarque centered the idea and experience of *mestiçagem* in his study of the formation of Brazilian society, seeking to understand some of the obstacles the country was facing along the road to consolidating democracy. While *Raízes* is most often cited for its foundational treatment of Brazilian "cordiality" and the sociopolitical consequences of the "cordial man's" difficulty in differentiating private and public spaces, Buarque's treatment of Brazil's racial composition was central to his analysis. Buarque argued that Brazilian *mestiçagem* was but a continuation of a much longer Lusophone phenomenon, as the Portuguese had already comprised a heterogeneous and deeply miscegenated society as early as the sixteenth century.

He noted that in 1551, for example, enslaved Africans already comprised one-fifth of the population of Lisbon—a percentage that would grow over the ensuing decades, not only in urban areas but, more importantly, across the country. In keeping with Freyre's examination of the role of race in Brazil's patriarchal social organization and more specifically, in familial life, Buarque argued that even formal barriers, including racist legal structures, were ultimately unsuccessful in preventing intimate proximity between whites and people of color, whether enslaved or free. Over generations, national society was therefore increasingly hybrid—racially, socially, and culturally. As he elaborated: "O escravo das plantações e das minas não era um simples manancial de energia, um carvão humano à espera de que a época industrial o substituísse pelo combustível. Com freqüência as suas relações com os donos oscilavam da situação de dependente para a de protegido, e até de solidário e afim. Sua influência penetrava sinuosamente o recesso doméstico, agindo como dissolvente de qualquer idéia de separação de castas ou raças, de qualquer disciplina fundada em tal separação" (The plantation and mining slave was not simply a source of energy, human coal waiting for the industrial age to replace him with fuel. Often his relations with his owners oscillated from the situation of dependent to that of protected, and even of solidarity and affinity.

His influence sinuously penetrated domestic recesses, dissolving any notion of separation of castes or races, or of any discipline based on such separation).[51] Unlike the Spaniards, Northern Europeans, and other predominantly white national communities, Buarque argued further, the Portuguese had suffered no "orgulho de raça," or racial pride. As a result: "a mestiçagem que representou, certamente, notável elemento de fixação ao meio tropical não constituiu, na América portuguesa, fenômeno esporádico, mas, ao contrário, processo normal. Foi, em parte, graças a esse processo que eles puderam, sem esforço sobre-humano, construir uma pátria nova longe da sua" (The racial mixing that certainly represented a remarkable element of fixation to the tropical environment was not, in Portuguese America, a sporadic phenomenon, but, on the contrary, a normal process. It was partly thanks to this process that they were able, without superhuman effort, to build a new homeland far from their own).[52]

Finally, Buarque's conceptualization of Brazilian *mestiçagem* was, like Freyre's, attentive to the fundamental role that Indigenous peoples played in the unique formulation of national society. But whereas Freyre was mostly preoccupied with racial and cultural mixture—the convergence into Brazilianness of what von Martius had one century earlier metaphorized as a powerful "river of Portuguese blood" with "tributaries of the Indian and Ethiopian [sic] races"[53]—Buarque was also attentive to the racialization of the Brazilian imaginary, where Native peoples still loomed large as figures of romanticized nationhood, despite their small numbers vis-à-vis the overall population. Nineteenth-century writers and artists had managed to employ Indigenous protagonists as symbols of freedom not only because of their physical distance from the dominant society, he noted, but also due to the reputed "intemperance" and the rejection of servility that had made it ineffectual for colonizers to exploit them en masse as unpaid laborers.[54]

In this regard, Buarque in 1936 was also building on the ideological and aesthetic incorporation of Native imagery into national culture and cultural production that the Brazilian modernists had transformed from romanticization to parody just one decade earlier, when turning colonial and colonialist fear and abhorrence of radical Otherness on its head, Oswald de Andrade's *Manifesto Antropófago* (Anthropophagous Manifesto) provided a cheeky conceptual framework for incorporating foreign ideas and cultural products into Brazilianness by "deglutition" rather than imitation.[55] In the 2020s, nearly a century later, the ongoing, widespread embrace of cultural and intellectual *antropofagia* still places it among the country's most recognized and employed tropes of national identity and identification, permeating Brazilian life and reinscribing in jest the sixteenth-century portrayal of Native savagery and godlessness.[56]

Constructing Nationhood on Pillars of Scientific Racism

Considering the baggage of nineteenth-century racialized discourses that they were carrying, the anthropophagous *modernistas* (modernists), like their racially "democratic" posterities, were among the vanguard of Brazilian sociocultural critique during the 1920s and 1930s. The French statesman Joseph Artur de Gobineau, for example, who much to his own displeasure lived in Rio de Janeiro from 1869 to 1870, was one of Brazil's best-known and most virulent nineteenth-century critics. Gobineau famously expressed disgust and loathing toward the whole of Brazilian society, largely due to the prevalence of races he deemed "inferior" among the country's predominantly miscegenated population, whom he characterized as "mulattoes of the lowest category . . . vitiated in blood and spirit."[57] The only redeeming aspect of Gobineau's yearlong residence in the South was, in fact, the close friendship he established with Emperor Pedro II, whom he judged to be "almost" pure Aryan, and with whom he communicated regularly until his death in 1882—just six years before Brazil abolished slavery (1888), and seven before the declaration of the first Republic (1889).[58]

Over years of correspondence, Gobineau expressed support for the emperor's desire to advance the cause of emancipation in Brazil despite trepidation over the massive social, economic, and political upheaval it would provoke. Still deeply mired in the scientific racism that inspired his infamous *Sur l'inegalité des races humaines* (On the Inequality of the Human Races, 1855), Gobineau sought enthusiastically to convince the emperor that the mass immigration of German Catholic agricultural workers would be beneficial for Brazil's "racial problem," as well as for the country's economic stability and development. In a letter to the emperor dated August 2, 1870, he queried:

> Não acha o Imperador que o Brasil teria um grande interesse em tomar medidas para chamar a si a emigração dessas populações catholicas, para a activar, a prender, a seduzir? Parece-me isto uma boa partida que, jogada convenientemente, tiraria o Brasil de seu grande isolamento no ponto de vista da emigração geral e lhe daria o que há de melhor e de mais desejável, isto é, colonos agrícolas. Eu veria nisto o corollario muito feliz do grande

trabalho de emancipação que occupa tão justamente o pensamento do Imperador. Ainda uma vez parece-me que esta questão conduzida com firmeza, decisão e, o que é essencial, uma grande honestidade, poderia ser como uma graça providencial nos destinos do Brasil.

Does the Emperor not think Brazil would have a great interest in taking measures to attract the emigration of these Catholic populations, to activate, to retain, to seduce them? It seems to me this is a good move that, if played properly, would take Brazil out of its great isolation from the point of view of general emigration, and would give it what is best and most desirable, that is, agricultural settlers. I would see in this [move] the very happy corollary of the great work of emancipation that so rightly occupies . . . [your] thoughts. Once again, it seems to me that this question, conducted with firmness, decision and, most essentially, great honesty, could be like a providential blessing in the destinies of Brazil.[59]

At the time Gobineau penned this letter to the emperor, German immigration to Brazil had been underway for over a half century. Fleeing the Napoleonic invasion of the Iberian Peninsula in 1807, the Portuguese Crown escaped Lisbon, first for Bahia, and then headed to Rio de Janeiro, where it would remain for thirteen years. New European immigrants began settling in Brazil the following year, when Pedro II's grandfather, D. João VI, made it legal for non-Portuguese subjects to own land. Although the earliest settlements in Bahia failed, purportedly due to the arduous climate, subsequent waves of immigrants headed south, founding four German settlements between 1824 and 1830 in Rio Grande do Sul, Paraná, and Santa Catarina—mostly intended for small-scale family agriculture.[60]

Imperial backing for white European immigration strengthened further after 1850, when the importation of enslaved Africans became officially illegal and new legislation—Lei No. 601, Regarding the Empire's Vacant Lands—transformed unsettled, unclaimed, or informally claimed or occupied territories into property by putting them up for sale, "both for private enterprises and the establishment of domestic and foreign colonies, with the Government authorized to promote foreign colonization in the manner indicated."[61] The immediate result and lasting legacy of the land law, then, was to limit ownership to the already-propertied classes and to those immigrants who had enough means to buy land, thus concentrating wealth and territory in the hands of a tiny white minority that was entirely unrepresentative of the population living inside Brazilian borders. Article 17 specified further that those immigrants who purchased land and made residence in Brazil could be naturalized after two years.

Despite the fact that Brazil's imperial slave regime would endure almost another four decades, the interests of abolitionism and pro-immigration became intimately connected post-1850 as the governing classes saw the need—anticipating Gobineau's suggestions to the emperor by two decades—to continue settling the country with industrious laborers while also endeavoring to "whiten" and "improve" the population. Adverse living conditions and a general lack of social infrastructure in the so-called vacant areas (*áreas devolutas*) made it difficult for the imperial regime to attract and retain significant numbers of "desirable" settlers, particularly after the 1850 law required that lands be attained through purchase and no longer through occupation.[62]

Two years after Gobineau's cordial appeal to the emperor, the country's first official census in 1872 counted the overall Brazilian population at 9,930,473 individuals: 84.8 percent free and 15.2 percent enslaved. A mere 3.8 percent of the total population were immigrants, while 46 percent of all immigrants were *africanos* (Africans), and 36 percent were *escravos*.[63] Among other significant immigrant groups counted that year were Portuguese (33 percent), Germans (10.5 percent), Italians (2.1 percent), and French (1.8 percent)—percentages that would change significantly over the ensuing sixty years.[64] Indigenous peoples were included that year among *caboclos* (mixed-raced people of Indigenous descent), who comprised a surprisingly large 3.9 percent of the population. Remarkably, they would not be counted again as Native peoples for well over a century, until after the 1988 Constitution gave them differentiated citizenship rights for the first time in national history.[65] Of course, it was also the 1988 Constitution, promulgated a century after the abolition of slavery, and 101 years after the declaration of the First Republic in 1889 that also recognized for the first time the descendants of *quilombos* as Brazilian citizens with differentiated land rights.

Terra (e Botocudos) à vista! (Land ho! And Botocudos!)

As this discussion brings to the fore, the colonial, colonialist, imperial, and imperialist enterprise of naming, categorizing, and counting the individuals, groups, and communities that make up the Brazilian people takes us from the early colonial period through present. At every historical juncture, we face unresolved and potentially unresolvable questions regarding who does the naming, categorizing, and counting, for whom, when, and why. The unresolvable nature of these questions does not mean, of course, that no answers were or are possible, but rather, that the answers both draw from and depend on social, cultural, political, and economic contexts that are constantly in flux, and thus complicated additionally by always-shifting regimes of power. As we have seen, dominant conceptualizations and uses of race, ethnicity, and color have always been tied to material resources, whether explicitly or implicitly. In 1500, 1808, 1850, 1888, 1988, and 2022, the most enduring and determinant of those resources has been land. Alas, the term *terras devolutas* of the 1850 land law never in fact meant that lands were "empty" or "unoccupied," but rather, that no one residing there was much worth counting.[66] In short, Indigenous and Black lives were—and for some, continue to be—a cheap price to pay for civilization and development.

Less than half a century earlier, scandalized by "horrible and atrocious scenes of the most barbaric anthropophagy," and incensed over the "tyrannical" Indians who refused to "live pacifically in villages under the protection of his laws,"[67] or contribute to the mining and agricultural activities he sought to promote, D. João VI declared an offensive holy war on the "Índios Botocudos,"[68] authorizing the "reduction" or imprisonment and enslavement of any Índio Botocudo possessing arms and the subsequent takeover of all known "Botocudo" lands. On May 13, 1808, as he wrote to Pedro Maria Xavier de Ataide e Mello, Governor of the Capitania de Minas Gerais: "Ordeno-vos que façais distribuir em seis districtos, ou partes, todo o terreno infestado pelos Indios Botocudos, nomeando seis Commandantes destes terrenos, a quem ficará encarregada pela maneira que lhes parecer mais profícua, a guerra offensiva que convém fazer aos Indios Botocudos" (I order you to distribute in six districts, or parts, all the terrain infested by the Botocudo Indians, naming six Commanders of these lands, who will be in charge of the offensive warfare that should be done against the Botocudo Indians in the manner that seems most profitable).[69] The communication stated further that those subjects willing to take over the territories previously "infested" by the Botocudo would get a ten-year tax break for making them permanently productive. Exportation and importation by way of the Rio Doce would likewise be tax-free, and those subjects already indebted to the Royal Treasury who might be willing to establish cultural and "auriferous" works on said terrain would be able to defer their payments for up to six years.[70] A bloody and tragic segue from the colonial takeovers of the sixteenth century to the Amazonian resource conflicts of the 2020s, the prince regent's war of extermination on the Botocudo would endure two decades, offering an extended material incentive for soldiers and mercenaries to labor on the side of God, empire, and civilization: land.

On August 24, after three months of ceaseless conflict, João VI authorized the expansion of military forces required to defeat the Botocudo, informing Governor Ataide e Mello of his willingness to provide all means necessary for the struggle to be successful.[71] After an additional six months, on December 2, he ordered the governor to resettle communities of any peaceful and law-loving Indians in *aldeias* that would be overseen by the Catholic Church, which would also provide them a civilizing education. Smaller groups of Indians were to be distributed among local farmers who were given the authority to exploit their labor for anywhere between twelve and twenty years, depending on how long it might take the Indians to achieve reasonable levels of civilization. In exchange for the free Indigenous toil, these loyal agrarian subjects were to educate the Natives held under their control in the Holy Religion and provide them with any necessary food, clothing, or medicine.[72] Having thus taken over the Botocudo territories and put any surviving Indians to work for the benefit of the Portuguese Crown in exile, productive commercial activity could resume safely along the Rio Doce. As Ailton Krenak has explained, that activity entailed destroying all remaining forest cover and leaving his surviving "Botocudo" ancestors entirely dispossessed, or as he put it ironically, *à vista* ("Botocudos"). So few of his people survived into the twenty-first century, in fact, that Krenak was compelled to pay a personal visit to Darcy Ribeiro in the 1980s, seeking greater security for his community, and to convince the ethnographer-cum-politician that he had made a big mistake in characterizing the Krenak people as extinct in his scholarly books.[73]

Still home to a small community of "Botocudo" descendants (Krenak) in the twenty-first century, the Rio Doce, along with the neighboring town of Mariana (Minas Gerais), would be devastated by the culmination of that nineteenth-century "commercial productivity" exactly 207 years after João VI declared his war of extinction on his "anthropophagous" enemies. In 2015, a tailings dam (Fundão) owned and operated by the Brazilian-Australian conglomerate Samarco suffered a catastrophic and lethal failure, pouring forty-four million cubic meters of toxic sludge into the river and creating the largest environmental disaster worldwide of the mining industry to date.[74] Reflecting five years later on the consequences of that tragedy, the community's most outspoken advocate, Ailton Krenak, concluded:

É a nossa vez agora de ser esmagado por esse tipo de capitalismo que destrói os ambientes e depois vai para outro país.... Nós estamos vivendo no mundo inteiro uma mudança climática que já deveria ter proibido a mineração.... Os combustíveis fosseis e a mineração são duas atividades primitivas.... Não podemos esquecer que Mariana é um povo histórico. Mariana e Ouro Preto... foram sedes do governo colonial, tão importante quanto Potosí.... Então, não é novo o histórico de abuso e de violência contra ... as comunidades indígenas, e depois os afrodescendentes e mesmo os africanos que foram trazidos como escravos para cá. É para não esquecer que a matriz da mineração no Brasil é escravocrata. Quem furou as lavras de ouro no século 17, 18, foram os negros escravos; foram os índios também, quando eles conseguirem manter os índios preso. Essa piada de que os índios não gostavam de trabalhar, ela nasceu da observação dos capatazes que viam que os índios se escapavam do controle deles porque conheciam o território.... Os negros demoraram para constituir as rotas de quilombo ... onde podiam fugir do controle dos capatazes. Eram capatazes da mineração. A mineração nasceu de mão de obra escrava. Ela não tem dignidade nenhuma, não. Ela paga salário porque é obrigada. Se pudesse, ela continuava escravizando as pessoas. Aqueles corpos não importam. Se a barragem passar em cima e matar todo mundo, não tem problema nenhum. Porque historicamente, esses corpos nunca existiram.

It's our turn now to be crushed by this kind of capitalism that destroys the environment and then moves on to another country.... We are experiencing a worldwide climate change that should have banned mining by now. ... Fossil fuels and mining are two primitive activities.... We can't forget that Mariana is an historical town. Mariana and Ouro Preto ... were seats of the colonial government, as important as Potosí.... So, the history of abuse and violence against Indigenous peoples, and then the Afro-descendants, and even the Africans who were brought here as slaves, is not new. Let's not forget that the matrix of mining in Brazil is slavery. Black slaves dug the gold mines in the seventeenth, eighteenth centuries; Indians, too, when they managed to keep the Indians captive. This ridiculous notion that Indians "didn't like to work" was born from the observation of [mining] foremen who saw that the Indians could escape from their control because the territory was familiar to them.... The mining [industry] was born of slave labor. It has zero dignity. They pay wages because they have to. If they could, they would continue enslaving people. Those bodies don't matter. If a dam spills and kills everyone, no problem. Because historically, those bodies never even existed.[75]

An Other Botocudo, or, Other Than Botocudo?

In April 1921, an artillery captain named Alípio Bandeira wrote an impassioned letter to President Epitácio Pessoa expressing deep concern regarding a troubling encounter he had experienced with a group of "pacified Botocudo" (Xokleng) Indians in the state of Santa Catarina. The community, he explained, had been living for some time under the supervision of a young employee of the Serviço de Proteção aos Índios (Indian Protection Service, or SPI) named Eduardo de Lima e Silva Hoerhann,[76] who had become an SPI photographer at the age of fifteen.[77] Hoerhann's concern for Xokleng welfare had deepened after witnessing years of intense land conflict with encroaching settlers, gradually leading him to assume increasing levels of responsibility for the community's safety. As a result, in 1920, he finally led them to relocate to a new territory along the River Plate, approximately seventy miles from the town of Blumenau. Hoerhann's intention in helping the community resettle had been threefold: First, he wanted to mitigate the long-standing violence between the "Botocudo" and ever-expanding colonies of German immigrants. Second, he sought to protect the community from the brutal *bugreiros*, or "Indian hunters," who had terrorized Indigenous communities across the south of Brazil for decades, oftentimes at the behest of the state. And finally, in keeping with the broad goals of the SPI, he aspired to facilitate Botocudo incorporation into a productive and modern market economy through rice farming, not unlike the process Darcy Ribeiro would some decades later call "ethnic transfiguration."[78]

While Hoerhann's benevolent intentions alongside the Botocudo would be called into question years later by some members of that community,[79] Bandeira's 1921 rendering of the indigenist's work offered respect and admiration. As an outspoken leader in Brazil's Positivist movement alongside SPI founder Cândido Mariano da Silva Rondon, Bandeira lauded Hoerhann's efforts to feed and clothe hundreds of people on a paltry SPI budget that was increasingly decimated by a heartless, tightfisted National Congress. His memo to Pessoa implored on behalf of Hoerhann and the community for the president's direct intervention in Santa Catarina to safeguard the Indigenous lands from the swelling Companhia Hanseática—a decades-old "Colonizing Society" representing the territorial and financial interests of German immigrants (Henkels)—and to provide the Botocudo with desperately needed material support. The latter request, he explained, had come directly from a group of Botocudo representatives who were weary of the endless violence and exasperated by the disease and freezing weather that were decimating their population. Whereas Congress seemed to have no trouble funding plenty of foreign priests who did nothing for Native peoples but exploit and infantilize them, Bandeira complained, the Serviço and its tutees in Santa Catarina were struggling for survival. He protested: "Funds proportional to the magnitude of the task at hand over the ten years this Republican institution has been in existence would have been sufficient to pacify and unify all the Indians of Brazil. With the funds approved by Congress, [however], fifty years will be insufficient to do what's necessary, and misery will extinguish the genuine Brazilian race."[80]

While it's unclear from the archival record if President Pessoa responded to Bandeira's heartfelt letter, the SPI worked over the years immediately following his petition to establish the Duque de Caxias Indigenous Reserve, which was eventually inaugurated in 1926. Disputes with immigrant communities over rightful possession to the impacted lands ensued, lingering into the 1950s, when Santa Catarina state ceded a parcel of the contested lands to commercial timber interests. Later, during the 1970s, Brazil's military dictatorship built the controversial Barragem Norte (Northern Dam) on the nearby Rio Hercílio, which polluted Native fishing waters and flooded areas of communal cultivation, making them unsuitable for agriculture. By the end of the twentieth century, unremitting invasion by outsiders aiming to capitalize on the natural wealth of the ever-dwindling communal lands—by then reduced to less than half the original territory—led Indigenous leaders and allies to advocate once more for the physical integrity of the reserve and to seek demarcation in accordance with their 1988 constitutional rights and the 1926 borders.[81] It was also at this time that members finally rejected the "always erroneous" labels imposed on them by generations of outsiders—including the colonial-era, generic name "Botocudo"—and began calling themselves Laklãnõ (gente do sol).[82] For Neuton Calebe Vaipão Ndili, who has written about the long-term impact of the Northern Dam on his community, these processes of self-identification and the perennial struggle for land were inseparable. "For our people," he explained in 2015, renaming "marked the moment we recovered our autonomy."[83] Six years later, the people of the Laklãnõ community found themselves at the center of a colonial-era land dispute and Supreme Court case that would decide not only their own future but also the future of Indigenous Brazil, the Amazon, and arguably, the world.[84]

Conclusion: Land as Proxy for Race

Despite the abundance of legislation that has passed over the last hundred years to consolidate the rights of nonwhite Brazilians in the national polity, the contested control of these lands and of the very names of the people who have the right to occupy them remain in many ways as unsettled in the 2020s as they were a century prior, when Alípio Bandeira penned his letter to the president on behalf of the beleaguered "Botocudo." As we have seen, the 1988 Constitution officially inaugurated a new legal era of recognition, differentiated citizenship, and territorial rights for Native peoples and *Quilombolas*; nonetheless, these many decades later, the social instability for many communities has not abated, and in fact, the intense polemicization of differentiated citizenship rights since the turn of the twenty-first century has made them ever more vulnerable. Racialized violence has increased in recent years, as anti-Indigenous and anti-Black rhetoric have taken on an invigorated political life—one that is fueled by, and fosters, ignorance, fear, and resentment—and one that has been incentivized by animosity and avarice at the very highest levels of governance.[85]

Since 2019, Native territories have been increasingly violated by fire, resource pirates, and economically driven deforestation that the world has witnessed in real time thanks, in large part, to the proliferation of social media. Dozens of unprotected *quilombos* have been demolished by state and private forces, leaving thousands of *Quilombolas* in a state of complete dispossession. In early 2022, at least 134 *quilombos* across the country were living under the constant threat of violence.[86] In a society still ruled by the white power of *mestiço* lore, land has in many ways become a proxy for race, and lest we forget the cost of building Ribeiro's *nova Roma*, racial politics is (still) necropolitics.[87]

Despite this bleak picture, and paradoxically, considering the antipathy that Jair Bolsonaro expressed for *Quilombolas*, the 2022 census included *quilombos* as such for the first time in the country's history. According to IBGE officials, the assessment surveyed 5,972 sites across Brazil (some recognized officially, the vast majority, not) to map territory, assess infrastructure, education, health care, and other key services, and to gather information on racial self-identification.[88] For the executive coordinator of CONAQ, Antônio João

Mendes, this new compendium of state-based assessments was crucial. As he put it: "Enfrentamos muitas dificuldades, pois o racismo estruturado nas instituições governamentais não deixava o diálogo fluir. Sabemos que a invisibilidade dessa população cumpre um papel importante na marginalidade do nosso povo ao acesso ao direito a viver de forma digna nos nossos territórios" (We have faced many difficulties because the structural racism of governmental institutions did not allow for dialogue. We know that the invisibility of this population plays an important role in keeping our people from accessing the right to live with dignity in our territories).[89] Official inclusion in the counting, we know too well from the decades-long experience of Indigenous peoples, is alone no solution. Nonetheless, putting people and their territories on the map is a crucial step—a necessary but insufficient condition—for creating greater security for them, and greater accountability for Brazil and for the world. Ensuring these spaces physically and metaphorically makes possible the ongoing work that the Quilombola philosopher, teacher, poet, and activist Antônio Bispo dos Santos (o Nêgo Bispo) denominated "countercolonialism"—a philosophical, cultural, and political movement grounded not in the "(un)sustainable developmentalism" of dominant discourse but in the "re-editing of natural resources" through the logic of what he called "bio-interaction."[90]

More than forty years have passed since the revolutionary scholar, artist, and politician Abdias Nascimento published his epistemological manifesto on *quilombismo*, planting seeds for racial equality that would barely begin to sprout during his lifetime. His thinking even before *Quilombola* and Indigenous rights gained protection under the 1988 Constitution, however, reflect the clear and enduring sense, shared by Bispo and other leaders in the twenty-first century *Quilombola* movement and the Indigenous movement alike, that humanity only stands to lose collectively by conceiving of itself as unconnected from the natural world, as separate from the land. As he wrote in 1980: "O quilombismo essencialmente é um defensor da existência humana e, como tal, ele se coloca contra a poluição ecológica e favorece todas as formas de melhoramento ambiental que possam assegurar uma vida saudável para as crianças, as mulheres e os homens, os animais, as criaturas do mar, as plantas, as selvas, as pedras e todas as manifestações da natureza" (*Quilombismo* is essentially a defense of human existence, and as such, it is against ecological pollution and favors all forms of environmental improvement that can ensure a healthy life for children, women and men, animals, sea creatures, plants, jungles, rocks and all manifestations of nature).[91] One might imagine, then,

Nascimento's reply—in concert with Sonia Guajajara, whose words introduced this essay—to Bolsonaro's assessment that like Indigenous peoples, *Quilombolas* "não fazem nada" (they do nothing) because they are not sufficiently rapacious in extracting profit from the Earth: "Vocês olham para quilombo e chamam de 'terra improdutiva.' Nós chamamos isso de vida" (You all look at Indigenous territory and call it "unproductive." We call that life).

NOTES

1. "You all look at Indigenous territory and call it 'unproductive.' We call that life."
2. The histories of Asian and Middle Eastern immigrants and their descendants will have to remain outside the scope of this chapter. Key contributions to these histories include Jeffrey Lesser, *Negotiating National Identity: Immigrants, Minorities, and the Struggle for Ethnicity in Brazil* (Durham, NC: Duke University Press, 1999); Ana Paulina Lee, *Mandarin Brazil: Race, Representation, and Memory* (Stanford, CA: Stanford University Press, 2018).
3. However, the Indigenous population tripled between 1991 and 2000, partly due to population growth in urban areas and partly due to the way pollsters asked about and accounted for the self-identification of their interlocutors. For an analysis of these changes, see Ricardo Ventura Santos et al., "The Identification of the Indigenous Population in Brazil's Official Statistics, with an Emphasis on Demographic Censuses," *Statistics Journal of the IAOS* 35, no. 1 (2019): 29–46.
4. One key indicator is election data. Between 2016 and 2020, for example, tens of thousands of candidates across the country switched their racial identification from white to Black.
5. The Estatuto da Igualdade Racial (Law No. 12.288) passed amid great controversy in 2010, aiming to guarantee equal opportunities for Afro-descendant Brazilians (*a população negra*) in all realms of life and to protect the individual and collective ethnic rights of their broader communities. The law conceptualized racial inequity as "any unjustified difference in access to, or enjoyment of goods and services in the public or private sphere due to race, color, or heritage," and established protection from all forms of discrimination or unequal treatment through affirmative action as an obligation of the Brazilian state. Henrique Eduardo Alves, "Apresentação," in *Estatuto da Igualdade Racial* (Brasília: Centro de Documentação e Informação, 2014), 8. The legislation created polemics around several issues, perhaps most notably the use of the term *negro* to include those identifying as *preto* and *pardo* (both official census categories, along with *branco, amarelo,* and *indígena*). For the complete statute and catalog of historical legislation promoting racial equity, see *Estatuto da Igualdade Racial* (Brasília: Centro de Documentação e Informação, 2014).
6. In keeping with the 2010 statue and in light of what is inevitably lost in translation, here I refer to Afro-Brazilians and the *população negra* as "Black" to mean those who self-identify as *preto* or *pardo*.
7. Giorgio Agamben, *Homo Sacer* (Stanford, CA: Stanford University Press, 1998), 18.
8. An outlier on this list of colors, *indígena* became an official census category in 1991, before which Indigenous peoples were counted (if and when they were counted) as *caboclos* (in 1872), and thereafter under the amorphous *pardo* category (brown).

9. Instituto Brasileiro de Geografia e Estatística (IBGE), "What Color Are You," in *The Brazil Reader: History, Culture, Politics*, ed. James N. Green, Victoria Langland, and Lilia Moritz Schwarcz (Durham, NC: Duke University Press, 2019), 475–478.
10. Recent commentary on the survey, including the edition cited, notes, however, that the majority of interviewees self-identified with one of the official categories.
11. See *Nação Mestiça*.
12. Carlos Borges, "Cotas, racismo e a destruição do Brasil," *Nação Mestiça*, November 17, 2013. All translations are my own.
13. The "one-drop rule" in the United States is consistent with the notion of hypodescent, meaning that so-called mixed-race people pertain socially to, and are defined by, the subordinate racial category of their ancestry (as opposed to hyperdescent, whereby they pertain to the dominant group). While comparative scholarship has tended to emphasize the importance of phenotype on racialized experiences in Brazil and "Latin" America, and to emphasize the impact of legal categories and legislation (e.g., the enactment of Jim Crow) in the United States, some legal scholars also attest to the varied experiences of mixed-race individuals in the United States for whom "one drop" categorization was mostly a formality. Daniel J. Sharfstein, "Crossing the Color Line: Racial Migration and the One-Drop Rule, 1600–1860," *Minnesota Law Review* 91 (2007), 592–656.
14. Nearly 5.5 million Africans arrived to Bahia, Pernambuco, the Amazon, and Rio de Janeiro between the 1570s and the 1850s. See the Slave Voyages database. The term *quilombo* derives from the Kimbundu word for "community" and has typically referred to a rural settlement of young warriors uprooted from their homes. Since the second half of the twentieth century, the referent has expanded in legal and popular parlance from its original meaning to include rural Black communities across the country, as well as formerly rural communities that have been enveloped by urban expansion. See CONAQ, "O que é Quilombo"; Antônio Bispo, *Colonização, Quilombos: Modos e significados* (Brasília: Instituto Nacional de Ciência e Tecnologia de Inclusão no Ensino Superior e na Pesquisa/ Universidade de Brasília, 2015), 63–77; and Elizabeth Farfán-Santos, *Black Bodies, Black Rights: The Politics of Quilombismo in Contemporary Brazil* (Austin, University of Texas Press, 2016).
15. Among Bolsonaro's infamous statements during a 2017 campaign event was that *Quilombolas* "did nothing" and were not fit to procreate. He also promised that not one centimeter would be demarcated for *quilombos* or Indigenous communities under his watch. See "Bolsonaro é acusado de racismo por frase em palestra na Hebraica," *Veja*, April 6, 2017; Fabiano Maisonnave et al., "Amazônia sob Bolsonaro: Os desafios para manter a floresta em pé," *Folha de São Paulo*, February 21, 2021.
16. Compare Ronald Stutzman's well-known essay, "El Mestizaje: An All-Inclusive Ideology of Exclusion," in *Cultural Transformations and Ethnicity in Modern Ecuador*, ed. Norman E. Whitten (Urbana: University of Illinois Press, 1981).
17. Jaime Amparo Alves, *The Anti-Black City: Police Terror and Black Urban Life in Brazil* (Minneapolis: University of Minnesota Press, 2018); Jan Hoffman French, "Rethinking Police Violence in Brazil: Unmasking the Public Secret of Race," *Latin American Politics and Society* 55, no. 4 (2013): 161–181; Maiquel Angelo Dezordi Wermuth, "Biopolítica e polícia soberana: A sociedade escravocrata como chave de compreensão da violência e da seletividade punitiva no Brasil," *Revista Direitos Fundamentais & Democracia* 23, no. 3 (2018): 285–309.

18. See Keisha-Khan Y. Perry, "'We Still Have a Lot of Struggles Ahead': A Conversation with Anielle Franco," *NACLA*, January 4, 2022.
19. Daniel Cerqueira, Helder Ferreira, and Samira Bueno, eds., *Atlas da violência 2021* (São Paulo: IPEA, 2021), 49. State-level statistics are even more revealing: In Alagoas, 99 percent of murder victims were Black, followed by Amapá (97 percent), Sergipe (96 percent), and Bahia (94 percent). In only three states (Paraná, Santa Catarina, Rio Grande do Sul) did white murder victims comprise the majority. Cerqueira, Ferreira, and Bueno, *Atlas da violência*, 52.
20. Pedro Lovisi, "Com menos verba, Incra não consegue desapropriar novas terras," *Folha de São Paulo*, July 7, 2021.
21. Katna Baran, "Governo Bolsonaro titulou só três quilombos, mesmo sob pressão da Justiça," *Folha de São Paulo*, August 23, 2021; CONAQ, *Quilombos and Quilombolas in Amazônia: The Challenges of Recognition*, ed. Katia dos Santos Penha, Givânia Maria Silva, and Meline Cabral Machado (Brasília: ECAM/CONAQ, 2021).
22. Rubens Valente, "Ordem da Funai que veda proteção a indígenas atinge mais de 274 terras," *UOL Notícias,* January 6, 2022.
23. For an overview of changes in administrative oversight of land titling, see Oswaldo Braga de Souza, "What Changes (or What's Left) for the Quilombos with President Bolsonaro's Reforms?" *Instituto Socioambiental*, February 1, 2019.
24. The oft-repeated phrase is "muita terra pra pouco índio" (lots of land for just a few Indians).
25. Carlos Alberto Lima Menna Barreto, *A farsa ianomâmi* (Rio de Janeiro: Biblioteca do Exército, 1995), 142–143; Tracy Devine Guzmán, *Native and National in Brazil* (Chapel Hill: University of North Carolina Press, 2013), 40.
26. Menna Barreto, *A farsa ianomâmi*, 29–36, 68–69, 107–111.
27. "What Brazil's President, Jair Bolsonaro, Has Said about Indigenous People," *Survival International*.
28. Tracy Devine Guzmán, "To Keep the Sky from Falling: The Epic of Indigenous Environmentalism in Brazil," in *The Epic World*, ed. Pamela Lothspeich (New York: Routledge, 2023).
29. Bárbara Oliveira Souza, *Aquilombar-se: Panorama sobre o Movimento Quilombola Brasileiro* (Curitiba, Brazil: Appris Editora, 2016).
30. CONAQ, *Quilombos and Quilombolas*; Rita Damasceno, Joana Chiavari, and Cristina Leme Lopes, *Direitos de propriedade no Brasil rural* (Rio de Janeiro: Omidyar Network, 2017), 19.
31. Constituição da República Federativa do Brasil de 1988.
32. Baran, "Governo Bolsonaro titulou só três quilombos"; CONAQ, *Quilombos and Quilombolas*; Souza, *Aquilombar-se*. For a detailed overview of the certification process see CONAQ, *Quilombos and Quilombolas,* 26.
33. Jan Hoffman French, *Legalizing Identities: Becoming Black or Indian in Brazil's Northeast* (Chapel Hill: University of North Carolina Press, 2009), 182. On *quilombos*, see Desirée Poets, *Un-Settling Brazil: Urban Indigenous and Black Peoples' Resistance to Dependent Settler Capitalism* (Tuscaloosa: University of Alabama Press, 2024), 63–101..
34. Damasceno, Chiavari, and Lopes, *Direitos de propriedade no Brasil rural*, 19.
35. Damasceno, Chiavari, and Lopes, *Direitos de propriedade no Brasil rural*, 29.
36. Aníbal Quijano, "Coloniality of Power and Eurocentrism in Latin America," *International Sociology* 15, no. 2 (2000): 215–232.
37. Benedict Anderson, *Imagined Communities* (London: Verso, 1983).
38. Charles Mills, *The Racial Contract* (Ithaca, NY: Cornell University Press, 1997).

39. "I am sure we have made a beautiful country. . . . We are better, because [we are] washed in Black blood, in Indian blood, improved, tropical. . . . We are Rome."
40. Darcy Ribeiro, *Mestiço é que é bom!* (Rio de Janeiro: Revan, 1997), 104.
41. Darcy Ribeiro, *O povo brasileiro: A formação e o sentido do Brasil* (São Paulo: Companhia das Letras, 1995), 13. This preoccupation appears often in Ribeiro's work, including in the final version of *O povo brasileiro: A formação e o sentido do Brasil*, which he wrote and rewrote over three decades. Typical of Ribeiro's colloquial and very Brazilian Portuguese, the phrase is roughly equivalent to "Why hasn't [the project of] Brazil worked out yet?" Or, more informally, "How come [the project of] Brazil still hasn't turned out right?"
42. Ribeiro, *Mestiço é que é bom*, 156–157.
43. Ribeiro, *O povo brasileiro*, 452.
44. See Lilia Moritz Schwarcz's foundational study of these discourses, *O espetáculo das raças, cientistas, instituições e questão racial no Brasil, 1870–1930* (São Paulo: Companhia das Letras, 1993).
45. See, e.g., the contributions of Peruvian J. Uriel García, *El nuevo indio* (Lima: Universo, 1973) and Mexican José Vasconcelos, *La raza cósmica* (Mexico City: Porrúa, 2010).
46. Gilberto Freyre, *Casa-grande e senzala* (Rio de Janeiro: Schmidt-Editor, 1938), 209. Here and throughout, I have maintained the original Portuguese spelling, which varies significantly during the nineteenth and twentieth centuries.
47. Freyre, *Casa grande*, 197.
48. Freyre, *Casa grande*, 220.
49. Freyre, *Casa grande*, 127.
50. Sérgio Buarque de Holanda, *Raízes do Brasil* (Rio de Janeiro: José Olympio, 1986).
51. Buarque de Holanda, *Raízes do Brasil*, 55.
52. Buarque de Holanda, *Raízes do Brasil*, 66.
53. The German naturalist Carl Friedrich Phillip von Martius wrote the iconic, winning essay for a contest on "how to write the history of Brazil," sponsored in 1840 by the nascent Brazilian Historical and Geographic Institute with the support of Pedro II. The essay is reproduced in James N. Green, Victoria Langland, and Lilia Moritz Schwarcz, eds., *The Brazil Reader: History, Culture, Politics* (Durham, NC: Duke University Press, 2019), 187–189.
54. Buarque de Holanda, *Raízes do Brasil*, 56.
55. See Andrade's 1928 "Manifesto Antropófago," *Revista de Antropofagia* 1, no .1 (1928): 3–7.
56. See, e.g., the famous images of anthropophagy created by Theodor De Bry in the 1590s, based on captivity accounts by German soldier Hans Staden in the 1550s. Lauren Kilroy-Ewbank, "Inventing 'America,' the Engravings of Theodore de Bry," *Smarthistory*, May 18, 2019. On the role of *antropogafia* in Brazilian popular culture see Alessia Di Eugenio, "Eternos retornos e reusos da Antropofagia oswaldiana," *Confluenze* 13, no. 2 (2021): 320–336.
57. Georges Raeders, *Le Compte Gobineau au Brésil* (Paris: Nouvelles Éditions Latines, 1934), 32. See also Sales Augusto dos Santos, "Historical Roots of the 'Whitening' of Brazil," *Latin American Perspectives* 29, no. 1 (2002): 61–82; José Honório Rodrigues, *Brazil and Africa*, trans. Richard A. Mazzara and Sam Hileman (Berkeley: University of California Press, 1965).
58. On this friendship, see Raeders, *Le Compte Gobineau*, and *O inimigo cordial do Brasil: O Conde de Gobineau no Brasil* (Rio de Janeiro: Paz e Terra, 1988).
59. Georges Raeders, ed., *Dom Pedro II e o Conde de Gobineau: Cartas inéditas* (São Paulo: Companhia Editora Nacional, 1938), 21–22.

60. For an overview of this question, see Giralda Seyferth, "German Immigration and the Formation of German-Brazilian Ethnicity," *Anthropological Journal on European Cultures* 2, no. 7 (1998): 131–154.
61. "Fornece sobre as terras livres no Império, e sobre aquelas que são possuídas por título de sesmaria sem preencher as condições legais, bem como por simples título de posse pacífica; e determina que, quando os primeiros são medidos e demarcados, serão designados a um preço, tanto para empresas privadas como para o estabelecimento de colônias nacionais e estrangeiras, com o Governo autorizado a promover a colonização estrangeira na forma indicada." For the complete language of the law, visit the website for the Presidência da República, Subchefia para Assuntos Jurídicos (http://www.planalto.gov.br/ccivil_03/leis/l0601-1850.htm).
62. Seyferth, "German Immigration."
63. Instituto Brasileiro de Geografia e Estatística (IBGE), *Censo demográfico 1872*; Daniel Mariani et al., "Censo de 1872: O retrato do Brasil da escravidão," *NEXO*, June 27, 2017. The counted immigrant population comprised 377,358 individuals. *Africanos* were divided into two groups: *escravos* (enslaved) (138,358) and *alforriados* (freed) (37,699).
64. By 1930, somewhere between 194,060 and 250,000 Germans called Brazil home, with the vast majority residing in the south. In comparative terms, this population was small, representing only 5–6 percent of "white" immigrants arriving from Europe over the same period: Italy (1,485,000), Portugal (1,321,000), and Spain (583,000). Official sources offer conflicting data on these numbers, in part, as Seyferth notes, because departures were not always counted. See Valdir Gregory, "Imigração alemã: Formação de uma comunidade teuto-brasileira," in *Brasil: 500 anos de povoamento*, ed. Magda Prata Coelho (Rio de Janeiro: IBGE, 2007); Seyferth "German Immigration"; IBGE, *Território brasileiro e povoamento: Alemães, migração alemã: Formação de uma comunidade teuto-brasileira, Brasil 500 anos* (Rio de Janeiro: IBGE, 2000).
65. IBGE, *Censo demográfico 1991*.
66. On the "empty landscape," see Mary Louise Pratt, *Imperial Eyes* (New York: Routledge, 1992).
67. "Carta Régia de 2 de dezembro de 1808," in *Colleção das leis do Brazil de 1808* (Rio de Janeiro: Imprensa Nacional, 1891), 171.
68. Beginning in the 1700s, the Portuguese used *Botocudo* as a generic term in reference to diverse Indigenous peoples of the Macro Jê linguistic family, many of whom had relocated south from Bahia to reside near the Rio Doce in the capitania of Minas Gerais, finding themselves victims of "just war" by João VI after the Cartas Régias of 1808. As I explain, other groups identified erroneously as Botocudo resided in Espiritu Santo and Santa Catarina. The name derived from the *botoques* (buttons or plugs) that many wore as lip and ear ornaments.
69. "Carta Régia de 13 de maio de 1808," in *Colleção das leis do Brazil de 1808* (Rio de Janeiro: Imprensa Nacional, 1891), 38–39.
70. "Carta Régia de 13 de maio de 1808."
71. "Carta Régia de 24 de agosto de 1808," in *Colleção das leis do Brazil de 1808* (Rio de Janeiro: Imprensa Nacional, 1891).
72. "Carta Régia de 24 de agosto de 1808," 173.
73. Marco Antônio Tavares Coelho and Ailton Krenak, "Genocídio e resgate dos 'Botocudo': Entreviste com Ailton Krenak," *Estudos Avançados* 23, no. 65 (2009): 197.

On Democratic Imaginaries in a Discriminatory Society 407

74. The collapse polluted almost seven hundred kilometers of waterways, from the Rio Doce to the Atlantic Ocean. See Fonseca do Carmo et al., "Fundão Tailings Dam Failures: The Environment Tragedy of the Largest Technological Disaster of Brazilian Mining in Global Context," *Perspectives in Ecology and Conservation* 15, no. 3 (2017): 145–151.
75. Ailton Krenak, "Crime da Vale em Mariana e a economia do desastre," YouTube video, uploaded by Brasil de Fato, November 6, 2020.
76. The SPI was founded by Cândido Mariano da Silva Rondon in 1910 as a consequence of his many years working to establish telegraph lines along Brazil's western frontiers, where encounters between settlers and uncontacted Indigenous peoples had often become violent. Given the bloody history of settler violence in their country, Brazilians considered the SPI and Rondon revolutionary in their progressive and pacific approach to "interracial" and interethnic contact and relations. The SPI motto was "Morrer se preciso for, matar nunca" (die if necessary, but never kill). Over nearly six decades of well-publicized work across the country, Rondon's organization played a contradictory and oftentimes controversial role in Brazilian politics and public life. For analyses of the SPI and the impact of Rondon's work, see Antônio Carlos de Souza Lima, *Um grande cerco de paz: Poder tutelar, indianidade e formação do estado* (Petrópolis, Brazil: Vozes, 1995); Todd Diacom, *Stringing Together a Nation: Candido Mariano da Silva Rondon and the Construction of a Modern Brazil* (Durham, NC: Duke University Press, 2004); Devine Guzmán, *Native and National*.
77. Alípio Bandeira, *Letter to Epitácio Pessoa, Presidente da República*, April 21, 1921, microfilm 334, Archive of the Serviço de Proteção aos Índios, Museu do Índio, Rio de Janeiro.
78. Darcy Ribeiro, *Os índios e a civilização* (São Paulo: Companhia das Letras, 1996), 241–284; Rafael Casanova de Lima e Silva Hoerhann, "O Serviço de Proteção aos Índios e os Botocudo: A política indigenista através dos relatórios, 1912–1926," MA thesis, Universidade Federal de Santa Catarina, 2005.
79. Neuton Calebe Vaipão Ndili, "Mudanças socioambientais na comunidade Xokleng Laklãnõ a partir da construção da Barragem Norte" (coursework, Universidade Federal de Santa Catarina, 2015), 15.
80. Bandeira, *Letter to Epitácio Pessoa*, 6.
81. Vaipão Ndili, *Mudanças socioambientais*, 16.
82. Vaipão Ndili explains that some community members also rejected the more recent name Xokleng, arguing that it too had been imposed on them by anthropologists. *Mudanças socioambientais*, 14. Other translations include "povo que vive onde nasce o sol" (people who live where the sun rises/is born) and "povo ligero" (light people). On the history of naming in this community, see Fiocruz (Fundação Oswald Cruz), "Povos indígenas Laklãnõ-Xokleng" on *Mapa de conflitos*; Braga de Souza, "What Changes (or What's Left) for the Quilombos."
83. Vaipão Ndili, *Mudanças socioambientais*, 14.
84. This complex case, which could set a precedent for pending land disputes across the country, explores the *marco temporal*, or "temporal framework," legal theory, which stipulates that only Indigenous communities who can prove occupation of their lands or litigation involving their lands as of October 5, 1988 (when the Constitution was promulgated), have the right to demarcation. However, many communities were dispossessed of their territories before or during the 1964–1985 dictatorship and have no means to demonstrate such occupation. Over one hundred communities that remain uncontacted by dominant

society are similarly unable to meet this burden of proof. In September 2023, despite a Supreme Court ruling that the *marco temporal* was unconstitutional, the Brazilian Senate passed the bill. President Lula vetoed it in October, and Congress overrode the veto in December, thereby enshrining the *marco temporal* into law. Since that time, Indigenous activists and allies have continued appealing to the Supreme Court to reaffirm its ruling that the law is unconstitutional.

85. "What Brazil's President."
86. Fiocruz (Fundação Oswald Cruz), *Mapa de conflitos*.
87. Achille Mbembe, *Necropolitics* (Durham, NC: Duke University Press, 2019).
88. At the time of writing, the 2022 Census had been postponed by the COVID-19 epidemic, and its findings were not yet available. However, as this book goes to press, the 2022 data corroborates my arguments regarding the continued expansion of the country's non-white population and the initial inclusion of *quilombo* residents in the national demographic database.
89. As cited in Dindara, "Quilombolas no Censo 2022: 'Invisibilidade nos tira o direito de viver de forma digna nos territórios,'" *Terra*, February 9, 2022.
90. Bispo, *Colonização, Quilombos*, 81–85, 100.
91. Abdias Nascimento, *Quilombismo* (Petrópolis: Vozes, 1980), 277.

BIBLIOGRAPHY

Agamben, Giorgio. *Homo Sacer*. Stanford, CA: Stanford University Press, 1998.

Alves, Henrique Eduardo. "Apresentação." *Estatuto da Igualdade Racial*. Brasília: Centro de Documentação e Informação, 2014.

Alves, Jaime Amparo. *The Anti-Black City: Police Terror and Black Urban Life in Brazil*. Minneapolis: University of Minnesota Press, 2018.

Anderson, Benedict. *Imagined Communities*. London: Verso, 1983.

Andrade, Oswald de. "Manifesto antropófago." *Revista de Antropofagia* 1, no. 1 (1928): 3–7.

Bandeira, Alípio. *Letter to Epitácio Pessoa, Presidente da República*. April 21, 1921, Microfilm 344, Archive of the Serviço de Proteção aos Índios, Museu do Índio, Rio de Janeiro.

Baran, Katna. "Governo Bolsonaro titulou só três quilombos, mesmo sob pressão da Justiça." *Folha de São Paulo*, August 23, 2021. https://www1.folha.uol.com.br/cotidiano/2021/08/governo-bolsonaro-titulou-so-tres-quilombos-mesmo-sob-pressao-da-justica.shtml.

Bispo, Antônio. *Colonização, Quilombos: Modos e Significados*. Brasília: Instituto Nacional de Ciência e Tecnologia de Inclusão no Ensino Superior e na Pesquisa/Universidade de Brasília, 2015.

"Bolsonaro é acusado de racismo por frase em palestra na Hebraica." *Veja*, April 6, 2017.

Borges, Carlos. "Cotas, racismo e a destruição do Brasil." *Nação Mestiça*, November 17, 2013. https://nacaomestica.org/blog4/?p=12410.

Braga de Souza, Oswaldo. "What Changes (or What's Left) for the Quilombos with President Bolsonaro's Reforms?" *Instituto Socioambiental*, February 1, 2019. https://site-antigo.socioambiental.org/en/noticias-socioambientais/what-changes-or-whats-left-for-the-quilombos-with-president-bolsonaros-reforms.

Buarque de Holanda, Sérgio. *Raízes do Brasil*. 18th ed. Rio de Janeiro: José Olympio, 1986.

"Carta Régia de 13 de maio de 1808." *Colleção das leis do Brazil de 1808*, 37–41. Rio de Janeiro: Imprensa Nacional, 1891.

"Carta Régia de 24 de agosto de 1808." *Colleção das leis do Brazil de 1808*, 107. Rio de Janeiro: Imprensa Nacional, 1891.

"Carta Régia de 2 de dezembro de 1808." *Colleção das leis do Brazil de 1808*, 171–174. Rio de Janeiro: Imprensa Nacional, 1891.

Casanova de Lima e Silva Hoerhann, Rafael. "O Serviço de Proteção aos Índios e os Botocudo: A Política Indigenista através dos Relatórios, 1912–1926." MA thesis, Universidade Federal de Santa Catarina, 2005.

Cerqueira, Daniel, Helder Ferreira, and Samira Bueno, eds. *Atlas da violência 2021*. São Paulo: IPEA, 2021.

Coelho, Marco Antônio Tavares, and Ailton Krenak. "Genocídio e resgate dos 'Botocudo': Entreviste com Ailton Krenak." *Estudos Avançados* 23, no. 65 (2009): 193–204.

CONAQ. "O que é Quilombo." http://conaq.org.br/coletivo/terra-e-territorio/.

———. *Quilombos and Quilombolas in Amazônia: The Challenges of Recognition*. Edited by Katia dos Santos Penha, Givânia Maria Silva, and Meline Cabral Machado. Brasília: ECAM/CONAQ, 2021.

Constituição da República Federativa do Brasil de 1988. https://www.mds.gov.br/webarquivos/legislacao/seguranca_alimentar/_doc/leis/1988/Constituicao%20Federal%20de%201988%20-%20Titulo%20X%20-%20Art%2068.pdf.

Damasceno, Rita, Joana Chiavari, and Cristina Leme Lopes. *Direitos de propriedade no Brasil rural: História, problemas e caminhos*. Rio de Janeiro: Omidyar Network, 2017.

Devine Guzmán, Tracy. *Native and National in Brazil*. Chapel Hill: University of North Carolina Press, 2013.

———. "To Keep the Sky from Falling: The Epic of Indigenous Environmentalism in Brazil." In *The Epic World*, edited by Pamela Lothspeich. New York: Routledge, 2023.

Dezordi Wermuth, Maiquel Angelo. "Biopolítica e polícia soberana: A sociedade escravocrata como chave de compreensão da violência e da seletividade punitiva no Brasil." *Revista Direitos Fundamentais & Democracia* 23, no. 3 (2018): 285–309.

Diacom, Todd. *Stringing Together a Nation: Candido Mariano da Silva Rondon and the Construction of a Modern Brazil*. Durham, NC: Duke University Press, 2004.

Di Eugenio, Alessia. "Eternos retornos e reusos da Antropofagia oswaldiana." *Confluenze* 13, no. 2 (2021): 320–336.

Dindara. "Quilombolas no Censo 2022: 'Invisibilidade nos tira o direito de viver de forma digna nos territórios.'" *Terra*, February 9, 2022. https://www.terra.com.br/diversidade/quilombolas-no-censo-2022-invisibilidade-nos-tira-o-direito-de-viver-de-forma-digna-nos-territorios,9e4ce81377b43fba05945a776acdcfbbrpclmhpe.html.

Estatuto da Igualdade Racial. 3rd ed. Brasília: Centro de Documentação e Informação, 2014.

Farfán-Santos, Elizabeth, *Black Bodies, Black Rights: The Politics of Quilombismo in Contemporary Brazil*. Austin: University of Texas Press, 2016.

Fiocruz (Fundação Oswald Cruz). *Mapa de conflitos*. http://mapadeconflitos.ensp.fiocruz.br.

Fonseca do Carmo, Flávio, et al. "Fundão Tailings Dam Failures: The Environment Tragedy of the Largest Technological Disaster of Brazilian Mining in Global Context." *Perspectives in Ecology and Conservation* 15, no. 3 (2017): 145–151.

French, Jan Hoffman. *Legalizing Identities: Becoming Black or Indian in Brazil's Northeast.* Chapel Hill: University of North Carolina Press, 2009.

———. "Rethinking Police Violence in Brazil: Unmasking the Public Secret of Race." *Latin American Politics and Society* 55, no. 4 (2013): 161–181.

Freyre, Gilberto. *Casa-grande e senzala.* 3rd ed. Rio de Janeiro: Schmidt-Editor, 1938.

García, J. Uriel. *El nuevo indio.* 1937. Lima: Universo, 1973.

Green, James N., Victoria Langland, and Lilia Moritz Schwarcz, eds. *The Brazil Reader: History, Culture, Politics.* Durham, NC: Duke University Press, 2019.

Gregory, Valdir. "Imigração Alemã: Formação de uma comunidade teuto-brasileira." In *Brasil: 500 anos de povoamento,* edited by Magda Prata Coelho, 141–157. Rio de Janeiro: IBGE, 2007.

Henkels, Henry. 2006. "Botocudos." https://sites.google.com/site/hhenkels/hist%C3%B3ria_sbs/botocudos.

Instituto Brasileiro de Geografia e Estatística (IBGE). *Censo demográfico 1872.* https://biblioteca.ibge.gov.br/biblioteca-catalogo?id=225477&view=detalhes.

———. *Censo demográfico 1991.* https://biblioteca.ibge.gov.br/biblioteca-catalogo?id=782&view=detalhes.

———. *Censo demográfico 2010.* https://censo2010.ibge.gov.br/resultados.html.

———. "Território brasileiro e povoamento: Alemães, migração alemã: Formação de uma comunidade teuto-brasileira." In *Brasil 500 anos.* Rio de Janeiro: IBGE 2000. https://brasil500anos.ibge.gov.br/territorio-brasileiro-e-povoamento/alemaes.html.

———. "What Color Are You." In *The Brazil Reader: History, Culture, Politics,* edited by James N. Green, Victoria Langland, and Lilia Moritz Schwarcz, 474–478. Durham, NC: Duke University Press, 2019.

Kilroy-Ewbank, Lauren. "Inventing 'America,' The Engravings of Theodore de Bry." *Smarthistory,* May 18, 2019. https://smarthistory.org/engravings-theodore-de-bry/.

Krenak, Ailton. "Ailton Krenak sobre Botocudos e o Rio Doce." YouTube video, uploaded by Selvagem: Ciclos de estudo sobre a vida, October 14, 2019, https://www.youtube.com/channel/UCJFxuy0nRF3Z9YvBW7vIjCA.

———. "Crime da Vale em Mariana e a economia do desastre." YouTube video, uploaded by Brasil de Fato, November 6, 2020, https://www.youtube.com/watch?v=QxTrrAOPoLk.

Lee, Ana Paulina. *Mandarin Brazil: Race, Representation, and Memory.* Stanford, CA: Stanford University Press, 2018.

Lesser, Jeffrey. *Negotiating National Identity: Immigrants, Minorities, and the Struggle for Ethnicity in Brazil.* Durham, NC: Duke University Press, 1999.

———. *Searching for Home Abroad: Japanese Brazilians and Transnationalism.* Durham, NC: Duke University Press, 2003.

Lovisi, Pedro. "Com menos verba, Incra não consegue desapropriar novas terras." *Folha de São Paulo,* July 7, 2021. https://www1.folha.uol.com.br/mercado/2021/07/com-menos-verba-incra-nao-consegue-desapropriar-novas-terras.shtml.

Maisonnave, Fabiano, et al. "Amazônia sob Bolsonaro: Os desafios para manter a floresta em pé." *Folha de São Paulo,* February 21, 2021. https://temas.folha.uol.com.br/amazonia-sob-bolsonaro/quilombos-da-selva/sob-bolsonaro-quilombos-tem-menor-orcamento-em-uma-decada.shtml.

Mariani, Daniel, et al. "Censo de 1872: O retrato do Brasil da escravidão." *NEXO*, June 27, 2017. https://www.nexojornal.com.br/especial/2017/07/07/Censo-de-1872-o-retrato-do-Brasil-da-escravid%C3%A3o.

Mbembe, Achille. *Necropolitics*. Durham, NC: Duke University Press, 2019.

Menna Barreto, Carlos Alberto Lima. *A farsa ianomâmi*. Rio de Janeiro: Biblioteca do Exército, 1995.

Mills, Charles. *The Racial Contract*. Ithaca, NY: Cornell University Press, 1997.

Nascimento, Abdias. *Quilombismo*. Petrópolis, Brazil: Vozes, 1980.

Perry, Keisha-Khan Y. "'We Still Have a Lot of Struggles Ahead': A Conversation with Anielle Franco." *NACLA*, January 4, 2022. https://nacla.org/news/2022/01/04/marielle-franco-anielle-solidarity.

Poets, Desirée. *Un-Settling Brazil: Urban Indigenous and Black Peoples' Resistance to Dependent Settler Capitalism*. Tuscaloosa: University of Alabama Press, 2024.

Pratt, Mary Louise. *Imperial Eyes. Travel Writing and Transculturation*. New York: Routledge, 1992.

Quijano, Aníbal. "Coloniality of Power and Eurocentrism in Latin America." *International Sociology* 15, no. 2 (2000): 215–232.

Raeders, Georges, ed. *Dom Pedro II e o Conde de Gobineau: Cartas Inéditas*. São Paolo: Companhia Editora Nacional, 1938.

Raeders, Georges. *Le Compte Gobineau au Brésil*. Paris: Nouvelles Éditions Latines, 1934.

———. *O inimigo cordial do Brasil: O Conde de Gobineau no Brasil*. Rio de Janeiro: Paz e Terra, 1988.

Ribeiro, Darcy. *Mestiço é que é bom!* Rio de Janeiro: Revan, 1997.

———. *O povo brasileiro: A formação e o sentido do Brasil*. São Paulo: Companhia das Letras, 1995.

———. *Os índios e a civilização*. São Paulo: Companhia das Letras, 1996.

Rodrigues, José Honório. *Brazil and Africa*. Translated by Richard A. Mazzara and Sam Hileman. Berkeley: University of California Press, 1965.

Santos, Sales Augusto dos. "Historical Roots of the 'Whitening' of Brazil." *Latin American Perspectives* 29, no. 1 (2002): 61–82.

Schwarcz, Lilia Moritz. *O espetáculo das raças: Cientistas, instituições e questão racial no Brasil, 1870–1930*. São Paulo: Companhia das Letras, 1993.

Seyferth, Giralda. "German Immigration and the Formation of German-Brazilian Ethnicity." *Anthropological Journal on European Cultures* 2, no. 7 (1998): 131–154.

Sharfstein, Daniel J. "Crossing the Color Line: Racial Migration and the One-Drop Rule, 1600–1860. *Minnesota Law Review* 91 (2007): 592–656.

Souza, Bárbara Oliveira. *Aquilombar-se: Panorama sobre o Movimento Quilombola Brasileiro*. Curitiba, Brazil: Appris Editora, 2016.

Souza Lima, Antônio Carlos de. *Um grande cerco de paz: Poder tutelar, indianidade e formação do estado*. Petrópolis, Brazil: Vozes, 1995.

Stutzman, Ronald. "El Mestizaje: An All-Inclusive Ideology of Exclusion." In *Cultural Transformations and Ethnicity in Modern Ecuador*, edited by Norman E. Whitten, 45–94. Urbana: University of Illinois Press, 1981.

Vaipão Ndili, Neuton Calebe. "Mudanças socioambientais na comunidade Xokleng Laklãnõ a partir da construção da Barragem Norte." Capstone project, Universidade Federal de Santa Catarina, 2015.

Valente, Rubens. "Ordem da Funai que veda proteção a indígenas atinge mais de 274 terras." *UOL Notícias*, January 6, 2022. https://noticias.uol.com.br/colunas/rubens-valente/2022/01/06/governo-bolsonaro-terras-indigenas-oficio-circular.htm?cmpid=copiaecola.

Vasconcelos, José. *La raza cósmica*. 1925. Mexico City: Porrúa, 2010.

Ventura Santos, Ricardo, et al. "The Identification of the Indigenous Population in Brazil's Official Statistics, with an Emphasis on Demographic Censuses." *Statistics Journal of the IAOS* 35, no. 1 (2019): 29–46.

"What Brazil's President, Jair Bolsonaro, Has Said about Indigenous People." *Survival International*. https://www.survivalinternational.org/articles/3540-Bolsonaro.

PART 3

CONCEPTUALIZING DIVERSITY

CHAPTER 15

From Creolization to *Créolité*

Creole Subjectivities and Racial Divisions in Caribbean Societies

ARIEL CAMEJO

The group of islands and coastal territories that circumscribe what was to be named the Caribbean Sea was the first place of encounter with the European endeavor to discover new commercial routes to Asia. From the late fifteenth century to the beginning of the nineteenth, the region experienced a complex process of exploration, colonization, extraction of natural resources, and geopolitical segmentations that transformed the area into what the Dominican intellectual Juan Bosch referred to as an "imperial border," a prolonged extension not just of Europe's metropolitan geographies but also of its permanent tensions and struggles within the logics of contemporary Estate capitalism and imperialism.[1]

The early and almost total annihilation of the islands' original populations, the continuous migratory waves arriving mainly from different European territories over four hundred years, the Atlantic slave trade and the introduction of indentured servants, as well as the internal migration patterns and various ethnic mixing processes within the region are some of the most relevant factors to consider in a first approach to "racial" cartographies of the Caribbean. The diversity of that map is a significant background for displaying the notion of Caribbean societies, as it encompasses relations of dependency and hegemonic cultural perspectives and knowledge(s), the articulation of national narratives and intellectual designs, and the modeling of statuses for citizenship and national identity. As a result, the notions of *criollo* and *creole*—neologisms used in the first instance to refer to those born in the "New World" and later to the languages and cultures resulting from the context of cultural contact—could be considered heterogeneous epistemic territories and spaces of resistance for ethnic, linguistic, and cultural recognition.[2]

This chapter examines how these terms emerged as a tool not just for class and racial classification throughout the Caribbean but also as a pedagogical perspective to produce knowledge about its ecology and even as a linguistic means of resistance. The question of the criollo or creole overlaps with the intrinsic variety of colonization patterns unfolded by Spanish, French, English, and Dutch metropolitan powers over their colonies, some of them shifting from one model to another during the colonial period, some still attached to postcolonial logics today, and the majority of them dealing with the effects of colonial intellectual designs that shaped the ways the body, its social space, and its linguistic behavior could regulate access to national and communitarian identities.

Territorial Logics within the Caribbean Worlds: Landscapes and Humanscapes

A distinctive element in the configuration of the Caribbean as a colonial space was the coexistence of diverse patterns of relation with the new territories under control of the flourishing European imperial powers. These patterns of colonization, slowly shaped and adapted from the sixteenth to the eighteenth centuries, were decisive in the modeling of Caribbean societies as long as they filtered the nature of political, cultural, and economic subjection to European values. In the case of the Caribbean, it is possible to isolate two basic patterns of colonization: colonies of settlement and plantation colonies.

Spain introduced the pattern of settlement from the first stages of colonization. During the sixteenth and seventeenth centuries, the islands under Spanish control were organized as a system of principal cities and villas, with a special focus on the model of port cities that could provide a secure harbor to the Spanish fleet in charge of transporting to Europe all the goods and minerals extracted from the continent. Under that design, urban development, even when it was not balanced throughout the islands, made possible the establishment of important human and trade environments in cities like

San Juan (Puerto Rico), Santo Domingo (Dominican Republic), Santiago de Cuba, and Havana (Cuba), which became nodal points of the Spanish imperial system. Minor cities and villages managed to survive under less restrictive politics of trade and were more open to informal contraband with pirates and ships coming from other colonies of the archipelago. The Spanish politics of settlement made possible early processes of ethnic mixing as long as the principal cities demanded the incorporation of labor forces for their ports, of specialized workers to develop urban infrastructure, and the consolidation of an agricultural hinterland around its peripheries, among other needs. At the same time, a solid autochthonous population took form with a very heterogeneous composition, led by successive generations of Spanish descendants. This social class developed a growing feeling of belonging to the islands and defined themselves as criollos, a social category that expressed their relation with the colonial soil even when their members were still attached to the logics and legal definitions of Spanish citizenship.[3] By the end of the eighteenth century, when Spanish colonies in the Caribbean transitioned to the plantation system as a direct effect of the Haitian Revolution, the social class of criollos already dominated spaces of symbolic production within colonial societies: local newspapers and social and literary magazines began to circulate, cultural and economic associations flourished, public institutions ensured education, and artistic practices like literature, music, and painting emerged with a particular emphasis on local landscapes and iconology (especially the customs chronicle and portrait). The criollo class was ready at the beginning of the nineteenth century to produce, within the borders of the colonial world, its own concept of nation and national identity. This process had significant peculiarities: criollos, as direct descendants of Spanish immigrants, had a privileged position in the colonies, benefited directly from the exploitation of the land—and later from the tobacco and sugarcane plantations sustained with a growing importation of enslaved Africans—and were directly linked to the legacies of Western culture. This was the social class in charge of mediating, reading, and interpreting the processes of ethnic configuration and cultural hybridization throughout the Spanish colonies in the Caribbean, which they read as a slow and nonproblematic path of transcultural synthesis.[4]

An alternative pattern was followed by other European monarchies, mainly the British, French, and Dutch, and on a smaller scale, the Danish and Swedish. This pattern consisted of plantation colonies developed during the seventeenth and eighteenth centuries. Those territories hardly experienced a process of intense settlement, which meant a lack of significant urban environments. The dominating structure was the plantation house of designated white European immigrants who were in charge of vast lands devoted to agriculture. Due to the early exhaustion of the original populations in these islands, the immigrants deemed it necessary to import enslaved people to work at the plantations. Strict policies prevented ethnic mixing between enslaved and enslaver, feeding the segregation over racial theories, and an abyss between whites and Blacks took form. Nevertheless, it was the ideal cultural context for the emergence of creole linguistic trends, as creole functioned as the only means of communication amid the social and historical disparities of the two human groups. European languages, which were living a moment of consolidation in Western states, established a linguistic bridge, an intermediate utilitarian form that merged with the heterogeneous dialectal map of the enslaved Africans. The history of creole language, then, is as variable as the trends and flows of the slave trade, which was always attached to ideological and economic disputes of imperial colonialism, triangulated between Europe, Africa, and the Caribbean, with occasional irruptions from Southeast Asia and the Middle East. The conditions of the slave trade and the plantation system changed abruptly in the shift from the eighteenth to the nineteenth century. The Haitian Revolution, but also the languishing of old European monarchies, transformed the economic evaluation of the colonial world and the cultural attitude regarding slavery. From the end of the eighteenth century, the slave trade began to be banned in the non-Hispanic Caribbean, where slavery was successively abolished during the nineteenth century: the British colonies in 1834, the French ones in 1848, the Dutch between 1848 and 1863, and due to political pressures, the Spanish territories between 1873 and 1886. The process was intertwined with constant slave revolts and, with the exception of a few maroon settlements in Jamaica and the surroundings of Cartagena (Colombia), the only successful uprising was that of Saint-Domingue, the former French colony baptized as Haiti in 1804 by the victorious previously enslaved people. The rest of the non-Hispanic territories experienced a slow process of entering into postslavery societies, which were carefully and ideologically designed to empower minoritarian creole elites, descendants of plantation owners or ethnically mixed bourgeoisies. They were favored by the structures of colonial power to maintain the social and cultural status quo throughout the regional dependencies.

The subversion of the traditional order that implied both slavery and plantation economy introduced a transformation in the colonial logics of territorial control. In the new context, the relations of dependency were imprinted not just in political or economic structures but also, and with more intensity, in the strategies that could guarantee the hegemony of Western cultural values. As a result, creole languages and cultures, which already had an expression in the ethnic and identity composition of Caribbean societies, turned out to be territories of resistance to Western hegemony.

These two patterns of colonization showed significant singularities in their development and in resulting models of societies and local cultures. But some general characteristics could be extracted to measure the impacts of the colonial experience at a regional level, the colonial fingerprints left in the region's physical and human landscapes. A common aspect was the almost total annihilation of the original populations of the islands, which explains the minoritarian ethnic and linguistic influence of those groups on the resulting cultures of the colonies.[5] In the case of the Arawak and Taíno, the groups left a reduced phenotypic mark through the islands of the northern arch of the Caribbean (mainly in the eastern mountains of Cuba, the Dominican Republic, Puerto Rico, and the Bahamas) and reduced lexical apportions associated with toponomy, crops, names of plants and animals, or dishes of their regular diet, like cassava. Even lesser was the inheritance that survived from the Caribs, whose only significant legacy was preserved with the Garifuna people, a mixed group that resulted from the contact between Caribs and enslaved Blacks in the islands of Saint Vincent and the Grenadines and was expelled by the British army after a territorial dispute with France over control of those islands. Garifunas were forced to relocate mainly to the island of Roatán, off the coast of Honduras, from where they spread along the coast of today's Belize to Nicaragua. Only in the territories along the eastern coast of Venezuela to French Guiana, including British Guyana and Suriname, did the original Amerindian cultures manage to survive the colonization process, which led to significant and peculiar creolization phenomena. Minor Amerindian groups along the Caribbean coast of Venezuela, Colombia, and Panama (such as the Wayu and Kuna people) have survived in relative isolation until today without experiencing processes of creolization.[6]

Thus, from the early sixteenth century, the demographic composition of Caribbean territories was structured by European immigrants and enslaved Africans, in a correlative proportion that could vary in terms of total population depending on each pattern of colonization and metropolitan internal regulations. While in the non-Hispanic territories the proportions of whites to slaves went from one in ten and could even reach one in fifty, in Cuba, for example, including the moment of maximum sugarcane production, the enslaved Afro-descendant population never outnumbered the white component (although the statistics did not consider free people of color). The end of the slave trade and slavery promoted the immigration of labor forces coming mainly from India and China, although Syrio-Lebanese and Korean workers also arrived in smaller numbers.

When talking about the demographic composition of the Caribbean, it is important to outline at least two elements. One of them is the spatial-temporal, linguistic, religious, and social-environmental differences that characterized these groups, arriving to the Caribbean islands during an extended process over four hundred years, some willingly, some forced, some by absolute chance. Some of them proceeded from structured cultures and languages, and some from cultures and societies in formation. Some traveled with their most valuable belongings and patrimonies, and some with no belongings or patrimonies at all. That was the case of enslaved Africans, whose only means of relation with Africa were their own bodies and memories. But all of them were impelled to build a space of their own within the aspirations and tasks of the colonial adventure and its rigorous systems of social classification, amid the reification of the Western culture. Introducing another degree of complexity, it is important to note that neither the European human component nor the African one were at all homogeneous. Only nationalist ideologies could commodify the resolution of that uneven equation where Europe and Africa functioned as monolithic entities. Where it was possible, creolization resulted in the dialectic model ("tidalectic" if we follow Kamau Brathwaite's proposal) to solve a perpetual system of differences between human groups within the reduced space of the islands.

The other element involves the new type of cultural contact that affected the colonial experience in the Caribbean. The authors of the *Éloge de la Créolité* used the neologism of "mondialization" to refer to that scenario and employed it anew in later works:[7] "The Caribbean was the melting-pot for a new 'mondialization' as it placed in brutal and permanent contact, for the first time in the history of mankind, almost all major civilizations of the world: the Amerindian, the European, the African and the Asian. These atavist millenary identities, accustomed not to living in total isolation but in contact with neighboring identities, had to confront themselves with radical foreign identities."[8] Facing that confrontation, the most disfavored human group was, with no doubt, the African one. As the slave trade across the Atlantic Ocean became a substantial component of the plantation economy, the enslaved African was incorporated into colonial schemes as a subaltern, in places habilitated to European cultural logics that asserted their hegemony over the coexisting social patterns. As Mervin Alleyne has pointed out, the colonial experience in the Caribbean reinforced the pejorative connotation of Blackness that could be traced to Greco-Roman antiquity. Thus, Black phenotypes turned out to be symbolically charged as wild, noncivilized, nonhuman, and so on.[9]

A strict system of social classification was established within the successful plantation society that came to be a colonialist hierarchy. The enslaved African was treated as a mere labor commodity, discursively presented as an alien to European values of civilization and enlightened tradition, as recent decolonial confrontations with Cartesian and Hegelian principles has demonstrated. Even the formulations of universal human rights by the French Revolution (*liberté, egalité, fraternité*) were issued while France owned vast territories in the Caribbean that were subjected to slavery. Enslaved Africans and their descendants, sometimes mixed with poor European peasants or ethnic minorities, had to face European cultural ethnocentrism and confront a racist social scheme at the same time they struggled with the trauma of the Middle Passage and the possibilities of keeping attuned to their ancestral knowledges, languages, and cultural values. Frantz Fanon described the kind of colonialist racism that was internalized by the enslaved African in his classic work *Black Skin, White Masks*, which resulted in a key element in the process of self-perception of Afro-descendants, especially after the abolition of slavery.[10] Nevertheless, the historical process of creolization functioned as a parallel way to undermine the colonial strategies of Black alienation, even though it was not until the twentieth century that creole consciousness would succeed as a space of social and cultural recognition.[11]

The Creole Subject: Creolization Processes in the Caribbean Islands

The emergence of both categories of criollo and creole—whether to signal a social class, a particular nature, or a linguistic means of communication—is a clear expression of a tension between local practices and the global experience of colonialism. Thus, we can speak about a creolization process where the agenda of colonialism collapses with the increasing demands of local territories and populations in terms of settlement, establishing a space for coherent linguistic exchange and defining a historical continuum for the new society.

If metropolitan colonial logics provided these territories with patterns of citizenship, linguistic behavior, social infrastructure, and cultural agendas, the

"New World" of the colonies contested that paradigmatic, hegemonic, and asymmetric design through intense processes of cultural hybridization that resulted in, at the least, a binary subject that is capable of answering at the same time, from a multilayered space, to the demands of both streams. What Paul Gilroy has referred to as "double consciousness" could be analyzed as a regional adaptation, in the particular terms of the Caribbean experience, of the ontological question "Who am I?"[12] As long as it is landed and displayed throughout the heterogeneity that characterizes colonial territories, this question could have been and was indeed confronted with the disruptive condition of a subject once understood as (my)self and now reintegrated as (an)other. Then "Who am I [now] [here]?" covers two different kinds of displacement: the loss of a particular relation with time (to, say, a regular and homogeneous cultural legacy) and space (a pattern of social and symbolic exchange with human groups and nature).

As has been pointed by Kamau Brathwaite in his anthological essay *The Development of Creole Society in Jamaica, 1770–1820*, the Caribbean creolization experiences implied a challenge to historical principles of cultural distinction and unitary origin because of the ethnic and cultural pluralism of its territories.[13] At the same time—and this is a clear difference when faced with the concept of hybridity—creolization has an open character as long as Caribbean societies are permanently exposed to phenomena of ethnic mixing, linguistic contact, or cultural dialogue. These elements sustained regional narratives of historical discontinuity and geographical and political fragmentation that have survived until today and lie at the very core of creoleness agendas.[14]

Brathwaite's definition of creolization somehow also contests Ortiz's concept of transculturation, which seems to accommodate in a less conflictive way the cultural narrative of Spanish Caribbean territories. To Brathwaite, creolization should always be perceived as "cracked, fragmented, ambivalent, not certain of itself, subject to shifting lights and pressures," as long as it is always exposed to new cultural, political, or economic transformations.[15]

It is impossible to refer to a single process of creolization in the Caribbean. The map of creole subjects and communities is as variable as creole languages throughout the Caribbean. The Trinidadian linguist Mervin Alleyne made a synthetic approach to some of the most relevant outputs of linguistic creolization.[16] In territories like Guyana, Antigua, Montserrat, Jamaica, and St. Kitts, different levels of language evolved, ranging from a creole speech or patois to intermediate forms of standard English. In Haiti and the French

West colonies, a French-based creole came to be spoken by a majority of the inhabitants and is also spoken in St. Lucia and Dominica, although English is the official language. The creole of Suriname drew its vocabulary primarily from English during the initial period of colonization and was later influenced by Dutch, eventually developing into dialects such as Saramaccan and Sranan. Conditions on Barbados favored a close approximation to English; thus Bajan, one of the Barbadian creoles, is quite similar to English. In Trinidad, a dialect derived primarily from English, a French-based creole, and a nonstandard Spanish evolved. Papiamento in the three Dutch islands of Curaçao, Aruba, and Bonaire inherited elements of Spanish and Portuguese languages. Other creole from English can be found in Belize and the Colombian islands of San Andrés and Providencia, where it coexists with standard English and Spanish. Due to the singularities of the Hispanic model of colonization, the Spanish language did not produce creole derivations, with the exception of Palenquero, the common language of Maroon slaves who survived in the Colombian region of Palenque.[17]

Although there are multiple theories about the origins of creole languages, whether they answer to previous processes of linguistic creolization in the Gold Coast of Africa during the first stages of the slave trade, and whether they were triggered by the conditions of slave plantations, it is important to recognize that creole languages flourished as a conscious and simultaneous production of both enslavers and enslaved people. Creole was the basic means that transmitted a certain coherence to the colonial experience of multilingual populations reunited in the Caribbean islands and coasts, and for newborn generations, it was treasured as a first sign of belonging to somewhere. But this anthropological process was soon disregarded by European ethnocentrism and cultural hegemonies. The so-called Black Code was issued in several legal documents to regulate the nature of human relationships in the colonial space, which resulted in the rise of both negrophobia and creolephobia, as has been stated in *Éloge de la Creolité*.[18]

This was to be the scope that regulated the lights and shadows of creole linguistic and cultural practices, associated ever since with Black populations and their descendants. Two critical moments would define the legacies and positions of creole ecologies in the Caribbean: the abolition of slavery during the nineteenth century and the process of "decolonization" in the twentieth century. Postslavery societies did not mean the end of colonial dependency. The former relation of property over the enslaved body was replaced by a complex mechanism of cultural control. Even when what has been recalled in the last decades as "coloniality of power-knowledge" was an active asset of colonial hegemony in previous periods, the metropolitan powers reinforced the strategies of control through the legitimation of local anti-creolist intellectual elites. The creole then remained as a separate and distant world that was recently romanticized or, in the most critical cases, in need of an anthropological restoration.[19]

In that sense, the early twentieth century demanded first the human and cultural reevaluation of the Black Self and its relationship with African heritage, more than the establishment of a clear creole aesthetics. For Caribbean intellectuals this was going to center the political and cultural struggles for recognition, even in the former Spanish colonies. The poetics of the Négritude movement, inspired by the authors of the Harlem Renaissance, especially Langston Hughes and Jamaica-born Claude Mackay, were coined by the Senegalese intellectual Léopold Sédar Senghor and followed by the Martinican poet Aimé Césaire and the Guianese author Léon-Gontran Damas, whose literary work had quick resonances in Caribbean Black and mestizo writers. At the same time, Nicolás Guillén, Emilio Ballagas and Regino Pedroso (Cuba), Manuel del Cabral (Dominican Republic), and Luis Palés Matos and Julia de Burgos (Puerto Rico) encircled what turned out to be one of the first regional agendas of anticolonial inspiration. Nevertheless, the creole world had to wait until the 1940s and 1950s and the beginnings of the process of decolonization to recall attention over its peripheral developments in Caribbean societies.

As it is known, decolonization was implemented in different degrees and legal forms depending on the logics of each metropolitan power. Many of the former British colonies obtained a status of relative independence or a special form of association, also valid for US possessions like the Virgin Islands and Puerto Rico; the French colonies turned into special overseas departments, while Dutch territories were reunited in the Netherlands Antilles. The new societies that emerged from the process of decolonization had to face, among numerous political and economic challenges, the question of the place of creole cultures and languages in this context. But once again, the racial prejudices around the use of creole undermined the possibility of its integration into the instruction policies or the new cultural and artistic infrastructure. It was not until the 1970s that regional conditions and the advancements in mechanisms of regional concertation were going to favor a revival of the creole, a true creoleness cultural agenda.

From Creole Agendas to Créolité Movement

As well as the authors of the *Éloge de la Creolité* have signaled the moment of "departmentalization" in former French colonies of the Caribbean as a second wave of depreciation of creole, it is important to recognize that in terms of regional developments, it is possible to trace a certain number of transformations that improved the place of creole languages and cultures for Caribbean societies in general. In that sense, it could be said that more than the projections of particular literary groups, which otherwise gave an extraordinary impulse to international recognition of creole through literature since the 1970s, there is a progressive change of perspective about creole inside and outside the region.

The index of access to education improved in most islands, and several universities were founded with a regional perspective (University of the West Indies, founded in 1948, has an open campus with its main strongholds in Jamaica, Barbados, and Trinidad and offices in many former British colonies; Université des Antilles et de la Guyane, founded in 1982, was also conceived as an open campus with strongholds in Guadeloupe, Martinique, and French Guiana). In 1973, the Caribbean Community (CARICOM) was created as a mechanism for regional development planning and to strengthen a common economic market. In 1972, the city of Georgetown, Guyana, celebrated de first edition of the Caribbean Festival of Arts (CARIFESTA), a cultural event that remains today a celebration of cultural traditions of the Caribbean People. In 1976, the Cuban institution Casa de las Américas integrated to its literary prize the category of Caribbean literature in English and Creole, which was going to alternate with Caribbean literature in French and Creole. In 1979, UNESCO designated October 28 as International Creole Day, and since 1984, Creole Heritage Month has been celebrated in many islands. With different intensities, the study of creole languages was incorporated to primary levels of education and recognized as official language in some islands. The international music industry was more open to incorporating genres such as reggae, calypso, konpa, zouk, biguine, and steel band, especially associated with the celebration of Caribbean carnivals. The flourishing tourism industry in the majority of the islands, though reinforcing traditional tropical stereotypes, reintegrated the creole cuisine and its local traditions. It could also be said that the framework of academic tendencies like postcolonial and cultural studies draws new perspectives on creole linguistics and the impact of creolization in regional literary traditions.[20] Finally, Caribbean diasporic communities found ways to relocate creole cultures in contemporary cultural markets through festivals, art fairs, and independent publishing houses.

To what extent these transformations feed a kind of postcolonial nationalism is yet to be settled, but it is undeniable that creole backgrounds of Caribbean societies were relocated in this new map of local developments and global exchange. Creoleness, as a direct consequence of creolization, couldn't be a reassertion of a Black culture, but of the complex social ecology that was born in the territories of the colonial world, the result of the colonial experience, the creative dialogue, tensions, and struggles between Amerindian, European, African, Middle Eastern and Asian peoples and cultures. As well as they could be registered in music, language, religion and food products, Caribbean literatures, theater, dance, painting and crafts experienced a process of adaptation, assimilation and transformation.

Following this path, the Négritude movement was a decisive predecessor for the legitimation of creole as would be the seminal works of Édouard Glissant, especially his *Caribbean Discourse* but also the ideas later resumed in his *Poetics of Relation*.[21] The *Éloge de la Créolité* initiated its journey animated by these two milestones: the reification of human and cultural landscapes of the Caribbean archipelago. The *Créolité* movement, as the first aesthetic elaboration of a creole poetics, cannot be understood without taking into account the decisive influence of Césaire and Glissant, but it tried to pass over the ethnic and geopolitical limitations of both *Négritude* and *Antilleanism*. With that purpose, it benefited, directly or not, from a growing field of regional poetics centered on the problems of the colonial experience and the impacts of eurocentrism in Caribbean aesthetics. The literary work of, among many others, Aimé Césaire, Alejo Carpentier, George Lamming, Wilson Harris, Kamau Brathwaite, and Dereck Walcott established a clear agenda of forms and themes directly connected with the regional history of colonialism. A further step was witnessed with the consolidation of a literature written directly in creole or participation of the spirit of creoleness. Haiti was a space of reference in that sense with the inaugural works of Frankétyèn, Georges Castera, and Anthony Phelps, followed by the next generation of Haitian writers, among them Maximilien Laroche, Lyonel Trouillot, and Louis-Phillipe Dalembert, just to mention a few. In Martinique and Guadeloupe, the previous creole explorations of Jack Corzani and the influence of the literary work and thinking of Édouard Glissant fertilized the literary ground for authors like Maryse Condé, Gisèle Pineau, Ernest Pépin, Max Rippon, and Daniel Maximin.

Looking at this scenario, it is easier to understand the momentum of both the "creolité movement" and the *Éloge*, which is at the same time synthetic and projective. Its place of enunciation also coincided with the implosion of the socialist world and the wave of compensative subaltern movements that returned critically over the cultural hegemonies of the colonial and postcolonial order, with particular emphasis on the strategies of cultural dependency. Contrary to many celebratory narratives that sustained the construction of national/local identities in the Caribbean, the *Éloge* assumes from a critical perspective the Euro-centered myths of universalism, monolingualism, and purity of origins to declare the open character of creoleness as a space of dialogue and rebirth of the Caribbean self.[22]

With this purpose as a guideline, the creoleness manifesto underlined three central elements: the return to an inner vision that could lead to self-acceptance, the layers of creoleness, and its future perspective in the global dynamics. The first covers the overarching horizon unfolded by Césaire and Glissant and draws the ways to escape from the desert of nonexistence where creole culture was incarcerated. "The rejection of our bilingual richness was preserved as a painful diglossia," the authors affirm.[23] Then it is time not for denial but to recognize the double and sometimes multiple trajectories of the creole peoples' existence, including those who oversaw the colonialist vigilance. As the second element entails, this task needs to be disaggregated into multiple streams: the rescue of the oral tradition where ancestral knowledge and strategies of reexistence were preserved (e.g., popular chants, proverbs, folk stories, testimonies); updating of the true memory of creole peoples, a reservoir of histories that were silenced and obscured by the history of Caribbean colonization; the wonder of revealing how the world is perceived from the perspective of this new self; the challenges of facing the complexities of the contemporary existence from the framework of creoleness; and the position of the creole subject vis-à-vis its multilingual background. In general terms, these elements established a poetic agenda foregrounded in immediate literary developments, and not without fierce debates within the French overseas departments, they suggested a certain model for artistic creation whose most exemplary case was Chamoiseau's novel *Texaco* published in 1992, which became an iconic piece of contemporary Caribbean literature.

The *créolité* movement confronted a certain criticism inside and outside the Caribbean intellectual space. From the first, it was questioned to what extent the manifesto promoted an essentialist, almost messianic conceptualization of the creole subject (as far as the text tends to homogenize the substantial core of creoleness despite its heterogeneous developments throughout the Caribbean, not to mention non-Caribbean colonial contexts). From a decolonial perspective, the inherent will to conceptualize a cultural subject and the kind of ontological synthesis it implies contradicts some of the ideological constructions within the *Éloge* when facing the colonial experience and European ethnocentrism. The aprioristic approach to creole languages and cultures that, as has been previously analyzed here, followed different paths of development, were exposed to multiple and variable degrees of social and intellectual rejection and/or legitimacy, and were or are still attached to the heterogeneity of Caribbean political map, has also been questioned. That could explain, for example, why the *créolité* aesthetic did not have significant resonance in countries like Haiti, where the use of creole language is substantial and where creole literary agendas were developed before the manifesto. Even between Martinique and Guadeloupe, both islands participating in the same political design of French overseas departments, there exists significant ideological components that mediate the legitimacy of using creole as the expression language (the *Éloge* itself was not only written in French but also is the resulting text of a conference held in Paris). Particularly in the French departments, *créolité* was evaluated in some literary circles with suspicion as it presumably could lead to a commercial strategy to relocate francophone Caribbean literature within the European literary map and the popular academic constellation of cultural studies.

Nevertheless, the *Éloge* had the merit of reactivating the postponed debate around creole legacies after the process of *départamentalization*, a complex scenario of political and cultural negotiation that intended to promote the assimilation of former colonial societies into French paradigms. That meant the obliteration of cultural traditions and linguistic practices of its population and, even worse, the preservation of the status quo in terms of racial and class-based patterns of colonial control. To the Euro-centered pulsion for universalism and confluence, the *Éloge* opposes its defense of "diversalism," a constant dynamic of self-comprehension within the shifting and interconnected experience of the world and under the scope of the inherited experience of colonialism. "But, what kind of humanist or democratic lessons do we have to learn from countries responsible for Amerindian genocide, for slavery, for the extermination of Jews, for the extinction of original populations, not to name, within their own dominions, the Inquisition, the massacre of Saint-Barthélémy, and two fierce wars they called World Wars?"[24] Diversalism, then, is the place where creole cultures could find a place to redefine notions of humanism. It is a new dimension of being human which is a permanent place of arrival and departure. A territory with multiple options of engagement: multiethnic, multilingual, multicultural, diversalism draws the possibility of delinking from historical ties to colonialism and its Western ideological frames, a possibility that is being denied with more or less intensity to the "former" colonial territories. Diversalism, rooted in a conscious creoleness, is also a political claim from a cultural experience that remains in denial of its very existence. The praise for creoleness, then, is not a mere attempt to design a poetic realm, but also a desperate cry for creole people being left to live: *Si Barbad ka viv, si Lil Moris ka viv, si Malt ka viv, si Séchel ka viv, eben nou tou, nou pé viv.*²⁵

NOTES

1. Juan Bosch, *De Cristóbal Colón a Fidel Castro: El Caribe, frontera imperial* (Havana: Editorial Ciencias Sociales, 1981), 3.
2. It is important to notice the intrinsic difficulty implied in the presentation of an overarching perspective about the question of creolization and creole identities throughout the Caribbean. Even when it has been widely recognized that there is a clear difference between the path of the "criollo" and "criollismo" in the former Spanish colonies and the developments of "creole" and "creoleness," especially in the Francophone and Anglophone Caribbean, it is necessary to remark on the heterogeneous history of the creole languages and identities, which have tended to acquire decisive singularities in each territory. As presented in this chapter, the evolution, intensification, or degradation of the notions of criollo and creole cannot be separated from the transformation of the Caribbean colonial cartographies, a map of constant shifting in terms of political dependency, economic design, or human composition. (As long as French term *créole* and English *creole* refers to the same phenomena, I use here creole as a synthetic form for both contexts).
3. Both terms, *criollo* and *créole*, come from the Portuguese *crioullo*, a word used to refer to the slave raised at the master's house and etymologically related to the Latin *creare* (to create), from which was derived the Portuguese *criar* (also to rear a child) and from which comes the Spanish *criado* (servant, but literally, raised). The terms designated in the first instance the population component that was born in the colonies, establishing a natural link with the soil over ethnic or cultural backgrounds.
4. The iconic expression of that continuum was the notion of mulatess that centered the cultural debate in Spanish-Caribbean territories during the nineteenth century (from the Dominican Republic *cuadros de castas* to the iconic Cuban novel *Cecilia Valdés*, passing by tobacco stamps). See José F. Buscaglia-Salgado, *Undoing Empire: Race and Nation in the Mulatto Caribbean* (Minneapolis: University of Minnesota Press, 2003). Entering the twentieth century, that cultural debate was conceptualized as a "transculturation" process in the classic book by Fernando Ortiz, *Cuban Counterpoint, Tobacco and Sugar*, trans. Harriet de Onis (Durham, NC: Duke University Press, 1995).

5. Antillean lexicography had established during the twentieth century a wide lexicon of Arawak, Taíno, and Carib vocabulary integrated to metropolitan and creole languages. Nevertheless, there is a significant debt with the study of the anthropological and cultural influence of the original cultures of the Caribbean in contemporary societies. During the Second Congress of Caribbean Writers held in Guadeloupe in 2009, the Dominican writer and anthropologist Marcio Veloz Maggiolo insisted on the importance of rescuing that buried past that fertilized the ways and modalities of interaction between human groups and the island environments. Recently, the Cuban academic Yolanda Wood drew attention to the legacies of the first inhabitants into the imageries of nature that were appropriated by visual arts. See Yolanda Wood, *Islas del Caribe: Naturaleza-arte-sociedad* (Havana: Universidad de la Habana, 2012).
6. The concept of creolization has a strong linguistic component as it refers to a process of naturalization of an intermediate linguistic form that rises from two or more languages in a contact situation. As one of these groups loses the possibility of maintaining its maternal language, it is substituted by the creole that in turn becomes the maternal language of new generations. The more radical the rupture with the former maternal language, the more intense the process of creolization will be. But due to the conditions of colonization, creolization means not just the acquisition of a new language but also the recognition of a cultural status.
7. Jean Bernabé, Patrick Chamoiseau, and Raphäel Confiant, *Éloge de la Créolité* (Paris: Gallimard, 1989). The French neologism has no equivalent term in English. The authors outlined with that term a process that differentiates from the more popular concept of globalization. "Mondialization," then, is a global-scale process of cultures in contact that, compared to globalization, is always open and nonregulated.
8. Raphaël Confiant, "Creolidad, diversalidad y mundialización," *Revista Iberoamericana* 82, nos. 255–256 (2016): 333. All translations are mine.
9. Mervyn Alleyne, *The Construction and Representation of Race and Ethnicity in the Caribbean and the World* (Kingston: University of the West Indies Press, 2002), 52.
10. Frantz Fanon, *Black Skin, White Masks* (London: Pluto Press, 1967).
11. Even though the first documents originally printed in creole languages can be dated to the eighteenth century, the Caribbean creoles were a tool for immediate communication and were signaled as a low-class manifestation. The pejorative evaluation of speaking in creole was a decisive instrument to consolidate the prestige and authority of European languages but, at the same time, was considered a primary source of mediation with the increasing population of African slaves. The impact and consolidation of creole languages throughout the Caribbean islands is clearly expressed in the translation of the Bible and catechism materials into the most important creoles based in French (Haitian Kréyol and French Antillean Créole), English (patois) and Portuguese (Papiamento). These texts had been of common and considerable use even prior to the stabilization of their cultural legitimacy.
12. Paul Gilroy, *The Black Atlantic: Modernity and Double Consciousness* (London: Routledge, 1994), 12.
13. Kamau Brathwaite, *The Development of Creole Society in Jamaica, 1770–1820* (Oxford, UK: Clarendon Press, 1971).
14. For example, the Caribbean shows one of the most variable maps of political statuses for a particular region in the world, encompassing a socialist state, islands associated with different commonwealths of the United States and United Kingdom, overseas depart-

ments, administrative dependencies, royal special territories, confederations, independent states, and colonial territories. See Jan Rogoziński, *A Brief History of the Caribbean: From the Arawak and Carib to the Present* (New York: Plume, 1999), 285.
15. Kamau Brathwaite, *Contradictory Omens* (Kingston: Savacou, 1974), 6.
16. Alleyne, *The Construction*.
17. See a closer approach to Spanish language and creoles in John H. McWhorter, *The Missing Spanish Creoles: Recovering the Birth of Plantation Contact Languages* (Berkeley: University of California Press, 2000).
18. Bernabé, Chamoiseau, and Confiant, *Éloge de la Créolité*.
19. That was the case of the outstanding work developed by early twentieth century Haitian intellectuals like Jean Price-Mars or Jacques Roumain; and the Martinican writer Gilbert Gratiant. In Cuba, Fernando Ortiz and Lydia Cabrera highlighted the deep and varied layers of ethnic and cultural apportions of African peoples to the Cuban and Caribbean societies.
20. See Elizabeth DeLoughrey, "Island Writing, Creole Cultures," in *The Cambridge History of Postcolonial Literature*, vol. 2, ed. Ato Quayson (Cambridge: Cambridge University Press, 2012).
21. Édouard Glissant, *Caribbean Discourse: Selected Essays*, trans. J. Michael Dash (Charlottesville: University Press of Virginia, 1989); Édouard Glissant, *Poetics of Relation*, trans. Betsy Wing (Ann Arbor: University of Michigan Press, 1997).
22. I prefer to highlight the alternatives between the notions of national and local, as far as many islands of the Caribbean or even territories within the borders on national constructions could hardly be thought in terms of national space. As Raphaël Confiant has pointed out, in the contemporary world order these territories are a kind of nonplace. "Creolidad, diversalidad y mundialización," 336.
23. Bernabé, Chamoiseau, and Confiant, *Éloge de la Créolité*, 40.
24. Confiant, "Creolidad, diversalidad y mundialización," 343–344.
25. Confiant, "Creolidad, diversalidad y mundialización," 339. "If Barbados could live, if Mauritius could live, if Malta could live, if Seychelles could live, then we could, we could live."

BIBLIOGRAPHY

Alleyne, Mervyn. *The Construction and Representation of Race and Ethnicity in the Caribbean and the World*. Kingston: University West Indies Press, 2002.

Bernabé, Jean, Patrick Chamoiseau, and Raphäel Confiant. *Éloge de la Créolité*. Paris: Gallimard, 1989.

Bosch, Juan. *De Cristóbal Colón a Fidel Castro: El Caribe, frontera imperial*. Havana: Editorial Ciencias Sociales, 1981.

Brathwaite, Kamau. *Contradictory Omens*. Kingston: Savacou, 1974.

———. *The Development of Creole Society in Jamaica, 1770–1820*. Oxford, UK: Clarendon Press, 1971.

Buscaglia-Salgado, José F. *Undoing Empire: Race and Nation in the Mulatto Caribbean*. Minneapolis: University of Minnesota Press, 2003.

Confiant, Raphaël. "Creolidad, diversalidad y mundialización." *Revista Iberoamericana* 82, no. 255–256 (2016): 331–344.

DeLoughrey, Elizabeth. "Island Writing, Creole Cultures." In *The Cambridge History of Postcolonial Literature*, edited by Ato Quayson, 2:802–832. Cambridge: Cambridge University Press, 2012.

Fanon, Frantz. *Black Skin, White Masks*. London: Pluto Press, 1967.

Gilroy, Paul. *The Black Atlantic: Modernity and Double Consciousness*. London: Routledge, 1994.

Glissant, Édouard. *Caribbean Discourse: Selected Essays*. 1981. Translated by J. Michael Dash. Charlottesville: University Press of Virginia, 1989.

———. *Poetics of Relation*. Translated by Betsy Wing. Ann Arbor: University of Michigan Press, 1997.

McWhorter, John H. *The Missing Spanish Creoles: Recovering the Birth of Plantation Contact Languages*. Berkeley: University of California Press, 2000.

Ortiz, Fernando. *Cuban Counterpoint, Tobacco and Sugar*. 1941. Translated by Harriet de Onis. Durham, NC: Duke University Press, 1995.

Rogoziński, Jan. *A Brief History of the Caribbean: From the Arawak and Carib to the Present*. New York: Plume, 1999.

Wood, Yolanda. *Islas del Caribe: Naturaleza-arte-sociedad*. Havana: Universidad de la Habana, 2012.

CHAPTER 16

Race Relations in Contemporary Central America

From State Violence to Indigenous Empowerment (1940s–2021)

PATRICIA ARROYO CALDERÓN AND
MARTA ELENA CASAÚS ARZÚ

This chapter approaches some of the most important events and sociopolitical processes that affected the multifarious experience of Indigenous peoples in Central America from the 1940s to the present. In particular, this chapter focuses on the ways in which Indigenous peoples constituted and reconstructed strong ethnic identities in spite of their historical invisibilization, negation, discrimination, marginalization, displacement, and even annihilation by states that, as shown in our previous chapter on Central America included in this book, coalesced around national imaginaries characterized by their racism, authoritarianism, and exclusion. For this reason, even if it is necessary to analyze the way in which state and economic violence disproportionately affected the Indigenous populations in the region, it is key to emphasize their capacity for resistance, their power of organization and mobilization, and their ability to imagine other possible futures.

This chapter is divided into two sections. The first addresses the very turbulent period between the 1940s and the 1980s. Those decades were marked by severe social and political upheavals, including the emergence of popular and revolutionary movements and their subsequent repression by the state, repression that reached a brutal peak with the genocide of Maya populations. The second part of this chapter focuses on the period after the 1990s, when the political conflicts in the region turned into a new kind of low-intensity warfare. This "postwar" era is characterized by the dissemination of violence across society, as well as by a series of neoliberal reforms that caused increased levels of inequality and economic exclusion. In this new conjuncture, Indigenous peoples have taken advantage of the spaces opened by the "democratic transitions" to obtain new collective rights, reconstruct the fabric of communities, reinforce ethnic-based social movements, and demand justice for the harm caused by past violence, thus managing to occupy more visible positions in the public sphere. In spite of these advances, the third decade of the twenty-first century already presents new challenges for Central American Indigenous populations, who are currently confronting heightened attacks on their ancestral territories by transnational companies, as well as the growing criminalization of activists dedicated to the defense of land, natural resources, and the right to life of native communities.

From Revolutionary Movements to the Maya Genocide, 1940s–1980s

The 1930s brought to the region—with the exception of Costa Rica—a return to a series of authoritarian regimes that maintained complex relations with Indigenous populations. In the case of Nicaragua, the family dictatorship initiated by Anastasio Somoza García in the mid-1930s did not significantly change the processes of appropriation of Indigenous communal lands, a tendency that had entered a new accelerated phase around 1925. In El Salvador, the military dictatorship of Maximiliano Hernández Martínez initiated an era of repression, terror, and silencing with significant effects in the western areas of the country, where the majority of the population was Nahua-Pipil.

In Guatemala, the relationship between dictator Jorge Ubico and the Maya peoples was more ambiguous. On the one hand, Ubico deepened the situation of dependency of a large sector of the Indigenous population in relation to seasonal labor in coffee haciendas and coastal plantations, reinstating by decree several forms of agricultural forced work that had existed since the end of the nineteenth century.[1] On the other hand, the Guatemalan dictator initiated a process of modernization of infrastructures to refloat the economic model of agro-exportation that had been heavily affected by the stock market crisis of 1929. This project involved, among other things, the expansion of the road network to facilitate the transportation of different products, a plan that required abundant manual labor. As such, Ubico promulgated new laws of road conscription geared to obtain Indigenous labor, at the same time that he patronized certain Maya elites and created new ethnic-based institutions, such as the Compañías Voluntarias (Company of Volunteers).[2]

By the end of Ubico's dictatorship, Guatemala would initiate the cycle of revolution, counterrevolution, and counterinsurgence that characterized the region during the period between the 1940s and the 1980s. As is well known, the 1944 revolution would end the liberal phase initiated in Guatemala in the last decades of the nineteenth century. This new stage, characterized by the democratization of the state, the redistribution of wealth and the means of production, and the incorporation of ample sectors of the population that had been traditionally marginalized, brought with it the desire for a more inclusive national project. However, as has been noted by authors such as Edgar Esquit (2019), Greg Grandin (2000), and Arturo Taracena (2004), the privileged place that the decade between 1944 and 1954 occupies in the region's political imaginary precludes a holistic understanding of the complexities and contradictions of the revolutionary project, particularly regarding the role of Indigenous populations during the period, as well as in regard to the specific impact that the reforms of 1944–1954 had on Maya communities.[3] Esquit has questioned historiographical perspectives that relegate Indigenous populations to a mere footnote, or that consider them a social sector that was "nonpoliticized" or "manipulated" during the revolutionary period. To avoid these tendencies—typical of both conservative and progressive historiography—Esquit proposes to review this period attending to the logics of communal politics; this shift in perspective would allow us to understand the limitations of the revolutionary project in relation to Indigenous peoples, but also to examine the ways in which a number of Maya communities appropriated the new legal and institutional tools instituted by Juan José Arévalo and Jacobo Árbenz to favor their own agendas.

One of the events that offers clear evidence to the limitations of the revolutionary project in relation to the Maya peoples is the massacre of Patzicía, committed during the initial five days of the Revolution of 1944. On October 22, in a series of events never sufficiently clarified, a Ladino man from Patzicía shot a Kaqchikel man in the market, killing him. This situation triggered an Indigenous revolt that ended in the deaths of fourteen Ladinos. In turn, this second event prompted a wave of repressive actions taken on by the troops sent by the new president, Juan José Arévalo. The soldiers were accompanied by a number of irregular militias composed of Ladino civilians who persecuted, cornered and killed between four hundred and nine hundred Kaqchikeles over several days. To understand the sequence of events that led to this massacre, Esquit analyzed the intricacies of local political struggles during the previous decades; by doing so, he has refuted dominant narratives in which Indigenous peoples were presented as mere pawns of post-Ubico reactionary tendencies. At the same time, Esquit has provided solid evidence that points to the inability of the October Revolution authorities to understand Indigenous populations as political actors in the process of reconfiguration of the Guatemalan state.[4]

Within this framework, it is possible to understand the conception of the "nation" that was prominent during the revolutionary period, as well as the institutionalization of a series of state organizations devoted to the study and resolution of the so-called Indian problem. As analyzed by Taracena, the debates that took place during the Constitutional Assembly in 1944–1945 demonstrate that the democratizing impulse that expanded the base of the electorate and inspired the reform of legislation, state institutions and economic structures, did not translate into a more plural conception of national identity. In general terms, the Maya communities of Guatemala continued being perceived by political and intellectual elites either as an obstacle to the nation's "progress" or as subaltern subjects without agency, ones whose problems should be "analyzed" by specialized institutions, such as the National Indigenista Institute or the Institute of Anthropology and History, and "resolved" by a paternalistic state. All these ideas emerged from monocultural and Ladino-centric notions about the nation, the state, and modernity. For this reason, it can be said that the new revolutionary authorities considered the processes of "de-Indianization" and the fight against "illiteracy" as necessary conditions for the "incorporation" of Indigenous populations to the new Guatemala. This progressive dissolution of Indigenous identities was attempted through plans of *castellanización* (basic education in Spanish), through the abolition of ethnically differentiated labor regimes, and through the conversion of the rural proletariat—composed to a great extent of Indigenous men—into a new class of small landowners.

The reforms adopted in the areas of labor and land ownership—particularly Árbenz's Decree 900, which initiated the Agrarian Reform of 1952— opened up an important opportunity for the participation of Indigenous populations in the reorganization of the economy and the State structure.[5]

However, as analyzed by Grandin, in the case of Quetzaltenango and the Valley of Palajunoj, not all Indigenous sectors reacted in the same way to the changes introduced by the Revolutionary governments.[6] In this area, the Agrarian Reform of 1952 introduced new tensions to the already-tense relations between a prosperous urban K'iche' elite devoted to commercial activities and the impoverished Indigenous peasantry who interpreted this process of reform as a convenient way to resolve historic demands for land control and communal power. Decree 900 opened the door for all Guatemalan peasants to claim private, state, and communal lands, and it established new mechanisms to adjudicate such claims at a local level, mainly through the Comités Agrarios Locales (Local Agrarian Committees). In the case of Quetzaltenango, this shift of power toward K'iche' peasants provoked the rejection not only of Ladino landowners who considered that their properties were now in danger but also of the Indigenous elites whose function as privileged mediator vis-à-vis the state was called into question. In this manner, some of the most important instances that had sustained the K'iche' elites' authority over the communities were eroded.[7] To sum up: in different areas of the country during the revolutionary decade, some of the demands for emancipation, autonomy, and land ownership that traditionally marginalized Maya sectors had claimed were satisfied through new institutions in the context of a democratizing state. At the same time, the local manifestations of such reforms generated a profound rejection among the Ladino landowner class, as well as among certain Indigenous elites. Both sectors would eventually end up forming an alliance with the counterrevolutionary and "anticommunist" forces that launched a successful coup d'état against the government of Jacobo Árbenz in June 1954, with the support of the United States, the Central Intelligence Agency, and the United Fruit Company.[8]

The increasing interventionism of the United States in Central America manifested in its support of authoritarian regimes that were complacent with the economic and geopolitical interests of the United States in the region. The increasing criminalization of all kinds of social protest by presenting it as a "communist threat"—especially since the victory of the Cuban Revolution in 1959—did not, however, preclude the reorganization of numerous popular movements, unions in particular, in the 1950s and 1960s. For instance, in 1954, Honduras was witness to the largest strike in the country's history, called by the workers of the Standard Fruit Company and the Tela Railroad Company, who were in charge, respectively, of producing and transporting the bananas grown in the northern coastal fields to the nearby ports. Something similar happened in Nicaragua, where numerous agrarian unions and peasant federations started to reorganize in different areas of the country at the beginning of the 1960s. According to Jeffrey Gould, many of the claims expressed by these organizations at a local level—particularly in regard to land claims against wealthy landowners—were linked to what he calls "memories of primitive accumulation," that is, the vivid awareness of the dispossession that Indigenous communities had suffered from the 1880s on.[9] Nevertheless, according to Gould, the ethnic specificity of these memories had by then been debilitated by decades of assault to the structures of civil and religious authority that gave cohesion to Native communities, by the robust internal migration of Ladino settlers, and by the effects of a national imaginary that emphasized mestizaje and stigmatized Indigenous peoples. In this manner, in spite of the strong Indigenous roots of the popular movement in Nicaraguan rural areas, the revolutionary movements that would emerge in the late 1960s and early 1970s enunciated their claims of social transformation in the name of a "peasant" popular subject that, by then, did not express any ethnically differentiated demands.[10]

Again, the case of Guatemala deserves special attention for two reasons. On the one hand, there existed a variety of opinions displayed by diverse revolutionary organizations around the relevance of the "ethnic question" for armed resistance; on the other hand, the conflict established between a profoundly racist state and a series of guerrilla groups that operated in areas of majority Indigenous population would end up in a genocide against the Maya peoples. The civil war started in Guatemala in 1960 with the revolt of a group of leftist members of the army, as well as with the emergence of FAR (Armed Rebel Forces) in the eastern area of the country, a guerrilla group formed by students, workers, and radicalized members of the Partido Guatemalteco del Trabajo (Guatemalan Workers' Party) who opposed the increasing repression of the military governments.

The conflict that confronted the state of Guatemala with the armed insurgency—and also with organized and nonorganized sectors of the civil population—notoriously worsened in the 1970s for a number of reasons. In the first place, during this decade the claims made by popular movements intensified, particularly in the increasingly frequent mobilizations of workers and students. It is important to emphasize that the organizational capacity in rural areas—especially in the western highlands inhabited mostly by Mayas—clearly grew during this period; it was channeled to a great extent through groups close to the doctrines of liberation theology, women's organizations, and above all, agricultural cooperatives and peasant organizations. Among the latter, the most important was CUC (Committee of Peasant Unity), an organization with an initial base in the Indigenous communities of El Quiché, created right after the devastating earthquake of 1976 and spearheaded almost exclusively by Maya leaders.[11] Second, in the 1970s, two additional revolutionary groups would emerge: the Ejército Guerrillero de los Pobres (EGP, The Guerrilla Army of the Poor) and the Organización del Pueblo en Armas (ORPA, Organization of the People in Arms).[12] Both groups established their areas of operation in zones of majority Indigenous population, and in particular the EGP aspired to extend the movement's reach by connecting it to the network of existing communal organizations.[13] This displacement of most of the guerrilla activities to the mountainous region in the west of the country and to the jungle areas in the northwest, forced the leaders of both armed organizations to reflect more systematically on the role that Indigenous peoples should play in the revolution, about the nature of the Guatemalan nation and state, and on the historical importance of racism and ethnic discrimination as the main forms in which relations of domination were expressed in Guatemala.[14]

According to different authors, the shock brought by the earthquake of 1976 and the exponential intensification of social movements after 1977 created a deep crisis in the military-oligarchic regime. The combination of high levels of Indigenous participation in popular protests, the displacement of guerrilla activities to the western highlands and the northwestern jungles, and the failure of the modernization plans promoted by the Guatemalan military governments since 1954 generated a perfect storm in which the state—an institution that, at the time, lacked legitimacy but possessed an excess of deadly weapons—implemented a genocide against the Maya populations.[15] According to Marta Elena Casaús Arzú, the response of military leaders and oligarchs to the political crisis consisted of the activation of the racist imaginaries that had dominated social relations in Guatemala since the Colonial period.[16] Once again, the stereotypes about "Indigenous inferiority," this time in conjunction with the principles of the doctrine of national security, became the ideological core of state institutions. The doctrine of national security—actualized in Central America after the victory of the Sandinista Revolution in Nicaragua—equated all types of social protest with "communist" or "subversive" activities against the interests of the state and against the geopolitical order in the continent. In the case of Guatemala, the fusion between racism and national security facilitated the identification of *all* Indigenous people as "internal enemies" that the military would attempt to eliminate through the unleashing of a series of indiscriminate "counterinsurgent" measures. To top it all off, during the presidency of Efraín Ríos Montt (March 1982–August 1983), neo-Pentecostal doctrines that proclaimed the idolatrous and sinful nature of "communist Indians" added yet another layer of anti-Indigenous sentiment to the Guatemalan state apparatus. The alignment of the aforementioned elements resulted in a genocide in which the Guatemalan army—with the support of paramilitary groups—destroyed more than 600 villages, killed more than 70,000 people, raped an estimated number of 45,000 Maya women, and provoked a diaspora of more than 1.5 million refugees.[17]

Research on the Maya genocide is abundant and covers an enormous variety of angles.[18] Because it is impossible to analyze here all of those aspects, this chapter focuses on two fundamental facets of the Maya genocide: the study of racism as the most notorious feature of the ideology of the Guatemalan state and army during the 1980s, and the prevalence of sexual violence against Maya women as a mechanism used for the destruction of Indigenous communities.

Efraín Ríos Montt's coup d'état in March 1982 brought with it new strategies for the massive and systematic annihilation of noncombatant civilians, a tendency that accelerated after the implementation of the Victoria 82 campaign plan.[19] According to Jennifer Schirmer,[20] the objective of the plan was to separate the guerrilla fighters from noncombatant civilians or, as Ríos Montt put it, to extirpate "evil" from Guatemala by "taking the water from the fish."[21] Victoria 82 identified a series of war zones—all located in Indigenous territories—in which the army should carry out two complementary activities: the first consisted in "extermination" tasks; the second, in "recuperation" duties. The first task materialized in a series of military tactics known as scorched earth, that is, the systematic and indiscriminate elimination of all the population located inside the perimeter of military zones, including guerrillas, Communities of People in Resistance, and noncombatant civilians residing in the villages in the area.[22] In practice, the strategy of scorched earth consisted of indiscriminate and massive massacres of Indigenous peoples who resided in rural and remote areas of the country. Such massacres of male and female adults, elders, and children were always accompanied by actions of extreme cruelty—including torture, executions, impalements, and public sexual assaults; extraction of fetuses from pregnant women; mutilations and public display of corpses; aerial bombardments of survivors; and many more atrocities—geared toward dehumanizing Indigenous peoples and terrorizing whole communities.[23]

It is undeniable that racism occupied a central place in Guatemala's genocide. As some military documents—like Operation Sofia—demonstrate, the inhabitants of the areas attacked by the army were systematically dehumanized through various strategies, including their objectification and their animalization. In a number of documents, Maya children assassinated by the troops are called "chocolates," while other civilian victims are referred as "undocumented elements," and "irregular local forces" (Fuerzas Irregulares Locales, FIL). In other cases, expressions such as "25 horses, 70 sheep, 35 cows and 15 FIL were eliminated" were used; as it can be seen, farm animals appear as more relevant than Indigenous people for the army officers in charge of registering the number of victims. Finally, it is also important to indicate that a good number of survivors' testimonies emphasize the racism and the dehumanizing practices used by the army in their attacks on the villages.[24]

Additionally, it is crucial to address a very relevant aspect of the Guatemalan genocide: sexual violence against Indigenous women.[25] As many testimonies offered by women survivors of different ethnicities demonstrate, one of the most common occurrences during the army attacks on the villages consisted in the public, repeated, and collective rape of Indigenous women of all ages. These rapes also continued in other contexts, particularly at military posts, where many women survivors were transported after the destruction of their villages.

This was the case in Sepur Zarco (El Estor, Izabal), where an undetermined number of Q'eqchi' widows were retained as sexual and domestic slaves, some of them for a period of up to six years, during the 1980s.[26] These women were forced to take "turns" in the military detachment in order to complete a series of tasks for the soldiers, like washing their uniforms and preparing tortillas and other meals. At the same time, they were systematically raped by the troops. The goal of these public and massive violations was threefold: to humiliate and annihilate Indigenous women, to break the basic bonds and structure of the communities, and to impede the reproduction of the Mayas by "killing the seed." The ways in which sexual violence against Maya women unfolded during the genocide—highly systematized, depersonalized, and following specific protocols—as well as its connection with other forms of physical and cultural destruction of Indigenous peoples, has inspired feminist anthropologists such as Rita Segato to define the actions as a "femigenocidio" (femigenocide).[27] Likewise, these same features prompted the Guatemalan courts to sentence that sexual violence, in conjunction with other attacks against Indigenous peoples, was deployed with the objective to eliminate Maya communities.

As this section has shown, the social and political conflicts that characterized the history of the isthmus since the 1950s reached their peak of violence in the 1980s. Nevertheless, it was also in the 1980s that the first negotiations between belligerent parties started, approaches that would eventually put an end to the internal wars in Nicaragua, El Salvador, and Guatemala between 1990 and 1996. Despite the fact that transitions to democracy in the region happened under very precarious conditions, it is also important to note that violence, particularly gross human rights violations, considerably diminished from the 1990s on. At the same time, some advances took place regarding the situation of refugees; three truth commissions—one in El Salvador, two in Guatemala—were established; new rights for women and Indigenous peoples were recognized; new spaces opened up in the political arena; and there was a noticeable increase in participation of Indigenous leaders and intellectuals in the region's public sphere. In any case, there is consensus among scholars about the limitations of Central American transitions, to the point that some authors have alluded to this postwar period as "low-intensity," "uncertain," or "incomplete" democracies.[28] These transitional deficits have no doubt contributed to a series of problems that currently plague Central American countries, among them the return of authoritarian, autocratic, and populist regimes; the co-opting of the state by powerful oligarchies, drug lords, and other criminal organizations; high levels of corruption, impunity, and daily violence; and widespread social conflicts, transnational migration, and environmental degradation caused by an economic model that relies heavily on extractive activities. Still, and in spite of the complexity of the Central American scenario, Indigenous and Afro-descendant populations have reemerged as central social and political actors since the 1990s, in conjunction with new and strong popular movements.

The next section of this chapter focuses on some of the most important demands advanced by Indigenous and Afro-descendant leaders in the region: the struggles for the recognition of specific rights; the fights for the adoption of plurinational state models, where plurilingualism and pluralism within the juridical system are respected; the struggles against impunity and corruption; and the defense of Indigenous territories, natural resources, the environment, and the right to life for all peoples.

The Reconstitution of Ethnic Identities in Central America, 1990s–2021

As in other Latin American contexts, the 1990s in Central America also represented a turning point with respect to the reconstitution of ethnic identities, as well as the reemergence of Indigenous peoples as powerful political, social, and cultural actors. Without a doubt, some of the factors that explain this resurgence are common to the whole continent: for instance, the internationalization of multicultural doctrines and the subsequent recognition of differential rights for Indigenous peoples by a number of Latin American states; the adoption of the International Labour Organization's Indigenous and Tribal Peoples Convention (No. 169) in 1989; the countercelebrations to the fifth centenary of the "discovery of America" launched in 1992 by Indigenous peoples under the slogan "five hundred years of resistance"; and the strengthening of popular organizing that resulted from the social crisis provoked by the implementation of neoliberal recipes across the continent. However, other reasons were specific to the Central American context, including the awarding of the Nobel Peace Prize to Rigoberta Menchú Tum in 1992; the end of the regional wars as a result of peace agreements that recognized a wide range of rights for Indigenous peoples; and the opening of political, social, and cultural spaces for a new generation of Indigenous leaders.[29]

In general terms, it can be said that this period has two phases. The first one corresponds to the decade of the 1990s and the early 2000s; this phase was characterized by the recognition of specific rights for Indigenous populations, by the debates on the need to rethink the nature of Central American nations and their relation with cultural diversity, by the denunciation of racism as a structural problem in the isthmus' societies, and by the Indigenous peoples' demands for territorial autonomy and self-government. The second phase corresponds to the twenty-first century, especially since 2010. This period is marked by the struggles in favor of collective memory and justice, against the corruption of Central American states, and against an increasingly predatory economic model based on extractive activities. It is also characterized by an intensification in the criminalization and repression of Indigenous leadership in the region and by the emergence of new platforms for plurinational and interclass popular alliances.

The decade of the 1970s brought with it some early attempts in Indigenous organizing, as well as the first state efforts in enacting specific laws geared toward the Native populations of the region; some examples include the articulation of diverse ethnic organizations in Guatemala and El Salvador, or the approval of the Indigenous Law in Costa Rica in 1977. Nevertheless, it was not until the late 1980s and early 1990s when Central American Indigenous populations would arise as primary actors in the social and political arena. In the case of Honduras, the transition from a military to a civil regime—initiated with the summons to form a Constitutional Assembly in 1980—opened new spaces for the reconstruction of the organizational capacity of Hondurans. Indigenous, Afro-Indigenous and Afro-descendant groups (particularly the Lencas, the Chortís, and the Garifuna) took advantage of these spaces to strengthen their ethnic and cultural identities, increase their presence in the public sphere, and put together common agendas and demands.[30] Between 1985 and 1998, Indigenous and Afro-descendant peoples put pressure on the state and succeeded in obtaining, among other things, the official recognition of Honduras as a multiethnic, pluricultural, and plurilingual nation; the approval of the ILO Convention No. 169; the expulsion of multinational logging companies interested in exploiting forests located in Miskito territory; the suspension of laws that would have endangered the integrity of Garifuna lands; and the interruption of megaprojects, particularly large hydroelectric dams, that would have affected the ancestral territories of different ethnic groups. In spite of several initial victories achieved by Indigenous and Afro-descendant "pilgrimages" to Tegucigalpa,[31] the Honduran state soon disregarded these commitments, particularly the agreements related to the implementation of protection mechanisms for ancestral territories, as well as to the right of Indigenous and Afro-Indigenous communities to be consulted about mining, hydroelectric, logging, and tourism development projects. This is why the conflict between Indigenous and Afro-descendant communities and the Honduran state started to escalate by the end of the 1990s, deteriorating even more after the coup d'état of 2009. In this new phase—characterized by the almost complete militarization of the country, as well as by high levels of violence, corruption, and impunity—social exclusion has increased and extractive activities have intensified, at the same time that popular, Indigenous, and Afro-descendant movements have resurged.[32] Today, these movements face very high levels of violence at the hands of national and transnational economic actors oftentimes connected to organized crime, while they also suffer different forms of criminalization and repression by the Honduran State. An illustrative example of the aforementioned dynamics was the assassination of Lenca leader Berta Cáceres in 2016. Her murder no doubt caused an enormous uproar in the global public opinion; however, cases such as Cáceres's are unfortunately far from being unique or isolated in the Central American isthmus.[33]

In the case of Nicaragua, an organized Indigenous movement emerged during the 1980s against the backdrop of the war between the Sandinistas and the "Contras." In that context, the armed mobilization of the Miskito population helped advance the project of autonomy and self-government for the territories located in the Atlantic region, mostly occupied by Miskito, Mayangna, Rama, and Kriol communities. However, similarly to the case of Honduras, the relations between Indigenous and Afro-descendant populations and the Nicaraguan state have notoriously deteriorated in the twenty-first century, particularly after the Frente Sandinista, this time led by President Daniel Ortega and Vice President Rosario Murillo, returned to power in 2006. Concretely, the leaders of the Miskito and Mayangna communities living in the autonomous areas of the Caribbean coast have been denouncing for years the harassment and illegal occupation of their lands by mestizo settlers, as well as the violence inflicted by miners, loggers, and cattle ranchers allegedly protected by the government.[34] The violation of ancestral territories and of the right of Indigenous communities to be consulted were also exposed in the context of the plans to construct a "Grand Interoceanic Canal" in Nicaragua. The canal, which was expected to be financed with Chinese capital, caused an uproar in Nicaraguan society, to the point that the project was eventually canceled. In any case, all these tensions—in conjunction with other high-profile events, such as the wildfire that destroyed the nature reserve of Indio Maíz, ancestral territory of several Rama and Kriol communities—motivated a number of Indigenous leaders and communities to ally with other sectors of the Nicaraguan population in the massive popular protests that rocked the Ortega-Murillo regime during the spring of 2018.

In El Salvador, the emergence of Indigenous organizations and demands took place after the signing of the Chapultepec Peace Agreements in 1992, which ended the civil war that devastated the country during its twelve years.[35] The agreements indicated the need to reconstruct the social, political, economic, and cultural fabric of the country and, above all, to guarantee the peaceful coexistence of former opponents. To this end, a series of programs were implemented, most of them financed by international institutions such as UNESCO and the European Union, with the objective of creating a "culture of peace." These transnational initiatives prompted the emergence of a series of new Indigenous organizations, such as the CCNIS (Nationwide Coordinating Council of Salvadoran Indigenous Peoples), a coalition created in 1994 with the goal of pressuring the Salvadoran state to ratify the ILO Convention No. 169 and to defend the rights of Nahua-Pipil, Lenca, and Cacaopera communities to strengthen their ethnic identities. However, according to Virginia Tilley, many factors conspired against the advancement of the Salvadoran Indigenous movement, including internal divisions, struggles among different organizations that competed for international funds, and the existence of important divergences between "Indigeneity" as experienced by specific communities in El Salvador and "Indigeneity" as understood by international organizations.[36] In any case, the advances in this country were modest: the organizations did not succeed in convincing the state to neither recognize the multiethnic, pluricultural and plurilingual nature of the nation, nor to ratify the Convention No. 169. Currently, Salvadoran Indigenous peoples confront high levels of discrimination, different forms of economic and social exclusion, lack of access to justice, environmental degradation, and loss of their ancestral territories.

The Indigenous peoples of Costa Rica, Panama, and Belize confront similar challenges to those presented to the Indigenous populations of Honduras, Nicaragua, and El Salvador. The Costa Rican state acknowledged the existence of eight different ethnicities in 1977, via the Indigenous Law, which recognized twenty-four ancestral territories inhabited by the Huetar, Maleku, Bribri, Cabécar, Brunka, Ngäbe, Bröran, and Chorotega peoples, and ratified the ILO Convention No. 169 in 1993. Despite these early legal achievements, Indigenous communities in Costa Rica suffer from disproportionate levels of poverty—in the case of the Cabécar, it has reached 94 percent of households—and the integrity of their territories is systematically violated by transnational companies and settlers alike. Since the 2010s, clashes between different communities and an assortment of mining and oil extraction projects have skyrocketed, while non-Indigenous settlers have multiplied their presence in Indigenous territories as a result of the boom in new agricultural commodities (e.g., pineapples, citrus fruits, palm oil) that rely on extensive farming to be profitable. The pressure of non-Indigenous settlers over Indigenous territories has, in many cases, led to violence, including death threats and the eventual assassination of communal leaders. The situation of Indigenous communities in Panama—a country that recognizes a series of Indigenous territories called *comarcas*, as well as some legal mechanisms that facilitate consultations in the communities—is somewhat similar to the one we have just described. Indigenous territories in Panama are under attack by mining companies, hydroelectric megaprojects, and practices of fraudulent land titling. The situation is further complicated in the Caribbean region, where the Ngäbe-Buglé communities have been pressured to abandon their lands and dwellings as a result of massive development projects oriented to attract North American and European short-term tourists and long-term residents (often senior citizens looking for a more affordable and comfortable retirement). In some cases, such as in the archipelago of Bocas del Toro, this touristification of the coastal areas has led to serious conflicts between the Ngäbe communities and transnational developers, but also to interethnic tensions between Indigenous peoples and some Afro-Panamanian communities and individuals who have benefited from the booming tourist industry or who have agreed to serve as fronts for the land-titling rackets. Other coastal Indigenous communities, however, face even greater challenges. This is the case of the Guna (or Kuna) peoples whose ancestral land, Guna Yala—a territory that includes more than thirty islands—is in the process of becoming uninhabitable due to rising sea levels and increasingly extreme weather in the Caribbean basin. Finally, a few words on the situation of the Indigenous peoples of Belize is in order, despite the fact that this country is seldom included in scholarly discussions on Central American Indigenous populations. Around 11 percent of the Belizean population is of Maya descent, with an ethnic majority of Q'eqchi,' and minorities of Mopan and Yucatec Mayas. Whereas the presence of Mayas in Belize dates back to the pre-Columbian period, this population experienced an important increase during the nineteenth century, as a result of the migration of Yucatec Mayas who were fleeing the Caste War in the Yucatán Peninsula, as well as to the substantive arrival of Maya Q'eqchi' who were escaping the harsh conditions that newly arrived German planters had implemented in the coffee haciendas of the Guatemalan Verapaces after the 1870s. Nowadays, and despite some legal advancements in the recognition of the rights of Belizean Mayas to live and work in the lands that they have traditionally used and occupied, Indigenous populations in this Central American country still suffer high levels of poverty, food insecurity, and land dispossession—in this case, due to the pervasiveness of logging and oil exploration in their territories.

We conclude this chapter by paying attention to the complex case of Guatemala. As has been stated in the previous section, in spite of the high degree of violence and repression experienced by the Mayas during the 1970s and especially the 1980s, Indigenous leadership successfully consolidated around a series of civic, peasant, cultural, and human rights organizations.[37] However, the real breakthrough in the Maya movement would arrive with the change of conditions in the mid-1990s: first, with the ratification of the AIDIPI (Agreement on Identity and Rights of Indigenous Peoples) in 1995 and later with the approval of the ILO Convention No. 169 and the signing of the peace accords in 1996. In particular, the AIDIPI opened up new spaces by recognizing individual and collective rights for Indigenous peoples and communities. At the same time, the Maya population, particularly women, was recognized as a central actor in the social movements and within civil society. This document also redefined the Guatemalan nation as multiethnic, pluricultural, and plurilingual; recognized the heterogeneity of Indigenous populations, including Garifunas, Xincas, and Mayas (this latter group being the largest and most diverse, with twenty-two different ethnicities); and focused on the struggle against ethno-racial discrimination. Additionally, the AIDIPI emphasized the rights of Indigenous women; recognized all twenty-two Maya languages and a series of cultural rights for Native peoples; presented interculturality as a basic principle; indicated the importance of increasing the levels of political, social, and economic participation of Indigenous peoples; recognized the validity of customary law; and proposed the restitution of communal lands.

To sum up, it can be said that during the decades of the 1990s and the early 2000s, the Indigenous peoples of Guatemala emerged as crucial political, economic, social, and cultural actors. As such, they managed to gain visibility in the public sphere;[38] they were able to exercise new rights (particularly those rights related to the study and preservation of Indigenous languages, to bilingual and intercultural education, and to the protection of Maya sacred spaces and spiritual practices); and they advanced the struggles for collective memory, truth, justice, reparations, and human rights. Additionally, most Indigenous communities were successful in reinforcing their social fabric, organizational capacity, and ethno-cultural identity through more than three hundred community consultations guided by ancestral authorities. However, in spite of all these accomplishments, many scholars and activists have pointed out several shortcomings derived from the Guatemalan state's reluctance to comply with agreements related to the restitution of communal lands and the application of Maya laws.

These aspects—the issue of land ownership, the question of territorial sovereignty, and the matter of juridical pluralism—are still central to the struggles of Indigenous peoples in Guatemala. In fact, the second decade of the twenty-first century has been, for the most part, unfavorable toward Indigenous peoples due to the intensification of an economic model based on extractive activities and land dispossession, the displacement of numerous communities, the contamination of rivers and soils, and the criminalization of the actions of land, environmental, and human rights defenders.[39] This onslaught against the living conditions of Indigenous peoples has been facilitated by the cooptation of state institutions at the hands of local oligarchies, transnational corporations, corruption networks, and organized crime.

All these entities have reactivated high levels of violence against Indigenous activists and communities and have fostered an atmosphere of impunity.[40]

The debates around the amendment of Article 203 of the Constitution of Guatemala—a piece of legislation that seeks the equal incorporation of Maya customary law to the national juridical system—happened in this context. During these discussions, Guatemalan political and economic elites did not hesitate to reactivate a racist repertoire that depicts "Indians" as "unrepentant," "vengeful," "cruel," and "resentful," thus rebooting the old colonial fears about "racial difference" for a twenty-first-century audience.[41] At the same time, the revival of these threatening tactics has motivated a new generation of Maya women intellectuals to center, once again, the reflections on racism as the foundation of the Guatemalan state, to denounce its negative effects on Indigenous subjectivities, and to point to its pernicious consequences for the living conditions of the communities, including high levels of violence, poverty, discrimination, and exclusion.[42]

In a similar fashion, the ascertainment of these processes of institutional degradation has prompted many Indigenous intellectuals, activists, and organizations to begin a debate on the nature of the state and of sovereignty. In this debate, organizations such as the Coordinación y Convergencia Nacional Maya Waqib' Kej (Nationwide Maya Coordination and Convergence Platform Waqib' Kej) have proposed the need to refound the Guatemalan state as a truly plurinational and democratic entity. In this framework, the new Guatemalan State should be put to the service of all, guaranteeing the welfare of the population, helping weave new relations among the diverse ethnoracial groups and different social sectors, and reformulating the relationship between human beings and Mother Nature. In parallel, other organizations such as CODECA also support the refoundation of the Guatemalan state and nation, considering this process as a first step that would culminate in the summons of a constitutional assembly destined to fully reconfigure the legal, political, and economic systems. Finally, the forty-eight *cantones* (districts) of Totonicapán propose a different approach focused on launching a sustained effort of popular and interethnic mobilizations with the goal of fighting corruption, as well as guaranteeing territorial sovereignty, legal pluralism, and the rights of Indigenous peoples. In any case, all these tendencies indicate that, currently, the Indigenous peoples of Guatemala are at the forefront of the popular movements that oppose extractive capitalism, institutional corruption, and the use of violent state repression as a tool to placate social discontent. Finally, it is important to mention that these movements are formulated around a non-Western episteme that places *buen vivir* ("living well" or "collective well-being") above all other criteria.[43]

This chapter shows how Native peoples resurged with great strength in Central America during the 1990s, taking advantage of a favorable international and local context. While Indigenous peoples have fought hard to reconstruct their ethnic identities and enforce their demands, the twenty-first century has come with new challenges in the forms of extreme violence and land dispossession, which threaten again the living conditions of the isthmus's communities. However, in spite of the onslaught of corrupt states, organized crime networks, and transnational companies, Central American Indigenous populations resist and—almost everywhere in the region—lead the struggles for a dignified life for all people.

NOTES

1. For example, Ubico instituted the Law against Vagrancy, which consisted of a series of regulations approved in 1934 through which all unemployed males who did not own land (or who owned smaller plots of land than those stipulated by the law) were obliged to secure employment in a farm at least one hundred days per year.
2. The Compañías Voluntarias were militias integrated exclusively by Indigenous men. In addition to their primary task of maintaining public order, the members of the companies had to work 150 days per year on private farms, as well as in the construction of roads. See Arturo Taracena, *Etnicidad, nación y estado en Guatemala* (Antigua, Guatemala: CIRMA, 2004), 2:33.
3. Edgar Esquit, *Comunidad y estado durante la revolución: Política comunal maya en la década de 1944-1954 en Guatemala* (Guatemala City: Tujaal, 2019); Greg Grandin, *The Blood of Guatemala: A History of Race and Nation* (Durham, NC: Duke University Press, 2000); Arturo Taracena, *Etnicidad, nación y estado*. Conservative historiography has defended the idea that the 1944 revolution constituted a radical communist project that had to be extirpated from the root. In turn, historiography "from the left" has sacralized this decade and considers the ruling of Arévalo Martínez and Árbenz as unequivocal referents of democracy and equality in Guatemala.
4. Esquit, *Comunidad y estado durante la revolución*, and Taracena, *Etnicidad, nación y estado*, have noted that the tension between the Ladino and Kaqchikel populations in Patzicía was already apparent before the triumph of the October Revolution in 1944, as a result of a series of conflicts around local power and resources, in particular as related to the use of arable lands and communal forests. The ethnic fractures were exacerbated during the very brief interim presidency of Federico Ponce Vaides (July-October 1944), whose actions contributed to a nationwide reactivation of the old colonial fears of *motines de indios* (Indigenous revolts).
5. Reforms included the abolition of forced labor in haciendas and roads, as well as the

enactment of the 1947 Labor Code that facilitated the creation of new workers' unions and organizations.
6. Greg Grandin, *The Blood of Guatemala*.
7. An important point of contention was the regulation of the use of communal lands and forest. This important task had previously been under the exclusive control of local Indigenous councilmen; after 1952, it fell under the purview of the Local Agriculture Committees. See Grandin, *The Blood of Guatemala*, 212.
8. The coup d'état against Jacobo Árbenz Guzmán is sadly known for being the first US intervention in Latin America that followed the new rationale of the Cold War. It is hard to overestimate the importance of this coup for Central American history, as the establishment of the military government of Carlos Castillo Armas—a colonel who enjoyed the full support of the US administration—marks the beginning of a new phase in the isthmus. The new period initiated in 1954 would be characterized by increased US meddling in the region, a growing presence of the military in the political arena, the authoritarian implementation of CEPAL-backed models of economic development, the enforcement of the national security doctrine to "fight against communism," and increased levels of repression toward a series of popular movements that emerged during the 1950s and gained traction in the 1960s and 1970s.
9. Jeffrey Gould, *To Die in This Way: Nicaraguan Indians and the Myth of Mestizaje, 1880–1965* (Durham, NC: Duke University Press, 1998).
10. This statement is also valid for the case of El Salvador, where a series of guerrillas—later unified as the Frente Farabundo Martí de Liberación Nacional (FMLN)—did not pay particular attention to issues related to race and ethnicity. Returning to the case of Nicaragua, the relations between the Frente Sandinista de Liberación Nacional (FSLN)—the guerrilla coalition that overthrew the Somoza dictatorship in July 1979—and the Indigenous peoples of the Atlantic coast were never smooth. This was particularly evident during the 1980s, when the FSLN was involved in a serious conflict with the Miskito and, to a lesser extent, Mayangna communities. In a nutshell, a substantial number of Miskito communities—disappointed when the degree of territorial autonomy offered by the new revolutionary authorities did not match their expectations—joined the counterrevolutionary efforts of the Contra Army, an armed group composed of former *somocista* troops that invaded Nicaragua with the blessing of the US administration. The conflict between the FSLN and the Indigenous communities of the Atlantic coast of Nicaragua remained open until 1987, when a new Statute of Regional Autonomy was agreed on.
11. The earthquake of February 4, 1976, had a magnitude of 7.5 on the Richter scale and caused around twenty-five thousand deaths. The aftermath of the earthquake revealed the extreme poverty affecting vast percentages of the Guatemalan population, particularly in Indigenous majority areas of the country.
12. EGP and ORPA, together with FAR and a very small fraction of the PGT, united in 1982 under the banner of the URNG (Guatemalan National Revolutionary Union).
13. While EGP leaders were inspired by the Vietcong's strategies of "popular revolutionary war," ORPA commanders favored the creation of a guerrilla army that would operate in parallel to the social movements, but that would be independent from them. See Carlota MacAllister, "A Headlong Rush into the Future: Violence and Revolution in a Guatemalan Indigenous Village," in *A Century of Revolution: Insurgent and Counterinsurgent Violence during Latin America's Long Cold War*, ed. Greg Grandin and Gilbert K. Joseph

(Durham, NC: Duke University Press, 2010); Julieta Carla Rostica, "El anticomunismo y el fracaso de la 'integración' del indio: Hacia la coyuntura crítica del genocidio en Guatemala, 1954-1978," *Revista THEOMAI: Estudios Críticos sobre Sociedad y Desarrollo*, no. 36 (2017): 24-42.

14. For a detailed analysis of these discussions within EGP and ORPA, see Marta Elena Casaús Arzú, *Racismo, genocidio y memoria* (Guatemala City: F&G Editores, 2019), 200-202; Rostica, "El anticomunismo y el fracaso de la 'integración' del indio," 36; Taracena, *Etnicidad, nación y estado*, 125-131.

15. The Permanent Peoples' Tribunal, created in 1979, and the Jesuit priest Ricardo Falla, in his book *Masacres de la selva, Guatemala, 1975-1982* (Guatemala City: Editorial Universitaria, 1993) were some of the first to use the term *genocide* when alluding to the events that had transpired in Guatemala.

16. Casaús Arzú, *Racismo, genocidio y memoria*.

17. The total number of victims of the Guatemalan Civil War has been estimated at two hundred thousand (83 percent of victims were Mayas of different ethnicities). Approximately seventy thousand of them were killed during the bloody eighteen months of Efraín Ríos Montt's presidency. Additionally, the civil war left around forty-five thousand disappeared, tens of thousands of tortured individuals, one million internal refugees—most of them resettled in the so-called model villages or in the shantytowns of Guatemala City—and half a million people who fled Guatemala. Most of these transnational refugees would end up living in a string of refugee camps placed along the Guatemalan border in Chiapas, Mexico, or in different parts of the United States. The reports produced by the Interdiocese Project for the Recovery of Historical Memory (Proyecto Interdiocesano de Recuperación de la Memoria Histórica), *Guatemala, nunca más: Informe*, 4 vols. (Guatemala City: ODHAG, 1998), and the Commission for Historical Clarification (Comisión para el Esclarecimiento Histórico), *Guatemala: Memoria del silencio*, 12 vols. (Guatemala City: CEH, 1999), state that more than 90 percent of human rights violations were committed by the Guatemalan army, aided by the national police and a series of associated paramilitary groups.

18. Most unfortunately, given the characteristics of this text, we are not able to provide an account of the myriad aspects related to the Maya genocide that have been well studied by scholars. For interested readers, some authors who have extensively explored different facets of this topic include Arturo Arias, Roddy Brett, Marta Elena Casaús Arzú, Allison Crosby and M. Brinton Lykes, Kate Doyle, Sofía Duyos, Ricardo Falla, Amandine Fulchirone, Beatriz Manz, Víctor Montejo, Diane Nelson, Carlos Paredes, Victoria Sanford, Jennifer Schirmer, and Manolo Vela Castañeda. This list of authors is by no means exhaustive.

19. Victoria 82 would be followed by other campaign plans such as Firmeza 83, Firmeza 83-1, and Operation Sofía. All these secret military documents have been recovered—oftentimes in the midst of bizarre circumstances—by human rights defenders committed to transitional justice processes. See Sofía Duyos, *Los papeles secretos del genocidio en Guatemala* (Madrid: GPS Ediciones, 2021). On a different note, we need to at least mention that the sheer brutality of these military actions would not have been possible without the active support of Ronald Reagan's administration. See Kate Doyle, "The Final Battle: Ríos Montt Counterinsurgency Campaign," *National Security Archive*, May 9, 2013.

20. Jennifer Schirmer, *The Guatemalan Military Project: A Violence Called Democracy* (Philadelphia: University of Pennsylvania Press, 1998).

21. The original expression in Spanish is "quitarle el agua al pez." This locution does not imply, as in English, to remove "the fish" (i.e., the guerrilla groups) from "the water" (the Indigenous communities) while still leaving the liquid intact but, rather, to throw away "the water" so that "the fish" can no longer survive. As can be seen, the expendability of Indigenous communities in the fight against the guerrillas is already embedded in Ríos Montt's phrase.
22. The Comunidades de Población en Resistencia (CPRs, or Communities of People in Resistance) were small and mobile settlements that emerged in the Ixil Triangle, Ixcán, and Petén as a result of the brutal attacks conducted by the Guatemalan army against Indigenous communities during 1981 and 1982. The CPRs were composed of survivors who had managed to flee from the massacres, as well as from the subsequent forced relocation of the Maya peoples to "model villages" controlled by the army.
23. Abundant testimonies of survivors can be read in Comisión para el Esclarecimiento Histórico, *Guatemala*; Carlos A. Paredes, *Te llevaste mis palabras* (Guatemala City: ECAP, 2006); Proyecto Diocesano para la Recuperación de la Memoria Histórica, *Guatemala, nunca más*. These reports have documented more than six hundred massacres in Guatemala, most of them committed in Achi, Ixil, K'iche', Mam, and Q'eqchi' areas.
24. Casaús Arzú, *Racismo, genocidio y memoria*, 44.
25. The study of sexual violence committed during the civil war and the Maya genocide started in the late 1990s, when the report produced by the Interdiocese Project for the Recovery of Historical Memory, *Guatemala, nunca más*, included a chapter fully dedicated to the issue. Since then, many works on the topic have been published; here, we highlight the studies completed by organizations such as Consorcio Actoras del Cambio, ECAP, Mujeres Transformando el Mundo, and UNAMG, that have accompanied and supported Maya women survivors. Among these latter works, *Tejidos que lleva el alma, memoria de las mujeres mayas sobrevivientes de violación sexual durante el conflicto armado*, a collective research directed by Amandine Fulchirone (Guatemala City: ECAP & UNAMG, 2009) stands out for the abundance of its testimonies, to the point that it has been informally termed "Guatemala's third truth commission report." Finally, the trials for the genocide of the Maya Ixil people (2013 and 2018) and the Sepur Zarco court case (2016) triggered the publishing of new scholarly works, as well as of a number of expert witnesses' reports on sexual violence.
26. An in-depth analysis of the Sepur Zarco trial and its implications for transitional justice in Guatemala is in Irma Alicia Velásquez Nimatuj, "Las abuelas de Sepur Zarco, esclavitud sexual y Estado criminal en Guatemala," in *En tiempos de muerte: Cuerpos, rebeldías, resistencias*, ed. Xochitl Leyva Solano and Rosalba Icaza (Rotterdam: CLACSO and The Hague Institute of Social Studies, 2019).
27. Rita Segato, *La guerra contra las mujeres* (Madrid: Traficantes de Sueños, 2016).
28. The first concept was coined by Edelberto Torres-Rivas; the notion of uncertain democracies belongs to Casaús Arzú, and the last term has been used by Ricardo Sáenz de Tejada.
29. Rigoberta Menchú, a very well-known K'iche' social and political leader, has been an instrumental actor in the national and international denunciation of the atrocities committed by the Guatemalan state against the Maya peoples, as well as in the fight of Central American Indigenous populations for truth, memory, justice, and reparation. Her *testimonio*, *Me llamo Rigoberta Menchú y así me nació la conciencia* (Havana: Casa de las Américas, 1983), tells the story of her life and activism since the mid-1970s until the early 1980s, when she had to flee to Mexico due to the targeting of her family by the Guatema-

lan Army, and more generally due to the horrific levels of violence unleashed against the Maya communities in the highlands. The publication—first in Spanish, then in English, then in ten other languages—revealed the gravity of the situation in Guatemala and mobilized the international community around the need to put an end to the genocide of the Mayas and to the civil war that had ravaged the country for almost thirty years. In parallel, Rigoberta's *testimonio*—and the subsequent attack that the veracity of her narrative received from North American anthropologist David Stoll—had an enormous impact on the field of Latin American studies during the 1980s and 1990s, when it prompted debates around the status of truth in testimonial narratives from the Global South, on the ethics of "speaking for" historically oppressed groups, and on the political role of Global North intellectuals in transnational struggles for peace and human rights. Additionally, Rigoberta Menchú has been instrumental in the advancement of transitional justice in Guatemala. As such, in December 1999, she filed a lawsuit at the Audiencia Nacional de Madrid, in Spain, thus initiating the first court proceedings against Efraín Ríos Montt for crimes that included terrorism, systematic torture, and genocide. Finally, Menchú has been the first Indigenous woman to run for president in Guatemala, as the leader of the ethnic-based party Winaq in 2007. Despite the fact that her results were poor and that she did not reach the second round in the national election, she opened up the door for other Indigenous women who have run more successful presidential campaigns, such as the Mam leader Thelma Cabrera in 2019.

30. The first ethnic-based Honduran organization, OFRANEH (Honduran Black Fraternal Organization), was created in 1978 and still functions as the main federation for the Garifuna communities of the Atlantic coast. Other organizations would later be created in the 1990s, such as COPINH, currently devoted to the defense of the Lenca people and their territories, natural resources, and environment.

31. These "pilgrimages" were adopted by Indigenous and Afro-descendant organizations as their preferred political strategy during the 1990s. They gathered thousands of people who walked together to Tegucigalpa, where they occupied—sometimes for a few days, sometimes for weeks on end—a number of symbolic public spaces, such as the National Congress. See Marvin Barahona, *Pueblos indígenas, estado y memoria colectiva en Honduras* (Tegucigalpa: Editorial Guaymuras, 2009), 246–258.

32. Political instability and widespread violence against human rights defenders, Indigenous leaders, and independent journalists skyrocketed in Honduras as a result of the US-backed coup d'état against president Manuel Zelaya. These tendencies intensified even more after the fraudulent reelection of Juan Orlando Hernández, a politician with links to drug trafficking, to the presidency in 2017.

33. Berta Cáceres was a Lenca leader focused on the defense of Indigenous, women's, land, environmental, and human rights. She was murdered in March 2016, and her assassination was directly linked to Cáceres's opposition to the construction of the Agua Zarca hydroelectric dam. The completion of this megaproject would have provoked substantial disruptions in the water and food supply of local Indigenous communities and would have also changed the course of the Gualcarque River, which is sacred to the Lenca peoples.

34. The communities residing in the Atlantic region have been especially vocal in denouncing a series of murders, kidnappings, and disappearances affecting local Indigenous and Afro-Indigenous young people. These communities have also denounced the polluting effects of gold mining for the rivers and the groundwater, the invasion of lands and the

destruction of forests caused by intensive farming and logging, the slow but steady disappearance of game and fish, and the massive migration of Nicaraguan Indigenous peoples to Honduras and Costa Rica as a result of all these problems.

35. The only Indigenous organization that predates this period is the controversial ANIS (National Association of Salvadoran Indigenous Peoples). See Virginia Q. Tilley, *Seeing Indians: A Study of Race, Nation, and Power in El Salvador* (Albuquerque: University of New Mexico Press, 2005).

36. According to Tilley, *Seeing Indians*, 229–230, Salvadoran Indigenous communities were at a disadvantage at the moment of presenting their projects and demands to international funding institutions because those entities conceived of "Indigenous peoples" as social groups that shared a distinct culture and that occupied a delimited territory. None of these conditions were fully applicable in El Salvador, a country where Indigenous communities had lost most of their lands during the late nineteenth century, where censuses completed after 1932 consistently negated the existence of Indigenous peoples, and where the state had disseminated a consistent national imaginary based on "mestizaje" that had intentionally tried to subsume the Nahua-Pipil, Lenca, and Cacaopera populations within the broader category of (non-Indigenous) "peasants."

37. Among the latter ones, we highlight two human rights organizations created by Indigenous women even before the war was over: CONAVIGUA (National Coordination of Guatemalan Widows), founded in 1988 by Maya women whose husbands had been disappeared or assassinated at the hands of the army; and Mamá Maquín, founded in 1990 in the refugee camps of Chiapas (Mexico), and focused on the defense of the rights of refugees and returnees.

38. After the peace accords, a new generation of Maya intellectuals emerged in Guatemala. Among them we can mention (without being exhaustive) Lina Barrios, Emma Chirix, Aura Cumes, Edgar Esquit, Emil' Keme, Irma Alicia Velásquez Nimatuj, Gladys Tzul, and Jovita Tzul. At the same time, a group of Indigenous intellectuals broadly affiliated to the "Pan-Maya" movement, and who were already active since the 1980s, gained saliency in the Guatemalan public sphere. This second group includes Rigoberto Quemé, Demetrio Cojtí Cuxil, Demetrio Raxche', Víctor Racancoj, Luis Enrique Sam Colop, Humberto Ak'abal, and Gaspar Pedro González.

39. Currently, the main sources of conflict in Guatemala are linked to the activities of hydroelectric companies, as well as to open-pit mining, oil extraction, and the production of sugarcane and palm oil. Some of the problems generated by these businesses include the pollution of rivers, groundwater, and soils; the appearance of new and yet incurable diseases; the substantial increase of miscarriages and fetal malformations; lack of access to water; and widespread food insecurity. These new circumstances have prompted the skyrocketing of Indigenous migration (both to urban areas within the country and, with increased frequency, to the United States), the impoverishment of Indigenous populations, and a stark increase in violence in the rural areas. As a result, Maya communities have ramped up organizing to resist the worsening of their living conditions; some strategies of collective action include demanding community consultations, occupying lands, marching, protesting, and blocking roads and highways.

40. Among the new forms of criminalization of social protest, we can mention the imprisonment of community authorities; the kidnapping, disappearance, and/or murder of Indigenous leaders; the orchestration of smear campaigns; the labeling of Maya activ-

ists as "terrorists"; and the mass killing of unarmed protesters, as happened during the massacre of Cumbre de Alaska in 2012.
41. Long-established forms of racism have been recently reactivated thanks to new mobile and virtual platforms, such as the comment sections in digital publications, social media platforms, and WhatsApp threads.
42. Some prominent Maya intellectuals and activists who have been particularly vocal in the denunciation of racism include Emma Chirix, Aura Cumes, Andrea and Lucía Ixchíu, Victoria Tubin, Irma Alicia Velásquez Nimatuj, and Sandra Xinico Batz, as well as the organizations Mujeres de Kaqla (Women of Kaqla) and Asociación Política de Mujeres Mayas (MOLOJ, Political Association of Maya Women). Oftentimes, these women have been the target of racist attacks, which tend to be ever more hostile due to their dual identities as Indigenous (and) women.
43. As studied by Carlos Fredy Ochoa, *Reforma política: La propuesta de las organizaciones indígenas* (Guatemala City: ASIES, 2017), 19–22, notions of collective well-being have a long history in Maya cultures, although their use within a political context is relatively recent. This concept is expressed differently in diverse Mayan languages (e.g., *utzilaj k'aslemal, raxnaqil, ral ch'och'*), but it always alludes to the elements that allow the reproduction of life and guarantee a respectful coexistence. According to Ochoa, some terms associated with the semantic field of "buen vivir" include *jelq'ab, wayab, bajkutx,* and *kolk'ex,* four notions that situate mutual aid ancestral practices at the center of the moral and philosophical conceptions of community life; *patq'um, q'umlab'ahil,* and *lajti,* three terms that emphasize the role that consultation processes, consensus, participation, and collective decision-making have in Maya communities; and *awas, pak'uch,* and *tzonoj,* three concepts that allude to healthy nutrition, the enjoyment of leisure, and the free expression of affects.

BIBLIOGRAPHY

Barahona, Marvin. *Pueblos indígenas, estado y memoria colectiva en Honduras*. Tegucigalpa: Editorial Guaymuras, 2009.

Casaús Arzú, Marta Elena. *Racismo, genocidio y memoria*. Guatemala City: F&G Editores, 2019.

Comisión para el Esclarecimiento Histórico. *Guatemala: Memoria del silencio*. 12 vols. Guatemala City: CEH, 1999.

Doyle, Kate. "The Final Battle: Ríos Montt Counterinsurgency Campaign." *National Security Archive,* May 9, 2013. https://nsarchive2.gwu.edu/NSAEBB/NSAEBB425/.

Duyos, Sofía. *Los papeles secretos del genocidio en Guatemala*. Madrid: GPS Ediciones, 2021.

Esquit, Edgar. *Comunidad y estado durante la revolución: Política comunal maya en la década de 1944–1954 en Guatemala*. Guatemala City: Tujaal, 2019.

Falla, Ricardo. *Masacres de la selva: Ixcán, Guatemala, 1975–1982*. Guatemala City: Editorial Universitaria, 1993.

Fulchirone, Amandine, et al. *Tejidos que lleva el alma: Memoria de las mujeres mayas sobrevivientes de violación sexual durante el conflicto armado*. Guatemala City: ECAP & UNAMG, 2009.

Gould, Jeffrey. *To Die in This Way: Nicaraguan Indians and the Myth of Mestizaje, 1880–1965.* Durham, NC: Duke University Press, 1998.

Grandin, Greg. *The Blood of Guatemala: A History of Race and Nation.* Durham, NC: Duke University Press, 2000.

MacAllister, Carlota. "A Headlong Rush into the Future: Violence and Revolution in a Guatemalan Indigenous Village." In *A Century of Revolution: Insurgent and Counterinsurgent Violence during Latin America's Long Cold War,* edited by Greg Grandin and Gilbert K. Joseph, 276–308. Durham, NC: Duke University Press, 2010.

Menchú, Rigoberta. *Me llamo Rigoberta Menchú y así me nació la conciencia: Testimonio.* Edited by Elisabeth Burgos-Debray. Havana: Casa de las Américas, 1983.

Ochoa, Carlos Freddy. *Reforma política: La propuesta de las organizaciones indígenas.* Guatemala City: ASIES, 2017.

Paredes, Carlos A. *Te llevaste mis palabras.* 2 vols. Guatemala City: ECAP, 2006.

Proyecto Interdiocesano de Recuperación de la Memoria Histórica. *Guatemala, nunca más: Informe.* 4 vols. Guatemala City: ODHAG, 1998.

Rostica, Julieta Carla. "El anticomunismo y el fracaso de la 'integración' del indio: Hacia la coyuntura crítica del genocidio en Guatemala, 1954–1978." *Revista THEOMAI: Estudios Críticos sobre Sociedad y Desarrollo,* no. 36 (2017): 24–42.

Schirmer, Jennifer. *The Guatemalan Military Project: A Violence Called Democracy.* Philadelphia: University of Pennsylvania Press, 1998.

Segato, Rita. *La guerra contra las mujeres.* Madrid: Traficantes de Sueños, 2016.

Taracena, Arturo. *Etnicidad, nación y estado en Guatemala.* Vol. 2. Antigua, Guatemala: CIRMA, 2004.

Tilley, Virginia Q. *Seeing Indians: A Study of Race, Nation, and Power in El Salvador.* Albuquerque: University of New Mexico Press, 2005.

Velásquez Nimatuj, Irma Alicia. "Las abuelas de Sepur Zarco, esclavitud sexual y Estado criminal en Guatemala." In *En tiempos de muerte: Cuerpos, rebeldías, resistencias,* edited by Xochitl Leyva Solano and Rosalba Icaza, 89–112. Rotterdam: CLACSO and The Hague Institute of Social Studies, 2019.

CHAPTER 17

Racializing Arabs in Latin America

BAHIA M. MUNEM

Problematic ideas of "racial mixture" have been revered (and contested) as the through line in the myths of multiracial democracies in Latin America.[1] The valorization of whiteness and the institutionalization of a paramount European white racial order by and for the elite, predicated on the legacy of imperial and colonial regimes, has long endured across the region. The logics in these legacies were foundational in the subsequent nascent modern nation-states. This can be seen in the emergent immigration policies across the region that privileged European stock, especially in juxtaposition to Blackness and Indigeneity, and held with suspicion those at the interstices of racial categorization. In this chapter, I examine how Arabs historically factored into the racialization frameworks, which are still ongoing, in Latin American nation-states and address how these processes are relationally determined in terms of desirability and racial categorizations that have been at times deployed as fixed or in flux.

Arabs arrived in Latin America in three significant migratory waves. Each resulted from various and intersecting push and pull factors from home locations and within the diaspora. In Latin America, the new arrivals were referred to as *Sirio-Libanés* (*Sírio-Libanês* in Brazil)—a term widely used to refer to the inhabitants of what was Greater Syria under Ottoman rule and today comprises Syria, Lebanon, and Palestine. While this label has been widely used in more formal discourse, the more colloquial and sometimes pejorative term *turco* emerged from the Ottoman documents with which the first mostly masculine and Christian wave traveled to the Americas in the late nineteenth and early twentieth centuries. The subsequent second wave in the mid-twentieth century, though still largely comprising men, was mostly Muslim. The third wave, beginning in the 1970s, was varied in gender and kin formation but still significantly Muslim.

Today, both *sirio-libanés* and *turco* are broad referents to Middle Eastern Arabs and evoke monolithic ideas of gender and Arabness. As such, this chapter addresses the racialization of Arabs in Latin America in varying historical moments with particular attention to the intersectional categories of gender, labor, class, and religion, in nation-building projects in countries such as Mexico, Brazil, Argentina, and others. In examining the political and economic ascendency broadly featured about Arab immigrants in specific contexts through the prism of these categories, it also challenges the Orientalist narratives about this population. It parses specific ethnicities nested into the category "Sirio-Libanés" and the integration challenges they endured in different migratory waves. In unpacking racialization as it applies to Arabs in Latin America, I bring together three theorizations to address their racial formation.

Michael Omi and Howard Winant's formulation of racialization was critical in unmooring race from conceptualizations of fixed biological essences in the humanistic social sciences. Instead, they proposed that race needed to be viewed as "an unstable and decentered complex of social meanings constantly being transformed by political struggle."[2] Thus, in their theoretical framing, assigning meaning to physical appearance and other characteristics tethered to alterity has always been contingent on sociohistorical and political processes and impacts social organization. They also emphasized the role of the state in these racializing dynamics. While the authors focused on the United States, we can see these logics in the broader Americas. David Theo Goldberg, in contrast, argues more pointedly that the modern nation-state and race were and are coarticulated. He insists: "Race marks and orders the modern nation-state . . . more or less from its point of conceptual and institutional emergence. The apparatuses and technologies employed by modern states have served . . . to fashion, modify and reify the terms of racial expression as well as racist exclusions and subjugation."[3] From the time of Spanish expansion, Goldberg maintains, "racial definition of modern states [was] elaborated with the 'voyages of discovery' . . . and the debate in the 1550s between Las Casas and Sepulveda over Indian enslavement."[4] While holding onto to these theoretical threads and considering the legacy of colonialism in making and marking racial categories, Molina, HoSang, and Gutiérrez put forth a relational formation of race. Moving beyond binary racial logics of white or European and other, they suggest that the racialization of minoritized groups occurs in relation to one another.[5] The authors "conceptualize racialization as a dynamic and interactive process" by which "group-based race constructions are formed not only in relation to whiteness but also to devalued and marginalized groups."[6] Within these intersecting and layered dynamics, I examine how the racialization of Arabs occurs—that is, through sociohistorical and political processes, as part and parcel of nation-state technologies and practices, and via relational racial configurations between and within minority groups in systems of white dominance.

The suspicion with which Arabs have been viewed historically across social strata, including as merchants and politicians, throughout Latin America cannot be denied. While it can be said that the ascendency of Arabs in business and politics (mostly elite cis men) is indisputable, there is a laden distrust and Orientalist gaze with which they have been held and imagined. This is further compounded if they had or have ties to Islam in what have historically been predominately Catholic countries. Some of these ideas have been reified in different types of cultural production throughout the region, such as television, literature, and other forms of media. These essentialist notions are also often echoed by those who themselves have origins in the Levant and are conveyed during average day-to-day interactional levels as well as in more formal sociopolitical spaces occupied by the elite. In short, this self-Orientalizing, tracing back to the beginning of the twentieth century, reproduces essentialist ideas of exceptional and conniving business acumen and propensity toward class ascendency, which not only is predicated on a lineage with provenance in the Middle East but also lays claims to inherent traits ("in the blood") that destines them to new socioeconomic heights by whatever means.

A Brazilian anthropologist labels this auto-Orientalizing dynamic as *orientalismo nativo* (native Orientalism).[7] In Brazil, this form of essentializing by Arab intellectuals themselves in the emergent twentieth century was offered as a counternarrative to the dominant racialized nativist discourses about foreign others. They were attempting to purge ideas of differing and multiple Arab cultural, class, religious, ethnic, and racial variations because this in-group heterogeneity would further emphasize alterity and jeopardize belonging, especially when homogenization (whitening) was the national project of the receiving nation-state. Instead, these intellectuals centered a valorized economic exceptionalism, which they perceived facilitated integration for

Middle Eastern immigrants. In concert with political and cultural discourses of representation, this has had an enduring effect on perceptions of Arabness.

Immigration Policies toward Undesirable Others

An examination of some of the immigration policies in the twentieth century in several countries in Latin America provides more insight into the ways in which Arabs were imagined and racialized. In postrevolutionary Mexico (1910–1920), for example, there was an increase in anti-Arab sentiment, which culminated in a 1927 decree by the populist president Plutarco Elías Calles. The president banned labor immigration of Middle Easterners. While economics served as the logic for not allowing Arabs and other undesirable immigrants into the country, Peter Wade asserts that eugenics also played a role: "Chinese and Arabs were seen as inferior additions to the Mexican mix, likely to provoke degeneration."[8] Despite immigrants once being considered a symbol of progress during Porfirio Díaz's (1884–1911) tenure, when many entered the country on the premise of being agricultural laborers, in postrevolutionary Mexico, they were seen as an impediment to advancement and nation building. This is also in line with the reification of essentialist racial categories in pseudoscience that informed state policies of immigration, where there was a commitment to maintaining white domination and through practices of whitening the population (*blanqueamiento*).

However, there were other important elements that raised suspicions about Middle Easterners. Instead of entering the agricultural and other manual labor markets as had been the government's intention in allowing them entry, through their own networks, many new Arab immigrants were able to establish credit with their fellow merchant countrymen who were more financially stable. On the one hand, this facilitated peddling work for the new arrivals because they would not need money upfront to purchase products, fill suitcases, and sell them to make a living. On the other hand, it brought much-needed goods to Mexicans who were outside of the reach of developed regions and city centers in the country in the early twentieth century. During the Mexican Revolution, this labor practice had not ceased. In fact, many Middle Easterners who were engaged in this form of labor capitalized on the collapse of institutions, such as the banking system. While some Arab peddlers with humble means had themselves been given credit, they extended credit to Mexicans who needed to purchase much-needed products and did not have the means. Merchants at the top of the chain and intermediary peddlers at once grew their financial resources and Mexicans' reliance on them.[9]

This not only gave Arabs a heightened visibility but also increased resentment toward them. Amid proliferating suspicion and distrust by Mexicans because of disagreements on repayment of credit where they felt they were being swindled, formal denouncements by individuals and organizations alike were made to the federal government.[10] With this growing intrigue and distaste toward the Arab and Middle Eastern community in the country, the 1927 law under Calles suspended the immigration of those with Armenian, Lebanese, Palestinian, Syrian, "Arabic and Turkish origins" with the exception of "legal" chain migration or family reunification. However, this migration was mired with Anti-Arab sentiment because it required that those who qualified "have an honest means of earning a living and are in a good financial position."[11] In short, Middle Easterners were not only undesirable for reasons Wade suggests; they were also broadly framed as suspicious and conniving because of the alleged degenerate ways they made a living through commerce—especially those Arab immigrants, irrespective of whether they had family affiliation in the country, who did not meet a wealth test at the outset. Otherwise, the assumption was that they would arrive in Mexico without capital and reproduce the disparaged cycle (peddlers to bricks-and-mortar business owners) that had earned them ill repute. At this time, their prospects in the country were therefore measured by their economic and class position upon entering Mexico and not by the potential they might have in building financial security and contributing to the economy after settling there.

Attempts to exclude racialized others from the body politic of nation-states were abundant, but so were exceptions or ambivalent deployments of these ideas in immigration regimes in order to fill specific labor needs. In Honduras, for instance, which today is home to the second-largest Palestinian diaspora in Latin America (second only to Chile), the Immigration Law of 1934 allowed for the conditional entry of Arabs into the country on the premise that they would engage exclusively in agricultural work. Article 14 of the 1934 law specified that "the entry of Arabs, Turks, Syrians, Armenians, Palestinians, Czechoslovaks, Lebanese and Poles may be permitted provided that they give a guarantee which proves to the satisfaction of the Immigration and Colonization Office that they come exclusively to devote themselves to agriculture or the introduction or improvement of new industries without prejudice of exacting other requirements established by the other laws in this respect."[12] These particular immigrants were obligated to engage in agricultural labor or begin new industries within six months, or else they would be deported.[13]

Additionally, as posited by Darío Euraque, although Czechs and Poles were not the preferred Western Europeans, they were generally acknowledged as being white, especially within a relational framework to less desirable Middle Easterners. Mentioning them in the law, however, was an effort to discourage Jews from immigrating to Honduras; at the time, many Eastern Europeans who were fleeing a burgeoning anti-Semitism in Europe had migrated to Central America. Furthermore, the specificity of Honduran immigration laws emerged from the government's preoccupation with undesirable migration into the nation that would mar the nation's whitening project. For instance, there was a sizable British immigrant population, predominantly compromising Black agricultural laborers from the British colonies of the Caribbean, which had become of concern. In turn, in relation to these Caribbean laborers, Arabs were more desirable. Apparent here is the dynamic relational racialization process of devalued and minoritized groups. Eastern Europeans, such as Czechs and Poles, were devalued because of their potential Jewishness. Arabs were devalued but preferred over Black people from the Caribbean. Other Latin American countries also had specific immigration policies that focused on labor. While not always denying entry of Middle Easterners outright, the hesitation toward them was clear.

In the port cities of Cartagena and Barranquilla, in which the latter is considered the seat of Colombia's Caribbean region, Arabs began to arrive in the late nineteenth century. Many emigrated in search of economic opportunities that had been foreclosed by the declining Ottoman Empire, ethnic conflicts, and forced conscription. The majority were Christian.[14] Similar to those of other Latin American nation-states, Colombia's immigration policies privileged Europeans. A 1923 immigration decree stressed the importance of bringing to the country elements of "biological superiority," of which Europeans were said to be constituted. In 1912, a little over ten years before this decree, an explicit national policy and series of laws restricted the entry of those who were considered "oriental" into the country, which included "Hindus, Chinese, and Arabs." Immigrants from these origins were considered undesirable as they would not be beneficial to the progress of the nation.[15] Despite Hindu being a creed, it points to the racialization of religion.[16]

In effect, those with origins in the geographically capacious and nebulous "orient" were considered the antithesis of modernity and progress at different turns in Latin America, bringing to bear the argument of modernity being the flipside of coloniality.[17] In Colombia, however, the economic rise of Arab immigrants led to a relaxation of laws, especially since the relational racialization of Arabs to Afro-Caribbeans led to a selection of the more desirable of the undesirables. Similar to Honduras, while Arabs were not of the preferred European stock in the State's racial hierarchy, given the region's anti-Blackness, they were given preference over Black Caribbeans.[18]

Importantly, Colombia did not receive the same influx of migration in the late nineteenth and twentieth centuries in comparison to other Latin American countries, like Brazil or Argentina. It therefore did not economically benefit in the same way from the migratory movements that marked this time period. The Caribbean region of the country, however, was where the largest settlement of immigrants occurred. Yet there, as in Mexico, in the early twentieth century, suspicions began to take hold about "los turcos" who were said to have the propensity to accumulate wealth in a short period of time, principally through ambulant vending. They also gained a reputation for illicit dealings. Even so, their early economic success gave rise to social and political capital that saw their insertion into "industry, agriculture, and even politics" in the Colombian Caribbean.[19] Although Colombia was not a much-sought-after place to immigrate for Arabs, as in Mexico and Brazil, a significant portion of the community who came to settle in the coastal area transcended their early beginnings as ambulant peddlers to establish businesses, the success of which varied.

The orientalist constructions of Arab or *turco* masculinities, in particular in Latin America broadly, often involve ideas of extraordinary propensity for success in commerce. The businesses in which Arabs were involved, however, varied in scope and scale, as did their socioeconomic class positionality. While there is no denying that the Middle Eastern community had an important role in the development of Cartagena and Barranquilla, they did encounter discrimination. Much of this came from prejudice but also resentment because of their perceived economic advancements. Despite some reaching notable financial heights, "their *denied* entry into establishments such as the exclusive clubs of Cartagena ... encouraged the proliferation of their own societies."[20]

These racialized exclusions then led to the establishment of Syrian-Lebanese social clubs in many cities in Latin America where there was a sizable presence of Arab immigrants and their progeny from the Levantine region. However, often, these clubs in prominent city centers were founded by those of Lebanese and/or Syrian origin, and Palestinians did not usually have visible leadership positions in them. El Club Alhambra, however, was founded as a social-cultural space in 1945 in Barranquilla by Lebanese and Palestinian immigrants, with Nicolás Saade (Lebanese) as president and Francisco Jassir (Palestinian) as vice president.[21] Some twenty years later, the club was renamed Club Campestre del Caribe (Caribbean Country Club) and is still in operation today.

Although Arabs felt compelled to carve out their own social and cultural institutional niches as a result of racialized exclusionary practices, there were fissures in the Colombian elite and political class that allowed some to transgress these dynamics. The success of physician-turned-politician Gabriel Turbay, the son of immigrants from Lebanon, on the national and international stage is one of those. He served as Colombia's ambassador to the United States in the 1930s and 1940s. Unsurprisingly, he had a failed bid for the presidency in the 1940s, but he remained a historical reference for those from similar lineage to reach notable political heights, including extended kin, in the decades to come. Julio César Turbay Ayala, who became Colombia's twenty-fifth president (1978–1982), was one.[22] His mother was Mexican and his father was a Lebanese immigrant from Tannourine, "Antonio" Amin Turbay, who had amassed significant wealth only to lose it all during the country's civil war at the turn of the twentieth century. That said, the heterogeneity of the Middle Eastern community in Colombia historically and contemporarily remains understudied.

The Political Class

The valorization and dominance of whiteness is undeniable in Argentina, often perceived by Argentineans as the Europe of the South. Perhaps nowhere in Latin America is this more apparent. As such, examining the controversial figure of Carlos Menem, the former president of Argentina (1989–1999), who was regularly referred to as "el turco," provides insight into the reception and rejection of Arabs in the country's economic and political spheres, especially when Islam is in the shadows. Carlos Menem was born to Syrian immigrant parents, raised Muslim (Sunni), and later converted to Catholicism. This was likely, in part, to align himself with the religious affiliation espoused by the vast majority of the population in the country as he pursued a career in politics—especially because at the time he ventured into the political arena, the chief executive of the country had to be of the Catholic faith to occupy the position. This requirement was not removed from the constitution until 1994, under Menem's administration. Most of the Arabs (Sirio-Libaneses) in the country, however, are of Christian heritage. Menem's conversion from Islam nearly two decades prior to helming the office of presidency was not necessarily highlighted, but his pejorative *turco* status was.

As Christina Civantos has suggested, his shortcomings as president, of which there were many (e.g., neoliberal economic policies, pardoning military dictators, arms deals, obstruction), were essentialized and widely attributed to his Arab or *turco* origins.[23] Along with Menem's political rise, there was a reinvigoration of a racialized anti-Arab sentiment in Argentina. The popular satirical political magazine *Humor*, in circulation in the last three decades of the twentieth century, often reproduced Orientalist images and discourses of and about Menem, while painting the Middle East and Islam as backward.[24] In the latter part of his tenure as president, a genre of Orientalist nonfiction featuring Menem was popularized with tropes of "Ali Baba" and "harem" in the titles, hearkening to the Orientalism in knowledge production that has been critiqued in Saidian postcolonial studies. However, Menem himself was engaged in both self-Orientalizing and Orientalizing the Middle East via televised appearances and his brand of flamboyancy. One telecast of note is his appearance with a belly dancer in a Syrian-Lebanese community party, which served to reify eroticized, gendered orientalist ideas of both men and women in and from the Middle East. Thus, Menem did not eschew but rather engaged in a performative excess of the "Orient."

Besides political cartoons emerging soon after he took office suggesting he would Islamicize Argentina,[25] one particular occurrence reignited Menem's ethno-religious heritage. In 1995, his eldest son, Carlos Jr., perished in a helicopter crash. Unlike a significant number of Arab Muslim immigrants and their children who intermarried with Catholics in the first half of the twentieth century in Latin America, the younger Menem's death showcased his endogamous ethno-religious lineage. All four of his grandparents were Syrian, Sunni Muslims.[26] Carlos Jr. had a Muslim service at the Buenos Aires Islamic Center and was also buried according to Islamic jurisprudence, where the body is interred the very next day in a Muslim cemetery. Meanwhile, the elder Menem maintained (at least in public) the practices of his converted faith by making the sign of the cross on himself before leaving the side of his son's casket and by also seeking council from a Catholic priest.[27] Menem's first wife and the younger Menem's mother, Zulema Yoma, however, maintained her Muslim faith throughout their marriage and publicly declared her Muslimness, while also raising their two children in the religious tradition (albeit more secular than orthodox).

When Carlos Menem Sr. died in February 2021, at the age of ninety, the former president also had a Muslim burial service, with only Quranic scripture, and was interred in the same cemetery as his son. Of course, this puts into question the veracity and legitimacy of Menem's conversion into Catholicism. What appears undeniable, however, is that Menem attempted to slough off what he suspected would be the most problematic part of his identity and an obstacle to his political rise in Euro-Argentina: his Muslimness. Thus, he himself engaged in a relational racialization by changing what he could (his religion) about his already questionable desirability as an Arab to be more palatable in the political arena. Despite his conversion, in the Argentine national imagination, he remained a *turco* nonetheless.

In Brazil, Arabs have also risen to the upper echelons of the political class but none with clear Muslim ties like Menem. In 1978, Paulo Salim Maluf, the son of rich Lebanese immigrants, rose to prominence as a populist governor of São Paulo—the most populated state in Brazil.[28] He served one term as governor, until 1982, and then became mayor (1993–1996) of São Paulo—Latin America's largest metropolis—after the country's democratization. Continuing the established pattern of casting Arabs as suspicious, Malouf too was accused of misconduct and corruption. His cunningness was at once muted and highlighted when the saying "Maluf rouba mas faz" (steals but gets things done) was used to characterize him.[29] He went on to be embroiled in various corruption scandals and his name became synonymous with misdeed. However, looking closely, corruption has been rampant in politics in Latin America and politics more broadly, irrespective of ethno-religious heritage. But the racialized and essentialized figure of the *turco* is reductively used to qualify wrongdoing.

More recently in Brazil's history, however, is the presidency of Michel Temer by default. The son of Lebanese Maronite Christian immigrants, he rose to the highest political office after Brazil's first woman president, Dilma Rousseff, was impeached and removed from office in August 2016.[30] In November 2018, while still in office, Temer, at an Arab-Brazilian Chamber of Commerce dinner in São Paulo, in partnership with the Federation of Muslim Associations of Brazil, said: "Arab presence in Brazil is part of our daily lives, in the arts, in literature, economics, medicine, architecture and politics. This deeply human connection is the foundation of our fluid dialogue with all Arab countries, and truly the foundation to an intense, fruitful economic exchange."[31] The chamber's president, Rubens Hannun, hearkened to Temer's Arab roots and the well-rehearsed grand narrative of (elite) Arabs in the country—the son of Lebanese immigrants, who had worked hard to obtain economic and political gains and had a direct role in growing exports to Arab countries, claiming a 12 percent growth during part of his presidency, between 2015 and 2017. These political economic regimes have contemporary popular appraisals of an ethnicized entrepreneurial class whose cosmopolitanism has made a significant contribution to a globalized economy. They also paint a romanticized story of assimilation and contribution to the formation of the modern Brazilian nation-state, dehistoricizing practices and policies that marginalized newcomers from the Middle East and the variations in socioeconomic class in this broad community in the country. In other words, these discourses simultaneously reproduce tropes of Brazilian plurality and multiplicity that sustain the much contested but still salient mythology of Brazil's racial democracy, while reifying stereotypes of Arabs having inherent business acumen that is attributed to their "*turco*-ness."

As in other places and other groups, and even during the course of one individual life, economic class status and social conditions are not necessarily fixed and can fluctuate. This does not stave off gendered and racialized monolithic ideas established about a group, where an innately entrepreneurial male subject is unquestionably destined for economic success, nor does it keep its own members from reproducing them. Looking at Palestinians in Brazil, for instance, offers some insight.

There is a particularity and distinction between Palestinians and the Syrian-Lebanese with whom they are often conflated. However, Palestinians cannot be monolithically constructed either. Those who migrated to Brazil have had variegated trajectories and social-economic and political experiences. Some have been economic migrants and others refugees. For instance, there are some Palestinians who have acquired different degrees of economic stability and success and those who intimate that remittances sent to family back home (Palestine), because of continued deteriorating conditions resulting from the Israeli occupation and land grabs from Zionist settler-colonial expansion, have compromised their ability to become more financially sound.

In an interview with Khalil, a Palestinian merchant in São Paulo in 2010, I asked about the much-lauded economic success of Syrians and Lebanese in national narratives and how Palestinians factored in these economic discourses. He indicated that Palestinians had not been as economically successful in Brazil because Syrians and Lebanese had been in the country far longer and in much greater numbers. The larger the number, he asserted, the better the chances of forming successful economic networks. Moreover, according to Khalil: "The Palestinian, as you know, has one foot here and the other in Palestine. Sometimes they take more [financially] than they should from here to provide there. This is why I think they have not grown as much. They send money back home to family. On the one hand this is good, but on the other hand, business wise, it is not because they stop growing here."[32]

Khalil did not explicitly discuss the economic effects that the geopolitical situation in Palestine has had on those living in the Middle East as well as those in the diaspora, but he made tacit connections when discussing the difficulty of forming an economic stronghold because of remittances sent back "home."[33] And although an older and larger migration of Syrians and Lebanese could in itself place Syrians and Lebanese in a privileged economic position, as the anthropologist John Karam has elucidated, for Palestinians, the Partition and subsequent Occupation of Palestine has had multiple and layered socioeconomic effects that heightened such differences. The majority of Palestinians who entered Brazil in the 1950s, for instance, did so because the economic situation in their home location had become exceedingly difficult as a result of dispossession from the formation of the Israeli nation-state. Thus, many who left, or were forced to leave, did so precisely to provide economically for the family members who remained behind.[34] There are still others who, after living in Brazil for multiple years, migrated once again to other countries, such as the United States, for better economic opportunities. Khalil's own brothers had done this and lived in New York.[35]

Another interviewee, Amin, who lived in the southernmost state of Brazil, Rio Grande do Sul, and was part of the older Palestinian community, discussed why he migrated to the country and his contribution to the family of eight he left behind. He owned a small department store in the center of the same small town to which he first migrated in 1955. Amin came from Ramallah, in the West Bank, but had become a refugee during the Nakba (catastrophe) in 1948 when he was fifteen years old. His ancestral town was in northern Palestine, near Haifa. Amin had a cousin who had made the journey to Brazil earlier and helped facilitate his migration. In 1960, after being in Brazil for five years, he returned to Palestine with the intention of staying, but the hardship his family was enduring there made it difficult:[36] "I saw my family, my siblings, going through very hard times (financially). I could not bear to see that and asked myself: 'Can I live here with a sense of well-being, while seeing my siblings suffering such difficulties?' I am not blind. We stayed in Palestine less than a year. I decided to return to Brazil to work and to help them out more. I did everything I could to help them."[37]

Amin thought he would be better able to financially assist his family in Palestine, through remittances, by going back to Brazil. In this way, his narrative is closely aligned with the generalization that Khalil, the São Paulo merchant, made about the Palestinian experience in Brazil. That is, the remittances sent to struggling family members compromise, in one way or another, the sender's financial stability in Brazil and may at times impede establishing a sound financial foundation.

While Amin and Khalil arrived in Brazil twenty-five years apart, the former in 1955 and the latter in 1980, both have been implicated in the economic and geopolitical situation in their original home location. When family members are unable to subsist or get ahead because of the ever-declining socioeconomic situation in Palestine, primarily as a result of the Occupation, settler colonialism, and ongoing dispossession, relatives in the diaspora often contribute financially.[38]

Notwithstanding the significant distinction between Palestinians and other groups of "Arabs," and considering the varying contrasts within these groups, Palestinians are also often absorbed into broader Brazilian national discourses about Arabs or *turcos* belonging to a successful entrepreneurial class. While there might be some merit to this broad description because of the visibility of the elite in commerce, trade, and politics, such as the former president, Michel Temer, more nuanced socioeconomic, political, and lived realities within and between groups are too often overlooked. Because there is a redeeming yet suspicious orientalist "model minority" aspect of this attribution, Arabs themselves often reproduce these stereotyped tropes.

Conclusion

While racial mixture has long been revered as the gateway to multiracial democracies, such as Vasconcelos's "cosmic race" in Mexico and Freyre's "racial democracy" in Brazil,[39] the valorization and privileging of whiteness in these countries and across the Americas has long endured. This is particularly prevalent in immigration policies and practices where hierarchies of desirability emerged, whether in the Colombian Caribbean (Barranquilla and Cartagena), São Paulo, Veracruz (Mexico), Buenos Aires, or San Pedro Sula (Honduras). In these disparate Latin American cities, the resounding commonality is the significance of their Arab and Arab-descended populations, which can be traced to different migratory waves, and the broad, racialized wariness about them. However, as I have shown, in each location, with its own set of circumstances and history, the suspicion with which Arabs have been held, especially as merchants and politicians (men in particular), cannot be denied.

Just as in other groups who are racialized, gender, labor, class, and even religion play an integral part in the racialization of Arabs in Latin America. The legacy of Arab masculinized labor in the form of pack peddling shores up ideas of a predisposed innate but devious business acumen. These ideas are enshrined in a simultaneously valorized and disparaged enterprising masculinity. My aim is not to provide a totalizing summation of how Arabs broadly have been racialized across the region, but to draw contrasts and comparisons in different locations through specific sociohistorical and political processes and temporalities within a relational hierarchy of undesirable "others." Moreover, the heterogeneous character of this broad group is subsumed under the homogeneous ideas of Arabness, but Arabs themselves have also played a part in these dynamics by way of self-Orientalizing. Former Argentine president Menem trafficked in these tropes, as have others who have wielded some form of political and social power and thus hypervisibility. There are indeed a multitude of variations despite the tropes about these arrivals in Latin America that have carried a racializing residue for well over a century. An analysis of Muslim Palestinians in Brazil, for example, who are often subsumed under the Syrian-Lebanese and *turco* label lends insight to important nuances. More research studies about Arabs in Latin America that address the intersection of nation with ethnic affiliation, gender, social-economic class, and religion will further elaborate nuances and contribute to the growing field of race and ethnic studies in Latin America.

NOTES

1. Racial mixture is problematic in that it traffics in ideas of racial purity. That is, for a mixture to occur, there had to have been "pure" races at the outset.
2. Michael Omi and Howard Winant, *Racial Formation in the United States: From the 1960s to the 1990s* (New York: Routledge, 1994), 55.
3. David Theo Goldberg, *The Racial State* (Oxford, UK: Blackwell Publishers, 2002), 4.
4. Goldberg, *The Racial State*, 4.
5. Natalia Molina, Daniel HoSang, and Ramón A. Gutiérrez, *Relational Formations of Race: Theory, Method, and Practice* (Oakland: University of California Press, 2019), 2.
6. Molina, HoSang, and Gutiérrez, *Relational Formations of Race*, 2-3.
7. Paulo Gabriel Hilu da Rocha Pinto, "Labirinto de Espelhos: Orientalismos, Imigração e Discursos sobre a Nação no Brasil," *Revista de Estudos Internacionales Mediterráneos (REIM)*, no. 21 (2016): 53.
8. Peter Wade, *Degrees of Mixture, Degrees of Freedom: Genomics, Multiculturalism, and Race in Latin America* (Durham, NC: Duke University Press, 2017), 11.

9. Theresa Alfaro-Velcamp, *So Far from Allah, So Close to Mexico: Middle Eastern Immigrants in Modern Mexico* (Austin: University of Texas Press, 2007), 77–78.
10. Alfaro-Velcamp, *So Far from Allah*, 100.
11. Alfaro-Velcamp, *So Far from Allah*, 103.
12. As cited in Darío A. Euraque, "The Arab-Jewish Economic Presence in San Pedro Sula, the Industrial Capital of Honduras: Formative Years, 1880s-1930s," in A*rab and Jewish Immigrants in Latin America: Images and Realities*, ed. Ignacio Klich and Jeffrey Lesser (London: Routledge, 1998), 105.
13. Euraque, "The Arab-Jewish Economic Presence," 105.
14. It is important to highlight that since migration by Muslims was for the most part banned by the Ottoman Empire, those who were Muslim and emigrated to the Americas did so clandestinely. Because of this, the historian Kemal Karpat suggested that the numbers were likely greater.
15. Ana Milena Rhenal Doria, and Francisco Flórez Bolivar, "Entre lo árabe y lo negro: Raza y inmigración en Cartagena, 1880-1930," *Revista Sociedad y Economía*, no. 15 (2008): 130.
16. This is reminiscent of the racial prerequisite cases that determined qualification for citizenship in the United States in the first few decades of the twentieth century. As documented by Ian Haney-López in *White by Law: The Legal Construction of Race* (New York: New York University Press, 2006); Bagat Singh Thind in *Thind v. The United States* (1923) was denied his petition for citizenship because, although he fulfilled the "Caucasian" racial classification, the federal government contested his claim to whiteness. This was in part because of his religious affiliation. The question posed by the government was, "Is a high caste Hindu of full Indian blood, born at Amrit Sar, Punjab, India, a white person?" Haney-López, *White by Law*, 87.
17. Aníbal Quijano, "Coloniality and Modernity/Rationality," *Cultural Studies* 21, no. 2 (2007): 168–178.
18. Important to note is the legacy of slavery in the country and region and not imply that all Black people there arrived as immigrants per se.
19. Louise Fawcett and Eduardo Posada-Carbo, "Arabs and Jews in the Development of the Colombian Caribbean: 1850–1950," *Immigrants & Minorities* 16, nos. 1–2 (1997): 58.
20. Fawcett and Posada-Carbo, "Arabs and Jews," 72.
21. Odette Yidi David, "Los árabes en Barranquilla," *Memorias: Revista Digital de Historia y Arqueología desde el Caribe Colombiano*, no. 17 (2012): 3.
22. Massimo Di Ricco, "Filling the Gap: The Colombo Árabes Emergence as Political Actors in Barranquilla and the Caribbean Region," *Revista de Derecho*, no. 41 (2014): 220.
23. Christina Civantos, "Ali Bla Bla's Double-Edged Sword: Argentine President Carlos Menem and the Negotiating of Identity," in *Between the Middle East and the Americas: The Cultural Politics of Diaspora*, ed. Evelyn Alsultany and Ella Shohat (Ann Arbor: University of Michigan Press, 2013), 108–129.
24. Civantos, "Ali Bla Bla's Double-Edged Sword," 116–120.
25. Civantos, "Ali Bla Bla's Double-Edged Sword," 118.
26. Gladys Jozami, "The Manifestation of Islam in Argentina," *The Americas* 53, no. 1 (1996): 67–68.
27. Jozami, "The Manifestation of Islam," 68.
28. John Tofik Karam, "Turcos in the Mix: Corrupting Arabs in Brazil's Racial Democracy," in *Between the Middle East and the Americas: The Cultural Politics of Diaspora*, ed. Evelyn Alsultany and Ella Shohat (Ann Arbor: University of Michigan Press, 2013), 82–83.

29. Karam, "Turcos in the Mix," 82–83.
30. Although Temer acknowledged being raised in the Maronite Christian tradition, he often declared that he followed the Roman Catholic Church like the majority of Brazilians. See "Vilarejo libanês do 'filho Michel Temer' Segue igreja ortodoxa grega," *Folha de São Paulo*, August 5, 2016.
31. "'We want much more,' Says Temer on Trade with Arabs," *ANBA: Brazil-Arab News Agency*, November 11, 2018.
32. Bahia Munem, and Sônia Hamid, "Diasporic Palestinian Communities in Brazil and Hierarchies of Belonging: A Perspective from Palestinian Iraq War Refugees," *Revista Territórios & Fronteiras* 13, no. 2 (2021): 202.
33. Munem and Hamid, "Diasporic Palestinian Communities," 202.
34. In her article, Denise Jardim indicates that the creation of the Israeli state made economic viability for her interlocutors difficult at best. As a result, they migrated to Brazil to work and help their families. See Denise Jardim, "'As mulheres voam com seus maridos': A experiência da diáspora palestina e as relações de gênero," *Horizontes Antropológicos* 15, no. 31 (2009): 189–217.
35. Munem and Hamid, "Diasporic Palestinian Communities."
36. Bahia M. Munem, "Expulsions and Receptions: Palestinian Iraq War Refugees in the Brazilian Nation-State" (PhD diss., Rutgers University, 2014), 116–117.
37. Munem, *Expulsions and Receptions*, 117.
38. The impediment of movement within and between Palestinian towns and territory as a result of checkpoints, roadblocks by the Israeli Defense Forces (IDF), and the separation wall, make economic viability difficult at best. The control over water by the Israelis in the West Bank, where running water is often cut off from Palestinian towns (for days at a time) and siphoned to settler-colonial settlements, considered illegal in international law, compromises the possibility of an agrarian economy. In many cases, the separation wall has been built on seized property and impedes access to Palestinians' own lands. Additionally, the air, land, and sea blockade of Gaza (often dubbed the "world's largest open-air prison") completely controlled by the Israelis, as are all the supplies that come into Gaza, makes economic feasibility difficult at best.
39. While "racial democracy" has been attributed to Gilberto Freyre's influential text, *The Masters and the Slaves* (1933), the term is not found in his book.

BIBLIOGRAPHY

Alfaro-Velcamp, Theresa. *So Far from Allah, So Close to Mexico: Middle Eastern Immigrants in Modern Mexico*. Austin: University of Texas Press, 2007.

Civantos, Christina. "Ali Bla Bla's Double-Edged Sword: Argentine President Carlos Menem and the Negotiating of Identity." In *Between the Middle East and the Americas: The Cultural Politics of Diaspora*, edited by Evelyn Alsultany and Ella Shohat, 108–129. Ann Arbor: University of Michigan Press, 2013.

Di Ricco, Massimo. "Filling the Gap: The Colombo *Árabes* Emergence as Political Actors in Barranquilla and the Caribbean Region." *Revista de Derecho*, no. 41 (2014): 211–241.

Euraque, Darío A. "The Arab-Jewish Economic Presence in San Pedro Sula, the Industrial Capital of Honduras: Formative Years, 1880s-1930s." In *Arab and Jewish Immigrants in*

Latin America: Images and Realities, edited by Ignacio Klich and Jeffrey Lesser, 94–124. London: Routledge, 1998.

Fawcett, Louise and Eduardo Posada-Carbo. "Arabs and Jews in the Development of the Colombian Caribbean: 1850–1950." *Immigrants & Minorities* 16, no. 1–2 (1997): 57–79.

Goldberg, David Theo. *The Racial State*. Oxford: Blackwell Publishers, 2002.

Haney-López, Ian. *White by Law: The Legal Construction of Race*. New York: New York University Press, 2006.

Hilu da Rocha Pinto, Paulo Gabriel. "Labirinto de espelhos: Orientalismos, imigração e discursos sobre a nação no Brasil." *Revista de Estudos Internacionales Mediterráneos*, no. 21 (2016): 48–57.

Jardim, Denise. "'As mulheres voam com seus maridos': A experiência da diáspora palestina e as relações de gênero." *Horizontes Antropológicos* 15, no. 31 (2009): 189–217.

Jozami, Gladys. "The Manifestation of Islam in Argentina." *The Americas* 53, no. 1 (1996): 67–85.

Karam, John Tofik. "Turcos in the Mix: Corrupting Arabs in Brazil's Racial Democracy." In *Between the Middle East and the Americas: The Cultural Politics of Diaspora*, edited by Evelyn Alsultany and Ella Shohat, 80–95. Ann Arbor: University of Michigan Press, 2013.

Molina, Natalia, Daniel HoSang, and Ramón A. Gutiérrez. *Relational Formations of Race: Theory, Method, and Practice*. Oakland: University of California Press, 2019.

Munem, Bahia M. "Expulsions and Receptions: Palestinian Iraq War Refugees in the Brazilian Nation-State." PhD diss., Rutgers University, 2014.

Munem, Bahia, and Sônia Hamid. "Diasporic Palestinian Communities in Brazil and Hierarchies of Belonging: A Perspective from Palestinian Iraq War Refugees." *Revista Territórios & Fronteiras* 13, no. 2 (2021): 192–213.

Omi, Michael, and Howard Winant. *Racial Formation in the United States: From the 1960s to the 1990s*. New York: Routledge, 1994.

Quijano, Aníbal. "Coloniality and Modernity/Rationality." *Cultural Studies* 21, no. 2 (2007): 168–178.

Rhenal Doria, Ana Milena, and Francisco Flórez Bolivar. "Entre lo árabe y lo negro: Raza y inmigración en Cartagena, 1880–1930." *Revista Sociedad y Economía*, no. 15 (2008): 123–144.

"Vilarejo libanês do 'filho Michel Temer' Segue igreja ortodoxa grega." *Folha de São Paulo*, August 5, 2016, https://www1.folha.uol.com.br/poder/2016/05/1769102-vilarejo-libanes-do-filho-michel-temer-segue-igreja-ortodoxa-grega.shtml.

Wade, Peter. *Degrees of Mixture, Degrees of Freedom: Genomics, Multiculturalism, and Race in Latin America*. Durham, NC: Duke University Press, 2017.

"'We want much more,' Says Temer on Trade with Arabs." *ANBA: Brazil-Arab News Agency*, November 11, 2018, https://anba.com.br/en/we-want-much-more-says-temer-on-trade-with-arabs/.

Yidi David, Odette. "Los árabes en Barranquilla." *Memorias: Revista Digital de Historia y Arqueología desde el Caribe Colombiano*, no. 17 (2012): 1–5.

CHAPTER 18

Ethno-Racial Landscapes in Argentina, Uruguay, Paraguay, and Chile

From Assimilation to Contestation

GONZALO AGUIAR MALOSETTI

This chapter provides a historical and cultural overview of the question of race and ethnicity in the Southern Cone, a region where historical and cultural narratives created alternative spaces for ideologies of mestizaje and Afro-descendant experiences of social and racial marginalization. These narratives can be traced back to a history of colonization that made the subjugation of Indigenous populations and the slave trade in the Viceroyalty of the Río de la Plata essential tools for the imposition of relations of domination, and whose manifestations are felt even today. Consequently, this chapter aims to engage with the ways in which racial projects were deployed in the Southern Cone through discourses of whiteness, Afro–Latin American Blackness, and indigeneity. It is worth mentioning that such racial expressions have historically been explained as purely based on socioeconomic causes, leaving out the role of intersectionality in Afro-descendants' contemporary struggles for social and political visibility.

In the unfolding of such racial and racist projects, a series of discourses featuring "scientific racism" were deployed in nineteenth-century Latin America.

Culturalist notions such as *raza chilena* (Chilean race) and *raza paraguaya* (Paraguayan race) prompted a representation of the nation as not only based on cultural and racial homogeneity but also based on a disavowal of the ethnic difference by these nations' intellectual elites. A century later, the 2000 Regional Conference of the Americas held in Santiago, Chile, became the starting point for contemporary forms of activism against racial discrimination and violence in Argentina, Paraguay, and Uruguay. In this sense, this chapter shows how different expressions of Afro militancy in these societies are connected to a construction of collective identities that do away with assimilationist policies in search of a reinvented relationship with the state. I am interested in how ideologies of multiculturalism permeated these societies at a time when demands for cultural and ethnic recognition were part of a generalized reaction against neoliberalism while tending to favor, albeit problematically, leftist governments' promotion of ethnic and cultural plurality in the region.

Argentina's Own Racialized Citizens

Recent ethnographic work conducted in Argentina underscores the ways the myth of the country's predominantly European ancestry has established racial hierarchies to the detriment of the Afro-Argentine population.[1] In other words, either through ethnic nicknaming performed in social interactions,[2] or through an intentional suppression of the "afroargentinidad" historically effected in the national imaginary,[3] Blackness has been rendered invisible by Argentina's hegemonic discourse. Just like the efforts of rewriting the nation's history seen in other regions of the Southern Cone, an analysis of Argentina's attitude toward race and racialization should start by looking at its historical experience with slave traffic from the sixteenth century until well into the nineteenth century. What this examination will mainly do is to recognize the historical, social, and cultural significance of the Afro-Argentine legacy to the nation's "whitened" past.[4]

Between 1595 and 1680, with Buenos Aires established as the main port of entry in the Río de la Plata region, enslaved people were smuggled in droves and directed to Paraguay, Chile, and Alto Perú (present-day Bolivia). Most came from West Africa, whereas others entered into Buenos Aires from Brazil.[5] The resulting slave trade was so significant to the demographic makeup of the port cities of Buenos Aires and Montevideo that around 30 percent of the population consisted of free and enslaved people of color by 1800.[6] New social types were created in Buenos Aires as a result of the resettlement of people of African descent, who came to be seen as increasingly important in the city's economy. This was particularly noteworthy when one considers how the urban enslaved were able to engage in skilled labor, not only benefiting their owners but also putting pressure on the competition, European artisans who arrived in Buenos Aires in the nineteenth century.[7] In spite of their relative freedom to develop job skills that set them apart from more restrictive ways of servitude in late-colonial and early republican Buenos Aires, Afro-Argentines nonetheless had to bear the brunt of several pieces of legislation aimed at curtailing their freedom. With little or no variation at all, this continued happening in Argentina even after the slave trade was outlawed in 1813.

The creation of the United Provinces of the Río de la Plata in 1810, and the concomitant struggle for power between Buenos Aires and the interior provinces during the age of revolution, was an important episode in how Afro-descendants' legal status changed over time. The 1813 Free Womb Act was enacted to allow the gradual abolition of slavery from the region. In short, the legislation ruled that all children born to enslaved mothers were to be declared *libertos* (free). Erika Denise Edwards maintains that such piece of legislation "marked a formative escape from blackness," thus empowering "freed African descendants [to achieve] a measure of whiteness that late-nineteenth-century intellectuals extolled as the ideal."[8] In reality, the act was just a small but sure step toward granting Afro-descendants rights and freedoms, a process that continued with the formal abolition of slavery in all provinces except Buenos Aires in 1853. The city would follow suit in 1861.

A period of civil and international conflicts in the region featured Black people suffering heavy casualties in the Independence wars and in the defense of Buenos Aires in 1806–1807.[9] George Reid Andrews has the theory that Afro-Argentines were also involved in processes of racial miscegenation,[10] which helps explain how later in the century the population was increasingly undercounted in census data. The fact that Afro-Argentines were slowly fading from the nation's ethno-racial landscape makes for a compelling case to understand new forms of Afro militancy taking place in contemporary Argentina. When understood in the context of mid- to late nineteenth-century Argentina, Andrews's thesis becomes all the more relevant in terms of how racial categories were manipulated to make certain groups disappear from the "white" nation. The historian has worked around the notion of *trigueño* (dark-skinned individual) as one of the dispositives (in the Foucauldian sense) deployed institutionally to shift descriptions of Afro-Argentines from the axis *pardo-moreno* to a more ambiguous—and socially acceptable—racial category. The term *trigueño* detours around the more compromising racial categories historically associated with African ancestry, including *mulatto* and *negro*.[11] For Afro-Argentines eager to be accepted in a *porteño* society, such a conceptual shift, along with other institutional mechanisms of civility and citizenship, such as public education and claims of Indigenous ancestry ratified in courts,[12] was the opportunity for them to be assimilated into a racially homogeneous society. As Lea Geler convincingly argues, it precluded any "excess of color" in the progressive invisibilization of Blackness and mestizaje in modern Argentina.[13]

Political uses of Blackness in Argentina were particularly effective in the documented alliance between caudillo and president of the Argentine Confederation Juan Manuel de Rosas (1793–1877) and Afro-Argentine people. Associating Afro-Argentines with backwardness, degeneracy, and barbarian habits was, in the minds of the Argentine liberal elite, further proof of the urgency to eradicate the remnants of the past. But they did so by implementing biopolitical means of control over Afro-Argentine and Indigenous populations, which have been documented extensively in history. What remains relevant here is the extent to which mechanisms of institutional legitimation were responsible for the suppression of Afro-Argentine cultural practices that would later become the basis of the nation's cultural identity, such as tango, milonga, and candombe. The goal of studying Afro-Argentines' contributions to national culture, according to Alejandro Solomianski, is to break away from an image of Argentina as a "racist space for oligarchic rule" and highlight the heterogeneity of the Afro-Argentine legacy to the nation's future.[14]

During the first half of the twentieth century, new approaches to Argentina's ethnic makeup obtained visibility and public recognition in the cultural field. In Argentine scholar Ezequiel Adamovsky's view, the *criollista* discourse, with its focus on the "authenticity" predicated on expressions of vernacular culture, made room for broader and more significant spaces of identity negotiation.[15] Carnival celebrations, theatrical performances, representations of the gaucho—the latter portrayed with the phenotypical traits of a mestizo individual—were some of the visual strategies deployed so as to produce an image of the people (pueblo) that served to delegitimize the whitening project promoted by the Argentine elite. Subalternity was not hidden but revealed in multiple and complex ways, thus showing the path for a democratization of culture that was also used in conjunction with political ends. *Pueblo*, semantically linked to race and class, became an increasingly important sociopolitical construct for populist discourses about the nation.[16] Such cultural manifestations showed that the notion of Blackness was at a certain point delinked from its association with Afro-Argentines to describe instead an increasingly powerful working class.[17] Class-based analysis explaining economic and social disparities in the region were predominant over the past century, thus neglecting the category of race as a determinant factor in the suppression of racialized bodies and spaces in Argentine society.[18]

With the return to democracy in the 1980s, and the adoption of celebratory ideologies of multiculturalism in the 1990s, Afro cultural and political militancy gained renewed attention in Argentina. On the one hand, the construction of an Afro-Argentine identity evidences multiple layers of political organization focused on dismantling logics of racial and social exclusion from the body politic. In a recent Zoom event hosted by Howard University, a group of Afro-Argentine intellectuals and activists laid out a plan of action developed over decades of militancy.[19] There is a set of initiatives targeting the historical invisibility of Afro-Argentines, a pressing issue now more relevant than ever after the results of the 2010 national census indicated that at least 150,000 people identify themselves as Afro-Argentines—a number that is more than likely to be higher according to Afro-Argentine sociologist Carlos Álvarez Nazareno. Other demands include passing legislation that effectively protect Afro-descendants and Africans living in Argentina from structural violence manifested in episodes of racial and social injustice, questionable policing practices, and exclusion from public spaces; all the while, the emphasis continues to be the expansion of a militant cultural and political identity to counter overt or underhanded expressions of racism.

On the other hand, calling attention to racist manifestations in language as well as in how artistic expressions by Afro-descendants are perceived in hegemonic discourses of whiteness (phenotypically and culturally speaking) are linked to the ways Afro-Argentine activism has refashioned itself in the past few decades.[20] The works by Alejandro Frigerio and Eva Lamborghini are particularly important in this regard. Both authors have pointed out that an excessive attention to cultural events celebrating minorities' rights for self-expression—a fitting multiculturalist concept that allows for the mainstream acceptance of candombe music in the capital city, for instance—may conceal the fact that celebrations alone do not actually improve Afro-Argentines' economic and social needs.[21] Such an observation is highly significant as it points to one of the political quagmires of the African diaspora in Argentina as well as in other parts of the region. Be that as it may, the implementation of new subject positions through political activism, coupled with strategic alliances with the Argentine state and the ongoing challenge to Eurocentric perspectives still entrenched in the cultural field, constitute stimulating developments toward a more inclusive and equitable society.

Afro-Uruguayan and Indigenous Counternarratives in a "White" Nation

Just like in other parts of the region, individuals of African descent had to negotiate their social and racial status during the transition from colonial rule to republican administration in present-day Uruguay. Once part of the United Provinces of the Río de la Plata, the nation faced similar challenges as to how to integrate their African and Afro-descendant populations at a time when the abolition of the slave trade in 1812 led to the enactment of the Free Womb Act a year later, thus freeing babies from following the same fate of their enslaved mothers.[22] Such historical episodes did not prevent African and Afro-Uruguayans from continuing endure processes of marginalization, invisibility, and social and cultural delegitimization that existed well into the twentieth century. As we will see, the complex institutional mechanisms with which the Uruguayan state negotiated with its Afro-Uruguayan population were instrumental in the latter's increasing visibility in the public sphere. This was partly due to a gradual acceptance of Afro-Uruguayan cultural expressions associated in the past with "the sociocultural and socioeconomic factors that influence the value placed on cultural products."[23] The assimilating process by which Afro-Uruguayan music was legitimized as one of the most important vernacular expressions of national identity helped define the contours of a Black culture that has precipitated the demise of a mythical narrative centered on Uruguay as a white nation.

The foundation of Montevideo in 1724 gave the port city a strategic location among the system of ports in the Río de la Plata, as well as an entry point to the slave traffic coming to the region.[24] Unlike plantation economies in need of intensive labor, enslaved Africans coming to the Río de la Plata were mainly put to work in cities as domestic servants, artisans, and workforce in low-intensive agriculture.[25] Even though the formation of such urban ecosystems—undeniably shaped by enslaved labor—was facilitated by a network of "trans-imperial cooperation" connecting the Portuguese and Spanish imperial economies in the Río de la Plata region functioning as one of the epicenters of the Atlantic slave trade, as pointed out by Borucki,[26] the most interesting aspect is how the Afro population was seen and unseen in colonial as well as republican Montevideo. In this sense, the lack of segregationist policies in Uruguay made racism a nonexistent problem in the minds of many of its citizens. A relevant study conducted by Mariana Trías Cornú demonstrates that only a data analysis concerning Afro-Uruguayans' access to housing, education, and health can tell a more complete story of both discrimination and hardships suffered by the community throughout Uruguay's history.[27]

Erasing the presence of Afro-populations in the nation's ethno-racial makeup, even after the 1805 census indicating that over one-third of the population was African and Afro-descendant,[28] started with Black and *pardo* soldiers enlisted in independence wars against imperial aggressors and in conflicts between Uruguay's traditional political parties, like the Guerra Grande civil war (1839–1851). A certified military service did not guarantee a full enjoyment of social and civil equality for Black people, though. Andrews argues that there was a clear expectation on the part of the Uruguayan society for Afro-Uruguayans to continue serving in the military compulsorily, which caused many of them to flee the country to Buenos Aires.[29] Another factor in the community's gradual invisibility was the assumption by Uruguay's *principistas* (a group of young, ideologically liberal intellectuals educated in the 1860s and 1870s) that Afro-descendants were closely tied to *caudillista* politics due to their involvement in preceding civil wars that had devastated the country and impeded its modernization. Such association with barbarism, backwardness, social chaos, and emotionally charged ways of doing politics (the now-infamous *política candombera*) did considerable damage to the overall reputation of Afro-Uruguayans attempting to establish citizenship rights in the nation. It would later extend to other social and cultural areas in which Afro-Uruguayans were allowed to express themselves, though outside the city's walls.[30]

Both Andrews and Trías Cornú have highlighted the cultural significance of the *Libro del Centenario del Uruguay* (1925), a book published by the Ministry of Public Instruction on the occasion of the centennial celebration of one of the official founding dates of Uruguay. In addition to boasting about the fact that no trace of Indigenous existence could be found in the country after the 1832 extermination of the Charrúa people (a topic I will return to), the publication states unequivocally that "Uruguay is populated by the white race of European provenance in its entirety."[31] The statement came to be understood as the triumph of a national narrative focused on highlighting the influence of European immigration in the nation's whitening process. It was also an implicit recognition of the "limits of black upward mobility" in a society that did not respect the contribution of Afro-Uruguayans to official policies of social, educational, and economic inclusion that made up for most of the country's reputation around the world.

A corollary to decades of demographic changes in Uruguay, during the first decades of the twentieth century, the Afro-Uruguayan population resettled in Barrio Sur, Palermo, and other popular neighborhoods in Montevideo. The spaces of sociability generated in those *conventillos* (large tenement buildings) were decisive in the construction of artistic expressions that later gained official recognition such as carnival celebrations and candombe music. They were also symbolic sites of resistance against racial discrimination and social marginalization, especially in the context of a de facto government in 1970s Uruguay. At the time, many *conventillos* with great historical and cultural significance were condemned by the military in power, and their occupants were forced out and resettled in low-income areas of the capital known as *cantegriles*.[32] George Reid Andrews explains: "In later years black activists and organizations charged that the forced evacuation of Medio Mundo, Ansina, and other *conventillos* were racist assaults on the Afro-Uruguayan population, motivated in part by a desire to profit from rising real estate values in the city's central neighborhoods and in part by a desire to disrupt foci of black political and cultural resistance to the dictatorship."[33]

At stake was the right to a fully participatory citizenship threatened by an authoritarian regime that made policies of social and spatial exclusion to Afro-Uruguayans, and the latter's historically restrictive access to formal education,[34] even worse. Yet Black organizations that have sustained a movement toward recognition and cultural and social legitimacy have been operating in the nation throughout the past and present centuries. They were active in the public sphere through a series of serial publications focused on highlighting a dynamic Afro-Uruguayan community participating fully in the construction of a national sense of belonging. Engaging with white members of the lettered elite, as the Black magazine *Vanguardia* did with Uruguayan poet and critic Ildefonso Pereda Valdés (1899–1996) at a time when artistic depictions of Blackness were in high demand in the Western World,[35] proved a fruitful alliance in the struggle for recognition within national circuits of cultural production.

The revalorization of Afro-Uruguayan cultural traditions has expanded to other areas in addition to cultural forms officially sanctioned in national celebrations.[36] Going beyond the centrality Andrews gives to Afro-Uruguayan music and dance in the formation of a strong Afro-Uruguayan collectivity,[37] Melva Persico calls attention to different expressions of a Black lettered city that challenges hegemonic representations by a predominantly white cultural elite.[38] Similarly, Chagas and Stalla effectively surveyed the contribution of Afro-descendants to sports and the creative arts so as to demonstrate the invigorating presence of affirmative identities performing Blackness within the "multi-ethnic and multicultural character of the Uruguayan society."[39] With 8.1 percent of the nation's population identifying themselves as Afro-descendants in the 2011 census,[40] the ongoing revision of Uruguay's past has been furthered by a series of interdisciplinary collaborations drawing attention to the imperative of incorporating the Afro-Uruguayan experience into counternarratives of the nation.[41]

Whatever Happened to the Charrúa People?

"To what extent can we Uruguayans claim the Charrúa people as our ancestors?" asks the Uruguayan anthropologist Daniel Vidart.[42] The quote may be prompted by an exercise in nostalgia about an Indigenous nation who inhabited present-day Uruguay, acted in alliance with the patriots during the Independence wars, but was nonetheless subjected to extermination in the early nineteenth century in horrific episodes of state racism.[43] Yet the question by Vidart also encloses some of the most pressing issues many scholars are facing nowadays by working with an analytical framework informed by decoloniality. In this sense, undoing forms of knowledge and epistemologies derived from a colonial matrix of power have become imperative to disentangle the subaltern from a network of colonial and neocolonial conceptualizations that still "otherize" their presence in the national community.

How, then, is it possible to vindicate in the here and now an Indigenous ethnicity that was supposed to be erased from the (white) national imaginary in nineteenth-century Uruguay? To what extent does a conceptual reformulation of traditional academic disciplines change a national narrative describing Uruguay as a "nation without Indians"? Don't we know already that contemporary debates on the conditions that made such a narrative possible in the first place continues to be haunted by Indigenous specters that are rejected with derision or plainly denied by certain sectors of the Uruguayan society?[44] As Gustavo Verdesio argues in a recent article, this may have to do with how Uruguayans have represented themselves over the course of their history, a self-fashioned identity that excludes any reference to an Indigenous past.[45] Such scarce interest demonstrated by a society shaped by settler colonialism is, in Verdesio's view, a slap in the face to a reemergent activism that is "trying to vindicate . . . a way of life, a way of understanding and practicing the territory."[46]

If nothing else, this reappearance of the Charrúa people has prompted many academic debates at a time when articulating alliances with activist groups helps articulate forms of knowledge production focused on dismantling colonial legacies in all areas of social life. Singling out the state's genocidal policies regarding its *pueblos originarios* (Native populations) becomes an act of resistance in itself for both academics and activists. It offers the opportunity to confront the state and its historical responsibility in the systematic extermination of Indigenous peoples at a time when the Uruguayan ruling class modeled the nation after European liberal experiments. Acknowledging the cultural legacy of the Charrúa people, then, becomes not a nostalgic reappropriation of a mostly romanticized past but a political reinterpretation of how Uruguay came to be imagined as the gradual invisibilization of minorities took place in a methodical fashion. More importantly, it represents an act of social justice that somewhat reverses the cultural death that the Charrúa people underwent after the massacres, a phenomenon described by Vidart as an "ethnocide" that is yet to be fully addressed in Uruguay.[47]

Guaraní People and Afro-Descendants in the Heartland of Paraguay

Paraguay is the only country in Latin America where the majority speaks an Indigenous language.[48] Unlike the language spoken by the Ayoreo people (northern Chaco Indians who have historically resisted any attempts by Spaniards and missionaries to change their way of life), Guaraní has been on the forefront for as long as Paraguay has existed.[49] This was partly due to how significant the language was in the Jesuit reductions during colonial times, where all the social interactions, and the proper language used in masses, were in Guaraní.

Any debate about the invisibility of Afro-descendants in contemporary Paraguay cannot be easily explained away by the nation's assimilation process known as mestizaje.[50] In fact, the decolonial argument that traces the suppression of Afro-Paraguayan presence back to Spanish colonial subjugation, followed by forms of coloniality of power in the Republican era, is already part of the vocabulary used in Spanish-language media devoted to social and racial issues in the region.[51] As far as the racial debates in the public arena are concerned, this is indeed a remarkable turn of events when it comes to denouncing how entrenched discourses of racial assimilation are in Paraguay's foundational accounts. Ultimately, what this latest development reveals is the imperative for Afro-Paraguayans to transition from a struggle for cultural recognition to the implementation of political strategies focused on effective and democratic representation in the public sphere.

This long struggle for recognition dates back to colonial times, well before the institution of the Viceroyalty of the Río de la Plata in 1776. Historical records indicate that the first royal permit to import slaves to the Río de la Plata region was issued in 1534.[52] Between the first foundation of the city of Buenos Aires in 1536 and the abrogation (at least formally) of the encomienda system in 1803, African people and their descendants were subjected, regardless of their legal status, to several forms of servitude in colonial Paraguay. The *amparo*, instituted around 1577, was a particularly insidious one.[53] It was a royal ordinance that allowed the imposition of taxes to all free Blacks and mulattoes. Following Josefina Pla's archival research, Shawn Michael Austin claims that the lack of existing currency in the region forced most free individuals of color to pay the tax in the form of personal service to Spaniards appointed by the governor. The fact that the *amparo* was paid through personal service leads Austin to conclude that "each master functioned like an encomendero who received free blacks as personal servants on their states."[54] This particular modality of forced labor lasted until the end of the eighteenth century, "probably because the amparo turned into forced conscription of blacks into military service."[55]

The region's split between the provinces of Buenos Aires and Paraguay in 1617 represented a watershed in the latter's history due to its losing access to the Atlantic. Still, the treatment given to enslaved people in both regions remained basically the same. In Argentina and Paraguay, Afro-descendants were considered a symbol of social status and financial success to the point that only the richest members of the Paraguayan society were able to afford them while less privileged Spaniards had to settle for Guaraní labor.[56] Furthermore, enslaved people were subject to different types of transactions in the economic market, including serving as guarantees for loans and mortgage operations.[57] Such commodification of people of African descent was complemented by attitudes toward preserving their lives in colonial and republican Paraguay. During Gaspar Rodríguez de Francia's tight rule over the nation (1814–1840), for instance, several enslavers were severely punished for wrongdoings committed against Afro-Paraguayans in their charge.[58] Policies and enforced rules like in the preceding example allowed Francia to count on the allegiance of the *gente de color* for agricultural activities and protection of the national borders against external hostility. When José Gervasio Artigas (Uruguay's national hero) was granted political asylum in Paraguay (1820), he brought with him a contingent of Blacks and *pardos* that constituted "the most significant influx of colored people in the history of independent Paraguay."[59]

The traditional scholarly assessment claiming that the institution of slavery in Paraguay was relatively milder in comparison to the one developed in plantation economies is an interesting topic to explore here. It is based on the fact that the domestic character of the servitude in Paraguay cannot be equated to the brutal conditions in which Africans and Afro-descendants worked, for instance, in colonial Brazil. Josefina Pla concludes that enslaved people in Paraguay were not treated as harshly in part because they were mostly engaged in urban-related work and able to create affectional bonds with the enslaver's family. Such "patriarchal tolerance" does not hide the fact that both enslaved and manumitted Afro-Paraguayans continued to have no legal or juridical protections because of their lesser status than whites and Amerindians.[60] Even after the enactment of the Free Womb Law in 1842, two years after Dr. Francia's death, the social status of Afro-Paraguayans did not change significantly as they were enlisted in the army by a decree issued by the new President of Paraguay, Carlos Antonio López (1792–1862).

Archival documentation has demonstrated that this paternalist vision of the Paraguayan nation toward their subjects failed to account for the fact that Amerindians, Afro-Paraguayans and *pardos* looked for ways to break free from their social and ethnic status to be considered "Spaniards."[61] The effort was facilitated by a policy of closed borders that prevented immigration into Paraguay for decades in the nineteenth century, thus allowing mestizaje to run its course in the nation. In this regard, Boccia Romañach resorts to a number of textual sources all pointing in the same direction, that of a "mestizo society" favored by strict border policies and sustained by Indigenous labor.[62]

The cultural turn of Paraguayan mestizaje was of the utmost importance in the early twentieth century. On the occasion of Paraguay's centennial celebration of the nation's independence in 1911, the intellectual elite (known as Generación del 900) devised a series of cultural strategies to highlight the positive virtues of the *raza paraguaya* (Paraguayan race), chief among them its resilience, heroism, and superiority over other "races."[63] Such rhetorical appeal with patriotic overtones was basically fueled by the collective trauma caused by the War of the Triple Alliance (1864–1870), which prompted intellectuals, politicians, and historians to rewrite the history of interethnic relations in the nation. Yet the fact remains that the elite's master narrative of postwar Paraguay kept concealing the social marginalization and juridical, economic, and religious discriminations suffered by Indigenous and Afro-descendant peoples throughout history.[64] It is interesting to note that both Telesca and Erika Edwards, despite being focused on different geographical areas and historical periods within the Southern Cone, share the same conclusion as to how important disguising their ethnicity was to Afro-Paraguayans to be accepted in mainstream society. For Afro-descendants, Telesca tells us about late-colonial Paraguay, "this was not a process of mestizaje but one of 'whitening': to be Spanish would be replaced by being Paraguayan, and both words were synonymous with being 'white.'"[65]

A few assumptions about the strategies used by *pardos* to pass as Spaniards (or Paraguayans) can be made here with respect to present-day Paraguay. Chiefly among them is the way such assimilationist practices by the ruling elite would jettison the recognition of a pluricultural society that is clearly there despite long-standing policies of border protection and idiosyncratic policies focused on showing the nation's singularity with respect to the rest of the Americas. Insularity has been a historical characteristic of Paraguayan society, yet the state's deployment of a supposedly homogeneous Paraguayidad without legitimizing the demands of ethnic minorities continues to be a major task for all the social and political actors involved in implementing change.[66]

Bilingualism in Paraguay denotes an exceptional situation across the West that has been used for intercultural but also political reasons at a time when the question of language and territorial sovereignty was revisited during the Chaco War against Bolivia (1932–1935). The heavy propaganda machine produced in Guaraní at the time uplifted the patriotic spirit of the Paraguayan people, and in many ways, it served as the corollary of a mestizo identity identified as "Guaraní."[67] It is worth remembering that attempts by the Spanish Crown to eradicate the Guaraní language proved to be unsuccessful in colonial Paraguay.[68] Consequently, the permanence of a language deeply embedded in the nation's collective identity represents a sense of belonging that is felt in their everyday lives as well as in national conversations about Indigenous political activists pursuing recognition of their social demands.

It was on April 30, 1992, that Paraguay's new constitution included a section on Indigenous rights. The move was supposed to further a social agenda that was imperfectly implemented with the promulgation of the Indigenous Rights Law 904 in 1981 and in response to human rights violations perpetrated by the Stroessner regime, deposed in 1989. The addition of that chapter represented the efforts of Indigenous movements to advance social, racial, and economic justice as the result of decades fighting authoritarian repression, man-made ecological disasters, and a transnational network created with other Indigenous organizations across the Americas.[69] Harder Horst summarizes the extraordinary events that preceded the drafting of the document by Paraguay's constitutional assembly:

> Indigenous people mobilized together as never before to claim the first constitutional recognition of their existence. . . . [Such] unprecedented gathering highlights the degree to which the struggle against the regime had forged a pan-Indigenous identity in Paraguay. By this time, Native peoples identified themselves as 'nations' that had existed prior to European arrival. Their appropriation of Western political terminology and the collective name 'the indigenous peoples of Paraguay' shows the degree to which the struggle to protect and recover lands had changed Native people, and exactly how aware they were of Indigenous organization and movements taking place elsewhere in the continent.[70]

Effecting change is, in this sense, a remarkable progress toward a thorough questioning of the social and ethno-racial markers which Native people were assigned in historical terms. However, Harder Horst aptly observes how such recently acquired legal status by Indigenous communities may be used to trap them into what Bolivian sociologist Silvia Rivera Cusicanqui encapsulates in the notion of the "authorized Indian."[71] In other words, the notion means obtaining consent from the Indigenous community in exchange for recognition of their rights to exercise their culture. Whatever the outcome of this national pact might be, Paraguay's Indigenous people will continue to face challenges on multiple fronts as they look for a brighter political future in a contained nation dealing with organized crime, political dysfunctionality, and the ongoing ecological disaster of the Gran Chaco deforestation.

The Mapuche Nation: Toward an Indigenous Ethno-Nationalism Pursuing Recognition and Autonomy

The Mapuche question is deeply intertwined with how Chile imagined itself as a nation over the historical development of an ethno-racial imaginary from the early republican era until the present. The 2002 census shows that, among the eight officially recognized Indigenous groups in Chile by 1993, the Mapuche people represent over 95 percent of the overall Indigenous population in the nation,[72] which ultimately proves the significance of their current demands for recognition and equity in both rural and urban areas. The data also suggest that a correlation between ethnicity and poverty may help the Chilean government to identify new criteria in resource distribution through antipoverty programs.[73] Stressing the ethnic factor seems to be a fitting idea after all. In theory, it would help allocate resources to address income inequality, housing conditions, and an overall deterioration of the quality of life among Indigenous communities. Still, as Foerster and Vergara maintain, an increased visibility of the Mapuche people in Chilean society has not necessarily translated into actual change. Indigenous rights are negotiated without taking into account the need of a holistic approach to the "historical debt" that the Chilean state has with their indigenous population.[74] Instead, a series of neoliberal administrations in the late twentieth century and the early twenty-first century have only paid lip service to a celebratory politics of difference that have left pressing economic issues—Mariátegui's now-classic "Indian problem"—mostly untouched.

There is virtually no dispute about the fact that contemporary struggles of the Mapuche people for recognition and sovereignty over their expropriated lands began in earnest in the nineteenth century. Bernardo Subercaseaux has analyzed in great detail some of the most important components of a national imaginary centered on suppressing the Mapuche cultural heritage in favor of theories of miscegenation. In particular, he focuses on republican experiments made with social Darwinism, eugenics, and other social and racial policies that were instrumental in producing a hegemonic notion of *raza chilena* (Chilean race).[75] The symbolic power of those representations of race and nation furthered notions of belonging that go beyond a mere political citizenship. In reality, it establishes a link between political sovereignty and an ethno-cultural discourse that shapes a nationalism based on white, masculine, and heteronormative values. Subercaseaux calls it a "nación patriarcal" (patriarchal nation),[76] which in many ways departs from the pluricultural makeup of the nation by ignoring racial, social, and economic realities fragmenting such imaginary representations of the Chilean nation.

The extent to which such nationalist discourses on race and nation have influenced Chile's republican life is hard to deny in the light of its devastating effects on the autonomy of the Mapuche people. By applying the then-trending dichotomy civilization-barbarism to the ethnic community, the state was guaranteeing an otherized status to the Mapuche people and justifying processes of exclusion and inclusion that turned them into what Nahuelpan Moreno calls "vidas despojables y sirvientes" (disposable, servient lives).[77] The loss of ancestral territories and ways of living associated with those lands under the rule of the Chilean state (Wigkün) have brought an increasing pressure on the Mapuche nation to assimilate to a form of "extraterritorial community" that accelerates processes of transculturation and alienation from their cultural roots.[78] This goes against current demands by the Mapuche people to return to their traditions and their own forms of socialization historically and culturally located in the Araucanía, Las Pampas, and Patagonia.

Truthfully, there are several obstacles in their way toward a better representativity in the public sphere, and a more cohesive collective action on the part of the community at large. Chief among them is the lack of a structured collective project that makes up for a fragmented community suffering from exploitation, social injustice, and cultural uprootedness. Also, the Mapuche people should rethink their subaltern dependency with respect to the Chilean state and adopt a more constructive and affirmative discourse of social responsibility toward society.[79] Finally, the Mapuche people should be front and center in the redefinition of the "national" when it comes to debating and eventually solving the ethnic conflicts that have characterized Chile's institutional life in the past few decades.[80]

The Mapuche people were the only indigenous group able to negotiate with the Chilean state the preservation of their political and territorial sovereignty.[81] This collective effort has been recently jeopardized by the complicity between the state and corporate interests aimed at dismantling a social pact that interferes with neoliberal interventionism in the nation's pluricultural nature. Institutional attempts to put forward a consistent land policy in Chile have to deal with a political and economic framework (neoliberalism) that places emphasis on subject formations regulated by the market. This resulting ecosystem is deployed as a set of individual choices made by consumers as opposed to organizing efforts to implement change through collective action. Kelly Bauer has observed that such a sociopolitical conundrum is part of the ongoing negotiations with Mapuche activists pursuing land restitution, which allows for multiple constructions of social actors positioned between ethnocultural demands and the state's rights for land redistribution. Bauer adds:

> Actors are simultaneously making and being made within the state's governing logic, creating the conceptual space for actors to subvert this logic. Bureaucrats are positioned in the middle space, representing discipline and

resistance, and policy outcomes are the visible outcome of the how bureaucrats work to strategically negotiate and maneuver between the ideals of the state's governing logic and discourser, and the local application of that governing logic. For Mapuche communities pursuing degrees of autonomy through territorial rights claims through Chile's Indigenous land policy, these outcomes of bureaucrats' work are consequential, particularly when considering the uneven extension of neoliberalism over space and time.[82]

The "contradictory nature of neoliberal governance through the work of government officials" is certainly exploited in the public arena to demonstrate how entrenched the interests of the power elite are when it comes to maintaining an hegemonic control of the Chilean territory.[83] The last decades of the twentieth century have certainly brought a state recognition of Indigenous cultural practices attached to land and customary laws. Yet the framework of what Nahuelpan Moreno and Antimil Caniupán call "republican colonialism" still persists in Chile.[84] The state's recognition of Indigenous rights is projected in the public sphere as part of neoliberal policies celebrating the nation's pluricultural society without effecting real change. Both authors contend that the historical resistance of the Mapuche community to assimilationist policies on the part of the Chilean state was decisive in preserving their culture and demanding social and political recognition.

Current modes of political activism have been focused on keeping tense, and sometimes conflicting, negotiations with other social actors. This is happening thanks in part to a new generation of Mapuche activists who are performing "multidimensional rebellions" against historical policies of aggression, extermination, and identity erasure through national inclusion.[85] The topic of land restitution is central to Mapuche demands for recognition without assimilation. Yet addressing structural racism, dispossession, and the extermination policies implemented over the course of the nation's history constitutes additional areas for debate that reveal the programmatic nature of a body of knowledge produced by a group of organic intellectuals of the Mapuche Nation.[86]

A plurality of perspectives within the Mapuche movement also means coordinating successfully a number of expectations toward debating the means and ends of the movement's common goals. To do so, constructing a reterritorialization of Mapuche demands, as Alvaro Bello observes in reference to the "multicentered structure" of Mapuche ethnopolitics,[87] should be part of a broader agenda aimed at uniting the Mapuche experience in rural as well as urban settings. The purpose is to meet the cultural and social horizons of the Mapuche migration to the cities, an experience that may set them apart from their cultural roots attached to Indigenous land. What is at stake is the preservation of a sense of belonging to the community that may be in danger by exposing migrant Mapuches to "processes of transculturation" in the cities.[88] Prioritizing the protection of Indigenous rights and culture does not mean essentializing a certain image of the Mapuche people, though. It is important to emphasize that a vindication of Mapuche rights to their land and to a full integration into Chile's political and social plurality implies a recognition of the ethno-cultural causes behind the data supporting the lack of access to education and upward mobility of the Mapuche people. Only after acknowledging this fact can the Chilean society start working toward a better outcome for intercultural relations in the nation.

In this context, it has become imperative to question an ideology of whiteness entrenched in institutional discourses while recognizing the social and ethno-racial heterogeneity of a nation that has upheld the ideology of the "Un solo Chile" (a unified Chile) for so long. Moreover, attempts to reconstitute the internal fragmentation of the Mapuche community, due in part to centuries of colonial and neocolonial forms of exploitation and alienation, have become a political task of the first order. Reassessing the legal and juridical status of the Mapuche people vis-à-vis an all-inclusive Chilean state means vindicating a right to self-determination that would accomplish a long-aspired-to autonomy as well as an official restitution of Indigenous land. Millalen Paillal claims that the creation of a "Mapuche national community" is based on a strong ethnonationalist impulse that will eventually constitute a Mapuche Nation once the internal fragmentation of the community is resolved.[89] This political goal is now more important than ever as Chile is set to begin drafting a new constitution that will erase the remnants of an authoritarian past.

Conclusion

As in the case of contemporary activists advocating for "Afroargentinidad," or Mapuche intellectuals striving for a cultural affirmation that removes their communities from the role of subalterns in Chilean society, this chapter has shown how both Indigenous peoples and Afro-descendants in the Southern Cone develop strategies to counter racialized spaces in which ideologies of whiteness have traditionally had a privileged access to notions of sovereignty, identity, representativity, and self-determination. By assessing the efforts of these communities to break away from external and internal modes of colonialism, their respective at-large societies had to adjust accordingly, thus allowing for an expansion and redefinition of what an intercultural public sphere looks like. Either through collective or dispersed political activism demanding change, these popular manifestations continue to be successful in reengaging institutional forces in the ongoing struggle for social and racial justice.

NOTES

1. Prisca Gayles, "¿De dónde sos? (Black) Argentina and the Mechanisms of Maintaining Racial Myths," *Ethnic and Racial Studies* 44, no. 11 (2021): 2093–2112.
2. Ezequiel Adamovsky, "Ethnic Nicknaming: 'Negro' as a Term of Endearment and Vicarious Blackness in Argentina," *Latin American and Caribbean Ethnic Studies* 12, no. 3 (2017): 273–289.
3. Alejandro Solomianski, *Identidades secretas: La negritud argentina* (Rosario, Argentina: Beatriz Viterbo Editora, 2003), 19.
4. "The 2010 census recorded about 150,000 people of African descent in Argentina, a nation of 45 million, but activists estimate the true figure is closer to 2 million following a surge of immigration—and because many Argentines have forgotten or ignore African ancestry," Christiana Sciaudone, "Argentine Movement Tries to Make Black Heritage More Visible," *AP News*, November 26, 2021.
5. George Reid Andrews, *The Afro-Argentines of Buenos Aires, 1800–1900* (Madison: University of Wisconsin Press, 1980), 27. See Alex Borucki for a nuanced discussion on how the slave traffic in the region created "black social networks" that were the product of "both transimperial commerce and contraband within the Americas, and the actions of enslaved people seeking freedom by running away across imperial borders." "Across Imperial Boundaries: Black Social Networks across the Iberian South Atlantic, 1760–1810," *Atlantic Studies* 14, no. 1 (2017): 12.
6. Alex Borucki, David Eltis, and David Wheat, "Atlantic History and the Slave Trade to Spanish America," *American Historical Review* 120, no. 2 (2015): 447; Borucki, "Across Imperial Boundaries," 14.
7. Andrews, *The Afro-Argentines*, 32.
8. Erika Denise Edwards, *Hiding in Plain Sight: Black Women, the Law, and the Making of a White Argentine Republic* (Tuscaloosa: University of Alabama Press, 2020), 4.
9. Solomianski, *Identidades secretas*, 26–27.
10. Andrews, *The Afro-Argentines*, 68.
11. Andrews, *The Afro-Argentines*, 83–87, 109.
12. Edwards, *Hiding in Plain Sight*, 7–10.
13. Lea Geler, "African Descent and Whiteness in Buenos Aires: Impossible Mestizajes in the White Capital City," in *Rethinking Race in Modern Argentina*, ed. Paulina L. Alberto and Eduardo Elena (Cambridge: Cambridge University Press, 2016), 213–214. Geler thus con-

tinues: "This image of Buenos Aires and by extension of Argentina as white-European is partly supported by the widely held belief in the total extermination of the indigenous population in late-nineteenth century wars, and by the conviction that the descendants of enslaved Africans gradually decreased in number over the course of that century until they disappeared" (214).

14. Solomianski, *Identidades secretas*, 61.
15. Ezequiel Adamovsky, "La cultura visual del criollismo: Etnicidad, 'color' y nación en las representaciones visuales del criollo en Argentina, c. 1910-1955," *Corpus* 6, no. 2 (2016): 6.
16. See Peter Wade, "Debates contemporáneos sobre raza, etnicidad, género y sexualidad en las ciencias sociales," in *Raza, etnicidad y sexualidades: Ciudadanía y multiculturalismo en América Latina*, ed. Peter Wade et al. (Bucaramanga: Universidad Nacional de Colombia, Facultad de Ciencias Humanas, 2008), 49-58, for a broader exploration of the role gender and sexuality play in nationalist discourses focused on the social and sexual reproduction of society.
17. Eva Lamborghini and Lea Geler, "Imágenes racializadas: Políticas de representación y economía visual en torno a lo 'negro' en Argentina, siglos XX y XXI," *Corpus* 6, no. 2 (2016): 3.
18. Jennifer Roth-Gordon's reading of this phenomenon involves recognizing "the structural racism that was fed not only by differences in wealth, opportunity, and the situation of one's birth, but also by notions of the superiority of whiteness and the inferiority of blackness," *Race and the Brazilian Body* (Berkeley: University of California Press, 2016), 15. See also Peter Wade for an analysis of the "coexistence of mestizaje and racism" as holding "the key to Latin American concepts of race." "Race in Latin America," in *A Companion to Latin American Anthropology*, ed. Deborah Poole (Malden, MA: Blackwell, 2008), 186.
19. The event was titled *Afro-Argentines: Past and Present* and was held on October 27, 2021 in partnership with the Embassy of Argentina in Washington, DC.
20. Regarding the employment of racist expressions in Argentine Spanish, especially the common appellative *negro* as it is used in the Río de la Plata region, see Adamovsky, "Ethnic Nicknaming," esp. 279-280.
21. Alejandro Frigerio and Eva Lamborghini, "Procesos de reafricanización en la sociedad argentina: Umbanda, candombe y militancia 'afro,'" *Revista Pós Ciências Sociais* 8, no. 16 (2011): 32-34; Alejandro Frigerio and Eva Lamborghini, "El candombe (uruguayo) en Buenos Aires: (Proponiendo) nuevos imaginarios urbanos en la ciudad 'blanca,'" *Cuadernos de Antropología Social*, no. 30 (2009): 111-113; Alejandro Frigerio and Eva Lamborghini, "Criando um movimento negro em um país 'branco': Ativismo político e cultural afro na Argentina," *Afro-Ásia*, no. 39 (2010): 178-179. For more on the historical and cultural significance of candombe, refer to the following section of this chapter.
22. Edwards, *Hiding in Plain Sight*, 4.
23. Melva M. Persico, "Afro-Uruguayan Culture and Legitimation: Candombe and Poetry," in *Black Writing, Culture, and the State in Latin America*, ed. Jerome C. Branche (Nashville, TN: Vanderbilt University Press, 2015), 214.
24. Alex Borucki, "The Slave Trade to the Río de La Plata, 1777-1812: Trans-Imperial Networks and Atlantic Warfare," *Colonial Latin American Review* 20, no. 1 (2011): 83.
25. Borucki, "The Slave Trade," 85.
26. Borucki, "The Slave Trade," 92.

27. Mariana Trías Cornú, "Afrodescendencia y ciudadanía (segunda mitad del siglo XIX y siglo XX)," in *Historia de la población africana y afrodescendiente en Uruguay*, ed. Ana Frega, Nicolás Duffau, Karla Chagas, and Natalia Stalla (Montevideo: Facultad de Humanidades y Ciencias de la Educación, Ministerio de Desarrollo Social, 2020).
28. George Reid Andrews, *Blackness in the White Nation: A History of Afro-Uruguay* (Chapel Hill: University of North Carolina Press, 2010), 23.
29. Andrews, *Blackness in the White Nation*, 34.
30. Karla Chagas and Natalia Stalla, "Vida cotidiana, sociabilidad y expresiones culturales de la población afrodescendiente (siglos XVIII a XXI)," in *Historia de la población africana y afrodescendiente en Uruguay*, ed. Ana Frega, Nicolás Duffau, Karla Chagas, and Natalia Stalla (Montevideo: Facultad de Humanidades y Ciencias de la Educación, Ministerio de Desarrollo Social, 2020), 202-203.
31. As cited in Trías Cornú, "Afrodescendencia y ciudadanía," 143. "Puebla el Uruguay la raza blanca, en su totalidad de origen europeo." The passage continues, making references to the complete erasure of the "Indigenous race" in the nation: "La raza indígena que habitaba esta región de América cuando el descubrimiento y la conquista, ya no existe, siendo el único país del continente que no cuenta en toda la extensión de su territorio tribus de indios, ni en estado salvaje, ni en estado de domesticidad" (143).
32. See Natalia Stalla for further data on the demographic distribution of Afro-Uruguayans in the capital according to the 2011 national census, "Afrodescendientes y africanos en el Uruguay actual: Múltiples identidades," in *Historia de la población africana y afrodescendiente en Uruguay*, ed. Ana Frega, Nicolás Duffau, Karla Chagas, and Natalia Stalla (Montevideo: Facultad de Humanidades y Ciencias de la Educación, Ministerio de Desarrollo Social, 2020), 34-35.
33. Andrews, *Blackness in the White Nation*, 142.
34. Stalla, "Afrodescendientes y africanos," 38.
35. Rodrigo Viqueira, *Negrismo, vanguardia y folklore: Representación de los Afrodescendientes en la Obra de Ildefonso Pereda Valdés* (Montevideo: Rebeca Linke Editoras, 2019).
36. National Day of Candombe, for instance, is celebrated every December 3 since 2006.
37. Andrews, *Blackness in the White Nation*, 23.
38. Persico, "Afro-Uruguayan Culture," 217-218.
39. Chagas and Stalla, "Vida cotidiana," 222.
40. Stalla, "Afrodescendientes y africanos," 30.
41. See also George Reid Andrews, *Afro-Latin America: Black Lives, 1600-2000* (Cambridge, MA: Harvard University Press, 2016), 90-91, for a further analysis of the national debates on racial inequality that took place in Uruguay in the 1990s and early 2000s.
42. Daniel Vidart, *El mundo de los charrúas* (Montevideo: Ediciones de la Banda Oriental, 2010), 14.
43. I am referring to the massacres of Salsipuedes and Mataojo that took place in 1831 during the presidency of Fructuoso Rivera, the first elected president in the new Republic of Uruguay. Although it may be tempting to blame the extermination of the Charrúa people on Rivera, Vidart, in *El mundo de los charrúas*, warns us that the whole Uruguayan society allowed the president to be "the trigger of a weapon" loaded long before the actual massacres (86).
44. Leo Lagos, "¿Por qué tanto miedo al indio en Uruguay?," *La Diaria*, October 31, 2020; Comisión Nacional Honoraria de Sitios de Memoria, "Adhesión a las Demandas del

Pueblo Charrúa en Uruguay" (Montevideo: Institución Nacional de Derechos Humanos y Defensoría del Pueblo, 2022).
45. Gustavo Verdesio, "Ethnic Reemergence in Uruguay: The Return of the Charrúa in the Light of Settler Colonialism Studies," in *Decolonial Approaches to Latin American Literatures and Cultures*, ed. Juan G. Ramos and Tara Daly (New York: Palgrave Macmillan, 2016), 168.
46. Verdesio, "Ethnic Reemergence," 173.
47. Vidart, *El mundo de los charrúas*, 94.
48. Miguel Ángel Verón Gómez, "The Bicentenary of Paraguayan Independence and the Guaraní Language," in *The Paraguay Reader: History, Culture, Politics*, ed. Peter Lambert and Andrew Nickson (Durham, NC: Duke University Press, 2013), 404.
49. For a current perspective on the Ayoreos' struggle to maintain their cultural identity, see Mateo Sobode Chiquenoi, "The Ayoreo People," in *The Paraguay Reader: History, Culture, Politics*, ed. Peter Lambert and Andrew Nickson (Durham, NC: Duke University Press, 2013).
50. The Afro-descendant population in what is known today as Paraguay was calculated between 11 percent and 13 percent according to many sources. See Ignacio Telesca, "Mujer, honor y afrodescendientes en Paraguay a fines de la colonia," *América sin Nombre*, no. 15 (2010): 34; Irene Ayuso Morillo, "Afroparaguayos, condenados a no existir," *Otramérica* 26 (October 2011).
51. Ayuso Morillo, "Afroparaguayos."
52. Andrews, *The Afro-Argentines*, 23. This date differs slightly from the one provided by Josefina Pla (1536) in her groundbreaking *Hermano negro: La esclavitud en el Paraguay* (Madrid: Paraninfo, 1972). For the sake of clarity, I follow the timeline that appears in Andrews's later scholarship on the subject in *The Afro-Argentines*.
53. Telesca, "Mujer, honor y afrodescendientes," 30.
54. Shawn Michael Austin, *Colonial Kinship: Guaraní, Spaniards, and Africans in Paraguay* (Albuquerque: University of New Mexico Press, 2020), 264.
55. Austin, *Colonial Kinship*, 264.
56. Pla, *Hermano negro*, 44; Andrews, *Afro-Argentines*, 31; Alfredo Boccia Romañach, *Esclavitud en el Paraguay: Vida cotidiana del esclavo en las Indias Meridionales* (Asunción: Servilibro, 2004), 216.
57. Pla, *Hermano negro*, 61.
58. Josefina Pla includes various cases extracted from her archival work documented in *Hermano negro*. See especially *Hermano negro*, 78–80.
59. Boccia Romañach, *Esclavitud en el Paraguay*, 233.
60. Pla, *Hermano negro*, 74, 84–85; Ignacio Telesca, "Paraguay en el Centenario: La creación de la nación mestiza," *Historia Mexicana* 60, no. 1 (2010): 173. See Efraím Cardozo for the legal consequences brought by the Libertad de Vientres Law (1842) to Afro-Paraguayans, *Paraguay independiente* (Asunción: Carlos Schauman, 1988). See also Barbara A. Ganson, "Introduction," in *Native Peoples, Politics, and Society in Contemporary Paraguay: Multidisciplinary Perspectives*, ed. Barbara A. Ganson (Albuquerque: University of New Mexico Press, 2021), 7.
61. Ignacio Telesca, "Paraguay a fines de la Colonia: ¿Mestizo, español o indígena?" *Jahrbuch für Geschichte Lateinamerikas* 46, no. 1 (2009): 275–279.
62. "Esta Sociedad mestiza ya estabilizada, se organizó sobre las bases de una economía de consumo fundamentada por entero en el esfuerzo del brazo indígena." Telesca, "Paraguay a fines de la Colonia," 227. See also Ignacio Telesca, "People of African Descent

in Paraguay," in *The Paraguay Reader: History, Culture, Politics*, ed. Peter Lambert and Andrew Nickson (Durham, NC: Duke University Press, 2013).
63. Telesca, "Paraguay en el Centenario," 154.
64. Telesca, "Paraguay en el Centenario," 176; Telesca, "People of African Descent," 410–411.
65. Telesca, "People of African Descent," 412.
66. "Although Paraguay is often referred to as the 'Guaraní nation' . . . the country's indigenous population remains quite small (less than 2 percent); 95 percent of the country's total population of seven million are mestizo." Ganson, "Introduction," 11.
67. See Bridget María Chesterton, *The Grandchildren of Solano López: Frontier and Nation in Paraguay, 1904–1936* (Albuquerque: University of New Mexico Press, 2013), 103–123, for an engrossing analysis of how nonelite Paraguayans serving in the Chaco War refashioned themselves as "soldier-agriculturalists."
68. Ganson, "Introduction," 6–7.
69. For a similar project centered on recognizing indigenous cultural rights in Argentina, see "Amerindian Rights: State Law of Indigenous Rights," in *The Argentina Reader: History, Culture, Politics*, ed. Gabriela Nouzeilles and Graciela Montaldo (Durham, NC: Duke University Press, 2002), 525–527.
70. René D. Harder Horst, "Indigenous People in Paraguay and Latin America's Move to Democracy," in *Native Peoples, Politics, and Society in Contemporary Paraguay: Multidisciplinary Perspectives*, ed. Barbara A. Ganson (Albuquerque: University of New Mexico Press, 2021), 29.
71. As cited in Horst, "Indigenous People," 31.
72. Claudio A. Agostini et al., "Poverty and Inequality among Ethnic Groups in Chile," *World Development* 38, no. 7 (2010): 1037.
73. Agostini et al., "Poverty and Inequality," 1041.
74. Rolf Foerster and Jorge Iván Vergara, "Etnia y nación en la lucha por el reconocimiento: Los mapuches en la sociedad chilena," *Estudios Atacameños*, no. 19 (2000): 11, 34–35.
75. Bernardo Subercaseaux, "Raza y nación: El caso de Chile," *A Contracorriente* 5, no. 1 (2007): 30–31.
76. Subercaseaux, "Raza y nación," 57.
77. Héctor Nahuelpan Moreno, "'Nos explotaron como animales y ahora quieren que no nos levantemos'. Vidas despojables y micropolíticas de resistencia mapuche," in *Awükan ka kuxankan zugu Wajmapu mew: Violencias coloniales en Wajmapu*, ed. Enrique Antileo Baeza et al. (Temuco, Chile: Ediciones Comunidad de Historia Mapuche, 2015), 272.
78. Álvaro M. Bello, "Migración, identidad y comunidad mapuche en Chile: Entre utopismos y realidades," *Asuntos Indígenas* 3, no. 4 (2002): 44.
79. Vergara and Foerster, "Etnia y nación," 42.
80. Vergara and Foerster, "Etnia y nación," 37.
81. Héctor Javier Nahuelpan Moreno and Jaime Anedo Antimil Caniupán, "Colonialismo republicano, violencia y subordinación racial mapuche en Chile durante el siglo XX," *Historelo: Revista de Historia Regional y Local* 11, no. 21 (2019): 215–216.
82. Kelly Bauer, *Negotiating Autonomy: Mapuche Territorial Demands and Chilean Land Policy* (Pittsburgh, PA: University of Pittsburgh Press, 2021), 11.
83. Bauer, *Negotiating Autonomy*, 13.
84. Nahuelpan Moreno and Antimil Caniupán, "Colonialismo republicano," 239.
85. Nahuelpan Moreno, "'Nos explotaron como animales,'" 274.
86. The Centro de Estudios e Investigaciones Mapuche, Comunidad de Historia Mapuche has

produced critical scholarship to understand how colonial violence has been deployed all along. Through the (re)presentation of affective dimensions to the stories told by informants who have experienced such violence firsthand, this scholarship maintains a relational attitude toward the material that overlaps the scholar's own family histories with the larger picture of the nation's traumatic colonial past. For a closer assessment of the type of scholarship made by this group of scholars, see the works cited in this chapter.

87. Bello, "Migración, identidad y comunidad mapuche," 44.
88. Bello, "Migración, identidad y comunidad mapuche," 46.
89. José Millalen Paillal, "Taiñ mapuchegen. Nación y nacionalismo Mapuche: Construcción y desafío del presente," in *Ta iñ fijke xipa rakizuameluwün: Historia, colonialismo y resistencia desde el país mapuche*, ed. Héctor Nahuelpan Moreno et al. (Temuco, Chile: Ediciones Comunidad de Historia Mapuche, 2015), 256–257; Bello, "Migración, identidad y comunidad mapuche," 46.

BIBLIOGRAPHY

Adamovsky, Ezequiel. "La cultura visual del criollismo: Etnicidad, 'color' y nación en las representaciones visuales del criollo en Argentina, c. 1910–1955." *Corpus* 6, no. 2 (2016): 1–14.

———. "Ethnic Nicknaming: 'Negro' as a Term of Endearment and Vicarious Blackness in Argentina." *Latin American and Caribbean Ethnic Studies* 12, no. 3 (2017) 273–289.

Agostini, Claudio A., et al. "Poverty and Inequality among Ethnic Groups in Chile." *World Development* 38, no. 7 (2010): 1036–46.

"Amerindian Rights: State Law of Indigenous Rights." In *The Argentina Reader: History, Culture, Politics*, edited by Gabriela Nouzeilles and Graciela Montaldo, 525–527. Durham, NC: Duke University Press, 2002.

Andrews, George Reid. *The Afro-Argentines of Buenos Aires, 1800–1900*. Madison: University of Wisconsin Press, 1980.

———. *Afro-Latin America: Black Lives, 1600–2000*. Cambridge, MA: Harvard University Press, 2016.

———. *Blackness in the White Nation: A History of Afro-Uruguay*. Chapel Hill: University of North Carolina Press, 2010.

Austin, Shawn Michael. *Colonial Kinship: Guaraní, Spaniards, and Africans in Paraguay*. Albuquerque: University of New Mexico Press, 2020.

Ayuso Morillo, Irene. "Afroparaguayos, condenados a no existir." *Otramérica*, 26 (October 2011), http://otramerica.com/comunidades/afroparaguayos-condenados-a-no-existir/720.

Bauer, Kelly. *Negotiating Autonomy: Mapuche Territorial Demands and Chilean Land Policy*. Pittsburgh, PA: University of Pittsburgh Press, 2021.

Bello, Álvaro M. "Migración, identidad y comunidad mapuche en Chile: Entre utopismos y realidades." *Asuntos Indígenas* 3, no. 4 (2002): 40–47.

Boccia Romañach, Alfredo. *Esclavitud en el Paraguay: Vida cotidiana del esclavo en las Indias Meridionales*. Asunción: Servilibro, 2004.

Borucki, Alex. "Across Imperial Boundaries: Black Social Networks across the Iberian South Atlantic, 1760-1810." *Atlantic Studies* 14, no. 1 (2017): 11-36.

———. "The Slave Trade to the Río de La Plata, 1777-1812: Trans-Imperial Networks and Atlantic Warfare." *Colonial Latin American Review* 20, no. 1 (2011): 81-107.

Borucki, Alex, David Eltis, and David Wheat. "Atlantic History and the Slave Trade to Spanish America." *American Historical Review* 120, no. 2 (2015): 433-461.

Cardozo, Efraím. *Paraguay independiente.* 2nd ed. Asunción: Carlos Schauman, 1988.

Chagas, Karla, and Natalia Stalla. "Vida cotidiana, sociabilidad y expresiones culturales de la población afrodescendiente (siglos XVIII a XXI)." In *Historia de la población africana y afrodescendiente en Uruguay*, edited by Ana Frega, Nicolás Duffau, Karla Chagas, and Natalia Stalla, 191-269. Montevideo: Facultad de Humanidades y Ciencias de la Educación, Ministerio de Desarrollo Social, 2020.

Chesterton, Bridget María. *The Grandchildren of Solano López: Frontier and Nation in Paraguay, 1904-1936.* Albuquerque: University of New Mexico Press, 2013.

Comisión Nacional Honoraria de Sitios de Memoria. "Adhesión a las demandas del pueblo Charrúa en Uruguay." Institución Nacional de Derechos Humanos y Defensoría del Pueblo, 2022. https://www.gub.uy/institucion-nacional-derechos-humanos-uruguay/tematica/documentos-interes.

Edwards, Erika Denise. *Hiding in Plain Sight: Black Women, the Law, and the Making of a White Argentine Republic.* Tuscaloosa: University of Alabama Press, 2020.

Foerster, Rolf, and Jorge Iván Vergara. "Etnia y nación en la lucha por el reconocimiento. Los mapuches en la sociedad chilena." *Estudios Atacameños*, no. 19 (2000): 11-42.

Frigerio, Alejandro, and Eva Lamborghini. "El candombe (uruguayo) en Buenos Aires: (Proponiendo) nuevos imaginarios urbanos en la ciudad 'blanca.'" *Cuadernos de Antropología Social*, no. 30 (2009): 93-118.

———. "Criando um movimento negro em um país 'branco': Ativismo político e cultural afro na Argentina." *Afro-Ásia*, no. 39 (2010): 153-181.

———. "Procesos de reafricanización en la sociedad argentina: Umbanda, candombe y militancia 'afro.'" *Revista Pós Ciências Sociais* 8, no. 16 (2011): 21-35.

Ganson, Barbara A. "Introduction." In *Native Peoples, Politics, and Society in Contemporary Paraguay: Multidisciplinary Perspectives*, edited by Barbara A. Ganson, 1-18. Albuquerque: University of New Mexico Press, 2021.

Gayles, Prisca. "¿De dónde sos? (Black) Argentina and the Mechanisms of Maintaining Racial Myths." *Ethnic and Racial Studies* 44, no. 11 (2021): 2093-2112.

Geler, Lea. "African Descent and Whiteness in Buenos Aires: Impossible *Mestizajes* in the White Capital City." In *Rethinking Race in Modern Argentina*, edited by Paulina L. Alberto and Eduardo Elena, 213-240. Cambridge: Cambridge University Press, 2016.

Harder Horst, René D. "Indigenous People in Paraguay and Latin America's Move to Democracy." In *Native Peoples, Politics, and Society in Contemporary Paraguay: Multidisciplinary Perspectives*, edited by Barbara A. Ganson, 19-36. Albuquerque: University of New Mexico Press, 2021.

Lagos, Leo. "¿Por qué tanto miedo al indio en Uruguay?" *La Diaria*, 31 October 2020, https://ladiaria.com.uy/ciencia/articulo/2020/10/por-que-tanto-miedo-al-indio-en-uruguay/.

Lamborghini, Eva, and Lea Geler. "Imágenes racializadas: Políticas de representación y economía visual en torno a lo 'negro' en Argentina, siglos XX y XXI." *Corpus* 6, no. 2 (2016): 1–14.

Millalen Paillal, José. "*Taiñ mapuchegen*: Nación y nacionalismo Mapuche: Construcción y desafío del presente." In *Ta iñ fijke xipa rakizuameluwün: Historia, colonialismo y resistencia desde el país Mapuche*, edited by Héctor Nahuelpan Moreno et al., 241–258. Temuco, Chile: Ediciones Comunidad de Historia Mapuche, 2015.

Nahuelpan Moreno, Héctor. "'Nos explotaron como animales y ahora quieren que no nos levantemos': Vidas despojables y micropolíticas de resistencia mapuche." In *Awükan ka kuxankan zugu Wajmapu mew: Violencias coloniales en Wajmapu*, edited by Enrique Antileo Baeza et al., 271–300. Temuco, Chile: Ediciones Comunidad de Historia Mapuche, 2015.

Nahuelpan Moreno, Héctor Javier, and Jaime Anedo Antimil Caniupán. "Colonialismo republicano, violencia y subordinación racial mapuche en Chile durante el siglo XX." *Historelo: Revista de Historia Regional y Local* 11, no. 21 (2019): 211–247.

Persico, Melva M. "Afro-Uruguayan Culture and Legitimation: Candombe and Poetry." In *Black Writing, Culture, and the State in Latin America*, edited by Jerome C. Branche, 213–236. Nashville, TN: Vanderbilt University Press, 2015.

Pla, Josefina. *Hermano negro: La esclavitud en el Paraguay*. Madrid: Paraninfo, 1972.

Roth-Gordon, Jennifer. *Race and the Brazilian Body*. Berkeley: University of California Press, 2016.

Sciaudone, Christiana. "Argentine Movement Tries to Make Black Heritage More Visible." *AP News*, November 26, 2021, https://apnews.com/article/immigration-entertainment-discrimination-migration-race-and-ethnicity-0d18920b22e0eab19f28202c591ef0ea.

Sobode Chiquenoi, Mateo. "The Ayoreo People." In *The Paraguay Reader: History, Culture, Politics*, edited by Peter Lambert and Andrew Nickson, 342–347. Durham, NC: Duke University Press, 2013.

Solomianski, Alejandro. *Identidades secretas: La negritud argentina*. Rosario, Argentina: Beatriz Viterbo Editora, 2003.

Stalla, Natalia. "Afrodescendientes y africanos en el Uruguay actual: Múltiples identidades." In *Historia de la población africana y afrodescendiente en Uruguay*, edited by Ana Frega, Nicolás Duffau, Karla Chagas, and Natalia Stalla, 26–57. Montevideo: Facultad de Humanidades y Ciencias de la Educación, Ministerio de Desarrollo Social, 2020.

Subercaseaux, Bernardo. "Raza y nación: El caso de Chile." *A Contracorriente* 5, no. 1 (2007): 29–63.

Telesca, Ignacio. "Mujer, honor y afrodescendientes en Paraguay a fines de la colonia." *América sin Nombre*, no. 15 (2010): 30–38.

———. "Paraguay a fines de la Colonia: ¿mestizo, español o indígena?" *Jahrbuch für Geschichte Lateinamerikas* 46, no. 1 (2009): 261–288.

———. "Paraguay en el Centenario: La creación de la nación mestiza." *Historia Mexicana* 60, no. 1 (2010): 137–195.

———. "People of African Descent in Paraguay." In *The Paraguay Reader: History, Culture, Politics*, edited by Peter Lambert and Andrew Nickson, 410–416. Durham, NC: Duke University Press, 2013.

Trías Cornú, Mariana. "Afrodescendencia y ciudadanía (segunda mitad del siglo XIX y siglo XX)." In *Historia de la población africana y afrodescendiente en Uruguay*, edited by Ana Frega, Nicolás Duffau, Karla Chagas, and Natalia Stalla, 139-189. Montevideo: Facultad de Humanidades y Ciencias de la Educación, Ministerio de Desarrollo Social, 2020.

Verdesio, Gustavo. "Ethnic Reemergence in Uruguay: The Return of the Charrúa in the Light of Settler Colonialism Studies." In *Decolonial Approaches to Latin American Literatures and Cultures*, edited by Juan G. Ramos and Tara Daly, 163-179. New York: Palgrave Macmillan, 2016.

Vergara, Jorge Iván, and Rolf Foerster. "Permanencia y transformación del conflicto Estado-mapuches en Chile." *Revista Austral de Ciencias Sociales*, no. 6 (2002): 35-45.

Verón Gómez, Miguel Ángel. "The Bicentenary of Paraguayan Independence and the Guaraní Language." In *The Paraguay Reader: History, Culture, Politics*, edited by Peter Lambert and Andrew Nickson, 404-409. Durham, NC: Duke University Press, 2013.

Vidart, Daniel. *El mundo de los charrúas*. 3rd ed. Montevideo: Ediciones de la Banda Oriental, 2010.

Viqueira, Rodrigo. *Negrismo, vanguardia y folklore: Representación de los Afrodescendientes en la Obra de Ildefonso Pereda Valdés*. Montevideo: Rebeca Linke Editoras, 2019.

Wade, Peter. "Debates contemporáneos sobre raza, etnicidad, género y sexualidad en las ciencias sociales." In *Raza, etnicidad y sexualidades: Ciudadanía y multiculturalismo en América Latina*, edited by Peter Wade et al., 41-66. Bucaramanga: Universidad Nacional de Colombia, Facultad de Ciencias Humanas, 2008.

———. "Race in Latin America." In *A Companion to Latin American Anthropology*, edited by Deborah Poole, 177-192. Malden, MA: Blackwell, 2008.

CHAPTER 19

Chicanos, Hispanos, and Latinos

BÁRBARA I. ABADÍA-REXACH

*Constructing the Ethno-Racial Other: From
Latin America to the United States*

Despite the inescapable scientific evidence that there is only one race, the human race, the conversation about the origin of races persists and is discussed from two central angles: the biological and the political. Typically, the human race is recognized biologically. However, politically, one speaks of more than one race, and from that perspective, categories are established and racial groups are hierarchized. Thus, for years, people have been classified according to their phenotypic traits despite how problematic it is to confine people due to diverse characteristics that may not make their association with a specific racial group visible. Although caste systems and numerous racial categories based on mixtures of people in Latin America were established to signal Blackness, there was no American practice of the one-drop rule. Even with the possibility of exploring, through archives and oral histories, how racial discourses have been articulated in Latin America, certain conservative factions in the academy avoid the study of race because it is assumed that it is a resolved issue. In any case, it is determined from the biological point of view. But the importance of the discussion about race cannot be dismissed from the political point of view. It is precisely from that place that it is worth exploring how the racial subject is constructed in the light of the addition of ethnic categories.

Although ethnic and racial categories are not recent inventions, there is still confusion among people regarding identifying themselves racially and ethnically. Precisely because of the scarcity of dialogues regarding race, in Latin America, there is a denial of the existence of anti-Black racism. Racism functions as a system of oppression and white privilege that has normalized violence and racial harassment. As it is not recognized how it manifests itself structurally, solutions to combat it are not articulated. Nor would it seem essential to include the variable race in statistics that would demonstrate social inequities based on race. That is why in Latin American countries that carry out population censuses in which race is asked about, the majority of the population racially identifies itself as white.

For example, in the Dominican Republic, the percentage of the population that self-identifies as Black is unknown because that question is not included in the census. Interestingly, Dominicans often refer to themselves as Indians and Clear Indians; Blacks are Haitians with whom they share the same geographic space on Hispaniola. In Mexico, the question for Afro-Mexicans to identify themselves as such appeared for the first time in the 2020 census. In the Constitution of Ecuador, the collective rights of Afro-descendant people, who make up 40 percent of the impoverished population, are recognized; however, the state of vulnerability of Black communities, environmental racism, labor abuse, and lack of access to justice are some of the ways what is written on paper is proven pro forma. Although proclaiming itself an Afro-descendant country is a step forward, there are no public policies to serve that population apart from good intentions.

The same occurs in Colombia, where 10 percent of the population is Afro-Colombian and lives in poverty.[1] In Costa Rica, the Afro–Costa Rican population amounts to 8 percent;[2] likewise, it suffers from institutional racism despite the campaigns against racism that have been led since the current government, especially with the figure of the first female Black vice president, Epsy Campbell-Barr (2018). Since the 1990s, the Afro–Costa Rican anthropologist and poet Shirley Campbell-Barr has denounced anti-Black racism through her award-winning poem "Rotundamente negra." In Cuba, official records estimate that less than 10 percent of the population is Afro-Cuban.[3] Interestingly, Cuban cultural, musical, and religious practices of undoubted African roots contradict that percentage.

It surprises many people that in Uruguay, 10.6 percent of the population claim to be Afro-descendant or Black.[4] In Panama, from the 41 percent of the Afro-descendant population, only 5 percent is Black; the remaining percentage is divided between "mulatos" and "zambos."[5] In Brazil, more than 50 percent of the population self-identifies racially as Black or mestizo.[6] However, under the national rhetoric of racial democracy, most of the population survives—hopefully—the anti-Black racism that mainly kills Black men at the hands of the police. The Black genocide in Brazil also manifests in the criminalization of Black bodies and the demonization and impoverishment of visibly Black populations. In the case of Peru, since the 1970s, the Afro-Peruvian activist, choreographer, and composer Victoria Santa Cruz has been expressing how racism is experienced in her country through the poem "They shouted me black." For its part, the fifty-year-old group Peru Negro, the singers Susana Baca and Eva Ayllón have done the same, although the historical national rhetoric is that there is no anti-Black racism in Peru because they reach only 4 percent of the total population.[7]

In Puerto Rico, according to data from the 2020 Census, administered by the United States Bureau of Census, 7 percent of the population self-identified as Black.[8] Being an American colony since 1898, Puerto Rico's census instrument is the same that is used in the United States, with the same racial and ethnic categories. Although in Puerto Rico the mixture of the three races—indigenous Taíno, white Spaniard, and Black African enslaved—is celebrated, people mostly choose one, the "white" option, when choosing racial categories. And thus, it is learned that Puerto Rico is the smallest of the Greater Antilles, the largest in the Lesser Antilles, and the whitest in the Caribbean. Although it seems laughable, in this way, the discussion of racism is diluted. The cases I have briefly mentioned are only examples to provide an overview of Latin American racial identification.

Governments are not trying to implement an educational plan or a media campaign to educate their populations about the difference between race and ethnicity. It is worth mentioning that in Peru, in 2017, the question of ethnic identification was introduced to recognize Indigenous and Afro-descendant populations. But it would be worth asking what it means to recognize the ethnic groups that survive in Peru. What are the motivations for asking the ethnicity question before asking about the race of Peruvians? I can argue that the question would provide results on cultural but not racial diversity.

When it comes to ethnicity, people often confuse it with race. Some evade answering the question of race under the premise that they have indicated that they are Mexicans, Dominicans, Puerto Ricans, and so on. The question of race would seem unnecessary if the one that people understand is that of ethnicity. On the other hand, they find it redundant. Under the idea that they do not know what to answer in the race question because they do not consider themselves a single race, a contradiction prevails since the tendency has been to choose a single racial category. Sometimes, in Latin America, ethnicity is associated with cultural practices linked to racial groups considered a minority and invisible.

The problem has been combining race and ethnicity as interchangeable categories. In Latin America, ethnicity serves to differentiate the supposed majority of the population from Indigenous people and Afro-descendants; in the United States, they seek to distance themselves from marginalized groups in their country of origin, even if they are challenged as part of them. In Latin America and the United States, the categories seem inflexible and monolithic and are understood as mechanisms of exclusion and marginalization. At times, they are thought of as political mechanisms of denunciation and visibility.

Although in 2001 the World Conference against Racism, Racial Discrimination, Xenophobia, and Related Intolerance was held in Durban, South Africa, and the use of *Afro-descendant* was incorporated to expand the fight against anti-Black racism, the pattern of whitening, of celebrating Blackness only from the folkloric point of view, of having a limited perspective on Africa and of the indissoluble association with slavery, contributes to assertions of the nonexistence of racism and to the fact that Black populations in Latin America are thought to be scarce. This continues to occur even as the United Nations announced the Decade for People of African Descent 2015–2024. During the twenty-first century, Latin America has not managed to coordinate or articulate a transnational discourse of Black identity that influences Latinos' racial and ethnic self-identification in the United States. So the Latin American rhetoric about a whitened race is extrapolated to the United States through the Latino communities that, at the same time, are negotiating their membership in a territory that excludes them and categorizes them as the Other, as inferior.

The racial constructions of the Other that take place in Latin America, in very varied historical contexts, are extrapolated to the United States and intersect with the racial categories imposed through a system of white supremacy. In this final chapter, after a historical and geographical tour throughout Latin America to explore how nonwhite bodies have been constructed and racialized, we land in the United States and stop to think about the Chicano, Hispanic, and Latino categories and how people from the Latin American diaspora have been brought together into a group. At the same time, this text invites reflection and gives continuity to the conversation about the current use of these categories and their resignifications.

Chicanos: A Crusade from Xicano to Chicanx

The history of Mexicans in the United States is marked by the struggle for belonging. From 1846 to 1848, the American Intervention was carried out in Mexico. The United States annexed the former Mexican territories now known as the states of Arizona, California, Colorado, Kansas, Nevada, New Mexico, Oklahoma, Texas, Utah, and part of Wyoming. The proximity between the United States and Mexico facilitated the process of invasion and appropriation of Mexican lands. That same condition of proximity between the two countries has allowed the continuous movement of Mexicans who cross the border into the United States, albeit sometimes illegally. Today, 60 percent of the Hispanic population in the United States,[9] is of Mexican origin. In some ways, it can be said that Mexicans have never abandoned their ancestral lands; their presence in the United States has not diminished. Nor has the violence that has been exercised in the United States against Mexicans decreased. From "Mexican" came the "Xican" nickname that has evolved with the times.

Xicano, from an ethnic category slur, was transformed into pride. To highlight the particularities of the Mexican American experience in the United States, in the 1960s, during the Chicano Movement, this ethnic category gained relevance. "El Movimiento" advocated social and political empowerment through Chicanismo and cultural nationalism by embracing their entire heritage. Instead of only recognizing their Spanish or European background, Chicanos started to celebrate their Indigenous and African roots. In 1967, Rodolfo "Corky" Gonzales, a Chicano boxer, political organizer, activist, and poet, wrote "I am Joaquin," an emblematic poem of the Chicano Movement, and through this excerpt he said:

> La raza!
> Méjicano!
> Español!
> Latino!
> Chicano!
> Or whatever I call myself,
> I look the same,
> I feel the same,
> I cry and sing the same . . . [10]

This recognition arises from the struggles for workers' rights, the request for educational reforms that would reverse the statistics that placed Chicano students at a disadvantage, and the claim to the right to ancestral lands. These denunciations of the systemic inequality of the 1960s made it possible to reaffirm the historical pattern of oppression that minority groups—particularly Mexicans and their descendants—have experienced in the United States. In 1969, in his "Letter from Delano," César Chávez, cofounder of the National Farm Workers Association, wrote: "We are men and women who have suffered and endured much, not only because of our abject poverty but also because we have been kept poor. The colors of our skin, the languages of our cultural and native origins, the lack of formal education, the exclusion from the democratic process, the numbers of our men slain in recent wars—all these burdens generation after generation have sought to demoralize us, to break our human spirit. But God knows that we are not beasts of burden, agricultural implements, or rented slaves; we are men."[11] In the framework of the struggles for civil rights (the 1960s) and the Vietnam War (1955–1975), the growing awareness of inequalities experienced by Mexican Americans led to the emergence of political organizations, artistic and cultural initiatives such as the nonviolent Crusade for Justice, conferences like the Chicano Youth Liberation Conference (1969), and academic programs of Chicano/a studies. The academic approach to Chicanismo, too, has required an intersectional analysis from a feminist perspective. Chicana feminists have raised the importance of looking at race, class, gender, and sexuality within the broad and diverse Chicana community.[12]

Self-proclaimed Chicano is not only a symbol of identity pride, a literary category, or a music genre label; it is a political reassurance tool for people experiencing treatment as second-class citizens and seeking the improvement of their social and economic conditions. For this reason, from being colonized by mainstream American society in the United States, the epithet *Xicano* became *Chicano*, a category to cluster and homogenize millions of Mexican Americans that, later, was the flag of a social justice movement, the Mexican American Civil Rights Movement. At the same time, the use of *Chicanx* is incorporated, which breaks with the (cis)heteronormative binary.

The crusade from *Xicano* to *Chicano* to *Chicana* to *Chicanx/Xicanx* shows how an ethnic identification label, used to mark and distance the American community from Mexican immigrants or their descendants, can be reversed as a political struggle. From the 1960s to the present day, Xicanxs have used various forms of expression to make themselves visible and stand out in the United States against all odds. They have incorporated models of political action from other marginalized sectors; in turn, they have served as an example for other communities because of their persistence. Thanks to the Xicanxs' struggles, the statistics reflect the growth in the number of this population; furthermore, its importance to the economic development of the United States while Mexican individuals continue to be deported from the United States to Mexico—and while the living conditions of those who remain in the United States can be plagued with sacrifices and disadvantages—simultaneously, the success stories, too, keep increasing. A new generation of Xicanxs emulate the bravery of those first Mexicans who returned to their native lands, not to be segregated; they were deprived of human rights and were disparagingly called Xicanos. The Xicana struggle continues to be, today, a battle for the human rights of all Mexicans in and outside of Mexico. As an exclusive ethnic category of Mexicans or their descendants in the United States, it reflects the power of this community.

Hispanos: Politicization, Classification, and Homogenization

The presence of citizens of Spanish-speaking countries in the United States dates back more than a century. The reasons for emigrating to the United States vary, but, for the most part, they have to do with the idea of living in better conditions than what could be achieved in their countries of origin. Political factors, too, have played an essential role in the decision to leave a Hispanic American country to land in the United States. The war against drugs, guns, and violence, among other circumstances, has been among the motivations for the United States to intervene in Hispanic countries—for example, Chile, Honduras, El Salvador, Panama, and Colombia, among others. Of course, the US link with the origin of these conflicts is not a secret, but it is rarely explained what benefits the United States obtains from the migration from Hispanic American countries. There is a cause-and-effect relationship that privileges governments, but not citizens who, due to conditions of excessive impoverishment and inequalities, determine that living in the United States is the best option for a better future. Political situations of another type—such as colonialism, in the case of Puerto Ricans, or aversion to a communist regime, in the case of Cubans—are other forces that have brought citizens of Latin America and the Caribbean to the United States.

On the one hand, Mexican Americans demanded equity; on the other, Puerto Ricans claimed political sovereignty. They were two groups of inhabitants in growth, not only at the demographic level but also in terms of social activism. It is important to add that Cubans in Miami were united against Fidel Castro's regime in Cuba. During the presidencies of John F. Kennedy (1961–1963), Lyndon B. Johnson (1963–1969), and Richard Nixon (1969–1974), strategies were articulated to win political support and appease the claims of these populations of Spanish origin. Although in 1930, "Mexican" was included as a race category, in the 1970 Census, the question about "Spanish origin" (Mexican, Puerto Rican, Cuban, Central or South American, Other Spanish) first appeared. Interestingly, in racial terms, they were considered White. Considering them racially White served the State to make invisible and deny the inequalities that these groups were manifesting. However, homogeneously agglutinating them by origin, such as Hispanics, continued to be problematic and did not solve the unequal treatment.

In 1976, under the presidency of Gerald Ford (1974–1977), the Congressional Hispanic Caucus was formed. The purpose of the caucus was to serve as a legislative organization. Through legislative, executive, and judicial actions, the caucus sought to monitor whether the needs of Hispanics were being met. Later, at the beginning of James Carter's presidency (1977–1981), in September 1977, National Hispanic Heritage Week was instituted; later, it was expanded from September 15 to October 15 as Hispanic Heritage Month.

In 1980, the Hispanic category appeared in the census, after negotiations between census scientists and Mexican American activists who insisted on the political use of the results. The promise of the state was to bring them together as a group, to categorize them in order to attend to their particular situations in the United States. In the media, renowned figures, mainly from the world of sports, urged Hispanics to choose that option in the census. The question, which a decade earlier had caused confusion and multiple errors, was formulated as follows: "Is this person of Spanish/Hispanic origin or descent?" The possible responses were: "No (not Spanish / Hispanic); Yes, Mexican, Mexican American, Chicano; Yes, Puerto Rican; Yes, Cuban; Yes, other Spanish / Hispanic."

According to the sociologist Cristina Mora, the Hispanic category is ambiguous by design.[13] In her book *Making Hispanics: How Activists, Bureaucrats, and Media Constructed a New American*, Mora analyzes how the institutional use of Hispanics, from the 1960s through the 1990s, shifts the politics of race and ethnicity in the United States. For her, bringing together all the people of Spanish origin constitutes a pan-ethnic Hispanic identity. The effort imposed by the federal government involved active mobilization from bureaucrats, political organizations, and the media.

Although the uncertainty provoked by the question and the confusion between ethnicity and race remained, in 2022, the US Census Bureau reported 62.6 million people identified as Hispanics,[14] representing 18.9 percent of the total population in the US. The increase was due to births, not immigration.[15] Forty years after the first appearance of the Hispanic category on the census to classify people of Spanish origin, its institutionalized use is still problematic precisely because the politics of homogenization works against the consistently increasing "minority."

The historical background of the Hispanic category is inescapably linked to purely political motivations. Behind the supposed intention of attending to the needs of minority groups in Latin America, who have been homogenized, lies the partisan political desire to have them as a captive mass. It could be theorized that the Hispanic ethnic category privileged the US government and the governments of Hispano-America who would benefit from having arrangements with the United States, knowing the unequal treatment that their compatriots will receive, and doing "cleaning" in their territories, in facing multiple governance challenges. However, given the circumstances that I mentioned at the outset of this chapter, where I argue that in the countries of Latin America and the Caribbean, there is a lack of institutional conversations about race and an understanding of the difference concerning ethnicity, such that it celebrates white European origin and ethnicity. The association that persists between the Hispanic ethnic category and Spanish roots makes it accepted and marked by a broad sector of people questioned under that line. So the whitening trend, too, operates from the Hispanic ethnic category. This fact favored the US government and has not provoked a comprehensive discussion to reject it because of its uselessness in favor of those who agglomerate.

Latinos: (Re)signifying and (Re)configuring Otherness?

From the "Chicano" ethnic category, which belongs to Mexicans and their descendants in the United States and was first used as an epithet shortening the word "Mexican," it was changed to "Hispanic." The US government intended to bring together, mainly, a trio of Spanish-speaking ethnic groups with a lot of presence and political mobilization, Mexicans, Puerto Ricans, and Cubans, to attend to their various claims and complaints. However, the Hispanic category diluted the particular requests of these groups. Hence, given the growth of the migratory movement to the United States from Latin America and the Caribbean, it was urgent to use a term to refer more broadly to migrants from that region. Although "Latino," as an ethnic category, manages to bring together people from more than twenty countries, it also obliterates their peculiarities and diverse historical contexts. However, its use, sometimes interchangeable with Hispanic, persists and has taken on new nuances that ensure that it attends to the population growth of the Latino community and its consequences in the United States.

What is the difference between Hispanic and Latino? From which countries do people fall into the Hispanic category? From which countries do people fall into the Latino category? These are recurring questions. In general terms, Hispanics are defined as people who come from countries colonized by Spain; in turn, they speak Spanish. With regard to Latinos, they are those people who come from a Latin American country. However, the number of countries that fall under these categories, Hispanic and Latino, varies. The list of Hispanic countries can total twenty-one:

1. Mexico
2. Colombia
3. Argentina
4. Peru
5. Venezuela
6. Chile
7. Ecuador
8. Guatemala
9. Cuba
10. Bolivia
11. Dominican Republic
12. Honduras
13. Paraguay
14. El Salvador
15. Nicaragua
16. Costa Rica
17. Panama
18. Uruguay
19. Spain
20. Philippines
21. Equatorial Guinea

Interestingly, as a US territory, Puerto Rico is left out, although Puerto Rico was a colony of Spain from 1493 to 1898 and the primary official language is Spanish. Meanwhile, "Latin" countries include regions of Central America, South America, and the Caribbean where the official languages are Romance (Spanish, French, and Portuguese). For this reason, Brazilians, Guianans, Haitians, Guadaloupeans, Martinicans, Maarteners, and Barthélemoises/St. Barths are included in the Latino category but not the Hispanic category. Similarly, Guyana (English), Suriname (Dutch), and Belize (English), countries whose official languages are Germanic, are not considered Hispanic or Latino. Even with these exclusions, the diversity within the Latino category is monumental, so the homogenization of multiple nationalities remains a questionable issue.

In summary, Latinos are "people of Latin American origin in the United States—[who] have historically come to be collectively racialized as a separate and distinct non-white racial group."[16] Given the reconfigured demographic composition in the United States, in the 2000 Census, the term *Latino* was added to the ethnicity question: "Is this person Spanish / Hispanic / Latino?" In 2010, the formula was reworded to "Yes, another Hispanic, Latino, or Spanish origin" ("Argentinean, Colombian, Dominican, Nicaraguan, Salvadoran, Spaniard, and so on"). Nevertheless, the increased popularity of Latinos is palpable, for the anthropologist Arlene Dávila, the popularity in the marketplace is simultaneously accompanied by their growing stereotyped representation, exotification, and invisibility.[17]

As with the Hispanic category, which was conceived for the benefit of the US government and had little to do with Hispanics, Arlene Dávila examines, in 2001's *Latinos, Inc.: The Marketing and Making of a People*, how the US consumer economic market is enriched by creating a Latino subject with needs that must be met.[18] Not only is a stereotyped and monolithic representation of various ethnic groups conglomerated under the same category exhibited through the media; in addition, they are built in the image and likeness of the ideal consumer who seeks the market. Latinos are restricted from debating and rethinking their own cultural identities and varied ideologies. For example, when in 2020, Robert Unanue, chief executive officer of the food company Goya, publicly praised former US President Donald Trump, it seemed that Latinos would lose their gastronomic, cultural identity if they supported the boycott against the company. The debate revolved around how the boycott would affect the corporation's employees, not on how the policies of the former president and his predecessors have harmed access to the workplace, working conditions, and salaries of the communities. With a similar perspective on the analysis of Latinx representation, Báez added the notion of citizenship to the way Latinas consume media productions that depict them.[19]

Although it seems contradictory to the above, Latino, as an ethnic category, is, in turn, transnational. The US-born category, too, thrives on the constant movement, coming and going, of Latinos. Even the unwavering contact that many Latinos have with their countries of origin and how they negotiate their place in the United States while maintaining national customs and traditions is another way to enrich the diversity of the ethnic category. The continuing immigration of Latin Americans to the United States keeps the Latino category alive and complex.

Although the concept of *Latinidad/es* arises from the Latino ethnic category, the term attempts to refer to the diversity of the attributes of the Latino community. Within "Latinity," there is room for the identity expressions of Latinos in the United States, the experiences in their Latin American countries, and the conglomeration of transnational networks. So, even though Latinidad, as an umbrella concept, does not necessarily emerge to reverse the monolithic notion embedded in the Latino ethnic category, it does provide terrain to explore the complexities of Latino subjects. Through Latinidad, the sense of belonging can be studied, addressing one issue that is relevant and stands out from the experience of many Latinos. For Latinos, it is complex to fit and accommodate in the American Latinity due to the negotiations and adaptations that this entails, which range from language and food to other issues of national identity, race, gender, politics, and so on.

Latinidad clashes with the idea of Pan-Latinidad that has historically been associated with decolonization processes. Also, Pan-Latinidad refers to a romanticized notion of natural cultural affinity between Latin Americans. Pan-Latinidad has been used as a flag of solidarity in the face of conflicts in Latin American countries, but this is problematic in diluting the allocation of responsibilities that should not fall on citizens. A punctual criticism that the Pan-Latinidad concept has received is that it dissolves significant historical differences and poses a threat to the hard-earned victories won by social movements based on national origins.

To this day, Latinidad is continuously gaining relevance, but it is seen from only particular aesthetics and social constructions. In her book *Latinx Art: Artists, Markets, and Politics*, Dávila explains that there is certain ignorance regarding the existence of Latinx art productions. Even though the Chicano Movement has been recognized for its art, the media continues to dictate what is admissible, and contemporaneously, the mainstream market leaves out many other manifestations of art. The varieties of art that benefit the recognition of the Latinx diversity are relegated.

To address the disparities between the various Latino communities, Quiñones-Rosado suggests: "The US Census Bureau and numerous systems and institutions, public and private, will undoubtedly continue to count Latinos and track our outcomes in education, health, law enforcement, judicial and penal systems, employment, income, and wealth for the immediate, and perhaps, for the foreseeable future. However, the historical ambivalence of race policy toward Latinos and the apparent attempt to racially assimilate large segments of the Latino population through current policy do not serve the well-being and development of this community, nor that of US society overall."[20] A standard and uniform policy-based practice to classify or categorize Latinos as a racial group, albeit a racialized ethnicity, is essential and still necessary to clearly and accurately document and track over time real outcomes of institutional practices. Such a policy across states and agencies by federal mandate would ensure a more accurate count of Latinos and racial disparities in the treatment and outcomes of Latinos and all people of color relative to whites.

Over time, the use of the Latino ethnic category has raised questions about the ethnic groups it encompasses. From being a category that advanced the conversation about the inequalities and rights of Mexicans, Puerto Ricans, and Cubans, who were under the Hispanic label, it seemed that it did not address the circumstances of people from other Latin American countries, including those in the Global South.[21] Through literary and audiovisual analyses, Falconi and Mazzotti emphasize the importance of decentralizing the ethnic category when observing Latin American migration into the United States from the Andes, Central America, and Brazil.[22] They even emphasize the generational approach that sheds light on how the negotiations of Latinos in the United States are reconfigured.

It is worth stating that the Latino ethnic category has allowed us to explore the hybrid and multiracial aspects of the experiences of being a Latino in the United States. At the same time, this analysis exhibits the hierarchies and power dynamics that, sometimes mediated by race and subordination by skin color, are extrapolated from Latin American countries to the interior and exterior of Latino communities in the United States. This is further complicated when Latin American descendants have an imaginary built by an ideal alien to realities and subjectivities about the country of ancestral origin.

With the accelerated growth of the Latino community in the United States, it is increasingly common to find mixed-Latino subjects with mixed nationalities. Frances Aparicio studies this phenomenon in her book *Negotiating Latinidad: Intralatina/o Lives in Chicago*.[23] The author makes an exploration of culture, hybridity, and transnationalism that points to a new category and a new Latino identity, the "Intralatina." Undoubtedly, the addition of new experiences evidences the complexity and diversity of Latin America, contained within an ethnic category in the United States. For this reason, the flexibility and elasticity of the label point to new ways of looking at Latinos, from recognizing their counternarratives and ways to evade categorizations.

For example, in the 2018 book *Latinx: The New Force in American Politics and Culture*, Ed Morales, in addition to focusing on young people who are embracing the label, states:

> The advent of the term *Latinx* is the most recent iteration of a naming debate grounded in the politics of race and ethnicity. For several decades the term *Latino* was the progressive choice over *Hispanic*; according to G. Cristina Mora's *Making Hispanics*, the latter was pressed into service by the Nixon administration in the 1970s, an apolitical attempt at an antidote to the "unrest" created by increasing activism in Latinx communities inspired by the African American civil rights movement. As he did with African Americans, Nixon promoted Hispanic entrepreneurship by appointing a Mexican American as the head of the Small Business Administration. *Hispanic* became a "pan-ethnic" category whose development was fostered by data researchers such as the Census Bureau, political "entrepreneurs" of both liberal and conservative stripes, and media marketers, who ultimately created the vast Spanish-language media.[24]

Morales adds: "*Hispanic* overtly identified Latinx with Spanish cultural, racial, and ethnic origins. Yet *Latino* carried with it the notion that Latin American migrants to the United States were not merely hyphenated Europeans, but products of the mixed-race societies and cultures south of the border who freely acknowledged that they were not 'white.' It has over the years become more widely accepted among liberals, while *Hispanic* still carries a strong weight among conservatives—including many who are Latinx."[25] The author argues that with Donald Trump's open and public demonstrations of white privilege and the accusations he made suggesting that undocumented people from Mexico and Central America are violent and criminal, the Latinx category joined the discussion about race in the United States. To the Black-White binary, we add the ways Latinos in general think of themselves in racial terms, favoring mestizaje and moving away from their Blackness. With a critical view from racialization, Latinos have to understand that being considered Others, nonwhites, disrupts their notions of Latin American whitening. He says: "*Latinx* is a book about a growing group of Americans who are injecting a different idea about race into the American race debate.... But I believe that the Latinx view of race, inherited from nation-building ideologies that lionized race-mixing in Latin America, poses narratives that challenge and resist Anglo-American paradigms."[26]

On this point, I disagree, because although the recognition of unequal treatment in the United States is a trigger toward indignation and mobilization, the racial identity ideologies that are upset are the Latin American ones, but not the Anglo-Saxon debate per se, that continues to use Manichaean categories and leaves little space for communities to feel comfortable with the imposed categories. For example, in Puerto Rico and in the Puerto Rican diaspora in the United States, the majority of Puerto Ricans have racially self-identified as white over the years. Although in two decades, from 2000 to 2020, there was a decrease in people who self-identified as white in the island territory as I mentioned before discussing the censuses. The changes occurred in the colony, and the hypothesis that the increase in Black people in Puerto Rico had to do with the inferior treatment, as second-rate citizens, that Puerto Ricans receive in the United States and under the conditions that are survived in the colony.

In *Inventing Latinos*, Laura Gómez not only explores the growth of the Latino population in the United States; she also analyzes its political participation and how and why Latinx identity became a distinctive racial identity.[27] Like Morales, Gómez understands that the Latino community does influence American society and its racial constructions. However, it seems pertinent to point out that American racial resignifications are widening the gap between Black and white and phenotype, and, despite the colorism, it is Latinos, like Others, who continue to affect themselves. Hence, the author reaffirms American racism.

What Gómez points out about paradigm changes has been exposed through the media. In turn, Avilés-Santiago adds that the developments in contemporary Latina/os media are the result not only of an exponentially growing Latina/o population in the United States but also of the synergy between transformations in the global political economy and the emergence of new media platforms for production, distribution, and consumption.[28] According to Avilés-Santiago, Spanish-language media has nevertheless acted as a cultural platform through which Latina/os from different national origins could unite under the umbrella of Latinidad, a cultural rubric used to refer to the assignment of Latina/o traits to people, culture, and habits.

Although for more than a decade,[29] the Afro-Latin@ category—authors started writing it this way—has been circulating in academic spaces, and has been used to explain the experience of Black Latinos, it remains a shaky ground for those who do not recognize their Blackness. This ethnic-racial category allows questions of Black identity and representation, transnationalism, and diaspora in the Americas. As I pointed out at the beginning of this chapter, in Latin America, there is hardly any talk of race; there is a celebration of mestizaje in national discourses, but racial inequalities are made invisible. In addition, given the impoverished and vulnerable circumstances of Black Latin Americans, it is more difficult for them to migrate to the United States. Censuses reveal that the Black Latino population, as is the case with the African American population, remains without much growth in the United States in comparison to other populations.[30] Even so, the recognition of Afro-descendants continues to gain adherents. For the reasons explained by Morales for using the *x* in *Latinx*, it is also incorporated into the Afro-Latinx label. Experiences in the United States make it imperative to pay attention to the tension between self-identification and state-ordained labeling.

In a relatively short time, the Latino ethnic category has become more flexible and has become a queer, open, and inclusive space. What is observed from the academy, with the transformations in Latino/a studies programs and the extensive production of texts on different aspects of the Latino, shows the importance of recognizing diversity, accepting it, and humanizing the understandings that are generated from their complex experiences. It is fascinating how a homogenizing ethnic category has transmuted after considering the experiences of Latinos (Latina/os, Latin@s) of the same national origin, studying inter-Latin relations, understanding the processes between intra-Latino subjects and even Black and trans people across Afro-Latinos and trans-Latinas.

Although Latinos continue to occupy the first place among minorities in the United States, in 2025, it is surprising every time that Latino persons are first identified in roles that are traditionally occupied by whites (e.g., Rita Moreno, Joseph Acabá, Sonia Sotomayor, Miguel Cardona). Knowing where Latinos have still not reached given the lack of access and inequities is troublesome. Irrespective of all the difficulties the journey toward Latino recognition has designated on the system as a whole, Latinos keep surpassing, (re)signifying and (re)configuring Otherness.

Conclusion

In 1925, when José Vasconcelos spoke of "the cosmic race" and imagined Universópolis, he envisioned a fifth race, a new civilization in which humanity would transcend race, nationalities, and ethnicities.[31] This utopia married very well with the political discourse of a candidate for the presidency of Mexico, such as Vasconcelos. The rhetoric of racial unity served as a foundation for many political leaders throughout Latin America. The notion of the mixture of races, the celebration of mestizaje, was inscribed. Under this premise of racial harmony, historically, systems of white racial supremacy have been entangled, which privilege some bodies over other nonwhites. Structural and systematic racism has naturalized oppressive practices that have served to dehumanize groups of people considered minorities.

When analyzing the racial construction of the other in Latin America, contemporary Black enslavement and anti-Black genocide are evident. Although the abolition of slavery is commemorated, for example, in 1873 in Puerto Rico, there are daily practices that tend to dehumanize, demonize, and criminalize Black and Indigenous bodies. In Latin America, the state impoverishes, imprisons, and murders nonwhite human beings disproportionately daily. However, this repetitive pattern that causes racism not to be discussed and its existence denied in Latin America migrates to the United States.

In negotiations for survival in a foreign space, sometimes it is preferred to remain silent and adapt to a system that will insist on questioning belonging. For this reason, in the twenty-first century, there are people who confess never having talked about race or ethnicity, although they know differently that it does not fit. However, it falters and follows the state's game that should reject racism and xenophobia while inventing categories to homogenize the supposed minority groups. Having been built as the Other in Latin America perpetuates the dissonance between feeling different but being faced with the dilemma of marking oneself on an instrument conceived from power.

Despite the fact that in the scenarios described above (what happens in Latin America and the United States) the construction of otherness places certain bodies in a state of subalternity, where resistance and marronage coexist. Through literature, poetry, music, arts, food, language—the production of academic texts on ethno-racial identities, the negotiations with politicians and strategists of the census, has to persist by putting into practice the agency and power of social movements as learned from the Xicanos of the 1960s through contemporary Latinx. The imposed institutionalized categories are guiding others in new directions toward new revolutionary paths such as Chicanx, Cholas, and AfroLatinx identities.

NOTES

1. Rebecca Bratspies, "'Territory Is Everything': Afro-Colombian Communities, Human Rights and Illegal Land Grabs," *Columbia Human Rights Law Review*, May 27 (2020): 290–323. Adriaan Alsema, on November 11, 2019, reported in a *Colombia Reports* article that Colombia lost 3 million Black people in the last Census (https://colombiareports.com/amp/did-colombia-lose-3-million-black-people/).
2. For 2022 Census, the University of Costa Rica developed numerous initiatives to discuss Costa Rican Afro-descendants, to increase the 8 percent of Black Costa Ricans from Census 2011. "La UCR Is Committed to the African Descent of Costa Rica," Universidad

de Costa Rica, August 30, 2022, https://www.ucr.ac.cr/noticias/2022/08/30/la-ucr-esta-comprometida-con-la-afrodescendencia-costarricense.html. Also, a law was established to promote ethno-racial equality for Afro-descendants in Costa Rica. "Firmada la ley que promueve la igualdad de afrodescendientes en Costa Rica," August 10, 2021, https://www.swissinfo.ch/spa/costa-rica-afrodescendientes_firmada-la-ley-que-promueve-la-igualdad-de-afrodescendientes-en-costa-rica/46857902#:~:text=%2D%20El%20presidente%20de%20Costa%20Rica,de%20los%20habitantes%20del%20pa%C3%ADs.

3. Omar Freixa, "Negritud y racismo en Cuba," *El País*, September 10, 2014, http://www.onei.gob.cu/sites/default/files/publicacion_completa_color_de_la_piel__0.pdf.
4. Lucía Scuro, "La población afrodescendiente en Uruguay desde una perspectiva de género," *Cuadernos del Sistema de Información de Género* (Instituto Nacional de las Mujeres, Uruguay), no. 1 (2010): 9.
5. Luis Oldemar Guerra, "Mayo: Mes de la etnia negra en Panamá," *Semanario La Universidad*, May 9, 2020. Interestingly, according to the Census 2010, 9.2 percent of the Panamanian population is Afro-descendant; they chose between "Negro colonial," "Negro antillano," and "Negro." INEC Panamá, *Diagnóstico de la población afrodescendiente en Panamá*, https://www.inec.gob.pa/archivos/P6541Afrodescendiente_Integrados.pdf.
6. In Brazil, the racial categories are "pardo" (Brown or Mixed race), "preto" (Black), "branco" (White), "amarelo" (Asian), and "indio" (Indian/Native). News commentaries pointed out that although more than 50 percent of the population identifies as Black, anti-Black racism persist and is mostly visible through criminalization and lack of representation in politics. "Brasil y el enquistado raciso que sigue asolando las bases de so sociedad," *France 24*, https://www.france24.com/es/am%C3%A9rica-latina/20221026-brasil-y-el-enquistado-racismo-que-sigue-asolando-las-bases-de-su-sociedad; "En Brasil el 56% de la pblación se declara negra, pero apenas ocupa el 26% de las bancas de la Cámara de Diputados," https://www.infoblancosobrenegro.com/nota/92066/en-brasil-el-56-de-la-poblacion-se-declara-negra-pero-apenas-ocupa-el-26-de-las-bancas-de-la-camara-de-diputados/.
7. In the Census 2017, only 3.6 percent of the Peruvian population declared their Afro-descendancy (negro, moreno, zambo, mulato, pueblo afroperuano or Afro-descendant). See INEI, "Capítulo 3.3: Población afroperuana," https://www.inei.gob.pe/media/MenuRecursivo/publicaciones_digitales/Est/Lib1642/cap03_03.pdf; Ministerio de Cultura, "Población afroperuana a nivel nacional, Censo 2017," May 2020, https://poblacionafroperuana.cultura.pe/sites/default/files/poblacion_afroperuana_nacional_censo_2017-daf.pdf; https://andina.pe/agencia/noticia-el-30-peruanos-se-identifica-como-indigena-o-afroperuano-724880.aspx.
8. Surprisingly, from 76 percent of White Puerto Ricans, the number dropped to 17 percent on the 2020 Census. America Counts Staff, "Puerto Rico Population Declined 11.8% from 2010 to 2020," Puerto Rico: 2020 Census, https://www.census.gov/library/stories/state-by-state/puerto-rico-population-change-between-census-decade.html#:~:text=Puerto%20Rico%20Population%20Declined%2011.8%25%20From%202010%20to%202020&text=Through%20interactive%20state%20and%20county,to%202020%20on%20five%20topics; https://censo.estadisticas.pr/node/499.
9. Jens Manuel Krogstad, Jeffrey S. Passel, Mohamad Moslimani, and Luis Noe-Bustamante, "Key Facts about US Latinos for Hispanic Heritage Month," September 22, 2023, https://www.pewresearch.org/fact-tank/2022/09/23/key-facts-about-u-s-latinos-for-national-hispanic-heritage-month/.
10. Rodolfo Gonzales, "I Am Joaquin," 1967, available at https://www.latinamericanstudies.org/latinos/joaquin.htm.

11. César Chávez, *Letter from Delano*, 1969, available at https://libraries.ucsd.edu/farmworkermovement/essays/essays/Letter%20From%20Delano.pdf.
12. Gloria Anzaldúa, *Borderlands/La Frontera: The New Mestiza* (San Francisco: Aunt Lute Books, 1987); Maylei Blackwell, *¡Chicana Power! Contested Histories of Feminism in the Chicano Movement* (Austin: University of Texas Press, 2011).
13. G. Cristina Mora, *Making Hispanics: How Activists, Bureaucrats, and Media Constructed a New American* (Chicago: University of Chicago Press, 2014).
14. The Hispanic population in the United States is growing significantly. US Census Bureau, "Hispanic Heritage Month 2022" (press release), September 8, 2022, https://www.census.gov/newsroom/facts-for-features/2022/hispanic-heritage-month.html.
15. Cary Funk and Mark Hugo Lopez, "A Brief Statistical Report of US Hispanics," Pew Research Center, https://www.pewresearch.org/science/2022/06/14/a-brief-statistical-portrait-of-u-s-hispanics/.
16. Raúl Quiñones-Rosado, "Latinos and Multiracial America," in *Race Policy and Multiracial Americans*, ed. Kathleen Odell Korgen (Bristol, UK: Policy Press, 2016), 2.
17. See Arlene Dávila, *Barrio Dreams: Puerto Ricans, Latinos, and the Neoliberal City* (Berkeley: University of California Press, 2004); Arlene Dávila, *Latino Spin: Public Image and the Whitewashing of Race* (New York: New York University Press, 2008); Arlene Dávila, *Latinx Art: Artists, Markets, and Politics* (Durham, NC: Duke University Press, 2020); Agustín Laó-Montes and Arlene Dávila, eds., *Mambo Montage: The Latinization of New York* (New York: Columbia University Press, 2001).
18. Arlene Dávila, *Latinos, Inc.: The Marketing and Making of a People* (Berkeley: University of California Press, 2001).
19. Jillian Báez, *In Search of Belonging: Latinas, Media, and Citizenship* (Urbana: University of Illinois Press, 2018).
20. Quiñones-Rosado, "Latinos and Multiracial America," 13.
21. Paul Ortiz, *An African American and Latinx History of the United States* (Boston: Beacon Press, 2018).
22. José Luis Falconi and José Antonio Mazzotti, *The Other Latinos: Central and South Americans in the United States* (Cambridge, MA: Harvard University Press, 2008).
23. Frances R. Aparicio, *Negotiating Latinidad: Intralatina/o Lives in Chicago* (Champaign: University of Illinois Press, 2019).
24. Ed Morales, *Latinx: The New Force in American Politics and Culture* (London: Verso, 2018), 6.
25. Morales, *Latinx*, 6.
26. Morales, *Latinx*, 5.
27. Laura E. Gómez, *Inventing Latinos: A New Story of American Racism* (New York: New Press, 2020).
28. Manuel G. Avilés-Santiago, "Latina/os in Media: Representation, Production, and Consumption," *Oxford Research Encyclopedia*, June 25, 2019.
29. Miriam Jiménez and Juan Flores, eds., *The Afro-Latin@ Reader: History and Culture in the United States* (Durham, NC: Duke University Press, 2010); Petra R. Rivera-Rideau, Jennifer A. Jones, and Tianna Paschel, eds., *Afro-Latin@s in Movement: Critical Approaches to Blackness and Transnationalism in the Americas* (New York: Palgrave Macmillan, 2016).
30. Christine Tamir, "The Growing Diversity of Black America," Pew Research Center, https://www.pewresearch.org/social-trends/2021/03/25/the-growing-diversity-of-black-america/.
31. José Vasconcelos, *The Cosmic Race*, trans. Didier T. Jaén (Baltimore: John Hopkins University Press, 1997).

BIBLIOGRAPHY

Anzaldúa, Gloria. *Borderlands/La Frontera: The New Mestiza*. San Francisco: Aunt Lute Books, 1987.

Aparicio, Frances R. *Negotiating Latinidad: Intralatina/o Lives in Chicago*. Champaign: University of Illinois Press, 2019.

Avilés-Santiago, Manuel G. "Latina/os in Media: Representation, Production, and Consumption." *Oxford Research Encyclopedia*, June 22, 2019. https://doi.org/10.1093/acrefore/9780190201098.013.389.

Báez, Jillian. *In Search of Belonging: Latinas, Media, and Citizenship*. Urbana: University of Illinois Press, 2018.

Blackwell, Maylei. *¡Chicana Power! Contested Histories of Feminism in the Chicano Movement*. Austin: University of Texas Press, 2011.

Bratspies, Rebecca. "'Territory Is Everything': Afro-Colombian Communities, Human Rights and Illegal Land Grabs." *Columbia Human Rights Law Review*, May 27 (2020): 290–323.

Chávez, César. *Letter from Delano*. 1969. https://libraries.ucsd.edu/farmworkermovement/essays/essays/Letter%20From%20Delano.pdf.

Dávila, Arlene. *Barrio Dreams: Puerto Ricans, Latinos, and the Neoliberal City*. Berkeley: University of California Press, 2004.

———. *Latinos, Inc.: The Marketing and Making of a People*. Berkeley: University of California Press, 2001.

———. *Latino Spin: Public Image and the Whitewashing of Race*. New York: New York University Press, 2008.

———. *Latinx Art: Artists, Markets, and Politics*. Durham, NC: Duke University Press, 2020.

Falconi, José Luis, and José Antonio Mazzotti. *The Other Latinos. Central and South Americans in the United States*. Cambridge, MA: Harvard University Press, 2008.

Freixa, Omar. "Negritud y racismo en Cuba." *El País*, September 10, 2014. https://elpais.com/elpais/2014/09/10/africa_no_es_un_pais/1410328800_141032.html.

Gómez, Laura E. *Inventing Latinos: A New Story of American Racism*. New York: New Press, 2020.

Gonzales, Rodolfo. "I Am Joaquin." 1967. https://www.latinamericanstudies.org/latinos/joaquin.htm.

Guerra, Luis Oldemar. "Mayo: Mes de la etnia negra en Panamá." *Semanario La Universidad*, May 9, 2020. https://launiversidad.up.ac.pa/node/1601#:~:text=En%20la%20actualidad%2C%20existe%20un,importante%20de%20la%20población%C3%B3n%20paname%C3%B1a.

Jiménez, Miriam, and Juan Flores, eds. *The Afro-Latin@ Reader: History and Culture in the United States*. Durham, NC: Duke University Press, 2010.

Laó-Montes, Agustín, and Arlene Dávila, eds. *Mambo Montage: The Latinization of New York*. New York: Columbia University Press, 2001.

Mora, G. Cristina. *Making Hispanics: How Activists, Bureaucrats, and Media Constructed a New American*. Chicago: University of Chicago Press, 2014.

Morales, Ed. *Latinx: The New Force in American Politics and Culture*. London: Verso, 2018.

Ortiz, Paul. *An African American and Latinx History of the United States*. Boston: Beacon Press, 2018.

Quiñones-Rosado, Raúl. "Latinos and Multiracial America." In *Race Policy and Multiracial Americans*, edited by Kathleen Odell Korgen. Bristol, UK: Policy Press, 2016.

Rivera-Rideau, Petra R., Jennifer A. Jones, and Tianna Paschel, eds. *Afro-Latin@s in Movement: Critical Approaches to Blackness and Transnationalism in the Americas.* New York: Palgrave Macmillan, 2016.

Scuro, Lucía. "La población afrodescendiente en Uruguay desde una perspectiva de género." *Cuadernos del Sistema de Información de Género. Instituto Nacional de las Mujeres, Uruguay*, no. 1 (July 2010).

Acknowledgments

We wish to thank the Center for the Humanities and the Center for the Study of Race, Ethnicity, and Equity, both at Washington University in Saint Louis, for their support for this volume. We also want to express our wholehearted gratitude to each of the contributors for their excellent contributions, hard work, and patience. Finally, we thank one another for the time and commitment each dedicated to this project.

Contributors

BÁRBARA I. ABADÍA-REXACH is an associate professor of Latina/Latino studies at San Francisco State University. Professor Abadía-Raxach's interests include Afro-Latinxs, Latinxs in US, Latin American studies, racialization, Blackness, identity formation, popular culture, music and race in Puerto Rico, media studies, the Black Hispanic Caribbean, and African diaspora. Her research has appeared in *Women Studies Quarterly* and *Afro-Hispanic Review*, among others.

GONZALO AGUIAR MALOSETTI is an associate professor of Spanish at the State University of New York, Oswego. Professor Aguiar Malosetti specializes in modern and contemporary Latin American literature and cultural studies. He is the author of *La modernidad refractada: Pensamiento, creación y resistencia en la historia intelectual de Argentina, Brasil y Uruguay, 1900–1935*. His research has appeared in several edited volumes.

PATRICIA ARROYO CALDERÓN is an associate professor of Spanish and Portuguese at the University of California, Los Angeles. Professor Arroyo Calderón specializes in Central American history, literature, and visual culture, with a focus in the late nineteenth and early twentieth centuries. Her forthcoming book is *Cada cosa en su sitio y cada uno en su lugar: Imaginarios de desigualdad en Guatemala, 1870–1900*. Her research has appeared in *Cuaderno de Profesores* and *Tradiciones de Guatemanala*, among others.

AMBER BRIAN is an associate professor of Spanish and Portuguese at the University of Iowa. Professor Brian's interests include colonialism, historiography, Indigenous intellectual history, and translation studies, and her publications address the movement of cultural knowledge and historical memory among Native individuals and communities as well as between those communities and the dominant political sphere in colonial Mexico. She is the author of *Alva Ixtlilxochitl's Native Archive and the Circulation of Knowledge in Colonial Mexico*. Her research has appeared in *Hispanic Review* and *Colonial Latin American Review*, among others.

ARIEL CAMEJO is an independent scholar. Dr. Camejo was formerly a professor of Caribbean and Latin American literature at the University of Havana. His research interests include national identity, creolité, digital literatures, and race and ethnicity. His latest book is *Objetos Textuales No Identificados: Narrativas emergentes en los nuevos entornos digitales de Cuba*.

MARTA ELENA CASAÚS ARZÚ is professor emerita of modern history at the Universidad Autónoma de Madrid. Professor Casaús Arzú is known for her research on Latin American elites, racism, and the Guatemalan genocide. She is the author of more than ten books, among them *Guatemala: Linaje y racismo* and *Las redes intelectuales centroamericanas: Un siglo de imaginarios nacionales (1820–1920)*.

MÓNICA DÍAZ is an associate professor of history at the University of Kentucky. Professor Díaz's research interests include Indigenous peoples and religion, race, coloniality, visual studies, gender and ethnic identity, cultural studies, Catholic studies, and Women's cultural production. She is the author of *Indigenous Writings from the Convent: Negotiating Ethnic Autonomy in Colonial Mexico*. Her research has appeared in *Ethnohistory*, *Hispanic Review*, and *Colonial Latin American Review*, among others.

CHRISTIAN ELGUERA is an assistant professor of Spanish and Latin American studies at Marist University. Professor Elguera focuses on contemporary Indigenous literatures. He has been a translator and Indigenous Literature correspondent for *Latin American Literature Today* (*LALT*). As a creative writer, he has received literary accolades in Peru, such as an honorable mention in the XXI Biennial Copé Short Story Award for his text "El extraño caso del señor Panizza" (2020), the Copé Silver Award for his short story "El último sortilegio de Fernando Pessoa" (2022), and the Copé Gold Award for his first novel, *Los espectros* (2023).

TRACY DEVINE GUZMÁN is an associate professor of Latin American studies at the University of Miami. Her research and teaching interests include cultural and intellectual history, social and political theory, and cultural production, especially as these fields intersect with questions of race/ethnicity, environmentalism, and animal studies. She is the author of *Native and National in Brazil: Indigeneity after Independence*. Her research has appeared in *Latin American Research Review* and the *Journal of Latin American Cultural Studies*, among others.

STEPHANIE KIRK is a professor of Hispanic studies at Washington University in Saint Louis. Professor Kirk's main teaching and research interests include the literature and culture of colonial Latin America with a focus on gender studies and religion. She is the author of two books, including *Sor Juana Inés de la Cruz and the Gender Politics of Knowledge in Colonial Mexico*. Her research has appeared in the *Publication of the Modern Language Association of America* (*PMLA*) and *Latin American Research Review*, among others.

RUTH HILL is a professor of Spanish and Portuguese and the Andrew W. Mellon Chair in the Humanities at Vanderbilt University. Professor Hill has written pioneering studies and essays on the history of science and the history of race in the Spanish world, including *Hierarchy, Commerce and Fraud in Bourbon Spanish America: A Postal Inspector's Exposé*. Her research has appeared in *Revista Canadiense de Estudios Hispánicos* and the *Journal of Early Modern Christianity*, among others.

ARIANA HUBERMAN is a professor of Spanish at Haverford College. Professor Huberman's research focuses on Latin American Jewish literature and culture. She has published articles and books that delve into cultural translation, immigration and diaspora, identity and nation, and travel narrative in Latin American literature. Her latest book is *Keeping the Mystery Alive: Jewish Mysticism in Latin American Cultural Production*. Her research has appeared in the *Hispanic Journal* and *Cincinnati Romance Review*, among others.

AGUSTÍN LAÓ-MONTES is a professor of sociology at the University of Massachusetts, Amherst. Professor Laó-Montes's fields of specialty include world-historical sociology and globalization, political sociology, social identities and social inequalities, and sociology of race and ethnicity, among others. His latest book is *Contrapunteos diaspóricos: Cartografías políticas de Nuestra Afroamérica*. His research has appeared in edited volumes and academic journals, including *Cultural Studies*.

IGNACIO LÓPEZ CALVO is a professor of Latin American literature and culture and the Presidential Endowed Chair in the Humanities at the University of California, Merced. Professor López Calvo's research interests include cultural production by and about Latin American authors of Asian descent, and literary and cultural representations of the relationship between human rights, racialization, gender, migration, and authoritarianism. His latest book is *Saudades of Japan and Brazil: Contested Modernities in Lusophone Nikkei Cultural Production*.

MARISELLE MELÉNDEZ is a professor of colonial Spanish American literatures and cultures and the LAS Alumni Distinguished Professorial Scholar at the University of Illinois at Urbana Champaign. Professor Meléndez's research focuses on issues of race and gender in colonial Spanish America with special interest in the eighteenth century, the cultural phenomenon of the Enlightenment, food studies, and environmental studies, as well as visual studies. Her latest book is *Deviant and Useful Citizens: The Cultural Production of the Female Body in Eighteenth-Century Peru*. Her articles have appeared in journals such as *Latin American Research Review*, *Colonial Latin American Review*, and *Bulletin of Spanish Studies*.

MABEL MORAÑA is the William H. Gass Professor in Arts and Sciences at Washington University in Saint Louis. Professor Moraña specializes in a number of topics, from the colonial times to the present: the baroque, nationhood and modernity, cultural criticism and cultural theory, contemporary Latin American narrative, postcolonial studies, intellectual history, and gender and violence, among others. Dr. Moraña is the author of more than twenty-seven books, most recently *Genero y bio/necro/poéticas latinoamericanas* and *Jacques Derrida (el ex-céntrico) y America Latina* and has edited more than fifty volumes.

BAHIA M. MUNEM is the director of undergraduate studies at the Center for the Study of Ethnicity and Race at Columbia University. Dr. Munem's scholarship bridges the fields of Latinx, Latin American, and Middle East studies by examining forced transnational migration and gendered and racialized modes of belonging in the Americas. Her current book manuscript, *(Un)Settling Muslim Refugees: Gender, Class, and the Racialization of War Migrants in Brazil*, is an ethnography of Muslim and Palestinian Iraq War refugees resettled in Latin America's largest democracy, Brazil.

IVÁN FERNANDO RODRIGO-MENDIZÁBAL is a professor of communication at the Universidad Andina Simón Bolívar. Professor Rodrigo-Mendizábal specializes in communication, semiotics, and Latin American science fiction. He is the author of numerous academic works, including *Máquinas de pensar* and *Imaginaciones científico-tecnológico letradas*.

CARLOS ALBERTO VALDERAMA RENTERÍA is a professor of sociology at the Universidad del Pacífico. Professor Valderama Rentería's research focuses on Afro-Colombian social movements, race and racism, critical Afro-Colombian thought, and political identities and subjectivities. His research has appeared in *Revista Colombiana de Antropología* and the *Journal of Latin American and Caribbean Anthropology*, among others.

MIGUEL A. VALERIO is an associate professor of Spanish and Portuguese at the University of Maryland, College Park. Professor Valerio is a scholar of the African diaspora in the Iberian world. His research has focused on Black lay Catholic brotherhoods or confraternities and Afro-creole festive practices in colonial Latin America, especially Mexico and Brazil. He is the author of *Sovereign Joy: Afro-Mexican Kings and Queens, 1539–1640*. His research has appeared in *Slavery and Abolition*, *Colonial Latin American Review*, and *Latin American Research Review*, among others.

JORGE DANIEL VÁSQUEZ is a Changemaker Postdoctoral Fellow in the School of International Service at American University. Dr. Vásquez's research integrates global and transnational sociology, historical sociology, sociology of race and ethnicity, and decolonial studies. He is the author of *Transforming Ethnicity: Youth and Migration in Southern Ecuadorian Andes* and is currently working on the book manuscript *The Sociology of the Global Color Line*.

MARCEL VELÁZQUEZ CASTRO is a professor of Peruvian and Latin American literature at the Universidad Nacional Mayor de San Marcos. Professor Velázquez Castro's research interests include the nineteenth century, modernity, press, and race. His latest book is *Cuerpos vulnerados: Servidumbre doméstica infantil y anticlericalismo en el Perú*. His research has appeared in *Anuario de historia de América Latina* and *Revista de estudios hispánicos*, among others.

www.ingramcontent.com/pod-product-compliance
Lightning Source LLC
Chambersburg PA
CBHW030316300825
31845CB00004B/103